Developmental Dyslexia

Developmental Dyslexia

Editor: Aria Harris

AMERICAN
MEDICAL PUBLISHERS
www.americanmedicalpublishers.com

AMERICAN
MEDICAL PUBLISHERS
www.americanmedicalpublishers.com

Cataloging-in-Publication Data

Developmental dyslexia / edited by Aria Harris.
p. cm.
Includes bibliographical references and index.
ISBN 979-8-88740-045-7
1. Dyslexic children. 2. Dyslexia. 3. Developmentally disabled children. 4. Dyslexics.
5. Developmental neurobiology. I. Harris, Aria.
RJ496.A5 D48 2023
618.928 553--dc23

American Medical Publishers,
41 Flatbush Avenue,
1st Floor, New York,
NY 11217, USA

ISBN 979-8-88740-045-7 (Hardback)

Contents

Preface

Developmental dyslexia, also known as dyslexia, is neurobiological disorder that causes severe problems in learning to read and interpret. It can be caused by heredity factors, other factors that affect the brain, and phonologic disability. There are four types of dyslexia, namely, phonological dyslexia, surface dyslexia, rapid naming deficit, and double deficit dyslexia. Phonological dyslexia, also called dysphonetic or auditory dyslexia, is a type of dyslexia in which the affected person experiences difficulty in processing the sounds of the individual letters and syllables. Surface dyslexia, also known as visual dyslexia, is another type of dyslexia that causes problem in recognizing complete words which results from visual processing difficulties in the brain. In rapid naming deficit, the affected person faces issues in processing and naming a letter, number, color, or object. A person with double deficit dyslexia faces both phonological and rapid naming deficit. This book provides significant information of this discipline to help develop a good understanding of developmental dyslexia. It consists of contributions made by international experts. Those in search of information to further their knowledge will be greatly assisted by this book.

This book has been the outcome of endless efforts put in by authors and researchers on various issues and topics within the field. The book is a comprehensive collection of significant researches that are addressed in a variety of chapters. It will surely enhance the knowledge of the field among readers across the globe.

It gives us an immense pleasure to thank our researchers and authors for their efforts to submit their piece of writing before the deadlines. Finally in the end, I would like to thank my family and colleagues who have been a great source of inspiration and support.

Editor

1

Modeling individual differences in text reading fluency: a different pattern of predictors for typically developing and dyslexic readers

Pierluigi Zoccolotti[1,2], Maria De Luca[2]*, Chiara V. Marinelli[2] and Donatella Spinelli[2,3]

[1] *Department of Psychology, Sapienza University of Rome, Rome, Italy*
[2] *Neuropsychology Unit, IRCCS Fondazione Santa Lucia, Rome, Italy*
[3] *Department of Human Movement Sciences and Health, University of Rome "Foro Italico", Rome, Italy*

***Correspondence:**
Maria De Luca, Neuropsychology Unit, IRCCS Fondazione Santa Lucia, Via Ardeatina 306, 00176 Rome, Italy
e-mail: m.deluca@hsantalucia.it

This study was aimed at predicting individual differences in text reading fluency. The basic proposal included two factors, i.e., the ability to decode letter strings (measured by discrete pseudo-word reading) and integration of the various sub-components involved in reading (measured by Rapid Automatized Naming, RAN). Subsequently, a third factor was added to the model, i.e., naming of discrete digits. In order to use homogeneous measures, all contributing variables considered the entire processing of the item, including pronunciation time. The model, which was based on commonality analysis, was applied to data from a group of 43 typically developing readers (11- to 13-year-olds) and a group of 25 chronologically matched dyslexic children. In typically developing readers, both orthographic decoding and integration of reading sub-components contributed significantly to the overall prediction of text reading fluency. The model prediction was higher (from ca. 37 to 52% of the explained variance) when we included the naming of discrete digits variable, which had a suppressive effect on pseudo-word reading. In the dyslexic readers, the variance explained by the two-factor model was high (69%) and did not change when the third factor was added. The lack of a suppression effect was likely due to the prominent individual differences in poor orthographic decoding of the dyslexic children. Analyses on data from both groups of children were replicated by using patches of colors as stimuli (both in the RAN task and in the discrete naming task) obtaining similar results. We conclude that it is possible to predict much of the variance in text-reading fluency using basic processes, such as orthographic decoding and integration of reading sub-components, even without taking into consideration higher-order linguistic factors such as lexical, semantic and contextual abilities. The approach validity of using proximal vs. distal causes to predict reading fluency is discussed.

Keywords: reading, individual differences, dyslexia, suppression effect, RAN, vocal reaction times

INTRODUCTION

Fluent reading of texts is an important requisite for school achievement. The present study was aimed at investigating the factors that modulate individual differences in this skill.

Fluent reading aloud requires the integration of multiple sub-components (or process them in a cascaded manner according to the terminology adopted by Protopapas et al. (2013). When a word is being fixated and decoded readers plan the next saccade (based on para-foveal pre-processing of text on the right) but keep information about the previous words of the text so that they are able to utter them; readers also have to understand and memorize the meaning of what they are reading. A measure of this multiple-processing task is the asynchrony between eye position and speech output, referred to as eye-voice span (Buswell, 1921) or eye-voice lead (Fairbanks, 1937); indeed, typically developing readers are able to scan and process words much in advance of the word they are actually uttering.

In adult proficient readers reading aloud occurs fluently and effortlessly, with maximum reading speed for texts (in standard conditions) estimated at approximately 300 words per minute (Carver, 1982). Notably, even higher estimates are obtained using paradigms such as the rapid serial visual presentation which control for the influence of eye movements (e.g., Rubin and Turano, 1992). However, this performance is the endpoint of several years of practice, indicating slow power-function improvement in fluency (Zoccolotti et al., 2009). Notably, increases in reading speed (see data in Carver, 1982), as well as in the size of the eye-voice span (Buswell, 1921), have been observed up to college age.

Many children fail to acquire adequate reading skills, a deficit referred to as developmental dyslexia. Children with dyslexia do not learn to read fluently (e.g., Wimmer, 1993), produce frequent paralexias and characteristically have a very small eye-voice lead (e.g., De Luca et al., 2013). The literature on this disorder is large, particularly that focused on interpreting the nature of reading errors (e.g., see Castles et al., 2006; Temple, 2006; Friedmann and Lukov, 2008; Hulme and Snowling, 2014). Here we focus on the speed deficit of dyslexic children, that is, the deficit in reading fluency that is especially noted in languages with regular orthography (Wimmer, 1993; Zoccolotti et al., 1999). Considering reading fluency as the end-point of the integration of multiple sub-components of reading, some key questions arise. Which components contribute to the reading slowness shown by dyslexic children and how can they be measured and characterized? Does the need to integrate multiple sub-processes also contribute to generating the reading deficit?

To understand individual differences in reading fluency in typically developing and dyslexic children, we started from the working hypothesis that at least two basic factors contribute to the ability of all children to read fluently. The first is efficient orthographic analysis, i.e., *orthographic decoding,* and the second is the ability to integrate decoding of the on-going stimulus with utterance of the target and programming of the next saccade, i.e., *integration of reading sub-components.* The present preliminary study was aimed at evaluating whether these two components explain a relevant portion of the individual differences in text reading fluency. To rationalize our focusing on these two processes we capitalize on two major lines of reading speed research. The first one characterizes the basic difficulty in orthographic processing encountered by dyslexic children. The second one features studies that contrasted discrete and multiple presentations of stimuli and provides information on the integration of reading sub-components in typically developing and dyslexic readers. Below, we briefly review these two lines of research.

ORTHOGRAPHIC DECODING DEFICITS IN DYSLEXIA

A vast literature shows that orthographic decoding is the key difficulty in developmental dyslexia. Indeed, very clear reading deficits are detected in reading single words, i.e., when the requirement to read is stripped of the need to place the stimulus within a sentence and to pronounce it (e.g., van den Broeck and Geudens, 2012).

One related question is whether a developmental deficit can also be reliably detected for single letters or short letter strings. It is generally held that children with dyslexia show deficits in reading words (e.g., Katz and Wicklund, 1971) but not in recognizing letters (e.g., Katz and Wicklund, 1972). Notably, this sparing has also been shown with methodologies that allow controlling for the general difficulty of the task. For example, Martelli et al. (2009) examined the contrast threshold to identify single letters and words and found that dyslexic and typically developing readers needed about the same amount of contrast to identify single letters but differed greatly in the case of long words. Bosse et al. (2007) found that dyslexic children were not impaired in identifying briefly presented letters but had severely impaired visual spans, i.e., they were unable to process a multi-element array of consonants in parallel. In a later study (Lassus-Sangosse et al., 2008), they showed that the string letter deficit was present only when the presentation of letters was simultaneous not when it was sequential. In a similar vein, De Luca et al. (2010) found that dyslexic children were only mildly affected in letter, bigram and two-letter syllable tasks but were severely affected in the case of both words and non-words. Performance in these latter tasks was well accounted for by a single global factor referred to as a "*letter-string*" factor to mark, on one hand, that it was present only in the case of multi-letter displays and, on the other, that it was independent from lexical activation.

The presence of this global letter-string factor has been confirmed in a number of studies that provide information about its characteristics (Zoccolotti et al., 2008; Paizi et al., 2011, 2013; Di Filippo and Zoccolotti, 2012). In particular, the global factor that marks the decoding deficit of children with dyslexia was present when they named orthographic but not pictorial stimuli (Zoccolotti et al., 2008) and when targets were presented visually but not acoustically (Marinelli et al., 2011). Notably, in all these studies the global factor accounted for a very large proportion of the variance in group differences between dyslexic and typically developing readers. Overall, children with dyslexia are severely impaired in decoding when the task requires the parallel processing of a string of letters presented visually regardless of whether the letter string represents a legal word or not. We proposed that this global factor indicates a deficit in a pre-lexical "grapheme description" independent of case, font, location or orientation (see Marsh and Hillis, 2005). Dehaene et al. (2005) proposed a neural model to account for the abstract ability to process words regardless of their location, font and size. According to the Local Combination Detector (LCD) model written words are encoded by a hierarchy of detectors tuned to increasingly larger and more complex word fragments (visual features, single letters, bigrams, quadrigrams and, possibly, words). Over years of practice, learning of local combination detectors allows portions of the left ventral occipito-temporal visual system (referred to as visual word form area, VWFA) to become attuned to the regularities of the writing system, yielding fast parallel processing in reading (Cohen et al., 2000, 2002). The construction of this mechanism seems defective in dyslexic children (Richlan et al., 2009; Pontillo et al., 2014). This mechanism fits well with the pre-lexical "grapheme description" we found defective in dyslexic children.

In the cited studies of dyslexic children (i.e., Zoccolotti et al., 2008; Marinelli et al., 2011; Paizi et al., 2011, 2013; Di Filippo and Zoccolotti, 2012), in agreement with the predictions of the rate and amount model (RAM, Faust et al., 1999) the presence of a letter-string factor was inferred through linear regression analysis on the basis of performance on a large variety of tasks (reading high- or low-frequency words of different lengths, making lexical decisions on words or pseudo-words, etc). Notably, the predictions of the RAM apply at both a group and individual level (Faust et al., 1999). Thus, one may use the parameters of the linear regression of the condition means of a given dyslexic child over those of the total group of readers to obtain estimates of the impairment of the child in terms of the global factor (for a discussion on this point see Kail and Salthouse, 1994). For example, van den Boer et al. (2013) recently showed that the slope and the intercept were expressing different reading processes: the slope indicated the degree of serial processing while the intercept expressed the overall reading speed of words and non-words. Based on the RAM, individual slopes calculated for reading words and pseudo-words using RTs (De Luca et al., 2010) or mean total reading times per item (Di Filippo and Zoccolotti, 2012) correlated significantly with reading speed (and accuracy) in a standard reading test.

However, when studying reading with a correlational approach as in the present study, the use of a single target task may prove advantageous to establish individual performance as compared to the extraction of a single index from a variety of experimental conditions. On the one hand, it is considerably more economical. On the other hand, it avoids the difficulty of obtaining reliable regression coefficients (i.e., slopes and intercepts) at an individual level. Indeed, these are typically based on relatively few conditions and few trials per condition on each observer; thus, individual outliers may occasionally be present for whom the linear regression accounts for only a small proportion of variance. As described in greater detail below, in the present study, we selected a task particularly apt to measure orthographic decoding ability i.e., reading visually displayed single pseudo-words with the instruction to read as fast as possible (ASAP). This task captures the critical characteristics of the letter-string factor because it is in the visual modality and it calls for the fast parallel processing of a string of graphemes without requiring direct access to the lexicon. At the same time, it does not imply the ability to deal with multiple items as this represents a separate factor contributing to reading fluency. Note that processing of a letter string requires dealing with multiple elements (i.e., a set of graphemes) in parallel. Thus, if parallel processing for string is not developed, such as when learning to read, integration processes are evident also within a single word, and, for example, this is indicated by multiple fixations on the string and/or parceled uttering of the target. In the present context with 6th graders, we only focus on the contrast between the orthographic decoding of a single (although in itself complex) target with the ability to integrate this processing with the decoding of other adjacent targets as typical of functional reading.

INTEGRATION OF READING SUB-COMPONENTS: DISCRETE- vs. MULTIPLE-STIMULUS PRESENTATION

Fluent reading requires the ability to integrate the decoding of the on-going stimulus with utterance of the target and programming of the next saccade. This ability implies various sub-components. Previous research has shown that sub-components, such as visual scanning or eye movements, are not affected *per se* in dyslexic children. Thus, scanning and eye movements appear largely unimpaired if non-linguistic stimuli are presented (e.g., Brown et al., 1983; Olson et al., 1983; De Luca et al., 1999). Similarly, no articulatory deficit is present (e.g., Di Filippo et al., 2005; Wimmer et al., 1998).

However, there is evidence suggesting that *integration of the subcomponents involved in reading* is defective in children with dyslexia also when they perform a non-orthographic task. This evidence comes from studies comparing the presentation of discrete- vs. multiple-stimulus displays. Indeed, several of these studies stemmed from research on the paradigm known as "rapid automatized naming" or RAN (Denckla and Rudel, 1974, 1976). In the typical display, the child has to name 50 stimuli (i.e., digits, patches of colors, drawings of objects, etc.) regularly placed on a sheet of paper. Only a few targets (usually five) are used for each trial. The children are trained so they have no uncertainty about the repeated target names. Denckla and Rudel (1976) reported that dyslexic children performed this task more slowly than typically developing readers but were relatively accurate. The nature of the dyslexic children's difficulty in this seemingly simple task has been debated.

Some authors see RAN as just another example of a phonologically laden task (e.g., Ramus et al., 2003). In this view, dyslexic children are slow because of their inefficiency in retrieving the color, digit or picture names. Some correlational evidence goes in this direction. Thus, performance on RAN tasks generally correlates with performance on other phonological awareness tasks (Katz, 1986; Wagner and Torgesen, 1987; Compton et al., 2001; Chiappe et al., 2002). An alternative interpretation was advanced by Wolf and Bowers (1999; see also Wolf et al., 2000). They proposed that RAN is highly correlated with reading as it reproduces its "*microcosm*," i.e., it involves all the sub-components comprising functional reading with the exception of orthographic decoding (see also Blachman, 1984). In this view, dyslexic children are impaired because they are slow in organizing a fluent stream of multiple processes. In this hypothesis, the comparison between discrete and multiple presentations of stimuli is crucial, as only the latter format should show a relationship with reading. By contrast, according to a phonological explanation inefficiency in retrieving color, digit or picture names is expected in both cases. Supporting Wolf and Bowers's view, much research has shown that if stimuli (i.e., digits, colors, pictures) are presented individually, correlations with reading skills are lower than with serial naming (e.g., Stanovich et al., 1983; Bowers, 1995; Chiappe et al., 2002; Logan et al., 2011).

Several studies have dealt with this issue in the last few years. de Jong (2011) examined the development of the relationship between RAN and reading fluency as a function of the format (i.e., discrete vs. serial stimulus presentation) in first, second and fourth grade children. The author found that similar formats of RAN and reading were more strongly related than dissimilar formats among "advanced readers" (i.e., children that read words by sight; almost all 2nd and 4th grade children). Discrete RAN was more related to discrete reading fluency of high-frequent one-syllable words than with the serial reading of these words, while serial RAN was more related to serial words reading fluency than with discrete word reading. Moreover, discrete RAN made a unique contribution in predicting discrete word reading among "advanced readers," whereas serial RAN did not. On the contrary, for "beginning readers" (i.e., those who still read such words serially), RAN was the strongest predictor (whereas the contribution of discrete RAN was negligible) in word reading irrespective of the serial-discrete format (see also de Jong, 2008). Note that serial RAN predicted a large amount of unique variance in serial word reading in both advanced and beginning readers. In a recent study, Georgiou et al. (2013) compared discrete and serial RAN in a variety of experimental conditions. They found that RAN was related to reading partly because it involved serial processing (no correlation with reading was present in the case of discrete naming) and partly because it required the oral production of the different names of the stimuli. In fact, the correlation with reading dropped when subjects were instructed to give fixed oral responses to target and non-target stimuli (i.e., yes or no, 2 or 5, and apple or chicken). Georgiou et al.'s (2013) findings indicate that the whole set of cognitive operations involved in reading is necessary to yield the relationship between RAN tasks and reading. In the same vein, it has been observed that scanning the same RAN targets to cross out a given target is not correlated with reading (see also Wimmer et al., 1998; Landerl, 2001; Di Filippo et al., 2005; Georgiou et al., 2013).

Logan et al. (2011) found that serial naming uniquely predicted reading and that the relation was stronger when isolated naming was controlled for, suggesting that isolated naming functioned as a suppressor variable in the relation between serial naming and reading. In the case of suppression an independent variable contributes little or no variance to the dependent variable but may have a sizeable beta weight because it "purifies" one or more independent variables of their irrelevant variance, thereby allowing their predictive power to increase (Capraro and Capraro, 2001). Notably, specific analyses are needed to show these suppression effects (typically not adopted in early research on serial-discrete RAN). Evidence for a suppressive effect was recently confirmed by Protopapas et al. (2013) who compared the performance on discrete and serial naming of digits, objects, and words of second and sixth grade Greek children. Discrete and serial word reading correlated highly in younger children but less in older children. A reading–naming dimension explained the data well for the younger children; by contrast, a dimension in terms serial-discrete processing emerged with older children. Thus, although RAN and reading are correlated at different ages the underlying structure of this relationship may actually change as a function of reading experience. So, younger children appeared to process stimuli predominantly as a series of isolated items while older children start using serial procedures in a cascaded manner effectively. Protopapas et al. (2013) also examined the contribution of naming tasks over and above that of the effect of discrete word reading through regression and communality analyses. The results for communality analyses are particularly relevant here as we used the same approach. For sixth graders, multiple RAN contributed unique variance to the prediction of serial words, while discrete word reading was a minor contributor. The reverse held for younger children; in this case there was a large contribution of discrete word reading and multiple RAN did not explain unique variance.

Notably, most research on discrete and multiple targets is correlational and direct experimental comparisons between these two types of presentation are very few (particularly in the case of reading tasks). One possible reason is that different (and not directly comparable) dependent measures are characteristically used in the two domains. Studying the reading of isolated words (and non-words) largely rests on the analysis of vocal reaction times (RT). Thus, only the time between stimulus onset and the beginning of the vocal response is measured; this putatively captures the decoding part of the response, whereas the actual pronunciation is usually considered as not interesting (but, for a recent analysis of the characteristics of the pronunciation component of the response see Davies et al., 2013; Martelli et al., 2014). By contrast, reading fluency with multiple stimuli, such as word lists or texts, is measured by calculating the time needed to entirely process each stimulus. Thus, the whole time needed to decode and utter a target is considered in this case. Analysing total reading time of discrete stimuli (i.e., the time from onset of the stimulus to the end of the pronunciation) allows for a direct comparison between reading of discrete vs. multiple words (or non-words).

Using this approach, we recently found that 12 years-old typically developing readers had a clear advantage on multiple over discrete items in both RAN and reading tasks (Zoccolotti et al., 2013). Thus, they were able to partially process the next visual stimulus while uttering the current target, producing the time advantage over discrete items. The children with dyslexia of the same age showed a smaller advantage for multiple stimuli in naming colors and digits but presented the opposite pattern in reading, i.e., they were faster when they read discrete than multiple targets. Accordingly, we proposed that dyslexic children's great impairment on multiple arrays indicates a selective difficulty in integrating the multiple subcomponents of the reading task (Zoccolotti et al., 2013). As stated above, direct comparisons of reading under discrete and serial conditions are lacking; thus, to the best of our knowledge, we cannot compare our data with those of other laboratories. Using a somewhat different paradigm, Jones et al. (2009) directly compared discrete and multiple RAN-type tasks and reported that dyslexic young adults showed a greater deficit for multiple than discrete items, whereas non-dyslexic individuals showed a marginal facilitation with this format.

Overall, it seems that the integration of multiple subcomponents (analogous to those implied in reading) is defective in dyslexic children over and above the basic nuclear deficit in decoding words (Zoccolotti et al., 2013). Thus, in the present study, we considered integration ability as a separate factor in predicting reading fluency.

PRESENT STUDY

The present study aimed to evaluate the factors that account for individual differences in the reading fluency of typically developing and dyslexic readers. As dependent measure we chose to examine reading of texts rather than single words because it has a clear functional value and includes dealing with both orthographic materials and multiple target displays. These two latter aspects correspond to the two critical factors we selected to account for children's ability to read fluently: (1) decoding strings of letters presented visually (referred to as *orthographic decoding*); and (2) integrating decoding of the on-going stimulus with utterance of the target and motor preparation of the next saccade, which requires parafoveal analysis of the future target (referred to as *integration of reading sub-components*). Both factors are active when children read a meaningful text. However, measuring reading fluency does not directly allow understanding which of them is responsible (and to what extent) for a reading delay because both factors are involved in the performance. Indeed, only one of them (or both but to a variable degree) may be inefficient. A model that separately evaluates the contribution of these two factors may offer, at least in principle, the basis for future investigations of selective disturbances of each factor and/or their interaction.

To measure these two factors separately, we selected single pseudo-word reading and a standard RAN task requiring the naming of digits (or colors). As stated above, single pseudo-word reading appears as a particularly appropriate measure of the ability to decode a string of letters. Critically, on one hand, this performance does not require integrating multiple subcomponents (as in standard reading) and on the other hand it does not involve the orthographic lexicon. The performance of digit (or color) RAN represents a particularly suited measure of the ability to integrate the various sub-components typically involved in reading except for orthographic decoding (and keeping lexical and semantic processing aside).

This proposal may be seen as a simplified schema of the processes involved in text reading fluency. As proposed above, the motivation to develop this model stems from the observation that dyslexic children's impairment on multiple stimuli cannot be entirely explained by their single word performance (Zoccolotti et al., 2013). Although they have many different key features, most accepted models of reading, such as the dual route model (Coltheart et al., 2001), the CDP+ model (Perry et al., 2007) or the triangle model (Plaut et al., 1996), focus on the word level; thus, they are only partially informative when examining dyslexic children's reading slowness on texts and more generally when the aim is to predict reading fluency.

Clearly, the proposed model is only a skeleton focused on the processes that, based on previous research, we expect to be closely related to individual differences in text reading fluency. A full model would require specifying all the processes involved in reading fluency (e.g., spelling out all the processes that converge to determine the "integration of the reading sub-components" factor); this enterprise is beyond the aims of the present study which was intended as a first step in this direction. At any rate, it is important to keep in mind that other factors may also play a role in predicting individual differences in text reading fluency. In particular, higher-order linguistic factors may moderate this relationship. These in turn should include efficiency in accessing the orthographic and the phonological lexicon as well as semantic and contextual abilities. In this present preliminary study, however, we were specifically interested in examining how much individual differences in reading fluency can be accounted for by relying only on basic reading processes.

One question concerns the relative independence of the two factors considered. For instance, to explain dyslexics' difficulties in RAN tasks Wolf et al. (2000) proposed that there are "*connections among processes underlying naming speed, automatic orthographic pattern recognition, word identification, and reading fluency*" (Wolf et al., 2000). According to this "connection" hypothesis, one would expect the two factors to be partially related in their influence on reading fluency.

Operationally, we tested whether two variables (discrete pseudo-word reading and multiple RAN) alone or in combination significantly predicted reading fluency on meaningful texts. For RAN, both digit and color stimuli were used. It has been proposed that these two sets of stimuli generate partially different patterns of response (e.g., van den Bos et al., 2002). Notably, naming digits requires the arbitrary mapping of visual stimuli into phonological labels and is expected to produce generally more automatic processing; naming colors is mediated by semantic activation and yields generally slower and less automatized responses than digit stimuli. Thus, we decided to analyze digit and color conditions separately. As a measure, we considered a unit (i.e., total reading time per item) that was directly comparable with both discrete and multiple stimulus presentations as well as reading and naming tasks. We expected both variables i.e., discrete pseudo-word reading and multiple RAN, to contribute unique variance to the prediction and evaluated whether they also shared a common portion of the variance. Moreover, we used an additional control task, i.e., naming times for the isolated presentation of digits (or colors) which, based on previous research, was expected to contribute to the variance indirectly by acting as a suppressor variable (Logan et al., 2011; Protopapas et al., 2013; Logan and Schatschneider, 2014). As we expected predictors to show varying degrees of inter-correlation we used commonality analysis, a type of multiple linear regression that allows partitioning the total variance explained by independent variables into variance unique to each variable and variance shared by a subset of independent variables (Pedhazur, 1982). Commonality analysis is particularly suited when collinearity of predictors is expected as well as the presence of suppression effects (Nimon and Reio, 2011). Based on previous research, we expected a suppression effect of the discrete naming variable (Logan et al., 2011; Protopapas et al., 2013).

First, we present data relative to a group of typically developing readers (Study 1); second, we present data relative to a group of dyslexic readers, highlighting possible differences in the weight of predictors between the two groups (Study 2). In the main text we report data using the digit conditions (both RAN and discrete naming); we synthetically report the same analyses for the color conditions for both typically developing and dyslexic children as Supplementary Materials.

STUDY 1: PREDICTING READING FLUENCY IN TYPICALLY DEVELOPING READERS

Below we present data from a group of 11- to 13-year-old children with typical reading development. At this age level acquisition of reading speed is almost complete (Zoccolotti et al., 2009). Furthermore, recent evidence indicates that in children in this age range the processing of multiple displays is well differentiated from that of isolated stimuli (Protopapas et al., 2013).

MATERIALS AND METHODS

Participants

Forty-three typically developing readers (20 males and 23 females; mean age 11.6 ± 0.4 years) participated in the experiment. Nonverbal IQ level was assessed using Raven's Colored Progressive Matrices. All children scored well within the normal limits according to the Italian norms (Pruneti et al., 1996); mean raw score was 28.8 ± 3.4; mean z score was −0.32 ± 0.80. Reading efficiency was assessed by the MT Reading test (Cornoldi and Colpo, 1995, see below). All participants had normal or corrected-to-normal visual acuity.

MT reading test

The child reads a passage aloud within a 4-min time limit. Reading time (s/syllable) and accuracy (number of errors, adjusted for the amount of text read) are scored (Cornoldi and Colpo, 1995). As for raw data, the average reading time per syllable was 0.23 s ($SD = 0.04$), and the mean number of errors was 6.2 ($SD = 3.6$). Mean z scores (based on normative values, Cornoldi and Colpo, 1995) were near zero for all parameters (0.02 and −0.09 for reading time and accuracy, respectively).

Note that, for the specific aims of the present study, the reading speed at the MT test was the dependent measure for estimating text reading fluency. As for all other measures (see below), an inverse transformation was applied to the data so that item/s was considered in the statistical analyses.

Reading pseudo-words

Twenty 5- and 20 7-letter pseudo-words (matched for initial phoneme across lengths) were derived from words by changing one (or two) letter(s) of each word (see Appendix). Words were selected from the LEXVAR database (Barca et al., 2002; http://www.istc.cnr.it/grouppage/lexvar) and were matched for frequency across length (mean log frequency = 1.4) as well as for bigram frequency (according to the children corpus of word frequency by Marconi et al., 1993). The mean number of syllables was 2.0 for five-letter items and 2.9 for seven-letter items.

Pseudo-words appeared in black lowercase Times New Roman on a white background. Center-to-center letter distance subtended 0.4° horizontally at a viewing distance of 57 cm. Items were singly presented on a PC screen in two blocks, separately for the two lengths.

Naming digits and colors

Stimuli were five digits (2, 4, 6, 7, and 9) and five colored squares (black, yellow, and the primary green, red, and blue, digitally defined according to the red, green and blue (RGB) triplets for standard colors) on a white background. Both digits and color names had a mean number of syllables of 1.8 (mean of letter length = 4.6 for colors and 4.4 for digits, respectively) and did not differ for bigram frequency (Marconi et al., 1993). Note that pseudo-words in the reading experiment did not differ from digit names for bigram frequency (Mann-Whitney U Test, $Z = -0.28$, n.s.), but differed for number of syllables (Mann-Whitney U Test, $Z = 6.18$, $p < 0.0001$) and letters (Mann-Whitney U Test, $Z = 5.54$, $p < 0.0001$); pseudo-words differed from color names for bigram frequency (Mann-Whitney U Test, $Z = -4.06$, $p < 0.0001$), number of syllables (Mann-Whitney U Test, $Z = 5.17$, $p < 0.0001$) and number of letters (Mann-Whitney U Test, $Z = 5.54$, $p < 0.0001$).

In the discrete stimulus condition, a single digit (color) appeared in the screen. Twenty-five digit- and 25 color-trials were given in two separate blocks. In the multiple stimuli condition (RAN), 100 digits and 100 colored squares were printed on separate sheets of A4 paper; there were two sheets for each stimulus type (for a total of four sheets), each containing an array of 50 items arranged in 10 rows of five columns.

Each digit (Helvetica, black) subtended 0.9° and each square 2.5°, horizontally, both in the discrete (at 57 cm viewing distance) and the multiple (at 40 cm viewing distance) conditions.

Procedure

Each participant was tested individually in a quiet room. All experiments were administered the same day with a pause after each condition.

In the discrete condition, both digit (color) stimuli and pseudo-words were displayed singly on a PC screen controlled by DMDX software (Forster and Forster, 2003) according to the following trial sequence: 15 ms acoustic tone, 400 ms blank field, 250 ms fixation cross, stimulus onset. The stimulus disappeared at pronunciation onset or after 4000 ms. Stimuli appeared in a pseudo-randomized fixed order in each block. The child was instructed to name the digit (or color name) or to read the pseudo-word aloud as fast and accurately as possible. Reaction time was measured and the whole utterance was digitally recorded.

In the multiple condition, a total of four sheets (two for each of the types of stimulus) were presented to the participant. The child was instructed to name the items aloud as fast and accurately as possible, progressing row-by-row and from left to right. The total time to complete the task was measured with a stopwatch and the errors were noted.

A short practice preceded task execution, separately for the different conditions. The order of conditions (discrete, multiple) as well as the order of type of stimulus (color, digits; five- or seven-letter pseudo-words) was counterbalanced across participants.

Data analysis

In the discrete condition, naming or reading times per item were the time between the onset of the stimulus and the offset of the vocal response (manually detected by means of Check Vocal software; Protopapas, 2007).

In the multiple condition, total naming times per lists were computed and divided by the number of stimuli in the arrays (100) to obtain a measure of naming time per item.

Preliminary analyses indicated some moderate tendency of the distribution of time scores to be skewed as often reported for this type of measures. In particular, the discrete digit naming condition deviated appreciably from normal distribution (Chi-Square goodness-of-fit test = 9.03, $p < 0.05$) although data from the other conditions did not deviate significantly (all $ps > 0.05$). Thus, inverse transformations for all measures were used, i.e., number of items/s. Normality tests indicated that none of these scores deviated from the normal distribution (all $ps > 0.05$ according to the Chi-squared goodness-of-fit test). So, this measure was adopted for all conditions.

Z scores were computed separately for digits and colors based on the group condition means and SDs. This was done separately for the discrete and multiple conditions. To obtain a single measure for pseudo-word reading performance in the discrete conditions, data for five- and seven-letter pseudo-words were collapsed. Z scores were computed based on the group condition means and SDs and averaged to obtain a single z score for pseudo-words.

To summarize, the final time measures entered in the analyses were: text reading (MT reading test), discrete pseudo-word reading, multiple digit (or color) RAN and discrete digit (or color) naming.

To test the influence of predictors on reading fluency in text reading we used commonality analysis, a method of variance partitioning designed to identify proportions of variance in the dependent variable that can be attributed uniquely to each of the independent variables, and proportions of variance that are attributed to various combinations of independent variables (Pedhazur, 1982; Nimon, 2010). To test our hypothesis that fluency in text reading can be effectively predicted by orthographic decoding and integration of reading sub-components, we first ran an analysis using only discrete pseudo-word reading and multiple digit (or color) RAN as predictors. Then we added the additional predictor "discrete digit (or color) naming" to see whether there was an increase in the explanatory power of the analysis.

RESULTS

Table 1 presents the matrix of inter correlations between all predictors and the dependent variable, i.e., fluency in text reading. A 0.003 *p* level (based on Bonferroni correction for multiple comparisons) was adopted. An inspection of the table identifies a number of major results:

- digit and color conditions are significantly correlated both in the case of multiple RAN and discrete naming but the latter correlation (between two typically ASAP tasks) is appreciably higher than on the RAN conditions;
- Performance on the multiple digit RAN task is correlated with text reading (the correlation for the multiple color RAN condition fails short of significance after correction for multiple comparisons);
- discrete digit or color naming show very low and insignificant correlations with text reading.
- multiple RAN (whether digits or colors) and discrete naming (digits or colors) are insignificantly correlated;
- multiple digit RAN is significantly correlated with discrete pseudo-word reading (the correlation for the multiple color RAN task fails short of significance after correction for multiple comparisons);
- finally, discrete naming (whether digits or colors) and discrete pseudo-word reading are significantly correlated.

Tables 2A,B presents the results of the multiple regression analysis using the digit conditions. **Table 2A** reports the commonality coefficients for the multiple digit RAN and discrete pseudo-word reading variables. As to the percentage of variance explained (see the rightmost column in **Table 2A**), the unique contributions of the "multiple digit RAN" (27.24%) and "discrete pseudo-word reading" (34.61%) variables are present as well as the commonality between the two predictors (38.15%).

Unique and common contributions are summarized in **Table 2B** along with other parameters of the analysis, including the total variance explained by the model (37%) and the standardized β coefficients (and their significance values). For the sake of presentation we refer to this model as "*Model 1*". The last column of the table reports the percentage of variance explained by the two factors considered (due to the presence of the common variance of the two factors the sum of the values exceeds 100%). By and large, results for the color conditions ("*Model 1 color*") are consistent with those for the digit conditions (see Supplementary Materials).

Tables 3A,B presents "*Model 2*," i.e., the commonality coefficients when the "discrete digit naming" variable is added as a predictor to the multiple regression analysis. Unique and common contributions are summarized in **Table 3B** along with the other parameters of the analysis, including the total variance explained by the model and the standardized β coefficients. Note that the total variance explained by "*Model 2*" increases substantially with respect to "*Model 1*," passing from 37 to 52%. This increase is due to the influence of the "discrete naming" variable; specifically, the effect of this variable is suppressive with regard to the influence of the "discrete pseudo-word reading" variable (coefficient: −0.14 corresponding to 27.52% of explained variance, **Table 3A**). Again, results for the color conditions were similar (see Supplementary Materials).

DISCUSSION

Both basic factors, i.e., orthographic decoding and integration of reading sub-components contributed significantly to the overall prediction of text reading fluency. Furthermore, the prediction was higher when discrete naming was added to the model than

Table 1 | Matrix of correlations between all predictors and the dependent variable, i.e., speed in text reading (MT test) for the group of proficient readers.

	Text reading	Multiple RAN (digits)	Multiple RAN (colors)	Discrete naming (digits)	Discrete naming (colors)	Discrete pseudo-word reading
Text reading (speed)	–	0.49*	0.36	0.03	0.04	0.53*
Multiple RAN (digits)		–	0.49*	0.16	0.19	0.38*
Multiple RAN (colors)			–	0.16	0.28	0.33
Discrete naming (digits)				–	0.81*	0.65*
Discrete naming (colors)					–	0.56*
Discrete Pseudo-word reading						–

*$p < 0.003$.

Table 2 | (A) Commonality coefficients and percentage of explained variance for predictors of text reading ("Multiple RAN" and "Discrete pseudo-word reading"): proficient readers (MODEL 1). (B) Unique and common contributions of "Multiple RAN" and "Discrete pseudo-word reading" to fluency measure: proficient readers (MODEL 1).

A Variables	Coefficient	Percent
Unique to "Multiple RAN"	0.10	27
Unique to "Discrete pseudo-word reading"	0.13	35
Common to "Multiple RAN" and "Discrete Pseudo-word reading"	0.14	38
Total	0.37	100

B	*R*	R^2	R^2 adj.	ß st.	*p*	Unique	Common	Total	% of R^2 (r_s^2)
Model	0.61	0.37	0.34						
Multiple RAN				0.35	0.015	0.10	0.14	0.24	65.4%
Discrete pseudo-word reading				0.39	0.006	0.13	0.14	0.27	72.8%

Adj., adjusted; St., standardized; Unique, predictor's unique effect; Common, predictor's common effects; Total, Unique + Common; % of R^2, Total/R^2.

Table 3 | (A) Commonality coefficients and percentage of explained variance for predictors of text reading ("Multiple RAN," "Discrete digit naming" and "Discrete pseudo-word reading"): proficient readers (MODEL 2). (B) Unique and common contributions of Multiple RAN, Discrete Naming and Discrete pseudo-word reading to fluency measure: proficient readers (MODEL 2).

A Variables	Coefficient	Percent
Unique to "Multiple RAN"	0.07	13
Unique to "Discrete digit naming"	0.15	28
Unique to "Discrete pseudo-word reading"	0.27	52
Common to "Multiple RAN" and "Discrete digit naming"	0.03	6
Common to "Multiple RAN" and "Discrete pseudo-word reading"	0.18	34
Common to "Discrete digit naming" and "Discrete pseudo-word reading"	−0.14	−27
Common to "Multiple RAN," "Discrete digit naming" and "Discrete pseudo-word reading"	−0.03	−6
Total	0.52	100

B	*R*	R^2	R^2 adj.	ß st.	*p*	Unique	Common	Total	% of R^2 (r_s^2)
Model	0.72	0.52	0.48						
Multiple RAN				0.29	0.023	0.07	0.18	0.24	47.1%
Discrete digit naming				−0.51	0.001	0.15	−0.14	0.00	0.1%
Discrete pseudo-word reading				0.75	0.000	0.27	0.00	0.27	52.4%

Adj., adjusted; St., standardized; Unique, predictor's unique effect; Common, predictor's common effects; Total, Unique + Common; % of R^2, Total/R^2.

when only the two original factors were considered. The general pattern of findings was similar for the digit and color conditions indicating that is the variance common to these two sets of stimuli to carry the relationship.

As to the orthographic decoding factor, performance in discrete pseudo-word reading exerted a large unique influence in the analyses with both the two- and three-factor models (i.e., "*Models 1* and *2*"). We proposed that this factor marks the individual efficiency of the pre-lexical graphemic description of the letter string (Zoccolotti et al., 2008).

As to the integration of the reading sub-components factor, the presence of a unique contribution of multiple RAN confirms that RAN tasks capture a proportion of variance (coefficient 0.07; about 13% of explained variance in "*Model 2*," **Table 3A**) which is different from that accounted for by orthographic processing. This is in keeping with the idea that the RAN paradigm captures a portion of variance related to the processing of multiple stimuli.

The two variables also exerted a substantial influence together. One might think that the degree of efficiency in dealing with orthographic analysis of a string of letters contributes to managing multiple stimuli. In this vein, the interaction between multiple naming and reading would change as a function of reading experience. There is some evidence that the correlation between RAN and reading increases with reading experience (Kirby et al., 2003). Furthermore, Protopapas et al. (2013) recently reported that the co-variance between reading and RAN is best expressed in terms of a reading-naming latent structure in younger children and in terms of a serial-discrete dimension in more experienced children.

These relationships are schematized in **Figure 1**. Note that orthographic decoding and integration of reading sub-components influence reading fluency directly (both singly and interaction between each other). An indirect influence is also presented in the figure; indeed, the discrete digit naming variable exerted a suppressive effect selectively on discrete pseudo-word reading (but not on multiple RAN). A suppressor variable is one that is not directly correlated with the dependent variable but acts indirectly through another predictor(s) (note the insignificant correlation in **Table 1** between reading fluency and digit or color naming). When added to the model the suppressive factor allows for a better overall prediction by accounting for some irrelevant variance in the predictor variables resulting in an increase of the relationship between the predictors and the outcome. This was clearly the case when we passed from the two-variable ("*Model 1*") to the three-variable analysis ("*Model 2*") and obtained an increase in explanatory power (from 37 to 52%; from 31 to 43%, in the case of the color conditions).

The idea that naming isolated non-orthographic items can have a suppressive effect in accounting for individual differences in reading was first conceived by Logan et al. (2011) and later supported by Protopapas et al.'s (2013) findings. Furthermore, Logan and Schatschneider (2014) recently re-analyzed seven different studies and confirmed that isolated naming acts as a suppressor variable in the relation of serial naming with reading. The present results are in part consistent with these previous studies and in part different. In considering the different outcomes it must be noted that Logan et al. (2011) only examined tasks with non-orthographic stimuli. By contrast, we observed ("*Model 2*") that the suppressive effect of the discrete digit naming variable was mostly on discrete pseudo-word reading (i.e., −27.52%) and was not detected directly on multiple RAN (a very small suppressive effect, i.e., −6.58%, was present on the variance common to discrete pseudo-word reading and RAN).

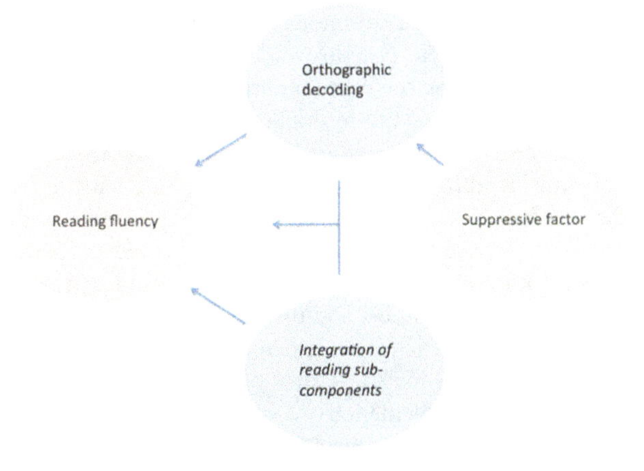

FIGURE 1 | Factors affecting individual differences in word fluency in typically developing readers. Note that the suppressive factor exerts an effect on reading fluency only indirectly through the orthographic decoding but not through the integration of reading sub-components factor.

This pattern of findings can be used to try to understand the nature of the suppressive effect. As this was unknown until recently, only tentative proposals can be advanced. For example, as their data indicated a suppressive effect over RAN, Logan et al. (2011) originally proposed that eye movements and parafoveal processing should be examined as possible targets of future research to explain the suppressive effect (for similar considerations see Logan and Schatschneider, 2014). In the present study the suppressive effect of discrete naming was on discrete pseudo-word reading, i.e., a condition with single, foveally presented orthographic stimuli; thus, Logan and co-workers' proposal would not easily fit the present data.

Another possibility is that what is being suppressed is naming speed. Within this idea, discrete naming taps the efficiency in the retrieval of phonological labels (whether directly linked to arbitrary mappings as in the case of digits or through semantic activation as in the case of colors). Efficient naming of discrete digit (or color) with ASAP instructions shares variance with discrete pseudo-word reading as it has in common the requirement to quickly retrieve and activate a phonological label after stimulus onset. By contrast, discrete naming is not directly related to reading fluency; thus, efficient phonological retrieval is not the reason that pseudoword decoding is related to text fluency. As stated above, one may envisage that the key factor for pseudo-word reading to predict reading is that it captures variance related to the processing of a (relatively long) string of graphemes.

Yet another, more general, alternative is that the portion of variance of the discrete naming variable which generates the suppressive effect is the requirement for a fast response to an externally triggered imperative stimulus under ASAP instructions. Indeed, this requirement is common to the discrete naming and discrete pseudo-word reading while it is not shared by discrete naming and text reading fluency (where is the subject to set his/her own pacing in proceeding through the text). In this vein, what is being suppressed by the discrete naming of colors/digits can be seen as expressing individual "cognitive speed." While this term may appear overly general, Faust et al. (1999) specify rather specific conditions to define this dimension and we refer to their formulation here. Accordingly, cognitive speed expresses the commonality that is present across many speeded decision tasks and that indicates the overall information processing rate characteristic of a given individual. Typical within this frame are studies of the general slowing observed with aging (e.g., Cerella, 1990). Faust et al. (1999) showed that commonality emerges quite clearly in factor analyses of tasks requiring a response under time constraints, i.e., in conditions in which the subject must respond ASAP to an external stimulus that triggers the response. In this perspective, cognitive speed marks the individual information processing rate across many tasks and modalities.

The present data are consistent with this interpretation although they cannot prove it. For this reason in the scheme of **Figure 1** we use the neutral term "suppressive factor," even though we feel that the "cognitive speed" factor represents a coherent and comprehensive framework to interpret it. Further comments on the suppressive factor will be advanced in the general discussion.

STUDY 2: PREDICTING READING FLUENCY IN DYSLEXIC CHILDREN

The development of reading progresses from early acquisition of orthographic decoding to a later ability to effectively integrate decoding with the other sub-components of reading. In the words of Buswell (1921): *"An immature reader ... tends to keep the eye and voice very close together, in many cases not moving the eye from a word until the voice has pronounced it. Reading of this type becomes little more than a series of spoken words because there is no opportunity to anticipate the meaning in large units."*

This pattern of reading was confirmed experimentally by Protopapas et al. (2013) examining discrete and serial naming of digits, objects and words in Greek second and sixth graders. Discrete and serial word reading correlated very highly in Grade 2 but only moderately in Grade 6. Protopapas et al. (2013) concluded that *"word fluency tasks in Grade 2 are apparently accomplished largely as a series of isolated individual word naming trials even though multiple individual letters in each word may be processed in parallel. In contrast, specifically serial procedures are applied in Grade 6, presumably via simultaneous processing of multiple individual words at successive levels."*

As young readers dyslexic children may be expected to process stimuli in an isolated fashion, as indicated by their smaller eye-voice lead (Buswell, 1921; Fairbanks, 1937; De Luca et al., 2013). According to the proposed model, this can be captured in part from their (defective) performance on the multiple RAN tasks; furthermore, one may believe that the orthographic decoding factor is particularly important in these children as compared to typically developing readers. This may be expressed as greater weight of this factor in the prediction or, alternatively, as a dominant role of this factor over and above the moderating influence of the discrete naming variable.

MATERIALS AND METHODS

Participants

Twenty-five children with dyslexia (14 males and 11 females; mean age 11.8 ± 0.8 years) participated in the experiment. Children were comparable for age and gender to the typically developing readers in Study 1. To assess non-verbal IQ levels, we used the scores obtained by 12 children with dyslexia on Raven's Colored Progressive Matrices. All children scored well within the normal limits according to Italian norms (Pruneti et al., 1996). Mean raw score was 27.3 ± 2.6; mean z score was −0.66 ± 0.62. Wechsler Intelligence Scale for Children (WISC) data were available for the other 13 children with dyslexia; scores were well within the normal range for both performance and verbal subscales (mean total score 96.2 ± 10.1). All participants had normal or corrected-to-normal visual acuity.

The children with dyslexia scored at least 1.65 standard deviations below the norm for either speed or accuracy on the MT Reading test (Cornoldi and Colpo, 1995). As for raw data, the average reading time per syllable was 0.51 s ($SD = 0.17$), and mean number of errors was 21.7 ($SD = 9.1$). Based on normative values (Cornoldi and Colpo, 1995), mean z scores were −2.50 and −2.97, for reading time and accuracy respectively.

As for typically developing children, an inverse transformation was applied to the data so that item/s was considered in the statistical analyses. So, reading speed at the MT test (in terms of word/s) was the dependent measure to estimate text reading fluency.

Experimental conditions procedure

All measures were computed as described above.

As for reading/naming time measures, the pseudo-word reading condition deviated appreciably from normal distribution (Chi-Square goodness-of-fit test = 12.78, $p < 0.001$) while data from all the other conditions did not deviate significantly (all $ps > 0.05$). Thus, inverse transformations for all measures were used, i.e., number of items/s, as for typically developing children. Normality tests indicated that none of these scores deviated from the normal distribution (all $ps > 0.05$ according to the Chi-squared goodness-of-fit test).

Data analysis

As described above.

RESULTS

Table 4 presents the matrix of inter correlations between all predictors and the dependent variable (i.e., speed in text reading), for the sample of children with dyslexia. A 0.05 significance level was adopted; as we were interested in comparing this pattern of results with those of typically developing readers no correction for multiple comparisons was considered in this case.

The general pattern of correlations is similar to that observed with typically developing children. One main difference emerges: discrete naming (both digits and colors) is correlated with text reading. This is at variance with what occurs for typically developing readers where no correlation was detected.

Table 5A presents the commonality coefficients for the multiple RAN and discrete pseudo-word reading variables for the dyslexic children using the digit conditions. There is a detectable unique contribution of the multiple RAN variable (10.16% of explained variance). The unique contribution of the discrete pseudo-word reading variable is large (36.41%). Finally, the two predictors share 53.43% of the variance. Unique and common contributions of the two variables are summarized in **Table 5B** along with other parameters of the analysis, including the variance explained by the model and the standardized β coefficients. Note that the total variance explained by the model (referred to as "*Model 3*") is high (69%). Results of the color conditions are again similar (see Supplementary Materials).

An additional multiple regression was carried out by adding the discrete digit naming predictor. The results of this analysis are presented in **Tables 6A,B**. Notably, the proportion of explained variance was the same after adding this variable (69%; "*Model 4*"). In the analysis the discrete digit naming variable shares some variance with the multiple RAN and pseudo-word reading variables

Table 4 | Matrix of correlation between all predictors and the dependent variable (text reading fluency), speed in text reading (MT test) for the group of dyslexic readers.

	Text reading	Multiple RAN (digits)	Multiple RAN (colors)	Discrete naming (digits)	Discrete naming (colors)	Discrete pseudo-word reading
Text reading (speed)	–	0.66*	0.42*	0.56*	0.54*	0.78*
Multiple RAN (digits)		–	0.70*	0.42*	0.36	0.55*
Multiple RAN (colors)			–	0.33	0.25	0.34
Discrete naming (digits)				–	0.86*	0.69*
Discrete naming (colors)					–	0.62*
Discrete Pseudo-word reading						–

*p <0.05.

Table 5 | (A) Commonality coefficients and percentage of explained variance for predictors of text reading ("Multiple RAN" and "Discrete pseudo-word reading"): dyslexic readers (MODEL 3). (B) Unique and common contributions of "Multiple RAN" and "Discrete pseudo-word reading" to fluency measure: dyslexic readers (MODEL 3).

A		
Variables	**Coefficient**	**Percent**
Unique to "Multiple RAN"	0.07	10
Unique to "Discrete pseudo-word reading"	0.25	36
Common to "Multiple RAN" and "Discrete pseudo-word reading"	0.37	54
Total	0.69	100

B	R	R^2	R^2 adj.	ß st.	p	Unique	Common	Total	% of R^2 (r_s^2)
Model	0.83	0.69	0.66						
Multiple RAN				0.32	0.036	0.07	0.37	0.44	63.6%
Discrete pseudo-word reading				0.61	0.000	0.25	0.37	0.62	89.8%

Adj., adjusted; St., standardized; Unique, predictor's unique effect; Common, predictor's common effects; Total, Unique + Common; % of R^2, Total/R^2.

but does not exert a suppressive effect (as in the sample of typically developing readers). The parallel results for the color conditions are reported Supplementary Materials.

DISCUSSION

In the case of children with dyslexia, the model with only two predictors i.e., "multiple RAN" and "discrete pseudo-word reading," accounts for a large proportion of variance (69%) and no increase in explanatory power is obtained by adding the corresponding discrete naming variable. A note of caution in interpreting these data is in order given the relatively small sample size of dyslexic children, particularly considering the type of statistical analyses. This suggests the importance that the pattern of results be replicated in a different, larger sample, before definite conclusions be drawn. At any rate, results similar to those obtained considering the digit conditions were found using the color conditions. This finding points to the stability of the pattern observed at least within the sample examined.

Notably, the general structure of the model is similar to that of typically developing readers (as schematized in **Figure 1**). In the case of children with dyslexia, however, no suppressive effect of the discrete digit (or color) naming variable was detected when this was added to the model. Thus, it appears that for these children discrete pseudo-word reading performance is so heavily loaded with orthographic decoding that no additional power can be obtained by considering the moderating effect of discrete naming, or individual "cognitive speed" as proposed above.

GENERAL DISCUSSION

To predict individual differences in text reading fluency in typically developing and dyslexic readers, we chose to evaluate factors that, based on previous research, clearly distinguished children with and without a reading deficit. We reasoned that the two selected tasks would selectively measure two different basic processes of reading fluency, i.e., the ability of the child to process a letter string and the ability to integrate this processing with on-going analysis of the text. For the time being, we have purposely ignored all higher-level linguistic processes, such as activation of lexical and semantic information and on-going syntactic processing, to determine how much individual reading rate depends on basic reading processing.

PREDICTING SPEED IN READING MEANINGFUL TEXTS

The main result of the study is that the ability to decode letter strings (measured by the pseudo-word reading variable) and the ability to integrate the various sub-components at work in

Table 6 | (A)Commonality coefficients and percentage of explained variance for predictors of text reading ("Multiple RAN," "Discrete digit naming" and "Discrete pseudo-word reading"): dyslexic readers (MODEL 4). (B)Unique and common contributions of Multiple RAN, Discrete Naming and Discrete pseudo-word reading to fluency measure: dyslexic readers (MODEL 4).

A		
Variables	**Coefficient**	**Percent**
Unique to "Multiple RAN"	0.07	10
Unique to "Discrete digit naming"	0.00	0
Unique to "Discrete pseudo-word reading"	0.16	23
Common to "Multiple RAN" and "Discrete digit naming"	0.00	0
Common to "Multiple RAN" and "Discrete pseudo-word reading"	0.15	22
Common to "Discrete digit naming" and "Discrete pseudo-word reading"	0.10	14
Common to "Multiple RAN", "Discrete digit naming" and "Discrete pseudo-word reading"	0.22	31
Total	0.69	100

B	R	R^2	R^2 adj.	ß st.	p	Unique	Common	Total	% of R^2 (r_s^2)
Model	0.83	0.69	0.65						
Multiple RAN				0.32	0.041	0.07	0.37	0.44	63.6%
Discrete digit naming				0.002	0.915	0.00	0.31	0.31	45.0%
Discrete pseudo-word reading				0.60	0.004	0.16	0.47	0.62	89.8%

Adj., adjusted; St., standardized; Unique, predictor's unique effect; Common, predictor's common effects; Total, Unique + Common; %of R^2, Total/R^2.

reading (measured by the RAN variable) jointly allow accounting for a sizeable amount of variance in reading fluency on meaningful texts. The reliability coefficient for our dependent measure, i.e., the MT Reading test time (Cornoldi and Colpo, 1995), is reported to be ca 0.90. Thus, the basic reading processes examined allow accounting for approximately two-thirds of the true variance in text fluency. This holds for both typically developing readers and dyslexic children although with a partially different pattern of predictors (see below). Notably, this high prediction occurs without considering higher level linguistic processes, which involve the activation of lexical, semantic and contextual information.

Below we discuss some specific, and partially open, questions related to the variables considered in the study; in the last section we speculate on the advantage of modeling reading deficits based on proximal rather than distal causes.

PSEUDO-WORD READING

Orthographic decoding contributed importantly to the prediction of reading fluency. The pseudo-word reading task putatively captures the ability to process a letter string and produce an appropriate phonological output. In the introduction, we presented evidence that children with dyslexia show a selective deficit when they have to deal with a letter string presented visually, the deficit being very similar whether the stimulus is a word or a pseudo-word (Zoccolotti et al., 2008; De Luca et al., 2010; Marinelli et al., 2011). We proposed that this deficit marks a prelexical impairment in forming a graphemic description of the stimulus, i.e., a deficit in the abstract representation of a letter string (Zoccolotti et al., 2008). In neural terms, the LCD model proposes that this ability rests on the output of a hierarchy of detectors tuned to increasingly larger and more complex word fragments (Dehaene et al., 2005). In this hypothesis the underlying factor refers essentially to visual perception.

Alternative hypotheses can also be considered to interpret this ability. One idea is that the phonological component of the processing is essential for generating the difference between dyslexic and control readers and in mediating the relationship with reading. Against a strict phonological interpretation, it has been shown that dyslexic readers' deficit is selective for the visual modality and the same stimuli presented acoustically are responded to flawlessly (Marinelli et al., 2011). Furthermore, clear deficits are present also when children have to process strings of consonants in tasks that minimize the influence of phonological activation (i.e., visual span paradigm; Bosse et al., 2007; Valdois et al., 2012). In the same vein, we recently completed a lexical decision experiment in which we used as foils either pronounceable pseudo-words (such as DASU) or unpronounceable non-words made of consonants (such as RNGM). Group differences in responses to words, pseudo-words and non-words were all accounted for by the same (letter-string) global factor indicating that pronounceability of the foil was not critical in mediating the deficit of dyslexic children (Marinelli et al., under revision). A more advanced hypothesis is that the binding between orthographic and phonological information is crucial in generating the dyslexic deficit (Ziegler et al., 2010a; van den Broeck and Geudens, 2012). Some recent neuroimaging evidence points in this direction. In a fMRI study, van der Mark et al. (2011) detected a significant disruption of the functional connectivity between the VWFA and left inferior frontal and left inferior parietal language areas in children with dyslexia. Therefore, the possibility must be considered that the critical underlying factor in the pseudo-word reading task is the need to connect a string of graphemes to the corresponding phonological output.

The possibility should also be considered that lexical activation contributes to performance of the pseudo-word reading task. On the whole, this hypothesis seems unlikely on several grounds. It has been proposed that pseudo-words may generate lexical effects or that parts of pseudo-words may be recognized holistically (e.g., Moll et al., 2009). However, this generally occurs under very specific conditions, such as when they are presented intermingled with words, but this did not occur in the present experiment. Furthermore, lexical attempts at reading pseudo-words are much more frequent among children learning to read an irregular orthography such as English than a regular orthography such as German (e.g., Wimmer and Goswami, 1994).

Overall, orthographic decoding plays an important role in the prediction of fluency in reading a text in a regular orthography such as Italian. Whether this performance essentially marks the efficiency of the graphemic processor of letter strings or of a mechanism binding the output of this processor to phonological processing is beyond the aims of the present study and is a question open to future research.

RAN

The finding that performance on the RAN tasks actually predicts reading fluency confirms much previous research (Wolf and Bowers, 1999; Wolf et al., 2000). Based on evidence summarized in the Introduction, we considered that RAN tasks selectively capture the ability to integrate the various sub-components necessary for effective reading but exclude orthographic decoding. Critical in this perspective is the finding that RAN correlates with reading only if the task requires serial processing and active production of specific names (Georgiou et al., 2013), as occurs in reading. The present results indicate that RAN tasks account for a sizeable amount of variance (more than 10% in both groups of children) over and above that accounted for by orthographic decoding, and that accounted in common by the two factors. This finding confirms previous observations by Protopapas et al. (2013) who found RAN to contribute unique variance over and above discrete word reading at least in 6 grade children. Overall, the RAN tasks capture individual variability linked to the ability to deal with multiple targets; note that this variability cannot be explained in terms of processing the same stimuli when presented in a discrete format (Georgiou et al., 2013; present data).

It is not clear at present whether these individual differences can be ascribed to a single identifiable mechanism. One hypothesis proposes that slowness in RAN tasks depends on a multiple, or domain-general, temporal processing deficit in dyslexic children (Farmer and Klein, 1995). However, a systematic check of this hypothesis failed to reveal any indication that a deficit in temporal processing *per se* underlies the reading deficit of dyslexic individuals (Chiappe et al., 2002). Alternatively, one can speculate that individual differences in the fluency to deal with multiple visual stimuli, such as digits or color, with the aim of naming them rest on a more specific skill. At least in part, this represents an individual trait present prior to school experience as it has been found that performance on RAN tasks at a pre-school stage significantly predicts later efficiency in reading (e.g., Bishop, 2003), However, this does not exclude that efficiency in RAN tasks is progressively tuned through reading itself (e.g., Torgesen et al., 1994). In fact, through reading training, children get much experience in integrating target identification with visual scanning, parafoveal pre-analysis and pronunciation. Thus, when we examine individual RAN speed in children who already attended school for a number of years, we measure a skill that has had received partial reinforcement from reading experience itself. In support of this view, the distinction between single-multiple stimuli processing becomes prominent in modulating the relationship with reading only after a number of years of schooling (Protopapas et al., 2013). Furthermore, while RAN tasks are correlated with reading across very different ages, the size of this correlation increases with reading experience (Kirby et al., 2003). Thus, the link in **Figure 1** between "orthographic decoding" and "integration of reading sub-components" sketches a relationship between the two factors that is bidirectional and may presumably change with age and reading experience.

In the same vein, note that a much more complex model could be proposed following the (not unlikely) view that reading experience affects fluency, and fluency may affect both integration and decoding. Feedback links should integrate the model and different analyses may contribute to evaluating the direction and weight of each influence; however, we see the present study only as a first step in modeling individual variations in reading fluency in Italian typically developing readers and dyslexic children.

SUPPRESSIVE FACTOR

The performance on the discrete digit or color naming task contributed as a third factor, and in a suppressive manner, to the prediction of reading fluency in typically developing but not in dyslexic readers. Above, we tentatively discussed a few alternative interpretations. Admittedly, the present data do not allow to persuasively select between a naming speed and a cognitive speed interpretation and only speculative considerations can be advanced at this point. However, as stated in the comments of study 1, cognitive speed seems to provide a theoretically sound interpretation and one that is potentially worth of further research.

Faust et al. (1999) define cognitive speed as the overall information processing rate characterizing a given individual across a variety of tasks (Faust et al., 1999). Indeed, in conditions with ASAP instructions the time measures of performance (RTs) on different tasks are always highly correlated. Due to this very large co-variation, if a standard factor analysis is applied to the data a single factor accounts for a large proportion of individual variability (Faust et al., 1999). At first glance, this finding contrasts with the well-known fact that RTs are particularly sensitive in picking up differences due to experimental manipulations. See, for instance, the effects of psycholinguistic variables (such as word frequency, orthographic neighbors, etc) on word recognition that typically reveal significant effects with differences of a few milliseconds. When testing the effects of experimental manipulations, this large co-variation is controlled for by the use of repeated measures designs (which essentially partial out the correlation between measures across experimental conditions). However, if one wants to examine individual differences (rather than the effects of experimental manipulations) one must face the fact that the time measures will all be highly correlated, particularly when the general format of task and response is kept constant (as in RT tasks in which the subject has to respond ASAP to an external imperative stimulus). In these cases, the presence of correlation will substantially modulate the relationships between the specific factors investigated. This represents a problem if, as in the present case, no correlation is actually expected between reading fluency and cognitive speed *per se* (as shown by Bonifacci and Snowling, 2008); however, measures of cognitive speed will correlate with other predictors provided that they share the general task format which may indeed be more important than the specific type of stimuli. In this vein, it is interesting that the discrete digit/color naming task has a large suppressive effect on pseudoword reading with which it shares a general format (i.e., an ASAP response), but has no detectable effect on the RAN tasks with which it shares the type of stimulus (digits or colors) but not the general format.

This framework may help placing the lack of an effect in dyslexic children. Based on readers' data, we should expect the cognitive speed factor to modulate pseudoword reading. However, this influence was not significant because the dramatic slowness of dyslexic children in orthographic decoding also implies huge individual differences at this level and dominates over the cognitive speed factor.

In the introduction and above we have cited evidence indicating that a global factor marks individual performance in speeded reading tasks and effectively discriminates between dyslexic and typically developing readers. However, the global factor that marks dyslexics' performance (Zoccolotti et al., 2008) and the cognitive speed factor described by Faust et al. (1999) are clearly distinct constructs. Dyslexic children are slow across many tasks, but only if they require the processing of orthographic strings. By contrast, according to Faust et al. cognitive speed refers to a more general construct, spanning across different stimuli and modalities.

MODELING INDIVIDUAL DIFFERENCES IN READING FLUENCY: PROXIMAL vs. DISTAL CAUSES

The present approach should be distinguished from several previous attempts to predict individual reading performance (e.g., Torgesen et al., 1997; Muter and Snowling, 1998; Compton et al., 2001; Kirby et al., 2003; Ziegler et al., 2010b; Landerl et al., 2012; Warmington and Hulme, 2012). In these studies, the authors aimed to predict reading using a variety of cognitive measures but without explicitly attempting to make a componential analysis of reading behavior. Characteristically, a spectrum of linguistic, meta-phonological, visual and also RAN measures are used jointly to examine which predictor(s) is (are) more strongly related to the reading dependent measure.

One way to distinguish this approach from the present one is to see it as focusing on distal (as opposed to proximal) causes of behavior. Within a proximal approach (such as in the present study), reading behavior is described in terms of the building blocks of the reading processes (see further comments below). By contrast, a distal approach has the more ambitious goal of searching for the ultimate origin of normal and disordered behavior. Thus, predictors are considered as inherently independent causes of behavior and, as such, the presence of uni-directional links between putative causes and effects is an essential tenet of this approach. However, this assumption is problematic when using cognitive markers as distal "causes" of individual variability in reading.

This point has been often discussed in relation to phonological awareness. One popular view considers phonological awareness as a critical ability for the beginning of reading and defective phonological awareness as a possible cause of dyslexia (for a review see Melby-Lervag et al., 2012). In this vein, phonological awareness is a distal cause of reading behavior, exerting a unidirectional relationship. However, this assumption is questioned by the observation that the critical learning for the conscious awareness of phonemes actually occurs during schooling (Morais et al., 1979). The influence of school experience is particularly clear in studies comparing later-schooled children (i.e., children who start school 1 or 2 years after the usual age) with children matched for age but differing for school experience, and children matched for schooling but differing for age (Alcock et al., 2010; Cunningham and Carroll, 2011; for similar data on Italian children see Scalisi et al., 2013). Thus, phonological awareness may be seen more as a consequence than a cause of reading. More complex interpretations have been advanced that propose the presence of a reciprocal relationship between phonological awareness and reading (e.g., Perfetti et al., 1987). However, even if this were appropriate, it would seriously undermine the validity of using phonological awareness as a distal, unidirectional predictor of reading.

Although this question has been often discussed in relation to phonological awareness, it presumably also refers to other general cognitive predictors, such as vocabulary breadth or visual scanning. Indeed, the same argument may well apply to RAN even though the change in performance after the beginning of schooling is not as abrupt as in the case of phonological awareness tasks (e.g., Scalisi et al., 2013). As stated above, it seems reasonable to envisage that children tune their ability to integrate scanning, identify and name visual targets mostly through reading experience and it is with reading experience that individual differences in the fluidity of carrying out such complex behaviors come out most clearly (Kirby et al., 2003; Protopapas et al., 2013).

Overall, for a distal approach to be effective it is crucial that cognitive predictors be independent from the behavior to predict, i.e., that the direction of causality be unidirectional. However, this assumption seems very difficult to hold in view of the strict bidirectional relationship that most of the cognitive abilities (as phonological abilities and integrating skills) typically entered in prediction studies hold with reading.

Another critical characteristic of the distal approach in the case of reading and dyslexia is that the nature of the relationship between the cognitive measures and reading are usually left under-specified in terms of actual processes. One can imagine, for example, various ways in which low short-term memory, small vocabulary or inefficient ability to segment or blend phonemes can indeed affect the acquisition of reading. Yet, no explicit relationship is typically formulated as to which specific cognitive deficiency should produce which selective effect on reading. Put in other terms, predictors do not have a specific place in the architecture of reading.

In the present study, we viewed the predictions about reading from the perspective of proximal causes. According to some influential authors, this approach has its own autonomy even in the absence of a full description of the distal causes of dyslexia, although these will eventually need to be investigated (e.g., Jackson and Coltheart, 2001, 2002). In the proximal approach, it is not critical that expertise in orthographic decoding and integration of reading sub-components are progressively tuned throughout schooling and, more generally, with reading experience, i.e., that they are not fully independent causes exerting a unidirectional influence on reading fluency. What is crucial is to spell out the building blocks of the reading process and evaluate their individual and interactive influence on individual reading fluency. In this view, note that here we qualify RAN performance as a measure of a specific component of the reading process, namely the integration of reading sub-components (see Georgiou et al., 2013), not as a general cognitive predictor. There is a long tradition of studies based on the proximal approach, particularly stemming from the dual route model (Coltheart et al., 2001). Most often, they have dealt with the analysis of single case studies. Here, we propose that a proximal approach may help to re-think the correlational studies predicting individual variability in text reading.

Finally, a novel methodological element of the approach used in the present study is the homogeneity of the measures adopted. By focusing specifically on reading speed, we used the same measure (i.e., total reading time per item) across both independent and dependent variables. Most previous studies on the prediction of reading used mixed measures and included reading accuracy as a dependent variable even in cases in which speed measures were used as predictors (Logan and Schatschneider, 2014). In these cases, variations in the format of the measures used might have unknown effects on the pattern of relationships found.

CONCLUSIONS

The results of the present study indicate that fluency in reading texts depends heavily on basic reading processes, i.e., the ability to decode letter strings and to integrate the various reading sub-components. This prediction occurs without considering the role of lexical, semantic and contextual information. Although these processes may also exert some influence, it seems that they can only complement the prediction in view of the large proportion of variance accounted for by basic reading processes. In typically developing readers, the prediction becomes more effective when the suppressive effect of stimulus-triggered naming speed under ASAP instructions is considered, suggesting a putative indirect role of individual cognitive speed.

ACKNOWLEDGMENTS

This work was supported by grants from the Department of Health and Sapienza University. We would like to thank Drs. Claudio Barbaranelli, Kim Nimon and Silvia Primativo for their advice and help with the statistical analyses, Maria Pontillo for help in data collection, and Claire Montagna for the linguistic revision of the text.

REFERENCES

Alcock, K. J., Ngorosho, D., Deus, C., and Jukes, M. C. H. (2010). We don't have language at our house: disentangling the relationship between phonological awareness, schooling, and literacy. *Brit. J. Educ. Psychol.* 80, 55–76. doi: 10.1348/000709909X424411

Barca, L., Burani, C., and Arduino, L. S. (2002). Word naming times and psycholinguistic norms for for Italian nouns. *Behav. Res. Methods Instrum. Comput.* 34, 424–434. doi: 10.3758/bf03195471

Bishop, A. G. (2003). Prediction of first-grade reading achievement: a comparison of fall and winter kindergarten screenings. *Learn. Disability Q.* 26, 189–200. doi: 10.2307/1593651

Blachman, B. A. (1984). Relationship of rapid naming ability and language analysis skills to and kindergarten first-grade reading achievement. *J. Educ. Psychol.* 76, 610–622. doi: 10.1037/0022-0663.76.4.610

Bonifacci, P., and Snowling, M. J. (2008). Speed of processing and reading disability: a cross-linguistic investigation of dyslexia and borderline intellectual functioning. *Cognition* 107, 999–1017. doi: 10.1016/j.cognition.2007.12.006

Bosse, M. L., Tainturier, M. J., and Valdois, S. (2007). Developmental dyslexia: the visual attention span deficit hypothesis. *Cognition* 104, 198–230. doi: 10.1016/j.cognition.2006.05.009

Bowers, P. G. (1995). Tracing symbol naming speed's unique contributions to reading disabilities over time. *Read. Writ.* 7, 189–216. doi: 10.1007/BF01027185

Brown, B., Haegerstrom-Portnoy, G., Adams, A. J., Yingling, C. D., Galin, D., Herron, J., et al. (1983). Predictive eye-movements do not discriminate between dyslexics and control children. *Neuropsychologia* 21, 121–128. doi: 10.1016/0028-3932(83)90078-7

Buswell, G. T. (1921). The relationship between eye-perception and voice-response in reading. *J. Educ. Psychol.* 12, 217–227. doi: 10.1037/h0070548

Capraro, R. M., and Capraro, M. M. (2001). Commonality analysis: Understanding variance contributions to overall canonical correlation effects of attitude toward mathematics on geometry achievement. *Mult. Lin. Regr. Viewp.* 27, 16–23.

Carver, R. P. (1982). Optimal rate of reading prose. *Read. Res. Quart.* 18, 56–88. doi: 10.2307/747538

Castles, A., Bates, T., and Coltheart, M. (2006). John Marshall and the developmental dyslexias. *Aphasiology* 20, 871–892. doi: 10.1080/02687030600738952

Cerella, J. (1990). "Aging and information-processing rate," in Handbook of the psychology of aging (3rd ed.). *The Handbooks of Aging, eds J. E. Birren and K. W. Schaie (San Diego, CA: Academic Press)*, 201–221.

Chiappe, P., Stringer, R., Siegel, L., and Stanovich, K. E. (2002). Why the timing deficit hypothesis does not explain reading disability in adults. *Read. Writ.* 15, 73–107. doi: 10.1007/s11145-009-9199-1

Cohen, L., Dehaene, S., Naccache, L., Lehéricy, S., Dehaene-Lambertz, G., Hénaff, M. A., et al. (2000). The visual word form area: spatial and temporal characterization of an initial stage of reading in normal subjects and posterior split-brain patients. *Brain* 123, 291–307. doi: 10.1093/brain/123.2.291

Cohen, L., Lehericy, S., Chochon, F., Lemer, C., Rivaud, S., and Dehaene, S. (2002). Language-specific tuning of visual cortex? *Functional properties of the visual word form area. Brain* 125, 1054–1069. doi: 10.1093/brain/awf094

Coltheart, M., Rastle, K., Perry, C., Langdon, R., and Ziegler, J. C. (2001). DRC: a dual route cascaded model of visual word recognition and reading aloud. *Psychol. Rev.* 108, 204–256. doi: 10.1037/0033-295X.108.1.204

Compton, D. L., De Fries, J. C., and Olson, R. K. (2001). Are RAN- and phonological awareness-deficits additive in children with reading disabilities? *Dyslexia* 7, 125–149. doi: 10.1002/dys.198

Cornoldi, C., and Colpo, G. (1995). *Nuove Prove di Lettura MT Per la Scuola Media Inferiore.* Firenze: O.S. Organizzazioni Speciali.

Cunningham, A. J., and Carroll, J. M. (2011). Reading-related skills in earlier- and later-schooled children. *Sci. Stud. Read.* 15, 244–266. doi: 10.1080/10888431003706309

Davies, R., Rodrìguez-Ferreiro, J., Suárez, P., and Cuetos, F. (2013). Lexical and sub-lexical effects on accuracy, reaction time and response duration: impaired and typical word and pseudoword reading in a transparent orthography. *Read. Writ.* 26, 721–738. doi: 10.1007/ s11145-012-9388-1

de Jong, P. F. (2008). Differences in the correlates of reading accuracy and speed in young Dutch readers. *Educ. Child Psychol.* 25, 37–48.

de Jong, P. F. (2011). What discrete and serial rapid automatized naming can reveal about reading. *Sci. Stud. Read.* 15, 314–337. doi: 10.1080/10888438.2010.485624

De Luca, M., Burani, C., Paizi, D., Spinelli, D., and Zoccolotti, P. (2010). Letter and letter-string processing in developmental dyslexia. *Cortex* 46, 1272–1283. doi: 10.1016/j.cortex.2009.06.007

De Luca, M., Di Pace, E., Judica, A., Spinelli, D., and Zoccolotti, P. (1999). Eye movement patterns in linguistic and non-linguistic tasks in developmental surface dyslexia. *Neuropsychologia* 37, 1407–1420. doi: 10.1016/S0028-3932(99)00038-X

De Luca, M., Pontillo, M., Primativo, S., Spinelli, D., and Zoccolotti, P. (2013). The eye-voice lead during oral reading in developmental dyslexia. *Front. Hum. Neurosci.* 7:696. doi: 10.3389/fnhum.2013.00696

Dehaene, S., Cohen, L., Sigman, M., and Vinckier, F. (2005). The neural code for written words: a proposal. *Trends Cogn. Sci.* 9, 335–341. doi: 10.1016/j.tics.2005.05.004

Denckla, M. B., and Rudel, R. G. (1974). Rapid "automatized" naming of pictured objects, colors, letters and numbers by normal children. *Cortex* 10, 186–202. doi: 10.1016/S0010-9452(74)80009-2

Denckla, M. B., and Rudel, R. G. (1976). "Rapid automatized naming" (R.A.N.): dyslexia differentiated from other learning disabilities. *Neuropsychologia* 14, 471–479. doi: 10.1016/0028-3932(76)90075-0

Di Filippo, G., Brizzolara, D., Chilosi, A., De Luca, M., Judica, A., Pecini, C., et al. (2005). Rapid naming, not cancellation speed or articulation rate, predicts reading in an orthographically regular language (Italian). *Child Neuropsychol.* 11, 349–361. doi: 10.1080/09297040490916947

Di Filippo, G., and Zoccolotti, P. (2012). Separating global and specific factors in developmental dyslexia: a study with the RAN paradigm. *Child Neuropsychol.* 18, 356–391. doi: 10.1080/09297049.2011.613809

Fairbanks, G. (1937). The relation between eye-movements and voice in the oral reading of good and poor silent readers. *Psychol. Monogr.* 48, 78–107. doi: 10.1037/h0093394

Farmer, M. E., and Klein, R. M. (1995). The evidence for a temporal processing deficit linked to dyslexia: a review. *Psychon. Bull. Rev.* 2, 460–493. doi: 10.3758/BF03210983

Faust, M. E., Balota, D. A., Spieler, D. H., and Ferraro, F. R. (1999). Individual differences in information processing rate and amount: implications for group differences in response latency. *Psychol. Bull.* 125, 777–799. doi: 10.1037/0033-2909.125.6.777

Forster, K. I., and Forster, J. C. (2003). DMDX: a windows display program with millisecond accuracy. *Behav. Res. Methods Instrum.* 35, 116–124. doi: 10.3758/BF03195503

Friedmann, N., and Lukov, L. (2008). Developmental surface dyslexias. *Cortex* 44, 1146–1160. doi: 10.1016/j.cortex.2007.09.005

Georgiou, G. K., Parrila, R., Cui, Y., and Papadopoulos, T. C. (2013). Why is rapid automatized naming related to reading? *J. Exp. Child Psychol.* 115, 218–225. doi: 10.1016/j.jecp.2012.10.015

Hulme, C., and Snowling, M. J. (2014). The interface between spoken and written language: developmental disorders. *Phil. Trans. R. Soc. B Biol. Sci.* 369, 1–8. doi: 10.1098/rstb.2012.0395

Jackson, N. E., and Coltheart, M. (2001). *Routes to Reading Success and Failure: Toward an Integrated Cognitive Psychology of Atypical Reading.* New York, NY: Psychology Press.

Jackson, N. E., and Coltheart, M. (2002). Distinguishing proximal from distal causes is useful and compatible with accounts of compensatory processing in developmental disorders of cognition. *Behav. Brain Sci.* 25, 758–759. doi: 10.1017/S0140525X02290135

Jones, M. W., Branigan, H. P., and Kelly, M. L. (2009). Dyslexic and nondyslexic reading fluency: rapid automatized naming and the importance of continuous lists. *Psychon. Bull. Rev.* 16, 567–572. doi: 10.3758/PBR.16.3.567

Kail, R., and Salthouse, T. A. (1994). Processing speed as a mental capacity. *Acta Psychol.* 86, 199–225. doi: 10.1016/0001-6918(94)90003-5

Katz, R. B. (1986). Phonological deficiencies in children with reading disability: evidence from an object naming task. *Cognition* 22, 225–257. doi: 10.1016/0010-0277(86)90016-8

Katz, L., and Wicklund, D. (1971). Word scanning rate for good and poor readers. *J. Educ. Psychol.* 62, 138–140. doi: 10.1037/h0030777

Katz, L., and Wicklund, D. (1972). Letter scanning rate for good and poor readers in grades two to six. *J. Educ. Psychol.* 63, 363–367. doi: 10.1037/h0033582

Kirby, J. R., Parrila, R. K., and Pfeiffer, S. L. (2003). Naming speed and phonological awareness as predictors of reading development. *J. Educ. Psychol.* 95, 453–464. doi: 10.1037/0022-0663.95.3.453

Landerl, K. (2001). Word recognition deficits in German: more evidence from a representative sample. *Dyslexia* 7, 183–196. doi: 10.1002/dys.199

Landerl, K., Ramus, F., Moll, K., Lyytinen, H., Leppänen, P. H., Lohvansuu, K., et al. (2012). Predictors of developmental dyslexia in European orthographies with varying complexity. *J. Child Psychol. Psyc.* 54, 686–694. doi: 10.1111/jcpp.12029

Lassus-Sangosse, D., N'Guyen-Morel, M. A., and Valdois, S. (2008). Sequential or simultaneous visual processing deficit in developmental dyslexia? *Vis. Res.* 48, 979–988. doi: 10.1016/j.visres.2008.01.025

Logan, J. A., and Schatschneider, C. (2014). Component processes in reading: shared and unique variance in serial and isolated naming speed. *Read. Writ.* 27, 905–922. doi: 10.1007/s11145-013-9475-y

Logan, J. A. R., Schatschneider, C., and Wagner, R. K. (2011). Rapid serial naming and reading ability: the role of lexical access. *Read. Writ.* 24, 1–25. doi: 10.1007/s11145-009-9199-1

Marconi, L., Ott, M., Pesenti, E., Ratti, D., and Tavella, M. (1993). *Lessico elementare. Dati Statistici Sull'italiano Letto e Scritto dai Bambini Delle Elementari.* Bologna: Zanichelli.

Marinelli, C. V., Angelelli, P., Di Filippo, G., and Zoccolotti, P. (2011). Is developmental dyslexia modality specific? A visual-acoustic comparison on Italian dyslexics. *Neuropsychologia* 49, 1718–1729. doi: 10.1016/j.neuropsychologia.2011.02.050

Marsh, E. B., and Hillis, A. E. (2005). Cognitive and neural mechanisms underlying reading and naming: evidence from letter-by-letter reading and optic aphasia. *Neurocase* 11, 325–337. doi: 10.1080/13554790591006320

Martelli, M., De Luca, M., Lami, L., Pizzoli, C., Pontillo, M., Spinelli, D., et al. (2014). Bridging the gap between different measures of the reading speed deficit in developmental dyslexia. *Exp. Brain Res.* 232, 237–252. doi: 10.1007/s00221-013-3735-6

Martelli, M., Di Filippo, G., Spinelli, D., and Zoccolotti, P. (2009). Crowding, reading and developmental dyslexia. *J. Vis.* 9, 1–18. doi: 10.1167/9.4.14

Melby-Lervag, M., Lyster, S. A., and Hulme, C. (2012). Phonological skills and their role in learning to read: a meta-analytic review. *Psychol. Bull.* 138, 322–352. doi: 10.1037/a0026744

Moll, K., Fussenegger, B., Willburger, E., and Landerl, K. (2009). RAN is not a measure of orthographic processing: evidence from the asymmetric German orthography. *Sci. Stud. Read.* 13, 1–25. doi: 10.1080/10888430802631684

Morais, J., Gary, L., Alegria, J., and Bertelson, P. (1979). Does awareness of speech as a sequence of phones arise spontaneously? *Cognition* 7, 323–331.

Muter, V., and Snowling, M. (1998). Concurrent and longitudinal predictors of reading: the role of metalinguistic and short-term memory skills. *Read. Res. Q.* 33, 320–337. doi: 10.1598/RRQ.33.3.4

Nimon, K. (2010). Regression commonality analysis: demonstration of an SPSS solution. *Mult. Lin. Regr. Viewp.* 36, 10–17.

Nimon, K., and Reio, T. (2011). Regression commonality analysis: a technique for quantitative theory building. *Hum. Resour. Dev. Rev.* 10, 329–340. doi: 10.1177/1534484311411077

Olson, R. K., Kliegl, R., and Davidson, B. J. (1983). Dyslexic and normal readers' eye movements. *J. Exp. Psychol. Hum.* 9, 816–825. doi: 10.1037/0096-1523.9.5.816

Paizi, D., De Luca, M., Burani, C., and Zoccolotti, P. (2011). List context manipulation reveals orthographic deficits in Italian readers with developmental dyslexia. *Child Neuropsychol.* 17, 459–482. doi: 10.1080/09297049.2010.551187

Paizi, D., De Luca, M., Zoccolotti, P., and Burani, C. (2013). A comprehensive evaluation of lexical reading in Italian developmental dyslexics. *J. Res. Read.* 36, 303–329. doi: 10.1111/j.1467-9817.2011.01504.x

Pedhazur, E. G. (1982). *Multiple Regression in Behavioral Research: Explanation and Prediction, 2nd Edn.* New York, NY: CBS College Publishing.

Perfetti, C. A., Beck, I., Bell, L. C., and Hughes, C. (1987). Phonemic knowledge and learning to read are reciprocal: a longitudinal study of first grade children. *Merrill Palmer Q.* 33, 283–319.

Perry, C., Ziegler, J. C., and Zorzi, M. (2007). Nested incremental modeling in the development of computational theories: the CDP+ model of reading aloud. *Psychol. Rev.* 114, 273–315. doi: 10.1037/0033-295X.114.2.273

Plaut, D. C., McClelland, J. L., Seidenberg, M. S., and Patterson, K. (1996). Understanding normal and impaired word reading: computational principles in quasi-regular domains. *Psychol. Rev.* 103, 56–115. doi: 10.1037/0033-295X.103.1.56

Pontillo, M., De Luca, M., Ellis, A. W., Marinelli, C. V., Spinelli, D., and Zoccolotti, P. (2014). Failure to learn a new format in developmental dyslexia. *Sci. Rep.* 4, 4869. doi: 10.1038/srep04869

Protopapas, A. (2007). CheckVocal: a program to facilitate checking the accuracy and response time of vocal responses from DMDX. *Behav. Res. Methods* 39, 859–862. doi: 10.3758/BF03192979

Protopapas, A., Altani, A., and Georgiou, G. K. (2013). Development of serial processing in reading and rapid naming. *J. Exp. Child Psychol.* 116, 914–929. doi: 10.1016/j.jecp.2013.08.004

Pruneti, C. A., Fenu, A., Freschi, G., Rota, S., Cocci, D., Marchionni, M., et al. (1996). Aggiornamento della standardizzazione italiana del test delle matrici progressive colorate di raven (CPM). *Bollettino di Psicologia Applicata* 217, 51–57.

Ramus, F., Rosen, S., Dakin, S. C., Day, B. L., Castellote, J. M., White, S., et al. (2003). Theories of developmental dyslexia: insights from a multiple case study of dyslexic adults. *Brain* 126, 841–865. doi: 10.1093/brain/awg076

Richlan, F., Kronbichler, M., and Wimmer, H. (2009). Functional abnormalities in the dyslexic brain: a quantitative meta-analysis of neuroimaging studies. *Hum. Brain Mapp.* 30, 3299–3308. doi: 10.1002/hbm.20752

Rubin, G. S., and Turano, K. (1992). Reading without saccadic eye movements. *Vis. Res.* 32, 895–902. doi: 10.1016/0042-6989(92)90032-E

Scalisi, T. G., Desimoni, M., and Di Vito Curmini, L. (2013). Age and schooling effects on the development of phonological awareness (PA) and rapid automatized naming (RAN) in Italian children aged 5-7 years. *J. Appl. Psycholinguist.* 13, 45–60.

Stanovich, K. E., Feeman, D. J., and Cunningham, A. E. (1983). The development of the relation between letter-naming speed and reading ability. *Bull. Psychon. Soc.* 21, 199–202. doi: 10.3758/BF03334686

Temple, C. M. (2006). Developmental and acquired dyslexias. *Cortex* 42, 898–910. doi: 10.1016/S0010-9452(08)70434-9

Torgesen, J. K., Wagner, R. K., and Rashotte, C. A. (1994). Longitudinal studies of phonological processing and reading. *J. Learn. Disabil.* 27, 276–286. doi: 10.1177/002221949402700503

Torgesen, J. K., Wagner, R. K., Rashotte, C. A., Burgess, S., and Hecht, S. (1997). Contributions of phonological awareness and rapid automatic naming ability to the growth of word-reading skills in second-to fifth-grade children. *Sci. Stud. Read.* 1, 161–185. doi: 10.1207/s1532799xssr0102_4

Valdois, S., Lassus-Sangosse, D., and Lobier, M. (2012). Impaired letter-string processing in developmental dyslexia: what visual-to-phonology code mapping disorder? *Dyslexia* 18, 77–93. doi: 10.1002/dys.1437

van den Boer, M., de Jong, P. F., and Haentjens-van Meeteren, M. M. (2013). Modeling the length effect: specifying the relation with visual and phonological correlates of reading. *Scient. Stud. Read.* 17, 243–256. doi: 10.1080/10888438.2012.683222

van den Bos, K. P., Zijlstra, B. J. H., and Spelberg, H. C. I. (2002). Life-span data on continuous-naming speeds of numbers, letters, colors, and pictured objects, and word-reading speed. *Sci. Stud. Read.* 6, 25–49. doi: 10.1207/S1532799XSSR0601_02

van den Broeck, W., and Geudens, A. (2012). Old and new ways to study characteristics of reading disability: the case of the nonword-reading deficit. *Cognitive Psychol.* 65, 414–456. doi: 10.1016/j.cogpsych.2012.06.003

van der Mark, S., Klaver, P., Bucher, K., Maurer, U., Schulz, E., Brem, S., et al. (2011). The left occipitotemporal system in reading: disruption of focal fMRI connectivity to left inferior frontal and inferior parietal language areas in children with dyslexia. *Neuroimage* 54, 2426–2436. doi: 10.1016/j.neuroimage.2010.10.002

Wagner, R. K., and Torgesen, J. K. (1987). The nature of phonological processing and its causal role in the acquisition of reading skills. *Psychol. Bull.* 101, 192–212. doi: 10.1037/0033-2909.101.2.192

Warmington, M., and Hulme, C. (2012). Phoneme awareness, visual-verbal paired-associate learning, and rapid automatized naming as predictors of individual differences in reading ability. *Sci. Stud. Read.* 16, 45–62. doi: 10.1080/10888438.2010.534832

Wimmer, H. (1993). Characteristics of developmental dyslexia in a regular writing system. *Appl. Psychol.* 14, 1–33. doi: 10.1017/S0142716400010122

Wimmer, H., and Goswami, U. (1994). The influence of orthographic consistency on reading development: word recognition in English and German children. *Cognition* 51, 91–103. doi: 10.1016/0010-0277(94)90010-8

Wimmer, H., Mayringer, H., and Landerl, K. (1998). Poor reading: a deficit in skill-automatization or a phonological deficit? *Sci. Stud. Read.* 2, 321–340. doi: 10.1207/s1532799xssr0204_2

Wolf, M., and Bowers, P. G. (1999). The double-deficit hypothesis for the developmental dyslexias. *J. Educ. Psychol.* 91, 415–438. doi: 10.1037/0022-0663.91.3.415

Wolf, M., Bowers, P. G., and Biddle, K. (2000). Naming-speed processes, timing, and reading: a conceptual review. *J. Learn. Disabil.* 33, 387–407. doi: 10.1177/002221940003300409

Ziegler, J. C., Bertrand, D., Tóth, D., Csépe, V., Reis, A., Faísca, L., et al. (2010b). Orthographic depth and its impact on universal predictors of reading a cross-language investigation. *Psychol. Sci.* 21, 551–559. doi: 10.1177/0956797610363406

Ziegler, J. C., Pech-Georgel, C., Dufau, S., and Grainger, J. (2010a). Rapid processing of letters, digits and symbols: what purely visual-attentional deficit in developmental dyslexia? *Dev. Sci.* 13, F8–F14. doi: 10.1111/j.1467-7687.2010.00983.x

Zoccolotti, P., De Luca, M., Di Pace, E., Judica, A., Orlandi, M., and Spinelli, D. (1999). Markers of developmental surface dyslexia in a language (Italian) with high grapheme–phoneme correspondence. *Appl. Psychol.* 20, 191–216. doi: 10.1017/S0142716499002027

Zoccolotti, P., De Luca, M., Judica, A., and Spinelli, D. (2008). Isolating global and specific factors in developmental dyslexia: a study based on the rate and amount model (RAM). *Exp. Brain Res.* 186, 551–560. doi: 10.1007/s00221-007-1257-9

Zoccolotti, P., De Luca, M., Lami, L., Pizzoli, C., Pontillo, M., and Spinelli, D. (2013). Multiple stimulus presentation yields larger deficits in children with developmental dyslexia: a study with reading and RAN-type tasks. *Child Neuropsychol.* 19, 639–647. doi: 10.1080/09297049.2012.718325

Zoccolotti, P., De Luca, M., Di Filippo, G., Judica, A., and Martelli, M. (2009). Reading development in an orthographically regular language: effects of length, frequency, lexicality and global processing ability. *Read. Writ.* 22, 1053–1079. doi: 10.1007/s11145-008-9144-8

2

Executive functions in developmental dyslexia

Pamela Varvara[1,2†], Cristiana Varuzza[1†], Anna C. P. Sorrentino[1], Stefano Vicari[1] and Deny Menghini[1*]

[1] Neuroscience Department, Children's Hospital Bambino Gesù, Rome, Italy
[2] Psychology Department, Libera Università Maria Ss. Assunta, Rome, Italy

***Correspondence:**
Deny Menghini, Neuroscience Department, Children's Hospital Bambino Gesù, Piazza Sant'Onofrio 4, Rome I-00165, Italy
e-mail: deny.menghini@opbg.net

†These authors have contributed equally to this work.

The present study was aimed at investigating different aspects of Executive Functions (EF) in children with Developmental Dyslexia (DD). A neuropsychological battery tapping verbal fluency, spoonerism, attention, verbal shifting, short-term and working memory was used to assess 60 children with DD and 65 with typical reading (TR) abilities. Compared to their controls, children with DD showed deficits in several EF domains such as verbal categorical and phonological fluency, visual-spatial and auditory attention, spoonerism, verbal and visual short-term memory, and verbal working memory. Moreover, exploring predictive relationships between EF measures and reading, we found that spoonerism abilities better explained word and non-word reading deficits. Although to a lesser extent, auditory and visual-spatial attention also explained the increased percentage of variance related to reading deficit. EF deficits found in DD are interpreted as an expression of a deficient functioning of the Central Executive System and are discussed in the context of the recent temporal sampling theory.

Keywords: developmental disabilities, working memory, central executive system, attention, phonological processing

INTRODUCTION

Executive functions (EF) are a set of high cognitive abilities that control and regulate other functions and behaviors (Welsh et al., 1991). They may involve abilities such as selectively processing information in the environment, retaining task-relevant information in an accessible state over time, making a plan by selecting a sequence of actions to achieve a goal, inhibiting a verbal or motor response, successfully adapting responses to changes in situations and environments, problem solving and self monitoring (Welsh et al., 1991; Pennington and Ozonoff, 1996; Friedman et al., 2006).

EF deficits have been described in several developmental disorders. Attention, working memory, inhibitory control, and flexible thinking deficits have been documented in individuals with attention and hyperactivity disorders (Sergeant et al., 2002; Corbett et al., 2009; Abad-Mas et al., 2011; Pani et al., 2013); inhibition of responses and planning deficits have been described in children with autism (Rinehart et al., 2001; Hill, 2004; Kenworthy et al., 2005; Robinson et al., 2009); planning and memory deficits have been reported in fetal alcohol spectrum disorder (Rasmussen, 2005; Green et al., 2009; Pei et al., 2011). Deficits in a set of EF have also been documented in genetic syndromes associated with intellectual disability (Costanzo et al., 2013). Moreover, a recent meta-analysis (Booth et al., 2010) has highlighted that children with reading disability have difficulties in several EF, including maintaining relevant information in WM, inhibition of irrelevant information, and accessing material in long-term memory.

Indeed, deficits in WM have been mainly investigated using span tasks and are considered one of the major defining characteristics of Developmental Dyslexia (DD) (Willcutt et al., 2005; Swanson et al., 2009, 2010; Bacon et al., 2013). Both verbal and visual-spatial components of WM have been found impaired in children (Poblano et al., 2000; Brosnan et al., 2002; Helland and Asbjørnsen, 2004; Martinussen and Tannock, 2006; Smith-Spark and Fisk, 2007; Menghini et al., 2011) and adults (Smith-Spark et al., 2003; Alloway and Alloway, 2013) with DD. In the light of Baddeley's model, the reduced performance of dyslexics in memory span tasks involving both verbal and visual-spatial modalities may be interpreted as an expression of deficient functioning of the Central Executive component of WM. The tripartite WM model (Baddeley and Hitch, 1974; Baddeley and Logie, 1999; Baddeley, 2000, 2001) includes a Central Executive System (CES) responding to different cognitive functions (e.g., attention, active-inhibition, planning, updating, maintenance and integration of information) and two peripheral slave systems devoted to the temporary storing and rehearsing of information pertaining to a single modality (visual-spatial sketchpad and articulatory loop). The CES coordinates the two slave systems, integrating their storage capacities and making available attentional resources for online processing of incoming information. It has been proposed that the CES may be analogous to the Supervisory Attentional System (SAS) described by Shallice and colleagues (Norman and Shallice, 1986; Shallice and Burgess, 1993). Indeed, the SAS is defined as a conscious control mechanism that resolves interference and allows attentional control over action. CES and SAS not only have a critical control function in WM, but are also involved in several processes requiring higher-order cognitive control. Accordingly, Kane and Engle (2002) define controlled attention as an executive control capability that can effectively maintain stimulus, goal, or context information in an active, easily accessible state in the face of interference, effectively inhibiting goal-irrelevant stimuli or responses (Kane et al., 2001).

Deficits in visual-spatial attention in DD have also been found using tasks which evaluate orientation, focusing, shifting attention and visual search (Helland and Asbjørnsen, 2000; Altemeier et al., 2008; Menghini et al., 2010). Deficits in auditory attention have also been found using discrimination speech tasks (e.g., Casco and Prunetti, 1996; Facoetti et al., 2000; Buchholz and McKone, 2004; Valdois et al., 2004; Dufor et al., 2007). Hari and Renvall (2001) and Laasonen et al. (2012) have suggested that children with DD may suffer from sluggish attentional shifting (i.e., engaging and disengaging attention) as revealed by tasks assessing sustained and divided attention, auditory saltation illusion, auditory pitch streaming sequence, and attentional blink.

Furthermore, studies in DD have documented deficits in categorical fluency, planning, monitoring and revising during problem solving, and response shifting using the flexibility task, the Go/No-go task, and the Tower of London task (e.g., Condor et al., 1995; Mati-Zissi and Zafiropoulou, 2001; Reiter et al., 2005; Swanson et al., 2006). Other authors have demonstrated that DD children were impaired in inhibition tasks such as the Stroop Test (Everatt et al., 1997; Brosnan et al., 2002; Reiter et al., 2005).

With few exceptions (Reiter et al., 2005; Willcutt et al., 2005; Swanson et al., 2006), the above-mentioned studies investigated each EF separately in DD.

However, in the last few years, a multifactorial deficit has been found, supporting the view that neurocognitive developmental dysfunctions in DD may not be limited to the linguistic brain areas, but may also involve a more multifocal cortical system (Pennington, 2006).

Recent functional neuroimaging findings provide evidence of a neurobiological signature for dyslexia, including two crucial posterior systems, one in the occipito-temporal regions and one in the parieto-temporal regions, as well as an anterior system, mainly located in the inferior frontal gyrus (Shaywitz et al., 2008).

The anterior system is implicated in the output of phonological and articulatory aspects, verbal working memory, and the semantic aspects of word reading (Price, 2000; Jobard et al., 2003; Gabrieli, 2009). It was recently suggested (Hoeft et al., 2007; Graves et al., 2010) that in both expert readers and dyslexics the contribution of this system to reading is primarily due to the attention, working memory and executive processes required by reading than to orthographical-phonological mapping *per se*.

The occipito-temporal system has a particularly important role in skilled, fluent reading (i.e., rapid and automatic identification of words) and encompasses the fusiform gyrus (Visual Word Form Area) and the middle and inferior temporal gyrus (Cohen et al., 2000; Vinckier et al., 2007). The parieto-temporal system includes the angular and the supramarginal gyri, and portions of the temporal lobe, such as the left superior temporal gyrus. This system is responsible for cross-modal relation of auditory and visual processes during reading and for the integration of letters and sounds.

To overcome the limitations of previous studies which evaluated each EF separately, the aim of the present study was to simultaneously test different EF domains in the same group of children with DD using numerous tasks.

Children with DD were then compared to children with typical reading (TR) abilities using a neuropsychological battery tapping several EF such as verbal phonological and categorical fluency, spoonerism abilities, visual-spatial and auditory attention, verbal, visual and spatial short-term memory, verbal WM, and visual shifting. To better understand the potential role of EF in reading, the relationships between EF measures and reading abilities were also explored.

MATERIALS AND METHODS

PARTICIPANTS

The study included 60 children and adolescents with DD (27 females) and 65 children with TR abilities (28 females) matched for chronological and mental age.

The chronological age range was 8–17 years for the DD group (mean 11.4 ± 1.9 *SD*) and 8 to 16 years for TR participants (mean 11.9 ± 1.6 *SD*). The diagnosis of DD was made when word or non-word reading speed and/or accuracy level was at least 2 standard deviations below the mean value for the scholar level. In a non-verbal intelligence test Colored Progressive Matrices (CPM; Raven, 1994) all DD participants had a performance level in the normal range (above 10th percentile; mean 29.28 ± 4 *SD*).

The presence of Attention Deficit Hyperactivity Disorder was excluded by means of DSM-IV recommendations (American Psychiatric Association, 2000) and confirmed by behavioral rating scales filled out by parents (Cornoldi et al., 1996; Re and Cornoldi, 2009). Furthermore, none of the children with DD underwent any intensive or specific reading training.

Criteria for inclusion in the TR group were: (i) no reading delay in word and non-word reading tests; (ii) normal or corrected visual acuity; (iii) no Attention Deficit Hyperactivity Disorder diagnosis. In the above-mentioned non-verbal intelligence test (Raven, 1994), TR children had a performance level in the normal range (above 10th percentile; mean 29.83 ± 3.53 *SD*).

DESIGN AND MATERIALS

Children with DD were evaluated in three testing sessions carried out on three different days at the Department of Child and Adolescent Psychiatry of the Bambino Gesù Children's Hospital in Rome. TR children were assessed in three testing sessions in a local primary school. All tasks included a practice phase during which the experimenter explained the task instructions. Tasks were administered in a pseudorandom manner (IQ and reading abilities were always assessed before testing began). All the children's parents gave written informed consent after an extensive description of the research study. The neuropsychological battery involved IQ, reading abilities and EF tasks.

GENERAL INTELLIGENCE

Non-verbal intelligence was measured using the CPM (Raven, 1994), which evaluate the ability to form perceptual relations and to reason by analogy, irrespective of language and formal schooling.

READING ABILITIES

Reading abilities were assessed using two subtests of a battery for the diagnosis of DD (Sartori et al., 1995). Participants were asked to read aloud lists of words and non-words. Speed (in seconds) and errors (each incorrect word or non-word was calculated as one error) were computed for each task. Also, inefficiency reading indexes were considered, calculating the ratio between reading speed and accuracy rate (number of words/non-words correctly read over the total number of words/non-words) for both word and non-word reading tasks.

EF TASKS

Verbal categorical fluency

The Category fluency test (Vicari, 2007) was used to measure verbal fluency. Participants were asked to generate words in a particular category (e.g., animals, clothes, fruits, toys). Deviations from the test rules, including repetitions (perseveration errors) and words not identifiable as an example of the category, were considered errors. All words generated by the participants were recorded by the examiner, and the number of valid responses produced during the time limit (60 s) was calculated (excluding repetitions and errors). The score is calculated as the sum of the number of words generated for each category and the total number of responses.

Verbal phonological fluency

The Phonological Fluency Test (Marotta et al., 2008) was used to evaluate the ability to recall several items using a phonological input. In this task, the child was asked to verbalize as many words as possible beginning with a given phoneme (F, A, and S) within 60 s for each of the three trials. The global score is the sum of the correct responses for the three trials.

Spoonerism

The Spoonerism Task (Marotta et al., 2008) was used to evaluate phonological awareness. The examiner pronounced two words aloud and the participant had to swap the initial phonemes to form two new real words. The child was asked to transpose the beginning sounds of the two words as quickly as possible (time limit to complete a single trial: 60 s; number of trials: 15). The score is the number of correct answers (maximum score: 30) and the time taken to complete the entire test (15 trials).

Visual-spatial attention

Selective visual-spatial attention was evaluated using the Map Mission. In this subtest of the Test of Everyday Attention for Children (Manly et al., 2001), a color-printed A3-laminated city map was presented. Eighty targets representing restaurants (i.e., small knife and fork symbols) were randomly distributed across the map. Distracting symbols of the same size were also present. Participants used a pen to circle as many targets as possible in 60 s. The performance score is the number of target symbols correctly marked by the participants (maximum score: 80).

Auditory attention

Sustained auditory attention was investigated using the Code Transmission task. In this task, which was also a subtest of the Test of Everyday Attention for Children (Manly et al., 2001), participants were asked to monitor a stream of monotonous digits (presented at a rate of one every 2 s) for the occurrence of a particular target sequence (e.g., 5, 5) and then to report the digit that occurred immediately before the target sequence. After a practice sequence to ensure comprehension, 40 targets were presented. The number of targets correctly detected is recorded as the measure of performance accuracy (maximum score: 40).

Verbal short term and working memory

To assess verbal short term memory and WM a verbal span task from an extensive memory battery was used (Vicari, 2007). The task consists of a list of eight, two-syllable low frequency words. In the first block, the examiner read aloud two words at a rate of one item per second. The participants were required to repeat the two words in the same order. Then, four additional strings of two words were presented. If the child was successful in at least three of the five sequences, a sequence one word longer was presented. If the child failed (less than three correct answers in a block), the task was discontinued. The same procedure was used for sequences of increasing length (up to a maximum of seven words). The score is computed by assigning 0.5 to each sequence of items correctly reproduced by the participant (maximum score: 17.5).

Moreover, a non-word repetition task (Vicari, 2007) was used to assess verbal WM. The number of non-words correctly repeated is recorded as a measure of performance accuracy (maximum score: 40).

Spatial short term and working memory

In the visual-spatial span task (Vicari, 2007), the material consisted of a non-verbalizable geometric shape that appears for 2 s in one of seven possible positions on the computer screen. Then, two empty cells were presented in the same spatial positions as before and the child had to indicate the order in which the stimuli appeared. If the child was successful in at least three of five two-position sequences, a sequence one block longer was presented. Also in this case, the same testing procedure was used for sequences of increasing length (up to a maximum of seven spatial positions). The score was computed by assigning 0.5 to each sequence of items correctly reproduced by the participant (maximum score: 17.5).

Visual short term and working memory

A similar procedure was used for the visual span task (Vicari, 2007). In this case, the experimental material consisted of seven complex geometric figures depicted in high contrast colors. Two figures were presented, one at time, for 2 s at the center of the computer screen. After the disappearance of the second figure, the two figures were presented aligned in the center of the screen in a random position and the participant was asked to indicate the order in which they appeared. Also in this case, if the child was successful in at least three of the five trials, a sequence one figure longer was presented and the task continued until a maximum of seven figures have been presented. The score is computed by assigning 0.5 to each sequence of items correctly reproduced by the participant (maximum score: 17.5).

Visual shifting

The Wisconsin Card Sorting Test (WCST; Heaton et al., 1993) is a neuropsychological test of set shifting and also involves cognitive flexibility function. The WCST consists of four stimulus cards and 128 response cards which differ in color (red, green, blue and yellow), shape (circle, star, cross, and star) and number (one, two, three, and four). The stimulus cards are one red triangle, two green stars, three yellow crosses, and four blue circles.

The child was given the response cards and instructed to place each consecutive card under one of the stimulus cards, according to which he/she considered correct. After each sort, the child was informed whether he/she was correct. The first sorting category was color, and after 10 consecutive correct sorts, the category changed to form, without forewarning, and then accordingly to number. Errors in shifting from one category to another and perseveration errors are registered as scores.

STATISTICAL ANALYSIS

Data were analyzed using the Statistical Program for Windows, Version 8.0 (StatSoft, Inc., Tulsa, OK, USA). Participants' performances were transformed into z-scores. Since the assumptions of normality were not met, comparisons between DD and TR children on EF measures were carried out by means of the Kruskal-Wallis non parametric test with Group as independent between-subjects factor. To correct for multiple comparisons, the level of significance was set at $p = 0.005$ using Bonferroni correction (10 comparisons).

Moreover, multiple regression analyses were computed to explore the linear relationship between EF measures (predictor variables) and reading abilities (criterion variable), using the stepwise method.

RESULTS

DD children obtained significantly lower scores (p always ≤ 0.005) than TR children in phonological and categorical fluency, spoonerism abilities, visual-spatial and auditory attention, verbal and visual short-term memory, and verbal WM. For the level of significance adopted ($p = 0.005$), the comparisons of spatial short-term memory and shifting abilities showed no significant results (see **Table 1**).

To determine predictive relationships between EF measures (predictor variables) and inefficiency reading indexes (criterion variables), multiple regression analyses were computed using the stepwise method. Thus, each EF measure was entered in sequence as predictor variable and its value assessed to determine its contribution to the success of the model; variables that did not significantly contribute were automatically removed.

Overall, the first regression model, which included only spoonerism abilities (speed in seconds), accounted for 49.2% of the variance (R^2 change $= 0.492$) in words reading inefficiency index. The inclusion of auditory attention resulted in an additional 4.2% of the variance being explained (R^2 change $= 0.042$). The addition of visual-spatial attention explained a further 2.8% of the variance (R^2 change $= 0.028$).

Similarly to non-words reading inefficiency, the first regression model included only spoonerism abilities, accounting for 49.2% of the variance (R^2 change $= 0.492$). The inclusion of auditory attention explained an additional 3% of the variance (R^2 change $= 0.03$), and the inclusion of visual-spatial attention accounted for a further 2% of the variance (R^2 change $= 0.02$). **Table 2** summarizes multiple regression analyses for words and non-words reading inefficiency index.

DISCUSSION

This study was aimed at testing simultaneously different EF domains in a group of DD children. Deficits in several aspects of EF such as spoonerism, verbal categorical and phonological fluency, visual-spatial and auditory attention, verbal and visual short-term memory, and verbal WM have been found. However, spatial short-term memory and visual shifting abilities were preserved.

Consistent with previous studies, we observed a deficit in verbal phonological fluency (Goswami, 2000; Snowling, 2000; Ramus, 2003; Ramus et al., 2013) and in verbal categorical fluency (Snowling, 2000; Ramus et al., 2003; Reiter et al., 2005). These tasks engage complex cognitive mechanisms, such as WM, self-monitoring, and flexible thinking (Troyer et al., 1998; Schwartz et al., 2003), and in addition require rapid access to words and strategic search through lexical/phonologic and conceptual/semantic memory (Baldo and Dronkers, 2006). Due to the several cognitive mechanisms involved, a large cortical network is required, including the dorsolateral prefrontal cortex and word associative fronto-temporal regions (Frith et al., 1991; Friston et al., 1991; Cilia et al., 2007; Kalbe et al., 2009).

We also found in children with DD a lower performance in the spoonerism task, which is generally used to assess phonological awareness. However, to interpret this result properly it is necessary to focus on the extra task demands and not only on phonological abilities (Wimmer et al., 2000). The child is first asked to segment the word into two parts, the first phoneme (onset) and

Table 1 | Performances of children with developmental dyslexia (DD) and with typical reading (TR) in executive functions tasks (after back-transformation to original measure units).

Measure	DD Mean (*SD*)	TR Mean (*SD*)	X^2	*p*
Phonological fluency (correct responses)	21 (8.26)	25.97 (6.61)	9.03	0.0027
Categorical fluency (correct responses)	43.40 (8.48)	50.97 (7.35)	19.74	<0.0001
Spoonerism (speed in seconds)	413.55 (162.81)	123.69 (76.60)	91.81	<0.0001
Visual-spatial attention (correct responses)	37.15 (10.43)	43.91 (11.69)	7.81	0.005
Auditory attention (correct responses)	34.05 (5.13)	38.22 (2.15)	17.49	<0.0001
Verbal short-term memory (span score)	3.55 (0.62)	4.08 (0.54)	9.76	0.0018
Visual short-term memory (span score)	3.10 (0.48)	3.68 (0.85)	11.20	0.0008
Spatial short-term memory (span score)	4.80 (0.80)	4.94 (0.79)	7.42	0.0064
Verbal working memory (correct responses)	31 (3.54)	37.18 (1.93)	58.09	<0.0001
Non-verbal shifting (errors)	73.18 (13.78)	75.51 (9.28)	0.01	1.0

Table 2 | Multiple regression analysis predicting words and non-words reading inefficiency (only significant relationships are shown).

	Words				Non-words			
Predictor variable	**β**	***t* for β**	***p***	**Adjusted R^2**	**β**	***t* for β**	***p***	**Adjusted R^2**
Spoonerism (speed in seconds)	−0.55	−7.956	<0.001	0.488	−0.575	−8.122	<0.001	0.488
Auditory attention (correct responses)	−0.204	−3.052	0.003	0.527	−0.171	−2.493	0.014	0.514
Visual-spatial attention (speed in seconds)	−0.181	−2.798	0.006	0.552	−0.152	−2.295	0.023	0.53

the remainder of the word (rime), and temporally store the onset and rime of the first word; the child repeats this segmentation for a second word, and then blends the first onset with the second rime, and the second onset with the first rime. Therefore, the spoonerism task requires blending as well as segmentation skills, but also involves short-term and WM abilities, close monitoring of the phonological manipulation, and inhibitory processes. These complex demands could explain the deficits in tasks such as spoonerism usually found in dyslexic children (Jeffries and Everatt, 2004; Berninger et al., 2008; Kibby and Cohen, 2008; Menghini et al., 2011). It is worth noting that the spoonerism task, which involves all of these functions, has an important predictive role for both global and analytic reading skills.

Moreover, our results concerning attention support the hypothesis that both phonological processing and non-verbal processing are impaired in DD. Indeed, significant differences between DD and TR children were found in auditory and visual-spatial attention domains. Although to a lesser extent, our results support the concept that auditory and visual-spatial attention explains an increased percentage of the variance related to reading disorders. A contribution of attention to reading, independent of the sensory modality considered, is then confirmed. Previous studies generally evaluated visual and auditory attention separately. Concerning visual attention, our results are consistent with reports of difficulties in rapidly focusing visual attention observed in individuals with DD (e.g., Brannan and Williams, 1987) as well as deficits in automatic control of visual attention (Facoetti et al., 2000, 2001, 2003; Hari and Renvall, 2001). Moreover, it was found that visual-spatial attention in preschoolers specifically predicts future reading acquisition (Franceschini et al., 2012), suggesting new approaches for early identification and efficient prevention of DD.

With respect to auditory attention, studies have clearly demonstrated auditory attentional deficits in DD (Asbjornsen and Bryden, 1998; Facoetti et al., 2000; Goswami, 2000; Ramus, 2003; Tallal, 2004; Ramus et al., 2013) which have been interpreted not only as a deficit in speech-sound perception (Cunningham et al., 2001) and in processing rapid sound sequences (Helenius et al., 1999), but also as a problem in shifting and focusing auditory attention (Renvall and Hari, 2002). The few studies assessing DD children on both modalities have documented multimodal (i.e., visual and auditory) attention deficits (Facoetti et al., 2000, 2003; Buchholz and McKone, 2004; Valdois et al., 2004; Dufor et al., 2007).

Furthermore, there is some evidence that in TR a visual dorsal pathway provides a mechanism for the early, preattentive visual analysis of words (Vidyasagar, 1999, 2001; Pammer et al., 2006; Vidyasagar and Pammer, 2010). An adequate parsing of a stream of text into grapheme guides the grapheme-phoneme correspondence and the sensory integration of visual signals. For the proper identification of the graphemes and the subsequent matching of graphemes with phonemes, an attentional mechanism is required. The multimodal integration of visual and auditory inputs mediates the synthesis of orthographic and phonological information (Pammer et al., 2006).

In our group of dyslexic children a general multimodal (verbal and visual) deficit in short-term memory and WM has also been found. The results are at variance with the theory that dyslexic children have an isolated verbal short-term deficit, possibly secondary to a deficit of phonological processing or the expression of a dysfunctional articulatory loop (Poblano et al., 2000; Willcutt et al., 2001; Jeffries and Everatt, 2004; Kibby et al., 2004). By contrast, our results concord with data showing deficits in individuals with DD in the temporary storage of visual-spatial as well as verbal material (Poblano et al., 2000; Brosnan et al., 2002; Helland and Asbjørnsen, 2004; Martinussen and Tannock, 2006; Smith-Spark and Fisk, 2007; Menghini et al., 2011). Our findings on WM can be interpreted as a deficient functioning of CES or SAS (Baddeley and Hitch, 1974; Norman and Shallice, 1986; Shallice and Burgess, 1993; Baddeley, 2000, 2001). Indeed, consistent with the model of WM, the failure of the CES to supervise the activity of both peripheral slave systems could fully account for poor performances in tasks involving different modalities as found in our dyslexic children.

Considering the several processes involved in the EF tasks adopted (e.g., attention, active-inhibition, temporary storage, maintenance, update and integration of information from several domain-specific codes) and their cross-modalities nature, deficits found in our dyslexic children could be the expression of a deficient functioning of CES/SAS. Therefore, we propose that a more global deficit in higher-order cognitive mechanisms might be a crucial feature of DD.

Additional support to this hypothesis is given by our findings which show that some EF tasks, primarily spoonerism but also auditory and visual-spatial attention, are strictly related to reading deficits in DD children. These data could confirm the contribution of the executive attention and domain-general attention control abilities (e.g., CES/SAS) to reading, irrespective of the sensory modality.

However, an additional hypothesis cannot be excluded. During recent years it has been proposed that DD arises from an abnormal auditory sampling (Goswami, 2011). Since cortical oscillations have been implicated in several aspects of human cognition, it has been assumed that the abnormal phonological processing observed in DD reflects a deficit in temporal sampling of speech by neuroelectric oscillation that encodes incoming information at different frequencies (Goswami, 2011). Indeed, temporal coding via the synchronous activity of oscillating networks of neurons at different frequency bands is crucial in the perceptual processing of speech (Luo and Poeppel, 2007). In dyslexics the auditory sampling might be altered, yielding phonemic representations of an unusual temporal format, with specific consequences for phonological processing and phoneme/grapheme associations (Lehongre et al., 2011).

Similarly, studying high-frequency auditory oscillations associated with verbal WM, Lehongre et al. (2011) found that dyslexics exhibited a supranormal entrainment of bilateral planum temporal to fast temporal modulations in the 50–70 Hz range. It has been hypothesized (Lehongre et al., 2011) that in dyslexics too fast low-gamma oscillations might flood the auditory system with overdetailed spectrotemporal information, thereby saturating theta-based auditory buffer capacity and verbal WM. However, the relationship between neuronal oscillations and non-verbal WM correlates is still an open issue in DD.

Finally, the cellular synchronization of oscillatory responses might be responsible for the above mentioned multimodal integration of visual and auditory inputs which mediates the synthesis of orthographic and phonological information (Gray et al., 1989). Indeed, changes in gamma-band signals have been implicated in cognitive integration of stimuli (Pulvermüller et al., 1997; Ward, 2003; Hermann et al., 2004) and alpha-band activity contributes to specific attentional processes such as attentional selection and filter. Moreover, alpha power is larger over visual cortices when attention is focused on the auditory part of a multimodal auditory-visual stimulus (Klimesch, 2012). So, different frequency domains might interact in terms of cross-frequency coupling of oscillations, with cross-modal knock-on effects. One possibility is that atypical cross-frequency coupling in DD might interfere with the attentional mechanism for the multimodal integration of visual and auditory inputs.

In conclusion, our findings support the hypothesis that DD is a multiple neurocognitive deficit and not solely related to a phonological system dysfunction. The relation of brain oscillation to EF networks remains to be explored and could be useful for the further development of current neurophysiological models of DD.

REFERENCES

Abad-Mas, L., Ruiz-Andrés, R., Moreno-Madrid, F., Sirera-Conca, M. A., Cornesse, M., Delgado-Mejía, I. D., et al. (2011). Executive function training in attention deficit hyperactivity disorder. *Rev. Neurol.* 52, 77–83.

Alloway, T. P., and Alloway, R. G. (2013). Working memory in the lifespan: a cross-sectional approach. *J. Cogn. Psychol.* 25, 84–93. doi: 10.1080/20445911.2012.748027

Altemeier, L. E., Abbott, R. D., and Berninger, V. W. (2008). Executive functions for reading and writing in typical literacy development and dyslexia. *J. Clin. Exp. Neuropsychol.* 30, 588–606. doi: 10.1080/13803390701562818

American Psychiatric Association (APA). (2000). *Diagnostic and Statistical Manual of Mental Disorders: Text Revision (DSM-IV-TR).* Washington, DC: American Psychological Association.

Asbjornsen, A. E., and Bryden, M. P. (1998). Auditory attentional shifts in reading-disabled students: quantification of attentional effectiveness by the attentional shift index. *Neuropsychologia* 36, 143–148. doi: 10.1016/S0028-3932(97)00090-0

Bacon, A. M., Parmentier, F. B., and Barr, P. (2013). Visuospatial memory in dyslexia: evidence for strategic deficits. *Memory* 21, 189–209. doi: 10.1080/09658211.2012.718789

Baddeley, A. D. (2000). The episodic buffer: a new component of WM? *Trends Cogn. Sci.* 4, 417–423. doi: 10.1016/S1364-6613(00)01538-2

Baddeley, A. D. (2001). Is working memory still working? *Am. Psychol.* 56, 851–864. doi: 10.1037/0003-066X.56.11.851

Baddeley, A. D., and Hitch, G. (1974). "Working memory," in *The Psychology of Learning and Motivation: Advances in Research and Theory*, ed G. H. Bower (New York, NY: Academic Press), 47–89.

Baddeley, A. D., and Logie, R. H. (1999). "Working memory: the multiple component model," in *Models of Working Memory: Mechanisms of Active Maintenance and Executive Control*, eds A. Miyake and P. Shah (New York, NY: Cambridge University Press), 28–61. doi: 10.1017/CBO9781139174909.005

Baldo, J. V., and Dronkers, N. F. (2006). The role of inferior parietal and inferior frontal cortex in working memory. *Neuropsychology* 20, 529–538. doi: 10.1037/0894-4105.20.5.529

Berninger, V. W., Raskind, W., Richards, T., Abbott, R., and Stock, P. (2008). A multidisciplinary approach to understanding developmental dyslexia within working-memory architecture: genotypes, phenotypes, brain, and instruction. *Dev. Neuropsychol.* 33, 707–744. doi: 10.1080/87565640802418662

Booth, J. N., Boyle, J. M., and Kelly, S. W. (2010). Do tasks make a difference? Accounting for heterogeneity of performance of children with reading difficulties on tasks of executive function: findings from a meta-analysis. *Br. J. Dev. Psychol.* 28, 133–176. doi: 10.1348/026151009X485432

Brannan, J. R., and Williams, M. C. (1987). Allocation of visual attention in good and poor readers. *Percept. Psychophys.* 41, 23–28. doi: 10.3758/BF03208209

Brosnan, M., Demetre, J., Hamill, S., Robson, K., Shepherd, H., and Cody, G. (2002). Executive functioning in adults and children with developmental dyslexia. *Neuropsychologia* 40, 2144–2155. doi: 10.1016/S0028-3932(02)00046-5

Buchholz, J., and McKone, E. (2004). Adults with dyslexia show deficits on spatial frequency doubling and visual attention tasks. *Dyslexia* 10, 24–43. doi: 10.1002/dys.263

Casco, C., and Prunetti, E. (1996). Visual search of good and poor readers: effects with targets having single and combined features. *Percept. Mot. Skills* 82, 1155–1167. doi: 10.2466/pms.1996.82.3c.1155

Cilia, R., Siri, C., Marotta, G., De Gaspari, D., Landi, A., Mariani, C. B., et al. (2007). Brain networks underlining verbal fluency decline during STN-DBS in Parkinson's disease: an ECD-SPECT study. *Parkinsonism Relat. Disord.* 13, 290–294. doi: 10.1016/j.parkreldis.2006.11.011

Cohen, L., Dehaene, S., Naccache, L., Lehericy, S., Dehaene-Lambertz, G., and Henaff, M. A. (2000). The visual word form area: spatial and temporal characterization of an initial stage of reading in normal subjects and posterior split-brain patients. *Brain* 123, 291–307. doi: 10.1093/brain/123.2.291

Condor, A., Anderson, V., and Saling, M. (1995). Do reading disabled children have planning problem? *Dev. Neuropsychol.* 11, 485–502. doi: 10.1080/87565649509540633

Corbett, B. A., Constantine, L. J., Hendren, R., Rocke, D., and Ozonoff, S. (2009). Examining executive functioning in children with autism spectrum disorder, attention deficit hyperactivity disorder and typical development. *Psychiatry Res.* 166, 210–222. doi: 10.1016/j.psychres.2008.02.005

Cornoldi, C., Gardinale, M., Masi, A., and Pettenò, L. (1996), *Impulsività e autocontrollo.* Trento: Erickson.

Costanzo, F., Varuzza, C., Menghini, D., Addona, A., Gianesini, T., and Vicari, S. (2013). Executive functions in intellectual disabilities: a comparison between Williams syndrome and Down syndrome. *Res. Dev. Disabil.* 34, 1770–1780. doi: 10.1016/j.ridd.2013.01.024

Cunningham, J., Nicol, T., Zecker, S. G., Bradlow, A., and Kraus, N. (2001). Neurobiologic responses to speech in noise in children with learning problems: deficits and strategies for improvement. *Clin. Neurophysiol.* 112, 758–767. doi: 10.1016/S1388-2457(01)00465-5

Dufor, O., Serniclaes, W., Sprenger-Charolles, L., and Démonet, J. F. (2007). Top-down processes during auditory phoneme categorization in dyslexia: a PET study. *Neuroimage* 15, 1692–1707. doi: 10.1016/j.neuroimage.2006.10.034

Everatt, J., Warner, J., and Miles, T. R. (1997). The incidence of stroop interference in dyslexia. *Dyslexia* 3, 222–228.

Facoetti, A., Lorusso, M. L., Paganoni, P., Cattaneo, C., Galli, R., and Mascetti, G. G. (2003). The time course of attentional focusing in dyslexic and normally reading children. *Brain Cogn.* 53, 181–184. doi: 10.1016/S0278-2626(03)00105-2

Facoetti, A., Paganoni, P., Turatto, M., Marzola, V., and Mascetti, G. G. (2000). Visual-spatial attention in developmental dyslexia. *Cortex* 36, 109–123. doi: 10.1016/S0010-9452(08)70840-2

Facoetti, A., Turatto, M., Lorusso, M. L., and Mascetti, G. G. (2001). Orienting of visual attention in dyslexia: evidence for asymmetric hemispheric control of attention. *Exp. Brain Res.* 138, 46–53. doi: 10.1007/s002210100700

Franceschini, S., Gori, S., Ruffino, M., Pedrolli, K., and Facoetti, A. (2012). A causal link between visual spatial attention and reading acquisition. *Curr. Biol.* 22, 814–819. doi: 10.1016/j.cub.2012.03.013

Friedman, N. P., Miyake, A., Corley, R. P., Young, S. E., De Fries, J. D., and Hewitt, J. K. (2006). Not all executive functions are related to intelligence. *Psychol. Sci.* 17, 172–179. doi: 10.1111/j.1467-9280.2006.01681.x

Friston, K. J., Frith, C. D., Liddle, P. F., and Frackowiak, R. S. (1991). Investigating a network model of word generation with positron emission tomography. *Proc. Biol. Sci.* 244, 101–106. doi: 10.1098/rspb.1991.0057

Frith, C. D., Friston, K. J., Liddle, P. F., and Frackowiak, R. S. (1991). A PET study of word finding. *Neuropsychologia* 29, 1137–1148. doi: 10.1016/0028-3932(91)90029-8

Gabrieli, J. D. (2009). Dyslexia: a new synergy between education and cognitive neuroscience. *Science* 17, 280–283. doi: 10.1126/science.1171999

Goswami, U. (2000). Phonological representations, reading development and dyslexia: towards a cross-linguistic theoretical framework. *Dyslexia* 6, 133–151. doi: 10.1002/(SICI)1099-0909(200004/06)6:2<133::AID-DYS160>3.0.CO;2-A

Goswami, U. (2011). A temporal sampling framework for developmental dyslexia. *Trends Cogn. Sci.* 15, 3–10. doi: 10.1016/j.tics.2010.10.001

Graves, L. E., Ridgers, N. D., Williams, K., Stratton, G., Atkinson, G., and Cable, N. T. (2010). The physiological cost and enjoyment of Wii Fit in adolescents, young adults, and older adults. *J. Phys. Act. Health* 7, 393–401.

Gray, C. M., König, P., Engel, A. K., and Singer, W. (1989). Oscillatory responses in cat visual cortex exhibit inter-columnar synchronization which reflects global stimulus properties. *Nature* 338, 334–337. doi: 10.1038/338334a0

Green, C. R., Mihic, A. M., Nikkel, S. M., Stade, B. C., Rasmussen, C., Munoz, D. P., et al. (2009). Executive function deficits in children with fetal alcohol spectrum disorders (FASD) measured using the Cambridge Neuropsychological Tests Automated Battery (CANTAB). *J. Child Psychol. Psychiatry* 50, 688–697. doi: 10.1111/j.1469-7610.2008.01990.x

Hari, R., and Renvall, H. (2001). Impaired processing of rapid stimulus sequences in dyslexia. *Trends Cogn. Sci.* 5, 525–532. doi: 10.1016/S1364-6613(00)01801-5

Heaton, R. K., Chelune, G. J., Talley, J. L., Kay, G. G., and Curtis, G. (1993). *Wisconsin Card Sorting Test (WCST) Manual, Revised and Expanded.* Odessa, FL: Psychological Assessment Resources.

Helenius, P., Uutela, K., and Hari, R. (1999). Auditory stream segregation in dyslexic adults. *Brain* 122, 907–913. doi: 10.1093/brain/122.5.907

Helland, T., and Asbjørnsen, A. (2000). Executive functions in dyslexia. *Child Neuropsychol.* 6, 37–48. doi: 10.1076/0929-7049(200003)6:1;1-B;FT037

Helland, T., and Asbjørnsen, A. (2004). Digit span in dyslexia: variations according to language comprehension and mathematics skills. *J. Clin. Exp. Neuropsychol.* 26, 31–42. doi: 10.1076/jcen.26.1.31.23935

Hermann, C., Munk, M., and Engel, A. (2004). Cognitive functions of gamma-band activity: memory match and utilization. *Trends Cogn. Sci.* 8, 347–533. doi: 10.1016/j.tics.2004.06.006

Hill, E. L. (2004). Executive dysfunction in autism. *Trends Cogn. Sci.* 8, 26–32. doi: 10.1016/j.tics.2003.11.003

Hoeft, F., Ueno, T., Reiss, A. L., Meyler, A., Whitfield-Gabrieli, S., Glover, G. H., et al. (2007). Prediction of children's reading skills using behavioral, functional and structural neuroimaging measures. *Neuroscience* 121, 602–613. doi: 10.1037/0735-7044.121.3.602

Jeffries, S., and Everatt, J. (2004).Working memory: its role in dyslexia and other specific learning difficulties. *Dyslexia* 10, 196–214. doi: 10.1002/dys.278

Jobard, G., Crivello, F., and Tzourio-Mazoyer, N. (2003). Evaluation of the dual route theory of reading: a metanalysis of 35 neuroimaging studies. *Neuroimage* 20, 693–712. doi: 10.1016/S1053-8119(03)00343-4

Kalbe, E., Voges, J., Weber, T., Haarer, M., Baudrexel, S., Klein, J. C., et al. (2009). Frontal FDG-PET activity correlates with cognitive outcome after STN-DBS in Parkinson disease. *Neurology* 72, 42–49. doi: 10.1212/01.wnl.0000338536.31388.f0

Kane, M. J., Bleckley, M. K., Conway, A. R., and Engle, R. W. (2001). A controlled-attention view of working-memory capacity. *J. Exp. Psychol. Gen.* 130, 169–183. doi: 10.1037/0096-3445.130.2.169

Kane, M. J., and Engle, R. W. (2002). The role of prefrontal cortex in working-memory capacity, executive attention, and general fluid intelligence: an individual-differences perspective. *Psychon. Bull. Rev.* 9, 637–671. doi: 10.3758/BF03196323

Kenworthy, L. E., Black, D. O., Wallace, G. L., Ahluvalia, T., Wagner, A. E., and Sirian, L. M. (2005). Disorganization: the forgotten executive dysfunction in high-functioning autism (HFA) spectrum disorders. *Dev. Neuropsychol.* 28, 809–827. doi: 10.1207/s15326942dn2803_4

Kibby, M. Y., and Cohen, M. J. (2008). Memory functioning in children with reading disabilities and/or attention deficit/hyperactivity disorder: a clinical investigation of their working memory and long-term memory functioning. *Child Neuropsychol.* 31, 1–22. doi: 10.1080/09297040701821752

Kibby, M. Y., Marks, W., Morgan, S., and Long, C. J. (2004). Specific impairment in developmental reading disabilities: a working memory approach. *J. Learn. Disabil.* 37, 349–363. doi: 10.1177/00222194040370040601

Klimesch, W. (2012). Alpha-band oscillations, attention, and controlled access to stored information. *Trends Cogn. Sci.* 16, 606–617. doi: 10.1016/j.tics.2012.10.007

Laasonen, M., Salomaa, J., Cousineau, D., Leppämäki, S., Tani, P., Hokkanen, L., et al. (2012). Project DyAdd: visual attention in adult dyslexia and ADHD. *Brain Cogn.* 80, 311–327. doi: 10.1016/j.bandc.2012.08.002

Lehongre, K., Ramus, F., Villiermet, N., Schwartz, D., Pressnitzer, D., and Giraud, A. L. (2011). Altered cortical entrainment to fast acoustic modulations reflect phonological and working memory deficit in dyslexia. *Neuron* 72, 1080–1090. doi: 10.1016/j.neuron.2011.11.002

Luo, H., and Poeppel, D. (2007). Phase patterns of neuronal responses reliably discriminate speech in human auditory cortex. *Neuron* 54, 1001–1010. doi: 10.1016/j.neuron.2007.06.004

Manly, T., Anderson, V., Nimmo-Smith, I., Turner, A., Watson, P., and Robertson, I. H. (2001). The differential assessment of Children's attention: the Test of Everyday Attention for Children (TEA-Ch), normal sample and ADHD performance. *J. Child Psychol. Psychiatry* 42, 1065–1081. doi: 10.1111/1469-7610.00806

Marotta, L., Trasciani, M., and Vicari, S. (2008). *Test CMF. Valutazione Delle Competenze Metafonologiche.* Trento: Erickson.

Martinussen, R., and Tannock, R. (2006). Working memory impairments in children with attention-deficit hyperactivity disorder with and without comorbid language learning disorders. *J. Clin. Exp. Neuropsychol.* 28, 1073–1094. doi: 10.1080/13803390500205700

Mati-Zissi, H., and Zafiropoulou, M. (2001). Drawing performance in prediction of special learning difficulties of kindergarten children. *Percept. Mot. Skills* 92, 1154–1166. doi: 10.2466/pms.2001.92.3c.1154

Menghini, D., Finzi, A., Benassi, M., Bolzani, R., Facoetti, A., Giovagnoli, S., et al. (2010). Different underlying neurocognitive deficits in developmental dyslexia: a comparative study. *Neuropsychologia* 48, 863–872. doi: 10.1016/j.neuropsychologia.2009.11.003

Menghini, D., Finzi, A., Carlesimo, G. A., and Vicari S. (2011). Working memory impairment in children with developmental dyslexia: is it just a phonological deficit? *Dev. Neuropsychol.* 36, 199–213. doi: 10.1080/87565641.2010.549868

Norman, W., and Shallice, T. (1986). "Attention to action," in *Consciousness and Self Regulation: Advances in Research and Theory*, eds R. J. Davidson, G. E. Schwartz, and D. Shapiro (New York, NY: Plenum), 1–18. doi: 10.1007/978-1-4757-0629-1_1

Pammer, K., Hansenc, P., Hollidayd, I., and Cornelissenb, P. (2006). Attentional shifting and the role of the dorsal pathway in visual word recognition. *Neuropsychologia* 44, 2926–2936. doi: 10.1016/j.neuropsychologia.2006.06.028

Pani, P., Menghini, D., Napolitano, C., Calcagni, M., Armando, M., Sergeant, J. A., et al. (2013). Proactive and reactive control of movement are differently affected in attention deficit hyperactivity disorder children. *Res. Dev. Disabil.* 34, 3104–3111 doi: 10.1016/j.ridd.2013.06.032

Pei, J., Job, J., Kully-Martens, K., and Rasmussen, C. (2011). Executive function and memory in children with fetal alcohol spectrum disorder. *Child Neuropsychol.* 17, 290–309. doi: 10.1080/09297049.2010.544650

Pennington, B. F. (2006). From single to multiple deficit models of developmental disorders. *Cognition* 101, 385–413. doi: 10.1016/j.cognition.2006.04.008

Pennington, B. F., and Ozonoff, S. (1996). Executive functions and developmental psychopathology. *J. Child Psychol. Psychiatry* 37, 51–87. doi: 10.1111/j.1469-7610.1996.tb01380.x

Poblano, A., Valadéz-Tepec, T., de Lourdes Arias, M., and García-Pedroza, F. (2000). Phonological and visuo-spatial working memory alterations in dyslexic children. *Arch. Med. Res.* 31, 493–496. doi: 10.1016/S0188-4409(00)00096-5

Price, C. J. (2000). The anatomy of language: contributions from functional neuroimaging. *J. Anat.* 197, 335–359. doi: 10.1046/j.1469-7580.2000.19730335.x

Pulvermüller, F., Birbaumer, N., Lutzenberger, W., and Mohr, B. (1997). High-frequency brain activity: its possible role in attention, perception and language processing. *Prog. Neurobiol.* 52, 427–445. doi: 10.1016/S0301-0082(97)00023-3

Ramus, F. (2003). Developmental dyslexia: specific phonological deficit or general sensorimotor dysfunction? *Curr. Opin. Neurobiol.* 13, 212–218. doi: 10.1016/S0959-4388(03)00035-7

Ramus, F., Marshall, C. R., Rosen, S., and van der Lely, H. K. (2013). Phonological deficits in specific language impairment and developmental dyslexia: towards a multidimensional model. *Brain* 136, 630–645. doi: 10.1093/brain/aws356

Ramus, F., Rosen, S., Dakin, S. C., Day, B. L., Castellone, J. M., White, S., et al. (2003). Theories of developmental dyslexia: insights from a multiple case study of dyslexic adults. *Brain* 126, 841–865. doi: 10.1093/brain/awg076

Rasmussen, C. (2005). Executive functioning and working memory in fetal alcohol spectrum disorder. *Alcohol Clin. Exp. Res.* 29, 1359–1367. doi: 10.1097/01.alc.0000175040.91007.d0

Raven, J. C. (1994). *CPM, Coloured Progressive Matrices, Series A, AB, B.* Firenze: Giunti Organizzazioni Speciali. (Italian Adaptation).

Re, A. M., and Cornoldi, C. (2009). Two new rating scales for assessment of ADHD symptoms in Italian preschool children. *J. Atten. Disord.* 12, 532–539. doi: 10.1177/1087054708323001

Reiter, A., Tucha, O., and Lange, K. W. (2005). Executive functions in children with dyslexia. *Dyslexia* 10, 1–16. doi: 10.1002/dys.289

Renvall, H., and Hari, R. (2002). Auditory cortical responses to speech-like stimuli in dyslexic adults. *J. Cogn. Neurosci.* 14, 757–768. doi: 10.1162/08989290260138654

Rinehart, N. J., Bradshaw, J. L., Moss, S. A., Brereton, A. V., and Tonge, B. J. (2001). A deficit in shifting attention present in high-functioning autism but not Asperger's disorder. *Autism* 5, 67–80. doi: 10.1177/1362361301005001007

Robinson, S., Goddard, L., Dritschel, B., Wisley, M., and Howlin, P. (2009). Executive functions in children with autism spectrum disorders. *Brain Cogn.* 71, 362–368. doi: 10.1016/j.bandc.2009.06.007

Sartori, G., Job, R., and Tressoldi, P. E. (1995). *Batteria per la Valutazione Della Dislessia e Della Disortografia Evolutiva.* Firenze: Giunti Organizzazioni Speciali.

Schwartz, S., Baldo, J., Graves, R. E., and Brugger, P. (2003). Pervasive influence of semantics in letter and category fluency: a multidimensional approach. *Brain Lang.* 87, 400–411. doi: 10.1016/S0093-934X(03)00141-X

Sergeant, J. A., Geurts, H., and Oosterlaan, J. (2002). How specific is a deficit of executive functioning for attention-deficit/hyperactivity disorder? *Behav. Brain Res.* 130, 3–28. doi: 10.1016/S0166-4328(01)00430-2

Shallice, T., and Burgess, P. W. (1993). "Supervisory control of action and thought selection," in *Attention: Selection, Awareness and Control*, eds A. D. Baddeley and L. Weiskrantz (Oxford: Clarendon Press), 171–187.

Shaywitz, S. E., Morris, R., and Shaywitz, B. A. (2008). The education of dyslexic children from childhood to young adulthood. *Annu. Rev. Psychol.* 59, 451–475. doi: 10.1146/annurev.psych.59.103006.093633

Smith-Spark, J. H., and Fisk, J. E. (2007). Working memory functioning in developmental dyslexia. *Memory* 15, 34–56. doi: 10.1080/09658210601043384

Smith Spark, J., H., Fisk, J., Fawcett, A. J., and Nicolson, R. I. (2003). Investigating the central executive in adult dyslexics: evidence from phonological and visuospatial working memory performance. *Eur. J. Cogn. Psychol.* 15, 567–587. doi: 10.1080/09541440340000024

Snowling, M. J. (2000). *Dyslexia: a Cognitive-Developmental Perspective.* Oxford: Blackwell.

Swanson, H. L., Howard, C. B., and Sáez, L. (2006). Do different components of working memory underlie different subgroups of reading disabilities? *J. Learn. Disabil.* 39, 252–269. doi: 10.1177/00222194060390030501

Swanson, H. L., Kehler, P., and Jerman, O. (2010). Working memory, strategy knowledge, and strategy instruction in children with reading disabilities. *J. Learn. Disabil.* 43, 24–47. doi: 10.1177/0022219409338743

Swanson, H. L., Zheng, X., and Jerman, O. (2009). Working memory, short-term memory, and reading disabilities: a selective meta-analysis of the literature. *J. Learn. Disabil.* 42, 260–287. doi: 10.1177/0022219409331958

Tallal, P. (2004). Improving language and literacy is a matter of time. *Nat. Rev. Neurosci.* 5, 721–728. doi: 10.1038/nrn1499

Troyer, A. K., Moscovitch, M., Winocur, G., Alexander, M. P., and Stuss, D. (1998). Clustering and switching on verbal fluency: the effects of focal frontal- and temporal-lobe lesions. *Neuropsychologia* 36, 499–504. doi: 10.1016/S0028-3932(97)00152-8

Valdois, S., Bosse, M. L., and Tainturier, M. J. (2004). The cognitive deficits responsible for developmental dyslexia: review of evidence for a selective visual attentional disorder. *Dyslexia* 10, 339–363. doi: 10.1002/dys.284

Vicari, S. (2007). *PROMEA. Prove di Memoria e Apprendimento per l'Eta Evolutiva. Una Batteria Globale di Valutazione Della Memoria per Bambini dai 5 agli 11 anni.* Firenze: Giunti Organizzazioni Speciali.

Vidyasagar, T. R. (1999). A neuronal model of attentional spotlight: parietal guiding the temporal. *Brain Res. Rev.* 30, 66–76. doi: 10.1016/S0165-0173(99)00005-3

Vidyasagar, T. R. (2001). From attentional gating in macaque primary visual cortex to dyslexia in humans. *Progr. Brain Res.* 134, 297–312. doi: 10.1016/S0079-6123(01)34020-7

Vidyasagar, T. R., and Pammer, K. (2010) Dyslexia: a deficit in visuospatial attention, not in phonological processing. *Trends Cogn. Sci.* 14, 57–63. doi: 10.1016/j.tics.2009.12.003

Vinckier, F., Dehaene, S., Jobert, A., Dubus, J. P., Sigman, M., and Cohen, L. (2007). Hierarchical coding of letter strings in the ventral stream: dissecting the inner organization of the visual word-form system. *Neuron* 55, 143–156. doi: 10.1016/j.neuron.2007.05.031

Ward, L. (2003). Synchronous neural oscillations and cognitive processes. *Trends Cogn. Sci.* 7, 553–559. doi: 10.1016/j.tics.2003.10.012

Welsh, M. C., Pennington, B. F., and Groisserc, D. B. (1991). A normative-developmental study of executive function: a window on prefrontal function in children. *Dev. Neuropsychol.* 7, 131–149. doi: 10.1080/87565649109540483

Willcutt, E. G., Pennington, B. F., Boada, R., Ogline, J. S., Tunick, R. A., Chhabildas, N. A., et al. (2001). A comparison of the cognitive deficits in reading disability and attention-deficit/hyperactivity disorder. *J. Abnorm. Psychol.* 110, 157–172. doi: 10.1037/0021-843X.110.1.157

Willcutt, E. G., Pennington, B. F., Olson, R. K., Chhabildas, N., and Hulslander, J. (2005). Neuropsychological analyses of comorbidity between reading disability and attention deficit hyperactivity disorder: in search of the common deficit. *Dev. Neuropsychol.* 27, 35–78. doi: 10.1207/s15326942dn2701_3

Wimmer, H., Mayringer, H., and Landerl, K. (2000). The double-deficit hypothesis and difficulties in learning to read a regular orthography. *J. Educ. Psychol.* 92, 668–680. doi: 10.1037/0022-0663.92.4.668

3

The intergenerational multiple deficit model and the case of dyslexia

Elsje van Bergen[1]*, Aryan van der Leij[2] and Peter F. de Jong[2]

[1] Department of Experimental Psychology, University of Oxford, Oxford, UK
[2] Research Institute of Child Development and Education, University of Amsterdam, Amsterdam, Netherlands

Correspondence:
Elsje van Bergen, Department of Experimental Psychology, University of Oxford, 9 South Parks Road, Oxford OX1 3UD, UK
e-mail: elsje.vanbergen@psy.ox.ac.uk

Which children go on to develop dyslexia? Since dyslexia has a multifactorial etiology, this question can be restated as: what are the factors that put children at high risk for developing dyslexia? It is argued that a useful theoretical framework to address this question is Pennington's (2006) multiple deficit model (MDM). This model replaces models that attribute dyslexia to a single underlying cause. Subsequently, the generalist genes hypothesis for learning (dis)abilities (Plomin and Kovas, 2005) is described and integrated with the MDM. Next, findings are presented from a longitudinal study with children at family risk for dyslexia. Such studies can contribute to testing and specifying the MDM. In this study, risk factors at both the child and family level were investigated. This led to the proposed intergenerational MDM, in which both parents confer liability via intertwined genetic and environmental pathways. Future scientific directions are discussed to investigate parent-offspring resemblance and transmission patterns, which will shed new light on disorder etiology.

Keywords: intergenerational multiple deficit model, generalist genes hypothesis, dyslexia, comorbidity, family risk, developmental disorders, intergenerational transmission

PROBLEMS FOR SINGLE DEFICIT ACCOUNTS OF DYSLEXIA

Research into dyslexia has been dominated by the quest for the Holy Grail: the single cognitive deficit that is necessary and sufficient to cause all behavioural characteristics of the disorder. The dominant hypothesis of this kind has been the phonological-deficit hypothesis (e.g., Wagner, 1986; Snowling, 1995). However, a single cognitive deficit model of dyslexia, as single deficit models of developmental disorders in general (see Pennington, 2006, for a comprehensive overview), has a number of shortcomings. First, there is no single cognitive deficit found that can explain all behavioural symptoms of all cases with dyslexia (e.g., Ramus and Ahissar, 2012). For example, not all individuals with dyslexia show a phonological deficit (e.g., Valdois et al., 2011; Pennington et al., 2012). Conversely, not all individuals with a phonological deficit have dyslexia (e.g., Snowling, 2008; van der Leij et al., under review). This questions a one-to-one mapping and points to the possibility that various constellations of underlying cognitive deficits can lead to the behavioural symptoms of dyslexia.

In addition, a single deficit model cannot readily explain the phenomenon of comorbidity. For instance, dyslexia co-occurs more often than expected by chance with other developmental disorders, including dyscalculia, specific language impairment (SLI), speech-sound disorder, and attention-deficit/hyperactivity disorder (ADHD). To illustrate this point, suppose disorder A and B each have a prevalence of 5% in the general population. If disorder A and B were independent, then 5% of the cases with A would also have B. However, comorbidity rates for developmental disorders are commonly in the order of 30%, for example between dyslexia and speech-sound disorder or dyslexia and ADHD (Pennington, 2006). The huge discrepancy between these figures (5 vs. 30%) implies that developmental disorders are not independent.

The single deficit model requires for each comorbidity (pair of disorders) a distinct account. Pennington (2006) discusses as an example the comorbidity between dyslexia and speech-sound disorder. Speech-sound disorder is defined by difficulties in the development of spoken language, especially problems with the intelligible production of speech sounds. Approximately 30% of children with early language or speech problems go on to develop dyslexia. A parsimonious single deficit model to explain this comorbidity is the severity hypothesis. The severity hypothesis states that speech-sound disorder and dyslexia have the same underlying phonological deficit, with speech-sound disorder being an earlier developmental manifestation of this deficit than dyslexia. Comorbid cases will have the most severe phonological deficit. If the phonological deficit is less severe, speech-sound disorder will not reach clinical boundaries but dyslexia will. To account for cases with early speech-sound disorder but without later dyslexia, the model must pose a subtype of speech-sound disorders that is caused by a phonological deficit distinct from the phonological deficit as seen in cases with dyslexia. Alternatively, the phonological deficit in such cases must be resolved by the time they come to the task of learning to read. However, Snowling et al. (2000) followed a group of former language-impaired children into adolescence. Those with early speech-sound disorder (isolated phonological impairments at 4 years of age) had normal reading skills at age 15, but continued to show phonological deficits. Similar results were obtained by Peterson et al. (2009). In their study many children with early speech-sound disorder went on to learn to read normally despite a lasting phonological deficit. Thus, in both studies the children with early speech-sound disorder had a phonological deficit similar to children with dyslexia. This conclusion is inconsistent with the single cognitive deficit severity hypothesis.

While research at the cognitive level of explanation was still searching for a single deficit, studies at the genetic level converged on the conclusion that the aetiology of dyslexia, as of other developmental disorders, is genetically complex (Pennington, 2006). So instead of a single gene determining dyslexia, many genes act probabilistically (i.e., polygenicity), each having only a small contributory effect to the etiology of dyslexia (Bishop, 2009). Moreover, behavioural genetic studies have shown for certain developmental disorders that the relation between two traits (like reading ability and inattention) is larger in monozygotic (MZ) twin pairs than in dizygotic (DZ) twin pairs (Willcutt et al., 2000). Such a bivariate heritability supports genetic overlap between the conditions, in this example between dyslexia and ADHD. The partly shared etiology of dyslexia and ADHD does not yet rule out the possibility of a distinct single cognitive deficit for each disorder. However, studies have demonstrated that a processing speed impairment is not only a characteristic of dyslexia, but also of ADHD (e.g., Willcutt et al., 2005), suggesting that processing speed is a shared cognitive risk factor (McGrath et al., 2011). The accumulating evidence for etiological and cognitive overlap between dyslexia and ADHD speaks against a single deficit model for explaining their frequent co-occurrence. Also for other dyslexia comorbidities, shared cognitive deficits are found, for example a phonological deficit in SLI (e.g., Bishop et al., 2009) and a processing-speed deficit in dyscalculia (e.g., van der Sluis et al., 2004).

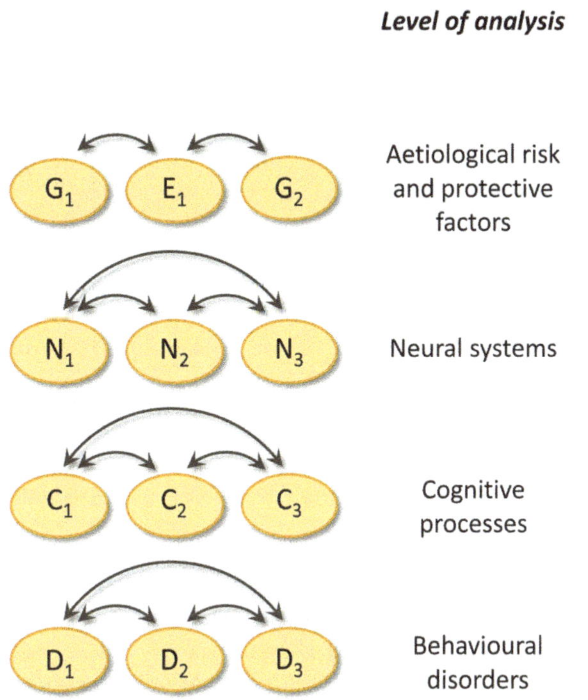

FIGURE 1 | Pennington's multiple deficit model. Double headed arrows indicate interactions. Causal connections between levels of analysis are omitted. G = genetic risk or protective factor, E = environmental risk or protective factor, N = neural system, C = cognitive process, D = complex behavioural disorder.

THE MULTIPLE DEFICIT MODEL

It seems that single deficit models are untenable and must give way to multiple cognitive deficit models for understanding developmental disorders. The multiple cognitive deficit model proposed by Pennington (2006) is depicted schematically in **Figure 1**. In his model, multiple genetic and environmental risk factors operate probabilistically by increasing the liability to a disorder; conversely, protective factors decrease the liability. These etiological factors produce the behavioural symptoms of developmental disorders by influencing the development of relevant neural systems and cognitive processes. Importantly, there is no single etiological or cognitive factor that is sufficient to cause a disorder. Instead, multiple cognitive deficits (each due to multiple etiological factors) need to be present to produce a disorder at the behavioural level. Some of the etiological and cognitive risk factors are shared with other disorders. As a result, comorbidity among developmental disorders is to be expected, rather than something that requires additional explanations. Finally, from Pennington's the multiple deficit model (MDM) it follows that "the liability distribution for a given disease is often continuous and quantitative, rather than being discrete and categorical" (Pennington, 2006, p. 404). Therefore, the threshold between affected and unaffected is rather arbitrary.

Note that there are other models out there to explain the co-occurrence of neurodevelopmental disorders or the covariance of their associated continuous traits. For instance, Pennington et al. (2005) and Pennington (2006) set out several models differing not only on the dimension of a shared or distinct cognitive deficit, but also of a shared or distinct etiology. The severity model discussed in the first section is among them; others are pleiotropy, cognitive phenocopy, synergy, and assortment. Disconfirmatory data for each of the models is given, leading to the proposed MDM.

Pennington (2006) concludes his paper by remarking that – in contrast to single deficit models – it remains challenging to test the multiple cognitive deficit model. The model is much more complex than single deficit models, which are attractively parsimonious, but this complexity is needed to account for the observations at the different levels of analysis. The model is universally applicable to developmental disorders, but therefore remains abstract. It is not specified which etiological factors, neural systems, and cognitive processes interact to produce a given disorder.

TESTING THE MDM

We argue here that a line of inquiry that can contribute to testing and specifying the MDM are family risk studies. In family risk studies, children are followed who are at risk of dyslexia by virtue of having an immediate dyslexic family member (usually a parent). Such studies have shown that 34–66% of them develop dyslexia (Scarborough, 1990; Elbro et al., 1998; Pennington and Lefly, 2001; Snowling et al., 2003; Torppa et al., 2010), depending on the stringency of the dyslexia criteria. The much higher prevalence of dyslexia among offspring of parents with dyslexia is consistent with twin studies showing moderate to strong heritability of dyslexia (e.g., Olson et al., 2014c).

From the MDM it follows that children at family risk experience at least some of the etiological risk factors: they inherit genetic risk factors and might experience a less rich literacy environment. Hence, it is hypothesized that at-risk children have a higher genetic and environmental liability than children without a family history of dyslexia (labeled control children). Furthermore, the at-risk children who go on to develop dyslexia are expected to show cognitive deficits (to varying degrees) in several processes. Some of these cognitive processes are expected to be affected even before the onset of reading instruction, as a consequence of etiological risk factors and deficient neural systems.

A key prediction of the MDM for family risk studies concerns the at-risk children who do not develop dyslexia. If liability to dyslexia were discrete (as would happen if only one factor, say a gene, were involved), at-risk non-dyslexic children would not differ from controls. However, according to the MDM, liability is continuously distributed. This also follows from the fact that reading ability is influenced by many genes of small effect, producing normal distributions of phenotypes (Plomin et al., 2008, p. 33). Consequently, the MDM predicts that at-risk children without dyslexia also inherit at least some disadvantageous gene variants from their dyslexic parents, giving them a higher liability than control children, although still lower than at-risk dyslexic children. At the behavioural and cognitive level this should translate into mild deficits in literacy skills and some of its cognitive underpinnings. When plotting mean performances of the three groups, a step-wise pattern (i.e., at-risk dyslexic < at-risk non-dyslexic < controls) would support a continuum of liability, one of the characteristics of the MDM.

Comparing the three groups of children on behavioural measures sheds light on cognitive deficiencies and behavioural symptoms, the bottom two levels in **Figure 1**. These three groups have also been compared on neural processing of visual and auditory stimuli (e.g., Regtvoort et al., 2006; Leppänen et al., 2010; Plakas et al., 2013), the second level of the MDM. Some family risk studies (e.g., Snowling et al., 2007; Torppa et al., 2007; van Bergen et al., 2011) have also examined aspects of the home environment, which belong to the etiological level. However, specific genetic risk factors remain hidden in family risk studies. As genetic screening of children for their dyslexia susceptibility is still far away, we propose an indicator of their genetic risk. Since reading ability is moderately to highly heritable and children receive their genetic material from their parents, we argue that cognitive abilities of parents can partly reveal their offspring's liability. One, but maybe even both parents of at-risk children will have weaker reading skills than those of control children, reflecting selection criteria in family risk studies. However, the key issue is whether the reading skills of parents of at-risk children *with* dyslexia differ from the reading skills of parents of children *without* dyslexia. Based on the MDM it is expected that at-risk children who develop dyslexia have inherited more genetic risk variants than at-risk children without dyslexia and that this difference can be revealed by lower reading performance of parents of the at-risk dyslexic children. In Section "Parents' literacy skills" we will elaborate upon parental effects.

Finally, the MDM predicts that some of the cognitive processes related to dyslexia are specific to dyslexia (or reading ability in general) and others are shared with comorbid neurodevelopmental disorders (and their accompanying continuous phenotype). In the following two paragraphs we will pursue the specificity matter, after which we return to the predictions for a family risk study laid out above.

THE GENERALIST GENES HYPOTHESIS

One of the aims of dyslexia research is to identify cognitive processes playing a role in the developmental pathways that lead to dyslexia. The MDM states that some cognitive deficits are shared among disorders. This raises the question of *which* cognitive precursors of dyslexia are distinct and which are shared with other disorders. With regard to learning abilities, like reading ability, there is a hypothesis that addresses this specificity issue: the generalist genes hypothesis (Plomin and Kovas, 2005; Kovas and Plomin, 2007).

The generalist genes hypothesis states that the same set of genes is largely responsible for individual differences in learning abilities (i.e., pleiotropy). It stems from behavioural genetic studies employing the twin design. The twin design is the major method to quantify genetic and environmental influences on a trait. If for a certain trait MZ twins are more similar than DZ twins, genetic factors must play a role. If there is no difference in resemblance heritability is negligible. Estimates for the heritability of reading ability are in the range of 0.47–0.84 (Taylor et al., 2010; Byrne et al., 2009, respectively).

As a side note, it should be borne in mind that the high heritability of reading performance does not imply at all that educational improvements are pointless. Instead, they positively impact on almost all children's reading achievement and raise the *average* of standardized scores of a class receiving effective reading intervention. Nonetheless, it is likely that individual *differences* among children remain largely genetically driven (Olson et al., 2009). This suggests that children with a genetic constraint on their reading development need increased reading instruction (as investigated by Zijlstra et al., under review).

Recently, the field of behavioural genetics has moved beyond quantifying genetic and environmental influences on a trait to studying genetic and environmental overlap between traits. For the three learning abilities reading, arithmetic, and language, empirical data have shown that the genes important for one learning ability largely overlap with the genes important for the other learning abilities. The genetic correlation is the measure that quantifies this: it indexes the extent to which genetic influences on one trait overlap with the genetic influences on another trait (independently of the heritability of the traits). The genetic correlation between learning abilities is about 0.70 (Plomin and Kovas, 2005; Kovas and Plomin, 2007). This suggests that roughly 70% of the genes associated with reading ability are generalists: they also influence other learning abilities. Hence Plomin and Kovas (2005) named their hypothesis the "generalist genes hypothesis." As genetic correlations are not 1.0, there are also specialist genes: genes that contribute to dissociations among learning abilities.

Observed differences in learning abilities among individuals are also partly due to differences between the environments in which individuals were born, were brought up and live. Behavioural genetics subdivides environmental influences into those that make family members similar (called shared environmental effects) and those that do not contribute to resemblance among family members (called non-shared environmental effects). Also for these environmental components statistics exist analogous to genetic correlation. Shared environmental correlations among learning abilities are as high as genetic correlations, so shared environmental effects are also largely general effects (Kovas and Plomin, 2007). In contrast, non-shared environmental correlations are low. This indicates that these effects primarily act as specialists, contributing to performance differences in learning abilities within a child (Kovas and Plomin, 2007).

THE HYBRID MODEL

The generalist genes hypothesis and the multiple cognitive deficit model complement each other well. The MDM is more general because it holds for all common developmental disorders, while the generalist genes hypothesis specifically pertains to learning abilities and disabilities. Furthermore, the MDM includes four levels of explanation, whereas the generalist genes hypothesis only explicitly models the etiological level. Although the MDM also comprises polygenicity and pleiotropy, the generalist genes hypothesis *quantifies* for learning abilities the degree of overlapping and unique influences in each of the three etiological components (genetical, shared environmental, and non-shared environmental influences). We have visualized the generalist genes hypothesis and incorporated it into the MDM, yielding the hybrid model depicted in **Figure 2.** In this model only the first and the fourth layer are further specified because the generalist genes hypothesis only deals with these two levels. The etiological factors of the first level influence the behavioural manifestations at the fourth level by acting through the second and third level.

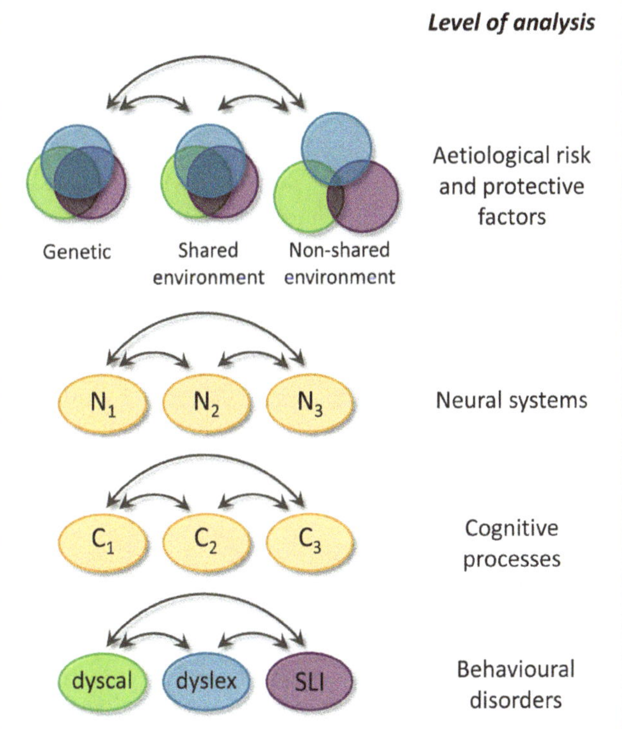

FIGURE 2 | Hybrid model for learning (dis)abilities, incorporating the generalist genes hypothesis (Kovas and Plomin, 2007) and the multiple deficit model (Pennington, 2006). Overlap at the aetiological level is graphically presented as Venn diagrams for each of the three sources of biometric variation. Double headed arrows indicate interactions. Causal connections between levels of analyses are omitted, N = neural system, C = cognitive process, dyscal = dyscalculia, dyslex = dyslexia, SLI = specific language impairment.

The hybrid model quantifies the overlap in etiological factors between learning abilities: genetic and shared environmental effects are largely shared by the three learning domains, whereas the non-shared environmental effects are largely distinct. These differential overlaps are visualized in the hybrid model as the degree of overlap between the circles. Despite this quantification of etiological overlap, the hybrid model does not specify, which etiological factors are relevant. Regarding genetic factors, molecular genetic studies will ultimately inform us which genes are implicated in dyslexia. Knowledge of specific genes contributing to dyslexia susceptibility promises to help bridge the gap from genes to neural systems, cognitive processes, and behavioural outcomes (Fisher and Francks, 2006).

Insight into which specific neural systems, cognitive skills, and behavioural symptoms are implicated in dyslexia can be gained from family risk studies. The hybrid model points to the opportunity to study reading in combination with arithmetic or language to increase insight into shared and distinct factors. We chose to focus on reading and arithmetic, both basic school skills are central during early primary school. As the model suggests, its disorders, dyslexia, and dyscalculia, indeed often co-occur (Landerl and Moll, 2010). Moreover, this pair of comorbidity is under-researched compared to the comorbidity of dyslexia with ADHD or language disorders. We aimed to study the comorbidity issue at the cognitive level of explanation. We investigated whether known precursors of reading are specific for reading or are shared between the development of reading and arithmetic.

FINDINGS FROM A FAMILY-RISK STUDY

As argued above, a study with children with and without a family history of dyslexia is valuable in relation to the MDM (or hybrid model), because specific testable hypotheses follow from the model. To reiterate, the following four hypotheses followed from Section "Testing the MDM":

1. Group comparisons on children's reading and reading related skills show a step-wise pattern (i.e., at-risk dyslexic < at-risk non-dyslexic < controls).
2. At-risk children with dyslexia exhibit more than one deficit.
3. Some deficits are reading specific and others are shared with e.g. arithmetic (dis)ability.
4. Group comparisons on parents' reading and reading related skills show a step-wise pattern.

The first three hypotheses pertain to the children, whereas the fourth hypothesis concerns the parents.

As an illustrative example we will present a family risk study that speaks to all four hypotheses. The family risk study is part of the Dutch Dyslexia Programme, abbreviated DDP (for an overview, see van der Leij et al., 2013). The study employs a prospective design, in which the progress of children ($N = 212$) at high and low family risk is followed. Children were considered at high family risk if (at least) one of their parents and another family member had dyslexia. After two and subsequently 3 years of reading instruction they were categorized as either dyslexic or non-dyslexic (below or above the 10th percentile cut-off on word-reading fluency, respectively). Subsequently, they were compared concurrently and retrospectively with each other and with typically developing children without such a family background. In the present paper, we will focus on the findings regarding reading and reading related (cognitive precursors and correlates of dyslexia) in parents and children (van Bergen et al., 2012, van Bergen et al., 2014a,b). We investigated the cognitive profile characteristic of the three groups of children and the impact of the cognitive profile of parents and the literacy environment parents create on children's reading outcome. An overview of the findings is given in **Table 1**.

CHILDREN'S (PRE)LITERACY SKILLS

The MDM predicts that normal reading children with a family risk do slightly poorer on reading and spelling than normal reading children without such risk. In addition, they are assumed to perform more poorly on reading related skills as there is evidence that these underlying cognitive processes of reading are also complex traits, influenced by multiple genetic and environmental factors (Petrill et al., 2006; Naples et al., 2009). Whether such a step-wise pattern was observed is indicated in the last two columns of **Table 1**.

At the end of Grade 2, the at-risk children with dyslexia were severely impaired compared to control children on all measures of accuracy and fluency of (pseudo)word reading (van Bergen et al., 2012; **Table 1**). In addition, they made many errors in spelling words. Although the at-risk group without dyslexia had literacy skills within the normal range for their age they read significantly less accurately and fluently than controls on all of these reading measures. The same step pattern was found for spelling. Thus, the MDM-based hypothesis about the at-risk no-dyslexia group taking up an intermediate position between the other two was confirmed.

Importantly, we also found a stepwise pattern in the frequency of the comorbid disorder of dyscalculia (van Bergen et al., 2014ca). Of the dyslexic children, 42% of the children performed below the 10th percentile on a calculation fluency test. In the FR-nondyslexic group this was 20%, which was significantly above the 8% in the group of control children. Such a stepwise pattern is to expected as, according to the MDM, comorbidity is due to shared risk factors of both disorders and, consequently, a familiar risk for one disorder also leads to an elevated risk for the other disorder.

With regard to the reading related skills, we included the most important precursors and correlates of dyslexia: phonological awareness (i.e., the blending and segmentation of speech sounds), rapid naming of familiar items (i.e., colors and digits) and letter knowledge. Letter knowledge was assessed at the end of kindergarten (age 5 or 6), before the start of reading instruction. The at-risk dyslexic group lagged behind on letter knowledge, whereas the at-risk children without later dyslexia showed a normal level of knowledge. The absence of a stepwise pattern is not in accordance with the MDM model. However, it could be argued that letter knowledge should be regarded as belonging to the symptom level, being a forerunner or autoregressor of reading.

Phonological awareness and rapid naming were assessed at the end of kindergarten (age 5 or 6) and at the end of Grade 2. On both occasions the findings were similar. The at-risk children without later dyslexia showed normal rapid naming, but performed below controls on phonological awareness. The at-risk dyslexic group was impaired on both skills as compared to the other two groups. Note that because the cognitive deficiencies in the dyslexic group were already in place in kindergarten, before the start of reading instruction, they are due to etiological factors rather than being the consequence of poor reading and less print exposure.

Apparently, phonological awareness is associated with both reading and risk status, while rapid naming is only related to reading status. The fact that rapid naming does not fit the MDM prediction in the DDP and in the family risk study of Moll et al. (2013) calls for an explanation. One possibility is that the at-risk children who go on to develop normal reading skills might do well despite their family risk because the efficiency of the processes that rapid naming tap might protect them against dysfluent reading. Their mild literacy problems could be due to their mild phonological awareness deficit. Another possibility is that, in contrast to the protective explanation, rapid naming is not a protective or risk factor, nor causally implicated, but an integral part of the reading system (see Section "The Intergenerational Multiple Deficit Model" for more on the reading system). On this view, Norton and Wolf (2012) conceptualize rapid naming as "a microcosm or mini-circuit of the later-developing reading circuitry" (p. 430).

We also examined the relation between more general abilities, verbal and nonverbal IQ, around the age of four, and reading outcome at the end of Grade 2 (see van Bergen et al., 2014cb). It was found that at-risk children who go on to become dyslexic were impaired relative to controls on both verbal and nonverbal IQ, with the gap being larger for verbal IQ. The at-risk children who do not become dyslexic showed good nonverbal abilities, but their verbal IQ was slightly but significantly lower than that of controls. For a discussion about the nature of the link between early IQ and subsequent reading the interested reader is referred to van Bergen et al. (2014b).

In the MDM comorbidity is explained by shared risk factors. To pursue this issue, it was examined whether children's skills before the onset of reading instruction were specifically related to reading. It appeared that nonverbal IQ was equally strongly related to later reading achievement (e.g., word-reading fluency) as to later arithmetic achievement (e.g., arithmetic fluency), while verbal IQ was specifically predictive of reading. With respect to the preliteracy skills, all were shown to be predictive of later arithmetic achievement as well. Rapid naming was equally strongly related to reading and arithmetic, but phonological awareness and letter knowledge were more specific precursors of reading (van Bergen et al. (2014a). Thus, some of the cognitive processes of importance to reading are also important for arithmetic, whereas others are distinct to reading. This is in line with the MDM (Pennington, 2006), the generalist genes hypothesis (Plomin and Kovas, 2005; Kovas and Plomin, 2007) and hence also with the hybrid model (**Figure 2**). Nonverbal IQ and rapid naming are shared and

Table 1 | Overview of the behavioural and cognitive findings from the DDP family risk study.

			Findings					
			Longitudinal predictor of reading[a]		Longitudinal predictor of arithmetic[a]			
Who	**When**	**Variable**	**On its own**	**After controlling for arithmetic**	**On its own**	**After controlling for reading**	**Group differences[b]**	**Support for MDM?**
Child	Age 4 - not yet in school	Nonverbal IQ[c]	✓	×	✓	×	FRD < FRND = C	×
		Verbal IQ[c]	✓	✓	✓	×	FRD < FRND < C	✓
	End kindergarten (age 5–6)	Rapid naming[d]	✓	✓	✓	✓	FRD < FRND = C	×
		Phonological awareness[d]	✓	×	✓	×	FRD < FRND < C	✓
		Letter knowledge[d]	✓	✓	✓	×	FRD < FRND = C	×
	End Grade 2 (age 8)	Rapid naming[e]	–	–	–	–	FRD < FRND = C	×
		Phonological awareness[e]	–	–	–	–	FRD < FRND < C	✓
		Word-reading accuracy[e]	–	–	–	–	FRD < FRND < C	✓
		Word-reading fluency[e]	–	–	–	–	FRD < FRND < C	✓
		Pseudoword-reading fluency[e]	–	–	–	–	FRD < FRND < C	✓
		Spelling[e]	–	–	–	–	FRD < FRND < C	✓
Dyslexic parent		Rapid naming[e]	–	–	–	–	FRD < FRND (< C)	✓
		Nonword repetition[e]	–	–	–	–	FRD = FRND (< C)	×
		Word-reading fluency[e]	–	–	–	–	FRD < FRND (< C)	✓
		Pseudoword-reading fluency[e]	–	–	–	–	FRD = FRND (< C)	×
		Spelling[e]	–	–	–	–	FRD = FRND (< C)	×
		Self-reported literacy difficulties[d]	–	–	–	–	FRD = FRND (< C)	×
Non-dyslexic parent		Self-reported literacy difficulties[d]	–	–	–	–	FRD < FRND (= C)	✓

[a] *Reading = word-reading fluency, arithmetic = arithmetic fluency.*
[b] *Dyslexia status was assessed using word-reading fluency at the end of Grade 2 or halfway Grade 3. Regarding the parents of the control children, the best-reading parent features in the non-dyslexic parent comparison, and the other in the dyslexic-parent comparisons.*
[c] *Reported in van Bergen et al. (2014b).*
[d] *Reported in van Bergen et al. (2014a).*
[e] *Reported in van Bergen et al. (2012).*
FRD = familial-risk dyslexia, FRND = familial-risk no-dyslexia, C = control, MDM = multiple deficit model.

therefore contribute to the correlation between arithmetic and reading. Likewise, at the lower end of the distribution, they contribute to the comorbidity between dyscalculia and dyslexia. Verbal IQ, phonological awareness, and letter knowledge were found to be skill-specific cognitive processes, contributing to the dissociation between arithmetic and reading. Rapid naming is an interesting case, as part of what it taps is shared between reading and arithmetic, but it also measures processes specific for each of the two academic domains (see **Table 1**).

FAMILY CHARACTERISTICS

In addition to predictors of dyslexia residing in children we examined possible predictors in their families. More specifically, we studied effects of home literacy environment and parental literacy skills on children's reading outcome.

Home literacy environment

In short, the three groups did not differ on cognitive stimulation by parents, but there was a tendency for parents of control children to own more magazines, newspapers and books. The two at-risk groups did not differ in any of the measures of home literacy environment (van Bergen et al., 2014a). Our findings are in agreement with findings from other family risk studies, which also failed to show effects of home literacy environment on children's reading outcome (Elbro et al., 1998; Snowling et al., 2007; Torppa et al., 2007; van Bergen et al., 2011). Thus, no environmental risk factors of substantial effect have been identified that would have been easy targets for intervention. Although behavioural genetic studies point to substantial heritability of reading, they also estimate that roughly 30% of individual differences is due to environmental factors (Petrill et al., 2006; Taylor et al., 2010; Olson et al., 2014c). The moderate total environmental influence and small to negligible shared-environmental influence do not leave much room to find effects of home literacy environment. Also other environmental factors warrant further investigation, such as pre- and perinatal factors and school and classroom characteristics.

Parents' literacy skills

The key innovating factor of the DDP family risk study is probably the inclusion of cognitive abilities of the parents. We went beyond using parental literacy for the sole purpose of dichotomizing children into high and low family risk samples by examining the relation between reading and reading-related skills of the parents and reading skills of their children. We had objective measures of the parents with dyslexia. Although all children in the at-risk sample have a parent with dyslexia, they might still vary in their degree of family risk for dyslexia. We tested this by comparing the groups of at-risk children with and without dyslexia on the reading skills of their parent with dyslexia. Since parents pass on their genes to their offspring and shape their environment, parental reading skills might be taken as an indicator of the offspring's liability to dyslexia.

In a previous family risk study (van Bergen et al., 2011) the dyslexia of the parents of the affected children was more severe than the dyslexia of the parents of the unaffected children, yielding the stepwise pattern predicted by MDM. This is a striking finding, because the affected parents read on average at the fifth percentile compared to national norms. Yet even in this restricted range group differences were observable.

In the DDP sample the difference between the at-risk children with and without dyslexia was replicated for the affected parent's word-reading fluency (see van Bergen et al., 2012). The two at-risk groups did not differ in parental pseudoword reading. They did not differ in spelling, and non-word repetition either, though both groups were impaired compared to controls. Interestingly, however, the parents of the at-risk dyslexia children were slower on rapid naming than those of the at-risk no-dyslexia children. This underscores the special role of rapid naming, at least in transparent orthographies.

In the two above mentioned studies data were reported of the parent with dyslexia. The study of van Bergen et al. (2014a) completes this by examining the influence of the parent *without* dyslexia for the first time. As hypothesized, also for the non-dyslexic parents there was a difference between the two at-risk groups: the parents of the affected children reported more literacy difficulties compared to those of the unaffected children.

The results concerning the unaffected parent further support the conclusion that children at family risk for dyslexia differ in their liability, as indicated by differences in parental reading skills between at-risk children with and without dyslexia. Moreover, differences between the two family risk groups in the severity of the dyslexia of the affected parent have now been replicated in Finnish. Torppa et al. (2011) showed differences in parental reading fluency, accuracy, and spelling.

Do the findings regarding precursors in families lend support for the MDM? According to this model, the etiology of dyslexia (and other developmental disorders) is multifactorial and probabilistic. Multiple genetic risk variants interact with each other and with multiple environmental risks to ultimately produce the disorder at the behavioural level. Some environmental factors were measured directly but did not have an effect. Genetic risk factors were not measured directly. Although there is now a huge body of evidence indicating that genes contribute importantly to individual differences in reading ability (Hayiou-Thomas et al., 2010; Olson et al., 2014c), the specific gene variants found thus far only explain a tiny part of these differences (see Bishop, 2009, for the example of the *KIAA0319* gene), despite substantive work in the field of molecular genetics (for a recent overview, see Carrion-Castillo et al., 2013). This phenomenon also applies to other common traits and is called the mystery of the missing heritability (see e.g., Manolio et al., 2009). Genetic screening is therefore not (yet) informative about a child's genetic vulnerability to dyslexia (Bishop, 2009). Instead, we propose that since parents pass on their genetic material to their offspring and shape their environment, cognitive abilities of parents could be used as an overall indicator of the genetic and environmental risk and protective factors in the MDM.

The DDP study provides two kinds of support for parental skills being an indicator for children's liability. First, as in other family risk studies, two samples of children were recruited based on having or not having a parent with dyslexia. The current and previous family risk studies (Scarborough, 1990; Elbro et al., 1998; Pennington and Lefly, 2001; Snowling et al., 2003; Torppa et al., 2010) found a large effect of having a family history on children's risk of becoming dyslexic. For example, in the DDP study it was found that the rate of dyslexia was 30% in the high-risk group and only 3% in the low-risk groups (van Bergen et al., 2012). Thus, having a parent with dyslexia increases the risk considerably. Secondly, within the at-risk sample it was found that affected *and* unaffected parents of the affected children had more literacy problems than those of the unaffected children. Moreover, when considering at-risk children's reading fluency on a continuous scale (rather than having or not having dyslexia), parental reading skills were significant predictors of children's reading skills.

Our findings thus support the view that skills of parents indicate their offspring's liability, which in itself is the combination of all genetic and environmental factors that affect reading development. Therefore, parental skills might shed light on the etiological level in the MDM. But based on parental skills it is not possible to disentangle the genetic and environmental contribution to the intergenerational transmission of skills. However, according to our data the transmission of risk seems to be mainly via genes, including gene-environment correlation (see also Figure 1 in Lyytinen et al., 1998). It is important to note that genes are inherited, not phenotypic traits. Thus, although the DDP data reinforce the view that parental skills are indicative of their offspring's liability, parental skills will never completely specify it.

THE INTERGENERATIONAL MULTIPLE DEFICIT MODEL

In our opinion there are two omissions in the MDM (Pennington, 2006) when applied to dyslexia. The first one – only touched upon here – relates to the reading system and the second to intergenerational transfer, which will be discussed in the remainder of this article.

First, when modeling reading ability and disability, the boxes at the level of cognitive processes in the MDM are typically thought of as precursors or correlates of reading, such as phonological awareness and rapid naming (e.g., Willcutt et al., 2010), or the cognitive components that each of these tasks tap. How these tasks and their components relate to reading outcome is extensively studied. In parallel, there is an extensive body of research into computational models of the reading system, in which visual word recognition is simulated (e.g., Coltheart et al., 2001; Peterson et al., 2013; Ziegler et al., 2014). Computational models are evaluated by how well they predict experimentally observed characteristics of the reading system, like lexicality and word length effects. The reading process is an important link between underlying cognitive process (such as phonological awareness and rapid naming) and the outcome of the reading process, reading accuracy and speed. Hence, in a MDM of reading (dis)ability, the cognitive level could be split up into underlying cognitive processes and the reading system (see Jackson and Coltheart, 2001). Research into underlying cognitive processes and into the reading system have developed separately, but van den Boer et al. (2013) recently made an important first step in linking these fields.

Secondly and applicable to all complex developmental disorders, intergenerational transmission of risk and protective factors is not explicitly present in the MDM, as it focusses on an individual child. Therefore, we propose an extension of the MDM: the intergenerational MDM (iMDM). Below we will elaborate on this model that is depicted in **Figure 3**. In the figure it can be seen that a top layer is added to Pennington's MDM, which represents characteristics of parents. The environment as created by parents is included in the top layer; other environmental factors are placed on the side. Note that again influences between child layers are omitted from the figure.

Cognitive abilities of parents, for instance reading ability, form part of their phenotype (PT in **Figure 3**). Their phenotype is the result of their genotype (GT) in interaction with their environment. Genes do not code for cognitive and behavioural traits but for the structure of proteins and the regulation of gene expression, which in highly complex ways and in interaction with the environment guides the building and maintenance of the brain (Fisher, 2006; Fisher and Francks, 2006). Despite this gap between genes and cognition, for traits that show genetic influences in behavioural genetic studies there must be a relationship between genotypic and phenotypic variation. In other words, for heritable traits parental phenotype is a proxy for their genotype. As both parents pass on half of their genes to their offspring, the genotype of both of them determines the genotype of their offspring. It follows that the phenotype of parents must be related to some extent to the genotype of children, which includes children's genetic risk and protective factors for a particular developmental disorder.

In addition to transmission of parental skills via genetic pathways, parental skills could be passed on via environmental pathways. Parents largely shape their children's childhood environment, which creates a relation between parents' characteristics and children's environment. This environment could exert a direct environmental effect (i.e., genetically unconfounded), referred to as *cultural transmission.* Hence, the cognitive phenotype of parents could be one of the factors that determines children's environmental risk and protective factors. The environment created by parents could also be correlated with the genotype of both parents and offspring, creating what is called (from the offspring's perspective) a *passive gene-environment correlation.* For example, good reading parents are more likely to spend a lot of time reading, thereby providing a role model to their children. Moreover, they appear to be better educated, and as a result, might live in better neighborhoods and might send their children to higher achieving schools. The family environment a child is exposed to can also be correlated with both generation's genotypes by parental behavior elicited by the child. Sticking with our reading-ability example, children genetically inclined to become fluent readers may be more likely to ask to be read to early on and ask for books and library visits later on. This phenomenon is termed *evocative gene-environment correlation.* Other aspects of the phenotype of parents might also be associated with or directly influence children's reading development. For instance, the behavior of parents and the interaction between them determines how structured or chaotic the household is, a factor that has been shown to be related to children's school performance (Hanscombe et al., 2011). Apart from genetic and cultural transmission, a third contributor to parent-child resemblance is shared *environmental confound* (D'Onofrio et al., 2003). In the case of reading, poverty could limit access to printed and digital reading material, which could affect reading ability in both generations. In conclusion, the phenotype of parents must also

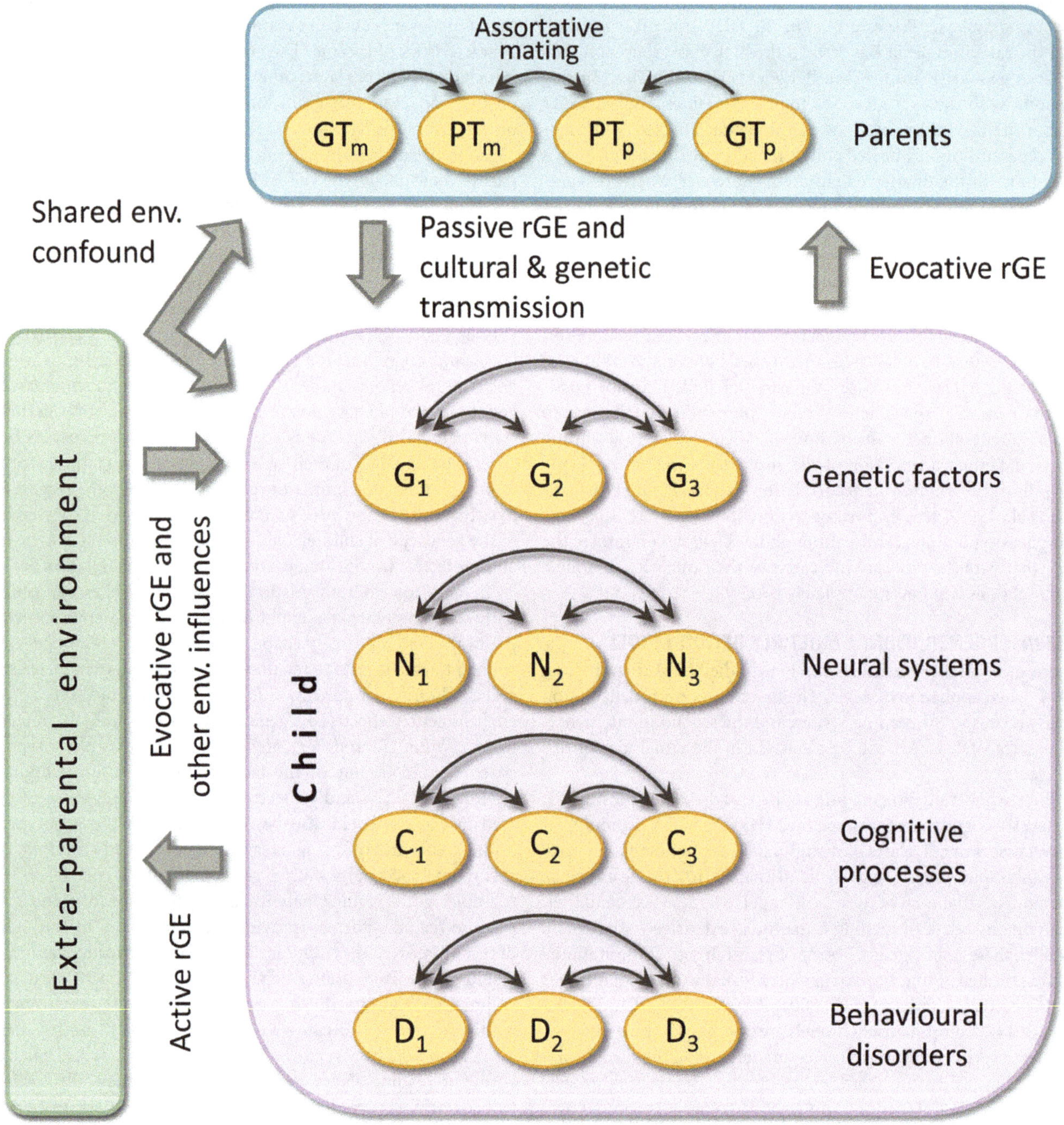

FIGURE 3 | The intergenerational multiple deficit model. Double headed arrows indicate interactions. Causal connections between levels of analyses are omitted. GT_m = maternal genotype, PT_m = maternal phenotype, GT_p = paternal genotype, PT_p = paternal phenotype, G = genetic risk or protective factor, N = neural system, C = cognitive process, D = complex behavioural disorder, env. = environmental, rGE = gene-environment correlation. Terminology: a *phenotype* is any measurable characteristic of an individual (e.g., reading ability or parenting style); a *genotype* is an individual's genetic makeup. There is *shared environmental confound* if an environmental factor influences both the parental and child phenotype. *Genetic transmission* refers to the genotypic factors passed down from parent to offspring that influence the phenotypes in both generations. *Cultural transmission* is the genuine environmental influence of parental characteristics on child outcome, so controlled for environmental and genetic confounds. *Assortative mating* is non-random mating. *Gene-environment correlation* (rGE) refers to the situation in which exposure to environments is not independent but correlated to the child's genotype (see the text for explanation about the three forms of rGE). The figure depicts the situation for one individual child and his/her (biological) parents. At the group level (i.e., multiple children), a second form of gene-environment interplay emerges: *gene-environment interaction*. That is, heredity depends on the environment, or sensitivity to the environment depend on genotype.

be related to a certain degree to children's environmental risk and protective factors. In addition, the mechanisms discussed highlight that measures of the environment that relate to child outcome may be attributable to familial confounding, rather than causation.

Given the above two lines of reasoning, the phenotype of parents is informative about children's genetic and environmental factors. Focussing on developmental disorders, this suggests that certain aspects of the phenotype of parents can inform us about a child's liability to a particular developmental disorder. Regarding dyslexia, the phenotypic aspects of parents that are expected to shed light on children's liability to dyslexia are skills in accurate and fluent reading, spelling, and their cognitive underpinnings like phonological awareness and rapid naming. Related skills (such as language and arithmetic) and their underlying cognitive abilities might also play a role. The ability of parents on each of the relevant continua can be conceptualized as a position in multivariate space. The position of father and mother in multivariate space is proposed to be indicative of a child's predisposition towards dyslexia.

Apart from environmental exposure closely linked to parental characteristics, children experience other environmental factors that influence their development. In **Figure 3** these extra-parental influences are put in the box on the side. They can influence all four child levels. In the case of reading, one can think of quality of the school and teacher, reading-instruction method, access to print and digital media, and factors related to child development in general, like (other) caretakers, peer influences, accidents, nutrition, and toxic threats.

Infants' environment is almost exclusively shaped by their parents, but as children grow older their environment becomes increasingly shaped independent by their parents. First, by gaining independence, running from acquiring locomotion to living independently. Second and related, by spending more and more time away from parents. This illustrates that children more and more actively select and create their environment. If this environmental exposure is correlated with the child's genotype, this is called *active gene-environment correlation.* For instance, children with a high genetic potential for good reading may actively seek out for opportunities to read. Children's genetically influenced abilities may also elicit environmental responses from others than their parents. For example, good readers may be given more difficult reading material by teachers, a form of *evocative gene-environment correlation.*

A form of gene-environment interplay not discussed so far is *gene-environment interaction.* This refers to a moderator phenomenon in which sensitivity to an environment depends on one's genotype (e.g., resilience to poor education), or the corollary, heritability depends on environmental exposure. An example of the latter in dyslexia research is a study by Friend et al. (2008) who found higher heritability of dyslexia among children from high compared to low socio-economic status. Gene-environment interaction is a group-level phenomenon and is therefore not depicted in the iMDM (**Figure 3**), which displays processes within the triad of an individual child and his/her (biological) parents, as well as the child-specific environment. As an illustration, the findings of Friend et al. would translate in an iMDM with strong genetic transmission for dyslexia predisposition in a child from a high socio-economic status family.

The iMDM is inspired by the described DDP study on dyslexia, but is generally applicable to other multifactorial developmental disorders with a genetic component. Examples of such disorders include ADHD, developmental coordination disorder, dyscalculia, SLI, and autism spectrum disorder. With respect to autism spectrum disorder, a number of studies (e.g., Happé et al., 2001; Bölte and Poustka, 2006; Losh et al., 2009) have studied the cognitive phenotype of parents of probands (as opposed to children of probands, as in family risk studies of dyslexia) and found in parents similar but milder impairments as in their children, indicating parent-child resemblance. A second example concerns SLI. Bishop's group found that language skills of probands and their parents were correlated (Bishop et al., 2012) and that a parent's non-word repetition ability was a predictor of whether the child would develop SLI (Bishop et al., 2012). These examples provide evidence of intergenerational transfer of cognitive skills other than reading.

The advantage of generally applicable MDMs comes however at a cost. First, the model is still empty and has to be specified for each particular (set of) developmental disorder(s). Candidate ingredients for the case of dyslexia are given throughout the current paper for the cognitive level. For the genetic level, the reader is referred to Carrion-Castillo et al. (2013), for the neural-system level to Richlan (2012), and for bridging these levels to Giraud and Ramus (2013). Second, the model (as depicted in **Figure 3**) is difficult to prove wrong. Still, the iMDM can inform the building of structural equation models for family data. Competing models can be tested to see which model best fits the observed data. Importantly, for (a) specific developmental disorder(s) the iMDM can therefore be falsified.

FUTURE AVENUES OF RESEARCH

Despite that Pennington's MDM as such is difficult to falsify, it has initiated a large body of research and our hope is that the intergenerational extension will further fuel this movement. Pennington's model has stimulated research in which more than one level of analysis is incorporated (vertical expansion) and has especially boosted horizontal expansion of studies, investigating more than one disorder simultaneously to understand comorbidity. By doing so, one can uncover shared and distinct risk factors at each of the levels of explanation. This not only helps to understand the origin of the comorbidity, but also the developmental paths leading to each of the disorders. For instance, a developmental disorder could develop secondary as a result of a primary disorder, or the two co-occur because of shared etiological factors (as evidenced by genetic correlations and environmental correlations). In examining the specificity of precursors for dyslexia we included arithmetic and dyscalculia in the DDP, but comorbidities with other developmental disorders were not investigated. Including more than just a single (dis)ability in future work will enhance our understanding.

From a practical point of view, the iMDM sheds light on an additional way to estimate disorder risk: not only an individual child's precursors to a certain disorder carry predictive power to identify young children at risk, also the cognitive and behavioural profile of their parents indicate risk. Studying intergenerational transfer and comorbidity can also be combined: parents might confer risks in different cognitive domains, like reading, language, and attention and additionally, parenting practices might not be optimal. Therefore, future studies are needed to test whether a more complete picture of parents' cognitive and behavioural profile yields a more reliable indication of their offspring's liability to a particular disorder. Reliable assessment of liability is of clinical importance: young children identified as at high risk can be enrolled in an intervention programe to ameliorate the risk. In the case of dyslexia, Zijlstra et al. (under review) showed in high risk children that trying to prevent reading difficulties works better than remediating once children lag behind substantially.

Apart from inspiring clinical work, the iMDM draws attention to an interesting area for future fundamental research: investigating transmission from one generation to the next. Research incorporating phenotypic characteristics of parents alongside one or more analysis levels in offspring is still sparse. We have discussed some family studies that revealed traits that show intergenerational correlations. Future family studies can further explore familial transmission patterns to identify relevant parental phenotypes and quantify phenotypic intergenerational associations. If both parents are assessed, one can test firstly whether this intergenerational association is moderated by the gender of parent and/or child. For example, van Bergen et al. (2014c) recently reported that paternal reading ability (as indicator for offspring's genetic liability) was a better predictor of offspring's reading ability for higher-educated fathers. Interestingly, this interaction was absent for mothers. The observed interaction for fathers is line with the gene-environment interaction between socio-economic status and heritability of dyslexia found by Friend et al. (2008). The differential pattern for fathers and mothers demonstrates that parental influences can be parent specific.

Secondly, if data on both parents are collected one can test whether there is *assortative mating* for the trait under study (see the correlation in **Figure 3** between maternal and paternal phenotypes). For level of education for example, the intuitive idea that people tend to choose a partner with similar academic attainment has been confirmed (e.g., Mare, 1991). Regardless of the iMDM it is important to establish the degree of assortative mating because it biases heritability estimates if not accounted for (Plomin et al., 2008, p. 160).

Genetically informed family studies can ultimately disentangle the contributions of causal genetic and environmental effects and gene-environment correlations to such an intergenerational correlation. Two examples of genetically sensitive family studies that rigorously investigate the mechanisms responsible for parent-offspring resemblance are studies which include MZ and DZ twin children plus their parents (nuclear twin-family design), or studies with adult MZ and DZ twins plus their offspring (children-of-twins design)[1]. Combining two such samples even allows for estimating cultural transmission and passive and evocative gene-environment correlation (Narusyte et al., 2008). That is, the direct environmental effect of parenting (or another parental trait) on children's outcome can be estimated while controlling for familial confounds. Regarding gene-environment correlation, the direction of effect (see **Figure 3**) can be revealed. We are unaware of such studies in the field of learning (dis)abilities, but see for an example on parental depression and offspring psychopathology Silberg et al. (2010).

The next step in a genetically sensitive family design would be to test whether parents differ in the relative quantity of cultural and genetic transmission. To start with cultural transmission, it may be expected that the parent who has the largest share in the child's upbringing exerts larger environmental influence. If parental involvement information is available, the structural equation models estimating cultural and genetic transfer could be rerun with parent couples subdivided based on involvement (rather than gender), or parental involvement could be included as a moderator. The amount of cultural transmission could also depend on the quality of the parent-child relationship and the gender of parent and child.

For genetic transmission, quantitative differences in transmission of paternal and maternal risk could arise from two mechanisms. First, if susceptibility genes show parent-of-origin effects [e.g., genomic imprinting, in which genes from mother and father have differential expression levels (Lawson et al., 2013)]. And second, if susceptibility genes would be carried on sex chromosomes (X and Y). Genetically informed family studies can estimate the total genetic risk that is passed down per parent. Hence, differences in transmitted genetic risk can be tested. Molecular genetic studies are needed to investigate the biological basis of possible maternal and paternal differences. Concerning dyslexia, the well-replicated candidate genes all lie on autosomal chromosomes, although there is some evidence for a locus on the X chromosome being implicated (Carrion-Castillo et al., 2013). Parent-of-origin effects have not yet been studied in relation to dyslexia (but see for a recent example on SLI Nudel et al., 2014).

To conclude, the iMDM encourages the inclusion of parent characteristics in future studies, which will enhance our prediction of risk and understanding of common neurodevelopmental disorders. The next exciting step is to conduct genetically informative family studies, in which genetic and environmental causal effects can be separated from familial confounding. This will bring us closer to elucidating causal chains underpinning disorder etiology.

ACKNOWLEDGMENTS

Elsje van Bergen is supported by a Rubicon Fellowship (446-12-005) of the Netherlands Organisation for Scientific Research (NWO) and a Junior Research Fellowship at Oriel College, University of Oxford. The Dutch Dyslexia Programme was supported by NWO grant 200-62-304. Elsje van Bergen thanks Dorothy Bishop for feedback and encouragement.

REFERENCES

Bishop, D. V. M. (2009). Genes, cognition, and communication. *Ann. N. Y. Acad. Sci.* 1156, 1–18. doi: 10.1111/j.1749-6632.2009.04419.x

Bishop, D. V. M., Hardiman, M. J., and Barry, J. G. (2012). Auditory deficit as a consequence rather than endophenotype of specific language impairment: electrophysiological evidence. *PLoS ONE* 7:e35851. doi: 10.1371/journal.pone.0035851

[1]The logic and modeling behind these approaches are beyond the scope of this article, but the interested reader is referred to D'Onofrio et al. (2003) for the children-of-twins design and D'Onofrio et al. (2013) for an overview of genetically informed family studies.

Bishop, D. V. M., Holt, G., Line, E., McDonald, D., McDonald, S., and Watt, H. (2012). Parental phonological memory contributes to prediction of outcome of late talkers from 20 months to 4 years: a longitudinal study of precursors of specific language impairment. *J. Neurodev. Disord.* 4, 3. doi: 10.1186/1866-1955-4-3

Bishop, D. V. M., McDonald, D., Bird, S., and Hayiou-Thomas, M. E. (2009). Children who read words accurately despite language impairment: who are they and how do they do it? *Child Dev.* 80, 593–605. doi: 10.1111/j.1467-8624.2009.01281.x

Bölte, S., and Poustka, F. (2006). The broader cognitive phenotype of autism in parents: how specific is the tendency for local processing and executive dysfunction? *J. Child Psychol. Psychiatry* 47, 639–645. doi: 10.1111/j.1469-7610.2006.01603.x

Byrne, B., Coventry, W. L., Olson, R. K., Samuelsson, S., Corley, R., Willcutt, E. G., et al. (2009). Genetic and environmental influences on aspects of literacy and language in early childhood: continuity and change from preschool to Grade 2. *J. Neurolinguistics* 22, 219–236. doi: 10.1016/j.jneuroling.2008.09.003

Carrion-Castillo, A., Franke, B., and Fisher, S. E. (2013). Molecular genetics of dyslexia: an overview. *Dyslexia* 19, 214–240. doi: 10.1002/dys.1464

Coltheart, M., Rastle, K., Perry, C., Langdon, R., and Ziegler, J. (2001). DRC: a dual route cascaded model of visual word recognition and reading aloud. *Psychol. Rev.* 108, 204. doi: 10.1037/0033-295X.108.1.204

D'Onofrio, B. M., Lahey, B. B., Turkheimer, E., and Lichtenstein, P. (2013). Critical need for family-based, quasi-experimental designs in integrating genetic and social science research. *Am. J. Public Health* 103, S46–S55. doi: 10.2105/AJPH.2013.301252

D'Onofrio, B. M., Turkheimer, E. N., Eaves, L. J., Corey, L. A., Berg, K., Solaas, M. H., et al. (2003). The role of the children of twins design in elucidating causal relations between parent characteristics and child outcomes. *J. Child Psychol. Psychiatry* 44, 1130–1144. doi: 10.1111/1469-7610.00196

Elbro, C., Borstrøm, I., and Petersen, D. K. (1998). Predicting dyslexia from kindergarten: the importance of distinctness of phonological representations of lexical items. *Read. Res. Q.* 33, 36–60. doi: 10.1598/RRQ.33.1.3

Fisher, S. E. (2006). Tangled webs: tracing the connections between genes and cognition. *Cognition* 101, 270–297. doi: 10.1016/j.cognition.2006.04.004

Fisher, S. E., and Francks, C. (2006). Genes, cognition and dyslexia: learning to read the genome. *Trends Cogn. Sci.* 10, 250–257. doi: 10.1016/j.tics.2006.04.003

Friend, A., DeFries, J. C., and Olson, R. K. (2008). Parental education moderates genetic influences on reading disability. *Psychol. Sci.* 19, 1124–1130. doi: 10.1111/j.1467-9280.2008.02213.x

Giraud, A., and Ramus, F. (2013). Neurogenetics and auditory processing in developmental dyslexia. *Curr. Opin. Neurobiol.* 23, 37–42. doi: 10.1016/j.conb.2012.09.003

Hanscombe, K. B., Haworth, C., Davis, O. S. P., Jaffee, S. R., and Plomin, R. (2011). Chaotic homes and school achievement: a twin study. *J. Child Psychol. Psychiatry* 52, 1212–1220. doi: 10.1111/j.1469-7610.2011.02421.x

Happé, F., Briskman, J., and Frith, U. (2001). Exploring the cognitive phenotype of autism: weak "central coherence" in parents and siblings of children with autism: I. Experimental tests. *J. Child Psychol. Psychiatry* 42, 299–307. doi: 10.1111/1469-7610.00723

Hayiou-Thomas, M. E., Harlaar, N., Dale, P. S., and Plomin, R. (2010). Preschool speech, language skills, and reading at 7, 9, and 10 years: etiology of the relationship. *J. Speech Lang. Hear. Res.* 53, 311–332. doi: 10.1044/1092-4388(2009/07–0145)

Jackson, N. E., and Coltheart, M. (2001). *Routes to Reading Success and Failure: Toward an Integrated Cognitive Psychology of Atypical Reading.* Ann Arbor, MI: Sheridam Books.

Kovas, Y., and Plomin, R. (2007). Learning abilities and disabilities: generalist genes, specialist environments. *Curr. Dir. Psychol. Sci.* 16, 284–288. doi: 10.1111/j.1467-8721.2007.00521.x

Landerl, K., and Moll, K. (2010). Comorbidity of learning disorders: prevalence and familial transmission. *J. Child Psychol. Psychiatry* 51, 287–294. doi: 10.1111/j.1469-7610.2009.02164.x

Lawson, H. A., Cheverud, J. M., and Wolf, J. B. (2013). Genomic imprinting and parent-of-origin effects on complex traits. *Nat. Rev. Genet.* 14, 609–617. doi: 10.1038/nrg3543

Leppänen, P. H. T., Hämäläinen, J. A., Salminen, H. K., Eklund, K. M., Guttorm, T. K., Lohvansuu, K., et al. (2010). Newborn brain event-related potentials revealing atypical processing of sound frequency and the subsequent association with later literacy skills in children with familial dyslexia. *Cortex* 46, 1362–1376. doi: 10.1016/j.cortex.2010.06.003

Losh, M., Adolphs, R., Poe, M. D., Couture, S., Penn, D., Baranek, G. T., et al. (2009). Neuropsychological profile of autism and the broad autism phenotype. *Arch. Gen. Psychiatry* 66, 518. doi: 10.1001/archgenpsychiatry.2009.34

Lyytinen, H., Ahonen, T., Aro, M., Aro, T., Narhi, V., and Rasanen, P. (1998). "Learning disabilities: a view of developmental neuropsychology," in *Reading Disability and More. A Tribute to Dirk J. Bakker,* eds R. Licht, A. Bouma, W. Slot and W. Koops (Delft: Uitgeverij Eburon), 29-54.

Manolio, T. A., Collins, F. S., Cox, N. J., Goldstein, D. B., Hindorff, L. A., Hunter, D. J., et al. (2009). Finding the missing heritability of complex diseases. *Nature* 461, 747–753. doi: 10.1038/nature08494

Mare, R. D. (1991). Five decades of educational assortative mating. *Am. Soc. Rev.* 15, 32.

McGrath, L. M., Pennington, B. F., Shanahan, M. A., Santerre-Lemmon, L. E., Barnard, H. D., Willcutt, E. G., et al. (2011). A multiple deficit model of reading disability and attention-deficit/hyperactivity disorder: searching for shared cognitive deficits. *J. Child Psychol. Psychiatry* 52, 547–557. doi: 10.1111/j.1469-7610.2010.02346.x

Moll, K., Loff, A., and Snowling, M. J. (2013). Cognitive endophenotypes of dyslexia. *Sci. Stud. Read.* 17, 385-397. doi: 10.1080/10888438.2012.736439

Naples, A. J., Chang, J. T., Katz, L., and Grigorenko, E. L. (2009). Same or different? Insights into the etiology of phonological awareness and rapid naming. *Biol. Psychol.* 80, 226–239. doi: 10.1016/j.biopsycho.2008.10.002

Narusyte, J., Neiderhiser, J. M., D'Onofrio, B. M., Reiss, D., Spotts, E. L., Ganiban, J., et al. (2008). Testing different types of genotype-environment correlation: an extended children-of-twins model. *Dev. Psychol.* 44, 1591. doi: 10.1037/a0013911

Norton, E. S., and Wolf, M. (2012). Rapid automatized naming (RAN) and reading fluency: implications for understanding and treatment of reading disabilities. *Annu. Rev. Psychol.* 63, 427–452. doi: 10.1146/annurev-psych-120710-100431

Nudel, R., Simpson, N. H., Baird, G., O'Hare, A., Conti-Ramsden, G., Bolton, P. F., et al. (2014). Genome-wide association analyses of child genotype effects and parent-of-origin effects in specific language impairment. *Genes Brain Behav.* 13, 418–429. doi: 10.1111/gbb.12127

Olson, R. K., Byrne, B., and Samuelsson, S. (2009). "Reconciling strong genetic and strong environmental influences on individual differences and deficits in reading ability," in *How Children Learn to Read,* eds K. Pugh and P. McCardle (New York: Psychology Press).

Olson, R. K., Keenan, J. M., Byrne, B., and Samuelsson, S. (2014). Why do children differ in their development of reading and related skills? *Sci. Stud. Read.* 18, 38-54. doi: 10.1080/10888438.2013.800521

Pennington, B. F., Willcutt, E., and Rhee, S. H. (2005). Analyzing comorbidity. *Adv. Child Dev. Behav.* 33, 263–304. doi: 10.1016/S0065-2407(05)80010-2

Pennington, B. F. (2006). From single to multiple deficit models of developmental disorders. *Cognition* 101, 385–413. doi: 10.1016/j.cognition.2006.04.008

Pennington, B. F., and Lefly, D. L. (2001). Early reading development in children at family risk for dyslexia. *Child Dev.* 72, 816–833. doi: 10.1111/1467-8624.00317

Pennington, B. F., Santerre-Lemmon, L., Rosenberg, J., MacDonald, B., Boada, R., Friend, A., et al. (2012). Individual prediction of dyslexia by single versus multiple deficit models. *J. Abnorm. Psychol.* 121, 212. doi: 10.1037/a0025823

Peterson, R. L., Pennington, B. F., Shriberg, L. D., and Boada, R. (2009). What influences literacy outcome in children with speech sound disorder? *J. Speech Lang. Hear. Res.* 52, 1175. doi: 10.1044/1092-4388(2009/08-0024)

Peterson, R. L., Pennington, B. F., and Olson, R. K. (2013). Subtypes of developmental dyslexia: testing the predictions of the dual-route and connectionist frameworks. *Cognition* 126, 20–38. doi: 10.1016/j.cognition.2012.08.007

Petrill, S. A., Deater-Deckard, K., Thompson, L. A., De Thorne, L. S., and Schatschneider, C. (2006). Reading skills in early readers: genetic and shared environmental influences. *J. Learn. Disabil.* 39, 48–55. doi: 10.1177/00222194060390010501

Plakas, A., van Zuijen, T., van Leeuwen, T., Thomson, J. M., and van der Leij, A. (2013). Impaired non-speech auditory processing at a pre-reading age is a risk-factor for dyslexia but not a predictor: an ERP study. *Cortex* 49, 1034–1045. doi: 10.1016/j.cortex.2012.02.013

Plomin, R., DeFries, J. C., McClearn, G. E., and McGuffin, P. (2008). *Behavioural Genetics,* 5th Edn. New York: Worth Publishers.

Plomin, R., and Kovas, Y. (2005). Generalist genes and learning disabilities. *Psychol. Bull.* 131, 592–617. doi: 10.1037/0033-2909.131.4.592

Ramus, F., and Ahissar, M. (2012). Developmental dyslexia: the difficulties of interpreting poor performance, and the importance of normal performance. *Cogn. Neuropsychol.* 29, 104–122. doi: 10.1080/02643294.2012.677420

Regtvoort, A. G. F. M., van Leeuwen, T. H., Stoel, R. D., and van der Leij, A. (2006). Efficiency of visual information processing in children at-risk for dyslexia: habituation of single-trial ERPs. *Brain Lang.* 98, 319–331. doi: 10.1016/j.bandl.2006.06.006

Richlan, F. (2012). Developmental dyslexia: dysfunction of a left hemisphere reading network. *Front. Hum. Neurosci.* 6:120. doi: 10.3389/fnhum.2012.00120

Scarborough, H. S. (1990). Very early language deficits in dyslexic children. *Child Dev.* 61, 1728–1743. doi: 10.2307/1130834

Silberg, J. L., Maes, H., and Eaves, L. J. (2010). Genetic and environmental influences on the transmission of parental depression to children's depression and conduct disturbance: an extended children of twins study. *J. Child Psychol. Psychiatry* 51, 734–744. doi: 10.1111/j.1469-7610.2010.02205.x

Snowling, M. J. (1995). Phonological processing and developmental dyslexia. *J. Res. Read.* 18, 132–138. doi: 10.1111/j.1467-9817.1995.tb00079.x

Snowling, M. J. (2008). Specific disorders and broader phenotypes: the case of dyslexia. *Q. J. Exp. Psychol.* 61, 142–156. doi: 10.1080/17470210701508830

Snowling, M. J., Bishop, D. V. M., and Stothard, S. E. (2000). Is preschool language impairment a risk factor for dyslexia in adolescence? *J. Child Psychol. Psychiatry* 41, 587-600. doi: 10.1111/1469-7610.00651

Snowling, M. J., Gallagher, A. M., and Frith, U. (2003). Family risk of dyslexia is continuous: individual differences in the precursors of reading skill. *Child Dev.* 74, 358–373. doi: 10.1111/1467-8624.7402003

Snowling, M. J., Muter, V., and Carroll, J. (2007). Children at family risk of dyslexia: a follow-up in early adolescence. *J. Child Psychol. Psychiatry* 48, 609–618. doi: 10.1111/j.1469-7610.2006.01725.x

Taylor, J., Roehrig, A. D., Hensler, B. S., Connor, C. M., and Schatschneider, C. (2010). Teacher quality moderates the genetic effects on early reading. *Science* 328, 512-514. doi: 10.1126/science.1186149

Torppa, M., Eklund, K., van Bergen, E., and Lyytinen, H. (2011). Parental literacy predicts children's literacy: a longitudinal family-risk study. *Dyslexia* 17, 339–355. doi: 10.1002/dys.437

Torppa, M., Lyytinen, P., Erskine, J., Eklund, K., and Lyytinen, H. (2010). Language development, literacy skills, and predictive connections to reading in finnish children with and without familial risk for dyslexia. *J. Learn. Disabil.* 43, 308–321. doi: 10.1177/0022219410369096

Torppa, M., Poikkeus, A., Laakso, M., Tolvanen, A., Leskinen, E., Leppänen, P. H. T., et al. (2007). Modeling the early paths of phonological awareness and factors supporting its development in children with and without familial risk of dyslexia. *Sci. Stud. Read.* 11, 73–103. doi: 10.1080/10888430709336554

Valdois, S., Bidet-Ildei, C., Lassus-Sangosse, D., Reilhac, C., N'Guyen-Morel, M. A., Guinet, E., et al. (2011). A visual processing but no phonological disorder in a child with mixed dyslexia. *Cortex* 47, 1197–1218. doi: 10.1016/j.cortex.2011.05.011

van Bergen, E., de Jong, P. F., Maassen, B., and van der Leij, A. (2014a). The effect of parents' literacy skills and children's preliteracy skills(on)the risk of dyslexia. *J. Abnorm. Child Psychol.* doi: 10.1007/s10802-014-9858-9 [Epub ahead of print].

van Bergen, E., de Jong, P. F., Maassen, B., Krikhaar, E., Plakas, A., and van der Leij, A. (2014b). IQ of(four)-year-olds who go on to develop dyslexia. *J. Learn. Disabil.* doi: 10.1177/0022219413479673 [Epub ahead of print].

van Bergen, E., van Zuijen, T., and de Jong, P. F. (2014c). Familial influences on reading ability. *Paper Presented at the International Conference of the British Dyslexia Association*, Guildford.

van Bergen, E., de Jong, P. F., Plakas, A., Maassen, B., and van der Leij, A. (2012). Child and parental literacy levels within families with a history of dyslexia. *J. Child Psychol. Psychiatry* 53, 28-36. doi: 10.1111/j.1469–7610.2011.02418.x

van Bergen, E., de Jong, P. F., Regtvoort, A., Oort, F., van Otterloo, S., and van der Leij, A. (2011). Dutch children at family risk of dyslexia: precursors, reading development, and parental effects. *Dyslexia* 17, 2–18. doi: 10.1002/dys.423

van den Boer, M., de Jong, P. F., and Haentjens-van Meeteren, M. (2013). Modeling the length effect: specifying the relation with visual and phonological correlates of reading. *Sci. Stud. Read.* 17, 243–256. doi: 10.1080/10888438.2012.683222

van der Leij, A., van Bergen, E., van Zuijen, T., de Jong, P. F., Maurits, N., and Maassen, B. (2013). Precursors of developmental dyslexia: an overview of the longitudinal dutch dyslexia programme study. *Dyslexia* 19, 191–213. doi: 10.1002/dys.1463

van der Sluis, S., de Jong, P. F., and Leij, A. V. D. (2004). Inhibition and shifting in children with learning deficits in arithmetic and reading. *J. Exp. Child Psychol.* 87, 239–266. doi: 10.1016/j.jecp.2003.12.002

Wagner, R. K. (1986). Phonological processing abilities and reading. *J. Learn. Disabil.* 19, 623–629. doi: 10.1177/002221948601901009

Willcutt, E. G., Betjemann, R. S., McGrath, L. M., Chhabildas, N. A., Olson, R. K., DeFries, J. C., et al. (2010). Etiology and neuropsychology of comorbidity between RD and ADHD: the case for multiple-deficit models. *Cortex* 46, 1345–1361. doi: 10.1016/j.cortex.2010.06.009

Willcutt, E. G., Pennington, B. F., and DeFries, J. C. (2000). Twin study of the etiology of comorbidity between reading disability and attention-deficit/hyperactivity disorder. *Am. J. Med. Genet.* 96, 293–301. doi: 10.1002/1096-8628(20000612)96:3<293::AID-AJMG12>3.0.CO;2-C

Willcutt, E. G., Pennington, B. F., Olson, R. K., Chhabildas, N., and Hulslander, J. (2005). Neuropsychological analyses of comorbidity between reading disability and attention deficit hyperactivity disorder: in search of the common deficit. *Dev. Neuropsychol.* 27, 35–78. doi: 10.1207/s15326942dn2701_3

Ziegler, J. C., Perry, C., and Zorzi, M. (2014). Modelling reading development through phonological decoding and self-teaching: implications for dyslexia. *Philos. Trans. R. Soc. Lond. B Biol. Sci.* 369, 1634. doi: 10.1098/rstb.2012.0397

4

Temporal sampling in vision and the implications for dyslexia

Kristen Pammer *

The Research School of Psychology, The Australian National University, Canberra, ACT, Australia

Correspondence:
Kristen Pammer, The Research School of Psychology, The Australian National University, Canberra, ACT 0200, Australia
e-mail: kristen.pammer@anu.edu.au

It has recently been suggested that dyslexia may manifest as a deficit in the neural synchrony underlying language-based codes (Goswami, 2011), such that the phonological deficits apparent in dyslexia occur as a consequence of poor synchronisation of oscillatory brain signals to the sounds of language. There is compelling evidence to support this suggestion, and it provides an intriguing new development in understanding the aetiology of dyslexia. It is undeniable that dyslexia is associated with poor phonological coding, however, reading is also a visual task, and dyslexia has also been associated with poor visual coding, particularly visuo-spatial sensitivity. It has been hypothesized for some time that specific frequency oscillations underlie visual perception. Although little research has been done looking specifically at dyslexia and cortical frequency oscillations, it is possible to draw on converging evidence from visual tasks to speculate that similar deficits could occur in temporal frequency oscillations in the visual domain in dyslexia. Thus, here the plausibility of a visual correlate of the Temporal Sampling Framework is considered, leading to specific hypotheses and predictions for future research. A common underlying neural mechanism in dyslexia, may subsume qualitatively different manifestations of reading difficulty, which is consistent with the heterogeneity of the disorder, and may open the door for a new generation of exciting research.

Keywords: reading, dyslexia, vision, temporal coding, oscillation, synchronisation, review

Developmental Dyslexia is a cognitive learning difficulty where a child demonstrates a specific problem in reading, with no obvious cause. A "definition by exclusion," it refers to a child that has experienced normal teaching and learning environments, has had normal social experiences, has no other comorbidities, and has a normal IQ, yet still demonstrates a specific reading difficulty (Scanlon, 2012). In reality, a dyslexic child quite often demonstrates comorbidities, or experiences impoverished social environments for example, and a child with a low (or high) IQ can still present as dyslexic. However, the definition by exclusion is important for researchers when trying to isolate biological bases for dyslexia, as it allows them to be more confident that the cognitive disorder the child is presenting with, is in fact likely to be dyslexia. Moreover, dyslexia is not just a childhood problem. Many adults who have suffered from developmental dyslexia as children never develop good reading skills (Hatcher et al., 2002). Those who do compensate for their reading difficulty and become good readers, invariably suffer from residual difficulties such as poor spelling and poor phonological coding (Lindgren and Laine, 2011).

The majority of children presenting with dyslexia demonstrate problems with phonics, where "phonics" is generally characterized as sensitivity to the subtle sounds of language. Tests of phonological awareness tend to be tests of how well an individual can understand, segment and manipulate speech and language sounds. Poor phonological coding precedes subsequent poor reading: most dyslexic children demonstrate some kind of difficulty in phonological coding, poor phonological coding remains when children grow into adulthood and develop compensated reading skills, and explicit training in phonics is the best strategy available with regard to a treatment for dyslexia (refer to Snowling, 2000 for a review). However, in regards to the latter point, phonics training is the best form of remediation as indicated by current evidence, but this could also be because research looking at other types of training such as visual training (e.g., Franceschini et al., 2013) or training grapheme-phoneme correspondences based on grain size (e.g., Kyle et al., 2013) is in its infancy. Thus dyslexia is often considered a form of language disorder as its basic aetiology may be in the form of deficits in auditory coding that make it difficult to develop stable phonological-graphemic relationships.

In addition to phonological coding, a large amount of research over the last 40 years has also demonstrated that many dyslexic readers have subtle visual deficits. Historically, dyslexia was considered a visual deficit, in the form of congenital word blindness; however, that dyslexic readers consistently demonstrated normal visual acuity, challenged the old "visual deficit" hypothesis in favor of deficits in phonological coding. Nevertheless, subsequent evidence suggests that many dyslexic readers appear to suffer from a deficit in coding visual information that is specific to the dorsal (or magnocellular) visual pathway (e.g., refer Stein, 2001; Pammer and Vidyasagar, 2005 for reviews).

THE MAGNOCELLULAR DEFICIT THEORY OF DYSLEXIA

At the subcortical level, the visual system consists of at least two pathways, magnocellular and parvocellular pathways, which carry visual information from the retina, through separate layers of the lateral geniculate nucleus (LGN) and project to distinct layers of primary visual cortex (V1). The two pathways run parallel to each other and consist of neurons which differ not only anatomically but also physiologically (Galaburda and Livingstone, 1993; Merigan and Maunsell, 1993; Zeki, 1993), suggesting that the they are specialized for processing different kinds of visual information. The magnocellular pathway demonstrates a high degree of sensitivity to low contrast, low spatial frequency, high temporal frequency, and achromatic visual information (Merigan and Maunsell, 1993). Consisting of large heavily myelinated neurons with fast conduction velocity, the magnocellular pathway responds maximally to rapid temporal changes, with magnocells responding at stimulus onset/offset rather than throughout the entire stimulus presentation. Conversely, the parvocellular pathway consists of small neurons that are sensitive to high spatial frequency, low temporal frequency, and color information, demonstrating sustained response activation throughout the entire duration of the stimulus (Goodale and Milner, 1992; Merigan and Maunsell, 1993).

From V1 the anatomical and functional dissociation of the magnocellular and parvocellular pathways becomes less clear, with visual information from the two streams interacting considerably as they project to extrastriate visual areas (Ferrera et al., 1992; Merigan and Maunsell, 1993; Nealey and Maunsell, 1994; Vidyasagar et al., 2002). Anatomical data indicates that the magnocellular and parvocellular systems may converge as early as layer 4 of V1 (Yabuta and Callaway, 1998), suggesting that higher order dorsal processing may not be entirely indicative of lower level magno functioning. Nevertheless two distinct cortical streams, the dorsal and ventral streams respectively, exist (Benardete et al., 1992; Zeki, 1993). The ventral (or "what") stream receives both magnocellular and parvocellular inputs as it projects to the inferotemporal cortex, an area specialized in extracting details relating to an object's shape and color (Zeki, 1993). This is in contrast to the magnocellular dominated dorsal (or "where") stream, which passes through V5 before projecting to the posterior parietal cortex, a selective spatial attention area specialized for processing the location of objects in space. Thus the dorsal pathway is considered to be responsible for visual qualities such as spatial awareness and movement, while the ventral pathway is considered to be responsible for qualities such as color processing and visual detail.

It is thought that dyslexic readers demonstrate difficulties transmitting visual information that is carried by the dorsal/magnocellular pathway. Here "dorsal" and "magnocellular" are somewhat different in that "magnocellular" refers to the cells that make up the dorsal visual pathway, and the dorsal pathway actually contains a small proportion of both parvocells and koniocells. However in the literature this distinction has frequently been blurred, and for the sake of brevity I will use "dorsal/magnocellular" to refer to theories and research that refer to both or either terminology. This Theory has become known as the "magnocellular deficit" hypothesis (Stein, 2001). Why the dorsal pathway is impaired in dyslexia, remains open to speculation, but may lie in the possibility that developmentally, the dorsal pathway is more vulnerable than the ventral pathway (Braddick et al., 2003). Numerous behavioral studies have demonstrated that; dyslexic readers are less sensitive to visual information that is carried by the dorsal/magnocellular pathway (e.g., Martin and Lovegrove, 1987; Pammer and Wheatley, 2001; Wright and Conlon, 2009), that sensitivity to dorsal/magnocellular tasks exist in children at risk for reading difficulties before they learn to read (Kevan and Pammer, 2008), that dorsal /magnocellular deficits predict subsequent reading ability in pre readers at risk for reading impairment (Boets et al., 2008; Kevan and Pammer, 2009), and that dorsal/magocellular sensitivity is correlated with reading ability (Witton et al., 1998; Pammer and Kevan, 2007). There is also good neurophysiological evidence to support a deficit in the dorsal/magnocellular pathways in dyslexic readers (Eden et al., 1996; Demb et al., 1998; Jednorog et al., 2011). Yet despite deficits in the dorsal pathway, visual coding in the ventral/parvocellular pathway in dyslexic readers remains normal. There is also substantial evidence to suggest that dyslexic readers have deficits in other sensory domains, such as auditory (refer to Hämäläinen et al., 2013 for a recent review) and motor processes (e.g., Thomson et al., 2006; Thomson and Goswami, 2008), prompting the suggesting that dyslexia might be a disorder that encompasses sensory systems more globally (Stein and Walsh, 1997).

However the view that dyslexic children demonstrate sensory coding deficits is not universal. For example, auditory processing deficits have not been found in all dyslexic children (Hill et al., 1999; Edwards et al., 2004; White et al., 2006). Halliday and Bishop (2006) compared dyslexic, normal readers and children with sensory hearing loss on auditory frequency modulation thresholds, they demonstrated that an amplitude modulated signal disrupted both low and high frequency coding, but only the children with sensorineural hearing loss differed from the normal readers, with no difference found between normal and dyslexic readers. Similarly, in some cases no differences have been found between dyslexic and non-dyslexic readers in the perception of speech signals (Messaoud-Galusi et al., 2011). Similar discrepant results have been found for visual processing (Ben-Yehudah et al., 2001; Stuart et al., 2001; Amitay et al., 2002; Olson and Datta, 2002; Ramus et al., 2003; White et al., 2006), where dyslexic readers have not been found to be different from normal readers. Refer to Skottun for comprehensive, alternative reviews of the magnocellular literature (e.g., Skottun, 2005; Skottun and Skoyles, 2007, 2008). Ramus et al. (2003) has suggested that sensory deficits may be characteristic of specific groups of dyslexic readers, such that deficits in different domains may be characteristic of different behavioral manifestations. This notion will be revisited in the "questions and hypotheses" section of this paper.

One important question regarding visual coding and dyslexia is to understand the link between dorsal/magnocellular processing, reading, and dyslexia. Because dorsal/magnocellular processing is not intuitively a natural candidate to support reading skill (its area of expertise is in coding spatial information, movement, and contrast), this link is not obvious. Some of the specific visual tasks that dyslexic readers have difficulties with, include: orienting attention (Facoetti et al., 2001, 2006), focusing attention (Facoetti et al., 2000, 2003), scanning cluttered environments

(Williams et al., 1987; Vidyasagar and Pammer, 1999; Sireteanu et al., 2008), and coding the locations of letters within words (Cornelissen et al., 1998). One interpretation of this evidence is that the dorsal/magnocellular pathway is important in the reading process by virtue of its role in attention (Hari et al., 1999; Iles et al., 2000; Vidyasagar and Pammer, 2010; Moores et al., 2011), specifically in the spatial coding and binding of letter and word features, letters within words, and directing saccadic movements across the page (Vidyasagar, 1999, 2004; Vidyasagar and Pammer, 1999). Problems with these processes would make it difficult for a young reader to generate stable visual representations of words, and move the eyes in a way to access the important visual qualities of text.

The notion that visual deficits in dyslexia may occur as a consequence of difficulties in binding the visual components of letters and words is consistent with what is known about the cortical processing of other visual objects. Object recognition is dependent on different parts of the cortex "binding" or synchronizing information to provide a coherent whole. For example, identifying a red bird flying from a tree requires at its very basic level, identifying the color of the bird, and the color of the leaves, identifying the bird-features and the tree-features, extracting the bird-object from the tree-object, and the movement of the bird, as distinct from the movement of the tree. This simple percept requires highly sophisticated cortical binding. For example, color needs to be bound to the locations of the various objects in space, which needs to be bound with the movement information. Moreover, all of this occurs within tens of milliseconds, and the visual system is extremely good at it; we would rarely—in the above example—perceive a green bird and red tree, suggesting that there are highly accurate and robust neural networks that communicate their information across time and space. Reading may be seen as an extension of this sophisticated cortical binding. Natural reading requires binding similar temporal and spatial information; letter features are to be bound into coherent letters, which are then placed within the correct locations within words, such that they can be identified, and the eye guided to the next location. Because the eye is moving very quickly across a page—fixations and saccades are in the order of 20 and 200 ms respectively—the spatio-temporal synchrony necessary to extract the letter, word, and sentence objects is really astounding.

However, like natural object recognition, these bottom-up processes do not occur in a linear, isolated fashion, but rather, are supported and sustained by top-down influences that facilitate recognition. For example, we demonstrated that "higher-level" cognitive functions in the reading network, such as language processing, are active within a few hundred milliseconds of the start of visual coding in the visual cortex. This was followed by both visual and language processing occurring in a dynamic, cascaded way, featuring feed-forward and feedback information flow (Pammer et al., 2004). This supports the notion that reading skills are dependent on a dynamic synthesis of both bottom-up and top-down information flow.

Thus, like other forms of object recognition, visual coding of text requires large populations of neurons to be synchronizing and synthesizing information extremely quickly, over disparate cortical areas to form coherent percepts.

TEMPORAL SAMPLING

Neuronal firing has a stochastic element, showing in their discharge, a large amount of variability and seemingly random firing patterns (e.g., Wang, 2010). However, behavior is not dependent on single cells firing at random, but rather on the coordinated, synchronous firing of thousands of cells in a neuronal population. That the brain demonstrates rhythmic discharge variations within neuronal populations has been known since the 20's with the first recordings of the alpha rhythm (Berger, 1929) and has resulted in hundreds of papers dedicated to understanding how and why such cortical rhythms occur. Indeed it is likely that unlocking the secrets of cortical rhythms will unlock many of the secrets of the brain.

In the current context, I will consider only rhythmic neural oscillations at the macroscopic level. Although oscillations have been observed for many years at the single-cell level (e.g., Hodgkin and Huxley, 1952; Llinas et al., 1991; Llinas and Steriade, 2006), the rhythmic cortical activity observable using EEG or MEG occurs when large populations of neurons synchronize to produce oscillations with a common frequency, amplitude and phase (Hämäläinen et al., 1993). In some cases, populations of neurons decouple from a common oscillation to synchronize at a different frequency or amplitude. This is referred to as Event Related Desynchronisation (ERD), and Event Related Synchronisation (ERS) occurs when local cell populations synchronize to form a coherently oscillating population (Pfurtscheller and Lopes da Silva, 1999). Moreover, populations of neurons in different areas of the brain can synchronize their oscillatory activity, which has been hypothesized to reflect cortical communication (Singer, 1999, 2009; Wang, 2010; Thut et al., 2012). It is this synchronisation of oscillatory behavior that is believed to underlie cortical binding, perception, cognition and behavior (Singer, 1999; Engel and Singer, 2001; Wang, 2010; refer to Siegel et al., 2012; Thut et al., 2012 for recent reviews).

Although it is assumed that cortical rhythms are causally related to behavior, it is possible that such cortical rhythms are simply epiphenomenal to information processing and behavior. However, there are a number of brain rhythms that have been associated with different cognitive or behavioral states, although there is a great deal of fluidity around the notion that particular cortical rhythms = cognitive function, and all the oscillatory rhythms that are generated by the brain have been demonstrated in one way or another with most cognitive functioning. Nevertheless, there is some broad consistency in the literature regarding some frequency ranges and cognitive/perceptual functioning. For example, theta rhythms (4–8 Hz) have been associated with maze navigation (Caplan et al., 2003; Kahana et al., 1999), episodic memory (Lega et al., 2012; Burke et al., 2013) and working memory (Sauseng et al., 2009; Moran et al., 2010). The alpha rhythm is one of the primary brain rhythms and frequently associated with various aspects of perception and cognition (e.g., Pfurtscheller and Klimesch, 1991). Beta rhythms (15–30 Hz) have been associated with motor preparation (Alegre et al., 2006; Cheyne et al., 2012) and control (e.g., Salmelin et al., 1995; Stancák and Pfurtscheller, 1996), and gamma rhythms (30–80 Hz) appear to be an index of attention (Jensen et al., 2007), feature binding (Tallon-Baudry et al., 1997) and object recognition (Tallon-Baudry and Bertrand, 1999; Martinovic et al., 2008; Friese et al., 2012). Some frequencies have been directly associated with changes in perception, for example, Fries et al. (2001) demonstrated that a gamma response in the visual cortex increases in response to attending to a behaviorally relevant stimulus. Connectivity at specific frequencies has also been demonstrated to reflect behavior. We demonstrated (Kujala et al., 2007) that unique areas of the brain synchronized at 8–12 Hz (alpha range) in response to different reading requirements. In this study, participants were presented with continuous text presented at rates that made comprehension easy, effortful, very difficult (only the general gist of the story was apparent), or impossible (random text). Left hemisphere cortical activations consistent with a reading network were activated at 8–12 Hz in a dynamic way that reflected the cognitive requirements of the reading task. Similarly, Hummel and Gerloff (2005) required participants to perform a visuo-tactile integration task, where a braille-like pattern was to be matched to a visual pattern on a computer screen. Long-range coherence between visual and motor areas, at the alpha frequency increased with better performance on the visuo-spatial integration task.

There are many examples of changes in oscillatory power or frequency in response to changes in information processing (refer Siegel et al., 2012 for a recent review), supporting the proposal that cortical oscillations, and the synchronisation of oscillations may represent a biological mechanisms for perception and cognition (e.g., Neuper and Pfurtscheller, 2001).

AUDITORY TEMPORAL SAMPLING IN DYSLEXIA

It has recently been suggested that poor phase-locking at low frequency theta and delta bands, (approximately 2–10 Hz), could be the proximal cause of dyslexia (Goswami, 2011). Phase-locking, also referred to as phase-synchrony (Lachaux et al., 1999), is the synchronisation of a brain signal at a specific frequency, reflecting the fact that the phase of the neural oscillation synchronizes with other neural oscillations, typically as fast evoked response to an external signal. Unstable auditory phase-locking at 2–10 Hz is believed to underlie the specific phonological impairments characteristic of dyslexia, and it has been suggested that such impairments may reflect a broader multi-sensory deficit, explaining some of the visual deficits also apparent in dyslexia (Goswami, 2011).

However, abnormal cortical oscillations in the auditory domain in dyslexia are not unique to theta or delta oscillations. For example, Lehongre et al. (2011) demonstrated abnormal auditory frequency dynamics in dyslexic readers in the gamma (25–35 Hz) frequency range. They presented dyslexic and normal readers with an auditory stimulus that was modulated linearly from 10 to 80 Hz. The associated auditory entrainment in the gamma range in normal readers was lateralized to the left hemisphere, specifically the superior temporal sulcus and planum temporale. They suggested that this neural signal is necessary for the fast formant transitions that occur in phonemic segregation. In dyslexic readers, however this gamma signal to the same stimulus was significantly reduced—providing a potential neurophysiological correlate of the common observation that dyslexic readers are impaired in phonological processing (Snowling, 2000). Moreover, dyslexic readers showed increased entrainment at 30 Hz in the right hemisphere—both compared to their left hemisphere, and compared to normal readers. This is also consistent with the evidence that dyslexic readers may develop compensatory right hemisphere reading networks, compared to normal readers (Leonard and Eckert, 2008), particularly for phonological output measures such as rapid automatized naming which requires left and right hemisphere integration (Eden et al., 2004). In addition, dyslexic readers show abnormally strong entrainment in the high gamma range (50–70 Hz) in the planum temporale of both hemispheres compared to controls.

Using sentences presented auditorily, Han et al. (2012) demonstrated that normal readers synchronize (normalized phase locking) high frequency gamma band (30–45 Hz) information bilaterally in the left and right auditory cortex, such that phonologically similar target words resulted in increased phase-locking, while phonologically dissimilar words resulted in decreased phase locking. Dyslexic readers however showed the opposite pattern of synchronisation. Since phonologically similar words require a more sophisticated analysis of phonemic information in order to distinguish between a "sensible" word, and a phonemically similar foil, the findings suggest better phonemic segmentation for heard words in normal readers compared to the dyslexic readers.

Clearly then cortical oscillatory activity in the auditory domain differs in dyslexia compared to normal reading. According to the temporal sampling hypothesis proposed by Goswami (2011), abnormal neural oscillatory activity may be responsible for dyslexia as a consequence of poor theta synchronisation to the sounds of language. There is also evidence for abnormal oscillatory activity in higher frequencies for dyslexic readers in response to auditory processing, which may also contribute to poor auditory temporal coding of language signals, making it difficult to develop good reading skills. However, reading is foremost a visual process, and dyslexia has also been associated behaviorally and physiologically with deficits in the dorsal visual pathway. Therefore, is there evidence for a visual correlate of the auditory temporal sampling hypothesis?

PHASE LOCKING OF SPEECH AND READING SIGNALS

Entrainment refers to oscillatory activity of neurons becoming synchronized with a repeated signal or perturbation (Pikovsky et al., 2003). External entrainment can occur by providing constant rhythmic stimuli such that neural assemblies phase-lock to the stimuli, synchronize their phase, and thus increase the neural signal (Thut et al., 2011). In this case, synchronizing and entrainment refer more-or-less to the same result—neural populations that have phase-locked to a signal and now oscillate at the same (or its harmonic Price and Ibbotson, 2001) frequency (refer to **Figure 1A**). One of the proposals of the temporal sampling hypothesis, is that auditory coding entrains to the temporal sampling of the speech signal—specifically its syllabic structure, and that this entrainment occurs at approximately the theta rhythm reflecting the temporal rhythm of syllabic structure (refer to **Figure 1B**). Dyslexia occurs when this phase-locking, entrainment and synchronisation are impaired, resulting in poor coding of speech, and thus a difficulty in generating

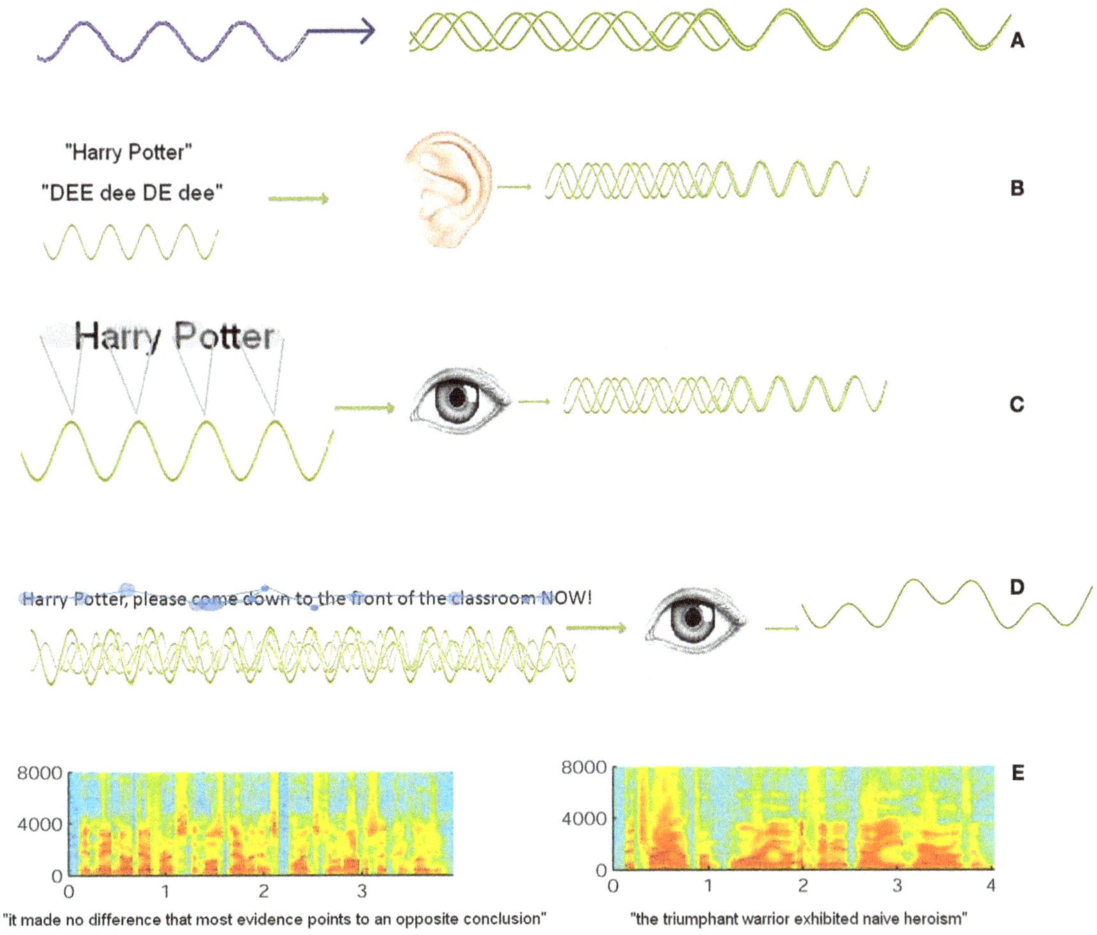

FIGURE 1 | (A) Is an illustration of how oscillatory signals—either external, or internal, can entrain a cortical oscillation, such that networks of neurons synchronize to oscillate at a critical frequency. It has also been suggested that the rhythmic nature of spoken language, such as "Harry Potter" in "dee's" (Goswami, 2011) can entrain an oscillatory cortical signal **(B)**. Moreover, the sequential spatial coding of words when reading lends itself to temporal sampling at much the same frequencies **(C)**. However, **(D)** is an example of how when reading, the unpredictable nature of fixations, saccades and regression might make it difficult to generate a single stable oscillatory signal, which in turn might make it difficult to entrain an associated oscillatory signal in the visual cortex. Here, the blue dots represent fixations of varying length and regressions. Similarly, when listening to speech, sentences have different spectral energy, **(E)** the sentence on the left has a spectral signature that is much more regular than that on the right. Nevertheless, Luo and Poeppel (2007) demonstrated entraining in the auditory cortex to both sentences (reproduced with permission from Luo and Poeppel (2007), supplementary material. Elsevier).

stable language-graphemic representations. Using the same arguments, it should also be possible for the visual system to entrain a visual signal that is phase-locked into the visual sampling of text.

Like the auditory coding of the speech stream, visual coding of text requires sequential sampling of words and text (refer to **Figure 1C**), and this sampling rate is consistent with the sampling rate of speech, i.e., approximately 2–10 Hz. In reading, fixations occur approximately every 200 ms (Rayner, 1998), and understanding the text requires the very fast sampling and concatenation of information from fixations to form a continuous, understandable percept—much like understanding speech. Moreover, it has been suggested that the temporal-spatial sampling of text is controlled by the magnocellular/dorsal stream, which then gates sampled information to the ventral pathways and other higher order cognitive mechanisms (Vidyasagar, 1998, 1999). If then, similar temporal mechanisms exist in both speech perception, and reading, it is possible that a common mechanism underlies both, and this would predict that dyslexic readers would be less sensitive to some of the visual equivalents of auditory signal processing.

It has been demonstrated that dyslexic readers are less sensitive to visual stimuli of low *spatial* frequency (Lovegrove et al., 1980; Badcock and Lovegrove, 1981; Slaghuis and Ryan, 1999), but the above hypothesis would predict that dyslexic readers would be less sensitive to visual signals that are presented at a regular temporal frequency, in much the same way they are impaired at processing auditory signals presented at a regular temporal frequency (refer to Goswami, 2011 for a review). However, "temporal coding" in vision in dyslexia can mean quite different things, and the research findings are highly variable. One interpretation of temporal coding is the speed at which the visual system can code visual information, another is the ability for the visual system to detect rapidly changing temporal events (e.g., refer to Farmer and

Klein, 1995; McLean et al., 2011), and the research literature rarely distinguishes between the two.

There is evidence to suggest that dyslexic children have difficulties in sequencing the temporal order of quickly presented stimuli (e.g., di Lollo et al., 1983; Brannan and Williams, 1988; Hari et al., 2001; Jaskowski and Rusiak, 2008; Liddle et al., 2009). These are typical Temporal Order Judgment (TOJ) tasks in which the participant is presented with a number of items (usually 2 or 3) in fast succession, and required to indicate their temporal order. The problem with TOJ tasks is that they can be quite difficult, and have quite a high memory load, so any differences between dyslexic and non-dyslexic readers could manifest from a number of different perceptual or cognitive causes. Similarly, the length of time it takes for a neural signal to decay in order to identify two discrete events, is Visible Persistence (VP). Dyslexic readers have been shown to require longer delays between signals (Badcock and Lovegrove, 1981; Slaghuis and Lovegrove, 1985; Lovegrove et al., 1986; Slaghuis and Ryan, 1999; Conlon et al., 2004), suggesting a longer period of neural persistence, although other studies have failed to find such a difference (e.g., Schulte-Körne et al., 2004). Temporal coding can also mean how quickly the visual system can deal with visual information i.e., processing speed. McLean et al. (2011) measured the temporal integration thresholds of the magnocellular and parvocellular pathways respectively. Here two isoluminant colored patches are alternated to "flicker." The temporal resolution of the flicker increases until the color merges, but the flicker is still noticeable—this is the parvocellular resolution limit. If the temporal frequency is increased further, then the colors not only merge, but the perceptual flicker goes away—this is the magnocellular resolution frequency. In this study, dyslexic children showed lower resolution thresholds compared to normal readers in their magnocellular, but not parvocellular thresholds.

If temporal coding in a language framework is predicated on the rhythmic frequency modulation of speech, and if temporal coding in reading is the rhythmic saccadic sequencing of visual information, then Attentional Blink (AB) may be a useful candidate to conceptualize visual temporal coding, and has the added bonus of at least one theoretical framework that is based on rhythmic pulses of neural signals. AB is a task that involves an RSVP stream of distractor stimuli (such as letters) in which are imbedded two targets (such as numbers); T1 and T2. Perception of T2 decreases when the delay between T1 and T2 is between 200–400 ms. The Boost and Bounce theory of AB (refer to Olivers and Meeter, 2008 for a comprehensive discussion of this theory) suggests that AB reflects a continuous, rhythmic sequence of visual signals. In dyslexia then if this fast temporal signaling is impaired (slower, or longer, less defined for example), then it might predict a number of outcomes: dyslexic readers should show less T1-sparing and lower detection of T1 because of a more prolonged signal from the distractor the precedes it. Although the research findings are mixed in AB and dyslexia, this is in fact one common finding (e.g., Hari et al., 1999; Visser et al., 2004; Facoetti et al., 2008). The dip in the "blink" might also be prolonged, and/or shifted to the right in dyslexic readers because the signal from T1 also lasts longer, which is consistent with some findings (Hari et al., 1999; Visser et al., 2004; Facoetti et al., 2008), although others have failed to find this effect (e.g., Lallier et al., 2010). Others have found no differences between dyslexic and normal readers (Badcock et al., 2008; McLean et al., 2010). One of the problems about AB is that there are multiple ways in which the dip can be analyzed and reported, which makes it difficult to compare results.

For the purposes of this paper, "temporal coding" is probably best conceptualized as both processing speed and the ability of the visual system to deal with information presented quickly, such as at the rate of saccadic and fixation sequences, or even faster. As in the auditory domain, temporal coding here really refers to the ability of the visual system to effectively process quickly presented information. Here "quickly presented information" comes about either because stimuli is presented quickly in sequence, such as in an RSVP (IB) task, or the visual system engages in a sequential temporal sampling process such as when reading. Thus, as an RSVP task presents the visual system with fast discrete visual percepts, so does reading when the bottom-up data acquisition during a fixation is separated by a "dwell time" caused by the saccade. The differences between the temporal processing tasks above and reading, is that the temporal component in the above tasks is procedural, caused by the stimuli itself and the eyes are static, compared to reading, where the temporal component is mechanical, caused by the fixations, saccades and eye movements, while the stimuli is static. A summary of some of the research regarding temporal coding in dyslexia is in **Table 1**. However, an important distinction here is that this is behavioral research, where "temporal coding" refers to the ability to process quickly presented information. It is still unclear the degree to which these studies inform the neural process of temporal coding which refers to the synchronisation of neural signals.

Conceptualizing visual temporal processing in this mechanical way also allows us to consider visual search and change detection. Here, like reading, the stimulus is static and the temporal information flow through to the visual system is mediated by fixations, saccades, and eye movements. There is a theoretical argument that links visual search to magnocellular/dorsal processing (Vidyasagar, 1998, 1999; Vidyasagar and Pammer, 1999, 2010), and studies have shown that dyslexic readers are worse than control readers at detecting a target in serial search and change detection (e.g., Vidyasagar and Pammer, 1999; Rutkowski et al., 2003; Jones et al., 2008; de Boer-Schellekens and Vroomen, 2012), and serial search predicts later reading ability in pre-readers (Franceschini et al., 2012).

Thus, many visual temporal coding tasks also draw on quite significant cognitive abilities, such as sequencing, judgment and memory, and although such mechanisms are also required in reading, it makes it difficult to use tasks such as these to explicitly isolate the neural components of visual coding in the temporal sampling process. Studies looking directly at the neural correlates of simple visual synchronisation and entrainment have not been done for normal or dyslexic readers, but would provide a good test of a visual example of the temporal coding hypothesis as has been developed in the auditory domain.

One potential confound for the proposal that visual oscillatory activity may be able to entrain to the temporal sampling rate when reading, is that entrainment or synchronisation is most

Table 1 | A summary of some of the behavioral evidence regarding visual temporal coding in dyslexia.

Study		Task details			Outcome	
Attentional blink		**Distracters**	**Targets**	**Timings**	**Magnitude of dip**	**Location of dip**
	Hari et al., 1999	Black letters	White letter	106 ms, no ISI	Dyslexics generally poorer at detecting the target	Shifted to longer durations for dyslexics
	Visser et al., 2004	Random dots	A shape (square, cross etc.)	40 + 60 ms ISI	Dyslexic generally poorer than controls, similar pattern as for reading matched controls	Shifted to longer durations for dyslexics compared to controls, same patters as for reading matched controls
	Facoetti et al., 2008	None. Only T1 and T2 were presented at varying intervals and each were masked	Letters, each had a pre and post-mask	T1 and T2 were each 100 ms	Shallower and longer for Dyslexic's	Shifted to longer durations
	Badcock et al., 2008	Black letters	T1 = white letter T2 = black X	100 ms	No difference between dyslexic and non-dyslexic adults after correcting for baseline sensitivity	No difference between dyslexic and non-dyslexic adults
	Lallier et al., 2010	Black digits	T1 = Red digit (1 or 5) T2 = black "0"	50 + 66 ms ISI	Lower detection for dyslexics at lag 4. However, no difference between dyslexic and controls. When using technique by Cousineau et al. (2006) Participants had to achieve a performance criteria	No difference between dyslexic and controls.
	McLean et al., 2010	1 of 4 arrows	A shape (square, cross, plus, diamond, circle, triangle)	26 + 80 ms ISI	Demonstrated an overall deficit for dyslexic children compared to controls that was not specific to any of the AB parameters	
Visible persistence		**Task**	**Details**		**Results**	
	di Lollo et al., 1983	Gap-detection	Line stimulus-gap-line stimulus. Duration of line = 20 ms Gap ISI = staircase threshold. Participants compared this to a "no-gap" stimulus. The task was to indicate which stimulus contained the gap		Dyslexic readers required longer ISI's to make accurate judgements to detect the gap between line stimuli	
		Pattern integration	Participants were to detect the presence of a missing dot over successively presented dots that form a matrix pattern		No difference between dyslexic and non-dyslexic participants	
	Badcock and Lovegrove, 1981; Slaghuis and Lovegrove, 1985	VP	grating-blank-grating sequence. Duration of gratings = 300 or 75 ms ISI blank period = staircase threshold. Participants to indicate if they had seen the blank period		Duration of VP was the duration at which the blank field was just visible. Dyslexic readers required longer durations to detect the blank period	

(Continued)

Table 1 | Continued

Visible persistence		**Task**	**Details**	**Results**
	Slaghuis and Ryan, 1999	Ternus apparent motion	3 squares in a row where the outermost square jumps from the left to the right side. Perception reflects the square jumping (element motion), or all 3 squares moving from left to right (group motion) 40 ms stimulus duration, 10-70 ms ISI. Participants were to indicate whether they saw "group" or "element" movement.	Dyslexic participants were less likely to perceive "group" movement. Suggesting that Dyslexic children demonstrated longer visible persistence
			120 ms stimulus duration	No differences between groups on the perception of group or element movement
	Conlon et al., 2004	Temporal counting	Adult dyslexic were required to count the count square targets presented as a RSVP	Dyslexic participants were significantly less accurate in counting rapidly presented stimuli compared to normal adults readers
	Schulte-Körne et al., 2004	VP	grating-blank-grating sequence. Duration of gratings = 300 ms ISI blank period = staircase threshold. Participants to indicate if they had seen the blank period	Duration of VP was the duration at which the blank field was just visible. Dyslexic readers were no different from dyslexic readers (indeed normal readers required longer durations to detect the blank period)
	Jones et al., 2008	Ternus apparent motion	3 squares in a row where the outermost square jumps from the left to the right side. Perception reflects the square jumping (element motion), or all 3 squares moving from left to right (group motion) 40 ms stimulus duration, 10-70 ms ISI. Participants were to indicate whether they saw "group" or "element" movement.	No difference between dyslexic and non-dyslexic children
Temporal order judgement		**Task details**		**Results**
	Brannan and Williams, 1988	3-letter words, or a symbol (and or #) were presented to the left or right of fixation. Stimuli = 900 ms ISI = variable staircase to achieve 75% threshold		Dyslexic readers required a significantly longer ISI to make accurate judgements regarding which order the stimuli appeared.
	Hari et al., 2001	Stimuli were presented in the left and right hemifield, participants were to indicate which stimulus appeared first. The ISI between stimuli was varied		Dyslexic participants required longer durations to determine which stimulus appeared first. However, results were asymmetric such that they showed a right visual field (left hemisphere) advantage
	Jaskowski and Rusiak, 2008	Pairs of rectangles where each were presented above/below or left/right of fixation. Participants had to indicate which rectangle appeared first—the left or the right, the top or the bottom. The ISI was varied between the stimuli presentations.		Dyslexic participants generally required a longer interval to make accurate judgements. However contra to Hari et al, there was no left/right asymmetry
	Liddle et al., 2009	Stimuli were presented in the left and right hemifield, participants were to indicate which stimulus appeared first. The ISI between stimuli was varied. Participants had to indicate whether the left or right stimuli appeared first. In Exp2 Participants had to indicate the shape of the stimuli that appeared first.		d' for accuracy showed significantly lower sensitivity for temporal order judgements for dyslexic adults compared to non-dyslexic adults. There was no left/right asymmetry
Visual search and change detection[a]		**Task**	**Details**	**Results**
	Vidyasagar and Pammer, 1999	Visual Search	Conjunction search using shape and color.	Dyslexic children became progressively less accurate compared to normal reading children, in more cluttered arrays

(Continued)

Table 1 | Continued

Visual search and change detection[a]		Task	Details	Results
	Rutkowski et al., 2003	Change detection	4 letters arranged in a square array around the fixation point. Followed by a blank period (250 ms), followed by another 4-letter stimuli arrangement. The stimuli alternated until a response was made.	Dyslexic children required longer presentation times compared to normal readers to determine whether the two 4-letter target stimuli were the same or different.
	Jones et al., 2008	Visual search	gratings in a circle around a fixation. 1 target + (2, 4, 8, or 16) distractors. Presentation = 100 ms. Target was an off-vertical grating. Distractors = vertical grating	Dyslexic children were less accurate over all set sizes except 2 items
	Franceschini et al., 2012	Visual search	Children scan left-to-right across lines of stimuli to circle specific targets. Children were young, identified as "at risk" at grade year 1.	Poor readers made significantly more errors. Search performance predicted later (1 year) pseudoword reading, text reading and letter naming.
	de Boer-Schellekens and Vroomen, 2012	Visual search	Distractors = Line segments (24 or 48 items) Target = horizontal or vertical line The target and distractors changed color dynamically red through green.	Dyslexic readers took significantly longer than normal readers to detect the target, particularly at the larger set size
	Tulloch and Pammer, submitted	Visual Search	Stimuli presented on a computer tablet were "game-like" bugs. Participants had to find the target bug always present on the screen (no memory component)	Search results significantly predicted reading rate for a group of children with a large range of reading ability.

[a]*Not typically considered a temporal task, but here I am considering the possibility of a static display, where the visual temporal quality occurs because of the "shutter-like" extraction of information at fixations as the eye scans across the page.*

easily studied in the context of a regular periodicy in the signal stream (refer to **Figure 1A**). An input signal that does not have a regular periodicy will not generate stable oscillations, because there simply is not a stable oscillatory signal to entrain to (refer to **Figure 1D**). Reading (like speech perception), is in fact highly variable. Smooth, effortless reading does involve spatial sampling at approximately the theta range, but the crucial word here is "approximately." Fixations vary considerably: they are longer and more frequent for more difficult words, or unexpected words, regressions are common, and saccade length can also determine the speed at which the text is sampled (refer to Rayner, 1998 for a review), and there are also cognitive confounds such as attention, anticipation, and decision making that could generate their own entrained signals (Thut et al., 2011) which could make it difficult for the system to entrain to the visual input signal. Similarly, in natural language the rhythmicity of the language itself can be quite variable (refer **Figure 1E**). Despite these reservations, entraining of theta signals to speech *has* been demonstrated (e.g., Luo and Poeppel, 2007), and the theta synchronisation was correlated with speech intelligibility. Furthermore, it is certainly possible that different oscillatory networks may entrain to different frequency components of the speech signal, and poor reading and/or language processing could result from differential impairments in specific frequencies in the overall spectral network, or the interaction of these networks.

If reading *can* be demonstrated to entrain a low-frequency oscillation in the visual domain as a consequence of temporal sampling in the reading process (refer to **Figure 1C**), then this may have enormous implications for dyslexia. Dyslexic readers' eye movements when reading, are dramatically different from those of normal readers (e.g., refer to Rayner et al., 2001 for a review), with more frequent fixations that are longer and less stable, as well as shorter saccades and more frequent regressions. Moreover it has been suggested that dyslexic readers also have problems in achieving stable binocular control (Stein et al., 2000). Therefore, consistent with Goswami (2011), if normal reading can entrain the visual system, then the highly unstable and variable eye movement behavior in dyslexic readers could very well result in a poor oscillatory coding, because of an inability to generate a systematic, rhythmic saccadic rhythm.

AN ARGUMENT FOR A TEMPORAL SAMPLING HYPOTHESIS IN VISION IN DYSLEXIA

Cortical frequency oscillations have long been considered to underlie visual perception (e.g., refer to Pfurtscheller and Lopes da Silva, 1999; Sewards and Sewards, 1999; Singer, 1999, 2009; Tallon-Baudry and Bertrand, 1999; Engel and Singer, 2001, for reviews). However the question of interest here is the role of cortical frequency oscillations in visual processing in the context of dyslexia. Specifically, do dyslexic readers differ from normal readers in oscillatory phase-locking in visual tasks related to reading. The most direct test of whether dyslexic children demonstrate temporal coding deficits in the visual domain, that are consistent with those found in the auditory domain, is to measure cortical frequency dynamics in dyslexic children for visual stimuli, and/or to evaluate cortical frequency dynamics in dyslexic children in the visuo-spatial areas of the brain. No studies have done this in the context of entrainment to a visual stimulus. Almost all research into cortical frequency dynamics in dyslexic readers, has used auditory stimuli, such as tones (Nagarajan et al., 1999; Ucles et al., 2009; Heim et al., 2011), sounds—such as white noise (Lehongre et al., 2011; Hämäläinen et al., 2012), phonological tasks (Rippon and Brunswick, 2000), or sentences (Han et al., 2012). One EEG study looking at visuo-spatial cuing in dyslexic adults found reduced coherence in the parietal cortex in dyslexic compared to normal readers (Dhar et al., 2010), however the results were only presented in the 8.5 Hz (alpha) range, and it is not known if differential impairments exist in other frequency ranges.

Some studies of linguistic processing in dyslexic readers have used visually presented words, which might allow the extraction of some vision-specific coding. Milne et al. (2003) found an increase in beta power in the posterior brain regions for dyseidetic dyslexic adults, and the reverse pattern, with an increase in beta signals anteriorly for dysphonetic dyslexic adults in a visual lexical decision task. However, only broad-spectrum beta (12–30 Hz) was analyzed, and the lack of spatial specificity inherent in EEG allowed only "posterior" or "anterior" descriptions of the results. Similarly, using EEG and visually presented words, letters or pseudowords, power changes have been demonstrated in theta (Klimesch et al., 2001a,b), as well as alpha and beta oscillations (Klimesch et al., 2001a,b) in dyslexic children. In the first study, differences in theta activity between dyslexics and controls were interpreted to result from difficulties in working memory encoding in dyslexic readers, and potentially more effortful coding for words in occipital sites. In the second study, changes in the patterns of alpha and beta activation were interpreted to reflect differential allocation of sustained attention in dyslexic compared to normal readers. However, in both studies the analysis period consisted of 5 sec after the presentation of a stimulus, making it unlikely that vision-specific coding of the stimuli could be specifically extracted. Other researchers have also presented word, or word-like stimuli visually, but their analyses have been in terms of the linguistic and not the visual coding of the stimuli such that ROI's are language-related areas rather than visual areas (e.g., Spironelli et al., 2008).

To summarize, while a number of studies have specifically looked at oscillatory activity in the auditory cortex of dyslexic readers, none has looked at oscillatory activity to visual temporal coding in the visual cortex of dyslexic readers. This provides two areas to explore: First, in the normal reading population, what is known about cortical oscillatory responses in vision and reading? Second, what is known about cortical responses in some of the visual tasks underlying reading? From these two explorations, a reasonable theoretical framework might be constructed of a role for temporal visual coding deficits in dyslexia.

The visual aspects of reading involve a number of complex and interrelated components, such as object recognition, visual search, extracting information from a cluttered array, guiding eye movements, feature binding, attentional shifting, and preattentive visual coding. Such tasks have been hypothesized to be mediated by the dorsal/magnocellular visual pathway (Vidyasagar, 1998, 1999, 2004), and many of these tasks involve synchronous gamma oscillations (refer to Sauve, 1999; Tallon-Baudry and Bertrand, 1999; Engel and Singer, 2001; Singer, 2009; Tallon-Baudry, 2009; Merker, 2013). Thus it is not at all unreasonable to predict that oscillatory gamma signals are apparent in reading in the way that they are in the perception of speech, and it remains to be seen whether differences in gamma oscillations also characterize dyslexia in the visual domain, like in the auditory domain.

TEMPORAL SAMPLING AND THE MAGNOCELLULAR PATHWAY

Given that a deficit in the magnocellular pathway appears to be found in many dyslexic readers, it would seem logical to ascertain whether the magnocellular pathway is selectively responsive to particular cortical frequencies.

Sewards and Sewards (1999) speculated that low frequency oscillations are characteristic of the parvocellular pathway, and high frequency gamma oscillations of the magnocellular pathway. They reached this conclusion from the following evidence: alpha signals are characteristic of stimuli that are static, and where the eyes are also static, whereas gamma *and* alpha oscillations occur when the stimulus itself moves or, with static stimuli when the eyes move. This is consistent with the observation that the magnocellular pathway is responsive to motion. Similarly, cell layers in the LGN that oscillate in the gamma range were found in the layers innervated primarily by retinal magnocellular cells (Livingston, 1996). However, Sewards and Sewards, also point out that Livingstone only measured gamma oscillations, making it difficult to assess the nature of other frequency oscillations in the LGN layers[1]. Sewards and Sewards also suggest that the physiological responses of the magnocells and parvocells are consistent with differential oscillatory activity, in that the fast magno cells are sensitive to temporal frequencies up to 50 Hz, but the slower-transmitting parvo cells have specific modulation frequencies of <10 Hz (Wiesel and Hubel, 1966). More recently, Fründ et al. (2007) demonstrated that low spatial frequency visual stimuli (1 cpd)—which would be transmitted primarily by the magnocellular pathway—generated an evoked gamma signal, whereas high spatial frequency stimuli (10 cpd)—which would be transmitted primarily by the parvocellular pathway—generated an evoked alpha signal.

Pammer et al. (2006) conducted an MEG study in which participants were to perform a lexical decision task that used words presented normally, and words in which the internal letters were shifted up or down relative to each other. The aim was to selectively activate the magno/dorsal pathway in reading, by manipulating the spatial configuration of the internal letters of the words. In this study we demonstrated strong gamma and

[1] It has also recently been demonstrated that low frequency rythms (<10 Hz) are characteristic of cells in the koniocellular layers of the LGN, not the magnocellular or parvocellular layers (Cheong et al., 2011).

alpha signals for the "shifted-words" condition, in the posterior parietal cortex—where we would expect magnocellular/dorsal activity. In addition, the time course of these signals was interesting, in that the first signal at approximately 150 ms was a gamma (35–40 Hz) signal, the second, at approximately 200 ms, an alpha signal, and the next signal at about 300 ms, again a gamma signal. It was argued that the initial gamma signal reflected a transient evoked signal—perhaps reflecting initial attentional mechanisms for spatial selection (Moran and Desimone, 1985; Motter, 1993; Vidyasagar, 1998, 1999; Martinez et al., 1999) and that the later gamma signal could be consistent with feature binding (Galambos, 1992; Başar-Eroglu et al., 1996; Pulvermüller et al., 1997; Tallon-Baudry and Bertrand, 1999; Hermann et al., 2004). The alpha signal that occurred between the early and late gamma signals was also associated with activation in a number of different cortical areas, possibly reflecting the recruitment of other cortical areas to support a relatively complex cognitive task.

Although projections of magnocellular and parvocellular neurons through the dorsal and ventral pathways respectively are not completely discrete, making it more difficult to isolate the two pathways, the evidence nevertheless suggests that high frequency neural oscillations could be a mechanism for binding the visual qualities of text, carried by the magnocellular/dorsal pathway. Thus a story is emerging that both high and low frequency signals may be important in visual coding in reading.

TEMPORAL CODING, VISION, AND READING

Very little research has been done to measure frequency oscillations specifically targeting the visual cortex in reading, and there is a tension between evidence for a theta deficit in dyslexia, and evidence that the magnocellular pathway is associated with gamma oscillations. However a few studies have found vision-specific coding to visually presented words and sentences, in the context of whole-cortex language networks. The results appear to be mixed, but suggest an interesting relationship between gamma and theta oscillations. In one study, Goto et al. (2011) conducted a time × frequency analysis for the reading network. In this study, participants engaged in a silent reading task, and the data was analyzed in five frequency bands (theta, alpha, beta, low gamma, and high gamma), using a 200 ms moving window technique up to 1550 ms post stimulus onset (see also Pammer et al., 2004 for a description of the methodology and an example of the reading network). **Figure 2A**, is adapted from Goto et al. (2011) and shows two spectrograms of interest. The first (a) is isolated in that part of the visual cortex responsible for the fast coding of the visual components of text. The associated spectrogram suggests that there is an early, transient increase in power (ERS) in the theta range, followed by a sustained decrease in power (ERD) in the beta and low-gamma range. If we map this to a similar spectrogram but in the auditory cortex (in fact the location of "c" in **Figure 2** is slightly below the auditory cortex), there is a similar theta ERS approximately 100 ms after the signal in the visual cortex, and then a similar sustained beta/low gamma ERD. It is possible that these signals may be functionally coupled, but this remains to be seen. Moreover, this visual theta signal is also transient, and may reflect quite different functionality to the sustained theta signals described in the auditory temporal coding hypothesis. For example, Bosman et al. (2010) using a visual search and detection task, found that a transient increase in visual theta was locked to stimulus onset when the stimuli was present, but sustained when the target was not present. It was suggested that the sustained response might reflect a sustained search, while the transient response might reflect a stimulus-locked, motor preparation. Thus it will be important to differentiate between transient and sustained signals in terms of functional consequence.

Similarly, we presented participants with nine-word sentences as a rapid serial visual presentation (RSVP) (*Pammer and Holliday, unpublished data*) and found a sustained theta signal. In this study we isolated two visual signals: one in the primary visual cortex, and the other in the posterior parietal cortex (**Figure 2C**). The former we considered to represent early visual coding, while the latter should involve the dorsal visual pathway and early attentional allocation (e.g., Shomstein and Behrmann, 2006). Like Goto et al., the activation in the primary visual cortex reflects ERS and occurs in the theta/alpha range, start very early, but in this case is sustained. It is likely that this sustained signal reflects the fact that the RSVP were word strings forming sentences, rather than single words as presented in Goto et al. However, whether this signal reflects a "higher-order" cognitive component such as memory, or is a simple visual entrained signal, remains to be seen. With respect to the activity in the posterior parietal cortex, again there was a fast, early theta/alpha signal, but there was also a high frequency gamma signal peaking at approximately 200 ms and then sustained for approximately 500 ms. These results are also consistent with Fitzgibbon et al. (2004), who found both theta and gamma signals in a naturalistic silent reading task. The increase in power relative to a control condition is in red (**Figure 2B**), and although this was an EEG study and thus lacks some temporal and spatial specificity, the signals are clearly concentrated in the occipital cortex. Other reading studies that have focused on particular frequency bands have also found significant gamma and theta signals (e.g., Bastiaansen et al., 2010) in visual areas in the context of the larger reading network.

In summary, an important and interesting consistency between these studies and the studies in the auditory domain is the presence of oscillatory signals in the theta and gamma range. Thus a coherent framework is beginning to develop that may link poor reading to both theta and gamma synchrony, and thus may start to provide a resolution of the conflict between a temporal coding deficit in dyslexia which is believed to be characterized by deficits in the theta range, and deficits in the magnocellular pathway, where the magnocellular pathway has been implicated in gamma oscillations.

PHYSIOLOGICAL MECHANISMS

The cortical networks involved in reading are highly complex, requiring a sophisticated interplay of temporally and spatially dynamic interactions. Thus, a common mechanism such as temporal sampling for normal reading, and by extension—abnormal reading, could be explained in two possible ways. On the one hand, auditory and visual signals—both necessary for successful reading—may involve unique and discrete phase-locking at the local level, such that deficits within one or

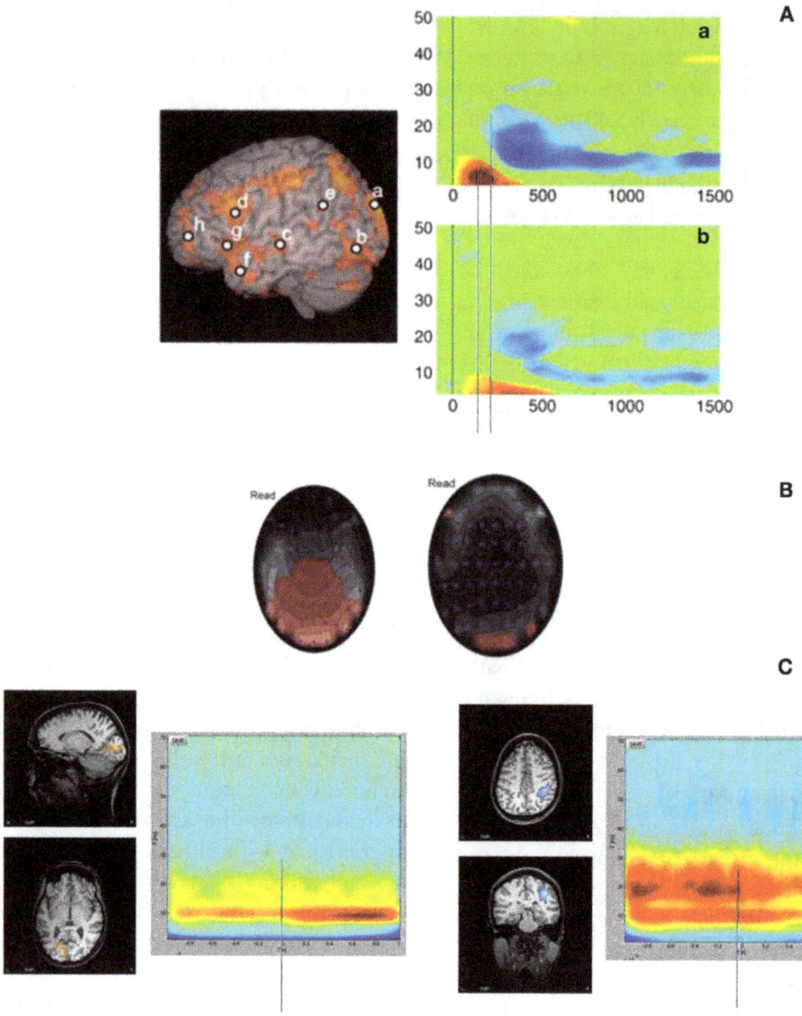

FIGURE 2 | Some illustrations of the potential relationship between low frequency and high frequency synchronisation in reading. (A) is adapted from Goto et al. (2011) demonstrating similar ERS and ERD interactions in the theta and gamma ranges in the visual and auditory cortices, refer to text for more detail **(A)** is partially reproduced with permission from Goto et al. (2011, p566, Elsevier). Similarly, Fitzgibbon et al. (2004) also demonstrate increases in gamma power (left) as well as theta (right) **(B)**. **(B)** is partially reproduced with permission from Fitzgibbon et al. (2004, p1806, Elsevier). The findings in **(A)** and **(B)** are consistent with results from our lab in which we demonstrate both gamma and theta/alpha signals to a RSVP reading task **(C)**. In this task, the stimuli were 8–9 word sentences presented RSVP at a rate of 102 ms per word, with a 16 ms ISI. Data was analyzed individually using SAM statistical mapping. SAM is a linear beamforming technique in which the MEG signal is passed through each channel, modified as a weighted linear function of the remaining channels (Vrba, 2002). SAM generates a statistical map by comparing and "active" period with a "control" period. In the current study, the reference control period for all comparisons was 1000 ms prior to the sentence onset. Montages were created for 5–40 Hz frequency bands, and the time × frequency spectrograms were created for two regions of interest that were apparent in all 10 subjects: the right PPc and the visual cortex. In the spectrograms, time includes the 1 sec pre-stimulus interval, and 1 sec sentence duration. Sentence onset is at 0 ms.

both modalities may manifest as a reading difficulty. Another possibility is the importance of long distance cross modal entrainment.

CROSS-MODAL MODULATION OF OSCILLATORY SIGNALS

One way in which cross modal modulation may manifest, is that the gamma and theta signals that are characteristic of language processing in dyslexia and implicated in visual coding in reading, are functionally coupled. One possibility is that the amplitude and/or phase of gamma oscillations are modulated or controlled by the phase of a theta oscillation (Siegel et al., 2012). The implications then are that a theta signal may provide a common regulatory mechanism for higher frequency signals in large-scale cortical networks. This makes intuitive sense in that any large scale neural network such as language perception, memory or reading requires a complex interplay of brain signals from disparate areas in the brain; communicating dynamically by various feed-forward and feedback interactions, with local networks synchronizing at different frequencies both within the network and between individual networks. That a lower-frequency signal may couple to these higher-frequency interactions provides a putative regulatory mechanism that would assist in guiding and adjusting phase and/or amplitude oscillations (e.g., Jensen and Colgin, 2007; Sauseng et al., 2008) between and within local neural networks.

Using direct sub-dural recordings during a number of different perceptual and cognitive tasks, Canolty et al. (2006) demonstrated that the power of very high frequency gamma oscillations (>75 Hz) as modulated by theta signals. Similarly, Doesburg et al. (2012) in an auditory cue task demonstrated significant increases in gamma synchronisation between the auditory and parietal cortex that were modulated by the phase of a concomitant theta signal. However, in both cases, these results could be the result of either within-modality, or within-site coupling. On the other hand, Demiralp et al. (2007) found theta/gamma coupling in a visual perception task, where the amplitude of an occipital gamma synchronisation was associated with a theta occipital as well as a frontal signal, suggesting the existence of more long range theta-to-gamma modulation.

There is also evidence for cross modal oscillatory phase setting such that an auditory signal entrains an oscillatory signal in the visual cortex, and importantly, increases perception for a visual signal (Romei et al., 2012). Although this was only demonstrated for alpha oscillations, it provides a principle to support the possibility that sensory stimuli, for example in the auditory domain, can entrain signals in the visual domain. This is important when considering reading, because the reading process is multi-modal. Behaviorally, reading and word recognition invariably generate a verbal code, and often an internal dialogue, and neuroimaging models of the reading network are consistent in involving visual, auditory and higher order language areas (Pammer et al., 2004).

If theta oscillations assist in coalescing discrete gamma oscillations into large-scale neuronal networks (Siegel et al., 2012), then the abnormal theta oscillations observed in language processing in dyslexia, may have an additional impact in the modulation of gamma synchronisation in the visual domain. Moreover, the abnormal theta oscillations observed may not be functionally important *per se* for the auditory coding of speech, or the visual processing of text, but instead modulate the higher frequency signals required in both the visual and auditory domains. For example, in reading and/or language, a gamma signal may be important for the fast sampling and coding of sensory events at the local level—in the visual domain such sensory coding may be controlled by the magnocellular pathway, while low frequency oscillations like theta may be responsible for more cognitive functions that are ubiquitous across modalities, such as working memory and/or attention, reflecting longer range interactions that mediate cognitive functions.

Lisman and Idiart (1995) were the first to propose that an interaction between low frequency brain waves such as theta oscillations and high frequency gamma oscillations may support short-term or working memory. Sensory—specific information may be coded at high frequencies, in spatially discrete networks (the visual or auditory cortex for example); then bound together in a short-term working memory mechanism coded through low frequency theta waves and via more long range networks, possibly via frontal and/or thalamic networks (refer to Jutras and Buffalo, 2010 for a review). For example, theta-gamma coupling is associated with working memory capacity (Moran et al., 2010), may be particularly important in maintaining temporal rather than spatial relationships (Roberts et al., 2013) and may specifically reflect retention in STM rather than encoding or recognition (Mizuhara and Yamaguchi, 2011).

Another candidate for a top-down theta mechanism, is attention, because both listening to a speech signal and reading require significant attentional input. However the evidence thus far suggests that gamma-theta coupling is specific to working memory, rather than sustained attention (Park et al., 2013). Moreover, attentional modulation of sensory signals appears to be characteristic of gamma and beta signals (refer to Siegel et al., 2012, for a recent review), rather than theta oscillations. Thus, both sensory coding and attentional modulation may be associated with oscillatory activity in the gamma range. It will be important in subsequent research to attempt to isolate attention from sensory coding, before making inferences about functionality. This will be particularly important in attention-intensive tasks like reading.

CONCLUSIONS, QUESTIONS, HYPOTHESES, AND PREDICTIONS

A substantial amount of research has been devoted to understanding coherent oscillatory activity in dyslexia, but most of this research has focused on the auditory domain. Similar research involving visual processing in dyslexia is virtually non-existent. Thus although I started out with the ambitious aim of describing a visual correlate of the auditory temporal coding hypothesis in dyslexia, this review has in the end attempted to weave together different strands of evidence to support the possibility of a common mechanism for both visual and language deficits in dyslexia. A targeted research program will be necessary to systematically analyse visual coding deficits in dyslexia in the context of temporal coding. Speculations here, suggest a number of hypotheses with clear predictions.

One question reflects the nature of hypothesized visual entrainment to reading. In language, the auditory entrainment occurs via amplitude modulation, but what is the physical visual signal that might entrain a theta rhythm? The first and simplest possibility is that the "shutter-like" quality of the saccade—fixation rhythm projects a rhythmic sequence of patterns at a frequency that will entrain a cortical response. If this was the case, then one should also be able to achieve the same cortical response using a simple RSVP task with patterns, letters or words. However, if cortical entrainment is coupled to the oculomotor behavior of the saccade-fixation rhythm, then maximum entrainment would be dependent on natural, contextual reading. Moreover, if this is the case, then the same signal should be able to be elicited by eye movements that simulate natural reading. Finally, if the cortical signal is in fact dependent on a memory code intrinsic to lexical access and the concatenation of current with previous lexical context when reading, rather than the actual saccade-fixation rhythm, then entrainment should occur in natural reading, but not simulated reading-like eye movements.

The temporal coding hypothesis as applied to auditory processing draws on a large amount of research which has investigated basic auditory coding, and suggests that dyslexic readers are less sensitive to some of the temporal coding aspects of speech, for example amplitude and frequency modulation at low frequencies.

A reasonable theoretical framework exists to implicate visual coding in much the same way; the temporal coding of reading mirrors in many ways the temporal coding of speech processing. Therefore, if poor phase locking and entrainment to an external signal forms part of the basis for dyslexia, then we should be able to show responses in the visual domain in dyslexic participants, which mirror those in the auditory domain. For example, if theta synchronisation is pervasive in visual and auditory processing, dyslexic readers should demonstrate reduced sensitivity also in visual tasks that modulate the input frequency in the theta range. For completeness, similar frequency modulations could be done at a range of frequencies in order to explore the possibility of differential sensitivities to different oscillations. Moreover, any sensitivity should also be correlated with reduced auditory sensitivity in the same theta frequency ranges.

Furthermore, exploring a temporal coding framework in other sensory domains from auditory coding, my give us some insight into the discrepancies that exist in the literature, where sensory deficits are not ubiquitous. While discrepant finding are well documented, once again we have little insight into why this might be the case. Thus, as I alluded to above, a temporal coding deficit in dyslexia may in fact be multi-modal, involving auditory, visual, and even motor kinaesthetic (e.g., Thomson and Goswami, 2008) elements. This is consistent with the behavioral literature, and theories suggesting that different manifestations of dyslexia, or different categories of dyslexia may reflect modality-specific differences in sensitivity (e.g., Hogben, 1996; Witton et al., 1998; Stein, 2001; Ramus et al., 2003). Moreover, there is no biological reason why this should not be the case, as multi-modal manifestations of temporal coding are well known, as described above. In the context of dyslexia then, it may be the case that temporal coding deficits may be weighted more heavily toward one or another modality in any individual. Here then, most dyslexic readers may show auditory temporal coding problems of varying degrees, consistent with the relatively stable findings of phonological deficits in dyslexia. However, individuals may also demonstrate visual temporal coding deficits which may manifest as dorsal coding deficits. If this were the case, then we should be able to show that the relative visual, auditory, and even kinaesthetic deficits in temporal coding are directly proportional to the behavioral manifestation of dorsal, auditory, and motor deficits in dyslexia.

Over 20 years of research suggests that there is a deficit in visual coding in dyslexia, and this deficit occurs as a consequence of abnormal visual coding in the magnocellular/dorsal pathway. The evidence reviewed here suggests that the magnocellular visual pathway generates high frequency gamma oscillations. Hence, dyslexic readers may have specific deficits in gamma synchronisation for tasks mediated by the magnocellular pathway, compared to normal readers.

One hypothesis that can be derived from the above discussion is that reading involves binding visual and spatial information in much the same way that occurs for general object recognition. Much of the research on object feature binding implicates gamma frequencies as an important cortical mechanism. Therefore, if dyslexic readers have problems in the binding of visual feature information in a way that is reflected in less stable synchronisation at gamma frequencies, then this should be reflected not only in word recognition, but also in other visual tasks that require feature binding.

The notion that high frequency cortical oscillations are the domain of the magnocellular visual pathway is still relatively speculative. Although good evidence attests to this suggestion, studies are still required to determine the exact spatio-temporal make-up of contrast sensitivity. A logical step here would be a replication of Fründ et al. (2007) but using MEG instead of EEG to allow better spatial mapping of the signals. Like Fründ et al., we would predict sensitivity to stimuli of a low spatial frequency to be associated with signals in the parietal cortex, and brain signals sensitive to higher spatial frequencies to be observed in the inferior temporal areas.

Studies using spatio-temporal mapping such as MEG would allow researchers to attribute oscillatory activity in different areas of the visual cortex to different functional components of the reading network. Such mapping is required at the very least in normal readers, and can then form a framework from which the causes of abnormal reading can be derived.

REFERENCES

Alegre, M., Imirizaldu, L., Valencia, M., Iriarte, J., Arcocha, J., and Artieda, J., (2006). Alpha and beta changes in cortical oscillatory activity in a go/no go randomly-delayed- response choice reaction time paradigm. *Clin. Neurophysiol.* 117, 16–25. doi: 10.1016/j.clinph.2005.08.030

Amitay, S., Ben-Yehudah, G., Banai, K., and Ahissar, M. (2002). Disabled readers suffer from visual and auditory impairments but not from a specific magnocellular deficit. *Brain* 125, 2272–2285. doi: 10.1093/brain/awf231

Badcock, D., and Lovegrove, W. (1981). The effects of contrast, stimulus duration, and spatial frequency on visible persistence in normal and specifically disabled readers. *J. Exp. Psychol. Hum. Percept. Perform.* 7, 495–505. doi: 10.1037/0096-1523.7.3.495

Badcock, N., Hogben, J., and Fletcher, J. (2008). No differential attentional blink in dyslexia after controlling for baseline sensitivity. *Vision Res.* 48, 1497–1502. doi: 10.1016/j.visres.2008.03.008

Başar-Eroglu, C., Struber, D., Schürmann, M., Stadler, M., and Başar, E. (1996). Gamma-band responses in the brain; a short review of psychophysiological correlates and functional significance. *Int. J. Psychophysiol.* 24, 101–112. doi: 10.1016/S0167-8760(96)00051-7

Bastiaansen, M., Magyari, L., and Hagoort, P. (2010). Syntactic unification operations are reflected in oscillatory dynamics during on-line sentence comprehension. *J. Cogn. Neurosci.* 22, 1333–1347. doi: 10.1162/jocn.2009.21283

Benardete, E. A., Kaplan, E., and Knight, B. W. (1992). Contrast gain control in the primate retina: P cells are not X-like, some M cells are. *Vis. Neurosci.* 8, 483–486. doi: 10.1017/S0952523800004995

Ben-Yehudah, G., Sackett, E., Malchi-Ginzberg, L., and Ahissar, M. (2001). Impaired temporal contrast sensitivity in dyslexics is specific to retain-and-compare paradigms. *Brain* 124, 1381–1395. doi: 10.1093/brain/124.7.1381

Berger, H. (1929). Über das Elektrenkephalogram des Menschen. *Arch. Psychiatry. Nervenkr.* 87, 527–570. doi: 10.1007/BF01797193

Boets, B., Wouters, J., van Wieringen, A., De Smedt, B., and Ghesquière, P. (2008). Modelling relations between sensory processing, speech perception, orthographic and phonological ability, and literacy achievement. *Brain Lang.* 106, 29–40. doi: 10.1016/j.bandl.2007.12.004

Bosman, C., Zamorano, F., and Aboitiz, F. (2010). Functional differences of low- and high-frequency oscillatory dynamics during illusory border perception. *Brain Res.* 1319, 92–102. doi: 10.1016/j.brainres.2010.01.004

Braddick, O., Atkinson, J., and Wattam-Bell, J. (2003). Normal and anomalous development of visual motion processing: motion coherence and "dorsal-stream vulnerability." *Neuropsychologia* 41, 1769–1784. doi: 10.1016/S0028-3932(03)00178-7

Brannan, J., and Williams, M. (1988). Developmental versus sensory deficit effects on perceptual processing in the reading disabled. *Percept. Psychophys.* 44, 437–444. doi: 10.3758/BF03210428

Burke, J., Zaghloul, K., Jacobs, J., Williams, R., Sperling, M., Sharan, A., et al. (2013). Synchronous and asynchronous theta and gamma activity during episodic memory formation. *J. Neurosci.* 33, 292–304. doi: 10.1523/JNEUROSCI.2057-12.2013

Canolty, R., Edwards, E., Dalal, S., Soltani, M., Nagarajan, S., Kirsch, H., et al. (2006). High gamma power is phase-locked to theta oscillations in human neocortex. *Science* 313, 1626–1628. doi: 10.1126/science.1128115

Caplan, J., Madsen, J., Schulze-Bonhage, A., Aschenbrenner-Scheibe, R., Newman, E., and Kahana, M. (2003). Human theta oscillations related to sensorimotor integration and spatial learning. *J. Neurosci.* 23, 4726–4736.

Cheong, S., Tailby, C., Martin, P., Levitt, J., and Solomon, S. (2011). Slow intrinsic rhythm in the koniocellular visual pathway. *Proc. Natl. Acad. Sci.* 108, 14659–14663. doi: 10.1073/pnas.1108004108

Cheyne, D., Ferrari, P., and Cheyne, J. (2012). Intended actions and unexpected outcomes: automatic and controlled processing in a rapid motor task. *Front. Hum. Neurosci.* 6, 237. doi: 10.3389/fnhum.2012.00237

Conlon, E., Sanders, M., and Zapart, S. (2004). Temporal processing in poor adult readers. *Neuropsychologia* 42, 142–157. doi: 10.1016/j.neuropsychologia.2003.07.004

Cornelissen, P., Hansen, P., Hutton, J., Evangelinou, V., and Stein, J. (1998). Magnocellular visual function and children's single word reading. *Vision Res.* 38, 471–482. doi: 10.1016/S0042-6989(97)00199-5

Cousineau, D., Charbonneau, D., and Jolicoeur, P. (2006). Parametizing the attentional blink effect. *Can. J. Psychol.* 60, 175–189.

de Boer-Schellekens, L., and Vroomen, J. (2012). Sound can improve visual search in developmental dyslexia. *Exp. Brain Res.* 216, 243–248. doi: 10.1007/s00221-011-2926-2

Demb, J., Boynton, G., and Heeger, D. (1998). Functional magnetic resonance imaging of early visual pathways in dyslexia. *J. Neurosci.* 18, 6939–6951.

Demiralp, T., Bayraktaroglu, Z., Lenz, D., Junge, S., Busch, N., Maess, B., et al. (2007). Gamma amplitudes are coupled to theta phase in human EEG during visual perception. *Int. J. Psychophysiol.* 64, 24–30. doi: 10.1016/j.ijpsycho.2006.07.005

Dhar, M., Been, P., Minderaa, R., and Althaus, M. (2010). Reduced interhemispheric coherence in dyslexic adults. *Cortex* 46, 794–798. doi: 10.1016/j.cortex.2009.09.006

di Lollo, V., Hanson, D., and McIntyre, J. (1983). Initial stages of visual information processing in dyslexia. *J. Exp. Psychol: Hum. Percept. Perform.* 9, 923–935. doi: 10.1037/0096-1523.9.6.923

Doesburg, S., Green, J., McDonald, J., and Ward, L. (2012). Theta modulation of inter-regional gamma synchronisation during auditory attention control. *Brain Res.* 1431, 77–85. doi: 10.1016/j.brainres.2011.11.005

Eden, G., Jones, K., Cappell, K., Gareau, L., Wood, F., Zeffiro, T., et al. (2004). Neural changes following remediation in adult developmental dyslexia. *Neuron* 44, 411–422. doi: 10.1016/j.neuron.2004.10.019

Eden, G. F., VanMeter, J. W., Rumsey, J. M., Maisog, J. M.,Woods, R. P., and Zeffiro, T. A. (1996). Abnormal processing of visual motion in dyslexia revealed by functional brain imaging. *Nature* 382, 66–69. doi: 10.1038/382066a0

Edwards, V. T., Giaschi, D. E., Dougherty, R. F., Edgell, D., Bjornson, B. H., Lyons, C., et al. (2004). Psychophysical indexes of temporal processing abnormalities in children with developmental dyslexia. *Dev. Neuropsychol.* 25, 321–354. doi: 10.1207/s15326942dn2503_5

Elliot, M., and Shanagher, L. (2010). Temporal event structure coding in developmental dyslexia: evidence from explicit and implicit temporal processes. *Psihologija* 43, 359–373. doi: 10.2298/PSI1004359E

Engel, A., and Singer, W. (2001). Temporal binding and the neuronal correlates of sensory awareness. *Trends Cogn. Sci.* 5, 16–25. doi: 10.1016/S1364-6613(00)01568-0

Facoetti, A., Lorusso, M. L., Paganoni, P., Cattaneo, C., Galli, R., and Mascetti, G. G. (2003). The time course of attentional focusing in dyslexic and normally reading children. *Brain Cogn.* 53, 181–184. doi: 10.1016/S0278-2626(03)00105-2

Facoetti, A., Paganoni, P., and Lorusso, M. L. (2000). The spatial distribution of visual attention in developmental dyslexia. *Exp. Brain Res.* 132, 531–538. doi: 10.1007/s002219900330

Facoetti, A., Ruffino, M., Peru, A., Paganoni, P., and Chelazzi. (2008). Sluggish engagement and disengagement of non-spatial attention in dyslexic children. *Cortex* 44, 1221–1233. doi: 10.1016/j.cortex.2007.10.007

Facoetti, A., Turatto, M., Lorusso, M. L., and Mascetti, G. G. (2001). Orienting of visual attention in dyslexia: evidence for asymmetrical hemispheric control of attention. *Exp. Brain Res.* 138, 46–53. doi: 10.1007/s002210100700

Facoetti, A., Zorzi, M., Cestnick, L., Lurusso, M. L., Molteni, M., Paganoni, P., et al., (2006). The relationship between visuo-spatial attention and nonword reading in developmental dyslexia. *Cogn. Neuropsychol.* 23, 841–855. doi: 10.1080/02643290500483090

Farmer, M., and Klein, R. (1995). The evidence for a temporal processing deficit linked to dyslexia: A review. *Psychon. B. Rev.* 2, 460–493. doi: 10.3758/BF03210983

Ferrera, V. P., Nealey, T. A., and Maunsell, J. H. R. (1992). Mixed parvocellular and magnocellular geniculate signals in visual area V4. *Nature* 358, 756–761. doi: 10.1038/358756a0

Fitzgibbon, S., Pope, K., Mackenzie, L., Clark, C., and Willoughby, J. (2004). Cognitive tasks augment gamma EEG power. *Clin. Neurophysiol.* 115, 1802–1809. doi: 10.1016/j.clinph.2004.03.009

Franceschini, S., Gori, S., Ruffino, M., Pedrolli, K., and Facoetti, A. (2012). A causal link between visual spatial attention and reading acquisition. *Curr. Biol.* 22, 814–819. doi: 10.1016/j.cub.2012.03.013

Franceschini, S., Gori, S., Ruffino, M., Viola, S., Molteni, M., and Facoetti, A. (2013). Action video games make dyslexic children read better. *Curr. Biol.* 23, 462–466. doi: 10.1016/j.cub.2013.01.044

Fries, P., Reynolds, J. H., Rorie, A. E., and Desimone, R. (2001). Modulation of oscillatory neuronal synchronization by selective visual attention. *Science* 291, 1560–1563. doi: 10.1126/science.1055465

Friese, U., Supp, G., Hipp, J., Engel, A., and Gruber, T. (2012). Oscillatory MEG gamma band activity dissociates perceptual and conceptual aspects of object processing: a combined repetition/conceptual priming study. *Neuroimage* 59, 861–871. doi: 10.1016/j.neuroimage.2011.07.073

Fründ, I., Busch, N., Körner, U., Schadow, J., and Herrmann, C. (2007). EEG oscillations in the gamma and alpha range respond differently to spatial frequency. *Vision Res.* 47, 2086–2098. doi: 10.1016/j.visres.2007.03.022

Galaburda, A., and Livingstone, M. (1993). Evidence for a magnocellular deficit in developmental dyslexia. *Ann. N. Y. Acad. Sci.* 682, 70–82.

Galambos, R. (1992). *A Comparison of Certain Gamma Band (40HZ) Brain Rhythms in Cat And Man*, Vol. Induced Rhythms in the Brain. Boston, MA: Birkauser.

Goodale, M. A., and Milner, A. D. (1992). Separate visual pathways for perception and action. *Trends Neurosci.* 15, 20–25.

Goto, T., Hirata, M., Umekawa, Y., Yanagisawa, T., Shayne, M., Saitoh, Y., et al. (2011). Frequency dependent spatiotemporal distribution of cerebral oscillatory changes during silent reading: A magnetoencephalographic group analysis. *Neuroimage* 54, 560–567. doi: 10.1016/j.neuroimage.2010.08.023

Goswami, U. (2011). A temporal sampling framework for developmental dyslexia. *Trends Cogn. Sci.* 15, 3–10. doi: 10.1016/j.tics.2010.10.001

Halliday, L., and Bishop, D. (2006). Is poor frequency modulation detection linked to literacy problems? A comparison of specific reading disability and mild to moderate sensorineural hearing loss. *Brain Lang.* 97, 200–213. doi: 10.1016/j.bandl.2005.10.007

Hämäläinen, M., Hari, R., Ilmoniemi, R., Knuutila, J., and Lounasmaa, O. (1993). Magnetoencephalography – theory, instrumentation, and applications to noninvasive studies of the working human brain. *Rev. Mod. Phys.* 65, 413–497. doi: 10.1103/RevModPhys.65.413

Hämäläinen, M., Rupp, A., Soltesz, F., Szucs, D., and Goswami, U. (2012), Reduced phase locking to slow amplitude modulation in adults with dyslexia: An MEG study. *Neuroimage* 59, 2952–2961. doi: 10.1016/j.neuroimage.2011.09.075

Hämäläinen, J., Salminen, H., and Leppanen, P. (2013). Basic auditory processing deficits in dyslexia; A systematic review of the behavioural and event-related potential field evidence. *J. Learn. Disabil.* 46, 413–427. doi: 10.1177/0022219411436213

Han, J., Mody, M., and Ahlfors, S. (2012). Gamma phase locking modulated by phonological contrast during auditory comprehension in reading disability. *Neuroreport* 23, 851–856. doi: 10.1097/WNR.0b013e32835818e1

Hari, R., Valta, M., and Uutela, K. (1999). Prolonged attentional dwell time in dyslexic adults. *Neurosci. Lett.* 271, 202–204. doi: 10.1016/S0304-3940(99)00547-9

Hari, R., Renvall, H., and Tanskanen, T. (2001). Left minineglect in dyslexic adults. *Brain* 124, 1373–1380. doi: 10.1093/brain/124.7.1373

Hatcher, J., Snowling, M., and Griffiths, Y. (2002). Cognitive assessment of dyslexic students in higher education. *Br. J. Educ. Psychol.* 72, 119–133. doi: 10.1348/000709902158801

Heim, S., Friedman, J., Keil, A., and Benasich, A. (2011). Reduced sensory oscillatory activity during rapid auditory processing as a correlate of language-learning impairment. *J. Neurolinguistics* 24, 538–555. doi: 10.1016/j.jneuroling.2010.09.006

Hermann, C., Munk, M., and Engel, A. (2004). Cognitive functions of gamma-band activity: memory match and utilization. *Trends Cogn. Sci.* 8, 347–533. doi: 10.1016/j.tics.2004.06.006

Hill, N., Bailey, P., Griffiths, Y., and Snowling, M. (1999). Frequency acuity and binaural masking release in dyslexic listeners. *J. Acoust. Soc. Am.* 106, 53–58. doi: 10.1121/1.428154

Hodgkin, A., and Huxley, A. (1952). A quantitative description of membrane current and its application to conductance and excitation in nerve. *J. Physiol.* 117, 500–544.

Hogben, J. (1996). A plea for purity. *Aust. J. Psychol.* 48, 172–177. doi: 10.1080/00049539608259526

Hummel, F., and Gerloff, C. (2005). Larger interregional synchrony is associated with greater behavioural success in a complex sensory integration task in humans. *Cereb. Cortex* 15, 670–678. doi: 10.1093/cercor/bhh170

Iles, J., Walsh, V., and Richardson, A. (2000). Visual search performance in dyslexia. *Dyslexia* 6, 163–177. doi: 10.1002/1099-0909(200007/09)6:3<163::AID-DYS150>3.0.CO;2-U

Jaskowski, P., and Rusiak, P. (2008). Temporal order judgement in dyslexia. *Psychol. Res.* 72, 65–73. doi: 10.1007/s00426-006-0093-z

Jednorog, K., Marchewka, A., Tacikowski, P., Heim, S., and Grabowska, A. (2011). Electrophysiological evidence for the magnocellular-dorsal pathway deficit in dyslexia. *Dev. Sci.* 14, 873–880. doi: 10.1111/j.1467-7687.2011.01037.x

Jensen, O., and Colgin, L. (2007). Cross-frequency coupling between neuronal oscillations. *Trends Cogn. Sci.* 11, 267–269. doi: 10.1016/j.tics.2007.05.003

Jensen, O., Kaiser, J., and Lachaux, J. (2007). Human gamma-frequency oscillations associated with attention and memory. *Trends Neurosci.* 30, 317–324. doi: 10.1016/j.tins.2007.05.001

Jones, M., Branigan, H., and Kelly, L. (2008). Visual deficits in developmental dyslexia: Relationships between non-linguistic tasks and their contribution to components of reading. *Dyslexia* 14, 95–115. doi: 10.1002/dys.345

Jutras, M., and Buffalo, E. (2010). Synchronous neural activity and memory formation. *Curr. Opin. Neurobiol.* 20, 150–155. doi: 10.1016/j.conb.2010.02.006

Kahana, M., Sekuler, J., Caplan, M., Kirschen, M., and Madsen, J. (1999). Human theta oscillations exhibit task dependence during virtual maze navigation. *Nature* 399, 781–784. doi: 10.1038/21645

Kevan, A., and Pammer, K. (2008). Making the link between dorsal stream sensitivity and reading. *NeuroReoprt* 19, 467–470. doi: 10.1097/WNR.0b013e3282f5f7ad

Kevan, A., and Pammer, K. (2009). Predicting early reading skills from pre-reading measures of dorsal stream functioning. *Neuropsychologia* 47, 3174–3181. doi: 10.1016/j.neuropsychologia.2009.07.016

Klimesch, W., Doppelmayer, M., Wimmer, H., Gruber, W., Röhm, D., Schwaiger, J., et al. (2001a). Alpha and beta power changes in normal and dyslexic children. *Clin. Neurophysiol.* 112, 1186–1195. doi: 10.1016/S1388-2457(01)00543-0

Klimesch, W., Doppelmayer, M., Wimmer, H., Schwaiger, J., Röhm, D., Gruber, W., et al. (2001b). Theta band power changes in normal and dyslexic children. *Clin. Neurophysiol.* 112, 1174–1185. doi: 10.1016/S1388-2457(01)00545-4

Kujala, J., Pammer, K., Cornelissen, P., Roebroek, A., Formisano, E., and Salmelin, R. (2007). Phase coupling in a cerebro-cerebellar network at 8-13 Hz during reading. *Cereb. Cortex* 17, 1476–1485. doi: 10.1093/cercor/bhl059

Kyle, F., Kujala, J., Richardson, U., and Lyytinen, H. (2013). Assessing the effectiveness of two theoretically motivated computer-assisted reading interventions in the United Kingdom: GG Rime and GG Phoneme. *Read. Res. Quart.* 48, 61–76. doi: 10.1002/rrq.038

Lachaux, J. P., Rodriguez, E., Martinerie, J., and Varela, J. (1999). Measuring Phase Synchrony in Brain Signals. *Hum. Brain Mapp.* 8, 194–208. doi: 10.1002/(SICI)1097-0193(1999)8:4<194::AID-HBM4>3.0.CO;2-C

Lallier, M., Donnadieu, S., and Valdois, S. (2010). Visual attentional blink in dyslexic children: Parametizing the deficit. *Vision Res.* 50, 1855–1861. doi: 10.1016/j.visres.2010.06.006

Landerl, K., and Willburger, E., (2010). Temporal processing, attention and learning disorders. *Learn. Individ. Differ.* 20, 393–401. doi: 10.1016/j.lindif.2010.03.008

La Roque, C., and Visser, T. (2009). Sequential object recognition deficits in normal readers. *Vision Res.* 49, 96–101. doi: 10.1016/j.visres.2008.09.027

Lega, B., Jacobs, J., and Kahana, M., (2012). Human hippocampal theta oscillations and the formation of episodic memories. *Hippocampus* 22, 748–761. doi: 10.1002/hipo.20937

Lehongre, K., Ramus, F., Villiermet, N., Schwartz, D., and Giraud, A.-L. (2011). Altered low-gamma sampling in auditory cortex accounts for the three main facets of dyslexia. *Neuron* 72, 1080–1090. doi: 10.1016/j.neuron.2011.11.002

Leonard, C., and Eckert, M. (2008). Asymetry and dyslexia. *Dev. Neuropsychol.* 33, 663–681. doi: 10.1080/87565640802418597

Liddle, E., Jackson, G., Rorden, C., and Jackson, S. (2009). Lateralized temporal order judgement in dyslexia. *Neuropsychologia* 47, 3244–3254. doi: 10.1016/j.neuropsychologia.2009.08.007

Lindgren, S.-A., and Laine, M. (2011). Cognitive linguistic performances of multilingual university students suspected of dyslexia. *Dyslexia* 17, 184–200. doi: 10.1002/dys.422

Lisman, J., and Idiart, M. (1995). Storage of 7 +- 2 short-term memories in oscillatory subcycles. *Science* 267, 1512–1515. doi: 10.1126/science.7878473

Livingston, M. (1996). Oscillatory firing and interneuronal correlations in squirrel monkey striate cortex. *J. Neurophysiol.* 75, 2467–2485.

Livingstone, M. S., and Hubel, D. H. (1988). Segregation of form, color, movement, and depth: anatomy, physiology, and perception. *Science* 240, 740–749. doi: 10.1126/science.3283936

Llinas, R., and Steriade, M. (2006). Bursting of thalamic neurons and states of vigilance. *J. Neurophysiol.* 95, 3297–3308. doi: 10.1152/jn.00166.2006

Llinas, R., Grace, A., and Yarom, Y. (1991). Invitro neurons in mammalian cortical layer 4 exhibit intrinsic oscillatory activity in the 10-Hz to 50-Hz frequency range. *Proc. Natl. Acad. Sci. U.S.A.* 88, 897–901. doi: 10.1073/pnas.88.3.897

Lovegrove, W., Heddle, M., and Slaghuis, W. (1980). Reading disability: Spatial frequency specific deficits in visual information store. *Neuropsychologia* 18, 111–115. doi: 10.1016/0028-3932(80)90093-7

Lovegrove, W., Martin, F., and Slaghuis, W. (1986). A theoretical and experimental case for a visual deficit in specific reading disability. *Cogn. Neuropsychol.* 3, 225–267. doi: 10.1080/02643298608252677

Luo, H., and Poeppel, D. (2007). Phase patterns of neuronal responses reliably discriminate speech in human auditory cortex. *Neuron* 54, 1001–1010. doi: 10.1016/j.neuron.2007.06.004

Martin, F., and Lovegrove, W. (1987). Flicker contrast sensitivity in normal and specifically disabled readers. *Perception* 16, 215–221. doi: 10.1068/p160215

Martinez, A., Anllo-Vento, L., Sereno, M., Frank, L., Buxton, R. B., Dubowitz, D. J., et al. (1999). Involevement of striate and extrastriate visual cortical areas in spatial attention. *Nat. Neurosci.* 2, 364–369. doi: 10.1038/7274

Martinovic, J., Gruber, T., and Müller, M. (2008). Coding of visual obect features and feature conjunctions in the human brain. *PLoS ONE:* 3:e3781 doi: 10.1371/journal.pone.0003781

McLean, G., Castles, A., Coltheart, V., and Stuart, G. (2010). No evidence for a prolonged attentional blink in developmental dyslexia. *Cortex* 46, 1317–1329. doi: 10.1016/j.cortex.2010.06.010

McLean, G., Stuart, G., Coltheart, V., and Castles, A. (2011). Visual temporal processing in dyslexia and the magnocellular deficit theory: The need for speed? *J. Exp. Psychol. Hum. Percept. Perform.* 37, 1957–1975. doi: 10.1037/a0024668

McLean, G., Stuart, G., Visser, T., and Castles, A., (2009). The attentional blink in developing readers. *Scientific Studies of Reading,* 13, 334–357. doi: 10.1080/10888430903001365

Merigan, W. H., and Maunsell, J. H. R. (1993). How parallel are the primate visual pathways? *Ann. Rev. Neurosci.* 16, 369–402. doi: 10.1146/annurev.neuro.16.1.369

Merker, B. (2013). Ortical gamma oscillations: the functional key is activation, not cognition. *Neurosci. Biobehav. Rev.* 37, 401–417. doi: 10.1016/j.neubiorev.2013.01.013

Messaoud-Galusi, S., Hazan, V. and Rosen, S. (2011). Investigating Speech perception in children with Dyslexia: is there evidence of a consistent deficit in individuals? *J. Speech Lang. Hear. Res.* 54, 1682–1701. doi: 10.1044/1092-4388(2011/09-0261)

Meyler, A., and Breznitz, Z. (2005). Visual, auditory and cross-modal processing of linguistic and nonlinguistic temporal patterns among adult dyslexic readers. *Dyslexia*, 93, 93–115. doi: 10.1002/dys.294

Milne, D., Hamm, J., Kirk, I., and Corballis, M. (2003). Anterior-posterior beta asymmetries in dyslexia during lexical decisions. *Brain lang.* 84, 309–317. doi: 10.1016/S0093-934X(02)00557-6

Mizuhara, H., and Yamaguchi, Y. (2011). Neuronal ensemble for visual working memory via interplay of slow and fast oscillations. *Eur. J. Neurosci.* 33, 1925–1934. doi: 10.1111/j.1460-9568.2011.07681.x

Moores, E., Cassim, R., and Talcott, J. (2011). Adults with dyslexia exhibit large effects of crowding, increased dependence on cues and detrimental effects of distractors in visual search tasks. *Neuropsychologia* 49, 3881–3890. doi: 10.1016/j.neuropsychologia.2011.10.005

Moran, J., and Desimone, R. (1985). Selective attention gates visual processing in the extrastriate cortex. *Science* 229, 782–784. doi: 10.1126/science.4023713

Moran, R., Campo, P., Maestu, F., Reilly, R., Dolan, R., and Strange, B. (2010). Peak frequency in the theta and alpha bands correlates with human working memory capacity. *Front. Hum. Neurosci.* 4, 1–12. doi: 10.3389/fnhum.2010.00200

Motter, B. (1993). Focal attention produces spatially selective processing in visual cortical areas V1, V2 and V4 in the presence of competing stimuli. *J. Neurophysiol.* 70, 909–919.

Nagarajan, S., Mahncke, H., Salz, T., Tallal, P., Roberts, T., and Merzenich, M. (1999). Cortical auditory signal processing in poor readers. *Proc. Natl. Acad. Sci. U.S.A.* 96, 6483–6488. doi: 10.1073/pnas.96.11.6483

Nealey, T. A., and Maunsell, J. H. R. (1994). Magnocellular and parvocellular contributions to the responses of neurons in macaque striate cortex *J. Neurosci. 14*, 2069–2079.

Neuper, C., and Pfurtscheller, G. (2001). Event related dynamics of cortical rhythms: frequency-specific features and functional correlates. *Int. J. Psychophysiol.* 43, 41–58. doi: 10.1016/S0167-8760(01)00178-7

Olivers, C., and Meeter, M. (2008). A boost and bounce theory of temporal attention. *Psychol. Rev.* 115, 836–863. doi: 10.1037/a0013395

Olson, R., and Datta, H. (2002). Visual temporal processing in reading-disabled and normal twins. *Read. Writ.* 15, 127–149. doi: 10.1023/A:1013872422108

Pammer, K., Hansen, P., Holliday, I., and Cornelissen, P. (2006). Attentional shifting and the role of the dorsal pathway in visual word recognition. *Neuropsychologia* 44, 2926–2936. doi: 10.1016/j.neuropsychologia.2006.06.028

Pammer, K., Hansen, P., Kringelbach, M., Holliday, I., Barnes, G., Hillebrand, A., et al. (2004). Visual word recognition: the first half second. *Neuroimage* 22, 1819–1825. doi: 10.1016/j.neuroimage.2004.05.004

Pammer, K., and Kevan, A., (2007). The contribution of visual sensitivity, phonological processing, and non-verbal IQ to children's reading. *Sci. Stud. Read.* 11, 33–53. doi: 10.1080/10888430709336633

Pammer, K., and Vidyasagar, T. R. (2005). Integration of the visual and auditory networks in dyslexia: a theoretical perspective. *J. Res. Read.* 28, 320–331. doi: 10.1111/j.1467-9817.2005.00272.x

Pammer, K., and Wheatley, C. (2001). Isolating the M(y)-cell response in dyslexia using the spatial frequency doubling illusion. *Vision Res.* 41, 2139–2147. doi: 10.1016/S0042-6989(01)00092-X

Park, J., Jhung, K., Lee, J., and An, S. (2013). Theta-gamma coupling during a working memory task as compared to a simple vigilance task. *Neurosci. Lett.* 532, 39–43. doi: 10.1016/j.neulet.2012.10.061

Pfurtscheller, G., and Klimesch, W. (1991). Event-related desynchronization during motor behaviour and visual information processing. *Electroencephalogr. Clin. Neurophysiol. Suppl.* 42, 58–65.

Pfurtscheller, G., and Lopes da Silva, F. (1999). Event-related EEG/MEG synchronization and desynchronization: basic principles. *Clin. Neurophysiol.* 110, 1842–1857. doi: 10.1016/S1388-2457(99)00141-8

Pikovsky, A., Rosenblum, M., and Kurths, J. (2003). *Synchronization A Universal Concept in Nonlinear Sciences*, 1st Ed. New York, NY: Cambridge University Press.

Price, N., and Ibbotson, M. (2001). Pretectal neurons optimized for the detection of saccade-like movements of the visual image. *J. Neurophysiol.* 85, 1512–1521.

Pulvermüller, F., Birbaumer, N., Lutzenberger, W., and Mohr, B. (1997). High frequency brain activity: its possible role in attention, perception and language processing. *Prog. Neurobiol.* 52, 427–445. doi: 10.1016/S0301-0082(97)00023-3

Ramus, F., Rosen, S., Dakin, S., Day, B., Castellote, J., White, S., et al. (2003). Theories of developmental dyslexia: insights from a multiple case study of dyslexic adults. *Brain* 126, 841–865. doi: 10.1093/brain/awg076

Rayner, K. (1998). Eye movements in reading and information processing: twenty years of research. *Psychol. Bull.* 124, 372–422. doi: 10.1037/0033-2909.124.3.372

Rayner, K., Foorman, B., Perfetti, C., Pesetsky, D., and Seidenberg, M. (2001). How psychological science informs the teaching of reading. *Psychol. Sci.* 2(Suppl. 2), 31–74. doi: 10.1111/1529-1006.00004

Rippon, G., and Brunswick, N. (2000). Trait and state EEG indices of information processing in developmental dyslexia. *Int. J. Psychophysiol.* 36, 251–265. doi: 10.1016/S0167-8760(00)00075-1

Roberts, B., Hsieh, L.-T., and Ranganath, C. (2013). Oscillatory activity during maintenance of spatial and temporal information in working memory. *Neuropsychologia* 51, 349–357. doi: 10.1016/j.neuropsychologia.2012.10.009

Romei, V., Gross, J., and Thut, G. (2012). Sounds reset rhythms of visual cortex and corresponding human visual perception. *Curr. Biol.* 22, 807–813. doi: 10.1016/j.cub.2012.03.025

Rutkowski, J., Crewther, D., and Crewther, S. (2003). Change detection is impaired in children with dyslexia. *J. Vis.* 3, 95–105. doi: 10.1167/3.1.10

Salmelin, R., Forss, N., Knuutila, J., and Hari, R. (1995). Bilateral activation of the human somatomotor cortex by distal hand movements. *Electroencephalogr. Clin. Neurophysiol.* 95, 444–452. doi: 10.1016/0013-4694(95)00193-X

Sauseng, P., Klimesch, W., Guber, W., and Birbaumer, N. (2008). Cross frequency phase synchronisation: a brain mechanism of memory matching and attention. *Neuroimage* 40, 308–317. doi: 10.1016/j.neuroimage.2007.11.032

Sauseng, P., Klimesch, W., Heise, K., Gruber, W., Holz, E., Karim, A., et al. (2009). Brain oscillatory substrates of visual short-term memory capacity. *Curr. Biol.* 19, 1846–1852. doi: 10.1016/j.cub.2009.08.062

Sauve, K. (1999). Gamma-band synchronous oscillations: recenet evidence regarding their functional significance. *Conscious. Cogn.* 8, 213–224. doi: 10.1006/ccog.1999.0383

Scanlon, D. (2012). Specific learning disability and its newest definition: which is comprehensive? And which is insufficient? *J. Learn. Disabil.* 46, 26–33. doi: 10.1177/0022219412464342

Schulte-Körne, G., Bartling, J., Deimel, W., and Remschmidt, H. (2004). Spatial-frequency and contrast dependent visible persistence and reading disorder: no evidence for a basic perceptual deficit. *J. Neural Transm.* 111, 941–950. doi: 10.1007/s00702-004-0135-x

Sewards, T., and Sewards, M. (1999). Alpha band oscillations in visual cortex: part of the neural correlate of visual awareness? *Int. J. Psychophysiol.* 32, 35–45. doi: 10.1016/S0167-8760(98)00062-2

Shomstein, S., and Behrmann, M. (2006). Objects modulate competition in human parietal and extrastriate cortices. *Proc. Natl. Acad. Sci. U.S.A.* 103, 11387–11392. doi: 10.1073/pnas.0601813103

Siegel, M., Donner, T., and Engel, A. (2012). Spectral fingerprints of large-scale neuronal interactions. *Nat. Rev. Neurosci.* 13, 121–134. doi: 10.1038/nrn3137

Singer, W. (1999). Neuronal synchrony: a versatile code for the definition of relations? *Neuron* 24, 49–65. doi: 10.1016/S0896-6273(00)80821-1

Singer, W. (2009). Distributed processing and temporal codes in neuronal networds. *Cogn. Neurodyn.* 3, 189–196. doi: 10.1007/s11571-009-9087-z

Sireteanu, R., Goebel, C., Goertz, R., Werner, I., Nalewajko, M., and Thiel, A. (2008). Impaired visual search in children with developmental dyslexia. *Ann. N. Y. Acad. Sci.* 1145, 199–211. doi: 10.1196/annals.1416.021

Skottun, B. (2005). Magnocellular reading and dyslexia. *Vision Res.* 45, 133–134. doi: 10.1016/j.visres.2003.09.039

Skottun, B., and Skoyles, J. (2007). The use of visual search to assess attention. *Clin. Exp. Optom.* 90, 20–25. doi: 10.1111/j.1444-0938.2006.00074.x

Skottun, B., and Skoyles, J. (2008). Coherent motion, magnocellular sensitivity and the causation of dyslexia. *Int. J. Neurosci.* 118, 185–190. doi: 10.1080/00207450601041872

Slaghuis, W., and Lovegrove, W. (1985). Spatial frequency dependent visible persistence and specific reading disability. *Brain Cogn.* 4, 219–240. doi: 10.1016/0278-2626(85)90071-5

Slaghuis, W., and Ryan, J. (1999). Spatio-temporal contrast sensitivity, coherent motion, and visible persistence in developmental dyslexia. *Vision Res.* 39, 651–668. doi: 10.1016/S0042-6989(98)00151-5

Snowling, M. (2000). *Dyslexia*. Oxford, UK: Blackwell publishers.

Spironelli, C., Penolazzi, B., and Angrilli, A. (2008). Dysfunctional hemispheric asymmetry of theta and beta EEG activity during linguistics tasks in developmental dyslexia. *Biol. Psychol.* 77, 123–131. doi: 10.1016/j.biopsycho.2007.09.009

Stancák, A. Jr., and Pfurtscheller, G. (1996). Event-related desynchronisation of central beta-rhythms during brisk and slow self-paced finger movements of dominant and nondominant hand. *Cogn. Brain Res.* 4, 171–183. doi: 10.1016/S0926-6410(96)00031-6

Stein, J., and Walsh, V. (1997). To see but not to read: the magnocellular theory of dyslexia. *Trends Neurosci.* 20, 147–152. doi: 10.1016/S0166-2236(96)01005-3

Stein, J. F. (2001). The magnocellular theory of developmental dyslexia. *Dyslexia* 7, 12–36. doi: 10.1002/dys.186

Stein, J., Richardson, A., and Fowler, M. (2000). Monocular occlusion can improve binocular control and reading in dyslexics. *Brain* 123, 164–170. doi: 10.1093/brain/123.1.164

Stuart, G., McAnally, K., and Castles, A. (2001). Can contrast sensitivity functions in dyslexics be explained by inattention rather than a magnocellular deficit? *Vision Res.* 41, 3205–3211. doi: 10.1016/S0042-6989(01)00176-6

Tallon-Baudry, C. (2009). The roles of gamma-band oscillatory synchrony in human visual cognition. *Front. Biosci.* 14, 321–332. doi: 10.2741/3246

Tallon-Baudry, C., and Bertrand, O. (1999). Oscillatory gamma activity in humans and its role in object representation. *Trends Cogn. Sci.* 3, 151–162. doi: 10.1016/S1364-6613(99)01299-1

Tallon-Baudry, C., Bertrand, O., Delpuech, C., and Pernier, J. (1996). Stimulus specificity of phase-locked and non-phase-locked 40Hz visual responses in human. *J. Neurosci.* 16, 4240–4249.

Tallon-Baudry, C., Bertrand, O., Delpuech, C., and Pernier, J. (1997). Oscillatory gamma-band (30-70 Hz) activity induced by a visual search task in humans. *J. Neurosci.* 17, 722–734.

Thomson, J., Fyer, B., Maltby, J., and Goswami, U. (2006). Auditory and motor rhythm awareness in adults with dyslexia. *J. Res. Read.* 29, 334–348. doi: 10.1111/j.1467-9817.2006.00312.x

Thomson, J., and Goswami, U. (2008). Rhythmic processing in children with developmental dyslexia: auditory and motor rhythms link to reading and spelling. *J. Physiol. Paris* 102, 120–129. doi: 10.1016/j.jphysparis.2008.03.007

Thut, G., Miniussi, C., and Gross, J. (2012). The functional importance of rhythmic activity in the brain. *Curr. Biol.* 22, 658–663. doi: 10.1016/j.cub.2012.06.061

Thut, G., Schyns, P., and Gross, J. (2011). Entrainment of perceptually relevant brain oscillations by non-invasive rhythmic stimulation of the human brain. *Front. Psychol.* 2, 1–10. doi: 10.3389/fpsyg.2011.00170

Ucles, P., Mendez, M., and Garay, J. (2009). Low level defective processing of non-verbal sounds in dyslexic children. *Dyslexia* 15, 72–85. doi: 10.1002/dys.360

Vidyasagar, T. R. (1998). Gating of neuronal responses in macaque primary visual cortex by an attentional spotlight. *Neuroreport* 9, 1947–1952. doi: 10.1097/00001756-199806220-00006

Vidyasagar, T. R. (1999). A neuronal model of attentional spotlight: parietal guiding the temporal. *Brain Res. Rev.* 30, 66–76. doi: 10.1016/S0165-0173(99)00005-3

Vidyasagar, T. R. (2004). Neural underpinnings of dyslexia as a disorder of visuo-spatial attention. *Clin. Exp. Optom.* 87, 4–10. doi: 10.1111/j.1444-0938.2004.tb03138.x

Vidyasagar, T. R., Kulikowski, J. J., Lipnicki, D. M., and Dreher, B. (2002). Convergence of parvocellular and magnocellular information channels in the primary visual cortex of the macaque. *Eur. J. Neurosci.* 16, 945–956. doi: 10.1046/j.1460-9568.2002.02137.x

Vidyasagar, T. R., and Pammer, K. (1999). Impaired visual search in dyslexia relates to the role of the magnocellular pathway in attention. *Neuroreport* 10, 1283–1287. doi: 10.1097/00001756-199904260-00024

Vidyasagar, T. R., and Pammer, K. (2010). Dyslexia: a deficit in visuo-spatial attention, not in phonological processing. *Trends Cogn. Sci.* 14, 57–63. doi: 10.1016/j.tics.2009.12.003

Visser, T., Boden, C., and Giaschi, D. (2004). Children with dyslexia: evidence for visual attention deficits in perception of rapid series of objects. *Vision Res.* 44, 2521–2535. doi: 10.1016/j.visres.2004.05.010

Vrba, J. (2002). Magnetoencephalography: the art of finding a needle in a haystack. *Physica C* 368, 1–9. doi: 10.1016/S0921-4534(01)01131-5

Wang, X.-J. (2010). Neurophysiological and computational principles of cortical rhythms in cognition. *Physiol. Rev.* 90, 1195–1268. doi: 10.1152/physrev.00035.2008

White, S., Milne, E., Rosen, S., Hansen, P., Sweltenham, J., Frith, U., et al. (2006). Therole of sensorimotor impairments in dyslexia: a multiple case study of dyslexic children. *Dev. Sci.* 9, 237–255. doi: 10.1111/j.1467-7687.2006.00483.x

Wiesel, T., and Hubel, D. (1966). Spatial and chromatic interactions in the lateral geniculate body of the rhesus monkey. *J. Neurophysiol.* 29, 1115–1156.

Williams, M., Brannan, J., and Lartigue, E. (1987). Visual search in good and poor readers. *Clin. Vision Sci.* 1, 367–371.

Witton, C., Stein, J., Stoodley, C., Rosner, B., and Talcott, J. (2002). Separate influences of acoustic AM and FM sensitivity on the phonological decoding skills of impaired and normal readers. *J. Cogn. Neurosci.* 14, 866–874. doi: 10.1162/089892902760191090

Witton, C., Talcott, J. B., Hansen, P. C., Richardson, A. J., Griffiths, T. D., Rees, A., et al. (1998). Sensitivity to dynamic auditory and visual stimuli predicts nonword reading ability in both dyslexic and normal readers. *Curr. Biol.* 8, 791–797. doi: 10.1016/S0960-9822(98)70320-3

Wright, C., and Conlon, E. (2009). Auditory and visual processing in children with dyslexia. *Dev. Neuropsychol.* 34, 330–355. doi: 10.1080/87565640902801882

Wu, H., Nagasawa, T., Brown, E., Juhasz, C., Rothermel, R., Hoechstetter, K., et al. (2011). Gamma-oscillations modulated by picture naming and word reading: intracranial recording in epileptic patients. *Clin. Neurophysiol.* 122, 1929–1942. doi: 10.1016/j.clinph.2011.03.011

Yabuta, N. H., and Callaway, E. M. (1998). Functional streams and local connections of layer 4C neurons in primary visual cortex of the macaque monkey. *J. Neurosci.* 18, 9489–9499.

Zeki, S., (1993). *Vision of the Brain.* Oxford, UK: Blackwell Scientific Publication.

5

Visual word learning in adults with dyslexia

Rosa K. W. Kwok and Andrew W. Ellis*

Department of Psychology, University of York, York, UK

Correspondence:
Andrew W. Ellis, Department of Psychology, University of York, York, YO10 5DD, UK
e-mail: andy.ellis@york.ac.uk

We investigated word learning in university and college students with a diagnosis of dyslexia and in typically-reading controls. Participants read aloud short (4-letter) and longer (7-letter) nonwords as quickly as possible. The nonwords were repeated across 10 blocks, using a different random order in each block. Participants returned 7 days later and repeated the experiment. Accuracy was high in both groups. The dyslexics were substantially slower than the controls at reading the nonwords throughout the experiment. They also showed a larger length effect, indicating less effective decoding skills. Learning was demonstrated by faster reading of the nonwords across repeated presentations and by a reduction in the difference in reading speeds between shorter and longer nonwords. The dyslexics required more presentations of the nonwords before the length effect became non-significant, only showing convergence in reaction times between shorter and longer items in the second testing session where controls achieved convergence part-way through the first session. Participants also completed a psychological test battery assessing reading and spelling, vocabulary, phonological awareness, working memory, nonverbal ability and motor speed. The dyslexics performed at a similar level to the controls on nonverbal ability but significantly less well on all the other measures. Regression analyses found that decoding ability, measured as the speed of reading aloud nonwords when they were presented for the first time, was predicted by a composite of word reading and spelling scores ("literacy"). Word learning was assessed in terms of the improvement in naming speeds over 10 blocks of training. Learning was predicted by vocabulary and working memory scores, but not by literacy, phonological awareness, nonverbal ability or motor speed. The results show that young dyslexic adults have problems both in pronouncing novel words and in learning new written words.

Keywords: word learning, reading, dyslexia, word length, repetition, working memory, phonological awareness

INTRODUCTION

The problems that dyslexic children and adults experience in reading and spelling have been well documented, even if there is continuing debate about the underlying causes of those difficulties (Snowling, 2001; Vellutino et al., 2004; Van den Broeck and Geudens, 2012). One aspect of reading skill that has received less attention than most in the literature, however, is how dyslexics learn new written words and how their ability to learn new words compares with that of normal readers (Reitsma, 1983; Ehri and Saltmarsh, 1995; Mayringer and Wimmer, 2000; Share and Shalev, 2004; Thomson and Goswami, 2010; De Jong and Messbauer, 2011). The current paper develops a methodology for studying basic aspects of word learning that we believe has considerable potential and applies it to understanding visual word learning in groups of dyslexic adults and normally-reading controls.

As children grow older, reading becomes an important source of new words that they must learn to recognize and understand if they are to function effectively (Cunningham et al., 2002; Cunningham, 2006; Nation, 2008, 2009). Nowhere is this more true than in higher education where, if students are to progress satisfactorily, they must learn new words connected with their academic studies that are often encountered first in written form (Mortimore and Crozier, 2006). Our concern in the present study is not with how dyslexics learn to associate new words with meanings, but rather with the process by which initially unfamiliar words become familiar through exposure and repetition, reaching the point where they can be recognized and processed as whole units rather than in piecemeal fashion.

The starting point for our investigation was a study by Weekes (1997) who asked skilled adult readers (undergraduate students at a UK university) to read aloud a mixture of familiar words and invented nonwords as quickly as possible. Naming latencies were measured as the time between a word or nonword appearing on the screen and the participant beginning to pronounce it. The words were either high frequency (e.g., bed, large) or low frequency (e.g., beg, latch): the nonwords were pronounceable sequences of letters that could be words but happen not to be (e.g., bam, lorge). Words and nonwords varied in length from 3 to 6 letters. In line with previous studies, naming latencies were substantially slower for the nonwords than for the familiar words (cf. Lupker et al., 1997; Rastle et al., 2003). Latencies for the nonwords increased substantially as letter length increased. In contrast, low frequency words showed only a small effect of length on naming speeds while high frequency words showed no significant effect at all. Stronger effects of length on naming latencies for nonwords than words in skilled readers have now been reported in English, German and French (Ziegler et al., 2001; Juphard et al., 2004; Valdois et al., 2006) while stronger effects of length on latencies for low than high frequency English words have been reported by Yap and Balota (2009) and others.

Weekes (1997) argued that slower reading of nonwords than familiar words, and larger effects of letter length for nonwords than words, could be explained within the dual-route (DRC) model of visual word recognition proposed by Coltheart et al. (2001). According to the DRC model, when an unfamiliar word or nonword is encountered for the first time, it is translated from written into spoken form through the application of letter-sound (grapheme-phoneme) conversion rules (referred to in the DRC model as the *nonlexical route*). The grapheme-phoneme conversion rules act in a serial, left-to-right manner, working systematically through a novel word from the beginning to the end until a pronunciation has been generated (Coltheart and Rastle, 1994). As a new word becomes familiar through repeated encounters, entries are created for that word in the mental lexicon. In the DRC model that process of lexicalization involves creating a representation of the written form of the word in an *orthographic input lexicon* and a representation of its spoken form in a *phonological output lexicon*. A route from print to sound becomes available for the newly-learned word through the two lexicons. This is known as the *lexical route*. Access to the orthographic input lexicon for familiar written words is both fast and parallel, with all of the component letters in a word being processed simultaneously. As a result, pronouncing a familiar word (lexical route) is faster than generating the pronunciation of an unfamiliar word or nonword (nonlexical route) and the impact of letter length is greatly reduced in familiar words (see Coltheart et al., 2001, pp. 238–239, where a simulation of the Weekes, 1997, results is presented). The more familiar a word is, the more its pronunciation will be captured by the lexical route, hence the progressively smaller effect of length seen in low and high frequency words.

If this account is broadly correct, it should be possible to observe the transition from nonlexical to lexical reading by presenting unfamiliar words or nonwords repeatedly. When the novel items are read for the first time, naming should reflect the operation of the nonlexical route: latencies should be slow and sensitive to the number of letters in the sequence. But as the novel words become familiar, lexical representation should be established and processing should make the transition from nonlexical to lexical reading, with naming latencies becoming become faster and less affected by length. Maloney et al. (2009) observed the beginnings of this transition. They took the 100 nonwords varying in length from 3 to 6 letters that were used by Weekes (1997) and presented them to skilled readers in four consecutive blocks of trials. Participants were instructed to read each one aloud as quickly as possible. As predicted, naming latencies became faster across the four blocks as the items became more familiar and the effect of length reduced.

In unpublished experiments we have replicated and extended Maloney et al.'s (2009) results. In one experiment we measured naming latencies for 4-letter, single-syllable nonwords and 7-letter, two-syllable nonwords. The nonwords were presented 10 times in consecutive blocks of trials, using a different random order of presentation in each block. Accuracy was very high across the experiment. In the first block, when all of the nonwords were new and unfamiliar, naming latencies were relatively slow and the effect of length was substantial. Reaction times (RTs) then reduced with repeated presentations and the impact of length diminished, becoming non-significant after five or six presentations of the nonwords. We obtained the same pattern of results in a second experiment using a different set of nonwords. In that experiment we also invited the participants back for a second testing session 7 days after the first session to assess the extent to which the learning effects persisted in the absence of any further experience with the nonwords. Naming latencies in block 1 of day 7 were a little slower than at the end of day 1, but much faster than at the start of day 1, demonstrating considerable retention of lexical knowledge about the newly-learned items. By the fourth block of day 7, the effect of length had completely disappeared: the nonwords had become familiar, created lexical entries, and been unitized to the point where they were read aloud in the same way as familiar words.

The present paper compares the performance of university and college students with a diagnosis of dyslexia with typically-reading controls on the same task. Nonwords composed of either 4 or 7 letters were presented 10 times in a first testing session, then 10 more times in a second testing session 7 days later. Accuracy of reading the nonwords aloud was assessed along with naming latencies. Bruck (1990) and Ben-Dror et al. (1991) found slower and less accurate reading of both words in nonwords in American college dyslexics than controls. Similar results have been reported for Polish (Reid et al., 2006) and Swedish (Wolff, 2009) dyslexic university students and controls. Less accurate reading aloud of both words and nonwords by student dyslexics than controls was reported by Snowling et al. (1997) and Hatcher et al. (2002) in very similar participant groups to those reported here (see also Callens et al., 2012; Deacon et al., 2012). These observations, combined with reports of less proficient reading of both nonwords and words by dyslexic children (Zoccolotti et al., 2005; Reid et al., 2006; Wolff, 2009; Paizi et al., 2013), led us to expect that the dyslexic students in our experiment would be slower and possibly less accurate than controls throughout the experiment, not only when the nonwords were presented for the first time, but even after multiple encounters.

We also expected that the adult dyslexics would show stronger effects of letter length on reading speed than the controls. There are two reasons why such a difference could come about. First, it has often been proposed that nonword reading presents particular problems for dyslexics (Rack et al., 1992; Herrman et al., 2006; though see Van den Broeck and Geudens, 2012). Wimmer (1996), for example, found that 10-year-old German dyslexic children read nonwords more slowly than younger normal readers who were matched to the dyslexics on the speed of reading familiar, high frequency words. If nonlexical reading is indeed differentially poor in many dyslexics, length effects should be greater in dyslexics than typical readers because the dyslexics will require more time per additional letter to convert that letter into sound.

Second, if dyslexics are slower than typical readers to create new lexical entries, then in the course of an experiment involving 20 presentations of each nonword across two separate sessions, the dyslexics may be slower than the controls to create orthographic and phonological representations for the novel items. The result would be that they spend more time reading nonlexically (with consequent length effects) and would be slower to switch to lexical reading (with reduced length effects). We are not aware of any studies of word learning in dyslexia that have involved adult participants, but research involving dyslexic children suggests problems learning both the spoken and the written forms of new words. Regarding the learning of spoken word-forms, Mayringer and Wimmer (2000) found that German-speaking dyslexic children were impaired at learning novel spoken words that were taught as the names of children shown in pictures. In contrast, the dyslexics were unimpaired at learning to associate familiar German names with pictures of children. The authors concluded from this that the dyslexic children's difficulty lay in learning the new spoken words rather than in associating names with people (see also Elbro and Jensen, 2005; Thomson and Goswami, 2010).

Mayringer and Wimmer (2000) suggested that if dyslexics have problems learning new written words, part of those problems could lie in learning the spoken (phonological) forms rather than their written (orthographic) forms. Visual word learning involves creating phonological as well as orthographic representations: difficulties in learning spoken word-forms would be expected to impact on visual word learning. The few published studies of visual (rather than spoken) word learning in dyslexia suggest, however, that dyslexics have problems learning new written word-forms over and above any problems they experience in learning spoken words (Reitsma, 1983; Ehri and Saltmarsh, 1995; Share and Shalev, 2004; De Jong and Messbauer, 2011; O'Brien et al., 2013). Reitsma (1983; Expt. 3) compared visual word learning in Dutch children with reading disabilities with learning in a group of younger normal readers. The children first practiced reading aloud novel words embedded in sentences. Three days later they were asked to read aloud the novel words as quickly as possible as they were presented individually on a computer screen. Half of the novel words were presented in exactly the same written form as in the training while the other half were presented in a form that had a different spelling but was pronounced the same. (An equivalent English example might be to train children to read *breet* then test them three days later on either *breet* or *breat*). The normal readers were faster to read aloud the versions of the novel words that they had been trained on three days earlier than the re-spelled version, though they were faster on both than on entirely new and untrained nonwords (so faster on *breet* than *breat* but faster on both of them than on *broat*). In contrast, the children with reading disability read both forms of the trained novel words (*breet* and *breat*) faster than the untrained items (*broat*) but showed no difference between the versions of the trained items that preserved the original spellings (*breet*) and the versions that changed those spellings (*breat*). The implication of these results is that the normal readers learned both the orthographic and phonological forms of the novel words in training and retained that knowledge through to the test three days later. The disabled readers remembered something of the phonological forms of the trained novel items across the retention interval but seemed not to retain any detectable orthographic information.

If dyslexic children combine less efficient nonlexical reading with slower creation of lexical entries, we would expect them to show larger length effects in nonword reading than typically-reading controls. We would also expect dyslexics to show larger effects of letter length in word reading arising from the fact that they are less efficient than controls at switching from nonlexical to lexical reading so read more words nonlexically than controls do. This prediction is supported by reports of stronger effects of letter length on naming latencies for real words in dyslexic children than controls in English, Dutch, German, Spanish and Italian (e.g., Ziegler et al., 2003; Marinus and De Jong, 2010; Paizi et al., 2011; Davies et al., 2013; Martelli et al., 2014).

Dyslexics may have difficulty learning new spoken and written word-forms but dyslexic Italian children have been reported to read words faster than nonwords (Paizi et al., 2013) thereby demonstrating some acquisition of word-specific knowledge. Paizi et al. (2013) also reported faster reading of high than low frequency words in dyslexic Italian children, indicating that regular exposure facilitates the creation of effective lexical entries in those readers. If dyslexics are capable of building up a vocabulary of words they can read in a relatively wholistic manner, albeit more slowly and effortfully than typical readers, that could explain the reduction in the impact of letter length on word reading with age that Zoccolotti et al. (2005) and De Luca et al. (2008) observed in both dyslexic Italian children and controls. Hence, on the basis of this admittedly incomplete literature, much of which is concerned with children rather than adults, we expected to see signs of word learning in the dyslexic participants in our experiment (i.e., faster naming latencies across blocks and a reduction in the impact of letter length with repeated exposure). We expected, however, that word learning would occur more slowly in the dyslexic participants than in controls (typical readers) and that if convergence between reading speeds for shorter and longer items was achieved, it would require more presentations of the nonwords.

Finally, our participants were given a short battery of tests to characterize their broader cognitive abilities. The cognitive profiles of dyslexic students at the same institution as many of the participants in the present study (the University of York, UK) were described a decade ago by Hatcher et al. (2002) and more recently by Warmington et al. (2013b). Hatcher et al. (2002) found that the student dyslexics performed at comparable levels to normally-reading controls on nonverbal ability (Raven's Advanced Progressive Matrices) but more poorly on a range of measures including verbal ability (WAIS-R vocabulary), word reading and spelling, forward and backward digit span, phonological tasks [object naming, digit naming and spoonerisms (exchanging sounds between words)] and mental arithmetic. Similar profiles were reported by Snowling et al. (1997) and Warmington et al. (2013b) for UK student dyslexics and Callens et al. (2012) for Belgian dyslexic students. A wider review and meta-analysis of dyslexia in adults is provided by Swanson and Hsieh (2009).

In addition to comparing the dyslexics and controls on the test battery, we used regression analyses to explore the ability of performance on the different cognitive tests to predict two aspects of performance in the experiment, namely initial reading speeds for the longer (7-letter) nonwords and the change in reading speeds across the 10 presentations in the first testing session. Initial reading speeds assess efficiency of converting unfamiliar letter sequences into sounds (in DRC terms, the efficiency of the nonlexical route), while the change in RTs across repetitions assesses the efficiency of word learning and the switch from nonlexical to lexical reading. Previous research has associated the speed and accuracy of reading nonwords or unfamiliar words with phonological awareness (Durand et al., 2005; Melby-Lervåg et al., 2012). For example, Pennington et al. (1990) documented persisting deficits in phonological awareness in adult dyslexics that were particularly linked to problems with nonword reading. Training studies have suggested, however, that phonological awareness must be linked to a knowledge of how letters map onto phonemes if improvements in phonological awareness are to be translated into improvements in reading (Hatcher et al., 1994; Melby-Lervåg et al., 2012).

Word learning has been more strongly associated with working memory than with phonological awareness (Gathercole et al., 1997, 1999; Avons et al., 1998). For example, Gathercole et al. (1999) reported an association between phonological working memory and vocabulary size in both 4-year-old and teenage children. Experimental studies by Jarrold et al. (2009) and Majerus and Boukebza (2013) reported a relationship between verbal working memory and ability to learn the form (rather than the referent) of new words by children and teenagers while Martin and Ellis (2012) found that word learning in an artificial second language by university students was predicted by performance on phonological short-term / working memory taks. Short-term and working memory have consistently been found to be impaired in dyslexia (Swanson et al., 2009) which may relate to the problems in word learning mentioned above.

MATERIALS AND METHODS

PARTICIPANTS

Participants were 30 students with a diagnosis of dyslexia (20 female, 10 male) and 30 typical readers who served as a control group (12 female, 18 male). The dyslexic students had a mean age of 21.5 years ($SD = 3.6$; range 17–36) while the controls had a mean age of 20.7 years ($SD = 3.2$; range 17–32). All were native speakers of English with normal or corrected-to-normal vision. The participants were students at the University of York ($n = 27$ per group), York Saint John University ($n = 1$ per group) and York College ($n = 2$ per group). The participants with dyslexia had all been diagnosed by a registered educational psychologist and supplied a copy of their diagnosis documents to the experimenters. Individuals with additional learning disabilities, a history of mental illness, epilepsy or other neurological disorders were excluded. Participants received either course credit or a small payment. The experiment was approved by the Ethics Committee of the Department of Psychology, University of York.

TEST BATTERY

The psychological test battery given to all the participants contained tests assessing vocabulary, reading and spelling, phonological awareness, working memory, nonverbal ability and motor speed. Published tests were scored according to the test manuals and the results are presented as standardized scores.

Vocabulary

Vocabulary was assessed using the Vocabulary subtest of the WASI which requires participants to define words verbally.

Word reading

Word reading was assessed using the reading subtest of the Wide Range Achievement Test (WRAT 4; Wilkinson and Robertson, 2006) which involves reading aloud single words of increasing length and difficulty (from see to synecdoche) and the Sight Word Efficiency subtest of the Test of Word Reading Efficiency (TOWRE SWE; Torgesen et al., 1999) which requires participants to read aloud as many words of increasing length and difficulty as possible in 45 s.

Nonword reading

Nonword reading was assessed using the Phonemic Decoding Efficiency (PDE) subtest of the TOWRE which requires participants to read aloud as many nonwords of increasing length and difficulty as possible in 45 s.

Word spelling

Word spelling was assessed using the Spelling Subtest of the WRAT 4 which requires participants to write single words to dictation.

Phonological awareness

Phonological awareness was measured using that part of the elision test from the Comprehensive Test of Phonological Processing (CTOPP; Wagner et al., 1999) in which a single initial, medial or final phoneme of a word must be deleted and the participant must say what remains (e.g., deleting the /k/ from "fixed" and responding "fist").

Working memory

Working memory was assessed using four tests from the Automated Working Memory Assessment (AWMA; Alloway, 2007). All the tests used span procedures in which sequence lengths were increased to the point where three or more errors were made within a block of trials. Standardized scores were calculated for each test. *Verbal short-term memory* was measured using immediate serial recall of lists of digits presented auditorily at a rate of 1/s. *Verbal working memory* was assessed using a test in which participants were presented with a sequence of spoken sentences. They were required to decide whether each sentence was true or false then recall the final words of each of the sentences at the end of the sequence. *Visuospatial short-term memory* was assessed using a dot matrix task in which a sequence of red dots appeared in squares of a 4 × 4 grid at a rate of one per 2 s. At the end of the sequence, the participant was required to touch the squares of the grid in the same order. *Visuospatial working memory* was measured using a spatial recall task. Participants were presented with pairs of shapes. The shape on the right always had a red dot in it. The shape on the left was either the same as the one on the right or different. The shape on the left could also be rotated with respect to the one on the right. The participant's task was first to say whether the two shapes were the same or different. After making those judgments to a sequence of pairs of shapes, the participant then had to indicate in the correct order where the red dot was positioned in each of the shapes on the right using a compass display with three points.

Nonverbal ability

Nonverbal ability was assessed using the matrix reasoning subtest of the Wechsler Abbreviated Scale of Intelligence (WASI; Wechsler, 1999).

Motor speed

Motor speed was assessed using a set of tapping tasks (Warmington et al., 2013a). Participants were asked to tap keys on a computer keyboard as many times as possible within 5 s. The start and end of each time interval was signaled both visually and auditory. The task consisted of three conditions with 6 trials in each condition. In Condition 1, the participants tapped one key using the index finger of their preferred hand as many times as possible. In Condition 2, the participants alternately tapped two keys using the index finger of their preferred hand as many times as possible. In Condition 3, the participants alternately tapped two keys using the first two fingers of their preferred hand as many times as possible. The score is the average time between taps across the three conditions.

EXPERIMENTAL STIMULI

The experimental stimuli were 12 4-letter, single-syllable nonwords and 12 7-letter, two-syllable nonwords. To reduce problems of voice key activation, none of the stimuli began with a voiceless fricative ("f," "s," "sh," or "th"). The 4- and 7-letter items were matched on naming accuracy from a pilot study involving typical student readers. They were also matched on mean log bigram frequency (4-letter mean = 3.28, range 2.72–3.57; 7-letter mean = 3.27, range 3.10–3.43; Duyck et al., 2004) and on initial letters and phonemes. The 4-letter experimental nonwords were: *brup, carg, dreb, jeph, lont, munt, nate, plin, relb, trok, varb,* and *zort.* The 7-letter experimental nonwords were: *blispod, coftrip, drentcy, joshule, larquof, mattoch, nelpoon, pronnet, roffler, trimsol, vushood,* and *zadroon.* Sixteen additional nonwords (8 4-letter and 8 7-letter) were selected for use in practice trials prior to the main experiment.

PROCEDURE

Participants attended for two sessions. The first session began with the participants reading and signing a consent form then completing the psychological assessment battery. That took approximately 45 min. After a break of around 10 min they began the experimental task. They were given practice at reading aloud 8 4-letter and 8 7-letter nonwords presented in a random order. That was followed by the 10 blocks of the experiment. Participants were seated approximately 60 cm from a computer screen on which the nonwords were displayed in black, lower case letters on a white background. The nonwords were presented in 18-point Times New Roman font with a height on the screen of approximately 10 mm. Each trial consisted of a centrally-presented fixation cross displayed for 1000 ms, followed by the nonword stimulus for 2000 ms, then a blank screen for 1000 ms before the next trial began. Participants were instructed to read each nonword aloud as quickly and as accurately as possible. The 24 nonwords were presented once in a random order. Participants were informed when the block was complete and pressed the space bar on a computer keyboard to initiate the next block when they were ready to continue. This process was repeated across 10 blocks with the stimuli being presented in a different random order in each block. Participants wore headphones with a high-sensitivity microphone connected to a voice key that was linked to the computer. Presentation of the stimuli and recording of naming latencies was controlled by E-prime experiment generator software (version 1.2; Schneider et al., 2002). The experimenter noted any trials in which the participant misread a nonword, hesitated or made a false start or other form of error.

Participants returned 7 days later for the second session which was a repeat of session 2 involving reading all the experimental nonwords aloud 10 more times in 10 blocks using a different random order in each block.

RESULTS

PERFORMANCE ON THE TEST BATTERY

Table 1 shows the results for the dyslexics and controls on the battery of tests together with the results of *t*-tests comparing the two groups along with the effect sizes (*r*; Field, 2009). Dyslexics performed significantly less well than the controls on every test except nonverbal reasoning. The effect sizes for the differences between the groups were largest for nonword reading, followed by spelling and word reading. The effect sizes for the differences between groups on verbal and visuospatial working memory tasks were similar.

PERFORMANCE ON THE EXPERIMENTAL TASK

Naming errors, hesitations and failures to activate the voice key were removed from the analysis of performance on the experimental task along with RTs less than 100 ms or longer than 2.5 *SDs* above the mean (defined separately for each participant in each block and for each length). Table S1 (Supplementary Materials) shows the full results (accuracy and mean RTs for correct, trimmed responses). Accuracy was very high (97.3% correct overall and never less than 95.5% correct for either group in any condition or block of trials). Given the high levels of accuracy in both groups, nonparametric Mann-Whitney *U* tests found no significant difference between dylexics and typical readers on overall accuracy across the two days for either 4-letter nonwords, $U_{(60)} = 464$, $Z = 0.208$, $p = 0.835$, or 7-letter nonwords, $U_{(60)} = 346$, $Z = -1.548$, $p = 0.122$. Wilcoxon matched pairs, signed ranks tests found no difference between accuracy for 4- vs. 7-letter nonwords across the two sessions for both groups of participants combined, $W_{(12)} = 23.0$, $Z = 1.26$, $p = 0.209$.

Naming latencies (RTs)

The main analyses focused on the RT data from the experimental task. **Figure 1** shows the pattern of RTs for correct, trimmed responses across blocks for the dyslexics (in red) and the controls (in blue). Inspection of the figure indicates that naming latencies were slower for the dyslexics than the controls throughout the experiment. At the start of the experiment, both groups were

Table 1 | Results of the dyslexic and typical readers on the psychological test battery.

	Dyslexics		Typical readers		*t*-tests and effect sizes (*r*)
	Mean	***SD***	**Mean**	***SD***	
VOCABULARY					
WASI Vocabulary	56.50	7.68	63.73	6.78	$t_{(58)} = 3.87, p < 0.001; r = 0.45$
WORD READING					
WRAT 4 Reading	99.00	7.44	117.30	12.80	$t_{(58)} = 6.77, p < 0.001; r = 0.66$
TOWRE-SWE	82.00	11.03	97.44	10.68	$t_{(58)} = 7.21, p < 0.001; r = 0.69$
NONWORD READING					
TOWRE-PDE	86.63	10.23	108.08	7.72	$t_{(58)} = 12.01, p < 0.001; r = 0.84$
SPELLING					
WRAT 4 Spelling	96.50	12.35	121.33	11.86	$t_{(58)} = 7.95, p < 0.001; r = 0.72$
PHONOLOGICAL AWARENESS					
CTOPP Elision	7.27	1.76	9.00	1.68	$t_{(58)} = 3.40, p < 0.001; r = 0.41$
WORKING MEMORY					
AWMA verbal STM	87.67	12.82	101.53	14.54	$t_{(58)} = 3.92, p < 0.001; r = 0.46$
AWMA verbal WM	93.00	13.86	105.97	14.55	$t_{(58)} = 3.53, p = 0.001; r = 0.42$
AWMA visuospatial STM	90.33	11.56	108.83	13.05	$t_{(58)} = 5.81, p < 0.001; r = 0.61$
AWMA visuospatial WM	95.87	16.09	106.89	11.92	$t_{(58)} = 3.02, p < 0.01; r = 0.37$
NONVERBAL ABILITY					
WASI Matrix reasoning	54.60	7.75	55.77	5.73	$t_{(58)} = 0.66, p = 0.510; r = 0.09$
Motor speed	267.66	55.54	224.26	35.11	$t_{(58)} = -3.54, p = 0.001; r = 0.42$

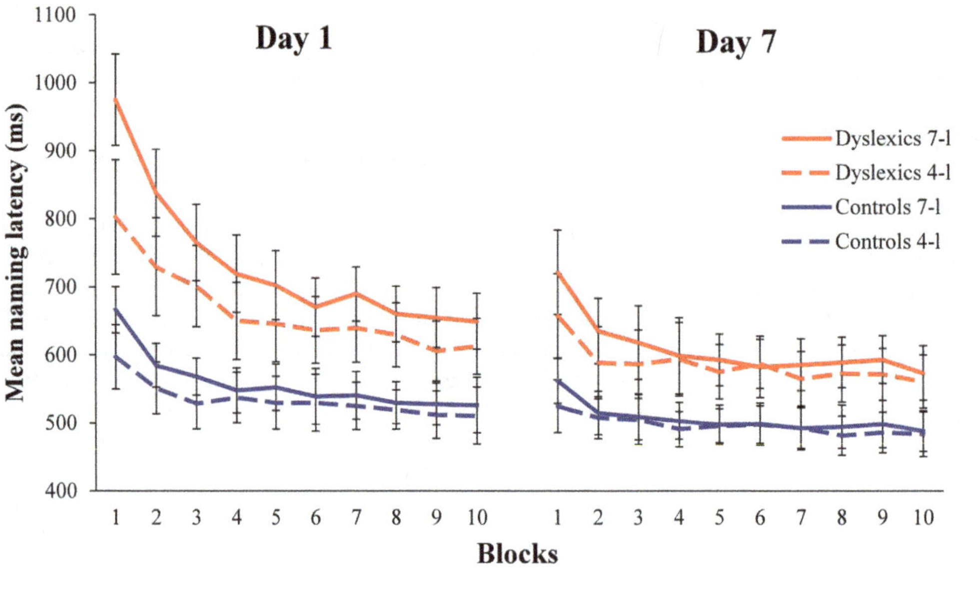

FIGURE 1 | Naming RTs to 4- and 7-letter nonwords in dyslexics and controls across two sessions (10 blocks per session). Error bars show 95% CIs.

slower to read aloud 7- than 4-letter nonwords. The difference in naming RTs for shorter and longer nonwords reduced with repetitions, but the dyslexic participants appear to have required more exposures to the nonwords before the RTs for shorter and longer items converged. These indications were explored in a series of ANOVAs. When Mauchly's test of sphericity was significant, the Greenhouse-Geiger correction was applied. Full details of the statistical analyses are presented in the Appendix (Supplementary Materials) where effect sizes are reported in terms of the partial eta squared statistic (η_p^2). We will summarize the important outcomes here.

Global analysis. The first ANOVA was a global analysis conducted on the RT data for both testing sessions with Group, Day, Blocks and Length as factors. There were significant main effects of Group (faster overall RTs for the controls than the dyslexics), Day (faster RTs on day 7 than day 1), Blocks (RTs becoming faster across blocks) and Length (faster overall RTs to 4- than 7-letter nonwords). All of the interactions were significant, including the interaction between Group and Length (larger length effects in the dyslexics than the controls) and Groups × Blocks × Length (the reduction in the length effect across blocks occurring more quickly in the controls than in the dyslexics). These results were explored further by means of separate analyses of RTs in day 1 and day 7, including separate analyses of the performance of the dyslexic and control groups on each day.

Day 1. Day 1 RTs were analyzed with Group, Blocks and Length as factors. There were significant main effects of Group (faster RTs in the controls than the dyslexics), Blocks (RTs becoming faster across blocks) and Length (faster RTs to 4- than 7-letter nonwords). All of the interactions were significant. Day 1 RTs were then analyzed separately for controls and dyslexics. The controls showed significant main effects of Blocks and Length with a Blocks × Length interaction. Bonferroni-corrected *t*-tests were used to compare RTs to 4- and 7-letter nonwords in blocks 1–10. The effect of length was significant for the controls in blocks 1, 2, and 3 but was no longer significant from block 4 onwards. The dyslexics also showed effects of Blocks and Length combined with a Blocks × Length interaction. In their case, Bonferroni-corrected *t*-tests found effects of length in blocks 1–5, 7, 9, and 10 with marginally significant effects in blocks 6 and 8 (see Appendix; Supplementary material).

In sum, nonword naming RTs in day 1 were slower for the dyslexics than the controls. Both groups showed significant effects of length in the first three blocks, but while the controls showed no difference in naming speed after block 3, the dyslexics continued to show longer RTs to 7- than 4-letter nonwords throughout day 1.

Day 7. The next set of analyses focused on RTs in day 7. As in day 1, there were main effects of Group (faster RTs in the controls than the dyslexics), Blocks (RTs becoming faster across blocks) and Length (faster RTs to 4- than 7-letter nonwords). A significant Blocks × Length interaction reflected an overall reduction in the effect of length across blocks. There were also significant Group x Blocks and Group × Length interactions reflecting more change across blocks and stronger effects of length in the dyslexics than the controls. The 3-way Group × Blocks × Length interaction was marginally significant ($p = 0.06$). These interactions were explored further by means of separate analyses of day 7 RTs for controls and dyslexics.

Controls showed effects of Blocks and Length on day 7 with a significant Blocks × Length interaction. Bonferroni-corrected *t*-tests found a difference in RTs to 4- and 7-letter nonwords in block 1 only. Dyslexics also showed effects of Blocks and Length with a Blocks × Length interaction. In their case, Bonferroni-corrected *t*-tests found effects of length in blocks 1, 2, and 3, but not from block 4 onwards.

In sum, the controls showed a small effect of length at the start of day 7, but that effect disappeared by block 2. Dyslexics required 3 or 4 presentations in day 7 before they began to show (for the first time) no significant difference between naming RTs to short and long nonwords.

PREDICTORS OF INTIAL NONWORD READING SPEED AND NOVEL WORD LEARNING

The final set of analyses brought together performance on the test battery with two aspects of the naming latency data. Nonlexical reading skill (decoding) was measured in terms of RTs to 7-letter nonwords in block 1 of day 1 while novel word learning was measured in terms of the change in RTs to 7-letter nonwords from block 1 to block 10 on day 1.

The number of predictor variables was reduced before the regression analyses were run, and some of the variables were transformed to improve the normality of their distributions. There were high correlations among the two word reading tests and the word spelling test ($rs = 0.67$–0.84, all p's < 0.001). A composite Literacy score was therefore calculated for each participant by averaging the standardized scores from the WRAT Reading, TOWRE word reading and WRAT Spelling tests. To avoid using nonword reading in one task to predict nonword reading in another task, performance on the TOREPDE nonword reading task was not included in the composite Literacy score. Substantial correlations were also observed among the four tests of working memory ($rs = 0.50$–0.56, all p's < 0.001). A composite Working memory score was therefore computed for each participant by averaging the standardized scores from the four working memory tasks.

Univariate normality was tested for each predictor and the dependent variables (RTs to 7-letter nonwords in blocks 1 and 10 of day 1). Phonological awareness, Nonverbal ability and Motor speed were found to violate the assumption of normality (Kolmogorov-Smirmov test of normality, $p < 0.05$). Distributions approximated normality most closely when Phonological awareness was reverse transformed (thereby reversing the normal direction of correlations) and Nonverbal ability and Motor speed were square root transformed. RTs were log transformed to reduce skew.

Reducing the number of variables helps to reduce the risks associated with multicollinearity (intercorrelation among the predictor variables). Multicollinearity among the final versions of the predictor variables was assessed using the variance inflation factor (VIF). VIF scores of less than 4 indicate that the result will not significantly influence the stability of the parameter estimates (Myers, 1990). VIF scores for the predictor variables ranged between 1.04 and 3.01.

Table 2 shows the correlations among the final predictor variables; also the correlations between the predictor variables and RTs to 7-letter nonwords in block 1 of day 1. There were significant correlations among all the predictor variables except Nonverbal ability which did not correlate significantly with any of the other predictors. All of the predictors except Nonverbal ability correlated significantly with RT, with Literacy showing the highest correlation, followed by Vocabulary, Working memory, Motor speed and Phonological awareness.

Linear mixed effects modeling was used to explore the ability of Vocabulary, Literacy, Phonological awareness, Working memory, Nonverbal ability and Motor speed to predict initial nonword reading speed and novel word learning. Linear mixed effects (LME) methods analyze all the available data and do not rely on averaging across participants or across items. They are

Table 2 | Correlations among the predictor variables, and between the predictor variables and naming RTs for 7-letter nonwords in block 1 of day 1.

Variable	1 Vocab	2 Literacy	3 Phon	4 Wkg mem	5 Nonverb	6 Mot	7 RT
1. Vocabulary	–						
2. Literacy	0.656**						
3. Phonological awareness	−0.403**	−0.571**	–				
4. Working memory	0.266*	0.520**	0.432**	–			
5. Nonverbal ability	−0.014	−0.127	−0.175	−0.247	–		
6. Motor speed	−0.319*	−0.452**	−0.336**	−0.418**	0.149	–	
7. Block 1, 7-letter RTs	−0.584**	−0.739**	−0.377**	−0.444**	0.001	0.409**	–

**p < 0.05, **p < 0.01. Note that phonological awareness was reverse transformed (thereby reversing the normal direction of correlations). Nonverbal ability and motor speed were square root transformed. RT was log transformed.*

particularly useful for analysing data from heterogeneous groups (such as individuals with dyslexia) because they allow differences in the baseline performance among participants and items (*random effects*) to be separated from the effects of the predictor variables (*fixed effects*) (Baayen et al., 2008; Jones et al., 2008). The analyses were conducted in R using the lme4 (Bates et al., 2012) and languageR (Baayen, 2009) packages.

Predicting initial nonword reading speed

The contribution of each predictor variable to predicting RTs for 7-letter nonwords presented in block 1 of day 1 was evaluated by using likelihood ratio tests to compare a model that contained all the fixed and random effects with a sequence of models in which different predictor variables were removed one at a time. These analyses showed that Literacy made a significant independent contribution to predicting nonword naming speed, $\chi^2_{(10)} = 16.12$, $p < 0.001$; $\beta = -0.005$, $t = -4.30$, $p < 0.001$. In contrast, Vocabulary, $\chi^2_{(10)} = 2.71$, $p = 0.096$, Phonological awareness, $\chi^2_{(10)} = 1.41$, $p = 0.235$, Working memory, $\chi^2_{(10)} = 1.53$, $p = 0.217$, Nonverbal ability, $\chi^2_{(10)} = 1.37$, $p = 0.243$, and Motor speed, $\chi^2_{(10)} = 1.12$, $p = 0.293$, made no independent contributions.

Predicting learning

Novel word learning was assessed in terms of the change in naming RTs for 7-letter nonwords between blocks 1 and 10 of day 1. RTs from both blocks were entered into the analysis. A categorical variable of Time was created to reflect the change in RTs between blocks 1 and 10. A set of predictor variables were then created which were the interactions involving Time with Vocabulary, Literacy, Phonological awareness, Working memory, Nonverbal ability and Motor speed. This makes it possible to evaluate the contribution of each independent variable to predict change in naming RTs to the 7-letter nonwords across blocks (Shek and Ma, 2011; Field, 2012). The effect of the categorical variable of Time was significant, $\chi^2_{(11)} = 516.29$, $p < 0.001$, reflecting the reduction in RTs from block 1 to block 10. The interactions of Time with Vocabulary, $\chi^2_{(17)} = 6.57$, $p < 0.05$; $\beta = 0.002$, $t = 2.57$, $p < 0.05$, and Time with Working memory, $\chi^2_{(17)} = 26.12$, $p < 0.001$; $\beta = 0.003$, $t = 5.14$, $p < 0.001$, were also significant. The interactions of Time with Literacy, $\chi^2_{(17)} = 0.71$, $p = 0.401$, Phonological awareness, $\chi^2_{(17)} = 1.79$, $p = 0.181$, Nonverbal ability, $\chi^2_{(17)} = 3.65$, $p = 0.100$, and Motor skill, $\chi^2_{(17)} = 0.10$, $p = 0.753$, made no independent contributions to predicting RT change across blocks.

In sum, reading latencies for the more difficult, 7-letter nonwords seen for the first time correlated significantly with all of the predictor variables except Nonverbal ability. The highest correlation was with Literacy. When the ability of each of the variables to predict naming RT was assessed in the context of the other variables (in analyses which took into account the differences between participants and items in overall naming speed), only Literacy was significant. Novel word learning was assessed as the change in RTs for 7-letter nonwords between blocks 1 and 10 of day 1. Only Vocabulary and Working memory predicted the degree of learning across blocks in session 1.

DISCUSSION

The adult dyslexics in the current experiment were all studying at university or in a college of higher education. They performed at a comparable level to typically-reading controls on a test of nonverbal ability (matrix reasoning) but had lower vocabulary scores, slower and less accurate reading and spelling of words, less efficient reading of nonwords, poorer phonological awareness, poorer performance on both verbal and nonverbal tests of span and working memory, and slower motor speed. These findings match other reports in the literature that dyslexics in higher education have cognitive problems that extend beyond reading and writing to wider aspects of linguistic, working memory and motor performance while typically sparing nonverbal reasoning (cf. Bruck, 1992; Gallagher et al., 1996; Snowling et al., 1997; Hatcher et al., 2002; Smith-Spark et al., 2003; Smith-Spark and Fisk, 2007; Callens et al., 2012; Warmington et al., 2013b). The working memory problems extend to visuospatial as well as verbal tasks (cf. Smith-Spark and Fisk, 2007; Menghini et al., 2011; Hachmann et al., 2014).

The largest difference between dyslexics and controls in the present study (as indicated by the effect size) was on the TOWRE Phonemic Decoding Efficiency test (Torgesen et al., 1999), a test of nonword reading. A great deal of effort is put into teaching phonic decoding skills to dyslexic children in the UK (Rose, 2009). The dyslexics who participated in our study had mastered the letter-sound correspondences of English sufficiently to enable them to read correctly nonwords like *drentcy* and *larquof* on the first encounter, but they were substantially slower than the controls. The results of the TOWRE-PDE indicate that pronouncing unfamiliar nonwords (and, by extension, unfamiliar real words) remains a problem for dyslexics in higher education (cf. Bruck, 1990; Ben-Dror et al., 1991; Reid et al., 2006; Wolff, 2009).

In the experimental task, the typical readers behaved very similarly to the participants in Maloney et al. (2009) who were drawn from a similar population. Letter length exerted a major effect on reading speeds for nonwords seen for the first time, but the impact of length declined as naming latencies reduced across blocks, becoming nonsignificant from block 4 of day 1. The results showed, therefore, that skilled adult readers can create representations of unfamiliar letter sequences after 4 or 5 presentations that allow them to recognize and pronounce the novel "words" quickly and to process their component letters in parallel.

The dyslexics were substantially slower at reading the nonwords throughout both sessions of the experiment. When the dyslexics read the 7-letter nonwords for the first time in block 1 of day 1, they did so with a mean latency that was over 300 ms slower than the controls. When performance on the 4- and 7-letter nonwords was compared, the dyslexics required 57 ms per letter in order to pronounce a nonword seen for the first time where the controls required just 23 ms per letter (less than half as much as the dyslexics). Ability at reading and spelling real words ("literacy") predicted decoding speed across the two groups. When the effect of literacy was taken into account there was no additional effect of vocabulary, phonological awareness or working memory on decoding speed for these particular readers.

The dyslexics in the present study were clearly capable of visual word learning. **Figure 1** shows that their naming latencies reduced across blocks and that their naming latencies to 4- and 7-letter nonwords eventually converged. Learning occurred considerably more slowly than in the dyslexics, however, than in the typical readers. Whereas the difference in RTs between shorter and longer nonwords became nonsignificant in the typical readers around the middle of session 1, the dyslexics showed slower naming of longer nonwords throughout session 1, only losing the length effect part-way into session 2 (day 7). The present study confirms, therefore, that the problems with word learning that have been documented in dyslexic children persist into early adulthood, even in high-functioning dyslexics (cf. Reitsma, 1983; Ehri and Saltmarsh, 1995; Mayringer and Wimmer, 2000; Share and Shalev, 2004; Elbro and Jensen, 2005; Thomson and Goswami, 2010; De Jong and Messbauer, 2011).

Importantly, the naming latencies for the dyslexics remained substantially longer than those of the typical readers through to the end of session 2. **Figure 1** suggests that the difference between the two groups had more or less stabilized by the second half of session 2. We know that dyslexic university and college students read familiar words aloud more slowly than normal readers (Bruck, 1990; Ben-Dror et al., 1991; Reid et al., 2006; Wolff, 2009): one interpretation of that finding and the present evidence is that no amount of exposure to individual words will allow dyslexic students to reach the point where they can convert them from print to sound as efficiently as typical readers.

In terms of the DRC model of reading (Coltheart et al., 2001), less efficient reading of nonwords in the TOWRE-PDE test and in the experimental task indicates less efficient functioning of the nonlexical route in undergraduate dyslexics than in typical readers. Slower convergence between RTs to shorter and longer nonwords in the dyslexics suggest that the creation of new lexical entries in the orthographic input lexicon and the phonological output lexicon occurs less efficiently in adult dyslexics than typical readers. This results in a slower switch-over from sublexical to predominantly lexical reading in the dyslexics. Finally, the fact that nonword reading remains slower in the dyslexics than the controls even at the end of session two, combined with the fact that adult dyslexics are slower than controls to read familiar words aloud, indicates that the lexical route also functions less efficiently in adult dyslexics than in typical readers. That could be due to slower operation of the two lexicons or the pathways between them, or it could also be due to less efficient functioning of the final stages involving activating phoneme sequences and converting those sequences into articulation. Problems at the phonological output stage in dyslexics that compromise the functioning of both the lexical and nonlexical routes would be compatible with other evidence for impairments in dyslexics at the speech output stage (see Coltheart, 2005; Ziegler et al., 2008; Hawelka et al., 2010, for discussions of developmental dyslexia within a DRC framework).

Across the two groups, the ability to learn novel words (measured here as the change in RTs to longer nonwords between blocks 1 and 10 of day 1) was predicted by vocabulary and working memory. Ricketts et al. (2007) found that vocabulary predicted the ability of normal 8–10-year-olds to read words with irregular or exceptional spellings but did not predict their ability to read nonwords. By definition, irregular words like *deaf* or *yacht* violate the grapheme-phoneme correspondences of English. Nonlexical procedures cannot read those words correctly: readers must rely instead on word-specific learning and the creation of lexical entries. The results of Ricketts et al. (2007) are therefore in line with the present findings, albeit for a younger group of readers.

If a reader has a larger vocabulary, novel words they encounter in reading are likely to have more orthographic and phonological neighbors; that is, familiar words that look and sound like the novel words, differing from them by only a few letters or phonemes. Storkel et al. (2006) taught adults novel spoken words paired with novel objects through stories and pictures. Learning was better for nonwords with many neighbors than for nonwords with few neighbors. In the DRC model, words that are already established in the orthographic and phonological lexicons support the processing of new words or nonwords which resemble them. This is done through interactions between the two lexicons and the systems that encode and represent letter and phoneme sequences. Those interactions allow the model to process nonwords with many neighbors more efficiently than nonwords with fewer neighbors. Lexical support for novel words during learning could explain the advantage for nonwords with many neighbors reported by Storkel et al. (2006) and the benefit of a larger vocabulary found by Ricketts et al. (2007) and in the present study.

As regards the contribution of working memory, we noted in the Introduction that studies of children and young adults by Jarrold et al. (2009), Majerus and Boukebza (2013) and Martin and Ellis (2012) found a relationship between working memory and the ability to learn novel words, with working memory apparently related more closely to acquiring new word-forms rather than their meanings. Those observations fit well with the present findings. The DRC model does not engage with the working memory literature directly, but an important part of working memory is the interaction between short- and long-term memory systems exemplified by the interaction between phoneme representations and lexical entries (the phonological output lexicon in the DRC model). Jarrold et al. (2009) and Martin and Ellis (2012) explained the relationship they observed between verbal short-term memory and word learning in terms of individual differences in the ability to maintain accurate phonological representations of novel words. Majerus et al. (2006) argued that maintaining information about the order of phonemes in words is particularly important for successful word learning. In that context, we note the report by Hachmann et al. (2014) that short-term recall of order information is particularly impaired in dyslexia, which may contribute to their word learning problems.

Phonological awareness did not emerge as a predictor of either initial naming RTs or learning when the contributions of the other predictors were taken into account. Research has established that phonological awareness alone is not enough to improve decoding skills: only when phonological training is combined with training on the mappings between letters and phonemes does reading improve (Hatcher et al., 1994; Melby-Lervåg et al., 2012). Knowledge of the links between letters and sounds may be better captured by the kind of measures of word reading and spelling that went into the Literacy variable in the present study than by phonological awareness based on spoken stimuli and responses.

In conclusion, our results show that adult dyslexics in the UK university and further education system continue to experience difficulty reading novel words and nonwords. They are slower to read nonwords aloud than typical readers, requiring more time per letter to pronounce unfamiliar sequences of letters. They show learning of novel words as a result of repeated exposures, but they require more exposures than typical readers before they establish effective lexical representations. Even after multiple presentations their speed of reading aloud is substantially slower than typical readers. They remain slower than typical readers even at reading familiar words aloud. Across both dyslexic and typical readers, decoding speed for nonwords was predicted by skill at reading and spelling real words ("literacy") while individual differences in word learning were predicted by vocabulary size and working memory. As others have also shown, the problems that adult dyslexics experience extend beyond reading and spelling to word learning, vocabulary, phonological awareness, working memory and even basic motor speed. Taken together, those problems will conspire to make it very challenging for adult dyslexics to function successfully within higher education.

ACKNOWLEDGMENTS

We thank Dr. Lisa Henderson and Dr. Meesha Warmington for advice on the design of the study and selection of the test battery. Jo Coulthard helped with recruiting participants while Carol Yuan and Madeline Croucher assisted with data gathering.

REFERENCES

Alloway, T. P. (2007). *Automated Working Memory Assessment.* London: Harcourt Assessment.

Avons, S. E., Wragg, C. A., Cupples, L., and Lovegrove, W. J. (1998). Measures of phonological short-term memory and their relationship to vocabulary development. *Appl. Psycholinguist.* 19, 583–601. doi: 10.1017/S0142716400010377

Baayen, R. H. (2009). *languageR: Data Sets and Functions with "Analyzing Linguistic Data: A practical introduction to statistics".* R package version 0.955.

Baayen, R. H., Davidson, D. J., and Bates, D. M. (2008). Mixed-effects modeling with crossed random effects for subjects and items. *J. Mem. Lang.* 59, 390–412. doi: 10.1016/j.jml.2007.12.005

Bates, D., Maechler, M., and Bolker, B. (2012). *lme4: Linear Mixed-effects Models Using S4 Classes.* R package v. 0.999999-0.

Ben-Dror, I., Pollatsek, A., and Scarpati, S. (1991). Word identification in isolation and in context by college dyslexic students. *Brain Lang.* 40, 471–190. doi: 10.1016/0093-934X(91)90144-P

Bruck, M. (1990). Word-recognition skills of adults with childhood diagnoses of dyslexia. *Dev. Psychol.* 26, 439–454. doi: 10.1037/0012-1649.26.3.439

Bruck, M. (1992). Persistence of dyslexics' phonological awareness deficits. *Dev. Psychol.* 28, 874–886. doi: 10.1037/0012-1649.28.5.874

Callens, M., Tops, W., and Brysbaert, M. (2012). Cognitive profile of students who enter higher education with an indication of dyslexia. *PLoS ONE* 7:e38081. doi: 10.1371/journal.pone.0038081

Coltheart, M. (2005). Analysing developmental disorders of reading. *Aust. J. Learn. Dis.* 10, 53–62. doi: 10.1080/19404150509546799

Coltheart, M., and Rastle, K. (1994). Serial processing in reading aloud: evidence for dual-route models of reading. *J. Exp. Psychol. Human.* 20, 1197–1211. doi: 10.1037/0096-1523.20.6.1197

Coltheart, M., Rastle, K., Perry, C., Langdon, R., and Ziegler, J. (2001). DRC: a dual route cascaded model of visual word recognition and reading aloud. *Psychol. Rev.* 108, 204–256. doi: 10.1037/0033-295X.108.1.204

Cunningham, A. E. (2006). Accounting for children's orthographic learning while reading text: do children self-teach? *J. Exp. Child Psychol.* 95, 56–77. doi: 10.1016/j.jecp.2006.03.008

Cunningham, A. E., Perry, K. E., Stanovich, K. E., and Share, D. L. (2002). Orthographic Learning during reading: the role of self-teaching. *J. Exp. Child Psychol.* 82, 185–199. doi: 10.1016/S0022-0965(02)00008-5

Davies, R., Rodgríguez-Ferreiro, J., Suárez, P., and Cuetos, F. (2013). Lexical and sub-lexical effects on accuracy, reaction time and response duration: impaired and typical word and pseudoword reading in a transparent orthography. *Read. Writ.* 26, 721–738. doi: 10.1007/s11145-012-9388-1

De Jong, P. F., and Messbauer, V. C. S. (2011). Orthographic context and the acquisition of orthographic knowledge in normal and dyslexic readers. *Dyslexia* 17, 107–122. doi: 10.1002/dys.427

De Luca, M., Barca, L., Burani, C., and Zoccolotti, P. (2008). The effect of word length and other sublexical, lexical and semantic variables on developmental reading deficits. *Cogn. Behav. Neurol.* 21, 227–235. doi: 10.1097/WNN.0b013e318190d162

Deacon, S. H., Cook, K., and Parrila, R. (2012). Identifying high-functioning dyslexics: is self-report of early reading problems enough? *Ann. Dyslexia* 62, 120–134. doi: 10.1007/s11881-012-0068-2

Durand, M., Hulme, C., Larkin, R., and Snowling, M. (2005). The cognitive foundations of reading and arithmetic skills in 7- to 10-year-olds. *J. Exp. Child. Psychol.* 91, 113–136. doi: 10.1016/j.jecp.2005.01.003

Duyck, W., Desmet, T., Verbeke, L. P. C., and Brysbaert, M. (2004). WordGen: a tool for word selection and nonword generation in Dutch, English, German, and French. *Behav. Res. Meth. Ins. C* 36, 488–499. doi: 10.3758/BF03195595

Ehri, L. C., and Saltmarsh, J. (1995). Beginning readers outperform older disabled readers in learning to read words by sight. *Read. Writ.* 7, 295–326. doi: 10.1007/BF03162082

Elbro, C., and Jensen, M. N. (2005). Quality of phonological representations, verbal learning, and phoneme awareness in dyslexic and normal readers. *Scand. J. Psychol.* 45, 375–384. doi: 10.1111/j.1467-9450.2005.00468.x

Field, A. (2009). *Discovering Statistics Using SPSS.* 3rd Edn. London: Sage Publications.

Field, A. (2012). *Discovering Statistics Using R.* 1st Edn. London: Sage Publications.

Gallagher, A. M., Laxon, V., Armstrong, E., and Frith, U. (1996). Phonological difficulties in high-functioning dyslexics. *Read. Writ.* 8, 499–509. doi: 10.1007/BF00577025

Gathercole, S. E., Hitch, G. J., Service, E., and Martin, A. J. (1997). Phonological short-term memory and new word learning in children. *Dev. Psychol.* 33, 966–979. doi: 10.1037/0012-1649.33.6.966

Gathercole, S. E., Service, E., Hitch, G. J., Adams, A.-M., and Martin, A. J. (1999). Phonological short-term memory and vocabulary development: further evidence on the nature of the relationship. *Appl. Cogn. Psych.* 13, 65–77. doi: 10.1002/1099-0720-199902

Hachmann, W. M., Bogaerts, L., Szmalec, A., Woumans, E., Duyck, W., and Job, R. (2014). Short-term memory for order but not for item information is impaired in developmental dyslexia. *Ann. Dyslexia.* doi: 10.1007/s11881-103-0089-5. [Epub ahead of print].

Hatcher, J., Snowling, M. J., and Griffiths, Y. M. (2002). Cognitive assessment of dyslexic: students in higher education. *Brit. J. Educ. Psychol.* 72, 119–133. doi: 10.1348/000709902158801

Hatcher, P., Hulme, C., and Ellis, A. W. (1994). Ameliorating reading failure by integrating the teaching of reading and phonological skills: the phonological linkage hypothesis. *Child Dev.* 65, 41–57. doi: 10.1111/j.1467-8624.1994.tb00733

Hawelka, S., Gagl, B., and Wimmer, H. (2010). A dual-route perspective on eye movements of dyslexic readers. *Cognition* 115, 367–397. doi: 10.1016/j.cognition.2009.11.004

Herrman, J. A., Matyas, T., and Pratt, C. (2006). Meta-analysis of the nonword-reading deficit in specific reading disorder. *Dyslexia* 12, 195–221. doi: 10.1002/dys.324

Jarrold, C., Thorn, A. S. C., and Stephens, E. (2009). The relationships among verbal short-term memory, phonological awareness, and new word learning: evidence from typical development and Down syndrome. *J. Exp. Child. Psychol.* 102, 196–218. doi: 10.1016/j.jecp.2008.07.001

Jones, M. W., Branigan, H. P., and Kelly, M. L. (2008). Dyslexic and nondyslexic reading fluency: rapid automatized naming and the importance of continuous lists. *Psychon. Bull. Rev.* 16, 567–572. doi: 10.3758/PBR.16.3.567

Juphard, A., Carbonnel, S., and Valdois, S. (2004). Length effects in reading and lexical decision: evidence from skilled readers and a developmental dyslexic participant. *Brain Cogn.* 55, 332–340. doi: 10.1016/j/bandc.2004.02.035

Lupker, E. J., Brown, P., and Colombo, L. (1997). Strategic control in a naming task: changing routes or changing deadlines? *J. Exp. Psychol. Learn.* 23, 570–590. doi: 10.1037/0278-7393.23.3.570

Majerus, S., and Boukebza, C. (2013). Short-term memory for serial order supports vocabulary development: new evidence from a novel word learning paradigm. *J. Exp. Child Psychol.* 116, 811–828. doi: 10.1016/j/jecp.2013.07.014

Majerus, S., Poncelet, M., Elsen, B., and Van der Linden, M. (2006). Exploring the relationship between new word learning and short-term memory for serial order recall, item recall, and item recognition. *Eur. J. Cogn. Psychol.* 18, 848–873. doi: 10.1080/09541440500446476

Maloney, E., Risko, E. F., O'Malley, S., and Besner, D. (2009). Tracking the transition from sublexical to lexical processing: on the creation of orthographic and phonological lexical representations. *Q. J. Exp. Psychol.* 62, 858–867. doi: 10.1080/17470210802578385

Marinus, E., and De Jong, P. F. (2010). Variability in the word-reading performance of dyslexic readers: effects of letter-length, phoneme length and digraph presence. *Cortex* 46, 1259–1271. doi: 10.1016/j.cortex.2010.06.005

Martelli, M., De Luca, M., Lami, L., Pizzoli, C., Pontillo, M., Spinelli, D., et al. (2014). Bridging the gap between different measures of the reading speed deficit in developmental dyslexia. *Exp. Brain Res.* 232, 237–252. doi: 10.1007/s00221-013-3735-6

Martin, K. I., and Ellis, N. C. (2012). The roles of phonological short-term memory and working memory in L2 grammar and vocabulary learning. *Stud. Second Lang. Acquis.* 34, 379–423. doi: 10.1017/S0272263112000125

Mayringer, H., and Wimmer, H. (2000). Pseudoname learning by German-speaking children with dyslexia: evidence for a phonological learning deficit. *J. Exp. Child Psychol.* 75, 116–133. doi: 10.1006/jectp.1999.2525

Melby-Lervåg, M., Lyster, S.-A. H., and Hulme, C. (2012). Phonological skills and their role in learning to read: a meta-analytic review. *Psychol. Bull.* 138, 322–352. doi: 10.1037/a0026744

Menghini, D., Finzi, A., Carlesimo, G. A., and Vicari, S. (2011). Working memory impairment in children with dyslexia: is it just a phonological deficit? *Dev. Neuropsychol.* 36, 199–213. doi: 10.1080/87565641.2010.549868

Mortimore, T., and Crozier, W. R. (2006). Dyslexia and difficulties with study skills in higher education. *Stud. High. Educ.* 31, 235–251. doi: 10.1080/030750706005 72173

Myers, R. H. (1990). *Classical and Modern Regression with Applications, 2nd Edn.* Boston, MA: PWS Kent.

Nation, K. (2008). Learning to read words. *Q. J. Exp. Psychol.* 61, 1121–1133. doi: 10.1080/17470210802034603

Nation, K. (2009). Form-meaning links in the development of visual word recognition. *Philos. Trans. R. Soc. B* 364, 3665–3674. doi: 10.1098/rstb.2009.0119

O'Brien, B. A., Van Orden, G. C., and Pennington, B. F. (2013). Do dyslexics misread a ROWS for a ROSE? *Read. Writ.* 26, 381–402. doi: 10.1007/s11145-012-9373-8

Paizi, D., Burani, C., De Luca, M., and Zoccolotti, P. (2011). List context manipulation reveals orthographic deficits in Italian readers with developmental dyslexia. *Child Neuropsychol.* 17, 459–482. doi: 10.1080/09297049.2010.551187

Paizi, D., De Luca, M., Zoccolotti, P., and Burani, C. (2013). A comprehensive evaluation of lexical reading in Italian developmental dyslexics. *J. Res. Read.* 36, 303–329. doi: 10.1111/j.1467-9817.2011.01504.x

Pennington, B. F., Van Orden, G. C., Smith, S. D., Green, P. A., and Haith, M. M. (1990). Phonological processing skills and deficits in adult dyslexics. *Child Dev.* 61, 1753–1778. doi: 10.1111/j.1467-8624.1990.tb03564

Rack, J. P., Snowling, M. J., and Olson, R. K. (1992). The nonword reading deficit in developmental dyslexia: a review. *Read. Res. Q.* 27, 29–53. doi: 10.2307/747832

Rastle, K., Kinoshita, S., Lupker, S. J., and Coltheart, M. (2003). Cross-task strategic effects. *Mem. Cogn.* 31, 867–876. doi: 10.3758/BF03196441

Reid, A. A., Szczerbinski, M., Iskierka-Kasperek, E., and Hansen, P. (2006). Cognitive profiles of adult developmental dyslexics: theoretical implications. *Dyslexia* 13, 1–24. doi: 10.1002/dys.321

Reitsma, P. (1983). Printed word learning in beginning readers. *J. Exp. Child Psychol.* 36, 321–339. doi: 10.1016/0022-0965(83)90036-x

Ricketts, J., Nation, K., and Bishop, D. V. M. (2007). Vocabulary is important for some, but not all reading skills. *Sci. Stud. Read.* 11, 235–257. doi: 10.1080/10888430701344306

Rose, J. (2009). *Identifying and Teaching Children and Young People with Dyslexia and Literacy Difficulties. Independent report by Sir Jim Rose to the UK Secretary of State for Children, Schools and Families, June 2009.* Available online at: http://www.interventionsforliteracy.org.uk/rose-review/

Schneider, W., Eschman, A., and Zuccolotto, A. (2002). *E-Prime User's Guide.* Pittsburgh, PA: Psychology Software Tools.

Share, D. J., and Shalev, C. (2004). Self-teaching in normal and disabled readers. *Read. Writ.* 17, 769–800. doi: 10.1007/s11145-004-2658-9

Shek, D. T., and Ma, C. (2011). Longitudinal data analyses using linear mixed models in SPSS: concepts, procedures and illustrations. *Sci. World J.* 11, 42–76. doi: 10.1100/tsw.2011.2

Smith-Spark, J. H., and Fisk, J. (2007). Working memory function in developmental dyslexia. *Memory* 15, 34–56. doi: 10.1080/09658210601043384

Smith-Spark, J. H., Fisk, J., Fawcett, A., and Nicolson, R. (2003). Investigating the central executive in adult dyslexics: evidence from phonological and visuospatial working memory performance. *Eur. J. Cogn. Psychol.* 15, 567–587. doi: 10.1080/09541440340000024

Snowling, M. J. (2001). *Dyslexia: A Cognitive Developmental Perspective, 2nd Edn.* Oxford: Basil Blackwell.

Snowling, M. J., Nation, K., Moxham, P., Galagher, A., and Frith, U. (1997). Phonological processing skills of dyslexic students in higher education: a preliminary report. *J. Read. Res.* 20, 31–41. doi: 10.1111/1467-9817.00018

Storkel, H. L., Armbrüster, J., and Hogan, T. P. (2006). Differentiating phonotactic probability and neighborhood density in adult word learning.

J. Speech Lang. Hear. Res. 49, 1175–1192. doi: 10.1044/1092-4388 (2006/085)

Swanson, H. L., and Hsieh, C.-J. (2009). Reading disabilities in adults: a selective meta-analysis of the literature. *Rev. Educ. Res.* 79, 1362–1390. doi: 10.3102/0034654309350931

Swanson, H. L., Zheng, X., and Jerman, O. (2009). Working memory, short-term memory and reading disabilities: a selective meta-analysis of the literature. *J. Learn Disabil.* 42, 260–287. doi: 10.1177/0022219409331958

Thomson, J. M., and Goswami, U. (2010). Learning phonological representations in developmental dyslexia: associations with basic auditory processing of rise time and phonological awareness. *Read. Writ.* 23, 453–473.

Torgesen, J., Wagner, R., and Rashotte, C. (1999). *Test of Word Reading Efficiency (TOWRE).* Austin, TX: Pro-Ed.

Valdois, S., Carbonnel, S., Juphard, A., Baciu, M., Ans, B., Peyrin, C., et al. (2006). Polysyllabic pseudo-word processing in reading and lexical decision: converging evidence from behavioral data, connectionist simulations and functional MRI. *Brain Res.* 1085, 149–162. doi: 10.1016/j.brainres.2006.02.049

Van den Broeck, W., and Geudens, A. (2012). Old and new ways to study characteristics of reading disability: the case of the nonword reading deficit. *Cogn. Psychol.* 65, 414–456. doi: 10.1016/j.cogpsych.2012.06.003

Vellutino, F. R., Fletcher, J. M., Snowling, M. J., and Scanlon, D. M. (2004). Specific reading disability (dyslexia): what have we learned in the past four decades? *J. Child Psychol. Psychiatry* 45, 2–40. doi: 10.1046/j.0021-9630.2003.00305.x

Wagner, R. K., Torgesen, J. K., and Rashotte, C. A. (1999). *Comprehensive Test of Phonological Processing.* Austin, TX: PRO-ED.

Warmington, M., Hitch, G. J., and Gathercole, S. E. (2013a). Improving word learning in children using an errorless technique. *J. Exp. Child Psychol.* 114, 456–465. doi: 10.1016/j.jecp.2012.10.007

Warmington, M., Stothard, S. E., and Snowling, M. J. (2013b). Assessing dyslexia in higher education: the York adult assessment battery-revised. *J. Res. Spec. Educ. Needs* 13, 48–56. doi: 10.1111/j.1471-3802.2012.01264.x

Wechsler, D. (1999). *Wechsler Abbreviated Scale of Intelligence.* San Antonio, TX: The Psychological Corporation.

Weekes, B. S. (1997). Differential effects of number of letters on word and nonword naming latency. *Q. J. Exp. Psychol.* 50A, 439–456. doi: 10.1080/713755710

Wilkinson, G. S., and Robertson, G. J. (2006). *Wide Range Achievement Test 4.* Lutz, FL: Psychological Assessment Resources.

Wimmer, H. (1996). The nonword reading deficit in developmental dyslexia: evidence from children learning to read German. *J. Exp. Child. Psychol.* 61, 80–90. doi: 10.1006/jecp.1996.0004

Wolff, U. (2009). Phonological and surface subtypes among university students with dyslexia. *Int. J. Disabil. Dev. Educ.* 56, 73–91. doi: 10.1080/103491208026 82083

Yap, M. J., and Balota, D. A. (2009). Visual word recognition of multisyllabic words. *J. Mem. Lang.* 60, 502–529. doi: 10.1016/j.jml.2009.02.001

Ziegler, J. C., Castel, C., Pech-Georgel, C., George, F., Alario, F.-X., and Perry, C. (2008). Developmental dyslexia and the dual route model of reading: simulating individual differences and subtypes. *Cognition* 107, 151–178. doi: 10.1016/j.cognition.2007.09.004

Ziegler, J. C., Perry, C., Jacobs, A. M., and Braun, M. (2001). Identical words are read differently in different languages. *Psychol. Sci.* 12, 379–384. doi: 10.1111/1467-9280.00370

Ziegler, J. C., Perry, C., Ma-Wyatt, A., Ladner, D., and Schulte-Körne, G. (2003). Developmental dyslexia in different languages: language-specific or universal? *J. Exp. Child Psychol.* 86, 169–193. doi: 10.1016/S0022-0965(03) 00139-5

Zoccolotti, P., De Luca, M., Di Pace, E., Gasperini, F., Judica, A., and Spinelli, D. (2005). Word length effect in early reading and developmental dyslexia. *Brain Lang.* 93, 369–373. doi: 10.1016/j.bandl.2004.10.010

6

Investigating the role of visual and auditory search in reading and developmental dyslexia

Marie Lallier[1]*, Sophie Donnadieu[2,3] and Sylviane Valdois[2,4]

[1] Basque Center on Cognition Brain and Language, Donostia-San Sebastian, Spain
[2] Laboratoire de Psychologie et NeuroCognition, UMR CNRS 5105, Grenoble-Chambéry, France
[3] Faculté de Psychologie, Université de Savoie, Chambéry, France
[4] Centre National pour la Recherche Scientifique, Paris, France

***Correspondence:**
Marie Lallier, Basque Center on Cognition Brain and Language, Paseo Mikeletegi 69, Planta 2, Donostia-San Sebastian, 20009, Spain
e-mail: m.lallier@bcbl.eu

It has been suggested that auditory and visual sequential processing deficits contribute to phonological disorders in developmental dyslexia. As an alternative explanation to a phonological deficit as the proximal cause for reading disorders, the visual attention span hypothesis (VA Span) suggests that difficulties in processing visual elements simultaneously lead to dyslexia, regardless of the presence of a phonological disorder. In this study, we assessed whether deficits in processing simultaneously displayed visual or auditory elements is linked to dyslexia associated with a VA Span impairment. Sixteen children with developmental dyslexia and 16 age-matched skilled readers were assessed on visual and auditory search tasks. Participants were asked to detect a target presented simultaneously with 3, 9, or 15 distracters. In the visual modality, target detection was slower in the dyslexic children than in the control group on a "serial" search condition only: the intercepts (but not the slopes) of the search functions were higher in the dyslexic group than in the control group. In the auditory modality, although no group difference was observed, search performance was influenced by the number of distracters in the control group only. Within the dyslexic group, not only poor visual search (high reaction times and intercepts) but also low auditory search performance (d') strongly correlated with poor irregular word reading accuracy. Moreover, both visual and auditory search performance was associated with the VA Span abilities of dyslexic participants but not with their phonological skills. The present data suggests that some visual mechanisms engaged in "serial" search contribute to reading and orthographic knowledge via VA Span skills regardless of phonological skills. The present results further open the question of the role of auditory simultaneous processing in reading as well as its link with VA Span skills.

Keywords: dyslexia, reading, visual search, auditory search, attention, temporal processing, visual attention span, phonology

INTRODUCTION

Developmental dyslexia is a neurocognitive disorder reflected by severe and persistent reading difficulties in individuals who have been provided with appropriate schooling, present a non-verbal IQ within the normal range, and do not suffer from any sensory or psychiatric disorders. A number of neuroimaging and behavioral studies now suggest that reading difficulties in dyslexia may not stem from a unique but rather multiple origins (Ramus and Ahissar, 2012; Koyama et al., 2013; van Ermingen-Marbach et al., 2013). Developmental dyslexia in this context is seen as a multifactorial and heterogeneous disorder. For example, the visual attention span (VA Span, hereafter) hypothesis describes at least two cognitive impairments (phonological and visual attentional) that can equally but independently lead to developmental dyslexia (Bosse et al., 2007). Looking at two large samples of French and English dyslexic children, Bosse et al. (2007) report that the reading difficulties of dyslexic children were either accompanied by a single phonological disorder (i.e., phonological awareness, phonological short term memory, phonological fluency), a single VA Span deficit (without phonological problems), or a combination of those two. Importantly, Peyrin et al. (2012) found that the biological bases for those two dyslexic cognitive subtypes were independent: they found that a dysfunction located within the left inferior frontal gyrus characterized dyslexia associated with a phonological disorder whereas a dysfunction of the superior parietal lobules bilaterally was seen in the VA Span dyslexic subtype.

The VA Span is defined as the number of visual elements that can be processed simultaneously (at a glance) in a visual multi-element array, regardless of the verbal or non-verbal nature of those elements (Lobier et al., 2012). VA Span skills are thought to tap into perceptual attention (i.e., attention skills which enhance perceptual encoding and its clarity) and be specifically critical for (i) processing simultaneously all the letters within whole-word visual forms, (ii) building-up lexical orthographic knowledge and (iii) enhancing the recognition of previously unfamiliar words

(Bosse and Valdois, 2009; Bosse et al., 2013). Moreover, VA Span skills have been shown to play a significant role at various stages of typical reading development by contributing to reading variance independently from phonological skills (Bosse and Valdois, 2009).

For the VA Span hypothesis, the simultaneous dimension of visual perceptual attention plays a central role in reading development independently of phonology. Contrastively, the sequential dimension of visual perceptual attention has been proposed as a significant contributor to dyslexia associated with phonological difficulties (sluggish attentional shifting theory of dyslexia, Hari and Renvall, 2001). Supporting the claims of both the VA Span and the sluggish attentional shifting theories, Lallier et al. (2010a) showed that a dyslexic adult with a severe phonological deficit but preserved VA Span skills was impaired on visual sequential attentional skills. This suggests that phonological, and visual sequential processing disorders can co-occur in dyslexia regardless of visual simultaneous processing problems, i.e., VA Span deficits. Along the same lines, some studies showed that dyslexic participants exhibited visual impairments on paradigms where stimuli were presented sequentially but not simultaneously (Ben-Yehudah and Ahissar, 2004; Conlon et al., 2004; Ram-Tsur et al., 2006), or the opposite (Yap and Van der Leij, 1993; Lassus-Sangosse et al., 2008).

These studies suggest that the dissociation between sequential and simultaneous visual processing deficits in dyslexia essentially depend on the stimulus presentation mode of the task. However, the link between sequential presentation paradigms and the sequential dimension involved in ecologic reading is rather indirect: orthographic units never appear and disappear sequentially at a unique fixation point (*externally driven* sequential processing). Rather, the self-paced visual attentional captures within and between words generate the sequential dimension present in the reading activity (*internally driven* sequential processing). Conversely, simultaneous visual processes such as VA Span skills are directly involved in ecologic reading since they reflect visual attention skills at play during an ocular fixation (Prado et al., 2007).

Visual search paradigms have been proposed to reflect both sequential (Vidyasagar and Pammer, 1999, 2010; Vidyasagar, 2004) and simultaneous (Marendaz et al., 1996) visual perceptual attention at play in reading. In those paradigms, participants are presented with a stimulus display where a target presented simultaneously with a set of distracters has to be detected as fast as possible. Within the framework of the "Feature Integration Theory" (Treisman and Gelade, 1980) two types of search tasks, in which the type of stimuli presented varies, are generally administered and require distinct visual processes. In the so-called "parallel" search, the target possesses only one feature which differentiates it from all the distracters (e.g., "Q" among "O"s). In this condition reaction times (RT) for target detection are not affected by the number of distracters: a pre-attentive "pop-out" effect for the target occurs because a battery of visual analyzers, specialized for detecting that unique feature, automatically captures the attentional focus. In the so-called "serial" search, the target is characterized by the conjunction of two features (e.g., "O" among "Q"s). In that case, RTs for target detection increase linearly as a function of the number of distracters because an effortful sequential screening, thought to engage controlled attention, occurs to search for the target. When assessed on visual search paradigms, dyslexic children (Casco and Prunetti, 1996; Marendaz et al., 1996; Vidyasagar and Pammer, 1999) and adults (Iles et al., 2000; Buchholz and McKone, 2004; de Boer-Schellekens and Vroomen, 2012) are repeatedly found to be impaired on the "serial" search condition, suggesting a visual attention deficit in this population. Typically, dyslexic participants present a higher search slope coefficient than skilled readers, indicating that they process a smaller amount of stimuli per second in the display.

To explain these deficits, two hypotheses regarding the nature of visual attention problems have been suggested: Marendaz et al. (1996) suggest the hypothesis of a reduction of the number of elements that dyslexic individuals can encode simultaneously under fixation whilst searching for the target (i.e., reduced VA Span). Alternatively and according to the feature integration theory of visual search, Vidyasagar (2004, Vidyasagar and Pammer, 1999), proposes that reading problems and difficulties on the visual "serial" search task in dyslexia are both caused by a failure in monitoring sequential spatial attentional shifts under fixation (see also Franceschini et al., 2012). This idea finds support from the neurophysiology of the visual system and the fact that visual information flux arriving from the retina to the visual primary cortex separates into two cortical pathways: (i) the dorsal or "magnocellular" pathway subtending fast/transient processing and object motion encoding and (ii) the dorsal or "parvocellular" pathway subtending slow/sustained visual processing and object identification mechanisms. According to Vidyasagar, the dorsal stream monitors rapid spatial attentional shifts screening serially each of the 7 or 8 letters falling under fixation, therefore facilitating their identification by the ventral system. Like the VA Span hypothesis, this proposal suggests that the key mechanism of visual attention for reading acquisition would occur within an ocular fixation and regardless of the phonological skills of participants (see Pammer et al., 2004, 2005; Vidyasagar and Pammer, 2010)[1].

In the present study, we present dyslexic and age-matched skilled reader children with a visual task and an auditory one that involve the simultaneous presentation of multiple stimuli. Our first aim was to determine whether deficits classically observed on the "serial" search task in developmental dyslexia were restricted to dyslexia associated with VA Span deficits. Our second aim was to investigate whether any impairment observed on the visual "serial" search task in dyslexia would also occur on an auditory search task. Indeed, since reading requires multimodal resources, it would not be surprising if perceptual attentional deficits in dyslexia were not restricted to only one sensory modality, but also tapped into an amodal pool of resources (Facoetti et al.,

[1]The theoretical nuance between the two theories is that Vidyasagar proposes that these visual attentional resources are serial (since it would be governed by the dorsal stream) whereas the VA Span hypothesis assumes that they are parallel (since they would be subtended by brain areas playing a role attention devoted to multi-element processing: Peyrin et al., 2012). Another difference between the two theories is that Vidyasagar defines the visual attentional resources in terms of spatiality whereas in the VA Span hypothesis, they are defined in terms of quantity.

2003, 2005, 2010; Lallier et al., 2009, 2010a,c). Moreover, a perceptual asymmetry, which is similar to the one found in visual search tasks, takes place in auditory search tasks. Cusack and Carlyon (2003) presented participants with a task in which a frequency modulated (FM) sound had to be detected among non-modulated sounds (steady sounds), and a task in which the opposite had to be done. No auditory pop-out effect was found for either of the two tasks; however, the participants' accuracy in detecting the FM sound among steady sounds was less affected by the number of distracters than their ability to accurately detect the steady sound among FM distracters was. The authors concluded that auditory search reflected systems specialized for certain auditory features, as well as the limited capacity of attentional resources to process the auditory set, and that the two conditions engaged various degrees of difficulty.

We reasoned that if search mechanisms require simultaneous perceptual attention, and simultaneous perceptual attention reflected in VA Span skills taps into an amodal pool of resources, poor VA Span skills should be associated with poor visual and auditory search performance. Support for this hypothesis comes from a recent study showing that dyslexic children with a VA Span disorder were impaired on simultaneous auditory attention assessed in a dichotic listening task designed to be comparable to the task measuring VA Span abilities (Lallier et al., 2012). Also found that simultaneous auditory attention was unrelated to the phonological awareness and short term memory skills of the participants. Here, we therefore expected that if detecting an auditory target presented simultaneously among auditory distracters involves simultaneous perceptual attention, performance should not be related to the phonological abilities of participants but rather to their VA Span skills.

MATERIALS AND METHODS

PARTICIPANTS

Thirty-two French children took part in the present study. A group of 16 dyslexic children (10 boys) was compared to a group of 16 control children (3 boys). All children attended school regularly and had French as native language. They had normal or corrected-to-normal vision, normal hearing level, and no history of neurological or psychiatric disorders.

The 16 dyslexic children were recruited at the "Reference Center for Specific Learning Disorders" of the Pediatric Department of the Hospital of Grenoble and the Neuropediatric Department of the Kremlin-Bicêtre Hospital in Paris where the diagnosis of developmental dyslexia was primarily established by practitioners in charge (i.e., neuropsychologists or neuropediatricians) using both inventories and testing procedures in accordance with the guidelines of the ICD-10 classification of Mental and Behavioral disorders. All the dyslexic participants had normal IQ (full IQ superior to 85 on the WISC-III or WISC-IV, or a score superior to the 25th percentile on the Raven's Progressive Matrices; Raven et al., 1998). Although the two groups were matched for age [controls: 128 ± 5 months; dyslexics: 133 ± 10 months, $t_{(30)} = 1.7$, $p = 0.09$], control children were older regarding reading age [139.2 ± 16 months; dyslexics: 85.7 ± 6.4 months, $z = 4.8$, $p < 0.001$] as measured by the "Alouette" reading test (Lefavrais, 1967).

READING SKILLS ASSESSMENT IN THE CONTROL AND THE DYSLEXIC CHILDREN

Reading performance of the 32 participants were assessed using reading lists including a list of 20 words, a list of 20 irregular words and a list of 20 pseudowords, taken from the ODEDYS battery (Jacquier-Roux et al., 2002). Items between lists were matched for letter and syllable lengths, grammatical class and frequency. The 20 pseudowords were legal pseudowords without lexical neighbors. Participants were instructed to read aloud each of the three lists as quickly and as accurately as possible. Both accuracy and reading rate were taken into account.

PHONOLOGICAL AND VA SPAN SKILLS SCREENING OF THE DYSLEXIC CHILDREN

Dyslexic children were presented with some additional tasks in order to determine the cognitive disorder associated to their dyslexia at the individual level. Phonological processing was quantified with two tasks: a phonemic deletion task (phonemic awareness) and a pseudoword repetition task (phonological short-term memory). The two phonological tasks were taken from the EVALEC battery (Sprenger-Charolles et al., 2005) in which pseudowords are presented to participants through headphones. The visual whole report and visual partial report tasks (e.g., Bosse et al., 2007; Bosse and Valdois, 2009) were further administered to dyslexic children in order to quantify their VA Span skills.

Phonemic awareness

Twelve pseudowords with a tri-phonemic consonant-consonant-vowel structure (CCV) were presented to the children via headphones. The children were instructed to remove ("eat") the first sound of the pseudoword and say the remaining part. The score corresponded to the percentage of correct answers.

Phonological short-term memory

Children were asked to repeat pseudowords as accurately as possible without any time constraint. The task included 24 pseudowords varying in length from three to six syllables. The score corresponded to the percentage of pseudowords accurately repeated.

VA span skills

Prior to the visual whole report task, children were administered a control letter identification task. Children were presented with a single letter (each of the 10 consonants presented for the two report tasks described below) in the center of the screen during varying durations (33, 50, 67, 84, and 101 ms) immediately followed by a mask. They were asked to name the letter immediately after being presented.

The whole report task included 20 black consonant strings (composed of 10 consonants, upper-case Arial font, 18 pt). The center-to-center distance between each adjacent consonant was 1.2° so that lateral masking effects were minimized. Stimuli did not include the same letter twice and were not French word skeletons (e.g., C M P T R for "compter"). At the start of each trial, a central fixation point was displayed for 1000 ms followed by a blank screen for 50 ms. Consonant strings were presented horizontally during 200 ms at the center of the screen. Immediately after the string presentation, participants had to recall as many letters as possible. The score corresponded to the percentage of letters accurately reported (identity not location).

In the partial report task, participants were required to orally report a single cued letter presented before briefly within a 5-consonant string. Fifty 5-letter strings were built from the same 10 consonants used in the whole report condition and with the same characteristics as the whole report task. The probe indicating the letter to be reported was a vertical bar presented for 50 ms, 1° below the target letter presented in the string. Each letter was used as target once in each position. Like in the whole report task, a central fixation point was presented for 1000 ms followed by a blank screen for 50 ms. The 5-letter string was then presented at the center of the screen for 200 ms. At the offset of the letter string, the bar probe appeared for 50 ms. Participants were asked to report the cued letter only and to be as accurate as possible and no time pressure. The score corresponded to the percentage of cued letters accurately reported.

VISUAL AND AUDITORY SEARCH TASKS

The two search tasks used in the present study were created from two tasks in the visual (Marendaz et al., 1996) and the auditory (Cusack and Carlyon, 2003, Experiment 3) modalities which previously showed a perceptual asymmetry for search performance as a function of target type and number of distracters.

Visual stimuli

As in Marendaz et al. (1996), the visual search configurations were composed of two types of capital letters (O and Q, Helvetica font, 28 pts) subtending an average angular size of 0.8°. The letter search display covered a surface of 10.2° by 11.4° (height and width) from a viewing distance of 45 cm. The minimum distance separating two stimuli was never twice as much as the letter size in order to avoid grouping effects. In the "parallel" search condition, children had to detect the target letter "Q" among distracter letters "Os" whereas in the "serial" search condition, they had to detect the target letter "O" among distracter letters "Qs."

Auditory stimuli

Following Experiment 3's procedure of Cusack and Carlyon (2003), the auditory search configurations were composed of 250 ms-long tones randomly distributed over a 1-s window [2] and across a logarithmic frequency scale (262–4192 Hz), with the constraint that two simultaneously occurring tones had to be separated from at least one third of an octave. In a first condition, children had to detect a FM tone target (described as a "moving sound"), which was modulated at a depth of 5% (0.84 semitones) among pure tones, and in a second condition, they had to detect a steady tone (described as a "non-moving sound") within FM tones. The sounds were presented over headphones (Earthquake, TS 800) at a level of 70 dB SPL approximately.

[2] In Cusack and Carlyon (2003, Experiment 3), the temporal window was 2 s long. We shortened this temporal window on purpose to favor the simultaneous processing of the tones.

Procedure

Henceforth, the two search conditions for each modality will be referred to as the "O target" and "Q target" conditions in the visual modality, and "FM target" and "Steady target" conditions in the auditory modality. In both the visual and the auditory tasks, eight search configurations of 4, 10, and 16 stimuli were created, yielding a total of 48 trials for each condition. For each condition, the configurations with various stimulus set sizes were presented randomly and the target was present in half of the trials. Children were instructed to determine whether the target was present or not: in the visual task, they had to press "P" on the keyboard as fast they could as soon as they detected the target, or press "A" when they did not detect any target. In the auditory task, they were instructed to wait until the 1-s auditory configuration finished before pressing the response key when a question about the presence or absence of the target appeared on a white screen.

In the visual modality (**Figure 1A**), children were first presented with a mask subtending the size of the following letter display for 2000 ms. Then, a blank screen was presented for 1000 ms followed by a fixation cross at the center of the screen for 900 ms. A blank screen then appeared for 200 ms and one of the eight visual configurations was presented. After the response of the subject a blank screen then appeared for 1000 ms before the presentation of the mask of the following trial. In the auditory modality (**Figure 1B**), a fixation cross appeared on a blank screen for 1000 ms and the auditory search configuration was displayed for 1000 ms whilst the cross remained on the screen. After the auditory sequence, a question appeared on the screen asking whether the target was present or not. Before the auditory search task, an identification task composed of 40 trials was administered to the children in order to make sure they could identify both types of sound. On this control task, all children were at ceiling,

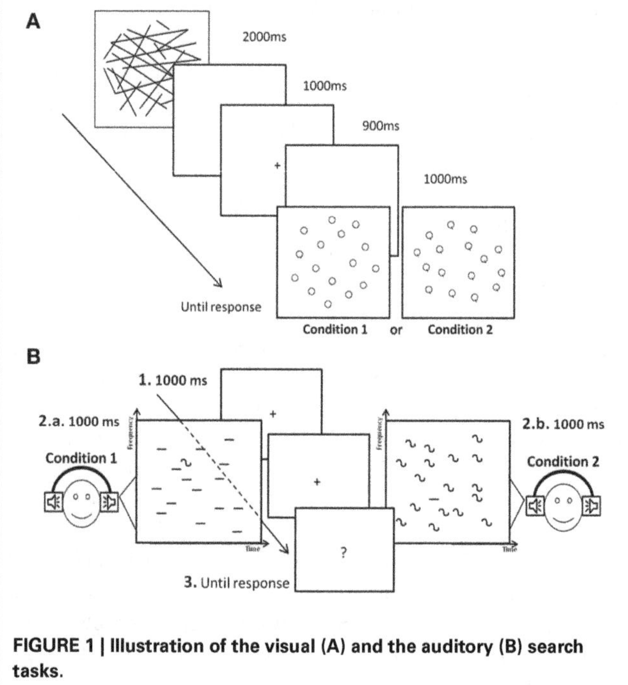

FIGURE 1 | Illustration of the visual (A) and the auditory (B) search tasks.

demonstrating good discrimination skills between FM and steady sounds. In both modalities, a training phase composed of 8 trials was administered prior to the test. The order of administration of the two conditions was counterbalanced between participants, as well as the order between the visual and the auditory tasks.

DATA ANALYSIS

Group differences on reading accuracy and speed were assessed by means of independent parametric *t*-tests (or non-parametric *U*-tests when the conditions for carrying out parametric analysis were not assumed) with group (control, dyslexic) as the between-subjects factor. Individual reading performance was compared to age-matched norms from which individual and group average *z*-scores were computed (Bosse and Valdois, 2009). Regarding the cognitive skills of the dyslexic children, individual *z*-scores were computed according to the age-matched corresponding norms for the two phonological tasks (Sprenger-Charolles et al., 2005) and for the VA Span tasks (Bosse and Valdois, 2009).

For the visual and the auditory search task separately, RTs for trials where the target was present and correctly detected, and d' scores were analyzed by means of mixed ANOVAs with group (control, dyslexic) as the between-subjects factor, and condition (O target/Q target; FM target/Steady target) as well as stimulus set size (4, 10, 16) as within subject factors. *Post-hoc* analyses were conducted using Bonferroni tests. In the case of non-homogeneity of variance or non-sphericity of the data, data transformation or Greenhouse-Geisser correction, respectively, were performed.

For partial correlation analyses (controlling for chronological age), we computed an additional search measure corresponding to the average measure of the search performance across the three stimulus set sizes for each modality.

RESULTS

READING SKILLS

As shown in **Table 1**, the performance of control children was significantly higher than the performance of dyslexic children on the three reading lists (for all *t* or *z* values, $ps < 0.001$, **Table 1**). All control children performed well within the norm, with all individual *z*-scores being above -1 on all the reading measures. The severe reading difficulties of the dyslexic children were illustrated by an average performance 2 SD below the norm on all the reading measures. Overall, the dyslexic group of the present study exhibited difficulties on both the global (irregular word reading) and analytic (pseudoword reading) reading procedures.

PHONOLOGICAL SKILLS AND VA SPAN SKILLS IN THE DYSLEXIC GROUP

Table 2 presents the performance of the dyslexic group regarding their phonological and VA Span skills. The dyslexic group was significantly worse at repeating pseudowords compared to the age-matched norm, which illustrated poor phonological short-term memory skills ($z = -1.84, p < 0.05$). In the CCV phonemic deletion task, the dyslexic group tended to exhibit poorer performance compared to the norm ($z = -1.54, p = 0.06$). On the visual control task of single letter identification, no deficit was found at any of the presentation times (33 ms: $z = -0.49$, 50 ms: $z = -0.59$, 67 ms: $z = -0.56$, 84 ms: $z = -0.67$ and 110 ms: $z = -0.67$, all *zs* n.s.), neither on the overall performance (104.4 letters identified out of 150 (±34), $z = -0.56$, n.s.). On the whole report task, the dyslexic group accurately reported 65.6% (±16.3) of the letters on average, indicating a deficit on that task ($z = -1.81, p < 0.05$). On the partial report task, as a group, the dyslexic children did not exhibit any deficit, reporting accurately 78% (±16.3) of the cued letters ($z = -0.88$, n.s.).

SEARCH TASKS

Search performance differences between the control and dyslexic groups

First, in the visual modality (**Figure 2A**), no effect involving the group was found on d' scores (all $Fs < 1$), indicating that there was no group difference on visual target detection sensitivity across all experimental conditions. In the auditory modality (**Figure 2B**), no effect was found on RTs (all $Fs < 1$) indicating that none of the factors (including the group) influenced the time to press the response button after the auditory configuration presentation.

Table 1 | Reading skills of the control group ($n = 16$) and the dyslexic group ($n = 16$).

	Control group		Dyslexic group		Group effect[b]
	M (SD)	*z*-score[a]	M (*SD*)	*z*-score[a]	
REGULAR WORDS					
Accuracy/20	18.8 (1.7)	0.04	13.9 (3.1)	−2.00*	$t_{(30)} = -5.2$***
Speed (s)	16.8 (4.8)	0.24	60.2 (36.5)	−4.70***	$z = 4.5$***
IRREGULAR WORDS					
Accuracy/20	17.6 (2.1)	0.58	7.1 (3.1)	−2.30*	$t_{(30)} = -10.8$***
Speed (s)	19.1 (5.9)	0.24	69.3 (37.6)	−4.50***	$z = 4.5$***
PSEUDOWORDS					
Accuracy/20	17.5 (1.9)	0.310	11.1 (3.9)	−2.40*	$t_{(30)} = -5.6$***
Speed (s)	24.3 (6.0)	0.08	57.3 (25.7)	−3.10**	$z = 4.8$***

[a] *Individual z-scores (one-tailed) computed according to age-matched norms (Bosse and Valdois, 2009).*
[b] *For speed measures, non-parametric Mann-Whitney U-tests were used (z statistics reported).*
*$p < 0.05$, **$p < 0.01$, ***$p < 0.001$.

Table 2 | Characteristics of the dyslexic group ($n = 16$).

	M (*SD*)	Range	*Z* score
PHONOLOGY			
Pseudoword repetition (%)[a]	45.5 (20)	19–79	−1.84*
CCV deletion (%)[a]	51.0 (27)	0–100	−1.54, $p = 0.06$
VISUAL ATTENTION SPAN[b]			
Whole report task (%)	65.6 (16.3)	35–91	−1.81*
Partial report task (%)	78.0 (13)	50–92	−0.88 n.s.

[a] *z scores computed from the age-matched norms of Sprenger-Charolles et al. (2005).*
[b] *z scores computed from the age-matched norms of Bosse and Valdois (2009).*
*$p < 0.05$.

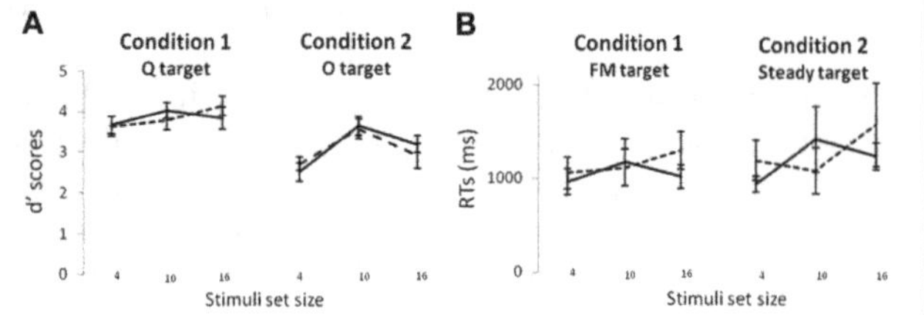

FIGURE 2 | Visual d′ scores (A) and auditory RT scores (B) in the control (solid line) and dyslexic (dotted line) children. Standard error bars are depicted.

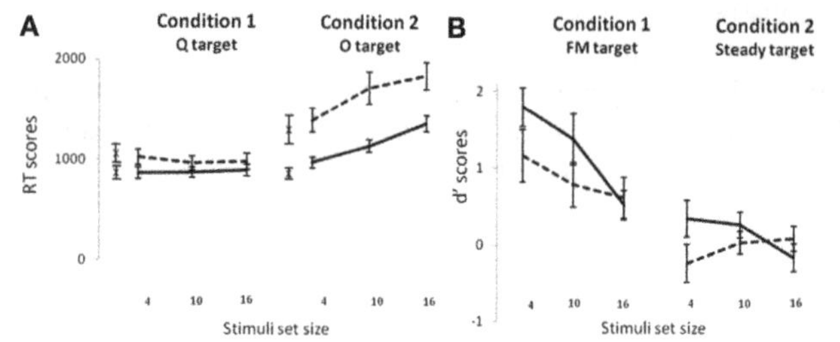

FIGURE 3 | Visual RT scores (A) and auditory d′ scores (B) in the control (solid line) and dyslexic (dotted line) children. Crosses represent the intercept values for the visual task. Standard error bars are depicted.

In the visual task (**Figure 3A**), there was a main effect of group on RTs [$F_{(1,\ 30)} = 4.90$, $p = 0.034$] that was modulated by the condition [$F_{(1,\ 30)} = 5.6$, $p = 0.02$], and that showed that dyslexic children were slower than control children in the O target condition (*post-hoc*: $p = 0.03$ but) but not in the Q target condition (*post-hoc*: $p > 0.9$). There was also a main effect of condition [$F_{(1,\ 30)} = 119.05$, $p < 0.001$] and stimulus set size [$F_{(2,\ 60)} = 22.3$, $p < 0.001$). These two factors interacted with each other [$F_{(2,\ 60)} = 26.2$, $p < 0.001$] indicating that the smaller the number of distracters, the faster the response, but only for the O target condition (*post-hoc*: all $ps < 0.001$; Q target condition, all $ps > 0.1$). RTs differences across stimulus set sizes in the O target condition could be explained by changes in participant's criteria (speed-accuracy tradeoff): Average d' scores and RTs indeed positively correlated in the whole sample ($r = 0.34$, $p < 0.05$) suggesting that the worse target sensitivity the child showed, the faster at responding they were. Importantly, since the two groups showed similar d' scores for all visual experimental conditions (see **Figure 2A**), speed-accuracy tradeoff variations between groups could not explain the aforementioned differences on RTs. As a follow-up of these significant effects on RTs, we computed intercept and slope values of the search functions. The group difference found in the O target condition on RTs was accompanied by a group difference on the search function intercepts (controls: 860 ± 213 ms; dyslexics: 1260 ± 520 ms; $t_{(30)} = -2.7$, $p < 0.05$), but not on the slopes (controls: 32 ± 18 ms/item; dyslexics: 37 ± 32 ms/item; $t < 1$). In the Q target condition, control and dyslexic children presented identical slopes (respectively, 2 ± 8 ms/item and -3 ± 16 ms/item, $t_{(30)} = 1.2, p > 0.05$) and intercepts (respectively, 860 ± 245 and 1037 ± 322 ms, $t_{(30)} = -1.7$, $p > 0.05$).

In the auditory task (**Figure 3B**), no main effect of group was found [$F_{(1,\ 30)} = 2.14$, $p = 0.15$] on d′ measures. There was a main effect of condition [$F_{(1,\ 30)} = 35$, $p < 0.001$] illustrating that participants were better in the FM target condition than in the Steady target condition. There was also an effect of stimulus set size [$F_{(2,\ 60)} = 5.3, p < 0.01$] showing that target detection performance was better for stimulus set size of four than 16 (*post-hoc* test: $p < 0.01$, other $ps > 0.05$). A condition by stimulus set size interaction [$F_{(2,\ 60)} = 4.2, p = 0.02$] revealed that the difference between the set sizes of 4 and 16 was true for the FM target condition (*post-hoc* test: $p < 0.001$), whereas in the Steady target condition, detection was equally hard for all set sizes (*post hoc* tests: all $ps > 0.10$). The condition by set size interaction was similar between groups ($F < 1$). Lastly, there was an interaction between group and stimulus set size [$F_{(2,\ 60)} = 3.4$, $p = 0.04$] showing that control children benefited of being presented with four compared to 16 stimuli (*post-hoc* test: $p < 0.005$) whereas dyslexic children did not, and this was not modulated by the condition ($F < 1$).

Search performance differences between dyslexic subgroups

In order to examine to what extent individual significant VA Span disorders in the dyslexic group were linked to search deficits, we ran subsequent subgroup analyses. We selected all the dyslexic children with a VA Span deficit, i.e., impaired on both the whole and partial report tasks (VASpan subgroup; all individual *z*-scores < -1.65, $n = 6$). We further selected all the dyslexic children with no impairment on any of the two report tasks (noVASpan subgroup: individual *z*-scores > -0.9, $n = 6$). Note that the four remaining dyslexic children exhibited poor performance on only one of the two report tasks and were not included in any of the subgroups. Both of the two subgroups presented the same reading delay compared to the level expected for their age (42 months for the VASpan subgroup and 48 months for noVASpan subgroup), which indicated similar impaired reading level in the two dyslexic subgroups (Mann Whitney *U*-test: $z = 1.26$ $p > 0.05$). Both dyslexic subgroups were impaired on phonological short term memory (VASpan: $z = -2.1$, $p = 0.018$; noVASpan: $z = -1.9$, $p = 0.029$), but only the noVASpan subgroup was significantly impaired on phonemic awareness (noVASpan: $z = -1.7$, $p = 0.045$; VASpan: -1.2, $p = 0.11$ n.s.). Kruskal-Walis tests were conducted with group as a between subject factor (VASpan, $n = 6$; noVASpan, $n = 6$; controls, $n = 16$) on the average performance in the visual O target condition and in the auditory FM target condition. On auditory search, the three groups presented similar performance overall [$H_{(2)} = 0.8$ $p = 0.66$]. On visual search, there was a main effect of group on RTs [$H_{(2)} = 11.1$ $p < 0.005$] that indicated slower target detection for the VASpan subgroup compared to the control group (multiple comparisons on mean ranks: $p < 0.005$, all other $ps > 0.05$). Note that no group effect was found on visual d' scores on the O target condition [$H_{(2)} = 0.59$ $p = 0.77$], suggesting no speed-accuracy tradeoff differences across groups. Although no group effect was found on the slope values [$H_{(2)} = 2.1$ $p = 0.33$], a group effect was found on the intercept values [$H_{(2)} = 6.8$ $p = 0.034$], which revealed higher intercepts for the VASpan group than the control group (multiple comparisons on mean ranks: $p = 0.04$, all other $ps > 0.05$).

PARTIAL CORRELATIONS ANALYSES

Within the whole sample

Following the results reported in section Search Tasks, an average d' obtained on the O target condition was controlled for in the correlations involving RTs for visual search in order to neutralize speed-accuracy tradeoff between participants. None of the reading measures correlated with any of the different search measures neither in the Q target condition for the visual task, nor in the Steady target condition for the auditory task. Therefore, all the subsequent analyses will focus on performance on the O target condition and the FM target condition.

Performance on these critical conditions correlated with each other (-0.33, $p < 0.05$, one-tailed, based on the *a priori* hypothesis of an amodal pool of resources for simultaneous processing, cf. Lallier et al., 2012) suggesting that they tapped into the same pool of amodal resources. As shown in **Table 3**, all reading *z*-scores significantly correlated with visual RTs, illustrating that the better reading (accurate and fast) the faster the search, for all stimulus set sizes. The reading scores also correlated with the intercept measures, but not with the slope measures, suggesting that the greater the intercept the poorer the reading skills. In the auditory modality, search performance (in particular for a set size of 10) significantly correlated with reading speed for all types of items and with real words only (regular and irregular) regarding accuracy, i.e., the higher the d', the faster and better the reading.

Within the dyslexic sample

We further ran partial correlation analyses in the dyslexic group in order to determine whether a low search performance in both modalities would contribute to their reading and/or cognitive deficits (i.e., phonological or VA Span difficulties). As seen in **Table 4**, auditory (d') and visual (RTs) search performance correlated with each other indicating that the higher the RTs in the visual task, the lower the d' score in the auditory task. Moreover, the higher the visual intercepts, the poorer the auditory search performance for a stimulus set size of 10.

Poor search skills of dyslexic children were associated with their poor reading skills. Visual search RTs and intercepts correlated with pseudoword and irregular word reading accuracy and auditory search d′ scores correlated with real word reading accuracy (regular and irregular) and reading speed for all items (**Table 5**). In particular, both visual (i.e., set sizes of 4, 10, and 16, average measure, intercepts) and auditory search performance (set size of 10 in particular) correlated strongly with irregular word accuracy (cf. **Table 5**; **Figure 4**). Visual slope values did not correlate with any of the reading measures.

Table 4 | Partial correlation coefficients visual and auditory search performance in the dyslexic sample ($n = 16$).

	Auditory search (d') FM target			
	SSS(4)	SSS(10)	SSS(16)	AVG
VISUAL SEARCH O TARGET				
RT—SSS(4)	−0.07	−0.68***	−0.30	−0.35
RT—SSS(10)	−0.05	−0.79***	−0.52*	−0.52*
RT—SSS(16)	−0.22	−0.75***	−0.68***	−0.65**
RT—AVG	−0.06	−0.79***	−0.52*	−0.53*
Slope	−0.37	0.01	−0.43	−0.33
Intercept	0.14	−0.60*	−0.17	−0.24

SSS, stimulus set size; AVG, average measure of the search performance across the three stimuli set sizes.

$^*p < 0.05$, $^{**}p < 0.01$, $^{***}p < 0.005$, one-tailed.

Table 3 | Correlation coefficients between reading *z*-scores and search tasks in the whole sample ($n = 32$).

	REG_Acc	REG_T	IRR_Acc	IRR_T	PW_Acc	PW_T
VISUAL SEARCH O TARGET						
RT—SSS(4)	−0.43**	−0.51***	−0.57***	−0.48***	−0.63***	−0.32*
RT—SSS(10)	−0.49***	−0.57***	−0.59***	−0.54***	−0.64***	−0.43***
RT—SSS(16)	−0.39*	−0.41*	−0.53***	−0.38*	−0.47**	−0.39*
RT—AVG	−0.46***	−0.53***	−0.60***	−0.50***	−0.61***	−0.40*
Slope	−0.01	0.07	−0.04	0.08	0.14	−0.15
Intercept	−0.40*	−0.49***	−0.52***	−0.47***	−0.62***	−0.27
AUDITORY SEARCH (d') FM TARGET						
SSS(4)	0.37*	0.30*	0.31*	0.17	0.10	0.36*
SSS(10)	0.34*	0.41*	0.33*	0.35*	0.27	0.36*
SSS(16)	0.29	0.08	0.02	0.04	0.18	0.09
AVG	0.41*	0.35*	0.30	0.25	0.23	0.35*

REG, regular words; IRR, irregular words; PW, pseudowords; Acc, accuracy; T, time; SSS, stimulus set size; AVG, average measure of the search performance across the three stimuli set sizes.

$^*p < 0.05$, $^{**}p < 0.01$, $^{***}p < 0.005$, one-tailed based on the a priori hypothesis of a relation between reading deficits and poor search performance.

Table 5 | Partial correlation coefficients between reading scores and search performance in the dyslexic sample ($n = 16$).

	REG_Acc	REG_T	IRR_Acc	IRR_T	PW_Acc	PW_T
VISUAL SEARCH O TARGET						
RT—SSS(4)	−0.31	0.24	−0.69***	0.32	−0.56*	0.19
RT—SSS(10)	−0.34	0.34	−0.79***	0.41	−0.48***	0.31
RT—SSS(16)	−0.18	0.11	−0.66**	0.15	−0.28	0.09
RT—AVG	−0.30	0.26	−0.76***	0.33	−0.48*	0.23
Slope	0.21	−0.19	0.14	−0.25	0.42	−0.15
Intercept	−0.32	0.25	−0.64**	0.33	−0.58*	0.20
AUDITORY SEARCH (d') FM TARGET						
SSS(4)	0.46*	−0.21	0.46*	−0.07	−0.02	−0.26
SSS(10)	0.53*	−0.51*	0.84***	−0.48*	0.32	−0.48*
SSS(16)	0.40	−0.10	0.52*	−0.10	0.24	0.09
AVG	0.57*	−0.33	0.74***	−0.26	0.20	−0.34

REG, regular words; IRR, irregular words; PW, pseudowords; Acc, accuracy; T, time; SSS, stimulus set size; AVG, average measure of the search performance across the three stimuli set sizes.

$^*p < 0.05$, $^{**}p < 0.01$, $^{***}p < 0.005$, one-tailed based on the a priori hypothesis of a relation between reading deficits and poor search performance.

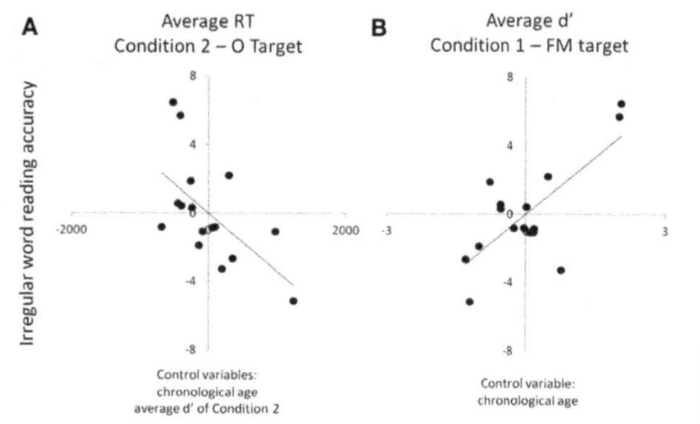

FIGURE 4 | Scatterplots depicting the partial correlations between irregular word reading accuracy (y axes) and visual (A) and auditory (B) search performance among the dyslexic children. For each panel, individual residual scores are represented, which stem from the two correlations between the factor(s) controlled for and (i) search performance, as well as (ii) irregular word reading accuracy.

Lastly, reduced VA Span skills were found to be associated with both poor visual (RTs and intercepts) and auditory (set size of 10) search performance (**Table 6**; **Figure 5**). No relation was found between search performance and any of the two phonological scores.

Table 6 | Partial correlation coefficients between cognitive skills and search performance in the dyslexic sample ($n = 16$).

	VA Span		Phonology	
	PARTIAL	**WHOLE**	**PSTM**	**PA**
VISUAL SEARCH O TARGET				
RT—SSS(4)	−0.37	−0.48*	−0.13	0.38
RT—SSS(10)	−0.47*	−0.60*	−0.12	0.34
RT—SSS(16)	−0.52*	−0.31	−0.05	0.26
RT—AVG	−0.48*	−0.51*	−0.11	0.35
Slope	−0.14	0.26	0.12	−0.20
Intercept	−0.30	−0.47*	−0.14	0.38
AUDITORY SEARCH (d') FM TARGET				
SSS(4)	0.04	0.28	0.33	0.11
SSS(10)	0.48*	0.61*	0.30	−0.20
SSS(16)	0.32	0.15	0.13	0.05
AVG	0.32	0.43	0.32	0.01

PSTM, phonological short term memory; PA, phonological awareness; SSS, stimulus set size; AVG, average measure of the search performance across the three stimuli set sizes. *$p < 0.05$.

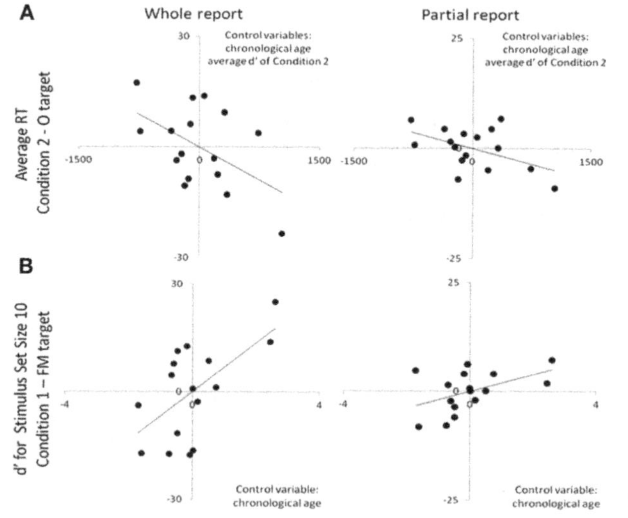

FIGURE 5 | Scatterplots depicting the partial correlations between VA Span skills (whole and partial report, y axes) and visual (A) and auditory (B) search performance (x axes) among the dyslexic children. For each panel, individual residual scores are represented, which stem from the correlations between the factor(s) controlled for and (i) VA Span skills, as well as (ii) search performance.

DISCUSSION

In the present study, we showed that dyslexic individuals are impaired in visual "serial" search paradigms. Dyslexic children were indeed slower than the control group to detect the letter O among Qs. This deficit was accompanied by a search function characterized by prolonged intercepts for the dyslexic group than the control group in the absence of difference on the search slope. Moreover, auditory search abilities were measured for the first time in children with and without developmental dyslexia. The condition where children had to detect a steady sound among FM sound distracters led to very low performance, suggesting that this task was too difficult for both the controls and the dyslexic groups. In both conditions, the control children's performance was enhanced when few auditory distracters were present, suggesting that stimulus set size influenced their perceptual attentional auditory load. No such modulation was observed in the dyslexic children, which might indicate that their auditory perceptual attention load is already "*at threshold*" for the processing of few stimuli, and might reflect a limitation of attentional resources allocated to auditory simultaneous processing. We will return to this point later. In favor of the amodality of perceptual attention at play in search mechanisms, fast visual "serial" search (O target) correlated significantly with good sensitivity to detect FM targets both in the whole group and within the dyslexic group of children.

Slow visual "serial" search and high intercepts were significantly associated with poor VA Span skills in the dyslexic group. More specific analyses of the individual cognitive profiles of the dyslexic children showed that only the children with a significant VA Span deficit (i.e., impaired on both the whole and the partial report tasks) exhibited slower RTs and higher intercepts on the visual "serial" search compared to controls. This result strongly suggests that the factor at play in both reading and our visual search task is linked to simultaneous visual attention, i.e., the number of visual elements that can be processed in parallel in one fixation. Importantly, we found no correlation between visual search skills and either phonological short term memory or phonemic awareness skills of the dyslexic children. Moreover, the dyslexic group with no VA Span impairment showed no deficit on the visual search task despite of being the only group impaired on phonemic awareness. This dissociation between phonological skills and visual search performance in the dyslexic group suggests that deficits in the "serial" search condition (O target) is unlikely to be driven by serial processing difficulties such as sluggish visual attentional shifting skills previously found to relate to poor phonological skills (Lallier and Valdois, 2012 for a review). This idea finds additional support in both the absence of group effect on the slope values and the absence of correlation between reading, VA Span and these slope values. Indeed, search slope values are thought to relate to serial attentional components of the search (Wolfe and Horowitz, 2008). In our study, the dyslexic children—in particular the subgroup with simultaneous visual processing deficits (VASpan subgroup)—did not exhibit any deficit in the visual sequential processing skills required for an efficient search (i.e., absence of atypically high slope values). This is reminiscent of the results of Lallier et al. (2010a,b,c) which show that simultaneous and sequential visual attentional deficits dissociate in developmental dyslexia. The dyslexic children in our study were rather impaired on components such as those determining the intercept of the search function. Intercept values have been related to factors linked to processes preceding or following search mechanisms *per se* (Woodman et al., 2001). The intercept values of the dyslexic children might therefore have been constrained by visual mechanisms that influenced their response, and that were possibly at play before the start of the attentional serial search (Jolicoeur and Dell'Acqua, 1999; Wolfe and Horowitz, 2008). We will discuss later on how such visual mechanisms could relate to VA Span skills.

In further support for the significant contribution of VA Span disorder to the visual search deficits of dyslexic children, we reported that their visual "serial" search performance (RTs and intercepts) and reading accuracy significantly correlated and especially strongly so for irregular words. In opaque languages like French, it is impossible to correctly read an irregular word using the most frequent grapheme-to-phoneme conversion rules: the only way to be accurate is to retrieve the phonological lexical form automatically from the whole-word visual form whose encoding depends on VA Span skills (Ans et al., 1998; Bosse and Valdois, 2009). Our results in the auditory modality were less clear due to an absence of difference between both the dyslexic and control groups as well as the VASpan and NoVASpan dyslexic subgroups. Still, like in the visual modality, a strong correlation was found between irregular word reading accuracy and auditory search performance (stimulus set size of 10) within the dyslexic group, suggesting that auditory simultaneous attention may also be important for lexical processing in dyslexia. For the irregular word list, dyslexic children had to read each item aloud, hence retrieve its phonological lexical form. Would auditory simultaneous attention mediate the access of auditory whole-word knowledge?

Studies have shown some links between auditory whole-word knowledge and the degree of divided attention engaged in a task. For example, dual-tasking seems to enhance the reliance of lexical knowledge strategies used in speech perception tasks: Mattys and Wiget (2011) showed that the reliance on lexical knowledge was stronger in high cognitive load settings simulating adverse speech perception conditions (dual task, divided attention) than in low cognitive load settings (see also Mattys et al., 2009)[3]. In the present study, the correlation between visual and auditory search performance and irregular word reading accuracy in the dyslexic group indicates that children with better phonological and orthographical whole-word knowledge (and good access to them) were those who could monitor better random increases of the load of perceptual attention for auditory search. According to (Mattys and Wiget, 2011, Experiment 6), the strong lexical knowledge reliance for speech processing in high cognitive load settings might stem from the need to cope with the sensory degradation of *temporal cues* important for phoneme identification. Similarly, Casini et al. (2009) showed that vowel duration was underestimated when participants had to perform a dual task. According to the hypothesis that the estimation of speech units' duration relies on registering the number of "temporal pulses" accumulated during speech unit intervals (e.g., Coull et al., 2004), Casini et al. (2009) proposed that sharing attentional resources between simultaneous tasks (or simultaneous stimuli in the present study) decreases the sampling rate allocated to each task (or stimulus). Such phonemic sampling reduction would thus lead to miss some pulses within phonemic intervals and the underestimation of their temporal features.

In favor of Casini et al. (2009)'s hypothesis and the hypothesis of a permanent "*dual-task-like*" mode of dyslexic individuals, Vandermosten et al. (2010, 2011) showed that dyslexic children exhibit poor phonemic identification skills relying on temporal cues. Lehongre et al. (2011) also showed that dyslexic adults exhibited less oscillatory neural entrainment than skilled readers at the phonemic sampling rate (30 Hz) in the left hemisphere, which further correlated to slow rapid automatized naming skills (phonological whole-word forms retrieval). This last result supports our idea that auditory whole-word knowledge relies on the quality of both phonemic-rate sampling (cf. Poeppel, 2003) and the monitoring of random increases of auditory perceptual attentional load (cf. **Figure 5**). The correlations highlighted between auditory/visual search and VA span skills suggest that dyslexic children with low VA Span skills may suffer from a permanent high perceptual load hindering visual and auditory processing. This should be particularly true when *several* stimuli have to be attended and encoded (like in "serial" search) since we did not report different intercepts between the dyslexic and control children when the attentional focus is automatically directed to *the* relevant target stimulus (such as in "parallel" search). In support of this idea, Woodman et al. (2001) reported an increase of the intercept but not the slope values of the visual "serial" search functions (like the performance of our dyslexic group) when participants had to maintain several visual elements in memory whilst performing the search. A VA Span reduction might therefore have a negative impact on perceptual attentional processing similar to the one generated by a cognitive overload stemming from dual-tasking.

[3]Even if we did not manipulate the cognitive load in our search tasks, perceptual load was. Perceptual and cognitive loads may further not be that independent in dyslexia since Lallier et al. (2012) showed that dyslexic children's scores on a dichotic listening dual-task (cognitive load) correlated with VA Span skills (perceptual attention load).

Interestingly, the auditory perceptual load generated by the simultaneous presentation of 10 stimuli was found to correlate with VA Span skills, intercept values and reading skills. Why this particular "signal-to-noise ratio" may be relevant for literacy development is an open question, but some studies looking at speech-in-noise deficits in developmental dyslexia could shed light on it (Ziegler et al., 2009; Dole et al., 2012). In particular, we found that auditory search performance was unrelated to phonological awareness (see also Lallier et al., 2012) which is supported by studies that show a relative independence between speech-in-noise deficits and other phonological deficits (Robertson et al., 2009; Ziegler et al., 2009; Messaoud-Galusi et al., 2011; Berent et al., 2012; Dickie et al., 2012). Speech-in-noise skills of dyslexic children also seem to dissociate from slow rate dynamic auditory processing linked to phonological awareness (Poelmans et al., 2011). Weak auditory entrainment to slow auditory frequencies (delta and theta) within speech streams—and critical for rhythm extraction—has been proposed as a cause of phonological awareness deficits in dyslexia (Goswami, 2011; Goswami et al., 2013; Hämäläinen et al., 2012). This weak auditory oscillatory entrainment at slow frequency bands might thus explain sluggish auditory attentional shifting, which appears to be restricted to dyslexia associated with phonological disorders (see Lallier et al., 2013), but is less likely to explain poor simultaneous processing abilities in auditory search. It is noteworthy that in the present study, we did not observe any significant deficit of the dyslexic group on our auditory search task. Although no strong conclusion about the role of auditory search in developmental dyslexia can be drawn at this point, the significant relationships highlighted between auditory search performance and reading skills as well as VA Span skills can still shed light on what this role might be.

Overall, we point out that different auditory perceptual attentional factors might contribute independently[4] to stable sound representations build-up (Hornickel and Kraus, 2013) and reading development. One of them could relate to speech processing in particular in high perceptual load situations (i.e., speech-in-noise, auditory search) and lexical knowledge, and would be linked to the simultaneous dimension of auditory processing (high frequency sampling). Another one would tap into slow modulations which are important for phonological awareness acquisition and that are carried by speech rhythm: this slow frequency sampling would tap into the sequential dimension of auditory processing[5]. We propose that a similar model could *a priori* hold true for the visual modality since perceptual attention deficits on one processing dimension (sequential or simultaneous) generally co-occur in audition and vision in the same dyslexic participants (Lallier et al., 2009, 2010a,c, 2012). We suggest that visual perceptual attention critical for reading acquisition requires both sequential (slow) and simultaneous (fast serial) mechanisms. First, a sequential visual attention mechanism would guide the attentional focus to engage and disengage over orthographic sequences, explaining sluggish visual attentional shifting and phonological disorders in dyslexia (Hari and Renvall, 2001; Facoetti et al., 2008; Lallier et al., 2009, 2010a,b). This visual mechanism would possibly trigger saccades in reading (Belopolsky and Theeuwes, 2009) and tap into parvocellular, hence relatively slow, temporal processing (Vidyasagar, 2004). A second mechanism, engaged in visual "serial" search (O target) would be in charge of screening the orthographic chunks falling under fixation and could be monitored by the magnocellular pathway, hence, characterized by a very high rate serial processing (Vidyasagar, 2004). The present results suggest that this second mechanism might be in part modulated by VA Span skills. Future studies will explore whether and how VA Span skills are monitored by a high frequency oscillatory visual system (gamma band) and whether this system dissociates from or depends on its coupling with a slow frequency oscillatory visual system (delta/theta bands).

CONCLUSION

In the present study, we assessed the search performance of a group of dyslexic children across the visual and the auditory modalities. Dyslexic children were slower than control children on the visual "serial" search condition only, which was accompanied by search function intercepts (but not slopes) that were higher in the dyslexic group than the control group. Despite the absence of deficit of the dyslexic group on the auditory search task, we showed that poor VA Span skills correlated to poor search performance not only in the visual but also in the auditory modalities. These results suggest that dyslexic children with a VA Span disorder may be under a permanent high perceptual load that hinders visual and auditory processing in particular in situations where several elements must be encoded simultaneously. Our results also suggest that limitations in simultaneous perceptual attention may preferentially affect the development of lexical reading (e.g., irregular word reading) and possibly the build-up of some phonological processes (first at the phoneme level, with consequences for auditory whole-word forms access). Finally, we stress the importance of taking into account the heterogeneity of the reading disorders at the cognitive level (e.g., phonological awareness, VA Span), since various time scales of processing might have different and potentially independent roles in literacy acquisition, and lead to different subtypes of developmental dyslexia.

ACKNOWLEDGMENTS

This research was supported by the CNRS (Center National de la Recherche Scientifique), the French Ministery of "Enseignement Supérieur et de la Recherche," and the European commission (Call ID FP7-PEOPLE-2010-IEF—Panel SOC—Proposal N°274352—Acronym: BIRD attributed to Marie Lallier). We thank Marie-Ange N'Guyen, Emilie Longeras, Catherine Billard, Camille Chabernaud and Luke Armstrong for their valuable help in this research and thank all the children and their family for their participation.

[4]Since the sampling frequencies characterizing speech streams are coupled and modulate each other, the independence of their respective contribution to reading and dyslexia may be relative and remains to be quantified.

[5]Most of the speech-in-noise deficits assessed in dyslexia reflect problems at lexical, syllabic or phonemic levels. Future studies should examine whether "speech streams"-in-noise perception shares any mechanisms with rhythm perception, phonological awareness and slow rate auditory entrainment.

REFERENCES

Ans, B., Carbonnel, S., and Valdois, S. (1998). A connectionist multiple-trace memory model for polysyllabic word read- ing. *Psychol. Rev.* 105, 678. doi: 10.1037/0033-295X.105.4.678-723

Belopolsky, A. V., and Theeuwes, J. (2009). When are attention and saccade preparation dissociated? *Psychol. Sci.* 20, 1340–1347. doi: 10.1111/j.1467-9280.2009.02445.x

Ben-Yehudah, G., and Ahissar, M. (2004). Sequential spatial frequency discrimination is consistently impaired among adult dyslexics. *Vision Res.* 44, 1047–1063. doi: 10.1016/j.visres.2003.12.001

Berent, I., Vaknin-Nusbaum, V., Balaban, E., and Galaburda, A. M. (2012). Dyslexia impairs speech recognition but can spare phonological compe- tence. *PLoS ONE* 7:e44875. doi: 10.1371/journal. pone.0044875

Bosse, M. L., Chaves, N., Largy, P., and Valdois, S. (2013). Orthographic learning during reading: the role of whole-word visual processing. *J. Res. Read.* doi: 10.1111/j.1467- 9817.2012.01551.x

Bosse, M. L., Tainturier, M. J., and Valdois, S. (2007). Developmental dyslexia: the visual attention span deficit hypothesis. *Cognition* 104, 198–230. doi: 10.1016/j.cognition. 2006.05.009

Bosse, M. L., and Valdois, S. (2009). Influence of the visual attention span on child reading performance: a cross-sectional study. *J. Res. Read.* 32, 230–253. doi: 10.1111/j.1467-9817.2008.01387.x

Buchholz, J., and McKone, E. (2004). Adults with dyslexia show deficits on spatial frequency doubling and visual attention tasks. *Dyslexia* 10, 24–43. doi: 10.1002/dys.263

Casco, C., and Prunetti, E. (1996). Visual search of good and poor readers: effects with targets hav- ing single and combined features. *Percept. Mot. Skills* 82, 1155–1167. doi: 10.2466/pms.1996.82.3c.1155

Casini, L., Burle, B., and Nguyen, N. (2009). Speech perception engages a general timer: evidence from a divided attention word identifica- tion task. *Cognition* 112, 318–322. doi: 10.1016/j.cognition.2009. 04.005

Conlon, E., Sanders, M., and Zapart, S. (2004). Temporal process- ing in poor adult readers. *Neuropsychologia* 42, 142–157. doi: 10.1016/j. neuropsychologia. 2003.07.004

Coull, J. T., Vidal, F., Nazarian, B., and Macar, F. (2004). Functional anatomy of the attentional modu- lation of time estimation. *Science* 303, 1506–1508. doi: 10.1126/sci-ence.1091573

Cusack, R., and Carlyon, R. P. (2003). Perceptual asymmetries in audition. *J. Exp. Psychol. Hum. Percept. Perform.* 29, 713–725. doi: 10.1037/0096-1523.29.3.713

de Boer-Schellekens, L., and Vroomen, J. (2012). Sound can improve visual search in developmental dyslexia. *Exp. Brain Res.* 216, 243–248. doi: 10.1007/s00221-011-2926-2

Dickie, C., Ota, M., and Clark, A. (2012). Revisiting the phonological deficit in dyslexia: are implicit non-orthographic representations impaired. *Appl. Psycholinguist.* 1, 1–24.

Dole, M., Hoen, M., and Meunier, F. (2012). Speech-in-noise perception deficit in adults with dyslexia: effects of background type and listening configuration. *Neuropsychologia* 50, 1543–1552. doi: 10.1016/ j.neuropsychologia.2012.03.007

Facoetti, A., Lorusso, M. L., Cattaneo, C., Galli, R., and Molteni, M. (2005). Visual and auditory atten- tional capture are both sluggish in children with developmental dyslexia. *Acta Neurobiol. Exp. (Wars)* 65, 61–72.

Facoetti, A., Lorusso, M. L., Paganoni, P., Cattaneo, C., Galli, R., Umiltà, C., et al. (2003). Auditory and visual automatic attention deficits in developmental dyslexia. *Cogn. Brain Res.* 16, 185–191. doi: 10.1016/S0926-6410(02)00270-7

Facoetti, A., Ruffino, M., Peru, A., Paganoni, P., and Chelazzi, L. (2008). Sluggish engagement and disengagement of non-spatial atten- tion in dyslexic children. *Cortex* 44, 1221–1233. doi: 10.1016/j.cortex. 2007.10.007

Facoetti, A., Trussardi, A. N., Ruffino, M., Lorusso, M. L., Cattaneo, C., Galli, R., et al. (2010). Multisensory spatial attention deficits are pre- dictive of phonological decoding skills in developmental dyslexia. *J. Cogn. Neurosci.* 22, 1011–1025. doi: 10.1162/jocn.2009.21232

Franceschini, S., Gori, S., Ruffino, M., Pedrolli, K., and Facoetti, A. (2012). A causal link between visual spa- tial attention and reading acquisi- tion. *Curr. Biol.* 22, 814–819. doi: 10.1016/j.cub.2012.03.013

Goswami, U. (2011). A temporal sam-pling framework for developmental dyslexia. *Trends Cogn. Sci.* 15, 3–10. doi: 10.1016/j.tics.2010.10.001

Goswami, U., Mead, N., Fosker, T., Huss, M., Barnes, L., and Leong, V. (2013). Impaired perception of syllable stress in children with dyslexia: a longitudinal study. *J. Mem. Lang.* 69, 1–17. doi: 10.1016/ j.jml.2013.03.001

Hämäläinen, J. A., Rupp, A., Soltész, F., Szücs, D., and Goswami, U. (2012). Reduced phase locking to slow amplitude modulation in adults with dyslexia: an MEG study. *Neuroimage* 59, 2952–2961. doi: 10.1016/j. neuroimage.2011.09.075

Hari, R., and Renvall, H. (2001). Impaired processing of rapid stimulus sequences in dyslexia. *Trends Cogn. Sci.* 5, 525–532. doi: 10.1016/S1364-6613(00)01801-5

Hornickel, J., and Kraus, N. (2013). Unstable representation of sound: a biological marker of dyslexia. *J. Neurosci.* 33, 3500–3504. doi: 10.1523/ JNEUROSCI.4205-12.2013

Iles, J., Walsh, V., and Richardson, A. (2000). Visual search performance in dyslexia. *Dyslexia* 6, 163–177. doi: 10.1002/1099-0909(200007/09)6:3<163..AID-DYS150>3.0. CO,2-U

Jacquier-Roux, M., Valdois, S., and Zorman, M. (2002). Odédys. Outil de dépistage des Dyslexies. Grenoble: Laboratoire cogni-sciences, IUFM de Grenoble. Jolicoeur, P., and Dell'Acqua, R. (1999). Attentional and structural con- straints on visual encoding. *Psychol. Res.* 62, 154–164. doi: 10.1007/ s004260050048

Koyama, M. S., Di Martino, A., Kelly, C., Jutagir, D. R., Sunshine, J., Schwartz, S. J., et al. (2013). Cortical signatures of dyslexia and reme- diation: an intrinsic functional connectivity approach. *PLoS ONE* 8:e55454. doi: 10.1371/journal. pone.0055454

Lallier, M., Donnadieu, S., Berger, C., and Valdois, S. (2010a). A case study of developmental phonologi- cal dyslexia: is the attentional deficit in the perception of rapid stim- uli sequences amodal? *Cortex* 46, 231–241. doi: 10.1016/j.cortex.2009. 03.014

Lallier, M., Donnadieu, S., and Valdois, S. (2010b). Visual attentional blink in dyslexic children: parameterizing the deficit. *Vis. Res.* 50, 1855–1861. doi: 10.1016/j.visres.2010.06.006

Lallier, M., Tainturier, M. J., Dering, B., Donnadieu, S., Valdois, S., and Thierry, G. (2010c). Behavioral and ERP evidence for amodal sluggish attentional shifting in developmental dyslexia. *Neuropsychologia* 48, 4125. doi: 10.1016/j.neuropsychologia. 2010.09.027

Lallier, M., Donnadieu, S., Thierry, G., Tainturier, M. J., Billard, C., Peyrin, C., et al. (2009). Auditory and visual stream segregation in children and adults: an assessment of the amodality assumption of the 'slug- gish attentional shifting' theory of dyslexia. *Brain Res.* 1302, 132–147. doi: 10.1016/j. brainres.2009.07.037

Lallier, M., Donnadieu, S., and Valdois, S. (2012). Developmental dyslexia: exploring how much phonological and visual attention span disorders are linked to simultaneous auditory processing deficits. *Ann. Dyslexia* 63, 97–116. doi: 10.1007/s11881- 012-0074-4

Lallier, M., Thierry, G., and Tainturier, M. J. (2013). On the importance of considering individual profiles when investigating the role of audi- tory sequential deficits in devel- opmental dyslexia. *Cognition* 126, 121–127. doi: 10.1016/j.cognition. 2012.09.008

Lallier, M., and Valdois, S. (2012). "Sequential versus simultaneous processing deficits in develop- mental dyslexia," in *Dyslexia – A Comprehensive and International Approach*, eds T. N. Wydell and Fern-Pollak, ISBN 978-953-51-0517-6, under CC BY 3.0 license.

Lassus-Sangosse, D., N'guyen-Morel, A., and Valdois, S. (2008). Sequential or simultaneous visual processing deficit in develop- mental dyslexia? *Vision Res.* 48, 979–988. doi: 10.1016/j.visres. 2008.01.025

Lefavrais, P. (1967). *Test de l'Alouette: Manuel.* Paris: Les éditions du Centre de Psychologie Appliquée.

Lehongre, K., Ramus, F., Villiermet, N., Schwartz, D., and Giraud, A. L. (2011). Altered low-gamma sampling in auditory cortex accounts for the three main facets of dyslexia. *Neuron* 72, 1080–1090. doi: 10.1016/j. neuron.2011.11.002

Lobier, M., Zoubrinetzky, R., and Valdois, S. (2012). The visual atten- tion span deficit in dyslexia is visual and not verbal. *Cortex* 48, 768–773. doi: 10.1016/j.cortex.2011. 09.003

Marendaz, C., Valdois, S., and Walch, J. P. (1996). Dyslexie développe- mentale et attention visuo-spatiale. *L'année psychologique* 96, 193–224. doi: 10.3406/ psy.1996.28893

Mattys, S. L., Brooks, J., and Cooke, M. (2009). Recognizing speech under a processing load: dissociating ener- getic from informational factors. *Cogn. Psychol.* 59, 203–243. doi: 10.1016/j.cogpsych.2009.04.001

Mattys, S. L., and Wiget, L. (2011). Effects of cognitive load on speech recognition. *J. Mem. Lang.* 65, 145–160. doi: 10.1016/j.jml.2011.04.004

Messaoud-Galusi, S., Hazan, V., and Rosen, S. (2011). Investigating speech perception in children with dyslexia: is there evidence of a consistent deficit in individuals? *J. Speech Lang. Hear. Res.* 54, 1682. doi: 10.1044/1092-4388(2011/09- 0261)

Pammer, K., Lavis, R., Cooper, C., Hansen, P. C., and Cornelissen, P.L. (2005). Symbol-string sensitiv- ity and adult performance in lexical decision. *Brain Lang.* 94, 278–296. doi:10.1016/j.bandl.2005.01.004

Pammer, K., Lavis, R., Hansen, P., and Cornelissen, P. L. (2004). Symbol- string sensitivity and children's reading. *Brain Lang.* 89, 601–610. doi: 10.1016/j.bandl.2004.01.009

Peyrin, C., Lallier, M., Demonet, J. F., Pernet, C., Baciu, M., Le Bas, J. F., et al. (2012). Neural dissociation of phonological and visual attention span disorders in developmental dyslexia: FMRI evidence from two case reports. *Brain Lang.* 120, 381–394. doi: 10.1016/j.bandl.2011.12.015

Poelmans, H., Luts, H., Vandermosten, M., Boets, B., Ghesquière, P., and Wouters, J. (2011). Reduced sensitivity to slow-rate dynamic auditory information in children with dyslexia. *Res. Dev. Disabil.* 32, 2810–2819. doi: 10.1016/j.ridd. 2011.05.025

Poeppel, D. (2003). The analysis of speech in different temporal and visual search: impact of the visual attention span. *Vision Res.* 47, 2521–2530. doi: 10.1016/j.visres. 2007.06.001

Ram-Tsur, R., Faust, M., and Zivotofsky, A. Z. (2006). Sequential processing deficits of reading dis- abled persons is independent of inter-stimulus interval. *Vision Res.* 46, 3949–3960. doi: 10.1016/j.visres. 2006.07.001

Ramus, F., and Ahissar, M. (2012). Developmental dyslexia: the dif- ficulties of interpreting poor performance, and the importance of normal performance. *Cogn. Neuropsychol.* 29, 104–122. doi: 10.1080/02643294.2012.677420

Raven, J. C., Court, J. H., and Raven, J. (1998). *Progressive Matrices Standard (PM38).* Paris: EAP.

Robertson, E. K., Joanisse, M. F., Desroches, A. S., and Ng, S. (2009). Categorical speech percep- tion deficits distinguish language and reading impairments in children. *Dev. Sci.* 12, 753–767. doi: 10.1111/j.1467-7687.2009. 00806.x

Sprenger-Charolles, L., Colé, P., Béchennec, D., and Kipffer-Piquard, integration windows: cerebral later- alization as 'asymmetric sampling in time' *Speech Commun.* 41, 245–255. doi: 10.1016/S0167-6393(02) 00107-3

Prado, C., Dubois, M., and Valdois, S. (2007). The eye movements of dyslexic children during reading A. (2005). French normative data on reading and related skills from EVALEC, a new computerized battery of tests (end Grade 1, Grade 2, Grade 3, and Grade 4). *Revue Européenne de Psychologie Appliquée/Eur. Rev. Appl. Psychol.* 55, 157–186. doi: 10.1016/j.erap. 2004.11.002

Treisman, A. M., and Gelade, G. (1980). A feature-integration the- ory of attention. *Cogn. Psychol.* 12, 97–136. doi: 10.1016/0010-0285 (80)90005-5

Vandermosten, M., Boets, B., Luts, H., Poelmans, H., Golestani, N., Wouters, J., et al. (2010). Adults with dyslexia are impaired in cat- egorizing speech and nonspeech sounds on the basis of tempo- ral cues. *Proc. Natl. Acad. Sci. U.S.A.* 107, 10389–10394. doi: 10.1073/pnas.0912858107

Vandermosten, M., Boets, B., Luts, H., Poelmans, H., Wouters, J., and Ghesquière, P. (2011). Impairments in speech and nonspeech sound categorization in children with dyslexia are driven by tempo- ral processing difficulties. *Res. Dev. Disabil.* 32, 593–603. doi: 10.1016/j.ridd.2010.12.015

van Ermingen-Marbach, M., Grande, M., Pape-Neumann, J., Sass, K., and Heim, S. (2013). Distinct neural signatures of cognitive subtypes of dyslexia with and without phono- logical deficits. *Neuroimage (Amst.)* 2, 477–490. doi: 10.1016/j.nicl.2013. 03.010

Vidyasagar, T. R. (2004). Neural under- pinnings of dyslexia as a disorder of visuo-spatial attention. *Clin. Exp. Optom.* 87, 4–10. doi: 10.1111/j. 1444-0938.2004.tb03138.x

Vidyasagar, T. R., and Pammer, K. (1999). Impaired visual search in dyslexia relates to the role of the magnocellular pathway in atten- tion. *Neuroreport* 10, 1283–1287. doi: 10.1097/00001756-199904260- 00024

Vidyasagar, T. R., and Pammer, K. (2010). Dyslexia: a deficit in visuo- spatial attention, not in phono- logical processing. *Trends Cogn. Sci.* 14, 57. doi: 10.1016/j.tics.2009. 12.003

Wolfe, J., and Horowitz, T. S. (2008). Visual search. *Scholarpedia* 3, 3325. doi: 10.4249/scholarpedia. 3325

Woodman, G. F., Vogel, E. K., and Luck, S. J. (2001). Visual search remains efficient when visual working memory is full. *Psychol. Sci.* 12, 219–224. doi: 10.1111/1467-9280. 00339

Yap, R., and Van der Leij, A. (1993). "Rate of elementary symbol pro- cessing in dyslexics," in *Facets of Dyslexia and its Remediation*, eds S. F. Wright, and R. Groner (Amsterdam: Elsevier Science), 337–347.

Ziegler, J. C., Pech-Georgel, C., George, F., and Lorenzi, C. (2009). Speech-perception-in-noise deficits in dyslexia. *Dev. Sci.* 12, 732–745. doi: 10.1111/j.1467-7687.2009.00817.x

7

Tracking orthographic learning in children with different profiles of reading difficulty

Hua-Chen Wang *, Eva Marinus, Lyndsey Nickels and Anne Castles

Department of Cognitive Science, ARC Centre of Excellence in Cognition and its Disorders, Macquarie University, Sydney, NSW, Australia

Correspondence:
Hua-Chen Wang, Department of Cognitive Science, ARC Centre of Excellence in Cognition and its Disorders, Macquarie University, Sydney, NSW 2109, Australia
e-mail: huachen.wang@mq.edu.au

Previous studies have found that children with reading difficulties need more exposures to acquire the representations needed to support fluent reading than typically developing readers (e.g., Ehri and Saltmarsh, 1995). Building on existing orthographic learning paradigms, we report on an investigation of orthographic learning in poor readers using a new learning task tracking both the accuracy (untimed exposure duration) and fluency (200 ms exposure duration) of learning novel words over trials. In study 1, we used the paradigm to examine orthographic learning in children with specific poor reader profiles (nine with a surface profile, nine a phonological profile) and nine age-matched controls. Both profiles showed improvement over the learning cycles, but the children with surface profile showed impaired orthographic learning in spelling and orthographic choice tasks. Study 2 explored predictors of orthographic learning in a group of 91 poor readers using the same outcome measures as in Study 1. Consistent with earlier findings in typically developing readers, phonological decoding skill predicted orthographic learning. Moreover, orthographic knowledge significantly predicted orthographic learning over and beyond phonological decoding. The two studies provide insights into how poor readers learn novel words, and how their learning process may be compromised by less proficient orthographic and/or phonological skills.

Keywords: orthographic learning, developmental dyslexia, subtypes, phonological decoding, orthographic knowledge

INTRODUCTION

Orthographic learning has been defined as the transition from the slow sounding out of an unfamiliar new word to the rapid automatic recognition of the same word. It is widely acknowledged that beginning readers need to make this transition in order to become proficient readers (e.g., Ehri and Wilce, 1983; Share, 1995; Castles and Nation, 2008). In this study, we explored orthographic learning in children with poor reading ability and investigated the factors that are associated with their success in acquiring new orthographic representations.

Most developmental theories propose that the sounding out of words, phonological decoding, is an important mechanism for reaching the final stage of automatic reading (for a review, see Ehri, 2005). Among these theories, the self-teaching hypothesis is associated with a strong claim for the importance of phonological decoding in orthographic learning (Share, 1995, 1999). It proposes that phonological decoding is the first and most important step of orthographic learning, providing an opportunity for this learning to take place. The act of phonological decoding is proposed to allow the reader access to a word's spoken form, as well as to draw their attention to the order and identity of the letters. This, together with repeated exposure to the new word, assists the reader in establishing an orthographic representation. According to the self-teaching hypothesis, although phonological decoding is crucial in orthographic learning, it is not the only factor: there is a secondary, orthographic processing component, which also determines the success of orthographic learning, although the nature of this mechanism is little understood (Share, 1995, 2011).

If phonological decoding is important for acquiring orthographic representations, proficient phonological decoding processes should increase the likelihood of successful orthographic learning. Conversely, impaired phonological decoding processes should be expected to lead to difficulties in orthographic learning. Indeed, abundant studies seem to support the view that deficits in phonological processing skills may be a primary cause of reading difficulties (e.g., Rack et al., 1992; Stanovich and Siegel, 1994) as well as orthographic learning difficulties (Share and Shalev, 2004).

However, a large body of evidence on heterogeneity within the dyslexic population and on the existence of different subtypes of developmental dyslexia suggests that the relationship between phonological decoding skills and orthographic learning may not be straightforward (Castles and Coltheart, 1993; Manis et al., 1996; Stanovich et al., 1997; Valdois et al., 2003; Castles et al., 2010b; Jones et al., 2011; McArthur et al., 2013; Peterson et al., 2013). The outcomes of these studies show that impairment in phonological decoding and impairment in automatic whole-word recognition can occur selectively—one aspect of reading can be impaired while the other develops normally. Namely, children with a *surface dyslexia* profile struggle to read irregular words (e.g., *yacht*) but are not impaired in reading nonwords (e.g., *grep*). This indicates that they are specifically impaired in recognizing whole words, whilst their phonological decoding skills are intact. Conversely, children with a *phonological dyslexia* profile show impairments in nonword reading but not irregular word reading, indicating a specific impairment in phonological decoding processes while being intact in sight word recognition skills. Note that children with these profiles are seen as falling at the ends of a normal continuum of ability on the relevant reading subskills, not as qualitatively distinct subtypes.

In sum, based on the view that phonological decoding is the primary factor in successful orthographic learning, the reading profiles of surface dyslexia and phonological dyslexia seem to be somewhat of a paradox. How are some beginning readers able to build up orthographic knowledge despite poor decoding skills (phonological dyslexics) and why do some children with proficient decoding skills fail to build up orthographic representations (surface dyslexics)? In order to address these questions we need to examine how orthographic learning occurs in these two subtype profiles.

To date, only two studies have explicitly contrasted differences in orthographic learning in children with phonological and surface dyslexia. Castles and Holmes (1996) found that, as expected by their specific reading profiles, children with a surface dyslexia profile were poorer at learning novel irregular words (measured by an orthographic choice task in which the child had to choose the target item from its distracters) than children with a phonological dyslexia profile. However, since the novel words in their study were all irregular, it may be that children with a surface profile performed more poorly than children with a phonological profile because their usual phonological decoding strategy is not effective for such items (e.g., how would one phonologically decode a word like "laugh"?).

Bailey et al. (2004) built on the results of Castles and Holmes (1996) by comparing orthographic learning of both regular and irregular words in children with profiles of phonological dyslexia and surface dyslexia. They found that overall, the two profiles were no different from each other, but were both more impaired than chronological age controls in orthographic learning (as measured by reading accuracy). In addition, they found that both children with a surface profile and the controls showed an advantage in learning regular words as compared to irregular words. In contrast, children with a phonological profile showed no difference between regular and irregular words, suggesting that phonological decoding was not relied on during orthographic learning. Although this study provided more insight into the orthographic learning processes of these two profiles of dyslexia, there are still some limitations. First, orthographic learning results were based on reading accuracy only[1]. Thus, the finding that children with a surface profile were more accurate in reading regular than irregular words may have been a function of the "decodability" of the words rather than orthographic learning *per se* (e.g., *cat* can be read correctly by phonological decoding, whereas this is not possible for *yacht*). Hence, to determine whether children with surface dyslexia are indeed better at acquiring (and not just decoding) regular orthographic representations than irregular ones, improved measures of orthographic learning with minimal influence from decoding ability are required. Second, selection of the subgroups was based on a relatively lax criterion. Instead of selecting children with a surface profile that were impaired on irregular word reading only, and phonological profile children that were impaired on nonword reading only, Bailey and colleagues based their selection on a discrepancy score between nonword and irregular word reading. Hence, for example, a phonological profile child in their study could have been poor on both nonword and irregular word reading, but with irregular word being relatively better than nonword reading. The design of the study presented here allows us to address these problems.

The first aim of the present study was to further extend our understanding of orthographic learning in children with surface and phonological profiles. By studying orthographic learning in these two subgroups we also aimed to bridge the gap between previous work on orthographic learning (mostly conducted with normal readers) and the extensive literature on subtypes in dyslexia. Building on the studies of Castles and Holmes (1996) and Bailey et al. (2004), we used a more stringent subgroup criterion in selecting participants and developed a novel paradigm to explore orthographic learning. Just like Bailey et al. we included a sample of typical readers as controls so that we could not only compare the performance of the children with different profiles, but also contrast their performance to that of normal readers.

We also included a broader range of measures of orthographic learning than in the previous studies. Given that spelling tasks are often difficult for poor readers, we included an orthographic choice task. Finally, we developed a new learning paradigm that assesses reading accuracy under both untimed and time-limited exposure conditions. Time-limited exposure reading accuracy is interpreted here as a fluency measure of item specific orthographic knowledge, as rapid recognition of words is considered a hallmark of the acquisition of orthographic representations (Yap and van der Leij, 1993; Marinus et al., 2012). This reasoning is similar to the idea that the time that is required to read a word is reduced when a word is read as a whole unit rather than by phonological decoding (e.g., Coltheart, 1983; Ehri, 2005). An additional benefit of this paradigm is that it allowed us to tap orthographic learning by tracking improvement of fluency over learning cycles. Hence, we were able to monitor orthographic learning in a dynamic and ongoing fashion. Finally, just like Bailey and colleagues, we included both regular and irregular words in order to see if we could replicate the regularity effect for children with a surface profile, and the absence of a regularity effect for children with a phonological profile.

In our novel word-learning paradigm, novel letter strings were assigned regular or irregular pronunciations and presented in three learning cycles. After each cycle, we measured reading accuracy under both untimed and time-limited stimulus exposure duration. After the three cycles were completed, traditional spelling and orthographic choice tasks were administered.

[1] Bailey et al. (2004) also used a spelling task to measure orthographic learning, however, due to the fact that accuracy of spelling was at floor, only reading accuracy results were discussed.

The untimed reading condition provided the opportunity for children to decode and build up orthographic representations of the novel words. In order to measure whether orthographic learning had taken place, each untimed reading block was followed by a time-limited exposure block in which items were presented for only 200 ms.

As mentioned earlier, this paradigm not only allows us to explore whether the two groups with contrasting reading profiles differ in their orthographic learning performance, but also to examine whether and to what extent orthographic learning improves with number of learning exposures. Previous studies examining the transition from decoding to rapid word recognition (as measured by increases in reading speed) have found that children with dyslexia need many more exposures to acquire novel word representations than typically developing readers (Reitsma, 1983; Manis, 1985; Ehri and Saltmarsh, 1995). Reitsma (1983, Experiment 3) reported that even six exposures to novel words was not enough to result in any increase in reading speed (taken as an index of orthographic learning) in a group of children with dyslexia. In contrast, in the same experiment, a group of younger readers without reading difficulties showed a steep increase in word reading speed. Note that none of these studies made a distinction between different profiles of reading difficulty. Hence, we used the current paradigm to monitor orthographic learning within two groups of poor readers with contrasting reading profiles.

Using the same paradigm, but with a larger sample of poor readers, we conducted a second study to explore to what extent different reading and language skills predict orthographic learning. For this purpose, we drew on an explicit model of component processes involved in skilled reading, the dual-route model of reading aloud (Coltheart et al., 1993, 2001). The six components of this model include: letter analysis; letter-sound conversion, phonemic buffer, orthographic lexicon, semantics, phonological lexicon. We used regression analyses to investigate the association between these components and orthographic learning. Reading and language skills mapping onto the six different components were used as predictors, and the orthographic learning results were used as outcome measures.

STUDY 1

As outlined in the Introduction, the existence of children with surface and phonological reading profiles challenges the role of phonological decoding in orthographic learning. The aim of Study 1 was to investigate how orthographic learning takes place in poor readers with contrasting reading profiles. Study 1 consisted of two parts. The first part aimed to validate the group membership of the phonological and surface profiles. In order to do this we measured language and reading skills involved in reading processes based on the dual-route model of reading aloud. In the context of the dual route model, we expect the children with a phonological profile to be impaired in the letter-sound knowledge process of the nonlexical route. In contrast, children with a surface profile are thought to be impaired in the lexical route, the orthographic lexicon in particular.

In the second part of Study 1, we used the novel word learning paradigm to investigate orthographic learning of the two profiles. The questions of interest were: (1) Are these children able to learn novel words at all? If so, is their learning rate slower than controls? This part of the study aimed to replicate previous studies suggesting that children with dyslexia are impaired at orthographic learning (Reitsma, 1983, 1989) (2). Will children with a phonological profile, having impaired phonological decoding skills, be less efficient at learning novel words than control children and those with a surface profile? Alternatively, will children with a phonological profile learn novel words faster than children with a surface profile as predicted by their subtype reading profiles? (3) Will children with phonological and surface profiles differ in the size of the regularity effect? Typically developing children have been shown to learn regular words better than irregular words as regular words are more "phonologically decodable" than irregular words (Wang et al., 2012). However, as suggested by Bailey et al. (2004), children with a phonological profile may show no effect of regularity on orthographic learning due to their impaired phonological decoding skill. Instead, they may learn novel words via some kind of rote association between the sound and the form of the novel words bypassing the phonological decoding process. Children with a surface profile, in contrast, may show a normal word regularity effect on orthographic learning as they have average phonological decoding skills.

PARTICIPANTS

Ninety-one poor readers (average age 9.3, range 7.2–12.3) were recruited from schools, clinics or via newspaper advertisements to participate in a reading training study at Macquarie University. Children were included in the study if they scored at least one standard deviation below average for their age on one or both subscales (irregular word and nonword reading) of the Castles and Coltheart 2 test (CC2; Castles et al., 2010a). All poor readers scored within the normal range on non-verbal IQ (Kaufman Brief Intelligence Test, K-Bit; Kaufman and Kaufman, 1990).

From this larger sample we selected two groups of poor readers: one with a surface profile and one with a phonological profile. We will from here refer to them as the "surface group" and the "phonological group." The criteria for a surface profile were performance within the normal range (z-score > -1.00) on nonword reading accuracy and below average performance on irregular word reading (z-score < -1.00, which is equivalent to the bottom 15% of the norms). In addition, to ensure a discrepancy in skills, the z-score difference between nonword and irregular word reading had to be more than 0.5. The same test was administered twice in two sessions that were 8 weeks apart. Only children with consistent reading profiles across the two sessions were included. Nine poor readers fitted our stringent criteria of a surface profile on both testing sessions. Next, we identified children showing consistent profiles of phonological dyslexia (nonword z-score < -1.00, irregular word > -1.00, with a difference of more than 0.5), resulting in a subsample of 22. From this sample we selected nine participants with a phonological profile, matching the surface group in age, IQ and level of impairment on the relevant reading subtest. Finally, we recruited nine age-matched typical readers that were participating in reading studies at Macquarie University as controls. The reading accuracy of these controls was within one standard deviation below the average range and 1.5 standard deviation above the average range scores on all three subscales of the CC2 (please see **Table 1** for the characteristics of the three groups).

SUBGROUP VALIDATION

In this first part of Study 1, we validated subgroup membership by examining the language and reading skills of the two groups with contrasting reading profiles. We designed tasks that aimed to tap different components of the dual route model of reading aloud (see **Figure 1**). This model proposes a *lexical* route through which words are directly recognized as whole units and a *nonlexical* route through which words are decoded phonologically.

As can be seen from **Figure 1**, each of these routes consists of a number of processing components, some shared across the routes and some separate. When a reader sees a printed word, the letters will first be recognized in the *letter analysis* component. Then in the nonlexical route, the graphemes of the word are phonologically decoded by the *letter-sound knowledge* component (also referred to as the "grapheme-to-phoneme conversion" component). In the lexical route, the orthography of known words is activated as a whole unit in the *orthographic lexicon*. Subsequently, in the *semantic system*, the meaning of the word is activated and then in the *phonological lexicon* the sound of the word is activated. The final component of the model is the *phonemic buffer* where phonemes are activated and temporarily stored before they are spoken.

Measures of reading processes

Each of the six basic components in the dual-route model was assessed with one test as described in the sections below. Test–retest reliability (Pearson's r) is reported for each measure based on scores over two testing sessions that are 8 weeks apart, with a sample of 115 children, aged 7–12 in a larger reading training study (McArthur et al., 2013).

Letter analysis

Letter analysis was measured with a cross-case copying task (McArthur et al., 2013). This task consists of 14 letters, 7 in upper case and 7 in lower case. For lower case letters the child was asked to write down the upper case of the same letters (e.g., t – T), and vice versa for upper case letters. Test–retest reliability, $r = 0.75$.

Letter-sound knowledge

The ability to convert letters or letter strings into sounds was tested with the Letter-Sound Test (LeST, Larsen et al., 2011). Each child was asked to produce the appropriate sound for 51 single-letter and multiletter graphemes. The items were presented on individual flash cards. The graphemes were selected as being consistent, in other words they had the same pronunciation in more than 75% of occurrences of that grapheme according to

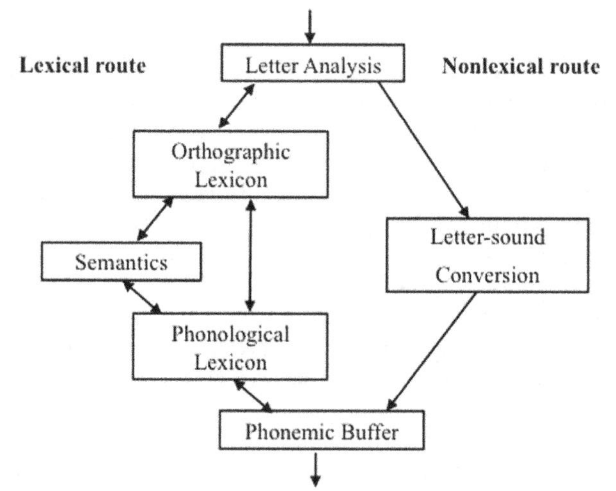

FIGURE 1 | The dual route model and its six basic components.

Table 1 | Characteristics and reading processing skills of the control, phonological, and surface groups.

	Controls	Phonological profile	Surface profile	Phon. vs. Surf.	
	Mean (*SD*)	**Mean (*SD*)**	**Mean (*SD*)**	***t***	***p* (2-tailed)**
CHARACTERISTICS					
Age	9.31 (1.52)	9.49 (1.35)	9.42 (1.62)	0.11	0.92
Nonverbal IQ (K-Bit, standardized score/100)	NA	105.22 (8.60)	101.44 (13.48)	0.71	0.49
Nonword reading (CC2, z-score)	0.15 (0.66)	−1.58 (0.25)**	−0.51 (0.44)*	−6.31	0.00**
Irregular word reading (CC2, z-score)	0.29 (0.55)	−0.57 (0.21)**	−1.53 (0.24)**	8.94	0.00**
READING PROCESSING SKILLS					
Letter analysis (Cross-case matching, raw score/14)	13.57 (1.13)	13.78 (0.44)	13.00 (1.58)	0.34	0.73
Letter-sound knowledge (LeST, raw score/51)	41.67 (3.61)	34.11 (7.22)*	40.78 (4.06)	2.42	0.03*
Orthographic lexicon (DOOR/DOAR, raw score/30)	22.89 (4.89)	24.44 (2.01)	18.89 (3.72)$^+$	3.94	0.00**
Semantics (PPVT, standardized score/100)	104.57 (13.97)	96.56 (7.99)	96.56 (12.82)	0.00	1.00
Phonological Lexicon (ACE, standardized score/10)	8.86 (2.04)	7.89 (1.54)	7.67 (2.96)	0.20	0.85
Phonemic Buffer (NEPSY, standardized score/10)	9.43 (3.65)	8.22 (2.22)	10.11 (1.45)	2.13	0.05$^+$

The asterisks in the "phonological profile" and "surface profile" columns indicate significant differences compared to control group.

$^*p < 0.05$, $^{**}p < 0.01$, $^+p < 0.1$.

the CELEX database (Baayen et al., 1993). Test–retest reliability, $r = 0.84$.

Orthographic lexicon

Word-specific orthographic knowledge was assessed with the DOOR/DOAR lexical decision test (McArthur et al., 2013). Thirty target words, ranging in frequency from 3 to 625 instances per million words, were selected from the Children's Printed Word Database (CPWD, Masterson et al., 2003). All words were selected to have alternative, homophonic spellings with adjustments of the vowel (e.g., FLAME changed to FLAIM) or a consonant (e.g., CURL changed to KURL). Each item was presented paired with its alternative homophonic spelling (e.g., DOOR and DOAR). The child was asked to circle the correct spelling. Test–retest reliability, $r = 0.57$.

Semantics

Semantic knowledge was measured with the Peabody Picture Vocabulary Test 4 (PPVT-IV, Dunn and Dunn, 2007). For each item the child was presented with four pictures and asked to point to the picture that was named by the tester. The administration of the test was stopped when the child made more than eight errors in a set of 12 items. Scores were standard scores with a mean of 100 and a standard deviation of 15. Test–retest reliability, $r = 0.84$.

Phonological lexicon

The ability to access the phonological lexicon was measured with the Naming subtest of the Assessment of Comprehension and Expression (ACE6–11 test; Adams et al., 2001). The child was asked to name 25 pictures. No stopping rule was applied. Test–retest reliability, $r = 0.87$.

Phonemic buffer

We tested the phonological output buffer with a standardized nonword repetition task, a subtest of the NEuroPSYchology (NEPSY) test (Korkman et al., 1998). In this task, the child was asked to listen to and orally repeat digitally recorded nonwords (e.g., crumsee). Scores were standard scores with a mean of 10 and a standard deviation of 3. Test–retest reliability, $r = 0.72$.

RESULTS: SUBGROUP VALIDATION

Table 1 presented the performance of the surface, phonological and control groups on the selection measures and the other measures of reading processing skills. The two groups were significantly different on the selection measures: nonword and irregular word reading accuracy. In addition, and as would be predicted, the phonological group performed significantly more poorly on the letter-sound knowledge test and the surface group performed significantly more poorly on the orthographic knowledge test (DOOR/DOAR). In addition, the difference on the nonword repetition test (NEPSY) approached significance ($p = 0.05$), with the surface group appearing to outperform the phonological group. However, as both groups still performed within the normal range on this task, this result is not discussed further. The two groups did not differ on any other measure. The results of the assessment of reading processing skills therefore confirmed that the phonological group had inferior letter-sound knowledge in the nonlexical route and the surface group showed lower proficiency of the orthographic knowledge in the lexical route.

ORTHOGRAPHIC LEARNING TASK

Materials

This task consisted of eight four to five-letter nonwords (e.g., *vack*), four of which were assigned with regular pronunciations and the other four with irregular pronunciations (please see Supplementary Material). The nonwords were created in the same way as the items used in Wang et al. (2011), but the items are not identical to Wang et al. due to differences in the experimental design. The regular items were pronounced according to a set of typical grapheme-phoneme correspondence rules (Rastle and Coltheart, 1999). "Typical" was defined on the basis that the pronunciation of the vowel occurred in more than 50% of words containing that vowel grapheme in both the CELEX database (Baayen et al., 1993) and the CPWD (Masterson et al., 2003). The irregular nonwords had pronunciations that did not follow typical letter-sound rules: the allocated pronunciation of the vowel in the target word occurred in fewer than 50% of words in the CELEX and the CPWD. All of the irregular pronunciations were nevertheless existing grapheme-phoneme correspondences in English. However, the pronunciations were infrequent and did not occur in the context of the vowels and the final consonants (bodies) of the irregular nonwords that were used in this task. For example, the nonword *cleap* was assigned a pronunciation "claip"; *ea* is pronounced this way in, for example, *great*, *break*, but is always pronounced "ee" when followed by *–p* (e.g., *heap*, *leap*).

Procedure

Children were tested individually in a quiet room. They learned four regular items followed by four irregular items. For both regular and irregular words, the same procedure was used an initial exposure phase, learning trials and two post-tests (see **Figure 2**).

During the initial exposure phase, the child was first presented with a picture with elves and was told they were going to learn the names of some of these elves. Next, the tester introduced the spoken forms of the four target nonwords ("elves names") to the children (initial exposure). This was necessary in order to expose the children to the pronunciations of the irregular nonwords. After this, the child was seated in front of a computer and the nonwords appeared on the screen one at a time. During the first presentation on the computer screen the tester said: "The name of this elf is ____." The children were not asked to read or repeat the novel words at this point and no accuracy was recorded. After a nonword had been introduced to the child orally and in print in the exposure phase, the first cycle of the learning trials began and reading accuracy was recorded. The four nonwords would appear on the screen one by one in a randomized order, and the child was asked to read them aloud. This was the untimed exposure reading. Feedback was provided regardless of whether the child read the target word correctly or not, to give an equal number of phonological exposures to each word. For example, after each response

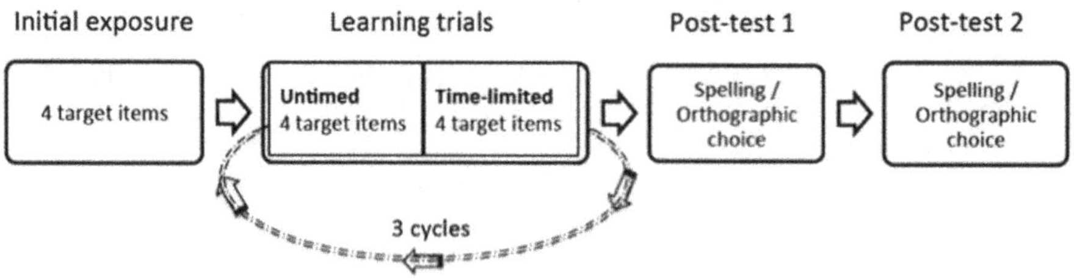

FIGURE 2 | Procedure of the orthographic learning task.

was given by the child, the experimenter said, "that's correct, it's a ferb" for correct responses; or "not quite, it is a ferb" for incorrect responses.

All three rounds of untimed reading were followed by a block of time-limited reading (200 ms presentation, with #### as backward masks) of the target words. This set up allows us to obtain an ongoing measure of orthographic learning (i.e., the ability to recognize words instantaneously) after each exposure (i.e., untimed reading with plenty of time to decode the word plus feedback). Again, all target words were presented in random order. This step was introduced to the child as the "speed reading game." One block of untimed reading followed by one block of time-limited exposure duration reading was considered a cycle, and this cycle was repeated three times.

Post-test measures

After the three learning cycles were completed, two post-tests were conducted to measure orthographic learning using both spelling and orthographic choice tasks. For the spelling task, the tester dictated all trained words in a random order. The children were asked to write down the elves' names exactly as they had learned them on the computer. For the orthographic choice task, each target item (e.g., *ferb*) was presented together with its homophonic foil (e.g., *furb*) and two visual distractors (e.g., *ferq*, *furq*) on one A4 sheet of paper. The children were asked to choose the correct spelling of the elf's name that they had learned from those four options. These two tasks were measured immediately after the learning trials and again after an hour to increase assessment reliability and statistical power. Thus, eight was the maximum score across two testing points for the orthographic choice task and spelling task for each word type—regular and irregular.

RESULTS: ORTHOGRAPHIC LEARNING

Learning cycles: untimed and time-limited exposure duration measures

Table 2 summarizes results of the orthographic learning trials for untimed and time-limited exposure duration reading for the two profiles of poor readers and the controls. We aimed to examine the improvement in learning over cycles for regular and irregular items between the three groups of children with different reading profiles. We ran a repeated measures ANOVA with cycle (1, 2, 3), regularity (regular items, irregular items), and exposure duration (untimed, time-limited) as within-subject factors, and group (phonological profile, surface profile, controls) as a between-subject factor. We specified two planned contrasts on the between-subject factor in order to compare the performance of the three different groups. The first contrast compared the performance of the two poor reader groups with the controls and the second contrast compared the performance of the two poor reader groups.

We found a main effect of cycle, $F_{(2,\ 25)} = 19.46$, $p < 0.01$, $\eta_p^2 = 0.45$, but no interaction between cycle and group, $Fs < 1$; nor were any of the higher level interactions between cycle and group with either regularity or/and exposure duration significant ($Fs < 1$). This indicates that across regular and irregular words, untimed and time-limited exposure conditions, all three groups improved over the learning cycles and that the degree of improvement did not differ between the groups.

The main effect of regularity was significant, $F_{(1,\ 24)} = 28.39$, $p < 0.01$, $\eta_p^2 = 0.54$, but the interaction between regularity and group was not, $F_{(1,\ 24)} = 1.79$, $p = 0.19$. All three groups performed better on regular words than on irregular words. However, the interaction between regularity and exposure duration was significant, $F_{(1,\ 24)} = 5.48$, $p = 0.03$, $\eta_p^2 = 0.19$. Considering the patterns of means across the conditions, this interaction indicated that for regular words, performance did not differ for untimed and time-limited exposure duration, $t_{(1,\ 26)} = 0.77$, $p = 0.45$. However, for irregular words, performance was be better under the time-limited condition than under the untimed exposure duration, $t_{(1,\ 26)} = -2.23$, $p = 0.03$. There was also an interaction between exposure duration and group, $F_{(2,\ 24)} = 4.33$, $p = 0.03$. The interaction reflected the fact that for the control and surface group, there were no differences between exposure duration [control: $t_{(1,\ 8)} = 0.54$, $p = 0.61$; surface: $t_{(1,\ 8)} = 1.04$, $p = 0.33$]; but for the phonological group performance was better in the time-limited condition compared to the untimed condition, $t_{(1,\ 8)} = 3.46$, $p < 0.01$.

Finally, there was a main effect of group, $F_{(2,\ 24)} = 8.56$, $p < 0.01$, $\eta_p^2 = 0.42$. The first planned contrast (both poor reader groups vs. controls) showed that, across conditions (regular/irregular, untimed/time-limited), the controls performed better than the poor reader groups, $F_{(1,\ 24)} = 17.12$, $p < 0.01$, $\eta_p^2 = 0.42$. However, there was no difference in overall performance between the two poor reader groups, $Fs < 1$.

It should be noted that the performance of the control group is at ceiling on the regular items at the later cycles and hence did not meet the statistical assumption of equal variance. Therefore, we ran a nonparametric randomization test that does not make

Table 2 | Reading accuracy across learning cycles.

Reading accuracy	Regular			Irregular		
	Phonological profile	Surface profile	Controls	Phonological profile	Surface profile	Controls
CYCLE 1 (RAW SCORE/4)						
Untimed	2.78 (1.20)	2.56 (1.13)	3.33 (0.71)	1.22 (0.83)	1.78 (1.20)	2.78 (0.97)
Time-limited	2.67 (1.41)	2.56 (1.13)	3.89 (0.33)	1.89 (0.78)	1.78 (1.56)	3.11 (1.05)
CYCLE 2 (RAW SCORE/4)						
Untimed	3.11 (1.17)	3.33 (0.71)	4.00 (0.00)	1.33 (0.87)	2.11 (1.17)	3.56 (0.53)
Time-limited	3.44 (0.73)	2.67 (1.00)	3.89 (0.33)	2.22 (0.44)	2.11 (1.36)	3.22 (0.83)
CYCLE 3 (RAW SCORE/4)						
Untimed	3.33 (0.87)	3.33 (0.71)	4.00 (0.00)	2.00 (1.12)	2.11 (1.36)	3.22 (0.97)
Time-limited	3.33 (1.12)	3.22 (0.97)	3.67 (0.50)	2.33 (1.32)	2.11 (1.17)	3.56 (0.53)
TOTAL (RAW SCORE/12)						
Untimed	9.33 (3.00)	9.33 (2.24)	11.33 (0.71)	4.56 (2.40)	6.00 (3.35)	9.78 (1.56)
Time-limited	9.44 (3.00)	8.44 (2.60)	11.44 (0.88)	6.44 (2.07)	6.00 (3.71)	10.00 (1.58)

any assumptions about the distribution of the data (Lunneborg, 2001). This randomization test was conducted for the regular as well as the irregular items on the main effect of group. The results confirmed that across cycle and exposure duration conditions, the controls performed better than the two poor reader groups (regular: $p = 0.03$; irregular: $p < 0.01$).

In summary, it was found that all three groups improved over learning cycles, but across learning cycles, the controls performed better than both poor reader groups. Importantly, the performance of the children with phonological and surface profiles did not differ. In addition, all three groups performed better on items with regular pronunciations than those with irregular pronunciations, and there was no difference in this regularity effect between the surface and phonological profiles. However, we need to interpret the results with caution as the controls were at ceiling for the regular items in the untimed reading condition. Lastly, it was found that for irregular words but not regular words, the performance was better under the time-limited exposure duration condition than under the untimed condition, particularly for the phonological group. This can be explained by the fact that the untimed condition provides an opportunity to decode a word, and in the case of irregular items, decoding results in incorrect responses. This result indicated that the timed condition has minimal influence from phonological decoding.

Table 3 | Accuracy on Spelling and Orthographic Choice Measured after the Learning Cycles (with SDs in brackets).

	Phonological profile	Surface profile	Controls
REGULAR ITEMS (RAW SCORE/8)			
Spelling	6.67 (1.58)	5.33 (2.00)	7.33 (1.12)
Orthographic choice	7.67 (0.50)	5.44 (1.94)	7.67 (0.71)
IRREGULAR ITEMS (RAW SCORE/8)			
Spelling	6.44 (0.88)	4.44 (2.19)	6.33 (1.12)
Orthographic choice	7.11 (1.05)	4.89 (2.15)	7.22 (0.97)

After learning cycles: spelling and orthographic choice measures

Table 3 summarizes results of the spelling and orthographic choice measures. We ran repeated measures ANOVAs with word regularity (regular items, irregular items) as a within-subject factor and group (phonological profile, surface profile, controls) as a between-subject factor. We specified the same two planned contrasts on the between-subject factor to compare the performance of the three different groups. Analyses were conducted separately for the spelling and orthographic choice tasks.

For the spelling task, the main effect of regularity approached significance, $F_{(1, 24)} = 4.20, p = 0.052, \eta_p^2 = 0.15$, and there was no interaction between regularity and group ($Fs < 1$). The main effect for group was significant, $F_{(2, 24)} = 6.11, p < 0.01, \eta_p^2 = 0.34$. The planned contrasts showed that this group main effect was reflecting the significantly lower performance of the surface group compared to the controls, $F_{(1, 24)} = 10.44, p < 0.01, \eta_p^2 = 0.30$, as well as the phonological group, $F_{(1, 24)} = 7.67, p = 0.01, \eta_p^2 = 0.24$. The phonological group on the other hand, performed equally as well as the controls, $Fs < 1$.

For the orthographic choice task, the difference between regular and irregular items was not significant, $F_{(1, 24)} = 2.61, p = 0.12$, nor was the interaction between word regularity and group, $Fs < 1$. As with spelling performance, there was a main effect of Group, $F_{(2, 24)} = 12.97, p < 0.01, \eta_p^2 = 0.52$. The planned contrasts showed that the surface group was worse on the orthographic choice task compared to the controls, $F_{(1, 24)} = 19.93, p < 0.01, \eta_p^2 = 0.45$, and compared to the phonological group, $F_{(1, 24)} = 18.97, p < 0.01, \eta_p^2 = 0.44$. Again, the phonological group performed at the same level as the controls, $Fs < 1$. An additional analysis confirmed that all three groups performed above chance level (25% accuracy), even the surface group, $t_{(1, 8)} = 7.54, p < 0.01$.

In summary, the pattern of results of the spelling task was consistent with that of the orthographic choice task. For both tasks, the phonological group did not perform differently from the controls whereas the surface group was worse than both the phonological group and the control group. However, in contrast to the findings of the learning trials, the children did not perform better on the regular items than on the irregular items for the orthographic choice task and the difference in performance only approached significance for the spelling task.

DISCUSSION

The first question of interest in Study 1 was whether children with reading difficulties are able to learn novel words at all or to learn at the same pace as typically developing readers. We found that, just like the controls, children with both types of reading profile showed learning over the learning cycles as evidenced by untimed and time-limited reading accuracy, and the rate of improvement was no different from controls. This is in contrast with previous studies that have found little or no evidence of orthographic learning in children with dyslexia (Reitsma, 1983, 1989; but also see Staels and van den Broeck, 2013). The difference between the results of the present and previous studies may be explained by the sensitivity of the measure of orthographic learning. In the current study orthographic learning was monitored online during the exposure trials, whereas Reitsma (1983, 1989) found that Dutch poor readers showed no evidence of orthographic learning measured by an orthographic choice task after learning took place. However, we found that although the two dyslexic groups showed evidence of orthographic leaning, their reading accuracy overall was worse than the controls, and this is in line with previous studies using a group of mixed dyslexics (e.g., Manis, 1985; Share and Shalev, 2004).

The second question of interest was to explore the contrasting predictions made by the hypothesis of phonological decoding as the primary factor in orthographic learning vs. that of the children's reading profiles. According to the phonological decoding hypothesis, the phonological group, with their impaired phonological decoding skill, would be predicted to perform less well than the controls and the surface group. In contrast, the subtype profiles of the two groups predict that the phonological group would be better at orthographic learning than the surface group based on their superior sight word reading ability. The results of the present study did not fully support either of the hypotheses but was more consistent with the children's subtype profiles. The performance of the two poor reader groups did not differ on either untimed or time-limited exposure duration reading accuracy. However, the phonological group was found to be no different from the control group and to outperform the surface group on the subsequent spelling and orthographic choice task. The surface group was also significantly worse than the controls on the spelling and orthographic choice tasks. It should be noted that both the control and the phonological group performed close to ceiling on the orthographic choice tasks, hence making the differences between the two groups hard to detect. Nevertheless, the orthographic learning results of these two groups were in line with the selective difficulties in their reading profiles within the framework of the dual route model. The results of Study 1 thus showed that the difference in phonological decoding skill between the two subtype profiles did not directly translate into differences in the ability to acquire novel word representations, which is in contrast with the hypothesis that phonological decoding is the primary determinant of successful orthographic learning.

It is important to note that the surface group did not outperform the phonological group on untimed reading accuracy and did perform worse than the control group. We did not expect this result as we preselected the surface group to have average phonological decoding skills. The finding that the two poor reader groups did not differ in untimed reading accuracy might be explained by the test items that were used. For this task we used only four, regular, four to five letter nonwords. It might be the case that the test was not sensitive enough and/or might not have had enough statistical power to differentiate between the two poor reader groups. In addition, the finding that the surface group was worse at decoding the novel words than the control group could be due to the superior decoding ability of the control group. That is, although the surface group was within the average range on the nonword reading selection measure ($z = -0.57$, $SD = 0.21$), they were still on average worse than controls ($z = 0.15$, $SD = 0.66$), $t_{(1,\ 17)} = -2.47$, $p = 0.03$.

The last aim of Study 1 was to examine the effect of word regularity on orthographic learning. All groups showed higher reading accuracy when learning regular items than when learning irregular items. This implies that phonological decoding *was* used by both poor reader groups, as well as the typical readers, during the orthographic learning process. Together these results suggest that phonological decoding plays a role in orthographic learning for both subtype groups, yet it is also clear that this skill is not sufficient to fully account for the success of orthographic learning.

If phonological decoding skill cannot fully explain successful orthographic learning then what are the other factors determining this learning process? In order to further explore orthographic learning in poor readers, the second half of this study investigated the predictors of orthographic learning beyond phonological decoding. It has been proposed that poor readers could be relying on alternative learning strategies in order to compensate for poor phonological decoding skills (Stanovich and Siegel, 1994; Siegel et al., 1995; Castles et al., 1999). For example, it is possible that for children who have difficulties with phonological decoding, vocabulary knowledge is relied on more heavily during orthographic learning. In support of this, previous studies have found that when decoding can only be partially successful, in the case of irregular novel words, contextual information and vocabulary knowledge play a role in orthographic learning (Wang et al., 2011, 2013; Duff and Hulme, 2012). Similarly, word meaning has also been found to assist the reading of irregular words (e.g., Nation and Snowling, 1998; Ouellette, 2006; Bowey and Rutherford, 2007; Ricketts et al., 2007; McKay et al., 2008; Nation and Cocksey, 2009).

In addition to phonological decoding skills and vocabulary knowledge, pre-existing orthographic knowledge has also been considered an important factor in orthographic learning (Cunningham et al., 2002; Conners et al., 2010). Share (1995) suggested that although phonological decoding is the primary component of orthographic learning, the secondary, orthographic component determines how quickly and accurately orthographic representations are acquired.

In sum, we aimed to develop a more detailed picture of the reading processes associated with orthographic learning by exploring the strengths of the relationship between different reading and language skills and orthographic learning of regular and irregular words.

STUDY 2

For the purpose of exploring how well different skills involved in reading predict orthographic learning of regular and irregular words within a larger group of poor readers, we again drew on the language and reading skills in the dual route model as we did for subgroup validation in Study 1 (see **Figure 1** earlier).

As noted earlier, phonological decoding is often assumed to be the key to orthographic learning. Based on this hypothesis, we predicted that skills reflecting nonlexical processing (phonological decoding in particular) would be important for orthographic learning of both regular words and irregular words. However, when accurate decoding is compromised or not possible (such as when phonological decoding skill is impaired or when words are irregular), knowledge of semantics, phonology or orthography may become more important.

METHODS

Participants

The same cohort of 91 poor readers screened in Study 1 participated in Study 2. As mentioned in Study 1, these children scored at least one standard deviation below average for their age on one or more of the two subscales (irregular word and nonword reading) of the Castles and Coltheart 2 word reading test (CC2; Castles et al., 2010a). On average, the children scored -1.59 ($SD = 0.65$) on nonword reading; and -1.40 ($SD = 0.67$) on irregular word reading.

Materials and procedure

We assessed the poor readers on tasks tapping the six basic components of the dual-route model. In addition, all children completed the same orthographic learning task described in Study 1. In order to increase statistical power for the analyses used in Study 2, we created another set of nonword stimuli, consisting of an additional four regular and four irregular items. The extra set of items was created in the same way as described in Study 1. The same procedure of the orthographic learning task was applied in a separate session 8 weeks after the first set of nonwords were learnt. Each child was tested individually in a quiet room, and the children took approximately 100–120 min to complete all the assessments. The results of the six reading and language skill measures were used as predictors, and the orthographic learning performances were used as outcome measures.

RESULTS

To investigate how well each reading subcomponent predicts orthographic learning, a set of correlations, followed by stepwise multiple regressions, was conducted with the dual route processing components as predictors, and the various orthographic learning measures as the dependent variables. Regressions were carried out in addition to correlations as the predictor tasks are themselves intercorrelated, in order to identify the relationship between these factors and orthographic learning outcomes when the intercorrelations between the variables are controlled.

Table 4 shows the results of a series of correlations and partial correlations controlling for age and non-verbal IQ between the outcomes of the orthographic learning task (outcome measures: no. 1–8) and the components involved in lexical, nonlexical, and both routes (predictors: no. 9–14). Before the effects of age and non-verbal IQ were partialled out, all of the components involved in the reading routes correlated with almost all measures of orthographic learning. After controlling for age and IQ, the main difference is that the associations between orthographic learning measures and semantic knowledge (PPVT), and phonological lexicon functioning (ACE) were no longer significant.

The results of the regression analyses are summarized in **Table 5**. In the first step, age and non-verbal IQ were entered, followed by all the other potential predictor variables at step 2. Overall, letter-sound knowledge and orthographic knowledge seemed to be the best predictors of orthographic learning. Untimed exposure duration reading accuracy was predicted by letter-sound knowledge and phonemic buffer efficiency. Time-limited exposure duration reading accuracy was predicted by letter-sound knowledge, phonemic buffer efficiency, and word-specific orthographic knowledge (functioning of orthographic lexicon). Spelling accuracy was predicted by letter-sound knowledge and orthographic knowledge, whereas orthographic choice accuracy was only predicted by orthographic knowledge. For irregular items, orthographic knowledge was the only significant predictor for all measures except untimed exposure duration reading accuracy, which was predicted by both orthographic knowledge and letter-sound knowledge.

It should be noted that although it seemed that letter-sound knowledge was a better predictor of performance for the regular items than the irregular items, and that orthographic knowledge was a better predictor for irregular items than regular items, these correlational differences between regular and irregular items did not reach significance. However, across the two predictors, orthographic knowledge was a significantly better predictor than letter-sound knowledge for scores on spelling and orthographic choice measures, regardless of word regularity (regular spelling: $z = -2.17$, $p = 0.03$; irregular spelling: $z = -2.30$, $p = 0.02$; regular orthographic choice: $z = -2.82$, $p < 0.01$; irregular orthographic choice: $z = -3.67, p < 0.01$).

DISCUSSION

The results showed that letter-sound knowledge predicted the outcomes of all measures assessing regular word learning except for orthographic choice. Letter-sound knowledge also predicted the untimed reading accuracy during irregular word learning, but it did not predict any other measures assessing irregular word learning. The ability to repeat nonwords was used as an index of phonemic buffer proficiency, and performance on this task predicted orthographic learning of regular words when learning was measured by accuracy in reading aloud (both timed and untimed).

Our measure of orthographic knowledge predicted success on our dynamic measures of orthographic learning of both regular and irregular words except for untimed reading accuracy of

Table 4 | Correlations of the outcome measures and the predictors with (below the diagonal line) and without (above the diagonal line) age and nonverbal IQ controlled.

		1	2	3	4	5	6	7	8	9	10	11	12	13	14	15	16
Regular	1. Untimed reading	–	**0.93**	**0.68**	**0.44**	**0.60**	**0.69**	**0.63**	**0.55**	**0.45**	**0.60**	**0.61**	**0.41**	**0.41**	**0.52**	**0.53**	**0.43**
	2. Time-limited reading	**0.89**	–	**0.71**	**0.52**	**0.56**	**0.69**	**0.65**	**0.59**	**0.46**	**0.55**	**0.64**	**0.40**	**0.43**	**0.48**	**0.52**	**0.40**
	3. Spelling	**0.57**	**0.65**	–	**0.60**	**0.42**	**0.61**	**0.71**	**0.62**	**0.48**	**0.47**	**0.65**	**0.35**	**0.32**	**0.38**	**0.45**	**0.45**
	4. Orthographic choice	**0.38**	**0.48**	**0.62**	–	**0.47**	**0.56**	**0.56**	**0.62**	**0.46**	**0.40**	**0.46**	0.19	**0.29**	**0.39**	0.17	**0.28**
Irregular	5. Untimed reading	**0.53**	**0.47**	**0.33**	**0.45**	–	**0.85**	**0.63**	**0.56**	**0.32**	**0.45**	**0.49**	**0.29**	**0.31**	**0.34**	**0.36**	0.18
	6. Time-limited reading	**0.58**	**0.58**	**0.53**	**0.53**	**0.83**	–	**0.73**	**0.65**	**0.50**	**0.47**	**0.58**	**0.36**	**0.36**	**0.41**	**0.44**	**0.28**
	7. Spelling	**0.48**	**0.53**	**0.59**	**0.52**	**0.60**	**0.69**	–	**0.73**	**0.53**	**0.53**	**0.62**	**0.37**	**0.31**	**0.32**	**0.40**	**0.46**
	8. Orthographic choice	**0.38**	**0.44**	**0.53**	**0.61**	**0.50**	**0.56**	**0.68**	–	**0.51**	**0.46**	**0.63**	**0.41**	**0.32**	**0.30**	**0.41**	**0.39**
Predictors	9. Letter analysis	**0.25**	**0.27**	**0.36**	**0.38**	0.21	**0.38**	**0.39**	**0.37**	–	**0.36**	**0.44**	**0.27**	**0.27**	**0.31**	**0.39**	**0.44**
	10. Letter-sound know.	**0.45**	**0.38**	**0.33**	**0.32**	**0.36**	**0.33**	**0.39**	**0.34**	0.19	–	**0.41**	**0.38**	**0.38**	**0.32**	**0.39**	**0.33**
	11. Orthog. lexicon	**0.41**	**0.47**	**0.52**	**0.44**	**0.35**	**0.43**	**0.49**	**0.51**	**0.27**	**0.22**	–	**0.52**	**0.49**	**0.41**	**0.55**	**0.38**
	12. Semantics	0.09	0.08	0.05	0.07	0.09	0.11	0.11	0.14	−0.01	0.20	**0.26**	–	**0.67**	**0.30**	**0.22**	**0.48**
	13. Phono. lexicon	0.09	0.11	0.07	0.17	0.14	0.13	0.03	0.06	−0.01	0.16	**0.24**	**0.50**	–	**0.31**	**0.49**	**0.44**
	14. Phonemic buffer	**0.51**	**0.44**	**0.39**	**0.35**	**0.30**	**0.36**	**0.28**	**0.24**	**0.25**	**0.26**	**0.39**	**0.25**	**0.23**	–	0.16	0.13
	15. Age	–	–	–	–	–	–	–	–	–	–	–	–	–	–	–	**0.48**
	16. Non-verbal IQ	–	–	–	–	–	–	–	–	–	–	–	–	–	–	–	–

Predictors 9–14 refer to the six reading components tested by: Cross-case copying (Letter Analysis, 9); Letter-sound test (Letter-sound knowledge; 10); Door/Doar Lexical Decision (Orthographic lexicon, 11); PPVT (Semantic knowledge, 12); ACE (Phonological lexicon, 13); NEPSY (Phonemic buffer, 14); Age (15); Non-verbal IQ (K-Bit, 16).

Values represent Pearson's correlation coefficients; numbers in bold indicate $p < 0.05$, 2-tailed.

regular words. The fact that orthographic knowledge predicted time-limited but not untimed accuracy in reading the regular items is interesting as it suggests that, when rapid and fluent access to the orthographic representation is required, orthographic knowledge may play a more important role than when reading is untimed. In addition, orthographic knowledge was a better predictor than letter-sound knowledge when orthographic learning was measured by spelling and orthographic choice tasks. Finally, in contrast to the prediction that poor readers may use alternative skills such as vocabulary knowledge when learning to read, better functioning of the semantic system and/or phonological lexicon did not predict better orthographic learning.

GENERAL DISCUSSION

In this paper we examined orthographic learning in poor readers. Study 1 focused on orthographic learning of regular and irregular novel words in children with surface and phonological reading profiles. We developed a novel paradigm to track orthographic learning online. Participants were first asked to read the presented novel words untimed, then the items were presented under time-limited exposure duration of 200 ms. This cycle was repeated three times and followed by spelling and orthographic choice tasks. This set up allowed us to track orthographic learning more dynamically (i.e., untimed and time-limited reading accuracy) than traditional measures (such as spelling and orthographic choice), that typically take place after learning has taken place. With our novel and traditional measures of orthographic learning, we aimed to examine the role of phonological decoding in orthographic learning.

More specifically, we wanted to investigate whether phonological decoding is primary in orthographic learning as is widely proposed (e.g., Brady and Shankweiler, 1991; Byrne, 1992, 1998; Share, 1995). In this context, the orthographic learning of two subgroups is particularly interesting: children with specific difficulties with phonological decoding (a phonological profile) and those with specific difficulties in orthographic knowledge (a surface profile). If phonological decoding is indeed primary to orthographic learning, this should result in poorer orthographic learning in children with a phonological profile and normal orthographic learning in children with a surface profile. In addition to our measures of orthographic learning, we also examined the degree to which the different poor reader groups relied on phonological decoding by comparing the difference in their performance on regular and irregular word learning.

We found that children with phonological and surface profiles showed the same amount of orthographic learning on the dynamic measures (scores on untimed and time-limited trials). However, orthographic learning was still less efficient overall compared to that of the age-matched controls. This finding is consistent with previous studies suggesting that poor readers take longer to learn to read novel words (e.g., Manis, 1985; Share and Shalev, 2004). The results of our study add evidence that this less efficient orthographic learning is already apparent during online learning trials. The finding that children with a surface profile have superior phonological decoding ability but did not outperform children with a phonological profile seems to be inconsistent with the view of phonological decoding as the primary factor for orthographic learning. However, a key feature of the self-teaching hypothesis can also explain this finding. According to this hypothesis, orthographic learning is item based. Consequently, what is relevant to the success of orthographic learning is the correct decoding of the items to be learnt rather than one's

Table 5 | Summary of regression results predicting orthographic learning of regular and irregular words from lexical and nonlexical processing components.

	Step	R^2	Beta							
			Age	Nonverbal IQ	Letter analysis	Letter-sound knowledge	Orthogr-aphic knowledge	Semantic knowledge	Phonological knowledge	Phonological buffer
REGULAR ITEMS										
Untimed reading	1	0.22	0.34*	0.23	0.17	0.43*	0.18	−0.19	0.14	0.34*
	2	0.66	0.20	0.04						
Time-limited reading	1	0.19	0.35*	2.57	0.11	0.34*	0.32*	−0.25	0.06	0.28*
	2	0.54	0.24	0.04						
Spelling	1	0.22	0.15	0.40*	0.05	0.27*	0.54*	−0.13	−0.10	0.17
	2	0.57	−0.07	0.29*						
Orthographic choice	1	0.15	0.05	0.37*	0.01	0.15	0.52*	−0.06	−0.07	0.15
	2	0.43	−0.16	0.28*						
IRREGULAR ITEMS										
Untimed reading	1	0.13	0.30*	0.12	0.21	0.29*	0.40*	−0.23	0.10	0.14
	2	0.46	0.15	0.00						
Time-limited reading	1	0.17	0.33*	0.16	0.11	0.18	0.37*	−0.12	0.20	0.21
	2	0.51	0.15	0.02						
Spelling	1	0.28	0.19	0.44*	0.10	0.20	0.50*	−0.04	0.00	0.07
	2	0.57	−0.06	0.31*						
Orthographic choice	1	0.31	0.25	0.42*	0.09	0.08	0.56*	0.05	0.01	−0.05
	2	0.59	−0.04	0.32*						

*$p < 0.05$.

phonological decoding ability in general. On the untimed trials in our dynamic measure, the children with a surface profile did not decode the words better than the children with a phonological profile. In other words: they did not show superior decoding skills on this task to start with. Hence, in this regard it is not surprising that they did not do better than the children with phonological dyslexia on the time-limited exposure duration trials.

Our findings on the traditional measures (spelling and orthographic choice) painted a different picture. Here the children with a surface profile performed more poorly than both the children with a phonological profile and the controls, which is consistent with what was found by Castles and Holmes (1996). This result is also consistent with the prediction based on the two groups' reading difficulties within the framework of the dual route model: the phonological group had normal sight word reading ability and the surface group had impaired sight word reading ability. Moreover, the children with a phonological profile performed as well as the controls despite their poorer performance on reading accuracy during the learning trials. This imbalance between decoding performance and orthographic learning results suggests again that orthographic learning ability cannot be explained by phonological decoding ability alone.

One possible explanation for the inconsistent performance of the phonological group across dynamic and traditional measures is that different task demands are imposed by the different orthographic learning tasks used for this study. More specifically, the dynamic measures (untimed and time-limited reading aloud) required verbal output whereas the traditional measures (spelling and orthographic choice) did not. As phonological impairment in reading is often associated with deficit in verbal output (Hulme and Snowling, 1992; Szenkovits and Ramus, 2005), it is not surprising that the phonological group performed worse than typical readers on measures requiring verbal output compared to those not requiring verbal output. This explanation is also consistent with findings from Study 2 (results will be discussed in more detail later), where performance on dynamic measures was more strongly associated with letter-sound knowledge and phonemic buffer functioning than was performance on traditional measures.

The role of phonological decoding in orthographic learning was also examined by manipulating word regularity. We found word regularity effects for the dynamic measures (untimed and time-limited reading) but not for the traditional post-test measures (spelling and orthographic choice). Moreover, these effects were the same for all groups. The regularity effect found in dynamic measures suggests that phonological decoding does play a role during the learning process, even for children with a phonological profile. However, the word regularity effect was not significant for any of the post-test measures. The absence of a regularity effect for spelling and orthographic choice is in line with outcomes of studies examining regularity effects in word recognition. These studies showed that regularity effects are restricted to tasks involving reading aloud and typically not found in word recognition tasks, such as lexical decision (e.g., Coltheart et al., 1979; Seidenberg et al., 1984; Schmalz et al., 2013; but see Parkin, 1982).

Study 2 explored to what degree the different skills that underlie reading predicted orthographic learning of regular and irregular words in poor readers. We selected the underlying component skills from the dual-route model of reading as predictors, and as outcome variables we used the dynamic and traditional orthographic learning measures. According to the view that phonological decoding is the primary factor to successful orthographic learning, we expected that skills reflecting nonlexical processing (letter-sound knowledge in particular) would be stronger predictors of orthographic learning of both regular and irregular words than skills reflecting lexical processing. We found that letter-sound knowledge is indeed a strong predictor of orthographic learning.

However, we did not find letter-sound knowledge to be a stronger predictor of orthographic learning than skills reflecting lexical processing. In fact, we found that orthographic knowledge, a lexical processing factor, was a good predictor of both regular and irregular word learning, and an even better predictor than letter-sound knowledge for spelling and orthographic choice. The association between orthographic knowledge and orthographic learning appeared to be particularly evident when the measure of learning directly tapped word-specific (spelling and orthographic choice) and fluent (timed-limited reading) access of orthographic representations.

Thus, both Study 1 and 2 showed that orthographic knowledge was associated with success in orthographic learning. In Study 1, we found that children with average phonological decoding skill but good orthographic knowledge showed normal orthographic learning on the traditional learning measures. In contrast, children with an opposite reading profile—impaired orthographic knowledge but good phonological decoding skill showed impaired orthographic learning. In Study 2, we found that orthographic knowledge significantly predicted orthographic learning even after phonological decoding skills were controlled for. Orthographic knowledge also appeared to be a stronger predictor than phonological decoding skill when orthographic learning was measured by traditional measures (spelling and orthographic choice). Together these findings suggest that orthographic knowledge is not only important in orthographic learning, but also that having impaired orthographic knowledge could be more detrimental than having impaired phonological decoding skill when learning new words. The importance of orthographic knowledge in orthographic learning has also been reported in previous studies with typically developing readers (Cunningham, 2006; Conners et al., 2010). Similarly, the self-teaching hypothesis suggests that, although phonological decoding provides the opportunity for orthographic learning to take place, orthographic knowledge is the secondary factor required for successful orthographic learning (Share, 1995, 2011). Our results support the view that orthographic knowledge is important in orthographic learning, but challenge the view that orthographic knowledge is a "secondary" factor. It seems that orthographic knowledge may actually be equally important or even more important than phonological decoding in building up orthographic representations.

However, it must be considered in this context that there are two alternative explanations as to why orthographic knowledge might be a significant predictor of orthographic learning. First, the way orthographic knowledge was measured in this study could be seen as a measure of the children's historic ability to acquire orthographic representations. Hence, the relationship between orthographic knowledge and orthographic learning could simply be that both are a reflection of the children's ability to acquire lexical representations: children with better abilities to acquire orthographic representations will be better at both the task tapping the orthographic lexicon (as a result of past orthographic learning) and at our orthographic learning task (current orthographic learning). Second, it could be that existing orthographic representations contribute to the actual process of acquiring new representations with children using this knowledge during the learning process. This might occur by using analogies of known words or utilizing familiarity of orthographic patterns. Further research is required to investigate how exactly existing orthographic knowledge assists orthographic learning of novel words.

As mentioned earlier, one might expect that for poor readers, the success of orthographic learning might rely on alternative skills, such as semantics, compensating for poor phonological decoding skills. In contrast to this prediction, this study did not find any evidence that pre-existing semantic and phonological knowledge (measured by PPVT-IV and ACE6-11) predicted orthographic learning of regular or irregular words. However, the orthographic learning paradigm in this study did not provide word-specific vocabulary (semantic and phonological) knowledge for the novel words. Hence, there was little opportunity for the children to use such skills. It would be interesting for future studies to explore whether word-specific vocabulary knowledge affects orthographic learning in poor readers. Further investigation using a design that provides vocabulary knowledge of the novel words prior to written exposure, such as that used in Wang et al. (2011, 2013), is needed.

There are a number of limitations of the present study that require further consideration. First, due to the manipulation of word regularity, the items were read to the children as an initial exposure before the learning cycles started, and during the learning cycles feedback was provided. Consequently, although after the initial exposure the children were asked to first read the target words by themselves to simulate a partial self-teaching paradigm, it was not an independent learning environment. Therefore, it is possible that the results would have been different had the children learned the words without the experimenter's input. For example, the children with a phonological dyslexia profile may have benefited from the input and feedback to compensate for their poor decoding of the regular items, resulting in their untimed and time-limited reading accuracy not being different from the children with a surface dyslexia profile. Although providing feedback is still ecologically valid, as children often receive feedback when learning to read, particularly with irregular words, we cannot interpret the results in the context of pure self-teaching.

Second, it is possible that factors beyond phonological decoding and orthographic knowledge influenced the pattern of impaired orthographic learning in surface dyslexia and normal orthographic learning in phonological dyslexia. According to the self-teaching hypothesis (Share, 1995), phonological decoding draws the reader's attention to the order and identity of the letters in the word, and produces the phonology. This then allows bonding to occur between the phonology and the orthography via some kind of associative learning procedure. It is possible that differences in the ability to establish associations between phonology and orthography are the source of the difference in orthographic learning skill between the two subtypes of dyslexia. In studies that did not make distinctions between subtypes, children with dyslexia were found to have difficulties in learning paired associations (Gascon and Goodglass, 1970; Vellutino et al., 1975; Messbauer and de Jong, 2003; Litt et al., 2013). In addition, other abilities may also contribute to individual differences in learning to read, such as mapping the output of letter-sound correspondences to existing phonology of a word (e.g., *was:* from/w..aa..ss/... to /woz/; Elbro et al., 2012), and capitalizing contextual and syntactic information (Tunmer et al., 1987; Tunmer and Chapman, 2004). Future studies are required to further investigate orthographic learning in children with subtypes of reading profiles.

In sum, Study 1 used a novel paradigm that allowed us to explore the role of phonological decoding and track orthographic learning in two groups of poor readers who had contrasting reading impairments. The two poor reader groups showed orthographic learning patterns that were consistent with their reading profiles, which suggested that phonological decoding skill alone is insufficient for acquiring orthographic representations. Study 2 was the first to break down components of reading processes based on the dual route model of reading and to use these components to explore factors associated with orthographic learning. The results of this study indicated that, in addition to phonological decoding (letter-sound knowledge), prior orthographic knowledge also predicted the success of orthographic learning. Together, the outcomes of the two studies suggest that phonological decoding plays a role in orthographic learning of both regular and irregular words, and for children with and without phonological decoding difficulties. Orthographic knowledge was also found to be important in orthographic learning, especially when the measures of learning directly tapped word-specific and fluent access to orthographic representations.

REFERENCES

Adams, C., Cooke, R., Crutchley, A., Hesketh, A., and Reeves, D. (2001). *Assessment of Comprehension and Expression 6-11 (ACE6-11)*. Windsor: Nelson Publishing Company Ltd.

Baayen, R. H, Piepenbrock, R., and van Rijn, H. (1993). *The CELEX Lexical Database (CD-ROM)*. Philadelphia, PA: Linguistic Data Consortium, University of Pennsylvania.

Bailey, C., Manis, F., Pedersen, W., and Seidenberg, M. (2004). Variation among developmental dyslexics: evidence from a printed-word-learning task. *J. Exp. Psychol.* 87, 125–154. doi: 10.1016/j.jecp.2003.10.004

Bowey, J. A., and Rutherford, J. (2007). Imbalanced word-reading profiles in eighth-graders. *J. Exp. Child Psychol.* 96, 169–196. doi: 10.1016/j.jecp.2006.11.001

Brady, S., and Shankweiler, D. P. (eds.). (1991). *Phonological Process in Literacy.* Hillsdale, NJ: Lawrence Erlbaum Associates, Inc.

Byrne, B. (1992). "Studies in the acquisition procedure for reading: rationale, hypotheses, and data," in *Reading Acquisition,* eds P. Gough, L. C. Ehri, and R. Treiman (Hillsdale, NJ: Lawrence Erlbaum Associates, Inc.), 1–34.

Byrne, B. (1998). *The Foundation of Literacy: The Child's Acquisition of the Alphabetic Principle.* Hove: Psychology Press.

Castles, A., and Coltheart, M. (1993). Varieties of developmental dyslexia. *Cognition* 47, 149–180. doi: 10.1016/0010-0277(93)90003-E

Castles, A., Coltheart, M., Larsen, L., Jones, P., Saunders, S., and McArthur, G. (2010a). Assessing the basic components of reading: a revision of the Castles and Coltheart test with new norms. *Aust. J. Learn. Dif.* 14, 67–88. doi: 10.1080/19404150902783435

Castles, A., Datta, H., Gayan, J., and Olson, R. K. (1999). Genetic influences on subtypes of developmental dyslexia. *J. Exp. Child Psychol.* 72, 73–94. doi: 10.1006/jecp.1998.2482

Castles, A., and Holmes, V. M. (1996). Subtypes of developmental dyslexia and lexical acquisition. *Aust. J. Psychol.* 48, 130–135. doi: 10.1080/00049539608259519

Castles, A., McLean, G. M. T., and McArthur, G. (2010b). Dyslexia (neuropsychological). *Wiley Interdiscip. Rev. Cogn. Sci.* 1, 426–432. doi: 10.1002/wcs.16

Castles, A., and Nation, K. (2008). Learning to be a good orthographic reader. *J. Res. Read.* 31, 1–7. doi: 10.1111/j.1467-9817.2007.00367.x

Coltheart, M. (1983). Phonological awareness: a pre-school precursor of success in reading. *Nature* 301:370. doi: 10.1038/301370a0

Coltheart, M., Besner, D., Jonasson, J. T., and Davelaar, E. (1979). Phonological encoding in the lexical decision task. *Q. J. Exp. Psychol.* 31, 489–507. doi: 10.1080/14640747908400741

Coltheart, M., Curtis, B., Atkins, P., and Haller, M. (1993). Models of reading aloud: dual-route and parallel-distributed-processing approaches. *Psychol. Rev.* 100, 589–608. doi: 10.1037/0033-295X.100.4.589

Coltheart, M., Rastle, K., Perry, C., Langdon, R., and Ziegler, J. (2001). DRC: a dual route cascaded model of visual word recognition and reading aloud. *Psychol. Rev.* 108, 204–256. doi: 10.1037/0033-295X.108.1.204

Conners, F., Loveal, S., Moore, M., Hume, L., and Maddox, C. (2010). An individual differences analysis of the self-teaching hypothesis. *J. Exp. Child Psychol.* 108, 402–410. doi: 10.1016/j.jecp.2010.09.009

Cunningham, A. (2006). Accounting for children's orthographic learning while reading text: do children self-teach? *J. Exp. Child Psychol.* 95, 56–77. doi: 10.1016/j.jecp.2006.03.008

Cunningham, A., Perry, K., Stanovich, K., and Share, D. (2002). Orthographic learning during reading: examining the role of self-teaching. *J. Exp. Child Psychol.* 82, 185–199. doi: 10.1016/S0022-0965(02)00008-5

Duff, F., and Hulme, C. (2012). The role of children's phonological and semantic knowledge in learning to read words. *Sci. Stud. Read.* 16, 504–525. doi: 10.1080/10888438.2011.598199

Dunn, L. M., and Dunn, D. M. (2007). *Peabody Picture Vocabulary Test, 4th Edn.* San Antonio, TX: Pearson.

Ehri, L. C. (2005). "Development of sight word reading: phases and findings," in *The Science of Reading: A Handbook*, eds M. S. Snowling and C. Hulme (Oxford, UK: Blackwell), 135–154.

Ehri, L. C., and Saltmarsh, J. (1995). Beginning readers outperform older disabled readers in learning to read words by sight. *Read. Writ.* 7, 295–326. doi: 10.1007/BF03162082

Ehri, L. C., and Wilce, L. S. (1983). Development of word identification speed in skilled and less skilled beginning readers. *J. Educ. Psychol.* 75, 3–18. doi: 10.1037/0022-0663.75.1.3

Elbro, C., de Jong, P. F., Houter, D., and Nielsen, A. (2012). From spelling pronunciation to lexical access: a second step in word decoding? *Sci. Stud. Read.* 16, 341–359. doi: 10.1080/10888438.2011.568556

Gascon, G., and Goodglass, H. (1970). Reading retardation and the information content of stimuli in paired associate learning. *Cortex* 6, 417–429. doi: 10.1016/S0010-9452(70)80006-5

Hulme, C., and Snowling, M. (1992). Deficits in output phonology: an explanation of reading failure? *Cogn. Neuropsychol.* 9, 47–72. doi: 10.1080/02643299208252052

Jones, K., Castles, A., and Kohnen, S. (2011). Subtypes of developmental dyslexia: recent developments and directions for treatment. *Acquir. Knowl. Speech Lang. Hear.* 13, 79–83.

Kaufman, A., and Kaufman, N. (1990). *Kaufman Brief Intelligence Test.* Circle Pines, MN: American Guidance Service, Inc.

Korkman, M., Kirk, U., and Kemp, S. (1998). *NEPSY: A Developmental Neuropsychological Assessment.* San Antonio, TX: Psychological Corporation.

Larsen, L., Kohnen, S., McArthur, G., and Nickels, L. (2011). *Letter Sound Test (LeST).* Available online at: http://www.motif.org.au/

Litt, R. A., de Jong, P. F., van Bergen, E., and Nation, K. (2013). Dissociating crossmodal and verbal demands in paired associate learning (PAL): what drives the PAL–reading relationship? *J. Exp. Child Psychol.* 115, 137–149. doi: 10.1016/j.jecp.2012.11.012

Lunneborg, C. E. (2001). Random assignment of available cases: bootstrap standard errors and confidence intervals. *Psychol. Methods* 6, 402–412. doi: 10.1037/1082-989X.6.4.402

Manis, F. (1985). Acquisition of word identification skills in normal and disabled readers. *J. Educ. Psychol.* 77, 78–90. doi: 10.1037/0022-0663.77.1.78

Manis, F. R., Seidenberg, M. S., Doi, L. M., McBride-Chang, C., and Petersen, A. (1996). On the basis of two subtypes of developmental dyslexia. *Cognition* 58, 157–195. doi: 10.1016/0010-0277(95)00679-6

Marinus, E., de Jong, P. F., and van der Leij, A. (2012). Increasing word-reading speed in poor readers: no additional benefits of explicit letter-cluster training. *Sci. Stud. Read.* 16, 166–185. doi: 10.1080/10888438.2011.554471

Masterson, J., Stuart, M., Dixon, M., and Lovejoy, S. (2003). *The Children's Printed Word Database.* Available online at: http://www.essex.ac.uk/psychology/cpwd

McArthur, G. M., Kohnen, S., Larsen, L., Jones, K., Anandakumar, T., Banales, E., et al. (2013). Getting to grips with the heterogeneity of developmental dyslexia. *Cogn. Neuropsychol.* 30, 1–24. doi: 10.1080/02643294.2013.784192

McKay, A., Davis, C., Savage, G., and Castles, A. (2008). Semantic involvement in reading aloud: evidence from a nonword training study. *J. Exp. Psychol. Learn. Mem. Cogn.* 34, 1495–1517. doi: 10.1037/a0013357

Messbauer, V., and de Jong, P. F. (2003). Word, nonword, and visual paired associate learning in Dutch dyslexic children. *Exp. Child Psychol.* 84, 77–96. doi: 10.1016/S0022-0965(02)00179-0

Nation, K., and Cocksey, J. (2009). The relationship between knowing a word and reading it aloud in children's word reading development. *J. Exp. Child Psychol.* 103, 296–308. doi: 10.1016/j.jecp.2009.03.004

Nation, K., and Snowling, M. J. (1998). Individual differences in contextual facilitation: evidence from dyslexia and poor reading comprehension. *Child Dev.* 69, 996–1011. doi: 10.1111/j.1467-8624.1998.tb06157.x

Ouellette, G. (2006). What's meaning got to do with it: the role of vocabulary in word reading and reading comprehension. *J. Educ. Psychol.* 98, 554–566. doi: 10.1037/0022-0663.98.3.554

Parkin, A. (1982). Phonological recoding in lexical decision: effects of spelling-to-sound regularity depends on how regularity is defined. *Mem. Cogn.* 10, 43–53. doi: 10.3758/BF03197624

Peterson, R. L., Pennington, B. F., and Olson, R. K. (2013). Subtypes of developmental dyslexia: testing the predictions of the dual-route and connectionist frameworks. *Cognition* 26, 20–38. doi: 10.1016/j.cognition.2012.08.007

Rack, J. P., Snowling, M. J., and Olson, R. K. (1992). The nonword reading deficit in developmental dyslexia: a review. *Read. Res. Q.* 27, 28–53. doi: 10.2307/747832

Rastle, K., and Coltheart, M. (1999). Serial and strategic effects in reading aloud. *J. Exp. Psychol. Hum. Percept. Perform.* 25, 482–503. doi: 10.1037/0096-1523.25.2.482

Reitsma, P. (1983). Print word learning in beginning readers. *J. Exp. Child Psychol.* 36, 321–339. doi: 10.1016/0022-0965(83)90036-X

Reitsma, P. (1989). "Orthographic memory and learning to read," in *Reading and Writing Disorders in Different Orthographic Systems,* eds P. G. Aaron and R. M. Joshi (Dordrecht/Boston London: Kluwer Academic Publishers), 51–73.

Ricketts, J., Nation, K., and Bishop, D. (2007). Vocabulary is important for some, but not all reading skills. *Sci. Stud. Read.* 11, 235–257. doi: 10.1080/10888430701344306

Schmalz, X., Marinus, E., and Castles, A. (2013). Phonological decoding or direct access? Regularity effects in lexical decisions of Grade 3 and 4 children. *Q. J. Exp. Psychol.* 66, 338–346. doi: 10.1080/17470218.2012.711843

Seidenberg, M., Waters, G., Barnes, M., and Tanenhaus, M. (1984). When does irregular spelling or pronunciation influence word recognition? *J. Verbal Learn. Verbal Behav.* 23, 383–404. doi: 10.1016/S0022-5371(84)90270-6

Share, D. (1995). Phonological recoding and self-teaching: sine qua non of reading acquisition. *Cognition* 55, 151–218. doi: 10.1016/0010-0277(94)00645-2

Share, D. (1999). Phonological recoding and orthographic learning: a direct test of the self-teaching hypothesis. *J. Exp. Child Psychol.* 72, 95–129. doi: 10.1006/jecp.1998.2481

Share, D. (2011). "The role of phonology in reading acquisition: the self-teaching hypothesis," in *Explaining Individual Differences in Reading: Theory and Evidence,* eds S. Brady, D. Braze, and C. Fowler (New York, NY: Psychology Press), 45–68.

Share, D., and Shalev, C. (2004). Self-teaching in normal and disabled readers. *Read. Writ.* 17, 769–800. doi: 10.1007/s11145-004-2658-9

Siegel, L. S., Share, D., and Geva, E. (1995). Evidence for superior orthographic skills in dyslexics. *Psychol. Sci.* 6, 250–254. doi: 10.1111/j.1467-9280.1995.tb00601.x

Staels, E., and van den Broeck, W. (2013). Orthographic learning and the role of text-to-speech software in Dutch disabled readers. *J. Learn. Disabil.* doi: 10.1177/0022219413487407. [Epub ahead of print].

Stanovich, K. E., and Siegel, L. S. (1994). The phenotypic perform- ance profile of reading-disabled children: a regression-based test of the phonological-core variable-difference model. *J. Educ. Psychol.* 86, 24–53. doi: 10.1037/0022-0663.86.1.24

Stanovich, K. E., Siegel, L. S., and Gottardo, A. (1997). Converging evidence for phonological and surface subtypes of reading disability. *J. Educ. Psychol.* 89, 114–127. doi: 10.1037/0022-0663.89.1.114

Szenkovits, G., and Ramus, F. (2005). Exploring dyslexics' phonological deficit I: lexical vs. sub-lexical and input vs. output processes. *Dyslexia* 11, 253–268. doi: 10.1002/dys.308

Tunmer, W. E., and Chapman, J. W. (2004). "The use of context in learning to read," in *Handbook of Children's Literacy,* eds T. Nunes and P. Bryant (Springer Netherlands), 199–212.

Tunmer, W. E., Nesdale, A. R., and Wright, A. D. (1987). Syntactic awareness and reading acquisition. *Br. J. Dev. Psychol.* 5, 25–34. doi: 10.1111/j.2044-835X.1987.tb01038.x

Valdois, S., Bosse, M. L., Ans, B., Carbonnel, S., Zorman, M., David, D., et al. (2003). Phonological and visual processing deficits can dissociate in developmental dyslexia: evidence from two case studies. *Read. Writ. An Interdisciplinary Journal* 16, 541–572. doi: 10.1023/A:1025501406971

Vellutino, F., Steger, J., Harding, C., and Philips, F. (1975). Verbal vs non-verbal paired-associates learning in poor and normal readers. *Neuropsychologia* 13, 75–82. doi: 10.1016/0028-3932(75)90050-0

Wang, H., Castles, A., and Nickels, L. (2012). Word regularity affects orthographic learning. *Q. J. Exp. Psychol.* 65, 856–864. doi: 10.1080/17470218.2012.672996

Wang, H.-C., Castles, A., Nickels, L., and Nation, K. (2011). Context effects on orthographic learning of regular and irregular words. *J. Exp. Child Psychol.* 109, 39–57. doi: 10.1016/j.jecp.2010.11.005

Wang, H.-C., Castles, A., Nickels, L., and Nation, K. (2013). Predictors of orthographic learning for regular and irregular words. *Sci. Stud. Read.* 17, 369–384. doi: 10.1080/10888438.2012.749879

Yap, R. L., and van der Leij, A. (1993). Word processing in dyslexics: an automatic decoding deficit? *Read. Writ.* 5, 261–279. doi: 10.1007/BF01027391

8

Does pronounceability modulate the letter string deficit of children with dyslexia? A study with the rate and amount model

Chiara V. Marinelli[1]*, Daniela Traficante[2,3] and Pierluigi Zoccolotti[1,4]

[1] *Neuropsychology Research Centre, IRCCS Santa Lucia, Rome, Italy*
[2] *Department of Psychology, Catholic University of Milan, Milan, Italy*
[3] *NeuroMI – Milan Center for Neuroscience, Milan, Italy*
[4] *Department of Psychology, Sapienza University of Rome, Rome, Italy*

***Correspondence:**
Chiara V. Marinelli, Neuropsychology Research Centre, IRCCS Santa Lucia, Via Ardeatina 306, Rome, Italy
e-mail: chiaravaleria.marinelli@uniroma1.it

The locus of the deficit of children with dyslexia in dealing with strings of letters may be a deficit at a pre-lexical graphemic level or an inability to bind orthographic and phonological information. We evaluate these alternative hypotheses in two experiments by examining the role of stimulus pronounceability in a lexical decision task (LDT) and in a forced-choice letter discrimination task (Reicher–Wheeler paradigm). Seventeen fourth grade children with dyslexia and 24 peer control readers participated to two experiments. In the LDT children were presented with high-, low-frequency words, pronounceable pseudowords (such as DASU) and unpronounceable non-words (such as RNGM) of 4-, 5-, or 6- letters. No sign of group by pronounceability interaction was found when over-additivity was taken into account. Children with dyslexia were impaired when they had to process strings, not only of pronounceable stimuli but also of unpronounceable stimuli, a deficit well accounted for by a single global factor. Complementary results were obtained with the Reicher–Wheeler paradigm: both groups of children gained in accuracy in letter discrimination in the context of pronounceable primes (words and pseudowords) compared to unpronounceable primes (non-words). No global factor was detected in this task which requires the discrimination between a target letter and a competitor but does not involve simultaneous letter string processing. Overall, children with dyslexia show a selective difficulty in simultaneously processing a letter string as a whole, independent of its pronounceability; however, when the task involves isolated letter processing, also these children can make use of the ortho-phono-tactic information derived from a previously seen letter string. This pattern of findings is in keeping with the idea that an impairment in pre-lexical graphemic analysis may be a core deficit in developmental dyslexia.

Keywords: developmental dyslexia, lexical decision, Reicher–Wheeler paradigm, pronounceability, global factor, letter string

INTRODUCTION

In lexical decision tasks (LDTs) participants are required to discriminate between real words and foils. The difficulty of the discrimination varies according to the characteristics of the foils: as orthographic and phonological overlap between words and foils increases, the LDT becomes progressively more difficult. Participants are faster and more accurate at rejecting unpronounceable illegal non-words (i.e., letter strings such as GLDT) than pronounceable pseudowords (i.e., nonsense strings of letters that respect the orthographic rules of a given language but have no semantic content such as RINAFO; e.g., Holcomb and Neville, 1990; Forster et al., 2003; Ratcliff et al., 2004). Evans et al. (2012) reported that, as foils become increasingly word-like, non-word ("no") responses became significantly slower and less accurate: reaction times (RTs) were shorter, and accuracy was higher, for consonant strings compared to pseudowords. Moreover, also real word ("yes") responses in the context of increasingly word-like foils were slower and less accurate. Passing from non-word to pseudoword foils there is a progressive increase in pronounceability as well as in orthographic and phonological similarity to real words. Moreover, as foils become more word-like and orthographic and phonological overlap increases, foils produce more activation of similar words (Harm and Seidenberg, 2004) and the discrimination becomes more difficult, indicating that a higher level of activation is required for a real word ("yes") decision to avoid false alarms.

Some authors investigated whether pronounceability influences the depth of processing required for lexical decision. James (1975) found that this task involves retrieval of semantic information (as highlighted by the concreteness effect) only in the presence of pronounceable distractors, while, decreasing the similarity between words and foils, the use of unpronounceable distractors makes the semantic retrieval unnecessary. Similarly, Evans et al. (2012) reported smaller effects of imageability and semantic priming as decision difficulty and RTs decreased from pseudohomophone, to pseudoword, and non-word foil contexts, with semantic effects minimized with unpronounceable foils. Moreover, semantic effects increased significantly as decisions became harder (and slower) with more word-like foils. Dimitropoulou et al. (2010) examined the masked onset priming effect (MOPE) by manipulating the primes' lexicality, frequency, and pronounceability. The MOPE indicates faster naming latencies when a target word (e.g., BREAK) is preceded by a briefly presented masked prime that shares its initial sound with the target (e.g., belly) compared to when it does not (e.g., merry) or when it rhymes with it (e.g., stake; Forster and Davis, 1991). This effect has been interpreted as an advantage in speech planning of the response or as evidence of prime processing by the non-lexical route. Dimitropoulou et al. (2010) found the MOPE for all types of stimuli but unpronounceable non-words, a result favoring the speech planning hypothesis. Finally, pronounceability has been examined also in terms of the facilitation present for repeated stimuli. In a LDT, the repetition priming was larger in experiments with pseudowords than in experiments with non-words (Ratcliff et al., 2004).

The effect of pronounceability has been evaluated not only in LDTs, but also with other experimental paradigms. Seidenberg et al. (submitted) examined whether pronounceabililty influences the reading aloud process. Participants had greater difficulty in naming non-words containing grapho-tactically illegal sequences of letters (e.g., JULBZ) as compared to grapho-tactically legal non-words containing digraphs (i.e., multi-letter graphemes that map onto a single phoneme, e.g., the "ee" in NEESH). These findings indicate that pronounceability is a key factor in determining naming latencies, with pronounceable pseudowords being responded to faster than unpronounceable non-words. Differences are also observed when participants have only to identify a single letter in the stimulus in a post-cued letter-in-string identification task. Thus, letter recognition is more accurate in the context of a pronounceable pseudoword than in the context of a consonant string, the so-called pseudoword superiority effect (PSE; e.g., Baron and Thurston, 1973; Spoehr and Smith, 1975; Grainger and Jacobs, 1994, 2005).

It is worth noting that when also reading proficiency is taken into account the framework becomes more complex. In fact, if two groups (e.g., dyslexic and proficient readers) vary in general speed of processing (hereafter referred to as the global factor), group differences in latencies would depend on both the difficulty of a given task and the general group differences in processing speed (Faust et al., 1999). Then, for groups showing global differences in performance, one should expect to find over-additivity effects; i.e., the absolute group differences in performance would tend to grow as a function of task difficulty over and above the characteristics of the specific experimental manipulations (Faust et al., 1999). The presence of over-additivity may induce overestimation or underestimation of the contribution of specific variables modulating reading performance. Therefore, it may not be easy to identify the presence of a deficit in processing unpronounceable stimuli because of differences in task difficulty across experimental conditions and their interaction with basic group differences in rate of information processing. Models such as the rate and amount model (RAM; Faust et al., 1999) reveal the presence and characteristics of the global factor in information processing by distinguishing between the performance of dyslexic and proficient readers and isolating the conditions in which children with dyslexia show specific deficits not ascribable to over-additivity (Zoccolotti et al., 2008).

In previous studies, we found that a single global factor accounted for a very large proportion of the impaired performance of children with dyslexia in making lexical decisions and reading words and pseudowords (Di Filippo et al., 2006; Zoccolotti et al., 2008; Marinelli et al., 2011). Other studies showed that the global factor was present for orthographic but not pictorial stimuli (Zoccolotti et al., 2008) and in the visual, but not the auditory, modality (Marinelli et al., 2011). The global factor did not emerge in a variety of letter and bigram tasks even though their general difficulty was made similar to that of letter strings (i.e., both words or pseudowords; De Luca et al., 2010). In fact, tasks mapping letter (and bigram) recognition loaded on a separate factor other than that accounting for words and non-words.

These studies indicate that children with dyslexia are selectively impaired in processing visually presented strings of letters with or without lexical value. We have proposed that this deficit has a pre-lexical graphemic locus (e.g., De Luca et al., 2010), i.e., marks an impairment in forming a graphemic description of the letter string (Zoccolotti et al., 2008). This idea is in keeping with other proposals based on imaging and lesional studies of the so-called "visual word form area" (VWFA; Cohen et al., 2000, 2002). The local combination detector (LCD) model (Dehaene et al., 2005) posits that written words are encoded by a hierarchy of detectors tuned to increasingly larger and more complex word fragments (visual features, single letters, bigrams, quadrigrams and, possibly, words). At the neural level, information from letter features and single letter converges on the VWFA; here, a posterior-to-anterior gradient is present with a progression in selectivity to increasingly word-like stimuli (e.g., Dehaene et al., 2004; Vinckier et al., 2007). Over years of practice, frequent combinations of letters are selected to be represented by dedicated neurons (Cohen et al., 2008), and the VWFA becomes attuned to the regularities of the writing system, yielding fast parallel processing in reading (Vinckier et al., 2007; Cohen et al., 2008). Importantly, several studies found that dyslexic individuals show selective hypo-activation of the VWFA (for a review see Richlan et al., 2009). In a similar vein, Marsh and Hillis (2005) proposed that this area is involved in the computation of a prelexical "grapheme description" independent of case, font, location, or orientation. Notably, such graphemic description does not require stored knowledge of spelling or spelling-sound correspondences. In this perspective, the reading impairment of children with dyslexia might be ascribed to a deficit at the level of graphemic analysis.

Another interpretation of the dyslexic deficit is that the impairment is related to the inability to bind orthographic and phonological information (Ziegler et al., 2010; van den Broeck and Geudens, 2012). Evidence in this direction comes from imaging studies indicating a close association between letter and speech sounds early in development (for a review see Blomert, 2011). Accordingly, effective letter–speech sound integration is an emergent property of learning to read supported by an interrelated network of visual, auditory, and heteromodal brain areas. There is evidence that dyslexic individuals are impaired in letter–speech sound integration. For example, in a functional magnetic resonance imaging (fMRI) study, Blau et al. (2009) reported that adult dyslexic readers showed underactivation of the superior temporal cortex for the integration of letters and speech sounds. In a further study, Blau et al. (2010) reported that, unlike control readers, cortical responses to speech sounds of dyslexic individuals were not modulated by letter–speech sound congruency. In a complementary line of research, it has been reported that proficient readers activate orthographic representations in phonological LDT while children with dyslexia do not (van der Mark et al., 2011). Thus, dyslexic individuals fail to activate orthographic representations during spoken language processing. Finally, also previously described results on the VWFA are not necessarily incompatible with an orthographic–phonological binding perspective. The presence of interactions between orthographic and phonological processing is suggested by evidence indicating connections between the VWFA and language areas (Cai et al., 2008; Greve et al., 2013). First, it has been noted that the VWFA shows a clear lateralization with only the left, linguistic, hemisphere that becomes specialized for reading (Cai et al., 2008); furthermore, it has been reported that asymmetries in the VWFA are correlated with the ear advantage in a dichotic listening task (Greve et al., 2013). Overall, it has been proposed that a deficit in orthographic–phonological binding may represent a proximal cause of the reading slowness in dyslexia and may also help understanding the deficit in reading fluency of these individuals (Blomert, 2011).

In the present research, we tested these alternative hypotheses by evaluating the role of stimulus pronounceability on accuracy and latency in two different tasks: a LDT (Experiment 1), and a two-alternative forced-choice task (the so-called Reicher–Wheeler paradigm: see Reicher, 1969; Wheeler, 1970; Experiment 2).

In the LDT we are interested in assessing whether the impairment shown by children with dyslexia in processing letter strings is present only for pronounceable words and pseudowords or it is also detectable (and of a similar size) with unpronounceable letter strings. The first outcome would favor an orthographic–phonological binding interpretation while the latter a pre-lexical graphemic locus of the reading deficit. In fact, strings of consonants are not pronounceable and, as such, would not activate orthographic–phonological binding to the same extent as words or pseudowords. Therefore, based on the orthographic–phonological binding hypothesis we would expect a smaller deficit for non-words as compared to words and pseudowords (once the effect of over-additivity is controlled for). Based on the hypothesis of a letter string graphemic deficit, no interaction between groups and item pronounceability would be expected. All condition means in the LDT (for words, pseudowords, and non-words) are supposed to fit, in the RAM, with the same letter string factor.

The Reicher–Wheeler paradigm proposes the same types of stimuli used in the LDT, i.e., words, pseudowords and non-words, but does not require the simultaneous processing of several letters. In fact, the decision is to be made on the discrimination between a target letter and a competitor in the context of a previously displayed letter string. Assuming that the main impairment of children with dyslexia has to do with simultaneous letter string processing and not with single letters, the lack of a global factor in the RAM model might be expected. However, examining the context effects (i.e., the lexicality and the pronounciability of the prime) it is possible to test whether children with dyslexia can gain advantage from lexical activation and pronounceability in graphemic processing as much as control children.

In particular, testing for the PSE (i.e., letter identification is more accurate in the context of a pseudoword than in the context of a unpronounceable non-word) would allow evaluating whether children can take advantage from a pronounceable letter string which forms a typical orthographic context in Italian. Furthermore, testing for the word superiority effect (WSE; i.e., letter identification is more accurate in the context of a word than in the context of a pronounceable pseudoword) would allow evaluating whether children can take advantage of the lexical activation triggered by a word context in the successive letter recognition. According to the orthographic–phonological binding hypothesis we would expect, for children with dyslexia, a lack of both PSE and WSE, while for skilled readers a role of lexicality and pronounceability of the context is expected. On the other hand, the letter string graphemic deficit hypothesis would predict no differences in the effect size of the WSE and PSE in relation to reading proficiency, as the task does not require any decision on the lexicality of a specific letter combination, but only the discrimination between a single target letter and a competitor one. Furthermore, as no selective deficit in orthographic–phonological interaction is envisaged, one would expect children with dyslexia to be able to take advantage of the ortho-phonotactic regularities of the language (i.e., they are expected to show a PSE).

In order to apply the RAM model to the data from both the LDT and Reicher–Wheeler paradigms, we examined the speed of processing of children with dyslexia in responding to these tasks. There is evidence that, even though most studies on the Reicher–Wheeler paradigm focused on accuracy, parallel effects have also been reported with time measures (RTs and visual evoked potentials; Ziegler et al., 1997; Martin et al., 2006). To test the global factor it is important to have a sizeable spread of performances across conditions (Faust et al., 1999). To this aim, in LDT we presented high-frequency words, low-frequency words, pseudowords and non-words, varying for length within each category (from 4 to 6 letters), for a total of 12 different conditions. Previous data on Italian children indicate that children with dyslexia show frequency (e.g., Barca et al., 2006) and lexicality (e.g., Zoccolotti et al., 2008) effects both in reading and LDT (Paizi et al., 2013). These effects tend to be greater in children with dyslexia than in typically developing children in raw data analyses but, typically, this group interaction disappears when over-additivity is controlled for (Di Filippo et al., 2006; Zoccolotti et al., 2008; Paizi et al., 2013). In the Reicher–Wheeler paradigm, primes were 4-letter high-frequency words, pseudowords and non-words, with the target letter in first, second, or third position, for a total of nine different conditions. Note that no data are yet available on this paradigm on Italian children.

EXPERIMENT 1

The first experiment examined the performance of children with dyslexia and typically developing readers in a LDT with non-words, pseudowords, low-frequency words, and high-frequency words presented intermixed.

METHOD

Participants

Participants were 41 fourth grade children with a normal intelligence (according to the Raven's Coloured Progressive Matrices; Pruneti et al., 1996) and adequate socio-educational conditions. In particular, there were 17 children with dyslexia (10 Male and 7 Female; mean age = 9.50 years, $SD = 0.30$) and 24 control readers (9 Male and 15 Female; mean age = 9.50 year, $SD = 0.30$). Children were selected by our psychology unit during a screening for learning disabilities carried out in local public schools of Rome. Parents were informed of the screening procedure and authorized their child's participation.

Children with dyslexia were selected for a marked reading delay (at least 2 *SD*s below normative data) in accuracy and/or speed in reading a text passage (MT reading test, Cornoldi and Colpo, 1998). None of the children had received treatment for their reading impairment. Criteria for inclusion in the control group included normal reading speed and accuracy on the MT reading test (Cornoldi and Colpo, 1998). Control participants were comparable to children with dyslexia for sex ($\chi^2 = 1.06$, n.s.), age ($t_{(40)} = 0.08$, n.s.), and Raven's test performance ($F_{(1,41)} = 0.04$, n.s.). On the MT reading test (Cornoldi and Colpo, 1998), mean *z* scores of control participants were near zero for all parameters (accuracy: –0.03, $SD = 0.80$; speed: –0.10, $SD = 0.57$). By contrast, children with dyslexia performed worse than control readers in reading accuracy (mean *z* score = –3.00, $SD = 1.20$; $t_{(40)} = 9.45$, $p < 0.0001$) and speed (mean *z* score = –1.75, $SD = 1.25$; $t_{(40)} = 5.71$, $p < 0.0001$). As a group, children with dyslexia showed only mildly defective performance in reading comprehension (mean *z* score = –0.27, $SD = 0.43$), but they scored lower than the control readers (mean *z* score = 0.04; $SD = 0.26$; $t_{(40)} = 2.84$, $p < 0.01$).

A number of other tests were used to qualify the reading and cognitive profile of children with dyslexia. **Table 1** reports the performance on the *Word and Non-word Reading Test* (Zoccolotti et al., 2005), a standard test of words and non-words reading (for basic characteristics of this and other tests please refer to the legends of the Tables). As it can be seen from the table, performance of the group of children with dyslexia was significantly lower than that of control readers across all conditions. The table reports also the proportion of children performing at least 2 *SD*s below normative data; across all conditions 16 children out 17 children showed a deficit in at least one subset of the test (the odd one out had a moderate impairment in this test, about –1 *SD*, across all conditions). Impairment appeared more marked for low-frequency (both short and long) words and long high-frequency words.

On the *Test for the Diagnosis of Orthographic Deficit in Childhood* (Angelelli et al., 2008; **Table 2**), children with dyslexia, as a group, showed impaired performance on all subtests, except for that on spelling regular words. About half of the children with dyslexia showed severely impaired performance in spelling. **Table 3** reports the performance of the two groups of children on phonological and visual attention span tests (for information on these tests please refer to the Table legend). As a group children with dyslexia showed lower performance than control readers in several of these tests, i.e., the *Visual Attention Span* (Bosse et al., 2007), the *Repetition of Non-words Series* (Marinelli, 2010), and at the *Blending test* (Di Filippo et al., 2005) in the pseudoword condition (only a trend was present for the word condition). No difference was present at the *Digit Span* test (Wechsler, 2006). At any rate, it may be noted that, in most cases, the impairment was mild and (with the exception of the pseudoword condition of the *Blending test*) very few children showed frankly impaired performance in these tests.

Materials

Ninety-six 4-, 5-, and 6-letter words were selected from the *EPOS 2* database (Baldi and Traficante, 2005), based on the ease of recognition (words recognized by more than 90% of subjects) and high familiarity (familiarity estimated higher than

Table 1 | Performance of children with dyslexia and control readers in the *Word and Non-word Reading Test* (Zoccolotti et al., 2005).

	ACCURACY							SPEED						
	Control readers		Children with dyslexia					Control readers		Children with dyslexia				
	M	*SD*	*M*	*SD*	% path. perf.	$t_{(40)}$	*p*	*M*	*SD*	*M*	*SD*	% path. perf.	$t_{(40)}$	*p*
Short HF words	0.36	0.41	−0.66	0.94	23.53	4.7	< 0.001	0.7	1.67	−1.36	1.06	52.94	4.46	< 0.001
Long HF words	0.42	0.75	−2	1.75	64.71	6.03	< 0.001	0.65	0.95	−2.48	1.26	88.24	9.01	< 0.001
Short LF words	0.36	0.63	−1.42	1.18	47.06	6.22	< 0.001	0.6	1.21	−2.3	1.47	58.82	6.89	< 0.001
Long LF words	0.25	0.84	−1.52	1.32	47.06	5.21	< 0.001	0.8	1.08	−1.91	1.18	70.59	7.57	< 0.001
Short pseudo-words	0.29	0.48	−1.03	1.17	35.29	4.96	< 0.001	0.17	1.33	−1.23	1.11	41.18	3.55	< 0.01
Long pseudo-words	0.29	0.97	−1.36	1.52	35.29	4.22	< 0.001	0.48	1.13	−1.45	1.36	47.06	4.93	< 0.001

Values indicate z scores as compared to normative values (negative values indicate lower performance). Path. perf., pathological performance; HF, high-frequency; LF, low-frequency. The test is made of six A4 sheets, one for each subset of stimuli. There are 30 stimuli in each subset. Short stimuli are 4-, 5-letter long, while long stimuli are 8-, 10-letter long. Pseudo-words were generated from high-frequency words.

Table 2 | Performance of children with dyslexia and control readers in the *Test for the Diagnosis of Developmental Dysgraphia* (Angelelli et al., 2008).

	Control readers		Children with dyslexia				
	M	*SD*	*M*	*SD*	% path. perf.	$t_{(40)}$	*p*
Regular words	−1.38	2.01	−2.93	3.85	41.18	1.68	n.s.
Regular non 1:1 words	0.05	0.60	−1.33	1.80	29.41	3.49	< 0.001
Ambiguous words	0.76	0.96	−1.04	1.36	23.53	4.98	< 0.001
Pseudo-words	−0.20	0.56	−1.73	2.55	35.29	2.86	< 0.01
Total	0.20	0.72	−2.04	1.80	47.06	5.50	< 0.001

*Values indicate z scores as compared to normative values (negative values indicate lower performance). Path. perf., pathological performance. Regular words (N = 70) were with complete one-sound-to-one-letter correspondence; Non 1:1 regular words (N = 10) were words containing sounds that require syllabic conversion rules {i.e., the orthographic transcription of a consonant is determined by the vowel that follows it; for example [k] followed by /a/o/u/ = CA, CO, CU [e.g., CASA (=home) and CUBO (=cube)]; while [k] followed by /i/e/ = CHI, CHE [e.g., CHIESA (=church)]}; ambiguous words (N = 55) were words with unpredictable transcription along the phonological-to-orthographic conversion route (e.g., [kwo] in [kwota], the quota: QUOTA but not *CUOTA); pseudo-words (N = 25) were stimuli without lexical status but with one-sound-to-one-letter correspondence.*

Table 3 | Performance of children with dyslexia and normal readers on visual attention and phonological/metaphonological tests.

Time	Control readers		Children with dyslexia				
	M	*SD*	*M*	*SD*	% path. perf.	$t_{(40)}$	*p*
Visual attention span	0.44	0.70	−0.14	0.43	0.00	3.01	< 0.01
Phonological span	0.61	1.21	0.06	0.66	1.65	1.65	n.s.
Repetition of pseudo-word series	0.87	1.15	0.17	0.85	2.12	2.12	< 0.05
Blending test: words	0.73	0.94	0.05	1.31	1.95	1.95	0.06
Blending test: pseudo-words	0.64	1.10	−0.53	1.21	23.52	3.21	< 0.01

For all tests, values indicate z scores based on normative values (negative values indicate lower performance). Path. perf., pathological performance.
The Visual Attention Span (Bosse et al., 2007) is a task in which children see on the PC screen for 200 ms an unpronounceable string of five consonants (e.g., R H S D M) that, as such, cannot be recoded phonologically and must report as many letters as possible. Each letter is presented 10 times appearing twice in each of the five positions. The task includes twenty items and was implemented by the E-prime 2 software. Normative data on Italian children are presented in Marinelli (2010).
Phonological span was assessed with the Digit span task of the WISC III (Wechsler, 2006).
In the Repetition of Non-word Series, ten lists of three bi-syllabic, 5-letter pseudo-words are read aloud by the examiner at a pace of about one every 2 s. The child is asked to repeat each list as accurately as possible immediately after presentation. Each correct non-word was awarded a point out for a maximum score of 30. Normative data on Italian children are presented in Marinelli (2010).
The Blending Test (Di Filippo et al., 2005) is a measure of phonological awareness. Words (or pseudo-words) are presented phoneme-by-phoneme through an audiotape at a rate of one per second. At the end of the sequence, the child has to repeat aloud the whole stimulus. Nineteen (five- to six-letter) words/pseudo-words are presented. For each stimulus, the correctly blended pairs of phonemes are counted, irrespective of whether repetition of the entire target is achieved. The maximum score is 83.

6 on a 7-point scale). Half of words were of high-frequency (mean = 215.4; *SD* = 142.2; range = 70–794) and half of low frequency (mean = 14.5, *SD* = 5.6; range = 7–28), according to the children words frequency corpus (Marconi et al., 1993). Both high- and low-frequency word subsets were made of 16 stimuli for each length (4-, 5-, and 6- letters). Subsets were matched for bigram frequency, contextual rules, presence of orthographic complexity (double consonants and cluster of consonants), familiarity (based on *EPOS 2*, Baldi and Traficante, 2005) and percentage of recognition (Baldi and Traficante, 2005). Words were also matched for neighborhood-size (Baldi and Traficante, 2005), but only within the subsets with the same number of letters (due to the high covariance between length and neighborhood-size characteristic of Italian).

For each subset, pronounceable strings such as DASU (16 stimuli for each length for a total of 48 items) were generated from half of the words, and unpronounceable stimuli such as RNGM (16 stimuli for each length for a total of 48 items) from the other half. Although unpronounceable, the letter stimuli were made only with bigrams really existing in the Italian orthography. Usually, studies compare a pronounceable non-word such as STRENG with a consonant string such as STPFM. However, in this example, not only is the first type of stimulus pronounceable and more orthographically similar to a real word than the second one, but it is also orthographically and phonologically regular, whereas the second is not. In the present study, we used only orthographically and phonologically regular bigrams in order to control for this aspect, at least at the bigram levels.

For example, bigrams in VRSN are, respectively, in the words *aVRemo* ("we will have"), *oRSo* ("bear"), *SNello* ("slim"). Digrams SC, GL, GN, CH, which correspond to a single sound, were avoided.

Pronounceable strings were obtained changing vowels with other vowels, while unpronounceable strings were obtained changing vowels with consonants. Overall, there was the same number of "yes" and "no" responses; i.e., 96 real words ("yes" responses) matched with 96 non-words ("no" responses: 48 pronounceable and 48 unpronounceable). Items were randomized and presented in four blocks of 48 stimuli. Words and respective derived pseudowords or non-words did not appear in the same block. The order of presentation of the stimuli was randomized for each subject.

Procedure

Tests were carried out individually in a quiet room at the school of the children. Children performed a LDT, in which they had to decide whether or not a string of letters formed a legal Italian word.

Stimuli were printed in upper-case Courier new font, size 18, with a white color on a gray screen. Each item was preceded by a fixation point, which disappeared after 500 ms. After the appearance of the stimulus (that remained on the screen until the subject responded), there was a 1000 ms inter-trial interval. When the letter string appeared at the center of the PC screen, children had to push the right button on the keyboard as quickly and as accurately as possible if the stimulus was a word and the left one if it was not a word. The other buttons of the keyboard were hidden by means of a cardboard. A brief practice with 12 stimuli preceded the experiment. No feedback was provided. Children were allowed brief pauses between blocks.

Stimulus presentation and data recording were controlled with the E-Prime 2 software. The program recorded RTs and errors.

Data analysis

Invalid trials (due to technical problems), RTs below 250 ms and outliers (i.e., RTs exceeding the individual mean plus or minus 3 *SDs*) were excluded from the analyses. The percentage of excluded RTs was very small (for control readers: 0.47, 2.18, and 1.06% for unpronounceable non-words, pronounceable pseudowords and words, respectively; for children with dyslexia: 0.29, 1.82, and 1.06%, respectively). The RTs corresponding to errors were excluded from the analyses.

RTs were examined in order to check for the presence of the global factor in the data. In particular, the RAM (Faust et al., 1999) makes a number of testable predictions to detect the presence of global factor(s) in the data (see Results). When two groups vary for some general processing speed factor, larger group differences are expected in more difficult conditions (and smaller ones in an easier condition) over and above the specific effect of a given experimental manipulation; this is referred to as over-additivity effect (Faust et al., 1999). Over-additivity may modulate the group by condition interactions when two groups differ in general ability (Faust et al., 1999), as is the case for dyslexic and control readers. According to Faust et al. (1999), this effect can be controlled for by using various data transformations, including a *z* score transformation. For each participant, *z* scores are obtained by taking the RTs in each condition, subtracting their overall mean, and dividing them by the standard deviation across conditions (therefore, each individual has an average of 0 across conditions and a $SD = 1$). This transformation rescales individual performance to a common reference; hence, it allows controlling for global differences in information processing (Faust et al., 1999) while preserving the information regarding individual variability across experimental trials and conditions. Note that this transformation is appropriate only to open-scale measures, such as time, but not closed-scale measures such as accuracy. Interactions that are significant in both the raw score and *z*-transformed score analyses indicate the selective influence of a given parameter; in contrast, interactions that are significant only in the raw data analyses, but not on those with the *z*-transformed values, indicate the presence of spurious interactions (due to over-additivity effects; Faust et al., 1999).

Three separate analysis of variances (ANOVAs) were carried out to examine the effect of pronounceability (non-words vs. pseudowords), frequency (high- vs. low-frequency words) and lexicality (pseudowords vs. words), respectively. In each of these analyses, group (dyslexic vs. control children) was entered as between-subject factor and length (4-, 5-, and 6-letter stimuli) as repeated measure. Separate ANOVAs were carried out on percentages of errors, RT raw data (r) and RT *z*-transformed data (z). For the sake of presentation, the two latter types of analyses will be presented together (using raw RT means to illustrate effects); this will allow highlighting which group by condition interactions are genuine and which can be ascribed to the over-additivity effect. Whenever appropriate, means were compared with the *a posteriori* Tukey HSD test.

RESULTS

Analysis of global factor(s)

The RAM (Faust et al., 1999) predicts a linear relationship between: (i) the condition means of two groups of children (e.g., dyslexic and control readers) who vary in overall information processing rate; (ii) the condition means of the overall group and the standard deviation in the same conditions (i.e., that more difficult conditions will generate greater variability).

As it can be seen in **Figure 1**, condition means for the dyslexic group were linearly related to those of control readers. This pattern indicates that a global factor (which explains a large proportion of variance, i.e., $r^2 = 0.89$) accounts well for the slowness of children with dyslexia across all experimental conditions; namely, condition means for high- and low-frequency words, pronounceable pseudowords and unpronounceable non-words were all well fit by the same regression line. The slope is 1.52, indicating that children with dyslexia were 52% slower than control readers in performing the task.

The test of the second prediction is presented in **Figure 2**; the means of the overall sample of children (dyslexic and control readers) for all experimental conditions are plotted against the respective standard deviation in the same conditions. A linear relationship between means and standard deviation (with a 0.40 slope) was present accounting for a substantial amount of variance ($r^2 = 0.83$).

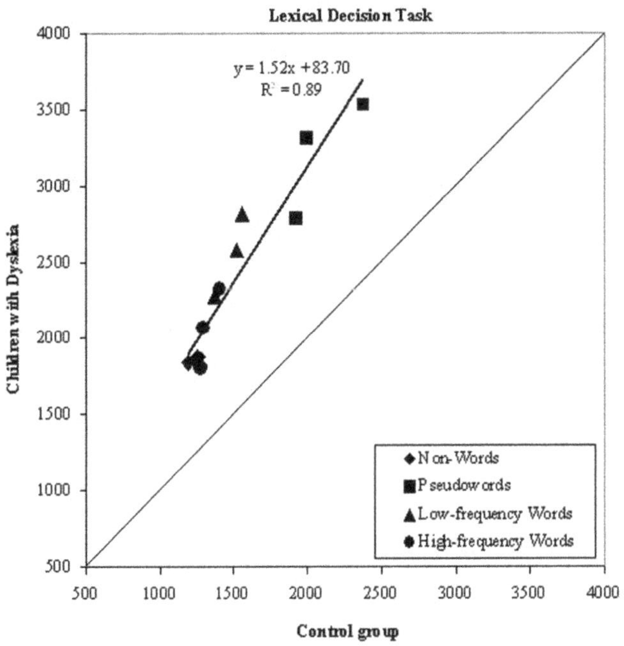

FIGURE 1 | Experiment 1. Dyslexics' condition means in the lexical decision task are plotted as a function of the control readers' means (symbols as described in the figure; the three symbols per condition represent word lengths). The diagonal line (slope = 1) represents equal RTs for dyslexic and control readers. Note that all data points lie above the diagonal line indicating that children with dyslexia were slower than controls in all conditions. All data points are well fit by a single regression line.

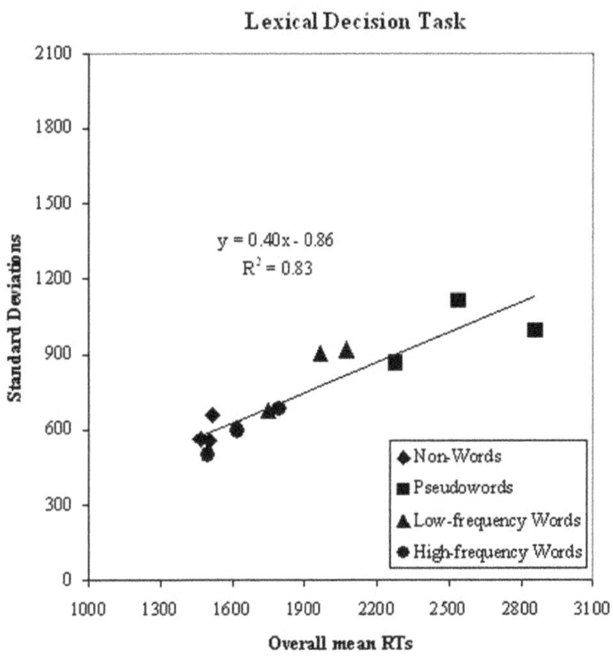

FIGURE 2 | Experiment 1. Condition means in the lexical decision task and standard deviation on the corresponding conditions are plotted against each other; data refer to the whole group of participants (dyslexic and control readers). Symbols are described in the figure; the three symbols per condition represent word lengths.

Due to the presence of a global factor in the data, in accordance with the RAM, the ANOVAs were performed also on *z*-transformed RTs in order to determine whether stimulus pronounceability, as well as frequency and lexicality, have a specific role in modulating group differences over and above the variance accounted for by the global factor.

Analysis of variance

Pronounceability. **Figure 3** shows the relevant means of the pronounceability effect in terms of errors, raw RTs and *z*-transformed RTs, separately for dyslexic and control readers.

The ANOVA on errors showed the main effect of pronounceability ($F_{(1,39)} = 45.9, p < 0.001$), with higher percentages of errors for pseudowords (15.8%) than non-words (3.4%). The length and group main effects as well as the interactions between these variables were all not significant (all *F*s about 1).

The ANOVAs on RTs showed the significance of the main effects of group ($F_{r(1,39)} = 28.0, p < 0.001$; the group effect is by definition nil in the analyses on *z*-transformed data), pronounceability ($F_{r(1,39)} = 100.1, p < 0.001$; $F_{z(1,39)} = 45.0, p < 0.001$), and length ($F_{r(2,78)} = 13.9, p < 0.001$; $F_{z(2,78)} = 8.9, p < 0.001$), with shorter RTs for control readers with respect to children with dyslexia (1671 vs. 2532 ms), for non-words compared to pseudowords (1546 vs. 2656 ms) and for shorter stimuli compared to longer stimuli (1938, 2101, and 2264 ms for 4-, 5-, and 6-letter stimuli, respectively). Pronounceability interacted with group in the raw data analysis ($F_{r(1,39)} = 5.1, p < 0.05$), but the effect was not significant in the analysis with *z*-transformed data ($F_{z(1,39)} = 1.9$, n.s.), indicating that the interaction with the raw data was due to the influence of over-additivity. All other interactions with the group factor were not significant. Pronounceability interacted with length ($F_{r(2,78)} = 8.5, p < 0.001$; $F_{z(2,78)} = 7.3, p < 0.001$): length effects were present for pseudowords (mean increase per letter = 301 ms), but not for non-words (mean increase per letter = 25 ms).

Frequency. The ANOVA on errors showed the significance of the main effects of group ($F_{(1,39)} = 23.8, p < 0.001$) and frequency ($F_{(1,39)} = 79.8, p < 0.001$), with higher percentages of errors for children with dyslexia (15.7%) than control (5.8%) readers and for low- (16.1%) than for high-frequency (5.4%) words. Frequency interacted with length ($F_{(2,78)} = 4.2, p < 0.05$), with a larger frequency effect for shorter than longer words: the difference between high- and low-frequency words was 13.9, 10.5, and 8.2% for 4-, 5-, and 6- letter words, respectively. Frequency also interacted with group ($F_{(1,39)} = 25.2, p < 0.001$), with a larger frequency effect for dyslexic than control readers (difference between low- and high-frequency words = 16.7 and 4.7% in the two groups, respectively), and a significant group difference for low- (15.9%, $p < 0.001$) but not high-frequency words (3.9%, n.s.).

The ANOVAs on RTs showed the significance of the main effects of group ($F_{r(1,39)} = 32.3, p < 0.001$), frequency ($F_{r(1,39)} = 65.9, p < 0.001$; $F_{z(1,39)} = 67.7, p < 0.0001$) and length ($F_{r(2,78)} = 20.6, p < 0.001$; $F_{z(2,78)} = 15.7, p < 0.001$), with shorter RTs for control readers than for children with dyslexia (1406 vs.

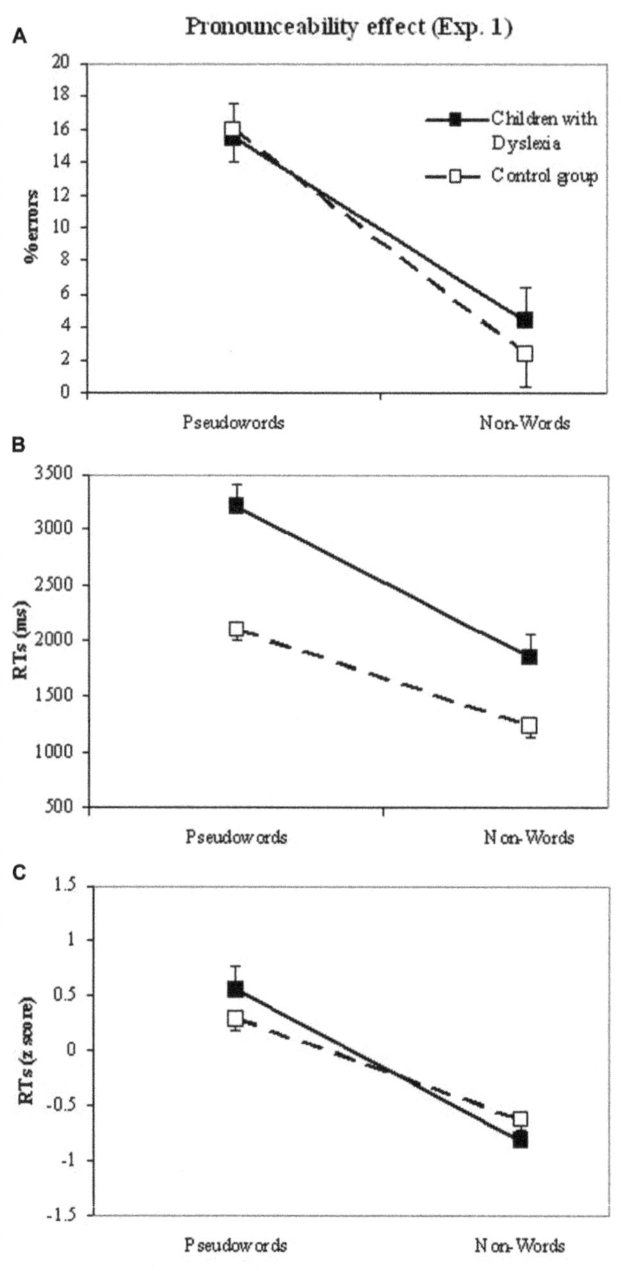

FIGURE 3 | Experiment 1. Performance on pseudowords and non-words (pronounceability effect) of dyslexic and control readers in the lexical decision task. The three plots report data in terms of errors (plot a), RT raw data (plot b) and *z*-transformed RT data (plot c).

2310 ms), for high- than low-frequency words (1695 vs. 2021 ms) and for shorter than longer words (1682, 1867, and 2024 ms for 4-, 5-, and 6-letter words, respectively). Group interacted with length and frequency in the raw data (respectively: $F_{r(2,78)} = 5.9$, $p < 0.01$; $F_{r(1,39)} = 17.3$, $p < 0.001$), but the interactions disappeared in the analysis on *z*-transformed data, indicating that they were due to over-additivity in the data. All other interactions with the group factor were not significant.

Lexicality. The ANOVA on errors showed the significance of the lexicality factor ($F_{(1,39)} = 5.2$, $p < 0.05$), with higher percentages of errors for pseudowords (15.8%) than words (10.8%). The group main effect approached significance ($F_{(1,39)} = 4.0$, $p = 0.053$) with a tendency for children with dyslexia to make more errors (15.6%) than control readers (10.9%). The lexicality by group interaction was significant ($F_{(1,39)} = 5.6$, $p < 0.05$) indicating the presence of a lexicality effect in control readers (difference between words and pseudowords = 10.1%, $p < 0.01$), but not for children with dyslexia (difference between words and pseudowords = –0.2%, n.s.). Groups had a similar performance in the case of pseudowords (16.0% of errors for control readers and 15.5% for children with dyslexia), while, in the case of words, control children produced fewer errors than children with dyslexia (5.8 vs. 15.7% respectively; $p < 0.05$).

The ANOVAs on RTs showed the main effects of group ($F_{r(1,39)} = 31.9$, $p < 0.001$), lexicality ($F_{r(1,39)} = 80.9$, $p < 0.001$; $F_{z(1,39)} = 1.79$, n.s.) and length ($F_{r(2,78)} = 23.6$, $p < 0.001$; $F_{z(2,78)} = 33.5$, $p < 0.001$). RTs were shorter for control (1753 ms) than dyslexic (2761 ms) readers, for words (1858 ms) than for pseudowords (2656 ms), and for shorter than longer stimuli (2019, 2261, and 2491 ms for 4-, 5-, and 6-letter stimuli, respectively). Group interacted with length ($F_{(2,78)} = 3.8$, $p < 0.05$), but the interaction disappeared in the *z* score analysis ($F_{z(2,78)} = 0.56$, n.s.), in keeping with the idea that it was due to over-additivity in the data. Group did not interact with lexicality (*F* about 1) in both raw and *z*-transformed data analyses, with similar lexicality effects for dyslexic and control readers (mean effect = 693 and 902 ms in the two groups, respectively).

DISCUSSION

Both groups of children were faster and more accurate at rejecting unpronounceable non-words than pronounceable pseudowords. This finding is consistent with previous studies (e.g., Holcomb and Neville, 1990; Forster et al., 2003; Ratcliff et al., 2004; Evans et al., 2012). As foils are more word-like (as in the case of pseudowords vs. non-words) the LDT proves more difficult. This might depend from several factors such as: (i) the increase of orthographic and phonological overlap between words and foils; (ii) foils producing more activation of similar words in the orthographic input lexicon; (iii) fewer sources of information being available to solve the task. In fact, for non-words, all procedures (semantic, lexical, and sub-lexical) are in favor of a "non-word" response (similarly to what happens for words for which all procedures are in favor of a "word" response). By contrast, in the case of pseudowords, the lexical and semantic routes favor a "no" response, while the sub-lexical procedure a "yes" response.

Pronounceability did not interact with group in the case of errors, indicating a similar pattern in the two groups. With regard to RTs, pronounceability interacted with group in the raw data, but not when over-additivity was taken into account in the *z*-transformed analysis: the larger effect of pronounceability among children with dyslexia was due to the presence of over-additivity in the data and the two groups showed a similar disadvantage in rejecting pseudowords compared to non-words.

Critically for the purpose of this study was to examine if performance on unpronounceable strings maps onto the global factor which accounts for the differences in performance between dyslexic and control readers. Consistent with the predictions of the RAM, condition means for the dyslexic group were linearly related to those of control readers. This pattern indicates that a single global factor accounts quite well for the slowness of children with dyslexia across all experimental conditions. Condition means for pronounceable pseudowords and unpronounceable non-words essentially showed the same result (i.e., they were all well fit by the same regression line). The children with dyslexia's impairment was evident when they had to process strings not only of pronounceable stimuli (such as words and pseudowords) but also unpronounceable stimuli (i.e., when they had to decide that a string of consonants was not a word), a deficit well accounted for by a single global factor.

Consistently with previous studies of Italian children with dyslexia using reading (e.g., Barca et al., 2006) and LDT (e.g., Marinelli et al., 2011), results highlighted a frequency effect among both children with dyslexia and control readers. This pattern indicates that children with dyslexia benefit from lexical activation in performing the task also in a highly regular orthography, such as Italian. The size of the frequency effect was actually larger for dyslexic than control readers but this difference disappeared when over-additivity was taken into account. The effect of lexicality did not interact with group in RTs (in both raw and z-transformed data), but only in errors, due to the absence of group differences for pseudowords (but only for words). Also this finding confirms previous evidence on Italian children with dyslexia (Zoccolotti et al., 2008).

EXPERIMENT 2

The first experiment supports the hypothesis that the difficulty in processing strings of letters accounts for a large amount of children with dyslexia's impairment, irrespective of the pronounceability of the strings. The second experiment, based on the Reicher–Wheeler paradigm, tests the ability of children with dyslexia to discriminate a target letter from a competitor in the context of strings of letters similar to the stimuli used with the LDT, i.e., words, pseudowords, and non-words. This task allows detecting the sensitivity of the two groups of children to use the prime pronounceability and lexical information to favor graphemic processing while responding is limited to the forced-choice discrimination of a target letter. If the difficulty of children with dyslexia is specifically linked to the ongoing simultaneous processing of a letter string (as in the LTD), no deficit should be present in this condition. At the same time, the possibility to test the sensitivity to context provides a further test of the distinction between a pre-lexical graphemic level and orthographic–phonological binding interpretation. Based on the orthographic–phonological binding hypothesis, the PSE (and the WSE) is expected for control children but not for children with dyslexia. Based on the letter string graphemic hypothesis, no difference in these effects is expected between the two groups of children.

METHOD

Participants

Same as Experiment 1.

Materials

Three groups of 4-letter stimuli were presented: 48 words (e.g., VISO, "face"), 48 pseudowords (e.g., VESI), and 48 letter strings (e.g., VRSN). Each derived pseudoword or non-word maintained two of letters from the original word.

All words had a CVCV structure and were selected from the Elementary lexicon by Marconi et al. (1993) and were high-frequency words ($M = 181/1$ million, $SD = 261$), with high rate of familiarity (Baldi and Traficante, 2005; $M = 6.8/7$ rating scale points, $SD = 0.08$), easy to recognize as real Italian words (wordlikeness; Baldi and Traficante, 2005; $M = 99.35\%$ of correct lexical judgment by adult proficient readers, $SD = 0.7$), and with a mean of four orthographic neighbors (Baldi and Traficante, 2005; $M = 3.9$, $SD = 1.7$).

Pseudowords were made from words, by changing the two vowels of the base stimulus. As mentioned above, letter strings were made of legal digrams, i.e., sequences of two letters that can be found in real Italian words. Target letters in first and third position were minimal phonological pairs (i.e., phoneme that differs for only one phonological feature, such as P–B, L–R, N–M) in order to emphasize the role of phonological decoding. The competitor letter was never in the multi-letter string and, in the case of substitution in the string, the competitor did not produce a lexical orthographic neighbor of target itself. The number of visually similar competitors (53%; e.g., P–B, N–M) was matched in each position. Target letters in second and fourth positions were vowels; so, in this case, it was not possible to use minimal pairs. Moreover, due to the ortho-phonotactic structure of Italian language, in which ending is always a vowel (a, e, i, o), stimuli with targets in fourth position were presented, but considered as fillers, because, in the case of words, they often produced other words, differently from the condition of consonant targets. However, they were presented to avoid children to focus their attention only on the first three letter positions.

For each stimulus type there were 16 targets in first, 16 in second, and 16 in third position, respectively, for a total of 48 stimuli per group and a grand-total of 144 stimuli. Filler stimuli with target in fourth position were eight in each group for a total of 24 stimuli. The overall number of stimuli was 168. Three blocks of stimuli were made, separated by a brief pause, in order to avoid attention decrease. Three blocks were matched for word frequency, familiarity, wordlikeness, and number of orthographic neighbors. In each block there was the same number of words, pseudowords, and non-words, equally distributed for each target letter position, avoiding that base-words and derived pseudowords and non-words were presented in the same block.

Procedure

Children made the task in a quiet room, sitting at about 54 cm from the screen. Stimuli were presented in Courier New, size 18 pt, in upper-case, in white foreground on gray background.

The trial sequence started with a get-ready display (500 ms), followed by the presentation of the multi-letter string (either word, pseudoword, or non-word) for 350 ms[1] and by the target letter display, which lasted until the forced-choice discrimination between target and competitor was made (**Figure 4**). The response was given by pressing one of two buttons of the keyboard: the "Up" button to choose the letter in the upper part of the display, the "Down" button for the letter in the bottom part. Correct responses were in half of the cases the "Up" choice.

Ten training stimuli were presented at the beginning of the experimental session. Three blocks of stimuli followed in a fully randomized order between blocks and within each block.

The program automatically recoded the responses of the participant; percentages of errors and RTs (only to correct responses) were used as dependent measures. Outliers (i.e., RTs 3 *SDs* below the mean) and invalid responses (i.e., responses faster than 250 ms or RTs not recorded correctly for technical problem) were excluded from the analysis.

RESULTS

Invalid responses and outliers were about 2.52% in children with dyslexia and 2.04% for typically developing children.

Analysis of global factor(s)

Before proceeding to the analysis of specific effects, we examined data for the possible presence of global components in the differences between the two groups of children (Faust et al., 1999). We first tested the prediction of a linear relationship between the means of the two groups for conditions that varied in overall information processing rate. Dyslexics' and skilled readers' condition means are plotted against each other in **Figure 5**, separately for each experimental condition in the Reicher–Wheeler paradigm.

Note that all data points are above the diagonal line (which indicates the benchmark for identical performance of the two groups); thus, children with dyslexia tended to be slower than typically developing readers across all conditions. In the Reicher–Wheeler paradigm, the percentage of variance accounted for by the regression line was moderate (59%) and the slope was less than unity ($b = 0.75$) indicating no over-additivity effect. Thus, in this case, the group differences appear entirely due to the intercept value (i.e., to a constant value).

Successively, we tested the prediction of a linear relationship between overall group means and standard deviation in the same conditions for the group as a whole. **Figure 6** reports the mean of the overall sample against the standard deviation for each corresponding experimental condition. The regression line was not very steep (0.35) and the percentage of variance explained for the conditions of the Reicher–Wheeler paradigm was moderate (69%).

As a global factor was not detected for the conditions of the Reicher–Wheeler paradigm, the *z* score transformation was not used and only standard RT analyses were carried out.

A mixed ANOVA with group (children with dyslexia vs. typically developing children) as a between-subject factor and context (words, pseudowords, and non-words) and position (first, second, and third position) as repeated measures was carried out on the percentages of errors in letter recognition. Significant interactions were explored with the *a posteriori* Tukey HSD.

The ANOVA showed the main effects of group ($F_{(1,39)} = 5.71$, $p < 0.05$), context ($F_{(2,78)} = 122.46$, $p < 0.001$), and position ($F_{(2,78)} = 26.75$, $p < 0.001$), as children with dyslexia made more letter recognition errors (17.9%) than typically developing children (10.6%), letters were recognized

[1]The exposure time of the multi-element strings was chosen on the basis of a previous pilot study, in which SOAs from 200 to 450 ms were tested. The duration of 350 ms was the time presentation that yielded 75% of accuracy in children with dyslexia.

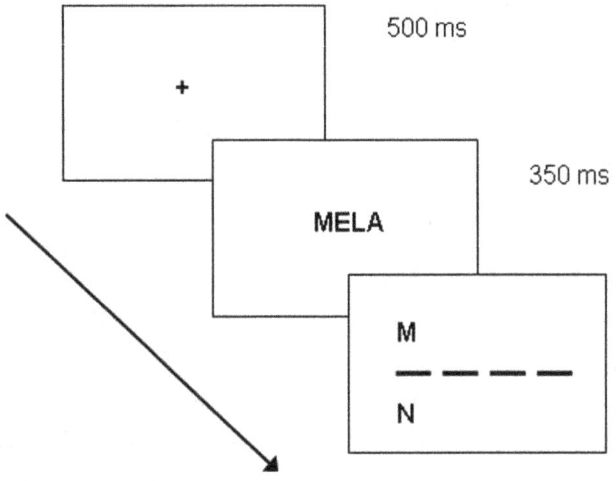

FIGURE 4 | Experiments 2. Time-course of the trial in the Reicher–Wheeler paradigm.

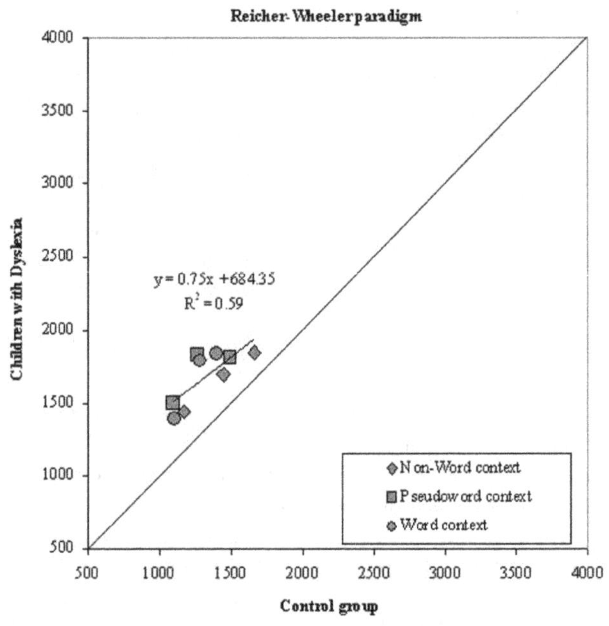

FIGURE 5 | Experiment 2. Dyslexics' condition means in the Reicher–Wheeler paradigm are plotted as a function of the control readers' means (symbols as described in the figure; the three symbols per condition represent letter positions). The diagonal line (slope = 1) represents equal RTs for dyslexic and control readers.

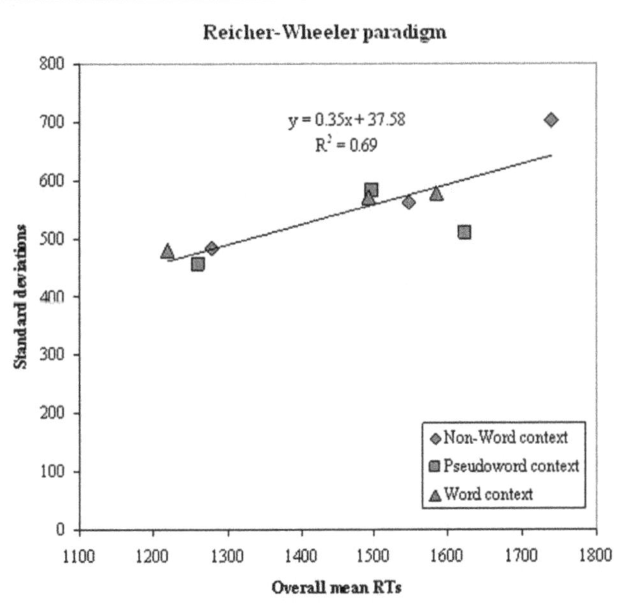

FIGURE 6 | Experiment 2. Condition means in the Reicher–Wheeler paradigm and standard deviation on the corresponding conditions are plotted against each other; data refer to the whole group of participants (dyslexic and control readers). Symbols are described in the figure; the three symbols per condition represent letter positions.

less well in the context of non-words (23.1%) than in the pseudoword (11.1%) and word (8.5%) contexts, and errors increased from first (9.5%) to second (15.3%) and third (18%) position.

All two-way interactions were significant. The group by context ($F_{(2,78)} = 16.26$, $p < 0.001$) indicated the presence of both the PSE (non-word context: 29.7%; pseudoword context: 14.3%; Tukey test: $p < 0.001$) and the WSE (word context: 9.5%; $p = 0.02$) in children with dyslexia. In typically developing children only the PSE reached the significance level (non-word context: 16.5%; pseudoword context: 7.8%; $p < 0.001$), while letter recognition errors in the word context (7.6%) did not differ from those in the pseudoword context. As for the group by position interaction ($F_{(2,78)} = 5.40$, $p < 0.01$), in children with dyslexia there was an increasing amount of letter recognition errors from the first (11.2%) to the second (18.9%) position ($p < 0.001$) and from the first to the third (23.5%) position ($p < 0.001$). For typically developing children the only significant difference was between the first (7.9%) and third position (12.4%; $p = 0.04$), while the second position (11.7%) did not differ from the others. The context by position interaction ($F_{(4,156)} = 9.36$, $p < 0.001$) indicated that in the non-word context there was an increasing amount of errors from the first (13.6%) to the second (25.2%) position ($p < 0.01$) and from the first to the third position (30.6%, $p < 0.01$), while the difference between the second and the third position did not reach significance level. In the pseudoword context, the first position was associated to a lower amount of errors (6.7%) than the third position (14%, $p = 0.02$), while percentage of errors in second position (12.5%) did not differ from the others. In the word context, letter recognition errors were low and similar in every position: 8.2% in first, 8.1% in second, and 9.3% in third position, respectively.

The ANOVA on RTs showed the main effects of group ($F_{(1,39)} = 6.01$, $p = 0.019$), and position ($F_{(2,78)} = 42.33$, $p < 0.0001$), with longer RTs for children with dyslexia (1681 ms) than typically developing children (1323 ms), and for letters in third (1676 ms) compared to second (1550 ms, $p < 0.001$) and first (1281 ms, $p < 0.01$) positions, but no main effect of context ($F_{(2,78)} = 2.19$, $p = 0.119$). Group interacted with context ($F_{(2,78)} = 4.24$, $p < 0.05$): there were smaller group differences in the non-word context (difference = 235 ms) compared to the pseudoword (difference = 427 ms) and word (difference = 411 ms) contexts. However, none of these differences reached significance at the *post hoc* analyses. In typically developing readers there was a detectable PSE (difference between the non-word and pseudoword contexts = 147 ms; $p = 0.05$), but no WSE (difference between pseudoword and word context = 15 ms). For children with dyslexia neither the PSE (difference between non-word and pseudoword contexts = −51 ms) nor the WSE (difference between pseudoword and word context = 39 ms) were present.

DISCUSSION

In the case of accuracy data, the results indicated a robust PSE in both groups of children, while the WSE was present only among children with dyslexia. Thus, accuracy in letter discrimination in young Italian readers, and remarkably also in children with dyslexia, was influenced by the ortho-phono-tactic regularity of the letter string. The results were generally less clear-cut in the case of RTs where the main effect of context was not significant. However, a significant PSE was detected in the case of typically developing children.

The present pattern of findings shares a number of similarities to the previous results on French children reported by Grainger et al. (2003). They found a large PSE effect in both dyslexic and reading-matched control children but no WSE for either group of children (while the WSE was present with the same type of stimulus materials in a group of adult readers). They proposed that the joint presence of PSE and absence of WSE favors a sublexical–orthographic interpretation, based on the greater familiarity of letter combinations in pseudowords compared to non-words. Pseudowords provide letter clusters which represent typical orthographic contexts for a given letter in a given position. Within this interpretation, children with dyslexia show a spared ability to use such sublexical–orthographic information to shape their performance in letter recognition. This pattern is at odds with the orthographic–phonological binding interpretation while it is consistent with a pre-lexical graphemic interpretation.

It is worth noting that in our study the facilitating role of lexical activation producing the WSE emerged just in children with dyslexia. This is in keeping with studies that found also in Italian, a language with a very consistent orthography, evidence of the activation of lexical representations in young readers. Several Italian studies (Barca et al., 2006; Paizi et al., 2013) showed lexical involvement in reading of children with and without dyslexia. The authors suggested that children might rely more on the lexical route when the non-lexical route is not automatized yet.

Results observed in children with dyslexia through the Reicher–Wheeler paradigm, in the present study, seem consistent with this hypothesis.

A general question addressed by Experiment 2 was whether performance in the Reicher–Wheeler paradigm would generate global group differences as reported for LDTs. The LDT used in Experiment 1 clearly yielded global differences in performance as previously reported with similar materials (e.g., Di Filippo et al., 2006; Paizi et al., 2013). In the case of the Reicher–Wheeler paradigm group differences were present although generally much smaller than those observed in the case of the LDT. Critically, when the RAM was applied to the time measures, group differences in RTs did not grow as a function of condition difficulty as expected in the case of a global factor (and an over-additivity effect). Indeed, the slope of the linear regression was smaller than unity. Thus, the small group differences were expressed by a constant value (intercept). How can this effect be explained? De Luca et al. (2010) noted that children with dyslexia have less practice with orthographic materials and proposed that this factor may be sufficient to explain the small deficit in letter-bigram tasks. The role of familiarity has been systematically tested by Valdois et al. (2012) who examined the performance on letter string, digit string, and color string processing; dyslexic children were impaired in the first two tasks but performed as controls in the color report task. This pattern is consistent with a familiarity account while is inconsistent with a visual-to-phonological-code interpretation. Overall, this pattern of findings is in keeping with the idea that a selective deficit in children with dyslexia is present only when the task requires the entire string of orthographic stimuli to be simultaneously processed. By contrast, it has repeatedly been shown that children with dyslexia are not (or minimally) impaired in the processing of single letters or bigrams (e.g., Bosse et al., 2007; Martelli et al., 2009; De Luca et al., 2010) or when the set of target letters is presented sequentially (Lassus-Sangosse et al., 2008).

GENERAL DISCUSSION

The results from the LDT in Experiment 1 indicated that a single global factor explained the performance with orthographic strings, independent from stimulus pronounceability, as well as frequency and lexicality. The children with dyslexia's impairment was evident (and of a comparable size) when they had to process strings, not only of pronounceable stimuli (such as words and pseudowords) as already reported in previous studies (e.g., Di Filippo et al., 2006; Marinelli et al., 2011; Paizi et al., 2013), but also of unpronounceable stimuli, a deficit well accounted for by the same global factor. Thus, the present study adds a new piece of information to the understanding of the nature of the global component affecting performance of children with dyslexia. Previous studies indicated that a single global factor explains the deficit of children with dyslexia in making lexical decisions and reading words and pseudowords, i.e., independent of word frequency and lexicality (Di Filippo et al., 2006; Zoccolotti et al., 2008; Marinelli et al., 2011), but not in dealing with pictorial stimuli (Di Filippo et al., 2006; Zoccolotti et al., 2008) or stimuli in the auditory modality (Marinelli et al., 2011). The present study adds to this picture that the global factor is independent not only from the lexical status of the stimulus, but also from the pronounceability of the letter string: when the over-additivity effect was controlled for, the deficit of children with dyslexia in the LDT was detectable, and of a comparable size, when rejecting pronounceable pseudowords or unpronounceable non-words. Therefore, the present findings are consistent with the proposal that an impairment in pre-lexical graphemic analysis (i.e., in forming a graphemic description of the letter string) is a core deficit in developmental dyslexia (Zoccolotti et al., 2008); by contrast, they do not support the idea that the deficit in dyslexia is due to an inability to bind orthographic and phonological information (Ziegler et al., 2010; van den Broeck and Geudens, 2012), not even in Italian, a language with very consistent orthography.

The RT data from the Reicher–Wheeler paradigm indicated that group differences in this task did not generate global differences between children with dyslexia and control readers. These data are generally in keeping with previous observations by De Luca et al. (2010) indicating that children with dyslexia were only mildly affected in tasks requiring the naming or matching of individual letters, bigrams or two-letter syllables and no over-additivity effect was present for these tasks. Therefore, it appears that the global factor accounting for the impairment of children with dyslexia is present when the child processes a (relatively long) string of letters in parallel, not when the task concerns isolated letters. The present results add to this picture that, even if the processing of a letter string is slowed down in these children, they can take advantage from the ortho-phono-tactic information deriving from such processing in discriminating a subsequent isolated target letter from a competitor; i.e., they showed a clear PSE (at least in the case of accuracy) in the Reicher–Wheeler paradigm. This differentiation can be appreciated most clearly by comparing the performance in making a lexical decision on pseudowords with that of recognizing a target letter in the presence of a pseudoword context. In the first condition, children with dyslexia were severely impaired in both accuracy and speed; in the second, they were more accurate than in the case of a four-letter non-word context (i.e., they had a PSE) and the group difference with typically developing children was quantitatively quite small. Therefore, when cognitive tasks (e.g., lexical decision, naming, semantic categorization, etc.) are to be applied to letter strings as a whole, children with dyslexia are in difficulty. On the contrary, when tasks involve isolated letter processing, also these children can make use of the ortho-phono-tactic information derived from a previously seen letter string. This spared ability appears inconsistent with the idea that children with dyslexia suffer from a selective deficit in orthographic–phonological binding. By contrast, it is consistent with a pre-lexical graphemic interpretation; according to this view, online simultaneous processing of multi-letter elements is generally impaired. However, if sufficient time is given for processing a letter string, children with dyslexia may effectively use its ortho-phono-tactic information to modulate orthographic processing of isolated letters.

The present findings are in keeping with the available information on the characteristics of the VWFA. Thus, neuroimaging studies indicate that the VWFA is activated not only by orthographically legal stimuli, such as words and pronounceable pseudowords, but also by illegal letter strings (e.g., Cohen et al.,

2002). There is clear evidence that event-related potentials (ERPs) recorded at posterior sites within the 150–250 ms time window at fronto-central, central, and temporo-parietal sites (typically in the form of the N200) are modulated by orthographic information. This finding is consistent with the hypothesis that the word form system analyzes visual linguistic stimuli at a pre-lexical level while information concerning lexical status and meaning is processed through additional neural systems (Bentin et al., 1999). In ERP studies, the VWFA does not generally differentiate between pseudowords and words (Hagoort et al., 1999) and no difference in N200 amplitude for these two stimuli is found (e.g., Tagamets et al., 2000 for a fMRI study). With regard to non-words, in some reports, the N200 was larger for non-words than for words (Compton et al., 1991; McCandliss et al., 1997), whereas, in others, the opposite pattern was reported (Cohen et al., 2000; Dehaene et al., 2002; Grossi and Coch, 2005) or no difference between legal and illegal orthographic letter strings was detected (e.g., Bentin et al., 1999). Some inconsistencies between studies may depend from differences in the experimental task. In fact, studies used several experimental paradigms: a letter search task (Ziegler et al., 1997), a letter-in-string identification task (Coch and Mitra, 2010), a LDT (Rosazza et al., 2009; Massol et al., 2011), and a rhyme judgment task (Bentin et al., 1999). In general, research comparing the processing of consonant strings and pronounceable pseudowords reports a divergence in the ERP waveforms as a function of target type only starting at around 200–250 ms post-target onset (Ziegler et al., 1997; Rosazza et al., 2009; Massol et al., 2012). This is in line with Grainger and Holcomb's (2009) proposal that processing up to around 200 ms post-target onset is largely identical for these two types of stimuli mostly involving parallel independent letter processing. Overall, it seems that the VWFA is activated by orthographic stimuli, independent from the lexical status or the pronounceability of the stimuli. In pinpointing a parallel between the present results and the characteristics of the VWFA it is important to observe that several studies reported a marked underactivation of this area in dyslexic individuals (for a review see Richlan et al., 2009).

A recent proposal which helps in placing the letter string deficit shown by children with dyslexia is the dual-route approach to orthographic processing proposed by Grainger and Ziegler (2011). According to this model, the initial mapping of visual features onto abstract letter identities operates in parallel and simultaneously for all the letters in the stimulus (e.g., see also Grainger and van Heuven, 2003; Adelman et al., 2010): "*...the alphabetic array codes for the presence of a given letter at a given location relative to eye fixation along the horizontal meridian. It does not say where a given letter is relative to other letters in the stimulus.... Thus, processing at the level of the alphabetic array is insensitive to orthographic regularity of letter string*" (Grainger and Ziegler, 2011, p. 2). The distinction between non-words, pseudowords, and words would turn out only later in the pathway, when the letter identity is referred to a specific position within the word (defined as a string of letters separated by spaces). Two different types of sublexical word-centerd orthographic representations develop in the reading acquisition process, according to the frequency of occurrence of given combinations of letters: (a) coarse-grained representations (open-bigram representations) that code for the presence of "ordered pairs of letters independently of their contiguity" (e.g., for the string WORD open-bigram representations are WO, WR, WD, OR, OD, RD); (b) fine-grained representations, that code for clusters of frequently co-occurring letter combination (e.g., multi-letter graphemes, syllables, morphemes, rhymes, etc.). The coarse-grained code offers diagnostic features for a rapid bottom-up activation of whole-word representations. However, for the correct identification of the target word is necessary the top-down activation from whole-word orthography level to coarse-grained orthography level. Only real words can activate this interactive process. In the case of pseudowords, the absence of top-down constrains makes the processing via the slower fine-grained route the only way to get disambiguating information on the letter string. Present findings highlight that the global factor explaining dyslexic's deficit is independent from pronounceability and lexicality of the stimulus. Then, according to the dual-route model (Grainger and Ziegler, 2011), it appears to indicate a deficit at an early stage of processing, i.e., when the initial mapping of visual features onto abstract letter identities is performed. In the subsequent stages of processing, children with dyslexia do not appreciably differ from control readers, as highlighted by the absence of the group by pronounceability or the group by lexicality interactions, once over-additivity was controlled for.

It is interesting to speculate on which mechanism may underlie the selective deficit in processing letter strings shown by children with dyslexia. As stated above, the deficit is confined to the simultaneous processing of several letters while it is much smaller or absent when the task regards single letters or bigrams (e.g., Bosse et al., 2007; Martelli et al., 2009; De Luca et al., 2010) or when the target letters are presented sequentially (Lassus-Sangosse et al., 2008). The present results indicate that children with dyslexia can actually use information from a letter string provided that responding is limited to a single letter presented subsequently to the letter string prime. Thus, the requirements for targets to be multiple and input to be simultaneous seem at the core of the group difference. One reasonable candidate to accommodate for these characteristics is visual crowding. Crowding refers to the decrease in recognizability of a letter surrounded by other letters placed closer than a critical distance (e.g., Pelli et al., 2004, 2007). In the case of letter strings, crowding affects the central letters much more than the initial or final ones (Bouma, 1970); thus, it seems to explain well the single-multiple dimension, as crowding between letters is only expected in the case of multiple displays and not with isolated letters. Further, as a perceptual mechanism, crowding can also easily account for the simultaneity requirement. Early evidence that children with dyslexia show enhanced sensitivity to crowding was presented by Bouma and Legein (1977). In the last years, several studies have shown results compatible with this interpretation (Spinelli et al., 2002; Martelli et al., 2009; Callens et al., 2013; Collis et al., 2013). For example, Martelli et al. (2009) found critical spacing to increase as a function of eccentricity with a greater proportionality for children with dyslexia than typically developing readers. Furthermore, particularly in the dyslexic group, degree of crowding appears to correlate significantly with reading (Martelli et al., 2009; Callens et al., 2013).

It is important to keep in mind that we examined the reading performance of children speaking a very regular language. It is well-known that orthographic consistency modulates the reliance on holistic reading processes (e.g., Ziegler et al., 2001; Ziegler and Goswami, 2006). For this reason, the present findings cannot be directly generalized to inconsistent orthographies, such as English or Hebrew. At any rate, it is interesting that several investigations based on children speaking French, a moderately irregular language, are in keeping with a visual-orthographic, as compared to a visual-to-phonology, impairment (e.g., Lobier et al., 2012a,b; Valdois et al., 2012). For example, Lobier et al. (2012a) reported that, in a visual categorization task with verbal and non-verbal stimuli, children with dyslexia were impaired independently of stimulus type, in keeping with the idea that the impairment was visual and not verbal. These findings suggest that a deficit in pre-lexical graphemic analysis may be present also in inconsistent orthographies, although this possibility certainly deserves further examination.

Overall, children with dyslexia were impaired when they had to process strings, not only of pronounceable stimuli but also of unpronounceable stimuli, a deficit well accounted for by a single global factor. By contrast, they were much less affected when they had to recognize an isolated letter (and no global factor was present) and could take advantage of a pronounceable context, effectively using the ortho-phono-tactic information derived from a previously seen letter string. Therefore, the present findings are in keeping with the proposal that an impairment in pre-lexical graphemic analysis is a core deficit in developmental dyslexia at least in a regular orthography (such as Italian) while they are inconsistent with the alternative view that orthographic–phonological binding may represent a proximal cause of dyslexia.

ACKNOWLEDGMENT

This work was supported by a grant from the Department of Health.

REFERENCES

Adelman, J. S., Marquis, S. J., and Sabatos-De Vito, M. G. (2010). Letters in words are read simultaneously, not in left-to-right sequence. *Psychol. Sci.* 21, 1799–1801. doi: 10.1177/0956797610387442

Angelelli, P., Notarnicola, A., Costabile, D., Marinelli, V., Judica, A., Zoccolotti, P., et al. (2008). *DDO Diagnosi dei Disturbi Disortografici in Età Evolutiva* [Diagnosis of Orthographic Deficits in Childhood]. Trento: Erickson.

Baldi, P. L., and Traficante, D. (2005). *EPOS 2. Elenco Delle Parole Ortograficamente Simili* [EPOS–2. List of Orthographically Similar Words]. Rome: Carocci.

Barca, L., Burani, C., Di Filippo, G., and Zoccolotti, P. (2006). Italian developmental dyslexic and proficient readers: where are the differences? *Brain Lang.* 98, 347–351. doi: 10.1016/j.bandl.2006.05.001

Baron, J., and Thurston, I. (1973). An analysis of the word superiority effect. *Cogn. Psychol.* 4, 207–228. doi: 10.1016/0010-0285(73)90012-1

Bentin, S., Mouchetant-Rostaing, Y., Giard, M. H., Echallier, J. F., and Pernier, J. (1999). ERP manifestations of processing printed words at different psycholinguistic levels: time-course and scalp distribution. *J. Cogn. Neurosci.* 11, 35–60. doi: 10.1162/089892999563373

Blau, V., Reithler, J., van Atteveldt, N., Seitz, J., Gerretsen, P., Goebel, R., et al. (2010). Deviant processing of letters and speech sounds as proximate cause of reading failure: a functional magnetic resonance imaging study of dyslexic children. *Brain* 133, 868–879. doi: 10.1093/brain/awp308

Blau, V., van Atteveldt, N., Ekkebus, M., Goebel, R., and Blomert, L. (2009). Reduced neural integration of letters and speech sounds links phonological and reading deficits in adult dyslexia. *Curr. Biol.* 19, 503–508. doi: 10.1016/j.cub.2009.01.065

Blomert, L. (2011). The neural signature of orthographic–phonological binding in successful and failing reading development. *Neuroimage* 57, 695–703. doi: 10.1016/j.neuroimage.2010.11.003

Bosse, M. L., Tainturier, M. J., and Valdois, S. (2007). Developmental dyslexia: the visual attention span deficit hypothesis. *Cognition* 104, 198–230. doi: 10.1016/j.cognition.2006.05.009

Bouma, H. (1970). Interaction effects in parafoveal letter recognition. *Nature* 226, 177–178. doi: 10.1038/226177a0

Bouma, H., and Legein, C. P. (1977). Foveal and parafoveal recognition of letters and words by dyslexics and by average readers. *Neuropsychologia* 15, 69–80. doi: 10.1016/0028-3932(77)90116-6

Cai, Q., Lavidor, M., Brysbaert, M., Paulignan, Y., and Nazir, T. (2008). Cerebral lateralization of frontal lobe language processes and lateralization of the posterior visual word processing system. *J. Cogn. Neurosci.* 20, 672–681. doi: 10.1162/jocn.2008.20043

Callens, M., Whitney, C., Tops, W., and Brysbaert, M. (2013). No deficiency in left-to-right processing of words in dyslexia but evidence for enhanced visual crowding. *Q. J. Exp. Psychol. (Hove)* 66, 1803–1817. doi: 10.1080/17470218.2013.766898

Coch, D., and Mitra, P. (2010). Word and pseudoword superiority effects reflected in the ERP waveform. *Brain Res.* 1329, 159–174. doi: 10.1016/j.brainres.2010.02.084

Cohen, L., Dehaene, S., Naccache, L., Lehericy, S., Dehaene-Lambertz, G., and Henaff, M. A. (2000). The visual word form area: spatial and temporal characterization of an initial stage of reading in normal subjects and posterior split-brain patients. *Brain* 123, 291–307. doi: 10.1093/brain/123.2.291

Cohen, L., Dehaene, S., Vinckier, F., Jobert, A., and Montavont, A. (2008). Reading normal and degraded words: contribution of the dorsal and ventral visual pathways. *Neuroimage* 40, 353–366. doi: 10.1016/j.neuroimage.2007.11.036

Cohen, L., Lehericy, S., Chochon, F., Lemer, C., Rivaud, S., and Dehaene, S. (2002). Language-specific tuning of visual cortex? Functional properties of the visual word-form area. *Brain* 125, 1054–1069. doi: 10.1093/brain/awf094

Collis, N. L., Kohnen, S., and Kinoshita, S. (2013). The role of visual spatial attention in adult developmental dyslexia. *Q. J. Exp. Psychol. (Hove)* 66, 245–260. doi: 10.1080/17470218.2012.705305

Compton, P. E., Grossbacher, P., Posner, M. I., and Tucker, D. M. (1991). A cognitive-anatomical approach to attention in lexical access. *J. Cogn. Neurosci.* 3, 304–312. doi: 10.1162/jocn.1991.3.4.304

Cornoldi, C., and Colpo, G. (1998). *Prove di Lettura MT Per La Scuola Elementare – 2. Manuale* [The MT Reading Test -2: User manual]. Florence: Organizzazioni Speciali.

Dehaene, S., Cohen, L., Sigman, M., and Vinckier, F. (2005). The neural code for written words: a proposal. *Trends Cogn. Sci.* 9, 335–341. doi: 10.1016/j.tics.2005.05.004

Dehaene, S., Jobert, A., Naccache, L., Ciuciu, P., Poline, J. B., Le Bihan, D., et al. (2004). Letter binding and invariant recognition of masked words. *Psychol. Sci.* 15, 307–313. doi: 10.1111/j.0956-7976.2004.00674.x

Dehaene, S., Le Clec', H. G., Poline, J. B., Le Bihan, D., and Cohen, L. (2002). The visual word form area: a prelexical representation of visual words in the fusiform gyrus. *Neuroreport* 13, 321–325. doi: 10.1097/00001756-200203040-00015

De Luca, M., Burani, C., Paizi, D., Spinelli, D., and Zoccolotti, P. (2010). Letter and letter-string processing in developmental dyslexia. *Cortex* 46, 1272–1283. doi: 10.1016/j.cortex.2009.06.007

Di Filippo, G., Brizzolara, D., Chilosi, A., De Luca, M., Judica, A., Pecini, C., et al. (2005). Rapid naming, but not cancellation speed or articulation rate, predicts reading in an orthographically regular language (Italian). *Child Neuropsychol.* 11, 349–361. doi: 10.1080/09297040490916947

Di Filippo, G., De Luca, M., Judica, A., Spinelli, D., and Zoccolotti, P. (2006). Lexicality and stimulus length effects in Italian dyslexics: role of the over-additivity effect. *Child Neuropsychol.* 12, 141–149. doi: 10.1080/09297040500346571

Dimitropoulou, M., Duñabeitia, J. A., and Carreiras, M. (2010). Influence of prime lexicality, frequency and pronounceability on the masked onset priming effect. *Q. J. Exp. Psychol. (Hove)* 63, 1813–1837. doi: 10.1080/17470210903540763

Evans, G. A. L., Lambon Ralph, M. A., and Woollams, A. M. (2012). What's in a word? A parametric study of semantic influences on visual word recognition. *Psychon. Bull. Rev.* 19, 325–331. doi: 10.3758/s13423-011-0213-7

Faust, M. E., Balota, D. A., Spieler, D. H., and Ferraro, F. R. (1999). Individual differences in information-processing rate and amount: implications for group differences in response latency. *Psychol. Bull.* 125, 777–799. doi: 10.1037/0033-2909.125.6.777

Forster, K. I., and Davis, C. (1991). The density constraint on form-priming in the naming task: interference effects from a masked prime. *J. Mem. Lang.* 30, 1–25. doi: 10.1016/0749-596X(91)90008-8

Forster, K. I., Mohan, K., and Hector, J. (2003). "The mechanisms of masked priming," in *Masked Priming. The State of the Art*, eds S. Kinoshita and S. J. Lupker (New York: Psychology Press), 3–37.

Grainger, J., Bouttevin, S., Truc, C., Bastien, M., and Ziegler, J. C. (2003). Word superiority, pseudoword superiority, and learning to read: a comparison of dyslexic and normal readers. *Brain Lang.* 87, 432–440. doi: 10.1016/S0093-934X(03)00145-7

Grainger, J., and Holcomb, P. J. (2009). Watching the word go by: on the time-course of component processes in visual word recognition. *Lang. Linguist. Compass* 3, 128–156. doi: 10.1111/j.1749-818X.2008.00121.x

Grainger, J., and Jacobs, A. M. (1994). A dual read-out model of word context effects in letter perception: further investigations of the word superiority effect. *J. Exp. Psychol. Hum. Percept. Perform.* 20, 1158–1176. doi: 10.1037/0096-1523.20.6.1158

Grainger, J., and Jacobs, A. M. (2005). Pseudoword context effects on letter perception: the role of word misperception. *Eur. J. Cogn. Psychol.* 17, 289–318. doi: 10.1080/09541440440000131

Grainger, J., and van Heuven, W. (2003). "Modeling letter position coding in printed word perception," in *The Mental Lexicon*, ed. P. Bonin (New York: Nova Science Publishers), 1–24.

Grainger, J., and Ziegler, J. C. (2011). A dual-route approach to orthographic processing. *Front. Psychol.* 2:54. doi: 10.3389/fpsyg.2011.00054

Greve, D. N., Van der Haegen, L., Cai, Q., Stufflebeam, S., Sabuncu, M. R., Fischl, B., et al. (2013). A surface-based analysis of language lateralization and cortical asymmetry. *J. Cogn. Neurosci.* 25, 1477–1492. doi: 10.1162/jocn_a_00405

Grossi, G., and Coch, D. (2005). Automatic word form processing in masked priming: an ERP study. *Psychophysiology* 42, 343–355. doi: 10.1111/j.1469-8986.2005.00286.x

Hagoort, P., Indefrey, P., Brown, C., Herzog, H., Steinmetz, H., and Seitz, R. J. (1999). The neural circuitry involved in the reading of German words and pseudowords: a PET study. *J. Cogn. Neurosci.* 11, 383–398. doi: 10.1162/089892999563490

Harm, M. W., and Seidenberg, M. S. (2004). Computing the meanings of words in reading: cooperative division of labor between visual and phonological processes. *Psychol. Rev.* 111, 662–720. doi: 10.1037/0033-295X.111.3.662

Holcomb, P. J., and Neville, H. J. (1990). Auditory and visual semantic priming in lexical decision: a comparison using event-related brain potentials. *Lang. Cogn. Process.* 50, 281–312. doi: 10.1080/01690969008407065

James, C. T. (1975). The role of semantic information in lexical decisions. *J. Exp. Psychol. Hum. Percept. Perform.* 104, 130–136. doi: 10.1037/0096-1523.1.2.130

Lassus-Sangosse, D., N'Guyen-Morel, M. A., and Valdois, S. (2008). Sequential or simultaneous visual processing deficit in developmental dyslexia? *Vision Res.* 48, 979–988. doi: 10.1016/j.visres.2008.01.025

Lobier, M., Zoubrinetzky, R., and Valdois, S. (2012a). The visual attention span deficit in dyslexia is visual and not verbal. *Cortex* 48, 768–773. doi: 10.1016/j.cortex.2011.09.003

Lobier, M., Peyrin, C., Le Bas, J. F., and Valdois, S. (2012b). Pre-orthographic character string processing and parietal cortex: a role for visual attention in reading? *Neuropsychologia* 50, 2195–2204. doi: 10.1016/j.neuropsychologia.2012.05.023

Marconi, L., Ott, M., Pesenti, E., Ratti, D., and Tavella, M. (1993). *Lessico Elementare: Dati Statistici Sull'italiano Scritto e Letto Dai Bambini Delle Elementari* [Elementary lexicon: Statistical Data for Italian Written and Spoken by Elementary School Children]. Bologna: Zanichelli.

Marinelli, C. V. (2010). *Reading and Spelling in Skilled and Dyslexic Children: A Cross-Linguistic Perspective.* Ph.D. thesis, Cognitive Neuroscience, Sapienza University of Rome, Rome.

Marinelli, C. V., Angelelli, P., Di Filippo, G., and Zoccolotti, P. (2011). Is developmental dyslexia modality specific? A visual-acoustic comparison on Italian dyslexics. *Neuropsychologia* 49, 1718–1729. doi: 10.1016/j.neuropsychologia.2011.02.050

Marsh, E. B., and Hillis, A. E. (2005). Cognitive and neural mechanisms underlying reading and naming: evidence from letter-by-letter reading and optic aphasia. *Neurocase* 11, 325–337. doi: 10.1080/13554790591006320

Martelli, M., Di Filippo, G., Spinelli, D., and Zoccolotti, P. (2009). Crowding, reading and developmental dyslexia. *J. Vis.* 9, 14, 14.1–14.18 doi: 10.1167/9.4.14

Martin, C. D., Nazir, T., Thierry, G., Paulignan, Y., and Démonet, J. F. (2006). Perceptual and lexical effects in letter identification: an event-related potential study of the word superiority effect. *Brain Res.* 1098, 153–160. doi: 10.1016/j.brainres.2006.04.097

Massol, S., Grainger, J., Midgley, K. J., and Holcomb, P. J. (2012). Masked repetition priming of letter-in-string identification: an ERP investigation. *Brain Res.* 1472, 74–88. doi: 10.1016/j.brainres.2012.07.018

Massol, S., Midgley, K. J., Holcomb, P. J., and Grainger, J. (2011). When less is more: feedback, priming, and the pseudoword superiority effect. *Brain Res.* 1386, 153–164. doi: 10.1016/j.brainres.2011.02.050

McCandliss, B. D., Posner, M. I., and Givon, T. (1997). Brain plasticity in learning visual words. *Cogn. Psychol.* 33, 88–110. doi: 10.1006/cogp.1997.0661

Paizi, D., De Luca, M., Zoccolotti, P., and Burani, C. (2013). A comprehensive evaluation of lexical reading in Italian developmental dyslexics. *J. Res. Read.* 36, 303–329. doi: 10.1111/j.1467-9817.2011.01504.x

Pelli, D. G., Palomares, M., and Majaj, N. J. (2004). Crowding is unlike ordinary masking: distiguishing feature integration from detection. *J. Vis.* 4, 1136–1169. doi: 10.1167/4.12.12

Pelli, D. G., Tillman, K. A., Freeman, J., Su, M., Berger, T. D., and Majaj, N. J. (2007). Crowding and eccentricity determine reading rate. *J. Vis.* 7, 1–36. doi: 10.1167/7.2.20

Pruneti, C. A., Fenu, A., Freschi, G., Rota, S., Cocci, D., Marchionni, M., et al. (1996). *Aggiornamento alla Standardizzazione Italiana del Test Delle Matrici Progressive Colorate di Raven (CPM)* [Update of the Italian standardization of Raven's Coloured Progressive Matrices]. *Boll. Psicol. Appl.* 217, 51–57.

Ratcliff, R., Gomez, P., and McKoon, G. (2004). A diffusion model account of the lexical decision task. *Psychol. Rev.* 111, 159–182. doi: 10.1037/0033-295X.111.1.159

Reicher, G. M. (1969). Perceptual recognition as a function of meaningfulness of stimulus material. *J. Exp. Psychol.* 81, 274–280. doi: 10.1037/h0027768

Richlan, F., Kronbichler, M., and Wimmer, H. (2009). Functional abnormalities in the dyslexic brain: a quantitative meta-analysis of neuroimaging studies. *Hum. Brain Mapp.* 30, 3299–3308. doi: 10.1002/hbm.20752

Rosazza, C., Cai, Q., Minati, L., Paulignan, Y., and Nazir, T. A. (2009). Early involvement of dorsal and ventral pathways in visual word recognition: an ERP study. *Brain Res.* 1272, 3–44. doi: 10.1016/j.brainres.2009.03.033

Spinelli, D., De Luca, M., Judica, A., and Zoccolotti, P. (2002). Crowding effects on word identification in developmental dyslexia. *Cortex* 38, 179–200.

Spoehr, K. T., and Smith, E. E. (1975). The role of orthographic and phonotactic rules in perceiving letter patterns. *J. Exp. Psychol. Hum. Percept. Perform.* 1, 21–34. doi: 10.1037/0096-1523.1.1.21

Tagamets, M. A., Novick, J. M., Chalmers, M. L., and Friedman, R. B. (2000). A parametric approach to orthographic processing in the brain: an fMRI study. *J. Cogn. Neurosci.* 12, 281–297. doi: 10.1162/089892900562101

Valdois, S., Lassus Sangosse, D., and Lobier, M. (2012). Impaired letter-string processing in developmental dyslexia: what visual-to-phonology code mapping disorder? *Dyslexia* 18, 77–93. doi: 10.1002/dys.1437

van den Broeck, W., and Geudens, A. (2012). Old and new ways to study characteristics of reading disability: the case of the nonword-reading deficit. *Cogn. Psychol.* 65, 414–456. doi: 10.1016/j.cogpsych.2012.06.003

van der Mark, S., Klaver, P., Bucher, K., Maurer, U., Schulz, E., Brem, S., et al. (2011). The left occipitotemporal system in reading: disruption of focal fMRI connectivity to left inferior frontal and inferior parietal language areas in children with dyslexia. *Neuroimage* 54, 2426–2436. doi: 10.1016/j.neuroimage.2010.10.002

Vinckier, F., Dehaene, S., Jobert, A., Dubus, J. P., Sigman, M., and Cohen, L. (2007). Hierarchical coding of letter strings in the ventral stream: dissecting the inner organization of the visual word-form system. *Neuron* 55, 143–156. doi: 10.1016/j.neuron.2007.05.031

Wechsler, D. (2006). "WISC-III Wechsler Intelligence Scale for Children–III," in *Italian Adaptation*, eds A. Orsini and L. Picone (Florence: O. S. Organizzazioni Speciali).

Wheeler, D. D. (1970). Processes in word recognition. *Cogn. Psychol.* 1, 59–85. doi: 10.1016/0010-0285(70)90005-8

Ziegler, J. C., Besson, M., Jacobs, A. M., Nazir, T. A., and Carr, T. H. (1997). Word, pseudoword, and nonword processing: a multitask comparison using event-related potentials. *J. Cogn. Neurosci.* 9, 758–775. doi: 10.1162/jocn.1997.9.6.758

Ziegler, J. C., and Goswami, U. (2006). Becoming literate in different languages: similar problems, different solutions. *Dev. Sci.* 9, 429–436. doi: 10.1111/j.1467-7687.2006.00509.x

Ziegler, J. C., Pech-Georgel, C., Dufau, S., and Grainger, J. (2010). Rapid processing of letters, digits and symbols: what purely visual-attentional deficit in developmental dyslexia? *Dev. Sci.* 13, F8–F14. doi: 10.1111/j.1467-7687.2010.00983.x

Ziegler, J. C., Perry, C., Jacobs, A. M., and Braun, M. (2001). Identical words are read differently in different languages. *Psychol. Sci.* 12, 379–384. doi: 10.1111/1467-9280.00370

Zoccolotti, P., De Luca, M., Di Filippo, G., Judica, A., and Spinelli, D. (2005). *Prova di Lettura di Parole e Non Parole* [*Word and Non-word Reading test*]. Rome: IRCCS Fondazione Santa Lucia.

Zoccolotti, P., De Luca, M., Judica, A., and Spinelli, D. (2008). Isolating global and specific factors in developmental dyslexia: a study based on the rate and amount model (RAM). *Exp. Brain Res.* 186, 551–560. doi: 10.1007/s00221-007-1257-9

9

Neural entrainment to rhythmic speech in children with developmental dyslexia

Alan J. Power*, Natasha Mead, Lisa Barnes and Usha Goswami

Department of Psychology, Centre for Neuroscience in Education, University of Cambridge, Cambridgeshire, UK

Correspondence:
Alan J. Power, Department of Psychology, Centre for Neuroscience in Education, University of Cambridge, Downing Street, CB23EB Cambridgeshire, UK
e-mail: ajp218@cam.ac.uk

A rhythmic paradigm based on repetition of the syllable "ba" was used to study auditory, visual, and audio-visual oscillatory entrainment to speech in children with and without dyslexia using EEG. Children pressed a button whenever they identified a delay in the isochronous stimulus delivery (500 ms; 2 Hz delta band rate). Response power, strength of entrainment and preferred phase of entrainment in the delta and theta frequency bands were compared between groups. The quality of stimulus representation was also measured using cross-correlation of the stimulus envelope with the neural response. The data showed a significant group difference in the preferred phase of entrainment in the delta band in response to the auditory and audio-visual stimulus streams. A different preferred phase has significant implications for the quality of speech information that is encoded neurally, as it implies enhanced neuronal processing (phase alignment) at less informative temporal points in the incoming signal. Consistent with this possibility, the cross-correlogram analysis revealed superior stimulus representation by the control children, who showed a trend for larger peak *r*-values and significantly later lags in peak *r*-values compared to participants with dyslexia. Significant relationships between both peak *r*-values and peak lags were found with behavioral measures of reading. The data indicate that the auditory temporal reference frame for speech processing is atypical in developmental dyslexia, with low frequency (delta) oscillations entraining to a different phase of the rhythmic syllabic input. This would affect the quality of encoding of speech, and could underlie the cognitive impairments in phonological representation that are the behavioral hallmark of this developmental disorder across languages.

Keywords: neural entrainment, developmental dyslexia, low frequency oscillations, temporal sampling, audio-visual

INTRODUCTION

Temporal coding is a critical aspect of speech processing and is fundamental to phonological representation, the mental representation of the sound structure of human languages. Temporal coding is thought to be accomplished in part by the synchronous activity of networks of neurons in auditory cortex that align their endogenous oscillations at different preferred rates with matching temporal information in the acoustic speech signal (Poeppel, 2003; Lakatos et al., 2008; Giraud and Poeppel, 2012). Speech involves auditory, visual and motor modalities, and both auditory and visual information in speech unfold over multiple timescales. Accordingly, oscillating networks of neurons in auditory *and visual* cortices are thought to "phase lock" or "phase align" their ongoing activity with matching modulation rates in the input (Luo et al., 2010). For human speech, the visuo-spatial information generated by face, cheek and mouth movements is temporally predictive of the production of speech sounds, and may "reset" auditory cortex to the optimal phase for processing succeeding vocalizations (Schroeder et al., 2008). *Multi-time resolution models* (MTRMs) of speech processing capitalize on these neurophysiological processes (e.g., Poeppel, 2003; Ghitza and Greenberg, 2009), and argue that the neural entrainment of these oscillatory networks is occurring at multiple temporal rates in both visual and auditory cortices, with hierarchical and interdependent cross-modal phase interactions, resulting in a coherent representation of the signal and enabling communication between human listeners.

A large literature suggests that temporal coding in both the auditory and visual modalities may be atypical in individuals with developmental dyslexia, a specific learning difficulty affecting reading and spelling that affects approximately 7% of children across languages (e.g., Witton et al., 1998; Snowling et al., 2000; Ziegler and Goswami, 2005; Lallier et al., 2009; Facoetti et al., 2010; Goswami et al., 2011; Hämäläinen et al., 2012a). Developmental dyslexia is not due to low intelligence, poor educational opportunities, or overt sensory or neurological damage. The primary cognitive difficulty found in dyslexia across languages is a difficulty in the accurate neural representation of phonology, the sound structure of words. Children with dyslexia are poorer than age- and reading-level matched controls at identifying and manipulating phonological units in words, for example, they are poorer at counting *syllables* (e.g., 3 syllables in "popsicle"), at identifying *rhymes* (e.g., "cat" and "hat" rhyme, "cat" and "hot" do not rhyme), and at recognizing shared *phonemes* (the smallest speech sounds that change meaning, e.g., "clip" and "quip" share the initial phoneme,/k/; see Ziegler and Goswami,

2005, for review). Children with dyslexia are also significantly impaired compared to younger reading level controls in prosodic awareness tasks, such as tasks requiring the identification of syllable stress (Goswami et al., 2013). These difficulties with phonology appear to precede learning to read (Lyytinen et al., 2001), and are also found in children with dyslexia who are learning non-alphabetic scripts. For example, Japanese Kana uses orthographic characters that represent syllables rather than phonemes, and Japanese children with dyslexia find syllable reversal tasks difficult (Kobayashi et al., 2003). Given the importance of neuronal oscillations for speech processing as revealed by multi-time resolution models, it is plausible that the phonological deficits found in dyslexia across languages could be related to impaired or atypical oscillatory mechanisms at one or more temporal rates in either auditory cortex, visual cortex or during audio-visual integration.

Accordingly, and building on the prior work noted above on MTRMs for speech processing, a "temporal sampling" framework (TSF) for developmental dyslexia has been proposed. The TSF suggests that the phonological deficit found in dyslexia across languages might be due in part to impaired or functionally atypical entrainment mechanisms for phonology in auditory cortex, particularly oscillations at the slower temporal rates (theta and delta) that are relevant to syllabic and prosodic processing (Goswami, 2011). As syllable awareness in children develops before phonological awareness of rhymes and phonemes (Ziegler and Goswami, 2005), and as syllables are the primary processing unit in all human languages (Greenberg et al., 2003), atypical entrainment mechanisms related to syllabic phonology would have effects throughout the phonological system in all languages, consequently affecting the phonological representation of smaller units such as rhymes and phonemes. According to multi-time resolution models of speech processing (Giraud and Poeppel, 2012), identification of phonetic segments is related to faster temporal modulations (gamma rate, 30–80 Hz), identification of syllables is related to slower modulations at the theta rate (4–10 Hz), and information relating to syllable stress and prosodic patterning is related to modulations at the delta rate (1.5–4 Hz). Here we provide the first direct test of the TSF with children with developmental dyslexia, utilizing a rhythmic speech paradigm previously developed for typically-developing children (Power et al., 2012b) to measure oscillatory entrainment to phonological information in dyslexia.

Oscillatory entrainment in humans has so far been measured by EEG in rhythmic paradigms, as by hypothesis endogenous oscillations should phase-reset their activity to the rhythmic information in the input, synchronizing cell activity so that peaks in excitation co-occur with stimulus delivery, thereby enhancing neural processing (Lakatos et al., 2005; Canolty et al., 2006). Whereas early studies of oscillatory entrainment in EEG utilized rhythmic streams of non-speech stimuli, such as tones or flashes of light (Lakatos et al., 2008; Stefanics et al., 2010; Gomez-Ramirez et al., 2011), we (Power et al., 2012b) designed a *speech* paradigm based on rhythmic repetition of the syllable "ba" by a female speaker. The repetition rate was 2 Hz, and participating 13-year-old children either saw a "talking head" so that both visual and auditory information was present (audio-visual or AV condition), saw the talking head without sound, so that only visual information was present (visual [V] condition), or heard the stimulus stream in the absence of visual stimulation (auditory [A] condition). The children were asked to detect occasional rhythmic violations in each condition (A, V, AV), when the syllable was slightly late and therefore out of time. We found significant entrainment at the stimulation rate (delta, 2 Hz) in all conditions, and also significant entrainment at the *theta* rate in the auditory and AV conditions. Consistent with the predictions of MTRMs of speech processing, therefore, theta entrainment was important in processing this syllabic input. Furthermore, individual differences in the strength of theta entrainment (measured by inter-trial coherence or phase consistency) were related to measures of phonological processing and reading in this typically-developing child sample. Higher phase consistency was associated with higher behavioral performance. Further, the preferred phase of auditory entrainment was altered by congruent visual information (AV condition), suggesting that visual speech information modulated auditory oscillations to the optimal phase for speech processing in these 13-year-old participants, consistent with Schroeder et al. (2008).

The TSF proposes that auditory oscillatory entrainment to phonological information at both delta and theta rates may by atypical in developmental dyslexia, and that atypical auditory entrainment might also have consequences for visual oscillatory entrainment to speech via cross-modal and cross-frequency phase alignment. The rhythmic speech paradigm that we developed (Power et al., 2012b) can also be used to study entrainment in children with dyslexia. Accordingly, we recruited a group of children with dyslexia, and matched their performance as a group to that of a sub-set of the typically-developing children who had participated in our previous study. The TSF enables a number of plausible predictions with respect to our dyslexic group. The simplest possibility is that the children with dyslexia should show significantly less entrainment to the auditory stimulus stream, at both delta and theta rates (reduced inter-trial coherence or phase consistency). Once cross-modal information is available, however, it is plausible that children with dyslexia may show strength of entrainment that is *equivalent* to typically-developing children (as visual information may modulate auditory oscillations to the optimal phase for speech processing). Indeed, children with dyslexia may rely *more* on visual speech information than typically-developing children, in order to *compensate* for their impaired auditory processing skills. A recent study of audio-visual processing of noise vocoded speech by adults with and without dyslexia produced some evidence for atypical visual processing of low frequency modulations in those with dyslexia in a non-rhythmic paradigm (Megnin-Viggars and Goswami, 2013). Nevertheless, the same study also produced some data suggestive of visual compensation. Other studies of rhythmic entrainment in adults with dyslexia have focused on the auditory modality.

In one relevant study utilizing MEG, we (Hämäläinen et al., 2012b) played amplitude-modulated white noise at 4 temporal rates (2, 4, 10, 20 Hz) to adults with and without dyslexia in an unattended listening paradigm (the participants were watching a silent video). On the basis of the TSF, we expected group differences in neuronal oscillatory entrainment at the slower AM rates (2 Hz, 4 Hz). The data showed significantly less entrainment by the participants with dyslexia in right hemisphere auditory networks to the 2 Hz rate only. There was also significantly weaker entrainment overall (adding across modulation rates) in the right hemisphere for those with dyslexia. As the right hemisphere is thought to prefer slower temporal rates (delta, theta, see Poeppel et al., 2008), these results were considered to be consistent with the TSF. Hamalainen et al. also found that the dyslexic group also showed significantly stronger entrainment to the 10 Hz rate in the *left* hemisphere, a finding which was not predicted. This could indicate compensatory entrainment at faster temporal rates. In a second study investigating dyslexia using EEG and an attended paradigm, we (Soltesz et al., 2013) compared rhythmic entrainment in adults with and without dyslexia to a tone stream delivered at 2 Hz (Soltesz et al., 2013). The task was to press a button whenever white noise replaced a tone in the stream, as in a standard auditory oddball paradigm. In this study, the strength of entrainment as measured by inter-trial coherence (ITC) was significantly reduced in the participants with dyslexia, even though they were as fast and as accurate as the controls in the button-press paradigm. Whereas response time in controls was significantly related to the instantaneous phase of the delta oscillation, with faster responses in the rising phase of the oscillation, participants with dyslexia showed no such relationship. This suggests that the oscillatory function of low frequency brain rhythms may be atypical in dyslexia (Soltesz et al., 2013).

However, an alternative oscillatory framework for dyslexia has been developed by Giraud and her colleagues, who have proposed that a single auditory anomaly, phonemic sampling in left auditory cortex, accounts for the three major aspects of impaired phonological processing in dyslexia (which are impaired phonological awareness, impaired rapid automatized naming [RAN], and impaired phonological memory, see Lehongre et al., 2011; Giraud and Poeppel, 2012). In a passive listening study with adults with dyslexia using MEG, Lehongre et al. (2011) presented amplitude-modulated white noise at rates that increased incrementally from 10 to 80 Hz, and measured the auditory steady state response (ASSR) while participants watched a silent video. Of particular theoretical interest were oscillations in the low gamma band (25–35 Hz), thought to reflect optimal phonemic encoding. Both dyslexic and control participants showed significant phase locking as measured by the ASSR, but hemispheric differences were found between groups, with left-dominant entrainment shown by the control participants only. When faster temporal rates were considered (>50 Hz), then those with dyslexia showed stronger entrainment bilaterally than controls. Lehongre and colleagues then computed the degree of leftward asymmetry shown by each participant at the low gamma rate for ASSR power, and correlated this measure with the phonological measures. Significant relations with phonological processing (a global construct measure made up of Spoonerisms, digit span and nonword repetition) and rapid naming were found when the dyslexics were considered alone, but not for controls alone nor for the total sample. Lehongre et al. (2011) argued that their data suggested a focal (left-lateralized) impairment of selective extraction and encoding of phonemic information, which would not be expected to affect global sensitivity to amplitude modulation. Phonemic oversampling was also proposed by Giraud and Poeppel (2012) to underpin the phonological "deficit" in dyslexia. The oscillatory nesting observed between theta/delta phase and gamma power (Schroeder and Lakatos, 2009; Canolty and Knight, 2010) was argued by Lehongre et al. (2011) to provide a means by which information at the phonemic (gamma) rate is integrated at the syllabic rate.

In the only neuroimaging study of which we are aware to *compare* slow rate (<10 Hz) and faster rate (20 Hz) oscillatory entrainment in dyslexia, the auditory steady state response was recorded to speech-weighted noise stimuli amplitude modulated at either 4 Hz, 20 Hz or 80 Hz (Poelmans et al., 2012). Participants were dyslexic and control adults, the task was passive listening, and EEG recordings were analyzed at parietal and mastoid electrodes only. No group differences were found for the ASSRs to the 80 Hz and 4 Hz stimuli, but a significant group × laterality effect was found for the 20 Hz stimulus. For 20 Hz AM noise, dyslexic adults showed less power at left hemisphere electrodes compared to controls. Phase coherence *between and within hemispheres* was also computed, and a main effect of group was found at the 20 Hz rate for both measures. Adults with dyslexia demonstrated lower inter- and intra-hemispheric coherence than controls. Note that this phase measure is not related to the stimulus *per se*, rather the between-hemisphere results show that the relationship between the phase pattern at the selected electrodes is less similar for participants with dyslexia. As the 20 Hz rate yielded the only significant group differences, Poelmans et al. (2012) concluded that cortical processing of phoneme-rate modulations was impaired in dyslexia.

However, a series of studies with dyslexic adults based on nursery rhymes (rhythmically-produced speech) by Leong and Goswami (2013) has compared rhythmic entrainment in dyslexia at slower and faster rates using behavioral measures (tapping or speaking to a beat). Using modeling developed by Leong (2012), these nursery rhyme studies explored the role of *phase relations* between amplitude modulation at different rates in the speech signal in the perception and production of rhythmic speech. Building on MTRMs of speech processing and the oscillatory hierarchy (Poeppel, 2003; Schroeder et al., 2008; Giraud and Poeppel, 2012), Leong (2012) modeled entrainment to different AM rates in the speech signal using an *amplitude modulation phase hierarchy* (AMPH) approach. Leong assumed that the modulation hierarchy within the speech signal followed the oscillatory hierarchy, with the slowest rates *highest* in the hierarchy. In Leong's models, the slower rates (delta and theta) hence temporally constrain entrainment at the faster rates, such as gamma (for detail regarding these novel AMPH models of the speech signal, see Leong, 2012). Leong and Goswami (2013) demonstrated that participants used the *phase relationship* between delta- and theta-rate AMs (2 Hz and 4 Hz AM rates) to calibrate their rhythmic behavior. Importantly, Leong and Goswami found that adults with dyslexia showed an *earlier* preferred phase angle for theta entrainment compared to control participants. Individual differences in both theta and delta preferred AM phase were correlated with phonological awareness in a Spoonerisms task, and with reading development.

Concerning rhythmic speech *production* (measured by asking participants to speak rhythmically in time with a metronome beat at 2 Hz), Leong and Goswami (2013) reported that the two groups showed equivalent *strength* of entrainment in terms of internal phase locking between delta- and theta-AMs, and between theta- and gamma-AMs (stressed syllable, syllable and phoneme rates, respectively). However, the participants with dyslexia again preferred a different phase alignment of the AMs conveying syllable and phoneme information, respectively (theta- and gamma-AMs). A difference in phase locking *angle* implies a difference in how speech information at different temporal rates is bound together in the final speech percept (Poeppel, 2003). Leong and Goswami (2013) argued that the significant difference in phase-locking angle between syllable- and phoneme-relevant information in speech was consistent with the large behavioral database indicating that phonological information is represented *differently* in the dyslexic mental lexicon.

In the current study, participants are also perceiving rhythmic speech in an attended paradigm, and neuronal oscillatory entrainment can be measured *directly* at both the delta and theta rates of AM (whereas when tapping and speaking in time are the dependent measures, the measurement of entrainment is necessarily indirect because of additional motor demands). Given the preferred phase angle differences found in the studies with adults (Leong and Goswami, 2013), it is therefore possible that the preferred *phase of entrainment* will differ between dyslexic and control children in the current study, at least in the auditory condition, for either delta or theta phase (or both). The phase of entrainment of neuronal oscillation relative to a presented stimulus has been shown to be central to stimulus processing. It has been shown that oscillations entrain to stimuli at differing preferred phases (anti-phase, in fact) depending on whether they are being attended to or being ignored (Lakatos et al., 2008; Besle et al., 2011; Horton et al., 2013). Furthermore, the phase of pre-stimulus delta activity has been shown to be related to reaction times in a task where the target probability was manipulated, suggesting that efficiency of stimulus processing is related to oscillatory phase (Stefanics et al., 2010). EEG phase patterns have also been shown to reflect the selectivity of neural firing with single neurons more likely to fire at specific phases in response to an auditory stimulus (Ng et al., 2013). *These studies suggest that there is an optimal or preferred phase of entrainment which is necessary for accurate and efficient stimulus processing.* If preferred delta and/or theta phase is different for participants with dyslexia, then speech units such as syllables will occur at a sub-optimal phase, and will not be processed optimally. The result will be a degraded representation or encoding of the speech stimulus.

In order to see whether such potential differences in preferred phase would be related to the quality of children's phonological representations, two strategies were employed. First, a phoneme deletion task was administered to participants as a measure of phonological awareness, and was correlated with the entrainment measures. Secondly, a correlogram approach was used to measure the fidelity of the neuronal representation to the envelope information in the speech signal. The speech stimulus is a stream of syllables repeated rhythmically enabling the stimulus envelope to be cross-correlated with the envelope of the averaged neural response. The peak *r*-value from the cross-correlogram gives us an estimate of the strength of stimulus representation in the EEG. The lag at which this peak occurs gives a measure of the timing of stimulus envelope processing (this is a similar approach to Abrams et al., 2009). If the brain is representing a speech syllable with high fidelity but at a different temporal phase with respect to entrainment to the ongoing stimulus, group differences in peak lag would occur, which would again have implications for the overall quality of the phonological representation via the binding together of temporal information at different rates in the speech signal.

To summarize, phase values (entrainment strength or ITC and phase angle), peak *r*-values (correlation strength), and peak lag values (temporal phase measure) might be expected to differ between dyslexic and control participants at delta and theta rates according to the TSF. According to the model based on anomalous temporal sampling at the low gamma rate proposed by Lehongre and colleagues, no such differences might be expected. In contrast, it has also been proposed that dyslexic children are developing high-quality mental representations of speech, and that the cognitive "phonological deficit" found in dyslexia arises as a result of problems in *accessing* the mental lexicon (see Ramus and Szenkovits, 2008). If the neural phonological representations themselves are precise, then on this "intact representations" hypothesis no group differences in these neural measures of representational quality would be expected.

MATERIALS AND METHODS

PARTICIPANTS

We studied 21 typically-developing children and 11 children with a history of developmental dyslexia (mean ages of 165.57 ± 12.71 months and 166.73 ± 13.72 months, respectively). All children were taking part in a longitudinal behavioral study of auditory processing (Goswami et al., 2011). All participants and their guardians gave informed consent for EEG in accordance with the Declaration of Helsinki, and the study was approved by the Psychology Research Ethics Committee of the University of Cambridge. All participants were free of any diagnosed learning difficulties aside from dyslexia (i.e., dyspraxia, ADHD, autistic spectrum disorder, speech and language impairments) and spoke English as their first language.

STANDARDIZED TESTS OF READING, NONWORD READING, VOCABULARY AND IQ

Psychometric tests were given for the purposes of group matching and also exploring possible relations between entrainment and the development of spoken and written language skills. The psychometric tests comprised the British Ability Scales (BAS) (single word reading, Elliott et al., 1996); the single word reading (SWE) and phonemic decoding efficiency (PDE) measure of non-word reading from the TOWRE (Torgesen et al., 1999); the British Picture Vocabulary Scales (BPVS receptive vocabulary, Dunn et al., 1982); and one subtest of the Wechsler Intelligence Scale for Children (WISC-III, Wechsler, 1992): picture arrangement. Performance on these measures is shown in **Table 1**.

EXPERIMENTAL PHONOLOGICAL TASKS

In order to see whether individual differences in entrainment would relate to individual differences in phonological processing between children, participants were administered a phoneme

Table 1 | Group differences in Age, IQ, and behavior.

Measure	CA	DY	$F_{(1, 30)}$	p
Age (months)	165.57 ± 12.71	166.73 ± 13.72	0.057	0.814
IQ	112.76 ± 13.31	114.64 ± 14.07	0.138	0.713
BAS standard score	109.29 ± 11.86	86.18 ± 15.5	22.729	<0.001
Reading age (months)	177.00 ± 20.7	134.55 ± 27.52	24.186	<0.001
TOWRE word reading	103.48 ± 10.33	87.91 ± 7.82	19.125	<0.001
TOWRE non-word reading	107.62 ± 11.21	81.55 ± 10.99	39.559	<0.001
BPVS not aligned	107.71 ± 13.28	100.1 ± 19.48	1.604	0.215
RAN TOTAL	34.67 ± 3.95	38.91 ± 8.88	3.5830	0.070
pSTM	45.81 ± 11.25	35.91 ± 12.55	5.170	0.03
Phoneme deletion	16.48 ± 3.17	12.91 ± 3.89	7.825	0.009

deletion task, an experimental measure of phonological short-term memory (PSTM) and an experimental measure of rapid automatized naming (RAN). Further details for each task are given in Power et al. (2012b).

RHYTHMIC ENTRAINMENT TASK

Rhythmic speech comprising multiple repetitions of the syllable "BA" was presented at a uniform repetition rate of 2 Hz. There were three conditions: auditory (A), visual (V), and audio-visual (AV). Further details of the task can be found in Power et al. (2012b). **Figure 1** summarizes the paradigm.

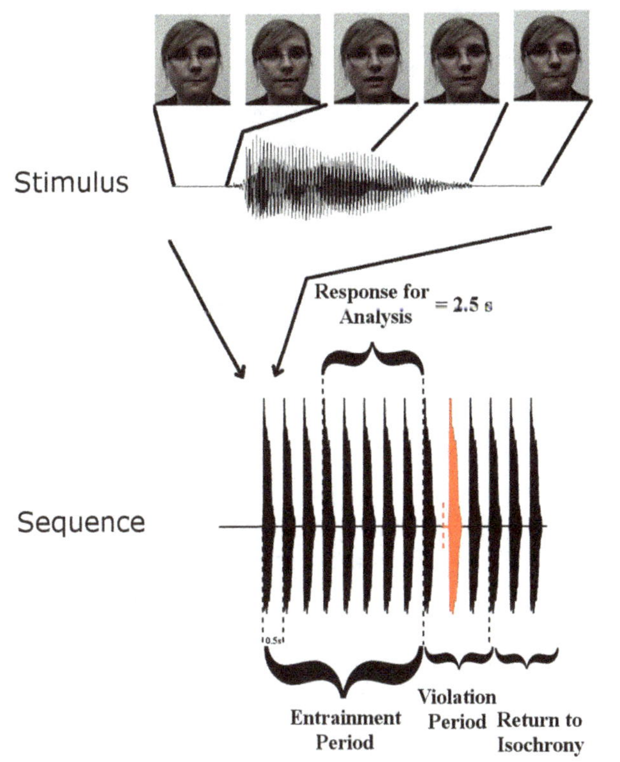

FIGURE 1 | Stimulus Setup: top panel shows one auditory "Ba" token and corresponding frames of the visual stimulus at five time points. Visual movement initiates 68 ms before auditory onset. The lower panel shows a stimulus sequence consisting of the entrainment period with SOA of 500 ms, and the violation period where SOA is disrupted, followed by 3 re-entrainment stimuli ("Return to Isochrony"). The red stimulus is the violator, whose position in the violation period is chosen at random (i.e., either the first, second, or third stimulus can violate the rhythm). The vertical dashed red line indicates where the stimulus would have onset if it had adhered to the isochronous stimulation rate. Also shown is the "Response for Analysis" period over which EEG responses were analyzed.

EEG PREPROCESSING

This was exactly as in Power et al. (2012b).

EEG ANALYSIS

For all analyses, the first three observations in each entrainment period were discarded to ensure that rhythmicity had been established (following the approach employed in Gomez-Ramirez et al., 2011). Here we are interested in entrainment to a uniform stimulus repetition rate, and so responses in the violation and "return to isochrony" periods (see **Figure 1**) were not analyzed. Furthermore, sequences in which a target was not detected were discarded, as were catch trials. As accuracy was ~79% and 75 target sequences were presented per condition, the analysis included ~60 trials per subject per condition. In order to identify frequency bands of interest we examined the phase-locked power (i.e., the power of sequence averages in the time period of interest) in the three conditions (see **Figure 2**). Phase locked power was obtained as in Power et al. (2012b). Given the peaks evident in the spectra, with the highest phase-locked power present for delta and theta, we deemed the delta (~2 Hz) and theta (~4 Hz) frequency bands to be of interest (for further details see *Results* and *Discussion*). Frequency band activity was obtained using FIR filters designed using the Parks-McClellan algorithm (Parks and McClellan, 1972). The delta band filter had corner frequencies of 1 and 3 Hz and the theta band filter had corner frequencies of 3 and 5 Hz. Both had a 40 dB attenuation in the stop band. In order to examine whether auditory entrainment differed for the A and AV conditions, we subtracted an estimate of phase-locked visual activity from each AV trial (AV-V), and compared the remaining A and (AV-V) activity. The estimate of visual activity was obtained from the time-locked average activity in the visual condition.

Power analysis

We wished to investigate possible differences in overall power between conditions and groups. This is important both in terms of potentially different EEG power in response to the various conditions, but also for interpreting differences in strength of phase locking. Higher inter-trial coherence (ITC) values may only be interpreted as improved phase consistency over trials if they are accompanied by no change in response power. If higher ITC is accompanied by a change in response power, it is possible that this is due to a stronger additive response as opposed to increased consistency over trials. To obtain the overall total power we calculated the FFT of the broadband responses for each trial for each subject and took the average. Thus, both phase-locked and non-phase locked power are included in the measure. Delta and theta power were extracted by taking the power at 2 and 4 Hz, respectively, from the overall broadband frequency representation.

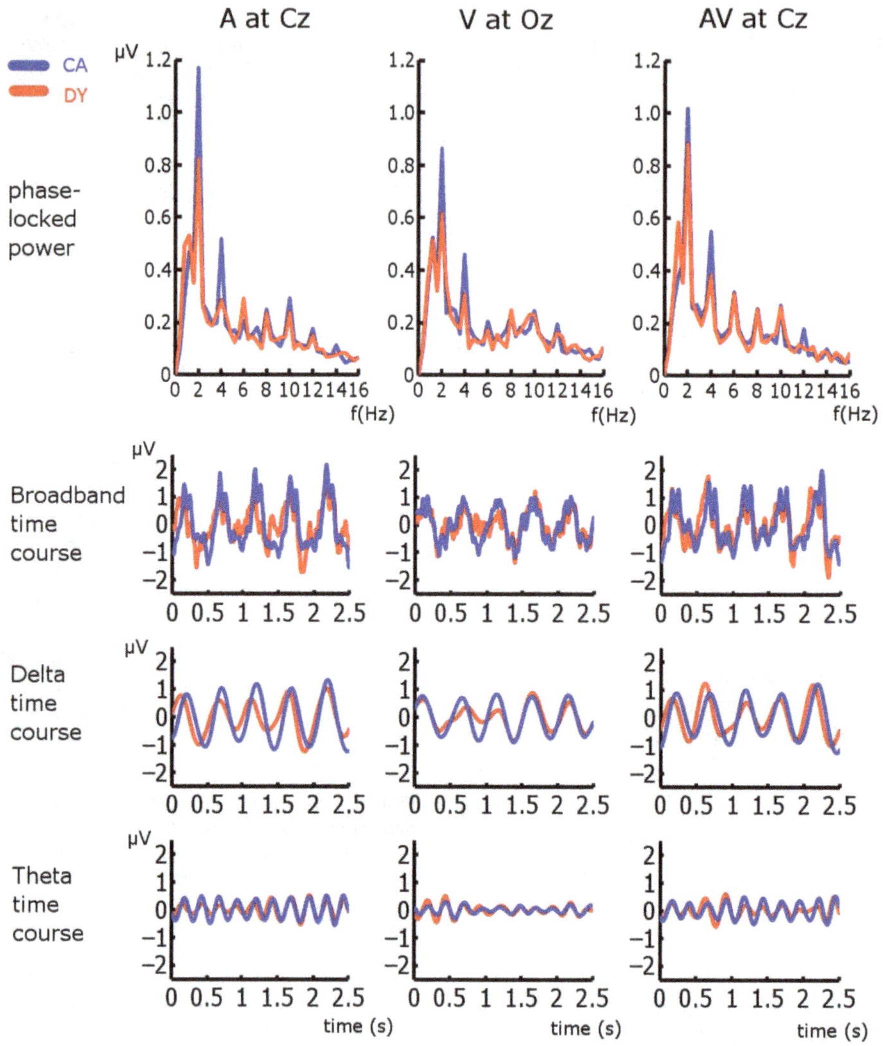

FIGURE 2 | Frequency spectra and broadband, delta, and theta time courses for all three conditions at representative electrodes. CA responses are in blue and DY response are in red.

Assessing phase-locking

The pre-stimulus phase of the last 5 stimuli in the entrainment period was obtained. The pre-stimulus phase is defined here as the phase at the onset of the visual element of the stimulus in the AV condition. This time point is kept consistent for all conditions (i.e., for the auditory condition phases are extracted at the time point where the visual stimulus would have onset, had the visual element of the stimulus accompanied the auditory information, this is 68 ms before auditory stimulus onset). Only sequences where the rhythmic violation was correctly identified are analyzed. These phase values were pooled across sequences and subjects. Given that 75 target sequences were presented to each subject and accuracy was ~79%, the number of phase observations was 6270, 6355, and 6155 (~60 sequences × 5 stimuli × 21 participants) observations for the control group for the auditory, visual and AV conditions, respectively. Similarly 3185, 3210, and 3250 observations were tested for the dyslexic group in the three conditions, respectively (~60 sequences × 5 stimuli × 11 participants). Pre-stimulus phase distribution histograms for each condition were obtained (see **Figure 3**). The phase values were extracted by obtaining the *analytic signal* of the filtered responses via the Hilbert transform. The *analytic signal* is complex, i.e., it has real and imaginary components, and thus the instantaneous phase can be extracted. To test if pre-stimulus phase distributions differed from uniformity, the distributions for the three conditions were tested against the null hypothesis of uniformity using the Rayleigh statistic at three representative electrodes (Fz, Cz, and Oz). A critical p-value of 0.001 was selected to minimize type I error. Statistical difference from uniformity suggests a preferred concentration of phase values, which is indicative of entrainment (Stefanics et al., 2010; Gomez-Ramirez et al., 2011).

Inter-trial coherence (ITC) was then used to compared strength of entrainment across groups, conditions, and channels. ITC is a measure of phase alignment and can have

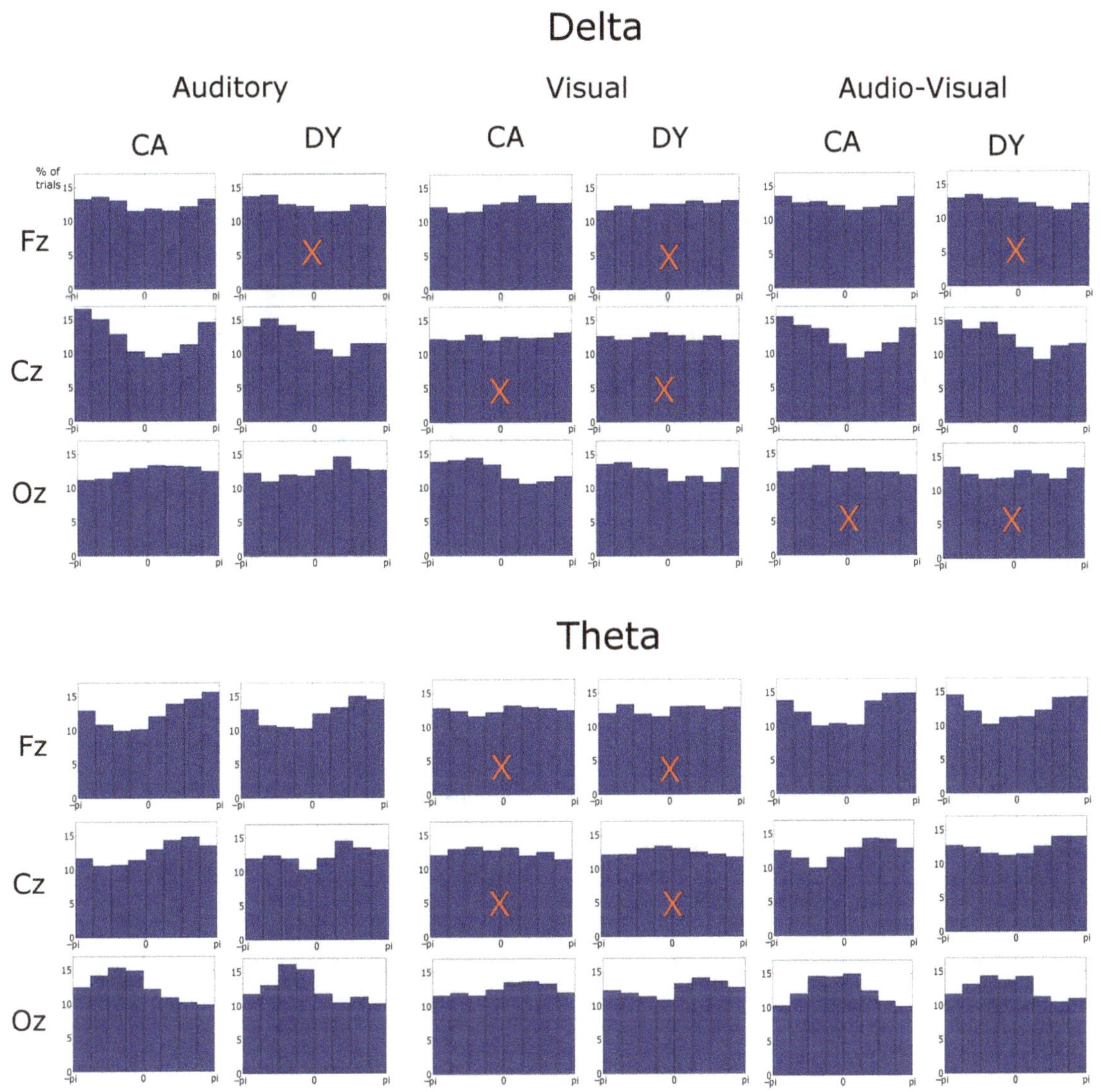

FIGURE 3 | Phase distributions at stimulus onset at representative frontal, central, and occipital electrodes in each condition, frequency band, and group. The *x*-axis is phase ranging from -π to π and *y*-axis represents the percentage of trials. Most distributions differed from uniformity when tested against the Rayleigh statistic at a critical *p*-value of 0.001. Distributions with a superimposed X did not result in significant entrainment.

values ranging from 0 to 1. 1 indicates perfect phase alignment and 0 indicates no phase alignment. ITC was calculated for the same pre-stimulus phase values that were submitted to the Rayleigh test. Preferred phase of entrainment between groups and conditions was also investigated (shown in **Figure 4**). The preferred phase of entrainment for each participant is obtained by calculating the mean pre-stimulus phase for that individual. Mean preferred phase for each group is then calculated for each condition (A, V, AV). If the phase at which the low frequency oscillations (delta, theta) entrain is different between the groups, this implies that the information encoded is different (neurons are firing at the "wrong" time, thus selectively encoding information at a sub-optimal point in the stimulus).

Cross-correlogram analysis of entrainment and laterality

Finally, in order to obtain converging evidence for entrainment, the relationship between the stimuli and the neural responses was also assessed using cross-correlations (see **Figure 5**). We then sought to relate measures of stimulus representation in the EEG data, obtained from these cross-correlations, to the behavioral data. To do this we employed peak *r*-values and the lags at which those peaks occurred. Peak *r*-values are a measure of the strength of stimulus representation in the EEG, and peak-lags are a measure of stimulus-response timing. We also tested potential hemispheric differences in the strength and timing of auditory encoding, following Abrams et al., 2009. To do this we found peak *r*-values and the lags at which those peaks occurred at three pairs of temporal electrodes. The temporal electrode

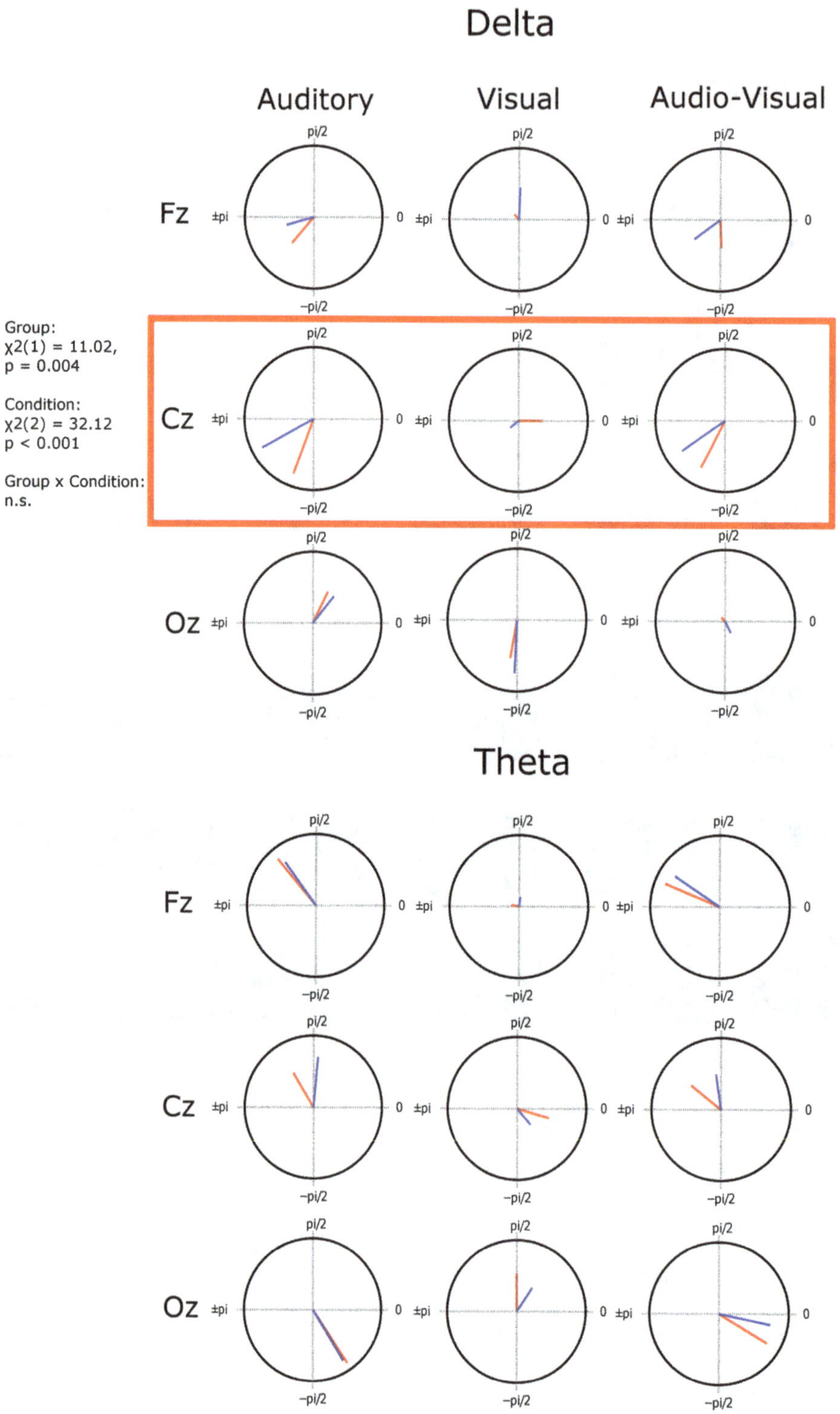

FIGURE 4 | Mean resultant vector plots indicating the coherency of preferred phase across subjects (the length of the vector) and the preferred angle of entrainment (the vector angle) plotted on a unit circle. A significant group difference in preferred angle was found in the delta band at electrode Cz.

pairs were electrodes at (T3, T4), (T5, T6) and (Tp7, Tp8) of the 10–20 system. The first electrode of each pair was in the left temporal region and the second was in the right temporal region.

Phase re-setting of auditory oscillatory activity by visual information

Finally, we sought to investigate the impact of the accompanying visual stimulation on auditory entrainment. The pre-stimulus phase values (at auditory stimulus onset) for the AV and (AV-V) responses were extracted in the same manner as outlined above for the separate conditions. We then looked at the topography of the strength of entrainment. To do this we plotted the pooled phase values at each electrode (shown in **Figure 7**). These topographies show a common region of strong entrainment, indicative of entrainment in auditory areas (see **Figure 7**). Subsequent analysis was thus confined to the pooled activity of electrodes in this region of interest (ROI). The electrodes chosen for this ROI are shown in **Figure 7**. We compared the extent of phase alignment as obtained using ITC and the preferred pre-stimulus phase. Once again an estimate of the preferred phase was determined for each subject by finding the mean pre-stimulus phase.

RESULTS

BEHAVIORAL ENTRAINMENT TASK

In order to assess whether there were significant behavioral differences between conditions, 2 Two-Way mixed design ANOVAs with a between-subject factor of Group and a within-subject factor of Condition were carried out. The dependent variables in the separate ANOVAs were the EEG task (79.4% accuracy) behavioral threshold in ms in each condition and response time (RT) in ms in each condition, respectively. If the assumption of sphericity was violated the Greenhouse–Geisser corrected degrees of freedom are reported. The ANOVA for *threshold* showed a main effect of Group that approached significance, $F_{(1,\ 30)} = 4.006, p < 0.054, \eta_p^2 = 0.118$. There was a significant main effect of condition, $F_{(1.57,\ 47.089)} = 97.9,\ p < 0.001,\ \eta_p^2 = 0.765$. *Post-hoc* inspection of the means (Bonferroni corrected) showed that the threshold for the visual condition was significantly higher than the thresholds for the auditory and AV conditions (both p's < 0.001). The thresholds in the auditory and AV conditions did not differ from each other ($p > 0.05$). The Group × Condition interaction approached significance [$F_{(1.57,\ 47.089)} = 2.602, p = 0.097$]. *A priori*, we had expected potential group differences in benefit accrued in presenting AV over A or V alone and also a possible differential benefit by group of A over V (those with dyslexia worse in A and better in V). Therefore, we carried out three planned exploratory *post-hoc t*-tests probing group effects in differences between conditions: (DY_A-DY_AV) vs. (CA_A-CA_AV), (DY_V-DY_A) vs. (CA_V-CA_A), (DY_V-DY_AV) vs. (CA_V-CA_AV). With Bonferroni corrections, a significance threshold of $p = 0.05/3 = 0.016$ was applied. Results of these *post-hoc* tests showed that dyslexics gained significantly more benefit in the AV condition compared to the auditory alone condition ($p = 0.014$). The difference in benefit from visual alone to AV did not differ between groups ($p = 0.057$). Therefore, the *post-hoc t*-tests suggest that dyslexics accrued more benefit than controls when stimuli were presented audio-visually rather than as auditory-alone. The same pattern was not found for AV presentation over visual-alone. The advantage of auditory alone over visual alone presentation was not significantly different between the groups ($p = 0.802$).

The ANOVA for *response time* showed a main effect of condition, [$F_{(1.638,\ 49.139)} = 39.24,\ p < 0.001,\ \eta_p^2 = 0.567$], but no significant group effects [$F_{(1,\ 30)} = 0.035, p > 0.05$] nor interaction [$F_{(1.638,\ 49.139)} = 0.118, p > 0.05$]. *Post-hoc* inspection of the significant condition effect (Bonferroni corrected) showed that RT in the visual condition was significantly faster than RT for the auditory and AV conditions (both p's < 0.001). Differences in RT between the auditory and AV conditions approached significance ($p = 0.054$), suggesting that although the AV condition did not result in an improved detection threshold over auditory information alone, some facilitation of RT was occurring. Performance on the behavioral entrainment task is shown in **Table 2**.

Table 2 | Response times and 79.4% detection threshold (in ms) for the EEG behavioral task.

	CA	DY
RT auditory (ms)	352.44 ± 45.48	358.52 ± 44.31
RT visual (ms)	303.27 ± 48.82	303.76 ± 43.45
RT audio-visual (ms)	337.71 ± 41.29	339.61 ± 40.02
EEG behavioral threshold auditory (ms)	51.39 ± 19.34	80.01 ± 62.15
EEG behavioral threshold visual (ms)	131.21 ± 26.44	138.56 ± 38.69
EEG behavioral threshold audio-visual (ms)	56.00 ± 17.85	62.41 ± 28.68

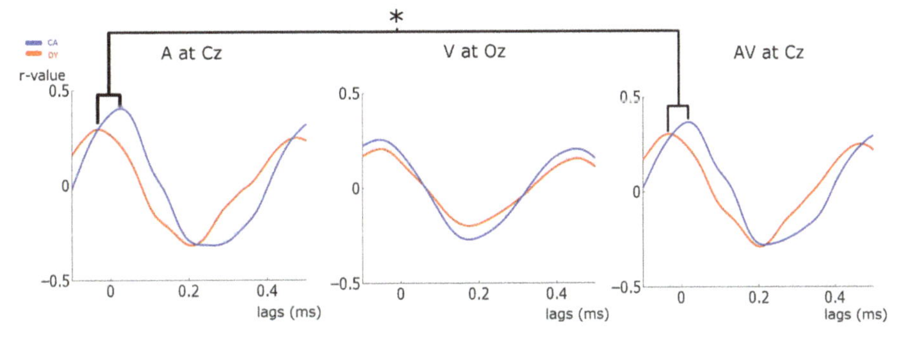

FIGURE 5 | Stimulus-Response cross-correlation analysis. The plots show the cross-correlation analysis between the stimulus and the responses at representative electrodes. Average CA data is plotted in blue and DYs in red. A very strong representation of the temporally extended stimulus is seen in the response. Significant peak timing differences are indicated. *$p < 0.05$.

Finally, to check that individual differences in the thresholds for the 3 conditions were correlated with the behavioral, reading, and phonological measures, partial correlations across all subjects controlling for age and IQ were computed (see **Table 3**). Most of the correlations were significant, suggesting that the task is tapping into mechanisms that are relevant to reading and reading development. The top panel of **Figure 6** shows a scatter plot and regression line of the auditory threshold in the EEG behavioral task plotted against performance in the phoneme deletion task.

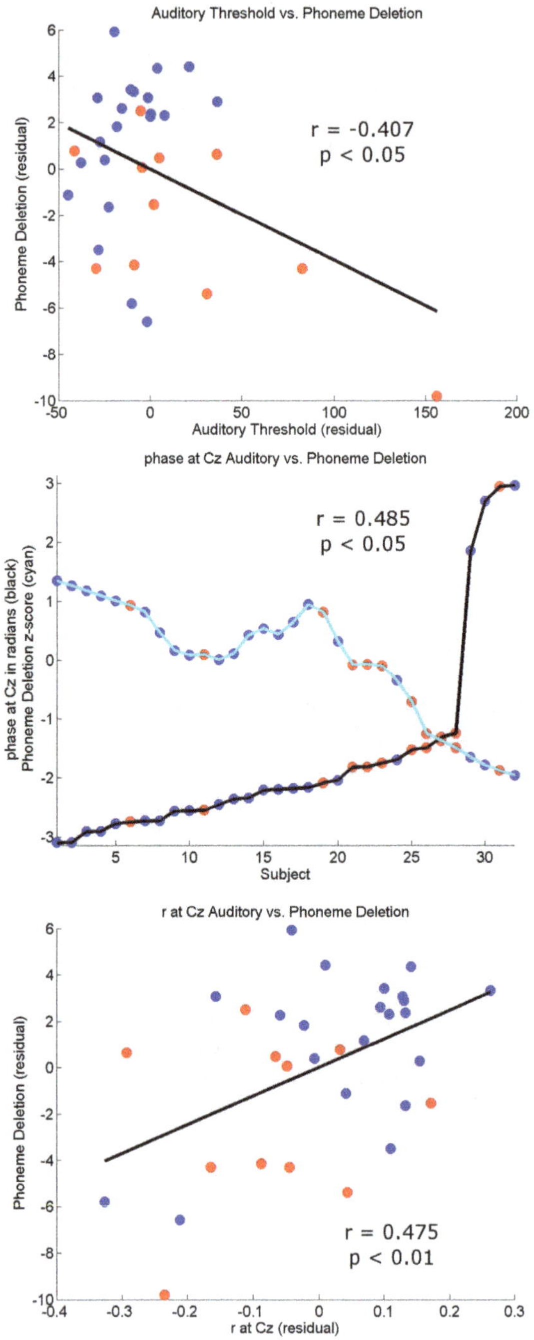

FIGURE 6 | Correlation plots. The **top panel** shows the partial correlation plot controlling for age and IQ of the Auditory Threshold on the EEG behavioral task with phonology (phoneme deletion). The **middle panel** shows the relationship between the circular variable preferred phase of entrainment (black trace) and the linear variable phoneme deletion *z*-score (cyan). For visualization purposes the phoneme deletion trace has been smoothed using a 12-point averaging window. Higher phoneme deletion scores occur when a subject has a preferred phase in the region $(-\pi, -\pi/2)$ and lower scores in the region $(\pi/2, \pi)$. The **bottom panel** shows the partial correlation plot controlling for age and IQ of strength of auditory stimulus representation at Cz (*r*) with phonology (phoneme deletion). Controls subjects are identified by blue dots and dyslexics by red dots in all panels.

EEG DATA: TOTAL RESPONSE POWER

To assess potential group differences in *total response power*, we carried out separate ANOVAs for each frequency band of interest (delta, theta) with the between-subject factor of group and within-subject factors of condition and channel. For the delta band ANOVA we found no main effect of group [$F_{(1, 30)} = 0.104$, $p = 0.75$, $\eta_p^2 = 0.003$]. There were significant main effects of condition [$F_{(2, 60)} = 9.932$, $p < 0.001$, $\eta_p^2 = 0.249$] and channel [$F_{(2, 60)} = 10.062$, $p < 0.001$, $\eta_p^2 = 0.251$]. The condition effect was driven by larger delta power in the A and AV conditions than the V condition. Power in the A and AV conditions did not differ. The main effect of channel was driven by higher delta power at Fz than at Cz and Oz. There was no difference in delta power between Cz and Oz. The was also a significant group × condition interaction [$F_{(2, 60)} = 3.428$, $p < 0.039$, $\eta_p^2 = 0.103$]. *Post-hoc* tests showed that this was driven by higher delta power in the A than V condition for controls, compared with no difference for those with dyslexia. In contrast, those with dyslexia had higher delta power for the AV condition than the V condition; this was not the case for controls.

In the theta band ANOVA we again found no main effect of group, suggesting that overall theta power was similar between the groups [$F_{(1, 30)} = 0.233$, $p = 0.633$, $\eta_p^2 = 0.008$]. Once again there were significant main effects of condition [$F_{(2, 60)} = 7.116$, $p = 0.002$, $\eta_p^2 = 0.192$] and channel [$F_{(2, 60)} = 3.875$, $p < 0.026$, $\eta_p^2 = 0.114$]. The condition effect was again driven by larger delta power in the A and AV conditions than in the V condition. Power in the A and AV conditions did not differ. The main effect of channel was driven by higher delta power at Fz

Table 3 | Partial correlations across all subjects controlling for age and IQ between EEG behavioral task thresholds and reading and phonology measures.

Measure	Auditory threshold	Visual threshold	Audio-visual threshold
BAS (SS)	*r* = −0.579**	*r* = −0.508**	*r* = −0.383*
Reading age	*r* = −0.522**	*r* = −0.475**	*r* = −0.305
TOWRE word reading	*r* = −0.434*	*r* = −0.441*	*r* = −0.306
TOWRE non-word reading	*r* = −0.538**	*r* = −0.533**	*r* = −0.389*
RAN	*r* = 0.193	*r* = 0.265	*r* = 0.216
pSTM	*r* = −0.044	*r* = −0.114	*r* = 0.153
Phoneme deletion	*r* = −0.407*	*r* = −0.123	*r* = −0.313

**$p < 0.01$, *$p < 0.05$.

than at Oz. There was also a significant group × channel interaction [$F_{(2, 60)} = 4.459, p < 0.026, \eta_p^2 = 0.129$]. *Post-hoc* testing revealed that this was driven by larger theta power at Fz than Cz for DYs only. There was also a significant channel × condition interaction [$F_{(2.974, 89.229)} = 5.036, p = 0.003, \eta_p^2 = 0.144$]. This is to be expected, as different channels should respond differently to different conditions e.g., Cz would respond more strongly to auditory than visual stimulation.

EEG DATA: PHASE CONSISTENCY

We next explored entrainment in the pre-stimulus phase distributions of the delta and theta activity (see **Figure 3**). Here three representative electrodes were chosen for analysis: Fz, Cz, and Oz, identifying responses from frontal, central, and occipital regions, respectively. Significant phase locking (i.e., significant differences from a uniform random distribution) were investigated using the Rayleigh statistic, and a critical *p*-value of 0.001 was chosen in order to minimize Type I errors.

In the *auditory* condition, significant entrainment was found at both delta and theta rates at all three channel locations, with one exception, the Fz channel for dyslexic participants (A_δ_DY_Cz: $Z = 36.76$, $p << 0.001$; A_δ_DY_Oz: $Z = 7.27$, $p << 0.001$; A_δ_CA_Fz: $Z = 14.30$, $p << 0.001$; A_δ_CA_Cz: $Z = 124.55$, $p << 0.001$; A_δ_CA_Oz: $Z = 36.76$, $p << 0.001$; A_θ_DY_Fz: $Z = 28.43$, $p << 0.001$, A_θ_DY_Cz: $Z = 9.60$, $p << 0.001$; A_θ_DY_Oz: $Z = 35.97$, $p << 0.001$; A_θ_CA_Fz: $Z = 73.58$, $p << 0.001$; A_θ_CA_Cz: $Z = 49.58$, $p << 0.001$; A_θ_CA_Oz: $Z = 75.38$, $p << 0.001$). Regarding delta activity at Fz for the dyslexics, the entrainment did approach significance (A_δ_DY_Fz: $Z = 6.73$, $p = 0.0013$). Therefore, as would be expected on MTRMs of speech processing, theta entrainment to the syllable stimulus was present in both groups and at all electrodes. Significant delta entrainment was also present in both groups at all electrodes, as would be expected in our paradigm.

In the *visual* condition, entrainment was significant in occipital areas only, as would be expected (V_δ_DY_Oz: $Z = 8.81$, $p << 0.001$; V_δ_CA_Oz: $Z = 46.28$, $p << 0.001$; V_θ_DY_Oz: $Z = 10.01$, $p << 0.001$; V_θ_CA_Oz: $Z = 13.30$, $p << 0.001$). No significant entrainment was found at Cz in either band (V_δ_DY_Cz: $Z = 0.56, p > 0.05$; V_δ_CA_Cz: $Z = 0.41, p > 0.05$; V_θ_DY_Cz: $Z = 3.78, p > 0.05$; V_θ_CA_Cz: $Z = 5.22, p > 0.05$). While significant entrainment was not found in either band at Fz for dyslexics (V_δ_DY_Fz: $Z = 0.70, p > 0.05$; V_θ_DY_Fz: $Z = 0.51$, $p > 0.05$), controls did show significant entrainment at Fz in the delta band (V_δ_CA_Fz: $Z = 13.09, p < 0.001$) but not the theta band (V_θ_CA_Fz: $Z = 2.04, p > 0.05$).

The pattern of entrainment for the *audio-visual* condition was somewhat more complex. Both groups showed significant entrainment in the theta band at Fz, Cz and Oz (AV_θ_DY_Fz: $Z = 21.10$, $p << 0.001$, AV_θ_CA_Fz: $Z = 75.50$, $p << 0.001$; AV_θ_DY_Cz: $Z = 9.78$, $p << 0.001$; AV_θ_CA_Cz: $Z = 35.83$, $p < 0.001$; AV_θ_DY_Oz: $Z = 21.03$, $p < 0.001$; AV_θ_CA_Oz: $Z = 66.55$, $p < 0.001$). In the delta band, however, both groups showed significant entrainment at Cz only (AV_δ_DY_Cz: $Z = 34.43$, $p << 0.001$; AV_δ_CA_Cz: $Z = 78.22$, $p < 0.001$). Controls also showed significant entrainment at Fz (AV_δ_CA_Fz: $Z = 9.50$, $p << 0.001$), whereas for the dyslexics entrainment only approached significance at Fz (AV_δ_DY_Fz: $Z = 6.64$, $p = 0.0013$). Neither group showed significant entrainment at Oz (AV_δ_DY_Oz: $Z = 1.58$, $p > 0.05$; AV_δ_CA_Oz: $Z = 2.11$, $p > 0.05$). The Oz data is likely due to volume conduction from auditory areas. As can been seen from **Figure 3**, activity at Oz in the auditory condition tends to entrain in opposite phase to the visual condition. This would lead to a balancing of the audio-visual phase distribution at Oz.

EEG DATA: PHASE LOCKING STRENGTH (ITC)

In order to examine potential group differences in the degree of phase locking *consistency* for each group we carried out separate mixed factor ANOVAs by group for each frequency band of interest. The with-in group factors were condition (A vs. V vs. AV), and channel (Fz vs. Cz Vs. Oz). Once again, if the assumption of sphericity was violated the Greenhouse–Geisser corrected degrees of freedom are reported. In the *delta band* ANOVA there was no main effect of group [$F_{(1, 30)} = 0.519$, $p = 0.477$, $\eta_p^2 = 0.017$], hence the strength of entrainment did not differ between the groups. There was a significant effect of condition [$F_{(2, 60)} = 8.294$, $p = 0.001$, $\eta_p^2 = 0.217$]. Bonferroni corrected *post-hoc* analysis showed this to be driven by stronger entrainment in the auditory and audio-visual conditions than in the visual condition. Strength of entrainment was equivalent between auditory and audio-visual conditions. There was also a main effect of channel [$F_{(2, 60)} = 14.74, p < 0.001, \eta_p^2 = 0.329$]. *Post-hoc* analysis found this to be driven by stronger entrainment at Cz then at either Fz or Oz. Finally, there was a significant condition × channel interaction [$F_{(4, 120)} = 9.474, p < 0.001, \eta_p^2 = 0.240$]. This interaction suggests that strength of entrainment at the electrodes depends on the experimental condition. This is to be expected, e.g., we would expect Cz to show stronger entrainment to the auditory and audio-visual stimuli than the visual stimulus. This can be seen in **Figure 4**. No other significant effects or interactions were found in the delta band.

In the theta band ANOVA the main effect of group approached significance [$F_{(1, 30)} = 3.264$, $p = 0.081$, $\eta_p^2 = 0.098$]. This suggests that the strength of theta entrainment tends to be greater for controls than those with dyslexia. A main effect of condition was also found [$F_{(2, 60)} = 5.916$, $p = 0.005$, $\eta_p^2 = 0.165$]. As in the delta band *post-hoc* analysis (Bonferroni corrected), entrainment in the auditory and audio-visual conditions was significantly stronger than in the visual condition. There was also a main effect of channel [$F_{(1.468, 44.031)} = 5.576, p = 0.013, \eta_p^2 = 0.157$]. Bonferroni *post-hoc* tests showed this to be driven by stronger entrainment at Oz than Cz, No significant interactions were found (all *p*'s > 0.05).

EEG DATA: PREFERRED PHASE OF ENTRAINMENT

Having assessed both presence of entrainment (significant phase locking, ITC) and potential differences in strength of entrainment for each group (degree of consistency in phase locking), we sought to investigate potential group differences in the *preferred phase* of entrainment. Although consistency of phase (strength of phase locking) did not differ between groups, this does not mean that both groups entrained at the *same* phase. The preferred phase of entrainment has been shown to be a crucial contributor to stimulus processing (Lakatos et al., 2008; Ng et al., 2013). Preferred phase angles can be seen in **Figure 4**. The length of the vector in **Figure 4** represents the inter-subject coherence; the greater the magnitude of the vector, the more similar the phase at which all subjects entrain. Conversely the shorter the vector, the less consistent (or more variable) the phase across subjects. In order to investigate whether preferred phase differed between groups, we carried out 6 group × condition ANOVAs, one for each frequency band/channel combination (Cz and delta, Cz and theta, Fz and delta, Fz and theta, Oz and delta, Oz and theta). This was done using the Harrison-Kanji two-factor ANOVA test (HK ANOVA) for circular variables (Harrison and Kanji, 1988). This test is not carried out using repeated measures. Also, the reported statistic depends on the width, or concentration factor kappa, of the Von Mises distribution applied to the data. If it is low (<2), a Chi-squared statistic is reported, but if it is high, an F-statistic is reported. A significant group effect was found only for Cz in the delta band ANOVA ($\chi^2_{(1)} = 11.02, p = 0.004$). A significant main effect of condition was also found in this ANOVA ($\chi^2_{(2)} = 32.12$, $p < 0.001$). The group × condition interaction was not significant ($p > 0.05$). Since the entrainment analysis and **Figure 3** showed that activity at Cz in the visual condition was not significantly entrained, and thus the preferred phase for this condition at this channel is not informative, we carried out a further exploratory group (CA vs. DY) × condition (A vs. AV) HK ANOVA for Cz and delta band activity, leaving out the potentially confounding visual condition. Again we found a significant main effect of group [$F_{(1, 63)} = 9.08, p = 0.0038$]. There was, however, no longer an effect of condition ($p > 0.05$) and no significant interaction ($p > 0.05$). This suggests that the two groups differ in their preferred phase of entrainment in the auditory and audio-visual conditions at Cz, and that the preferred phase for each group does not differ between these conditions. Activity at Cz is broadly indicative of auditory processing in this task.

SUMMARY OF EEG DATA

Regarding our hypotheses about potential group differences in entrainment, these data suggest that there were no overall group differences in response power or in the consistency of phase across trials (ITC). However, there were important group differences in the *preferred phase of entrainment*, which differed at Cz in the delta band in the Auditory and AV conditions. This points toward a potentially very important difference between the groups in the oscillatory processes supporting speech encoding, one that may have significant implications for the quality and type of information that is encoded. In particular, if the different preferred phase of entrainment has a negative effect on speech encoding by children with dyslexia, this should be reflected in relationships between individual differences in preferred phase and the behavioral measures of reading and phonology. To investigate whether this was the case, circular-linear correlations between the preferred phase of delta entrainment and the behavioral measures were computed, and are shown in **Table 4**. For the auditory condition, significant correlations are shown for all the measures of reading and for phoneme deletion, with a trend toward significance ($p < 0.10$) for the phonological memory and rapid naming measures. Clearly, preferred phase is significantly related to the quality of the phonological representations in the mental lexicons of our participants. A plot outlining the relationship between preferred phase of entrainment at Cz in the auditory condition and performance in the phoneme deletion task can be seen in the middle panel of **Figure 6**. This important result is considered further in the Discussion.

Table 4 | Circular-linear correlation between preferred delta phase of entrainment and reading and phonology measures.

Measure	Preferred phase for A at Cz	Preferred phase for V at Oz	Preferred phase for AV at Cz
BAS(SS)	0.532*	0.322	0.322
BAS(AS)	0.570**	0.213	0.294
Reading age	0.388*	0.245	0.356
TOWRE word reading	0.510*	0.200	0.323
TOWRE non-word reading	0.465*	0.324	0.271
RAN (combined)	0.405+	0.290	0.447*
pSTM combined	0.412+	0.312	0.424+
Phoneme deletion	0.485*	0.144	0.389+

The pattern of correlations mirrors that of the peak lag correlations in this table emphasizing that both measures tap into similar mechanisms (that is the timing of the EEG activity in response to the stimulus). **$p < 0.01$, *$p < 0.05$, +$p < 0.1$.

QUALITY OF THE STIMULUS REPRESENTATION: CROSS-CORRELOGRAMS

The analyses conducted so far have investigated differences in EEG responses between the groups. Now we investigate the direct relationship between the EEG response and the entraining stimulus for each group. To ascertain this relationship, we calculated the cross-correlogram between the stimulus envelope and the neural response. Following Abrams et al. (2009), we did not partition the EEG into sub-bands for this analysis, but used the broadband response. The peak r-values of the cross-correlogram indicate the strength of stimulus envelope representation in the EEG response. The lags at which the peak r-value occurs indicate the timing/phase at which the greatest representation of the stimulus occurs. Given the significant differences in preferred phase found in the EEG, peak lag values in particular might be expected to differ between those with dyslexia and the control group.

The strength of stimulus representation was investigated using a mixed factor ANOVA with the between-subject factor of group (CA vs. DY) and the within-subject factors of condition (A vs. V vs. AV) and channel (Fz vs. Cz vs. Oz). The dependent variable was the peak r-values. The main effect of group approached significance [$F_{(1, 30)} = 2.999, p = 0.094, \eta^2_p = 0.091$]. There was a significant main effect of condition [$F_{(2, 60)} = 6.675, p = 0.002, \eta^2_p = 0.182$]. Bonferroni corrected *post-hoc* analysis showed that this was driven by larger r-values in the A and AV conditions than in the visual condition ($p = 0.024$ and $p = 0.016$, respectively). The peak r-values in the A and AV conditions did not differ ($p > 0.05$). There was also a significant effect of channel [$F_{(2, 60)} = 11.328, p = 0.001, \eta^2_p = 0.274$]. *Post-hoc* analysis revealed this to be driven by larger r-values at Cz than at both Fz and Oz ($p < 0.001$ and $p = 0.01$, respectively). A significant condition × channel interaction was also found [$F_{(4, 120)} = 7.304$, $p < 0.001$, $\eta_p^2 = 0.196$]. This would be expected, as stimulus representation should differ at each channel in different experimental conditions. The stimulus-response cross-correlation has a period of ~500 ms (see **Figure 5**). This suggests that it is dominated by delta band activity.

To investigate the *timing* of maximal response representation, we extracted the lags for which peak *r*-values occurred for each participant at each channel and in each condition (a subset of which is plotted in **Figure 5**). We then took the lags at each channel as the dependent variable in 3 separate ANOVAs, each with the between-subject factor of group and the within-subject factor of condition (A vs. V vs. AV). The ANOVA for Fz showed a main effect of condition [$F_{(2, 60)} = 59.09$, $p < 0.001$, $\eta_p^2 = 0.653$]. There was no significant effect of group, nor was there a significant group × condition interaction. Similar results were found for the Cz ANOVA [main effect of condition: $F_{(2, 60)} = 33.808$, $p < 0.001$, $\eta_p^2 = 0.53$]. However, given that the analysis of entrainment had shown that visual activity at Cz was not significantly entrained, we also carried out an exploratory Two-Way ANOVA for Cz omitting the visual condition, with factors of group (CA vs. DY) and condition (A vs. AV). Here we found a significant main effect of group [$F_{(1, 30)} = 5.859$, $p = 0.022$, $\eta_p^2 = 0.163$], paralleling the results found at Cz for the preferred phase of entrainment analysis. *Post-hoc* analysis of the group effect revealed that it was driven by controls having a *longer* peak-lag than the dyslexic group. Although the timing of peak stimulus representation (as identified by the peak lags) does not measure the same thing as preferred pre-stimulus phase, both are measures of the timing of the relevant oscillatory response activity. Indeed, the results of this peak-lag analysis mirror those of the preferred phase of delta entrainment analysis carried out above, as both analyses point to atypical timing of response entrainment and atypical response representation in participants with dyslexia. Both the strength of stimulus representation and response timing are likely to be crucial factors in phonological development.

Converging evidence for a potentially important role for the neural timing of auditory responses in phonological development and reading development was sought by exploring correlations between these two measures of the quality of stimulus representation and the behavioral measures. Peak *r*-values and peak lags at Cz in the three conditions were correlated with the various reading and phonology measures, partialling out age and IQ (see **Table 5**). A series of significant correlations were found, most notably in the Auditory condition, and the correlations were positive, suggesting that a stronger stimulus representation (higher peak *r*-value) and a longer peak lag were related to higher scores on the behavioral tasks. As shown in **Table 5**, peak *r*-values were significantly correlated with reading age, non-word reading and phoneme deletion in the Auditory condition, while peak lag was significantly correlated with reading standard score and reading age (The bottom panel of **Figure 6** shows a scatter plot and regression line for the relationship between peak *r*-values at Cz in the auditory condition vs. performance in the phoneme deletion task) For the AV condition, peak *r*-values were significantly correlated with phonological awareness, while individual differences in peak lag were significantly correlated with reading age and RAN. As those with dyslexia showed *shorter* lags than controls, the more *"control-like"* the peak lag, the better the behavioral performance.

Overall, the partial correlations suggest that the typically-developing children had stronger neural representations of the speech stimulus "ba," and that the strongest representation occurred later in time compared to those with dyslexia. These results provide converging evidence for the importance of the *phase* of low frequency oscillations in stimulus encoding. The participants with dyslexia appear to be entraining to a sub-optimal phase, and this is reflected in both timing differences in their neural responses and also a difference in the quality of stimulus representation as measured by the correlograms.

To investigate potential effects of hemisphere on the strength of auditory stimulus representation and timing, we subjected the peak *r*-values and lags to separate 2 × 3 × 2 ANOVAs with a between-subject factor of group and within-subject factors of electrode pair (T3,T4 vs. T5,T6 vs. Tp7,Tp8) and hemisphere (left vs. right). The peak *r*-value ANOVA found no significant effects, suggesting that the strength of auditory stimulus representation does not differ by group in temporal regions.

Table 5 | Partial correlations across all subjects controlling for age and IQ between reading and phonology measures and peak *r*-value and peak lag at Cz in the Auditory condition, Oz in the visual condition, and Cz for the audio-visual condition.

Measure	*r*-value for A at Cz	Peak lag for A at Cz	*r*-value for V at Oz	Peak lag for V at Oz	*r*-value for AV at Cz	Peak lag for AV at Cz
BAS(SS)	0.402*	0.409*	0.076	−0.003	0.182	0.308
BAS(AS)	0.401*	0.429*	0.079	0.008	0.171	0.31
Reading age	0.324+	0.388*	0.088	0.038	0.116	0.373*
TOWRE word reading	0.281	0.356+	0.068	0.07	−0.043	0.354+
TOWRE non-word reading	0.385**	0.356+	0.131	−0.087	0.033	0.241
RAN	−0.167	−0.322+	−0.111	−0.006	0.193	−0.467**
pSTM	−0.054	0.060	0.127	−0.133	−0.2	0.357+
Phoneme deletion	0.475**	0.229	0.094	0.064	0.466*	−0.107

**$p < 0.01$, *$p < 0.05$, +$p < 0.1$.

Furthermore, no hemispheric difference or interactions were found, suggesting that the strength of stimulus encoding is similar in both hemispheres. The lag ANOVA showed a main effect of Group [$F_{(1, 30)} = 4.37, p = 0.045, \eta_p^2 = 0.127$]. No other contrasts resulted in significant effects. This timing difference was again driven by children with dyslexia having a shorter peak lag than children in the control group.

PHASE RESETTING: EFFECTS OF VISUAL STIMULATION ON AUDITORY ENTRAINMENT

Following Power et al. (2012b), our final question was whether there would be group differences in the degree to which visual speech information would reset the phase of auditory oscillations so that they were optimally timed to encode the speech signal. Given behavioral data (e.g., Megnin-Viggars and Goswami, 2013), we expected that the dyslexic group might accrue greater benefit from visual phase-resetting than controls. Following Power et al. (2012b), **Figure 7** shows ITC topographies for the A and (AV-V) conditions averaged across groups. The fronto-central distribution in both conditions is indicative of entrainment in auditory cortical areas. **Figure 7** also shows the phase distributions for delta and theta for the pooled activity in the ROI for both groups and conditions. Rayleigh tests revealed significant entrainment in both conditions at both frequencies (A_δ_DY: $Z = 403.43$, $p << 0.001$; AV-V_δ_DY: $Z = 265.87$, $p << 0.001$; A_θ_DY: $Z = 441.16$, $p << 0.001$; AV-V_θ_DY: $Z = 376.69$, $p << 0.001$; A_δ_CA: $Z = 1247.30$, $p << 0.001$; AV-V_δ_CA: $Z = 684.82$, $p << 0.001$; A_θ_CA: $Z = 1220.5$, $p << 0.001$; AV-V_θ_CA: $Z = 704.96$, $p << 0.001$). This would be expected given the way in which the ROI was determined.

To assess possible group differences in the effects of visual speech cues on the auditory oscillations, we first investigated whether the level of auditory entrainment (inter-trial coherence, ITC) was affected by the visual cues. The ITC values were submitted to two 2 × 2 ANOVAs (one each for delta and theta), with the between-subject factor of group (CA vs. DYS) and within-subject factor of condition [A vs. (AV-V)]. The ANOVAs showed no main effect of group nor condition in either frequency band (all p's > 0.05), suggesting that the strength of auditory phase locking in both bands was similar whether visual cues were present or not. There was also no significant group × condition interaction in either band (both p's > 0.05).

Mirroring the previous ITC analysis, we next carried out a similar 2 × 2 ANOVA for each frequency band taking the overall response power as the dependent variable. In the delta band, we found no main effect of group, but a significant group × condition interaction [$F_{(1, 30)} = 5.809, p = 0.022, \eta_p^2 = 0.162$]. *Post-hoc* inspection revealed that the interaction was driven by higher delta power in the A than in (AV-V) for the control children only. There was no difference in power between the two conditions for those with dyslexia. The theta band ANOVA showed similar results, with no main effect of group, but a significant group × condition interaction [$F_{(1, 30)} = 5.048$, $p = 0.032$, $\eta_p^2 = 0.144$]. *Post-hoc* inspection revealed that this was again driven by higher power in A than AV-V for the control children only.

Taking these results together, typically-developing children showed a significant difference between auditory oscillatory activity to auditory stimuli alone (A) and auditory oscillatory activity when visual cues were present (AV-V), in both delta and theta power. The children with dyslexia did not. This may indicate that

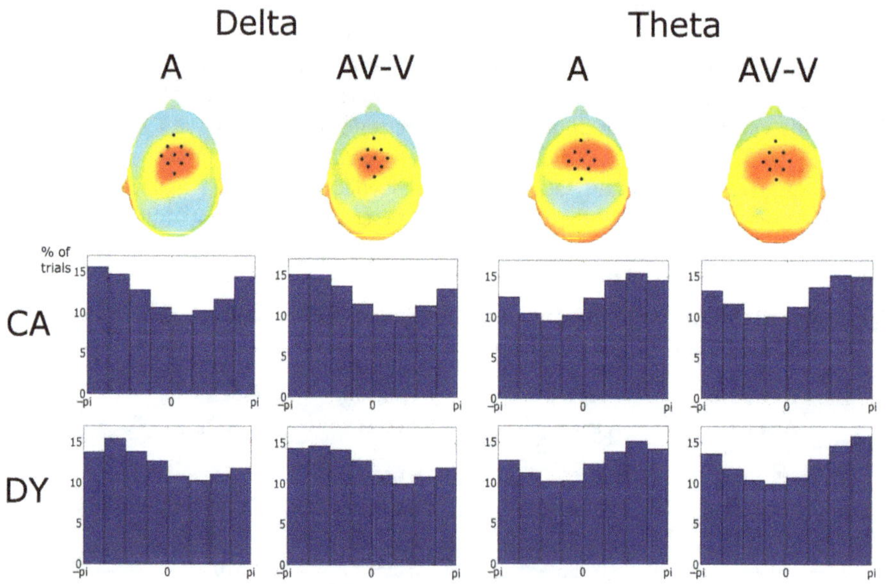

FIGURE 7 | Upper Panel: Topographies of the ITC for phase at stimulus onset. The similarity of these topographies established a particular fronto-central region of interest coinciding with the area of strongest entrainment. **Lower Panel:** phase distributions for the conditions and frequency bands in the region of interest (ROI). Activity in the ROI showed significant entrainment, as tested using the Rayleigh statistic, in both frequency bands and for both response types and both groups. Tests on the preferred phase of entrainment showed that auditory delta phase differed between groups. Auditory theta phase differed between conditions and was thus affected by visual cues.

auditory cortex in typical development does not have to work as "hard" to process speech stimuli when they are presented multimodally. The results also show that the consistency of auditory phase is not affected for either group by whether stimuli are only auditory or whether they are audio-visual.

PREFERRED PRE-STIMULUS PHASE

To assess whether the information from visual speech affected the phase of auditory entrainment similarly for each group, we tested for preferred phase differences in each frequency band using two 2-way circular ANOVAs (HK ANOVA as before). Each ANOVA had group as the between-subjects factor (CA vs. DY) and condition [A vs. (AV-V)] as the within-subjects factor. In the delta band ANOVA there was a significant main effect of group [$F_{(1, 63)} = 11.06$, $p = 0.0015$]. This mirrors the differences in preferred phase found by group at Cz for the auditory condition. There was no significant effect of condition ($p > 0.05$) and there was no significant interaction ($p > 0.05$). In the theta band ANOVA we found a significant main effect of condition [$F_{(1, 63)} = 7.97$, $p = 0.0065$] but no significant main effect of group ($p > 0.05$) and no significant interaction ($p > 0.05$). This suggests that for theta the preferred auditory phase in the ROI is altered by audio-visual information. The absence of a significant interaction with group in both ANOVAs suggests that the preferred phase of entrainment in both frequency bands is similarly affected by visual speech information in both groups, with no phase alteration in the delta band but a significant phase alteration in the theta band. Nevertheless, the preferred delta phase at which auditory responses entrain is different between the groups. Overall these data suggest that for theta band entrainment, which by hypothesis is primary in syllable-level processing (Poeppel, 2003), accompanying visual speech information does alter the preferred phase of entrainment, for both groups. Therefore, accompanying visual information results in a more optimal theta phase than when auditory information is presented alone, and both groups are *similarly* affected by visual speech information. There is no evidence for enhanced use of visual speech information by participants with dyslexia. In contrast, group differences in the preferred delta band phase persist in spite of the visual speech information. This suggests that *sub-optimal phase of entrainment* still occurs in the AV condition for participants with dyslexia.

DISCUSSION

Here we compared neuronal oscillatory entrainment in children with and without dyslexia in the delta and theta bands to a rhythmic speech stimulus, the syllable "ba" repeated at a 2 Hz (delta) rate. The speech stimulus was either presented in the auditory modality only, the visual modality only, or audio-visually (AV). On the basis of the temporal sampling framework for developmental dyslexia (TSF, Goswami, 2011), we predicted group differences in entrainment in the auditory modality. Given the prior literature on oscillatory entrainment in dyslexia (adult studies, Hämäläinen et al., 2012b; Soltesz et al., 2013), delta band oscillations seemed the most likely to reveal group differences in the current study. On the basis of previous behavioral studies of entrainment (tapping measures) with adults and children, we again expected group differences in the delta band (Thomson et al., 2006; Thomson and Goswami, 2008). Finally, on the basis of recent studies of behavioral entrainment in adults with dyslexia to rhythmic speech, we predicted possible group differences in preferred phase alignment (Leong and Goswami, 2013).

Here the data in the auditory entrainment condition showed no difference in phase consistency (ITC) over trials between the groups, and no difference in response power between groups. However, significant differences were indeed found in the *timing* of auditory stimulus encoding. Timing differences were revealed both by a significant group difference in the *preferred phase* of neuronal entrainment in the delta band, in both the auditory and AV conditions, and by the timing of maximal stimulus encoding as measured by cross-correlating the stimulus envelope with the neural response. The cross-correlation approach revealed a significant group difference in peak lag value, with typically-developing children showing later peak lags than children with dyslexia. There was also a trend toward higher *r*-values in controls, indicating better stimulus envelope representation. Regarding laterality, we found no differences in peak *r*-values by group or hemisphere, although longer peak lags were found in both hemispheres in controls. This is discussed further below. Individual differences in both the preferred delta phase measure and the cross-correlation measures were significantly correlated with behavioral measures of reading and phonology (**Tables 4, 5**). The preferred delta phase measure in the auditory condition showed a particularly consistent set of relations, with significant correlations for all the measures of reading and the phoneme deletion measure.

The suboptimal phase of encoding demonstrated for the participants with dyslexia in the delta band is likely to have significant consequences for the quality of their phonological representations. According to MTRMs of speech encoding (e.g., Luo and Poeppel, 2007; Ghitza and Greenberg, 2009), speech input is encoded most efficiently by the brain when endogenous cortical neuronal oscillations phase-align with temporal modulations (amplitude or frequency modulations) in the input signal, so that maximal neuronal responses occur at the most informative points. If the phase of peak neural responding is consistently misaligned with the modulation peaks in the input, then the signal will be encoded in suboptimal fashion. This will result in differently-specified phonological representations for words in the mental lexicon. The cross-correlation analyses in the current study (which cross-correlated the neural response with the stimulus envelope) provided congruent evidence for significantly different neural timing (peak lag measure) and lower quality neuronal representation of the speech envelope for "ba" (peak *r*-value measure) by the children with dyslexia. These delta band findings suggest that the highest level in the amplitude modulation hierarchy, the delta band, which carries information about prosodic structure, is encoded less efficiently by the dyslexic brain. This would have cascading effects for the encoding of the other levels of phonological structure that are nested within the delta band, including syllable-level (theta band) AM information and phoneme-level (gamma band) AM information. The difference in preferred phase in the current study was 12.8 ms between groups (0.1613 radians at 2 Hz). Acoustic changes in this timescale would be in the gamma range, suggesting that the consistent timing difference in preferred delta phase shown by our participants with dyslexia would have cascading consequences for the optimal encoding of gamma-rate or phonetic information. Some of these faster gamma transitions would be occurring in a suboptimal temporal window, contributing to the impairments in phonological encoding found at every grain size (prosodic, syllabic, onset-rhyme and phonemic) in developmental dyslexia (Snowling et al., 2000; Ziegler and Goswami, 2005; Goswami et al., 2013).

Hemispheric differences were not found in the cross-correlation measures, in contrast to an earlier study by Abrams et al. (2009). Abrams and colleagues employed three stimulus types: clear speech, conversational speech and compressed speech. A right hemisphere dominance in stimulus encoding (peak r-value) was found for the clear and conversational speech in good and poor readers, whereas for time-compressed speech (a more challenging listening condition), the right hemisphere dominance was only found for good readers. Encoding was represented symmetrically across hemispheres for the poorer readers. Although we found no hemispheric differences in encoding, there are some possible reasons for the differing results. Crucially, Abrams et al. (2009) employed a paradigm in which stimuli were presented to the right ear only. Subjects were instructed to ignore the sentences and to attend to a movie whose soundtrack was presented to the left ear. It has been shown that spatial attention in a speech environment suppresses the neural representation of the ignored stimulus (Horton et al., 2013). It has also been reported that stronger speech suppression takes place in the left hemisphere than in the right under such conditions Power et al. (2012a). The interplay between attention and hemispheric bias is not addressed in Abrams et al. (2009), and it is possible that attentional influence may contribute to the reported right hemisphere bias. For example, the fact that the stimulus is being actively ignored may suppress stimulus representations in the left hemisphere more than in the right. The fact that our stimuli are presented rhythmically, and thus timing is entirely predictable from syllable to syllable, is a further important difference with Abrams et al. (2009), where the speech stimulus envelope was not periodic. Indeed, the fact that the Group × Hemisphere interaction was only seen in their compressed speech condition suggests that the hemispheric interaction effect may be only apparent when the auditory system attempts to entrain to a taxing stimulus whose envelope is variable.

Abrams et al. (2009) also found a significant group × hemisphere interaction for peak lags in all three speech conditions. Poor readers had earlier r-value peaks in the left hemisphere and later peaks in the right hemisphere. It is of note that our results mirror the left hemisphere timing findings of Abrams et al. (2009). The lack of Group × Hemisphere interactions in our study may be due in part to the predictable nature of our stimuli. If the right hemisphere does preferentially encode low frequency activity, as hypothesized by Poeppel (2003), and if this right hemisphere encoding network is the primary impairment in dyslexia, as hypothesized by our group (Goswami, 2011), then we can argue that in a case where the right hemisphere network's capacity to follow low frequency fluctuations is not heavily taxed (as with a rhythmic and predictable stimulus), hemisphere differences may not be found. However, when difficulty increases (such as with non-periodic speech), the unaffected right hemisphere of control participants can facilitate processing, resulting in a decreased peak lag. In contrast, the impaired right hemisphere network of participants with dyslexia will struggle to cope, and so the peak lag increases. Taken together, the results of both studies converge in showing impaired processing of low frequency information by poor readers, both in terms of strength of stimulus representation and response timing. Further research is required, however, to tease apart the delicate contributions of attention and stimulus parameters.

Indeed, a recent study exploring how new acoustic representations are learned by the adult brain (Luo et al., 2013) has shown that neuronal phase patterns in *low-frequency oscillatory responses* below 8 Hz (i.e., in the delta and theta bands) are critical to the learning process. Distinguishably-different low-frequency oscillatory phase patterns were shown by Luo and colleagues to form gradually over learning time, thereby differentiating novel noise patterns as individual auditory objects for successful learners. If a similar learning mechanism underpins the learning of the acoustic patterns which are words, then the phase differences in dyslexia in the delta band revealed here would have serious consequences for the quality of the phonological representations of word forms developed by affected children. Oscillatory phase patterns may be more important than oscillation amplitude in terms of informational encoding. Ng et al. (2013) used natural animal sounds to investigate the encoding of acoustic stimuli in macaque auditory cortex, examining neural firing directly by recording local field potentials inside the brain. Ng and colleagues showed that stimulus-selective firing patterns imprinted on the *phase* rather than the *amplitude* of slow oscillations (<8 Hz), with phase patterns rather than oscillation power carrying discriminative information. A comparable result was reported for human EEG to the same naturalistic stimuli, and Ng and colleagues noted that these naturalistic stimuli could be discriminated on the basis of their phase patterns *without* any increases in oscillatory power. The emerging importance of phase suggests that the brain capitalizes on both power (firing rate) and phase (the timing of firing) when encoding and developing neuronal representations for a complex stimulus like human speech. Therefore, the neural timing differences revealed in the current study could carry important implications for the *quality* of phonological encoding. Note that earlier ASSR studies measuring differences in response *power* between adult participants with and without dyslexia did not measure phase consistency across trials (Lehongre et al., 2011; Poelmans et al., 2012). The identified difference in grand averaged power in those studies may hence be due to inconsistent phase alignment across trials. Both firing rates and phase patterns tend to be sensitive to the same acoustic features (Ng et al., 2013). Hamalainen et al. did investigate both phase and power in their ASSR study, and in their MEG study the group differences between participants with dyslexia and controls at 2 Hz were caused by differential phase consistency and not by differential response power. Note further that in the non-speech study reported by Soltesz et al. (2013), phase *was* examined, and those with dyslexia did show an earlier preferred phase in the 2 Hz entrainment condition compared to the control group; however, this effect was not significant. Nevertheless, it is important to note that none of these earlier dyslexic studies used the speech signal as input.

Contrary to prediction, we did not find any significant differences in *visual entrainment* between children with dyslexia and control children. As noted earlier, differences between dyslexic and control children have been found in visual attention shifting tasks (e.g., Facoetti et al., 2010) and in visual attention span measures (e.g., Lallier and Valdois, 2012), while adults with dyslexia have been reported to show *superior* perception of and memory for low-frequency visual features in natural scenes (Schneps et al., 2012). Our task explored the neural processing of natural dynamic visual cues to speech perception, which incorporate both low-frequency (e.g., jaw movement) and high-frequency (e.g., lip shape) visuo-spatial information, and by hypothesis should be directly related to the quality of phonological encoding. However, in the visual alone condition, dyslexics and controls showed equivalent entrainment strength and equivalent preferred phase, while in the AV condition the dyslexic group again showed an earlier preferred phase in the delta band compared to control participants, mirroring the findings for the auditory alone condition. When we explored how visual speech information affected the phase of auditory entrainment, we found that in the theta band visual information did alter preferred auditory phase, but to the same extent for both groups. Visual speech information is thought to reset auditory theta phase to the optimal alignment for processing upcoming speech (Schroeder and Lakatos, 2009). The only significant group difference was again in the delta band. As in the auditory alone condition, when computed for (AV–V), preferred phase of entrainment was significantly earlier for the dyslexic group. Hence despite the accompanying visual information, in the AV condition the participants with dyslexia were again entraining to a suboptimal phase. As previously, this suggests that the slower delta oscillations are not providing the dyslexic brain with an efficient temporal reference frame for auditory information encoding. In the theta band, by contrast, both groups showed efficient phase resetting of auditory oscillatory activity by congruent visual information.

In fact, given the earlier study by Power et al. (2012b) using the current paradigm, which reported a significant relationship between theta power and reading development in typically-developing children, the absence of significant group differences in theta band entrainment in the current study is somewhat surprising. Theta entrainment is thought to be central to speech processing on multi-time resolution models (syllable-level entrainment, e.g., Luo and Poeppel, 2007). However, our failure to find group differences in theta power or phase could be task-related. The participants were required to process a delta-rate rhythm (2 Hz), and to detect violations of that rhythm, and thus task demands did not focus on theta entrainment or phase. If stimuli had been delivered instead at a rhythmic rate within the theta band (e.g., 5 Hz), group differences in theta activity may have emerged. Nevertheless, the current violation detection task is likely to be more informative than the passive entrainment tasks used in prior studies with adult dyslexics (Lehongre et al., 2011; Hämäläinen et al., 2012b; Poelmans et al., 2012). With a passive listening paradigm it is impossible to quantify how the different groups are approaching the task, for example whether those with dyslexia and controls are using similar processing strategies. Furthermore, prior oscillatory studies suggest that when a stimulus is continuous (rather than rhythmic, as utilized here), the brain uses a continuous mode of processing, which maximizes gamma activity (e.g., Schroeder and Lakatos, 2009). Hence the gamma findings in prior studies using non-speech and continuous stimuli (Lehongre et al., 2011; Poelmans et al., 2012), indicating that gamma power was significantly lower in the dyslexic group when processing AM noise, could reflect task demands rather than stimulus-specific processing differences between participants with dyslexia and controls.

In conclusion, this study provides direct neural evidence for the "phonological representations" hypothesis of developmental dyslexia, according to which the neural representations underpinning word recognition in children with dyslexia are impaired or atypical in their phonological characteristics. The current study suggests that one mechanism contributing to atypical development of the dyslexic mental lexicon is auditory oscillatory entrainment to speech at a different preferred phase of the delta band, which consequentially affects the quality of the information encoded at all phonological levels including the phonemic level. Concurrent visual speech information as in natural listening conditions is not sufficient to ameliorate this difference in preferred auditory phase, as shown by the AV condition in the current study. Nevertheless, converging evidence is required regarding the developmental salience of delta band information for developing high-quality phonological representations, ideally investigating the entrainment to, and encoding of, auditory and speech stimuli in the dyslexic brain under various task demands.

ACKNOWLEDGMENTS

We would like to thank all the children and their parents for agreeing to take part in this study. This work was supported by the Medical Research Council, grant number G0902375. Our sponsor played no role in the design of the study nor in the collection, analysis, and interpretation of the data. Correspondence should be addressed to Alan Power (alan.j.pow@gmail.com) or Usha Goswami (ucg10@cam.ac.uk).

REFERENCES

Abrams, D. A., Nicol, N., Zecker, S., and Kraus, N. (2009). Abnormal Cortical Processing of the Syllable Rate of Speech in Poor Readers. *J. Neurosci.* 29, 7686–7693. doi: 10.1523/JNEUROSCI.5242-08.2009

Besle, J., Schevon, C. A., Mehta, A. D., Lakatos, P., Goodman, R. R., McKhann, G. M., et al. (2011). Tuning of the human neocortex to the temporal dynamics of attended events. *J. Neurosci.* 31, 3176–3185. doi: 10.1523/JNEUROSCI.4518-10.2011

Canolty, R. T., Edwards, E., Dalal, S. S., Soltani, M., Nagarajan, S. S., Kirsch, H. E., et al. (2006). High gamma power is phase-locked to theta oscillations in human neocortex. *Science* 313, 5793, 1626–1628. doi: 10.1126/science.1128115

Canolty, R. T., and Knight, R. T. (2010). The functional role of cross-frequency coupling. *Trends Cogn. Sci.* 14, 506–515. doi: 10.1016/j.tics.2010.09.001

Dunn, L. M., Dunn, L. M., Whetton, C., and Pintilie, D. (1982). *British Picture Vocabulary Scale.* Windsor: NFER-Nelson.

Elliott, C. D., Smith, P., and McCullogh, K. (1996). *British Ability Scales: Second Edition.* Windsor: NFER-Nelson.

Facoetti, A., Corradi, N., Ruffino, M., Gori, S., and Zorzi, M. (2010). Visual spatial attention and speech segmentation are both impaired in preschoolers at familial risk for developmental dyslexia. *Dyslexia* 16, 226–239. doi: 10.1002/dys.413

Ghitza, O., and Greenberg, S. (2009). On the possible role of brain rhythms in speech perception: intelligibility of time-compressed speech with periodic and aperiodic insertions of silence. *Phonetica* 66, 113–126. doi: 10.1159/000208934

Giraud, A. L., and Poeppel, D. (2012). "Speech perception from a neurophysiological perspective," in *Human Auditory Cortex*, ed D. Poeppel, T. Overath, A. N. Popper, and R. R. Fay (New York, NY: Springer), 225–259.

Gomez-Ramirez, M., Kelly, S. P., Molholm, S., Sehatpour, P., Schwartz, T. H., and Foxe, J. J. (2011). Oscillatory sensory selection mechanisms during intersensory attention to rhythmic auditory and visual inputs: a human electrocorticographic investigation. *J. Neurosci.* 31, 18556–18567. doi: 10.1523/JNEUROSCI.2164-11.2011

Goswami, U. (2011). A temporal sampling framework for developmental dyslexia. *Trends Cogn. Sci.* 15, 3–10. doi: 10.1016/j.tics.2010.10.001

Goswami, U., Mead, N., Fosker, T., Huss, M., Barnes, L., and Leong, V. (2013). Impaired perception of syllable stress in children with dyslexia: a longitudinal study. *J. Mem. Lang.* 69, 1–17. doi: 10.1016/j.jml.2013.03.001

Goswami, U., Wang, H.-L., Cruz, A., Fosker, T., Mead, N., and Huss, M. (2011). Language-universal sensory deficits in developmenta dyslexia: English, Spanish and Chinese. *J. Cogn. Neurosci.* 23, 325–337. doi: 10.1162/jocn.2010.21453

Greenberg, S., Carvey, H., Hitchcock, L., and Chang, S. (2003). Temporal properties of spontaneous speech: a syllable-centric perspective. *J. Phon.* 31, 465–485. doi: 10.1016/j.wocn.2003.09.005

Hämäläinen, J. A., Salminen, H. K., and Leppänen, P. H. (2012a). Basic auditory processing deficits in dyslexia: systematic review of the behavioral and event-related potential/field evidence. *J. Learn. Disabil.* 46, 413–427. doi: 10.1177/0022219411436213

Hämäläinen, J. A., Rupp, A., Soltész, F., Szücs, D., and Goswami, U. (2012b). Reduced phase locking to slow amplitude modulation in adults with dyslexia: an MEG study. *Neuroimage* 59, 2952–2961. doi: 10.1016/j.neuroimage.2011.09.075

Harrison, D., and Kanji, G. K. (1988). The development of analysis of variance for circular data. *J. Appl. Stat.* 15, 197. doi: 10.1080/02664768800000026

Horton, C., D'Zmura, M., and Srinivasan, R. (2013). Suppression of competing speech through entrainment of cortical oscillations. *J. Neurophysiol.* 109, 3082–3093. doi: 10.1152/jn.01026.2012

Kobayashi, M., Kato, J., Haynes, C., Macaruso, P., and Hook, P. (2003). Cognitive-linguistic factors in Japanese children's reading (Yoji no yominoryoku ni kakawaru ninchigengoteki noryoku). *Jpn. J. Learn. Disabil.* 12, 259–267.

Lakatos, P., Karmos, G., Mehta, A. D., Ulbert, I., and Schroeder, C. E. (2008). Entrainment of neuronal oscillations as a mechanism of attentional selection. *Science* 320, 110–113. doi: 10.1126/science.1154735

Lakatos, P., Shah, A. S., Knuth, K. H., Ulbert, I., Karmos, G., and Schroeder, C. E. (2005). An oscillatory hierarchy controlling neuronal excitability and stimulus processing in the auditory cortex. *J. Neurophysiol.* 94, 1904–1911. doi: 10.1152/jn.00263.2005

Lallier, M., Thierry, G., Tainturier, M. J., Donnadieu, S., Peyrin, C., Billard, C., et al. (2009). Auditory and visual stream segregation in children and adults: an assessment of the amodality assumption of the 'sluggish attentional shifting' theory of dyslexia. *Brain Res.* 1302, 132–147. doi: 10.1016/j.brainres.2009.07.037

Lallier, M., and Valdois, S. (2012). "Sequential versus simultaneous processing deficits in developmental dyslexia," in *Dyslexia - A Comprehensive and International Approach*, eds T. N. Wydell and L. Fern-Pollak, (Rijeka: InTech), 73–108. doi: 10.5772/39042

Lehongre, K., Ramus, F., Villiermet, N., Schwartz, D., and Giraud, A.-L. (2011). Altered low-gamma sampling in auditory cortex accounts for the three main facets of dyslexia. *Neuron* 72, 1080–1090. doi: 10.1016/j.neuron.2011.11.002

Leong, V. (2012). *Prosodic Rhythm in the Speech Amplitude Envelope: Amplitude Modulation Phase Hierarchies (AMPHs) and AMPH Models.* Cambridge, UK: PhD Thesis.

Leong, V., and Goswami, U. (2013). Assessment of rhythmic entrainment at multiple timescales in dyslexia: evidence for disruption to syllable timing. *Hear. Res.* doi: 10.1016/j.heares.2013.07.015. [Epub ahead of print].

Luo, H., Liu, Z., and Poeppel, D. (2010). Auditory cortex tracks both auditory and visual stimulus dynamics using low-frequency neuronal phase modulation. *PLoS Biol.* 8:e1000445. doi: 10.1371/journal.pbio.1000445

Luo, H., and Poeppel, D. (2007). Phase patterns of neuronal responses reliably discriminate speech in human auditory cortex. *Neuron* 54, 1001–1010. doi: 10.1016/j.neuron.2007.06.004

Luo, H., Tian, X., Song, K., Zhou, K., and Poeppel, D. (2013). Neural response phase tracks how listeners learn new acoustic representations. *Curr. Biol.* 23, 968–974. doi: 10.1016/j.cub.2013.04.031

Lyytinen, H., Ahonen, T., Eklund, K., Guttorm, T. K., Laakso, M. L., Leinonen, S., et al. (2001). Developmental pathways of children with and without familial risk for dyslexia during the first years of life. *Dev. Neuropsychol.* 20, 535–554. doi: 10.1207/S15326942DN2002_5

Megnin-Viggars, O., and Goswami, U. (2013). Audiovisual perception of noise vocoded speech in dyslexic and non-dyslexic adults: the role of low-frequency visual modulations. *Brain Lang.* 124, 165–173. doi: 10.1016/j.bandl.2012.12.002

Ng, B. S. W., Logothetis, N. K., and Kayser, C. (2013). EEG phase patterns reflect the selectivity of neural firing. *Cereb. Cortex* 23, 389–398. doi: 10.1093/cercor/bhs031

Parks, T. W., and McClellan, J. H. (1972). Chebyshev approximation for nonrecursive digital filters with linear phase. *IEEE Trans. Circuit Theory* 2, 189–194. doi: 10.1109/TCT.1972.1083419

Poelmans, H., Luts, H., Vandermosten, M., Boets, B., Ghesquière, P., and Wouters, J. (2012). Auditory steady state cortical responses indicate deviant phonemic-rate processing in adults with dyslexia. *Ear Hear.* 33, 134–143. doi: 10.1097/AUD.0b013e31822c26b9

Poeppel, D. (2003). The analysis of speech in different temporal integration windows: cerebral lateralization as 'asymmetric sampling in time'. *Speech Commun.* 41, 245–255. doi: 10.1016/S0167-6393(02)00107-3

Poeppel, D., Idsardi, W. J., and van Wassenhove, V. (2008). Speech perception at the interface of neurobiology and linguistics. *Philos. Trans. R. Soc. Lond. B Biol. Sci.* 363, 1071–1086. doi: 10.1098/rstb.2007.2160

Power, A. J., Foxe, J. J., Forde, E. J., Reilly, R. B., and Lalor, E. C. (2012a). At what time is the cocktail party? A late locus of selective attention to natural speech. *Eur. J. Neurosci.* 35, 1497–1503. doi: 10.1111/j.1460-9568.2012.08060.x

Power, A. J., Mead, N., Barnes, L., and Goswami, U. (2012b). Neural entrainment to rhythmically presented auditory, visual, and audio-visual speech in children. *Front. Psychol.* 3:216. doi: 10.3389/fpsyg.2012.00216

Ramus, F., and Szenkovits, G. (2008). What phonological deficit? *Q. J. Exp. Psychol.* 61, 129–141. doi: 10.1080/17470210701508822

Schneps, M. H., Brockmole, J. R., Sonnert, G., and Pomplun, M. (2012). History of reading struggles linked to enhanced learning in low spatial frequency scenes. *PLoS ONE* 7:e35724. doi: 10.1371/journal.pone.0035724

Schroeder, C. E., and Lakatos, P. (2009). Low-frequency neuronal oscillations as instruments of sensory selection. *Trends Neurosci.* 32, 9–18. doi: 10.1016/j.tins.2008.09.012

Schroeder, C. E., Lakatos, P., Kajikawa, Y., Partan, S., and Puce, A. (2008). Neuronal oscillations and visual amplification of speech. *Trends Cogn. Sci.* 12, 106–113. doi: 10.1016/j.tics.2008.01.002

Snowling, M., Bishop, D. V. M., and Stothard, S. E. (2000). Is preschool language impairment a risk factor for dyslexia in adolescence? *Journal of Child Psychology and Psychiatry* 41, 587–600. doi: 10.1111/1469-7610.00651

Soltesz, F., Szücs, D., Leong, V., White, S., and Goswami, G. (2013). Differential phase entrainment of neuroelectric delta oscillations in developmental dyslexia. *PLoS ONE* 8:e76608. doi: 10.1371/journal.pone.0076608

Stefanics, G., Hangya, B., Hernádi, I., Winkler, I., Lakatos, P., and Ulbert, I. (2010). Phase entrainment of human delta oscillations can mediate the effects of expectation on reaction speed. *J. Neurosci.* 30, 13578–13585. doi: 10.1523/JNEUROSCI.0703-10.2010

Thomson, J. M., Fryer, B., Maltby, J., and Goswami, U. (2006). Auditory and motor rhythm awareness in adults with dyslexia. *J. Res. Read.* 29, 334–348. doi: 10.1111/j.1467-9817.2006.00312.x

Thomson, J. M., and Goswami, U. (2008). Rhythmic processing in children with developmental dyslexia: auditory and motor rhythms link to reading and spelling. *J. Physiol. Paris* 102, 120–129. doi: 10.1016/j.jphysparis.2008.03.007

Torgesen, J. K., Wagner, R. K., and Rashotte, C. A. (1999). *Test of Word Reading Efficiency (TOWRE).* Austin, TX: Pro-Ed.

Wechsler, D. (1992). *Wechsler Intelligence Scale for Children, Third Edition (WISC – III).* Kent: The Psychological Corporation.

Witton, C., Talcott, J. B., Hansen, P. C., Richardson, A. J., Griffiths, T. D., Rees, A., et al. (1998). Sensitivity to dynamic auditory and visual stimuli predicts non-word reading ability in both dyslexics and controls. *Curr. Biol.* 8, 791–797. doi: 10.1016/S0960-9822(98)70320-3

Ziegler, J. C., and Goswami, U. (2005). Reading acquisition, developmental dyslexia, and skilled reading across languages: a psycholinguistic grain size theory. *Psychol. Bull.* 131, 3–29. doi: 10.1037/0033-2909.131.1.3

10

Reading the dyslexic brain: multiple dysfunctional routes revealed by a new meta-analysis of PET and fMRI activation studies

Eraldo Paulesu[1,2,3]*†, Laura Danelli[1,2]† and Manuela Berlingeri[1,2]

[1] *Department of Psychology, University of Milano-Bicocca, Milan, Italy*
[2] *NEUROMI- Milan Center for Neuroscience, University of Milano-Bicocca, Milan, Italy*
[3] *fMRI – Unit, Istituto di Ricovero e Cura a Carattere Scientifico Galeazzi, Milan, Italy*

Correspondence:
Eraldo Paulesu, Dipartimento di Psicologia, Università degli Studi di Milano-Bicocca, Pzza dell'Ateneo Nuovo, 1, 20126 Milano, Italy
e-mail: eraldo.paulesu@unimib.it

†These authors have shared first co-authorship.

Developmental dyslexia has been the focus of much functional anatomical research. The main trust of this work is that typical developmental dyslexics have a dysfunction of the phonological and orthography to phonology conversion systems, in which the left occipito-temporal cortex has a crucial role. It remains to be seen whether there is a systematic co-occurrence of dysfunctional patterns of different functional systems perhaps converging on the same brain regions associated with the reading deficit. Such evidence would be relevant for theories like, for example, the magnocellular/attentional or the motor/cerebellar ones, which postulate a more basic and anatomically distributed disorder in dyslexia. We addressed this issue with a meta-analysis of all the imaging literature published until September 2013 using a combination of hierarchical clustering and activation likelihood estimation methods. The clustering analysis on 2360 peaks identified 193 clusters, 92 of which proved spatially significant. Following binomial tests on the clusters, we found left hemispheric network specific for normal controls (i.e., of reduced involvement in dyslexics) including the left inferior frontal, premotor, supramarginal cortices and the left infero-temporal and fusiform regions: these were preferentially associated with reading and the visual-to-phonology processes. There was also a more dorsal left fronto-parietal network: these clusters included peaks from tasks involving phonological manipulation, but also motoric or visuo-spatial perception/attention. No cluster was identified in area V5 for no task, nor cerebellar clusters showed a reduced association with dyslexics. We conclude that the examined literature demonstrates a specific lack of activation of the left occipito-temporal cortex in dyslexia particularly for reading and reading-like behaviors and for visuo-phonological tasks. Additional deficits of motor and attentional systems relevant for reading may be associated with altered functionality of dorsal left fronto-parietal cortex.

Keywords: developmental dyslexia, meta-analysis, fMRI, PET, ALE, hierarchical clustering

INTRODUCTION

Developmental dyslexia (DD), the inability of acquiring fluent reading skills notwithstanding normal intelligence, adequate socio-cultural conditions, and preserved elementary sensory skills (DSM-IV, American Psychiatric Association, 1994; ICD-10, World Healt Organization, 1993), often co-occurs with phonological deficits (Snowling, 2001) that persist in adult life (Paulesu et al., 2001; Ramus et al., 2003). While it is fairly clear which classes of phonological tasks are more sensitive in bringing about a deficient performance in dyslexics (e.g., spoonerism tasks; see for example, Pennington et al., 1990), the fine-grained nature of cognitive deficits underlying these faulty performances remains to be established fully (Frith, 1999).

Subjects with DD may present a more complex behavioral profile (Menghini et al., 2010), the reading and phonological difficulties being sometimes accompanied by attentional, visual- and auditory-magnocellular and/or motor-cerebellar impairments (Facoetti et al., 2000; Nicolson et al., 2001; Stein, 2001; Gaab et al., 2007); these are hereafter called "*additional deficits*"[1]. The prevalence of the *additional deficits* may vary from sample to sample fuelling the debate on whether a core dyslexia syndrome exists together with a core underlying cognitive deficit. Indeed, the variable importance given to the *additional deficits* by different authors is one strong motivation for the presence of competing interpretations of dyslexia as a syndrome. The matter is complicated by the fact that the studies on co-morbidity in dyslexia have been run in groups selected with very different criteria: the range spans from studies on highly compensated adult university students in some cases (Ramus et al., 2003; Reid et al., 2007) to

[1]This labeling is used for convenience only without ideological positions about the importance of these deficits in dyslexia.

unselected young kids in other cases (Heim et al., 2008; Menghini et al., 2010). Studies in adult dyslexics have the advantage of permitting the assessment of a relatively stable neurocognitive system and to minimize the observation of co-occurring deficits due to delayed maturation; studies in kids are more prone to the uncertainties due to the—not necessarily synchronous—development of the multiple systems involved in reading and to the changing neuropsychological patterns that may place a given kid in the dyslexic or in the normal population range, depending on the year of testing (see for example, Shaywitz et al., 1992). Of course, studies in kids have the advantage of giving information relevant for the developmental process while the reading skill is being acquired.

There have been great hopes that functional anatomical studies of dyslexia could contribute to a better understanding of the disorder: it has been reasoned that if a well-defined malfunctioning brain system was identified, one could make stronger inferences on the nature of dyslexia at the cognitive level as well. This would have had obvious consequences in the field of rehabilitation (Demonet et al., 2004).

Indeed, brain imaging has had the merit of giving a demonstration that dyslexia has neurological bases. However, this demonstration has come sometimes in contrasting ways, giving further breath to the debate on the nature of dyslexia and on whether different forms of dyslexia exist and their relative weight.

By the time of the completion of the data collection for this paper, there have been more than 50 functional imaging papers on dyslexia that one could use for a formal review of the literature with a meta-analysis.

This previous literature can be grouped in few broad classes of activation studies: studies with tasks involving primarily reading (including lexical decision tasks, phonological awareness tasks or semantic tasks); lexical retrieval for visual stimuli, as in picture naming; studies on auditory phonological processes; studies on motor tasks and motor learning; studies on visual perception (picture or face oriented) or on visuo-spatial attention; studies on early visual or auditory processes, including stimuli tackling the magnocellular systems.

After such a huge experimental effort in the field, any review of the data based on a conventional verbose discussion of what is nominally described by the authors would prove insufficient, confusing, and sometimes contradictory. This is also because a nominal reference to a given brain structure, and the ensuing discussions, is deprived of much value and sometimes misleading when the precise stereotactic location of a statistical effect may point to more specific cortical or subcortical regions: congruence and incongruence of different data may only appear such because of this impreciseness[2].

In addition, the relative weight of a given study, based on the sample sizes and statistical thresholds adopted, is often impossible to deal with. Having clearly in mind the aforementioned limitations of *verbose*, that is, non-quantitative, reviews, we mention hereafter those that seem to be the most solid findings for reading related tasks. To make this illustration, we use some of the raw data that were entered into a formal meta-analysis in the paper. Much of this discussion will hopefully be superseded by the results of the present meta-analysis whose aim was in fact to shed further light in the dyslexia imaging literature by showing findings that truly replicate across studies of the same class and perhaps across studies of different classes.

STUDIES ON THE CORE SYMPTOMS: READING AND PHONOLOGICAL PROCESSING

The studies involving single-word reading in some form indicate dysfunction of both left occipito-temporal (ventral) (see Paulesu et al., 2001; Shaywitz et al., 2002 and more 20 studies from those listed in **Table 1**) or left temporo-parietal (dorsal) cortex (see for example Rumsey et al., 1992, 1997a). In particular, it has been proposed that the dorsal temporo-parietal cortex might be associated with an early dysfunction of phonological processing, emerging in the initial stage of learning process (Turkeltaub et al., 2003; Sandak et al., 2004), while the ventral occipito-temporal region may be associated with perturbed maturation of the word recognition systems (Paulesu et al., 2001; Sandak et al., 2004), a finding that generalizes across different alphabetic orthographies (Paulesu et al., 2001) and even Chinese (Hu et al., 2010).

A first look on the highly replicated finding for the left ventral occipito-temporal cortex can be seen in **Figure 1A**, where the location of the local maxima of significant hemodynamic response reduction was described for dyslexics. In the figure we visualize the peaks of reduced activations in dyslexia for all tasks that involved reading from the papers listed in **Table 1**.

A further look to the distribution of the areas of reduced activations for any task involving reading in dyslexia (see **Figure 1B**), however, provides a more complex picture that clearly justifies the urge for a formal re-assessment of the data.

Are these patterns age dependent? Are some of them task dependent? What is the role of the right hemispheric hypoactivations for a behavior like reading that is highly dependent on a left-lateralized neural system (Cattinelli et al., 2013a; Taylor et al., 2013)? More importantly, what is the level of replication of the findings of any given paper? Is this seemingly highly distributed pattern of malfunction undermining our understanding of the biology and the cognition of dyslexia? These are all questions that are still in search of some formal answer.

In fact, the situation appears immediately more complex if one also considers phonological tasks, both visual and auditory. As one major theory of dyslexia predicates a phonological deficit it becomes logical to expect a great anatomical congruence between findings based on reading and findings based on phonological tasks. The way these focal effects (regional hypoactivations in dyslexia) overlap with the reading ones is illustrated by **Figure 1C** (dots in blue and dots in green). Clearly there is some degree of overlap between the three sets of findings.

However, there are also quite a few discrepancies. The same unsolved questions listed before apply here.

[2]One obvious historical such example can be the parietal region involved in phonological short-term memory: identified at the temporo-parietal junction by Paulesu et al. (1993, 1995), it was re-discovered, so to speak, two cm above by Smith et al. (1998). This is just one of the many obvious limitations of reviews based on qualitative approaches (for more discussions, see Fox et al., 1998; Cattinelli et al., 2013b).

Table 1 | List of papers included in the metanalysis.

Authors	Year	Tecnique	Sample size (Controls/ Dyslexics)	Age of subjects	Modality presentation of stimuli	Experimental task
Bach et al.	2010	fMRI	18/11	Children	Visual	Letter substitution
Backes et al.	2002	fMRI	8/8	Children	Visual	Line orientation, string comparison, non-word reading, semantic judgment
Beneventi et al.	2009	fMRI	13/11	Children	Visual	Sequential verbal working memory task
Beneventi et al.	2010b	fMRI	14/12	Children	Visual	Working memory n-back task
Beneventi et al.	2010a	fMRI	13/11	Children	Visual	Working memory n-back task
Booth et al.	2007	fMRI	39/39	Children	Auditory, visual	Word-pair semantic judgment
Brambati et al.	2006	fMRI	11/13	Adults	Visual	Word and pseudoword reading
Brunswick et al.	1999	PET	6/6	Adults	Visual	Word and pseudoword reading
Cao et al.	2006	fMRI	12/12	Children	Visual	Word rhyming
Cao et al.	2008	fMRI	14/14	Children	Visual	Word rhyming
Conway et al.	2008	fMRI	11/11	Adults	Auditory	Auditory pseudoword segmentation
Desroches et al.	2010	fMRI	12/12	Children	Auditory	Auditory rhyming task
Dufor et al.	2007	PET	16/14	Adults	Auditory	Phoneme categorization
Eden et al.	2004	fMRI	19/19	Adults	Auditory	Word repetition, phoneme delection
Gaab et al.	2007	fMRI	23/22	Children	Auditory	Sound discrimination
Georgiewa et al.	1999	fMRI	17/17	Children	Visual	Non-word reading, frequent word reading, phonological manipulation
Grande et al.	2011	fMRI	25/20	Children	Visual	Picture naming, reading aloud of words
Grunling et al.	2004	fMRI	21/17	Children	Visual	Slash pattern matching, letter strings matching, pseudoword matching, frequent word matching, pseudoword rhyming
Heim et al.	2010	fMRI	20/16	Children	Auditory, visual	Phoneme discrimination, motion detection, attention shifting, auditory discrimination of verbal and non-verbal stimuli
Hoeft et al.	2006	fMRI	20/10	Children	Visual	Word rhyming
Ingvar et al.	2002	PET	9/9	Adults	Visual	Word and pseudoword reading
Kast et al.	2011	fMRI	13/12	Adults	Auditory, visual	Lexical decision
Kovelman et al.	2011	fMRI	12/12	Children	Visual	Word matching, word rhyming
Kronbichler et al.	2006	fMRI	15/13	Children	Visual	Sentence reading
Kronschnabel et al.	2013	fMRI	22/13	Children	Visual	Word and pseudoword reading
Landi et al.	2010	fMRI	13/13	Children	Visual	Word rhyming, semantic categorization
MacSweeney et al.	2009	fMRI	7/7	Adults	Visual	Picture matching, word Rhyming
Maurer et al.	2011	fMRI	16/11	Children	Visual	Word matching, pseudoword matching, picture matching
McCrory et al.	2000	PET	8/6	Adults	Auditory	Word and pseudoword repetition
McCrory et al.	2005	PET	10/8	Adults	Visual	Word reading, pitcure naming
Menghini et al.	2006	fMRI	14/14	Adults	Visual	Implicit motor learning
Meyler et al.	2008	fMRI	12/23	Children	Visual	Sentence judgment
Monzalvo et al.	2012	fMRI	23/23	Children	Visual	Houses, faces, word and checkboard perception, sentence listening in native and foreign language
Nicolson et al.	1999	PET	6/6	Adults	Auditory	Sequence motor learning
Olulade et al.	2012	fMRI	12/9	Adults	Visual	Word and pseudoword rhyming, Spatial rotation
Paulesu et al.	1996	PET	5/5	Adults	Visual	Syllable rhyming, verbal short-term memory task
Paulesu et al.	2001	PET	36/36	Adults	Visual	Word and non-word reading
Pecini et al.	2011	fMRI	13/13	Adults	Audiovisual	Rhyme-generation task
Pekkola et al.	2006	fMRI	10/10	Adults	Audiovisual	Perception of matching and conflicting audio-visual speech
Peyrin et al.	2011	fMRI	12/12	Children	Visual	Letter matching
Reilhac et al.	2013	fMRI	12/12	Adults	Visual	Letter string comparison
Richlan et al.	2010	fMRI	18/15	Adults	Visual	Phonological lexical decision

(Continued)

Table 1 | Continued

Authors	Year	Tecnique	Sample size (Controls/ Dyslexics)	Age of subjects	Modality presentation of stimuli	Experimental task
Rimrodt et al.	2009	fMRI	15/14	Children	Visual	Word recognition, sentence judgment
Ruff et al.	2002	fMRI	11/6	Adults	Auditory	Implicit categorial perception of phonemes
Rumsey et al.	1997b	PET	14/17	Adults	Visual	Irregular word and pseudoword reading, phonologial and ortographic lexical decision
Schulz et al.	2008	fMRI	22/12	Children	Visual	Sentence judgment
Schulz et al.	2009	fMRI	30/15	Children	Visual	Sentence judgment
Steinbrink et al.	2012	fMRI	16/17	Adults	Auditory	Same-different judgment of vowel duration
Temple et al.	2000	fMRI	8/10	Adults	Auditory	Sound discrimination
Temple et al.	2001	fMRI	15/24	Children	Visual	Letter matching, letter rhyming
van der Mark et al.	2009	fMRI	24/18	Children	Visual	Phonological lexical decision
Vasic et al.	2008	fMRI	13/12	Adults	Visual	Verbal working memory task
Wimmer et al.	2010	fMRI	19/20	Adults	Visual	Phonological lexical decision

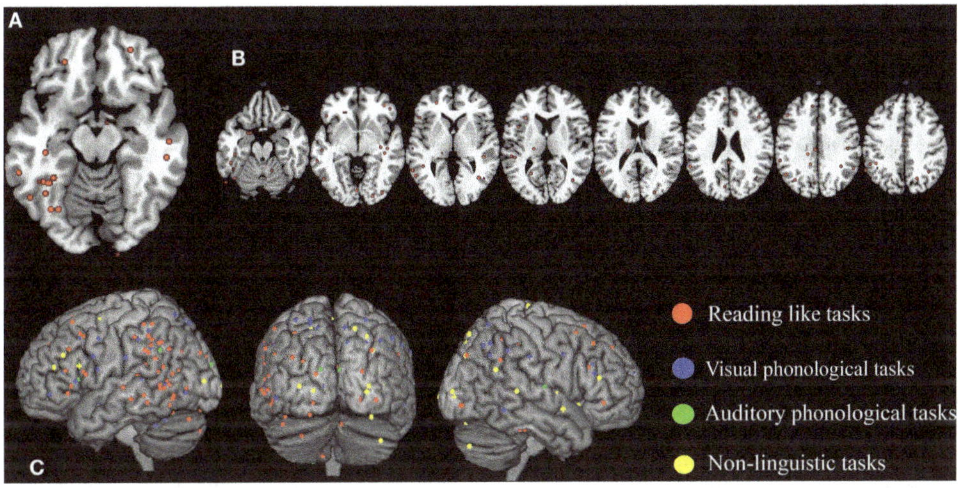

FIGURE 1 | Peaks of reduced activations in dyslexia for all tasks that involved reading (circles in red), for visual or auditory phonological tasks (circles in blue and in green, respectively) and for non-linguistic tasks (circles in yellow). (A) Show the highly replicated reduction of dyslexics at the level of the left ventral occipito-temporal peaks reported in literature. In **(B)** all the peaks of reduced activations observed in dyslexics during reading tasks included in our meta-analysis are reported. Finally, in **(C)** all the peaks of reduced activations observed in dyslexics during reading, phonological and non-linguistic tasks included in our meta-analysis are reported.

ASHES TO ASHES, NOISE TO NOISE: THE CONTRIBUTION OF THE IMAGING FINDINGS ON THE ADDITIONAL DEFICITS IN DYSLEXIA

Studies on what we call the additional deficits of dyslexia investigated the neural dysfunction of more basic abilities such as those of the magnocellular (visual or auditory) system, of the spatial attention system and of motor control with particular attention to the functions of the cerebellum.

The case of the visual magnocellular and visuo-motion perception system is an exemplar one: a dysfunction of this system is suggested by evidence that dyslexic may have reduced contrast sensitivity at the low spatial frequencies and low luminance levels (stimuli favored by the magnocells; Stein and Walsh, 1997), reduced visual-motion sensitivity, in particular for coherent motion (Cornelissen et al., 1995), that correlates with impaired letter position encoding (Cornelissen et al., 1998); the same deficit may explain greater crowding effects in dyslexic subjects (Zorzi et al., 2012). In addition, subjects with dyslexia may have subtle signs of a dysfunctional visuo-spatial attentional system (Facoetti et al., 2000) that may be more severe for the left hemispace in a sort of mini-neglect (Hari and Renvall, 2001; Liddle et al., 2009). This evidence was supported initially by ERP data (Galaburda and Livingstone, 1993) who found reduced VEPs in 5 dyslexics for low contrast reversing checkerboard stimuli (a finding not replicated by others—see Johannes et al., 1996) and a disorganized magnocellular subdivision of the lateral geniculate nucleus.

Initial fMRI evidence pointing to a dysfunctional magnocellular system was provided by Eden et al. (1996) followed by Demb et al. (1998) in two small samples of subjects: they found reduced activation of the visual motion area MT/V5, a result that was lately not confirmed by MEG data, as Vanni et al. (1997) found normal MT/V5 activation for moving stimuli.

Notwithstanding that the contribution of the magnocellular and visuo-motion perception system in normal reading remains contentious (no involvement of MT/V5 is seen for single word reading in normal subjects), the aforementioned results have been seen as a imaging evidence of the malfunction of the visual magnocellular system in dyslexia. Indeed, the magnocellular hypothesis remains a much pursued research avenue in dyslexia. Similar considerations may apply to the cerebellar hypothesis and its investigation.

To make this brutal introductory overview even more dismaying, **Figure 1C** (dots in yellow) shows how focal hypo-activations spread all over the brain if one considers non-linguistic tasks for either the visual modality or the motor one. This picture is quite similar with what would emerge if the scars and dyslaminations originally described by Galaburda et al. (1985) were superimposed onto the lateral surface of the brain in stereotactic space.

It should be noted that in these examples, we illustrate only voxels showing significant differences between groups. There is much more to be displayed if one considers as we did in the paper, also within group effects.

Clearly, such body of data cannot be assessed and summarized by a mere discussion of what has found paper X as opposed to paper Y. The obvious alternative to qualitative reviews is provided by formal meta-analyses, as their quantitative approach makes them more rigorous and less prone to subjective bias. In brain imaging, meta-analyses are generally used to identify groups of regional effects that fall sufficiently close in stereotactic space to be interpreted as reflecting a common functional-anatomical entity (Fox et al., 1998; Wager et al., 2007; Cattinelli et al., 2013b). The functional significance of any of these entities then needs to be analyzed, on the basis of the background information about the experiments that generated the activation peaks constituting them. Several meta-analytic studies, differing in the specific technique employed and the investigated cognitive domain, have appeared in the literature in recent years (Salimi-Khorshidi et al., 2009; Kober and Wager, 2010; Radua and Mataix-Cols, 2012). Quantitative meta-analytic approaches were also recently used to determine consistency across neuroimaging studies and to identify regions reported as dysfunctional in developmental dyslexia (Maisog et al., 2008; Richlan et al., 2009). In particular, two studies, using the Activation Likelihood Estimation (ALE) method (Maisog et al., 2008; Richlan et al., 2009), analyzed the neural differences between controls and dyslexics during reading and reading-related tasks, i.e., letter matching, rhyming, semantic judgment, and lexical decision tasks. In both articles, the authors suggested that developmental dyslexia is associated with the hypoactivation of the left occipito-temporal, temporo-parietal, and inferior frontal regions. No evidence for a systematic hyperactivation in the dyslexics was found (for the left inferior frontal cortex, nor for the cerebellum, as initially suggested by Shaywitz et al. (1998).

To provide information on the developmental progression of neural dysfunction in dyslexia, Richlan et al. (2011) performed a second meta-analysis and separated adult-related activations and children-related activations while comparing controls and dyslexics. They observed that the left occipito-temporal and temporo-parietal hypoactivation was present in the studies on adults. A hypoactivation was also observed in the anterior portion of the left occipito-temporal cortex for dyslexic children.

AIMS OF THE STUDY

These previous meta-analyses were focused on the task of reading or on reading-like behaviors. Aim of this study was to further assess the dysfunctional anatomical correlates of dyslexia, to approach the issue of co-occurrence of neural dysfunction dyslexia and test the hypothesis that, beyond well replicated findings (the lack of commitment to reading of the left ventral occipito-temporal cortex), other functional anatomical deficits might be present. The usual logic used to test this hypothesis in previous studies has been to assess the presence of focal hypoactivations in non-reading tasks, for example, in motor learning (Nicolson et al., 1999; Menghini et al., 2006) or visual motion perception (Eden et al., 1996). Conversely, the logic behind our study is similar to the one of Danelli et al. (2013) for normal reading: given the vast literature supporting the involvement of multiple systems in dyslexia (Frith, 1999; Nicolson et al., 2001; Snowling, 2001; Stein, 2001; Reid et al., 2007; Pernet et al., 2009), and given that these systems normally intersect in the brain into higher order cortices (Danelli et al., 2013), we expected that, on top of differences in brain areas that are highly specific for reading, dyslexics may also show a more limited functional anatomical intersection between different systems normally overlapping in skilled readers. This would be revealed in the present meta-analysis by reduced presence of regional effects from dyslexic groups in clusters showing a mix of peaks from reading-like and non-reading-like behaviors in normal controls.

In the present study this hypothesis was tested using a meta-analytical approach based on the optimized hierarchical clustering (HC) algorithm of Cattinelli et al. (2013b), complemented by the ALE algorithm (Turkeltaub et al., 2002; Eickhoff et al., 2009).

Hierarchical clustering has the advantage of permitting *post-hoc* statistical assessments of the functional or group assignations of individual clusters without the constraint of considering super-homogenous tasks at the stage of cluster identification, as when using ginger-ALE alone.

However, hierarchical clustering does not provide a statistical test of the spatial significance of a given cluster against a random reference distribution of regional effects. This is permitted by the ALE approach (Turkeltaub et al., 2002; Eickhoff et al., 2009) that we used to complement our analyses. A schematic flowchart diagram is now reported in **Figure 2**. A previous example of this combined approach can be found in Crepaldi et al. (2013), where, in addition to the dual meta-analytical procedure, the clusters were assessed *post-hoc* not only for simple effects but also for interaction effects, as in the present study.

By considering all imaging studies on dyslexia, no matter the neurocognitive domain under investigation, we hoped to detect the existence of a systematic co-occurrence of dysfunctional patterns of different functional systems and to evaluate whether these involve different system specific brain regions or rather multimodal regions that normally show intersections of multiple

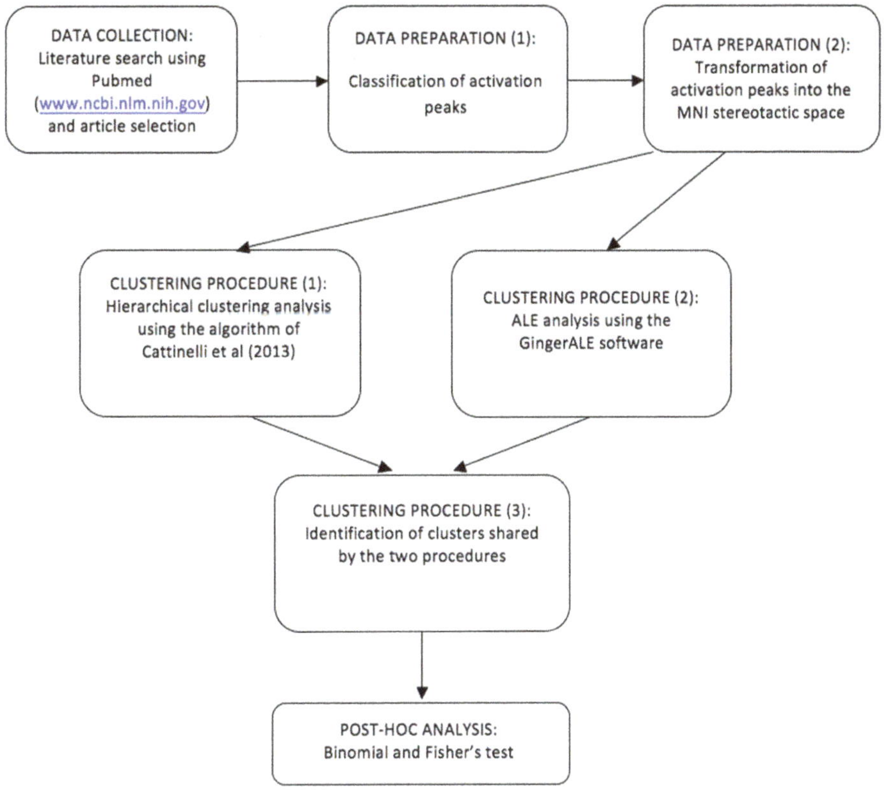

FIGURE 2 | A schematic flowchart diagram showing the procedure by which data are selected, clusters are estimated, tested and classified using HC and ALE.

systems. The face validity of the latter hypothesis was also assessed by comparison with the data of Danelli et al. (2013).

METHODS

DATA COLLECTION AND PREPARATION

Our meta-analysis is based on 53 neuroimaging articles investigating the anatomofunctional dysfunction of developmental dyslexia using PET or fMRI in both children and adult subjects published to September 2013.

Studies were selected through PubMed database (http://www.ncbi.nlm.nih.gov/pubmed/) running five queries. The search keys were: "Dyslexia AND fMRI," "Dyslexia AND PET," "Dyslexia AND neuroimaging," "Dyslexia AND functional Magnetic Resonance Imaging," and "Dyslexia AND Positron Emission Tomography." These queries returned 544, 34, 462, 267, and 45 entries, respectively.

After removing duplicates, we included only studies that did satisfy the following inclusion criteria: (1) sample population composed of both normal controls and subjects with developmental dyslexia; (2) imaging technique: PET or fMRI; (3) whole brain voxel based data-analyses using stereotactic conventions; region-of-interest analyses were not considered nor multiple single case analyses restricted to few regions, as, for example, in Eden et al. (1996); (4) presence of data for either within group comparisons, or between group comparisons or both.

For the suitable studies, in the meta-analysis we used data derived from (i) within group *simple effects* and (ii) between *group comparisons*. We incorporated also the within group data to have a more complete survey on whether a given brain region was differentially activated across groups, while still being active in each a group above a given conventional threshold, or whether the region, besides being significantly associated with one group, it never reached statistically significant effects in the other group. In any event, for the interaction group-by-task effects we only considered 1st order interactions.

Only data emerging from univariate statistical analyses were considered.

By applying such criteria, we included 2360 stereotactic activation loci, 1402 associated with controls and 958 associated with subjects with dyslexia. Thirty-nine foci were excluded by the analyses because they were outside of the boundaries the MNI stereotactic space.

The main characteristics of the 53 experiments included in this meta-analysis are reported in **Table 1**.

CLASSIFICATION OF THE RAW DATA PRIOR TO CLUSTERING ANALYSES

For each activation peak, we recorded all relevant information about the statistical comparison that generated it. We therefore determined a list of classification criteria to characterize each peak of activation included in the dataset (**Table S1** of the Supplementary Materials). These classifications were used for initial *post-hoc* statistical comparisons on the clusters that passed the ginger-ALE test for spatial significance.

- *Subjects*: we classified each peak on the basis of the age of the subjects. In particular, we considered as separate categories in this variable: (i) *children* when sample age was under the age of 18, (ii) *adults* when sample age was above the age of 18.
- *Stimulation modality*: (i) *auditory* or (ii) *visual.*
- *Nature of the experimental task*: for the sake of simplicity, the data were grouped in the following two broad categories: (i) *reading-like tasks* included orthographic tasks as letter matching or string comparison, reading, visual lexical decision, visual phonological tasks as rhyming, word manipulation or verbal short-term memory tasks, visual semantic tasks as written sentence comprehension or semantic judgment; because of its functional analogy (see McCrory et al., 2005) with the reading behavior and the documented reduced activations in reading-related brain areas in developmental dyslexia, picture naming was included in this group (ii) *non-reading-like tasks* included auditory perception task as sound, vowel or speech discrimination, motor tasks, visual perception and visuo-spatial attention tasks and lip reading for single vowel sounds[3].

For each peak we also completed our database with information about the variables listed below.

- *Scanning Technique* (PET or fMRI),
- *Stereotactic template* (*MNI* or *Tailarach and Tournoux* template),
- *Staistical thresholds* and *nature of the correction* for multiple comparisons.

To make it possible a combination of data coming from studies based on different stereotactic spaces, the stereotactic coordinates of studies in which activation peaks were reported in terms of the Talairach and Tournoux atlas (Talairach and Tournoux, 1988) were transformed into the MNI (Montreal Neurological Institute) stereotactic space (Mazziotta et al., 1995); the transformation was done using the software GingerALE, using MatthewBrett's script (http://imaging.mrc-cbu.cam.ac.uk/imaging/MniTalairach).

CLUSTERING PROCEDURE

First, we performed a hierarchical clustering analysis (HC) of the activation peaks as described in Cattinelli et al. (2013b): the analysis allowed us to extract the principal clusters of regional effects from the database. Hierarchical clustering was performed by using functions implemented in MATLAB 7. After computation of squared euclidean distances between each pair of the input data, clusters with minimal dissimilarity were recursively merged using Ward's (1963) criterion which minimizes total intracluster variance after each merging step. As described in Cattinelli et al. (2013b) and Crepaldi et al. (2013), "this procedure results in a tree, whose leaves represent singletons (i.e., clusters formed of a single activation peak), and whose root represents one large cluster including all the activation peaks submitted to the algorithm. Each level of the tree reports the clusters created by the algorithm at a specific processing step, as it progresses from individual activation peaks at the lowest level to the all-inclusive final cluster at the top of the tree". The procedure was continued until the average standard deviation around the cluster centroids of the individual peaks, in the *x*, *y*, and *z* directions, remained below 7.5 mm. This measure roughly mimics the spatial resolution of fMRI studies. As hierarchical clustering may be sensitive to the order in which the individual data are processed, and may generate alternative clustering trees (Morgan and Ray, 1995), an optimal clustering solution was identified by accepting the solution with maximized the between cluster error sum of squares (see Cattinelli et al., 2013b).

The mean coordinates of each cluster included in the final set were then passed as an input to a MATLAB script to automatically label the anatomical correspondence of the stereotactic coordinates of the centroids of each cluster. This procedure implied a query of the Automatic Anatomical Labeling (AAL) template available in the MRIcron visualization Software (Rorden and Brett, 2000).

HC analyses have the advantage of permitting *post-hoc* assessment of the functional meaning of a given cluster (see for example, Cattinelli et al., 2013a; Crepaldi et al., 2013) or, as in the present study, its assignation to a class of subjects (e.g., clusters specific or preferentially associated with controls rather than clusters associated with dyslexics).

However, HC does not quantify the significance of each individual cluster with reference to the probability of a spatially distributed statistical process. To protect ourselves from considering clusters of limited biological significance, the spatial distribution of the clusters identified by HC was compared with the results of a different meta-analytical method, namely the Activation Likelihood Estimation technique as implemented in the GingerALE software (Eickhoff et al., 2009; Turkeltaub et al., 2012). Only clusters also present in the GingerALE analyses were further considered (the threshold was set at $p < 0.05$ with FDRpN correction).

POST-HOC STATISTICAL ANALYSES ON THE RESULTING CLUSTERS

Group, age, or task preferential associations were assessed with the binomial test as follows.

For the group effect, we tested whether the distribution of control- and dyslexic-related peaks within each cluster was significantly different from the overall proportion of control- and dyslexic-related peaks included in the whole sample of coordinates ($1382/2321 = 0.59543$ for controls and $939/2321 = 0.40457$ for dyslexics). To this end, we used the binomial distribution and computed the probability of observing a specific number of peaks associated with a given group as the number of successes in a series of independent randomly-distributed trials: when this

[3]The rationale for using the two broad categories reading- and non-reading-like tasks, was dictated by the need to statistically assess the meaning of the clusters along a parsimonious, admittedly reduced, number of categories. The finer grained description of the more numerous yet broad classes of studies was left to the descriptive assessment of the composition of the clusters that proved significant for the two main categories. For example, once a cluster proved to be significantly associated with reading-like tasks, a qualitative exploration of the individual tasks that contributed to that effect allowed us to make some additional finer grained statement. See for example the case of clusters L5 and L6 in the results section.

probability was below 0.05, the cluster was considered to be associated with either the control or dyslexic groups.

Similar analyses were implemented in these clusters to test their association with either reading-related or non-reading related tasks and with either children or adult group. The proportion of non-reading and reading-related peaks included in the whole sample of coordinates was 406/2321 (=0.17492) and 1915/2321 (=0.82508), respectively, while the proportion of children- and adult-related peaks included in the whole sample of coordinates was 1144/2321 (=0.49289) and 1177/2321 (=0.50711), respectively[4].

We also assessed whether there were interactions effects within each cluster: the group-by-task and group-by-age interactions were tested with Fisher's exact test (Fisher, 1970); this estimates whether the distribution of one categorical variable (group) varies according to the levels of a second categorical variable (experimental task or age class), thus revealing clusters that were associated with either group in one task (e.g., reading-like tasks in controls), but with the opposite group in another task (e.g., dyslexic in non-reading-like tasks).

The odds ratio under the null hypothesis of the Fischer's test on the individual clusters was corrected to reflect the distribution of the categories under examination in the entire dataset. The odd ratio for group-by-task interaction was 1.09, for group-by-age interaction was 0.81 and for task-by-age interaction was 1.27.

Some of the interaction effects were tested to replicate previous analyses published in other meta-analytical papers: for example, the age-by-group interaction described by Richlan et al. (2013). We believe that describing these results, even if not all discussed in detail later on, leaves an important trace behind this paper for future assessments.

Finally, clusters that did not show a significant group preferential association were assigned to a class called undifferentiated. Among these clusters, we attempted to highlight those having higher probability of actually being completely non-specific, by performing binomial tests along the group axis. In particular, we assumed that clusters whose one-tailed *p*-value was greater than 0.5 for both groups are of high chance of being genuinely non-specific.

All post-clustering statistical analyses were performed using the free statistical software *R* (the code is available upon request to Manuela Berlingeri).

COMPARISON WITH DANELLI ET AL. (2013) MAPPING OF READING AND SYSTEMS INVOLVED IN DYSLEXIA

The results of the clustering analyses were also compared with the independent fMRI data described by Danelli et al. (2013). In that paper, the authors described fMRI patterns of intersection between the normal reading system and the auditory phonological system, or the visual motion/magnocellular system, or the motor/cerebellar system: they also reported reading per-se activations, that is, areas activated for single pseudowords reading, once any trend for the other aforementioned tasks was excluded by the analysis[5]. Comparison with this independent data-set helped in the interpretation of the functional relevance of the data of the present meta-analysis.

ADDITIONAL ANALYSES

The paucity of data on MT/V5 due to the lack of group-based data would inevitably dismiss the MT/V5 finding: to avoid this, we identified the average MT/V5 of the normal controls in Eden et al. (1996) and looked for the closest cluster in the meta-analysis.

Finally, the data of the regional effects associated with non-reading-like tasks (e.g., motor tasks, attentional tasks, visual perception tasks etc.) were also submitted to a separate meta-analysis. This additional meta-analysis was motivated by the desire of excluding the possibility that the overwhelmingly larger number of peaks from the reading-like experiments (# of peaks: 1915) could have masked the manifestation of specific clusters from the *non-reading-like* data (# of peaks: 406)[6]. As above, we tested whether the distribution of control- and dyslexic-related peaks within each cluster was significantly different from the overall proportion of control- and dyslexic-related peaks included in the whole sample of coordinates (0.58 for controls and 0.42 for dyslexics). To this end, we used the binomial distribution and computed the probability of observing a specific number of peaks associated with a given group as the number of successes in a series of independent randomly-distributed trials: when this probability was below 0.05, the cluster was considered to be associated with either the control or dyslexic groups. These analyses were performed only on clusters that showed a spatial congruence in the HC and ALE procedures.

RESULTS

The hierarchical algorithm identified a total of 193 clusters (**Figure 3A**)—96 clusters in the left hemisphere and 97 ones in the right hemisphere—with 2 to 51 peaks each, from 2 to 18 different studies; mean standard deviation along the three axes were 4.54 mm (x-axis), 4.83 mm (y-axis), and 4.76 mm (z-axis).

After the comparison of these results with ALE maps (**Figure 3B**), only 92 out of 193 clusters (**Figure 3C**) were considered for subsequent analyses.

GROUP-PREFERENTIAL CLUSTERS

When we indicate a cluster as "related to" or "preferential for" a group, we imply that there was a significantly greater proportion of peaks in one group as opposed to the other. This would

[4]To make some justice of the fine-grained variability of the tasks that contributed to each cluster, beyond the two broad categories described above, each cluster was explored qualitatively (the raw data are available in the supplementary materials).

[5]In Danelli et al. (2013) reading was tested with a pseudoword silent reading task; the visual magnocellular/visual motion system with a visual motion perception task using Gabor low-frequency patches; the auditory phonological system was tested with a rhyming task for syllabic sounds; the motor cerebellar system was tested with a finger tapping sequence learning task.

[6]The idea here is that the cloud of peaks from the reading-like experiments may operate as geometrical attractors in the clustering procedure and mask spatial effects coming from the less numerous data-set from non-reading-like experiments. The separate meta-analysis should have protected us from this hypothetical confound.

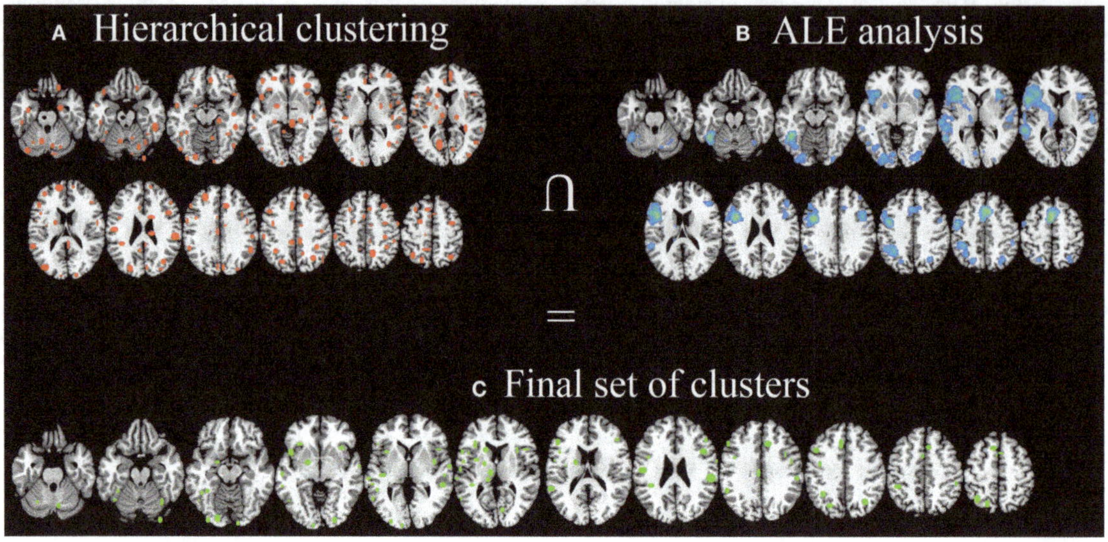

FIGURE 3 | Clusters identified with HC (A), clusters identified using ALE approach (B) and the final data-set of clusters, identified in both HC and ALE meta-analyses and considered for *post-hoc* statistical analyses (C).

correspond to the terminology suggested by Pernet et al. (2007), the so-called "preferential response" for brain regions with a comparatively greater response in a given condition/group, with no zero response in the control condition/control group. Nine clusters were preferentially associated with controls, while five clusters were associated with dyslexics (**Table 2**). The peaks distribution for each significant cluster is reported in the contingency tables in Supplementary Materials (**Table S2**).

Clusters associated with normal readers

There was a distributed left ventral occipito-temporal network involving the infero-temporal (clusters L6, L23) and fusiform (cluster L5) regions (areas in red in **Figure 4**). Within this network, peaks coming from lexical decision tasks were present in cluster L23 only, while all other reading-like behaviors were fairly evenly present in the entire set of the three left occipito-temporal clusters. Once compared with Danelli et al. (2013) statistical maps, the cluster L5 fell in the reading network while L6 fell in a region of the shared activations by an auditory phonological task and reading. L23 fell in between these two regions.

Moving toward more dorsal regions, there were two areas in the middle temporal and supra-marginal gyri (L86 and L89; areas in blue in **Figure 4**) that were associated with the normal controls for a mixture of tasks including reading but also active phonological manipulation tasks, involving some working memory demands.

Even more dorsally, we also found a left hemispheric network involving the posterior part of the supplementary motor cortex, the superior parietal cortex, the dorsal portion of the inferior parietal lobule (areas in green in **Figure 4**): these clusters included peaks from tasks involving phonological manipulation (e.g., phonological short-term memory), but also motoric or visuo-spatial perception/attention. A comparison with Danelli et al. (2013) data confirmed the mixed nature of the functional properties of these regions, which were involved in motoric tasks and, for the superior parietal region, in the visual motion perception task as well.

Clusters associated with dyslexic readers

These included the left basal ganglia (head of the caudate; pallidum), the right anterior cingulate, right precentral cortex and the right inferior parietal lobule (areas in cyan in **Figure 4**). While the left subcortical regions were brought about by reading-like tasks, the right hemispheric ones were associated with a variety of tasks, often of the non-reading-like kind.

Detailed description of group-related clusters is reported in **Table 2**.

TASK-PREFERENTIAL CLUSTERS

Four clusters, located in the opercular parts of the left inferior frontal gyrus, in the left insula and in the posterior portion of the left inferior temporal gyrus, were preferential for reading-like group, while five clusters, located in the right superior and inferior parietal lobule, in the superior temporal cortex, bilaterally, and in the left middle temporal gyrus, were significantly related with non-reading-like tasks.

AGE-PREFERENTIAL CLUSTERS

Fifteen clusters were preferentially associated with adults, while 10 clusters were associated with children. In particular, adult-related clusters were located in the left SMA, in the opercular part of the inferior frontal gyrus, bilaterally, in the left insula, in the left superior and inferior temporal gyrus, in the cerebellum, bilaterally, in the left pallidum and caudate nuclei, and in the left thalamus.

Children-related clusters were located in the pre-SMA, bilaterally, in the left middle frontal cortex, in the left superior temporal gyrus, in the left superior and right inferior occipital gyri, in the lingual gyri, bilaterally.

Table 2 | Clusters with significant group specificity.

	Cluster I.D.	Area	X	Y	Z	SD x	SD y	SD z	Co/D	p	R/NR	p	Ch/A	p	Congruence with Danelli et al. (2013) maps
Control-related clusters	L5	Fusiform gyrus	−41	−60	−18	3	3	4	11/1	0.018	10/2	n.s.	4/8	n.s.	Reading map
	L23	Inf. temporal gyrus	−45	−49	−15	3	4	4	26/1	<0.001	26/1	0.037^{R}	6/21	0.004^{A}	Reading per-se and reading and phonology maps
	L6	Inf. temporal gyrus	−50	−61	−9	3	3	6	10/1	0.028	11/0	n.s.	3/8	n.s.	Reading and phonology map
	L86	Mid. temporal gyrus	−58	−58	6	3	6	5	14/2	0.017	14/2	n.s.	9/7	n.s.	–
	L89	Supramarginal gyrus	−55	−47	35	5	6	3	14/1	0.005	14/1	n.s.	9/6	n.s.	–
	L30	Inf. parietal lobule	−43	−40	46	7	4	4	19/4	0.017	16/7	n.s.	10/13	n.s.	Reading and motor learning maps
	L38	Precentral gyrus	−41	−5	42	4	7	3	16/3	0.021	18/1	n.s.	9/10	n.s.	Reading map
	L34	Sup. parietal lobule	−19	−67	54	4	6	5	14/1	0.005	10/5	n.s.	7/8	n.s.	Visual motion and motor learning maps
	L16	SMA	−5	−4	62	3	3	5	9/0	0.009	5/4	n.s.	3/6	n.s.	Motor learning map
Dyslexic-related clusters	L80	Pallidum	−20	−3	14	4	5	7	8/17	0.005	24/1	n.s.	6/19	0.009^{A}	–
	L85	Caudate	−18	18	8	5	5	4	3/8	0.032	9/2	n.s.	0/11	$<0.001^{A}$	–
	R71	Inf. parietal lobule	50	−35	48	2,7	4	4	3/9	0.017	5/7	0.002^{NR}	4/8	n.s.	–
	R27	Mid. cingulum	14	17	43	4	6	3	2/7	0.027	7/2	n.s.	8/1	0.018^{Ch}	–
	R16	Precentral gyrus	42	−23	60	5	2	5	0/6	0.044	4/2	n.s.	4/2	n.s.	Motor learning map

Co, controls; D, Dyslexics; NR, non-reading-like tasks; R, reading-like tasks; A, Adults; Ch, Children.

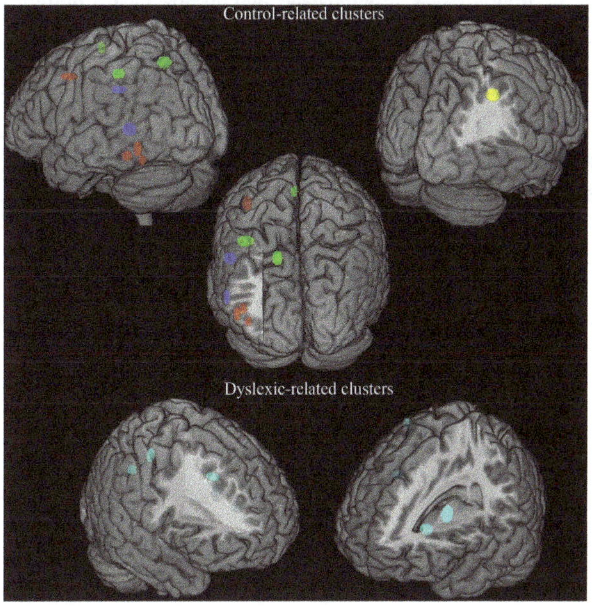

FIGURE 4 | Distribution of group-related clusters that showed a spatial congruence in the HC and ALE procedures. The red dots represent the control-related clusters that fell in reading and phonological specific activations in Danelli et al. (2013), the blue dots represent the control-related clusters that were not observed in Danelli et al. (2013) and the green dots represent the control-related clusters fell in visual motion and motoric activations in Danelli et al. (2013). The right yellow dots represent the control-related cluster identified by the meta-analysis restricted to the non-reading-like tasks. Finally, dyslexic-related clusters are reported in cyan.

INTERACTION EFFECTS

Task-by-age interactions

Three clusters, located in the left middle frontal and middle temporal cortex and in the left lingual gyrus, showed a task-by-age interaction effect (see **Table 3**). The former cluster was associated with reading-like tasks in children, the latter two clusters with reading-like tasks in adults.

Group-by-task interactions

Three clusters, located in the left superior and middle temporal gyri and in the right inferior parietal lobule, showed a group-by-task interaction effect (see **Table 3** and **Figure 5** for details). The former two were associated with the normal controls for reading-like tasks, the third with the dyslexics for the non-reading-like tasks.

Group-by-age interactions

Three clusters, located in the opercular part of the left inferior frontal gyrus, in the triangular part of the right inferior frontal gyrus and in the right precentral gyrus, showed a group-by-age interaction effect (see **Table 3** and **Figure 5** for details). The former two clusters were associated with adult controls, the third with young controls.

UNDIFFERENTIATED CLUSTERS

Seven clusters, located in the pre-SMA, bilaterally, in the triangular part of the right inferior frontal gyrus, in the right insula, in the

Table 3 | Group-by-task, group-by-age, and task-by-age distribution of the activation peaks included in each of the four clusters showing significant interaction between two factors.

		Controls	Dyslexics	
LEFT MIDDLE TEMPORAL GYRUS (B.A. 37; CLUSTER ID: L86); *x* = −58, *y* = −58, *z* = 6				
Task	Reading-like	14	0	14
	Non-reading-like	0	2	2
		14	2	16
			p-value	0.008
LEFT SUPERIOR TEMPORAL GYRUS (B.A. 42; CLUSTER ID: L87); *x* = −60, *y* = −44, *z* = 16				
Task	Reading-like	18	6	24
	Non-reading-like	0	3	3
		18	9	27
			p-value	0.028
RIGHT INFERIOR PARIETAL LOBULE (B.A. 2; CLUSTER ID: R71); *x* = 50, *y* = −35, *z* = 48				
Task	Reading-like	3	2	5
	Non-reading-like	0	7	7
		3	9	12
			p-value	0.045
LEFT INFERIOR FRONTAL GYRUS, PARS OPERCULARIS (B.A. 44; CLUSTER ID: L57); *x* = −56, *y* = 15, *z* = 12				
Age	Children	3	8	11
	Adults	12	2	14
		15	10	25
			p-value	0.004
RIGHT INFERIOR FRONTAL GYRUS, PARS TRIANGULARIS (B.A. 45; CLUSTER ID: R57); *x* = 45, *y* = 32, *z* = 14				
Age	Children	3	3	6
	Adults	10	0	10
		13	3	16
			p-value	0.036
RIGHT PRECENTRAL GYRUS (B.A. 6; CLUSTER ID: R73); *x* = 47, *y* = −1, *z* = 34				
Age	Children	7	0	7
	Adults	2	4	6
			4	13
			p-value	0.021
		Children	**Adults**	
LEFT LINGUAL GYRUS (B.A. 18; CLUSTER ID: L84); *x* = −20, *y* = −88, *z* = −12				
Task	Reading-like	11	15	26
	Non-reading-like	5	0	5
		16	15	31
			p-value	0.04
LEFT MIDDLE TEMPORAL GYRUS (B.A. 21; CLUSTER ID: L14); *x* = −65, *Y* = −26, *z* = 6				
Task	Reading-like	1	9	10
	Non-reading-like	4	2	6
		5	11	16
			p-value	0.04

(Continued)

Table 3 | Continued

		Children	Adults	
LEFT MIDDLE FRONTAL GYRUS (B.A. 44; CLUSTER ID: L44); *x* = −47, *y* = 16, *z* = 38				
Task	Reading-like	13	2	15
	Non-reading-like	2	4	6
		15	6	21
			p-value	0.03

x, y, and z refer to stereotactic coordinates of the centroid of each cluster.

right middle cingulum, and in the right inferior occipital gyrus, did not showed a group-related preferential association ($p >$ 0.5 in the binomial test) and were classified as undifferentiated activations (see **Table 4** for details).

ADDITIONAL ANALYSES

Because of the historical importance of the theories behind the scenes of the MT/V5 and cerebellar findings, *ad-hoc* special analysis was made for these two sets of findings.

MT/V5

We first identified "group" average stereotactic coordinates from Eden et al. (1996) from their eight normal subjects. This was done by using the same hierarchical clustering software of the meta-analysis. The centroid stereotactic locations of the MT/V5 region were located at $X = -52$; $Y = -75$; $Z = 7$; the SDs were: 11, 8, 5 mm in the three directions; on the right, the stereotactic coordinates were $X = 50$; $Y = -70$; $Z = 5$; the SDs were: 8, 8, 3 mm (areas in orange in **Figure 6**). As expected, Eden's et al. (1996) clusters fell within the statistical maps for visual motion perception described in Danelli et al. (2013).

We explored the anatomical congruence of these clusters with those that proved significant in the comparisons of controls and dyslexics in the meta-analysis. We also compared the Eden's MT/V5 location with the distribution of the raw data of the activations that were significantly larger in controls than in dyslexia. None of these analyses showed a systematic overlap of Eden's et al. (1996) MT/V5 and the data from other experiments on dyslexia.

We also compared the clusters associated with controls or dyslexics in the present study (see **Table 2**) with the mapping of the magnocellular system as identified by Danelli et al. (2013). There was one area of overlap (shared with an overlap for the motor learning task of Danelli et al., 2013) in one cluster located in the left superior parietal lobule (cluster L34). The experiments that generated these clusters in the data-set considered in this paper were based on phonological tasks, on a motor task in one case and on a visuo-spatial attentional tasks.

Cerebellum

There were five clusters identified by the general meta-analysis in the cerebellum (see **Table 5** and **Figure 7**). These regions were identified by a variety of reading-like tasks (66 peaks overall) and non-reading-like tasks (11 peaks), with no specific association with either normal controls or developmental dyslexics for any of these clusters. Of the 77 peaks, only three peaks came from a comparison controls > dyslexics, 8 came from the comparison

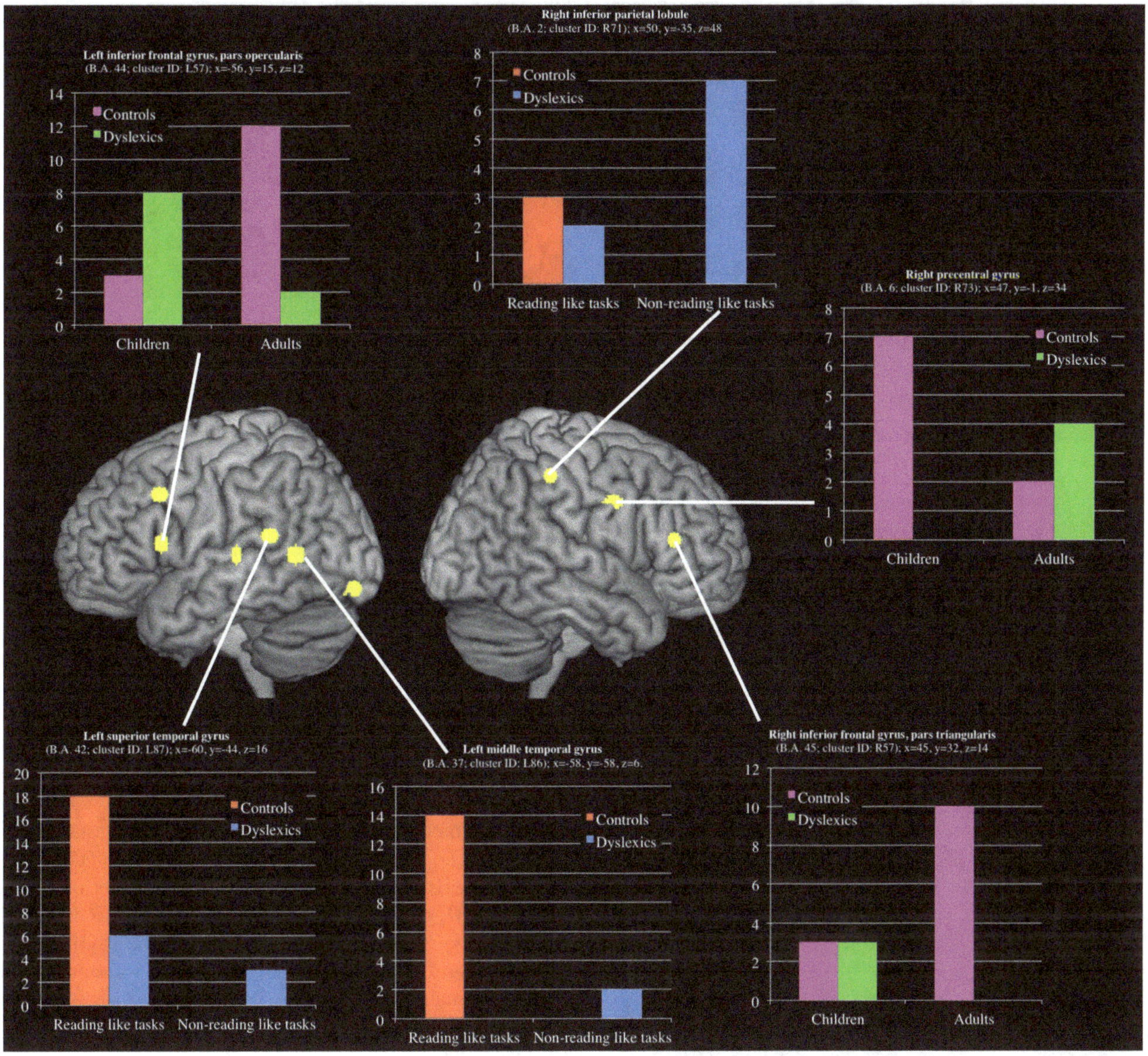

FIGURE 5 | Clusters that showed a significant group-by-task and group-by-age interaction effect. For each clusters a histogram describe the peak distribution across group/conditions.

Table 4 | List of the undifferentiated clusters.

Cluster ID	Brain area	*X*	*Y*	*Z*	*SD x*	*SD y*	*SD z*	Controls	Dyslexics
UNDIFFERENTIATED CLUSTERS ACROSS NORMAL OR DYSLEXIC READERS GROUPS									
R59	Right inferior occipital gyrus	23	−91	−2	5	6	5	10	7
R68	Right middle cingulum	10	26	33	6	5	5	11	8
R65	Right insula	34	21	−5	5	3	4	11	7
L90	Left inferior frontal gyrus, pars triangularis	−49	28	16	4	5	4	16	11
L47	Left SMA	−4	7	46	3	5	2	8	6
R52	Right SMA	2	3	65	3	4	3	7	4
R53	Right SMA	3	12	55	4	2	3	8	6

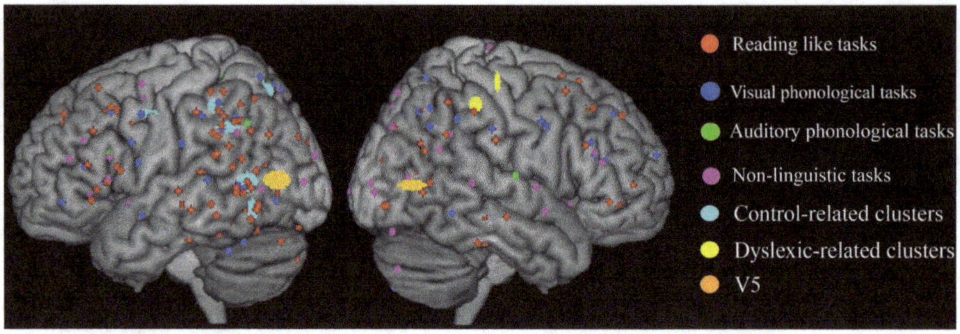

FIGURE 6 | Overlap of raw data, group-related clusters and the MT/V5 region of interest extracted from activations reported by Eden et al. (1996) in normal controls.

Table 5 | Clusters emerged in the cerebellum.

Cluster I.D.	Area	*X*	*Y*	*Z*	*SD x*	*SD y*	*SD z*	Co/D	*p*	R/NR	*p*	Ch/A	*P*
L45	Left cerebellum (lobule 6)	−26	−63	−27	4	3	3	5/9	n.s.	12/2	n.s.	2/12	0.007[A]
L93	Left cerebellum (crus I)	−42	−55	−30	4	5	4	15/9	n.s.	22/2	n.s.	5/19	0.004[A]
R70	Vermis (lobule 7)	8	−69	−27	4	5	4	12/9	n.s.	9/20	n.s.	1/20	<0.001[A]
R26	Right cerebellum (lobule 6)	34	−63	−19	3	6	4	6/5	n.s.	5/8	n.s.	2/9	0.063
R3	Right cerebellum (lobule 6)	24	−62	−31	2	3	4	2/5	n.s.	5/4	n.s.	2/5	n.s.

Co, controls; D, Dyslexics; NR, non-reading-like tasks; R, reading-like tasks; A, Adults; Ch, Children.

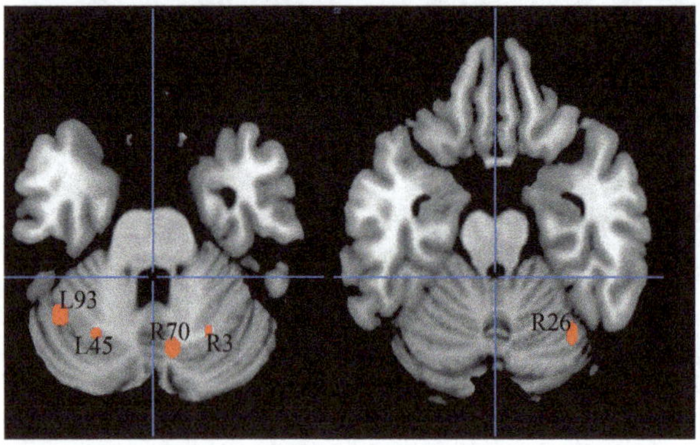

FIGURE 7 | Cerebellar clusters identified in both HC and ALE meta-analyses. In none of these there was a significant association with normal controls.

dyslexics > controls, 37 came from simple effects in the controls and 29 from simple effects in the dyslexics. Three of such clusters were significantly associated with data coming from adult volunteers.

Meta-analysis restricted to the non-reading-like tasks

The hierarchical algorithm identified a total of 85 clusters with 2–10 peaks each, and had mean standard deviation along the three axes of 4.56 mm (x-axis), 5.21 mm (y-axis) and 5.09 mm (z-axis). After the comparison of these results with ALE maps, 40 out of 85 clusters were considered for subsequent analyses.

The *post-hoc* analyses identified only one cluster that could be associated with the normal controls to a statistically greater ($p = 0.05$) degree than with dyslexics: the cluster (centroid coordinates: $X = 35$; $y = -41$; $Z = 41$; the SDs were: 5, 6, 7 mm) was located in the right inferior parietal cortex. The cluster included peaks from motor tasks (#3), auditory perception tasks (#3) and three dimensional visual discrimination tasks (#3). The centroid of this cluster is very close to that of cluster R86 (centroid coordinates: $X = 37$; $y = -45$; $Z = 43$; the SDs were: 5, 5, 7 mm) of the general analysis in which again specificity for controls (i.e., lack of activation for dyslexics) was seen. This cluster was not observed in the ALE analysis.

DISCUSSION

The problem of co-occurrence of neural dysfunctions in dyslexia remained not explored by meta-analytic studies to date; it remained to be seen whether, besides the well replicated finding of a left occipito-temporal hypoactivation, there is a systematic co-occurrence of dysfunctional patterns of different functional systems, perhaps converging on the same brain regions associated with the reading deficit. Such evidence would be relevant for theories like, for example, the magnocellular or the cerebellar ones, which postulate a more basic and possibly more broadly distributed disorder in dyslexia.

In the present study this issue was tested by submitting to the meta-analysis all the suitable data[7] from the literature on dyslexia, published up to September 2013, independently from the nature of the task, the materials, and the age-groups. Functional interpretation of the regional effects was made by direct exploration of the cluster compositions, by looking at

[7] See inclusion criteria for the raw data in the methods section.

the group or task that generated one effect, and appropriate *post-hoc* statistical tests, when possible, for broad categories. In addition, our evaluations of the results were also based on a direct comparison with the functional mapping of the reading, auditory phonological, visual magnocellular and visual motion, motor/cerebellar systems, and their intersections, as described by Danelli et al. (2013) for normal subjects using fMRI.

Our meta-analysis confirms one major milestone of previous empirical imaging studies and previous meta-analyses on dyslexia: the commitment to reading in normal controls for left occipito-temporal cortex (Paulesu et al., 2000; Cohen et al., 2002; Price et al., 2003), and the lack of such commitment in the same region for dyslexics (Shaywitz et al., 1998; Paulesu et al., 2001; Maisog et al., 2008; Richlan et al., 2009).

Because of the finer grained analysis afforded by our method, and thanks to the comparison with the independent fMRI data of Danelli et al. (2013), the same left occipito-temporal region identified by previous meta-analyses using ALE (Maisog et al., 2008; Richlan et al., 2009), was fractionated into three different clusters preferentially associated with the normal controls (L5, L6, and L23): clusters L5 and L23 are most likely associated with initial visual processing of the orthographic strings, while cluster L6 with the integration orthography with phonology.

By comparison with the data of Cohen et al. (2004) these corresponded to the visual-word form area (L5, VWFA), to the lateral inferior temporal multimodal region (L6; LIMA), and to an intermediate area (L23) that, to the best of our knowledge, has not been further characterized in the literature as yet.

There was more in our new data. The two more dorsal regions in the middle temporal and supra-marginal gyri (L86 and L89), were associated with the normal controls for a mixture of tasks including reading but also active phonological manipulation tasks, involving some working memory demands. These were not identified in the intersection paper of Danelli et al. (2013) most likely because the auditory phonological task had minimal demands in terms of manipulation and working memory processes.

Further up more dorsally, there was a new set of left hemispheric regions with different functional associations in parietal and premotor cortices and the supplementary motor area: these were brought about by a mix of reading, motor, phonological manipulation and visual attention tasks. Interestingly, once compared with Danelli et al. (2013) maps, some clusters overlapped with motoric regions (inferior parietal and SMA), while the left superior parietal lobule cluster overlapped with an intersection of motor learning and visual motion perception maps.

It is also worth noting that the meta-analysis restricted to the non-reading-like tasks revealed a right hemispheric inferior parietal cluster (R86; centroid coordinates: $X = 37; y = -45; Z = 43$; the SDs were: 5, 5, 7 mm) preferentially associated with normal readers, that is not present in developmental dyslexics. However, a more lateral right parietal cluster was preferential for the dyslexics (see **Figure 4**). There is overwhelming evidence of a role of the right parietal cortex in spatial attention (for review see Vallar et al., 2003; Corbetta and Shulman, 2011). The disorganized response in the right inferior parietal cortex of dyslexics (in some cases "more active," in other cases "less active") may be evidence for an anatomically grounded dysfunctional right hemispheric spatial attentional system in dyslexia.

On the other hand, no evidence was found either for a cerebellar dysfunction, nor for a left inferior frontal cortex hyperactivation in dyslexics, as in the previous meta-analyses (Maisog et al., 2008; Richlan et al., 2009).

In addition, we could not find evidence for the visual/magnocellular hypothesis of dyslexia, if this was to be benchmarked by a reduced recruitment of area V5/MT (Eden et al., 1996).

These findings expand previous evidence on the presence of functional anatomical deficits in dyslexia and identify a ventral to dorsal functional gradient with the more ventral areas, normally involved in the decoding aspect of reading (from orthography to phonology), the intermediate middle temporal and supra-marginal areas being related to reading-like behaviors or phonological processing and the more dorsal group being involved in reading but also in motoric or visual motion perception aspects of functional anatomy. We argue that the more dorsal left parietal and premotor cortex might be normally associated with eye-movement control or with visuo-spatial attention in language specific tasks. These would be functionally associated with the left hemispheric network of reading in normal controls but not in subjects with dyslexia.

This evidence brings new fuel for those believing in the existence of multiple dysfunctional systems in dyslexia without implying the need for focal and highly localized hypo-activations, preferentially associated with single classes of non-reading-like tasks. Rather, this new evidence speaks in favor of a distributed set of local malfunctions in "associative" regions normally involved in more than one behavior/cognitive domain. At a quantitative level, the number of peaks that contributed to the identification of these group-specific clusters was fairly balanced: 50 peaks for the occipito-temporal clusters, 31 for the intermediate network and 66 for the more dorsal network. It is worth noting that the more dorsal clusters appear group "specific", or preferentially associated with normal readers, only if one considers the entire data-set rather than the non-reading-like behaviors on their own (data not shown). This result speaks in favor of our strategy of merging the data from multiple classes of tasks to reach a critical mass of observations.

COMPARISON WITH THE PREVIOUS LITERATURE WITH PARTICULAR REFERENCE TO META-ANALYSES

There are other quantitative meta-analyses on the neural bases of developmental dyslexia in literature (Maisog et al., 2008; Richlan et al., 2009, 2011). In particular, these studies were focused on the task of reading or of reading-like behaviors, excluding auditory-verbal or non-linguistic tasks. Moreover, they included only peaks derived from group-by-task comparisons and used the ALE method (Maisog et al., 2008; Richlan et al., 2009). The potential advantages of our approach have been already commented upon.

Our findings are only partially consistent with the meta-analytic work published in literature. Indeed, control-related clusters emerged not only at the level of the left occipito-temporal and temporo-parietal regions, but also in the left middle temporal and parietal areas and in the supplementary motor cortex. Consistent with previous meta-analyses are also the more frequent subcortical effects for the dyslexics in the basal ganglia, for reading tasks.

Contrary to what described by Maisog et al. (2008) and Richlan et al. (2009), we could not find a reduced recruitment for the dyslexic group at the level of the left inferior frontal gyrus. However, it is worthy to note that a significant group-by-age interaction emerged in this area showing an association of this region with adult-control activations (as reported also by Richlan et al., 2011). The same area shows a "difficulty effect in phonological retrieval" in Cattinelli et al. (2013a) and Taylor et al. (2013) meta-analyses of reading, whereby the inferior frontal region is more active when reading non-words or low-frequency irregular words. An interaction effect emerged also for the right inferior frontal gyrus in the present study, while an association with control-children in the right precentral gyrus was observed.

A final difference with Richlan et al. (2011) is the lack of group by age interactions in the left parietal and occipito-temporal cortex. While not significant, technically speaking, at a statistical level, we note that an age effect in the left ventral occipito-temporal cortex was present and it was driven by adult normal readers (20 peaks for the controls, 1 peak for dyslexics) rather than by young readers (young controls: 6 peaks; young dyslexics: 0 peaks) and it is worth recalling that overall the number of "adult" and "young" peaks is balanced across the entire data-set. This is consistent with the idea that time is needed before the occipito-temporal cortex develops a neural expertise for reading (Dehaene et al., 2010).

Recently, Richlan et al. (2013) described a ALE-based meta-analysis of VBM data from dyslexia studies. The paper was mainly concerned with gray matter effects, as the papers that reported white matter abnormalities were only two (Eckert et al., 2005; Silani et al., 2005). The main trust of the paper is that there are reproducible reductions of gray matter in the left superior temporal sulcus; one of the coordinates described by them is consistent with the centroid of our cluster L86. The fact that functional imaging data show broader differences between normal controls and dyslexics when compared with the VBM ones, is a further argument in favor of the hypothesis that an abnormally wired cortex, rather than a focally damaged one, may better explain the functional disorder of dyslexia (see Silani et al., 2005, for further discussion; see also Paulesu et al., 1995; Klingberg et al., 2000).

VISUAL MAGNOCELLULAR AND CEREBELLAR THEORIES: CHASING THE WRONG USUAL SUSPECTS?

As discussed in the introduction there is a non-negligible evidence of a visuo-perceptual deficit in children with dyslexia and some evidence for motoric deficits. The neural counterpart of these deficits has been sought by using visual motion perception tasks or motor learning tasks. The visual motion perception experiment of Eden et al. (1996) is the one that sits less comfortably with our results as we could not find a cluster in V5/MT, and of course, nor a group specific effect there. This difficulty may in part arise by the fact that the testing of the visual-magnocellular/attentional hypothesis has somewhat limited attention in the literature or by the fact that the main replication of the V5/MT finding was made using region of interest analyses (Demb et al., 1998), which were not included in our study.

Our attempt to test the V5 hypothesis by all means (see the results section) failed to identify a congruence with any of the effects described in the dyslexia literature, Eden et al. (1996) and Demb et al. (1998) excluded. However, our finding is consistent with more recent evidence on area V5. In a recent study, again based on a region of interest analysis of the data (preceded by a localizer experiment) Olulade et al. (2013) were able to show that if the dyslexics and the controls are equated for reading age rather than by age per-se, a significant difference in V5/MT cannot be found. A rehabilitation program on reading had a carry-over effect on V5/MT response (Olulade et al., 2013).

However, the visual magnocellular V5/MT hypothesis could be reformulated as a spatial attentional hypothesis. If so, activity in V5/MT may not be the best benchmark as discussed elsewhere (see Danelli et al., 2013, p. 2682). If the magnocellular hypothesis may still give an account for oculomotor control difficulties, there are better anatomical targets to be explored, for example, the dorsal premotor and parietal areas that we found less frequently activated in dyslexia. In the same vein, the evidence for a disorganized recruitment of the right inferior parietal lobule in dyslexia in non-linguistic tasks is a potentially revealing finding for all the theorists of attentional hypotheses in dyslexia.

Similar considerations apply for the cerebellar hypothesis. This could be easily reformulated in terms of deficient fine-grained motor control/learning without an a-priori commitment to the cerebellum. Indeed, none of the tasks whose deficit is attributed to the cerebellum by the believers in the cerebellar hypothesis, can be univocally and exclusively attributed to that organ: posture tasks, walking tasks, subtle finger coordination or bimanual tasks, motor learning tasks all depend on widely distributed neural systems in which the cerebellum is just one of the players (Kandel et al., 2012).

We found reduced recruitment of a series of motor regions in which there was a mixture of peaks derived from reading-like and non-reading-like tasks. Observation of these focal effects may contribute to a re-evaluation of motoric disorders in developmental dyslexia. Of course, fresh new experiments are needed to further address this hypothesis.

THE CONTRIBUTION OF FUNCTIONAL CONNECTIVITY APPROACHES AND THE DISCONNECTION HYPOTHESIS OF DYSLEXIA

Finally, our data could be discussed in the context of a more network based approach, such as that provided by functional or effective connectivity analyses. It has been repeatedly suggested that dyslexia could be associated with a failure of the functional interaction between distant brain regions that subserve diverse, perhaps elementary, cognitive operations needed for the task of reading and the like (Paulesu et al., 1995; Horwitz et al., 1998). These regions should have greater functional and effective connectivity in normal controls. Even though this disconnection hypothesis of dyslexia is particularly dear to us (Paulesu et al., 1995; Klingberg et al., 2000; Silani et al., 2005), the number of the connectivity studies is still limited and therefore our analysis was concentrated on classical studies based on univariate assessments of regional effects. There are two classes of such connectivity studies: task-based and resting state studies. Task-based studies reported reduced functional connectivity between reading-related areas like the left angular gyrus and the occipito-temporal cortex (Horwitz et al., 1998) or the occipito-temporal cortex and the frontal cortex (van der Mark et al., 2011; Finn et al., 2013; Schurz et al., 2014)[8]. In one study (Finn et al., 2013), a stronger right hemispheric connectivity for dyslexics was described. In the lone dynamic causal modeling (DCM) study performed on developmental dyslexia to date (Cao et al., 2008), reduced modulatory effects and connectivity were demonstrated in a temporo-parietal network for visual rhyming trials with conflicting orthography/phonology. It is worthy to note that task-based connectivity studies have an important limitation: the connectivity patterns explored are task dependent, the number of connections explored are limited in some cases (e.g., when using DCM), and different patterns could be produced by different reading tasks (see for example Levy et al., 2009); as a consequence, different dysfunctional patterns could emerge from the comparison between controls and dyslexics depending on the task under examination (Pugh et al., 2000). Resting-state connectivity studies, independent component analysis (ICA) studies (Wolf et al., 2010) or the technique proposed by Finn et al. (2013), may be more task-independent[9] and better suited to test broader dysfunctions: while the ICA studies (Wolf et al., 2010) are difficult to interpret because one has to make assumptions on the functional meaning of the identified components and their comparability across different groups, the seed-based resting state functional connectivity studies have shown a reduction of connectivity between reading specific areas and regions not strictly involved in reading tasks, like, for example, between the left inferior parietal lobule and the left dorsal middle frontal areas (Koyama et al., 2013).

Taken together, these results are in line with the present findings, as they support the hypothesis that dyslexia could be the consequence of the co-occurrence of distributed dysfunctional patterns of different functional systems (see also Schurz et al., 2014): our data, however, also suggest a more limited degree of convergence of the multiple systems on high-level regions involved in reading-like as much as in non-reading-like tasks, particularly for the dorsal network identified here. Similar conclusions have not been made on the basis of a single study, even if based on a connectivity analysis. However, a more explicit demonstration of this general principle in the same sample of subjects is still in need.

[8]Finn et al. (2013) is a task-based study in which the weight of the task was regressed out. There are studies, however, in which reduced of connectivity was not found in dyslexics (Richards and Berninger, 2008). Here, an enhanced connectivity between the left inferior frontal gyrus and the right homolog was reported.

[9]The resting state condition, with the vaigue instructions attached, remains a task on its own.

CONCLUSIONS

Taken together our results provide a partial reconciliation of different accounts of dyslexia, those more concerned with the decoding problem of dyslexia, the underlying phonological deficit and the deficit in the conversion from orthography to phonology, and those more focused on motoric and visuo-attentional problems. Interestingly, the more dorsally one moves within the system identified here, the more the contribution of non-reading-like tasks becomes relevant with a mixture of phonological awareness tasks and motoric/attentional tasks.

In at least one cluster, it was possible to make an indirect reference to a likely component of the magnocellular cortical network thanks to its intersection with the visuo-motor perception maps and motor learning maps of Danelli et al. (2013). The same cluster was observed in an independent meta-analysis on reading by Cattinelli et al. (2013a), the cluster being associated with reading tasks that are more demanding (e.g., as in pseudoword reading) because the stimuli seek greater visuo-attentional resources and require a finer grained control of eye-movement. The right inferior parietal cluster is also giving support to a multidimensional account of dyslexia. It would have been hard to make these conclusions on the basis of a single experiment or with a conventional meta-analysis based on ultra-specific and similar tasks. Yet, as we value the original contributions of the colleagues who produced the 53 papers submitted to a meta-analysis here, we urge the readers to refer to that original work for further discussions of the functional anatomical patterns of dyslexia.

ACKNOWLEDGMENTS

We are grateful to all the colleagues who performed the hard work of collecting the empirical direct evidence on normal and dyslexic readers in the 53 papers included in this meta-analysis, or, indeed, previous meta-analyses. Even if it proved impossible to discuss their individual findings and their opinions in detail, at the very least their work is faithfully cited in the reference list of the manuscript. We are grateful to Silvia Brambilla for an initial contribution to this work for her master degree dissertation.

SUPPLEMENTARY MATERIAL

Table S1 | For each peak we reported the MNI coordinates (MNIx,y,z), the name of the first author, the journal and the year of publication of the article, the technique (PET or fMRI) and the stereotactic space used, the mean age of participants and the composition of the sample, the nature of the task, the nature of the functional contrast from which the peak was extracted. Moreover, we reported, for each peak, the corresponding cluster ID and the cluster label. In particular, for each cluster we reported the coordinates of the centroid (Mean MNIx,y,z) and the standard deviation on the three axes (SDx,y,z), the corresponding anatomical area. Finally, we reported, for each peak, the binomial classifications (non-reading or reading-like task; children or adults, controls or dyslexics) used for the *post-hoc* analyses.

Table S2 | Peak distribution in group-related clusters.

REFERENCES

American Psychiatric Association. (1994). *Diagnostic and Statistical Manual of Mental Disorders*. 4th Edn. Washington, DC: American Psychiatric Association.

Bach, S., Brandeis, D., Hofstetter, C., Martin, E., Richardson, U., and Brem, S. (2010). Early emergence of deviant frontal fMRI activity for phonological processes in poor beginning readers. *Neuroimage* 53, 682–693. doi: 10.1016/j.neuroimage.2010.06.039

Backes, W., Vuurman, E., Wennekes, R., Spronk, P., Wuisman, M., van Engelshoven, J., et al. (2002). Atypical brain activation of reading processes in children with developmental dyslexia. *J. Child Neurol.* 17, 867–871. doi: 10.1177/08830738020170121601

Beneventi, H., Tonnessen, F. E., and Ersland, L. (2009). Dyslexic children show short-term memory deficits in phonological storage and serial rehearsal: an fMRI study. *Int. J. Neurosci.* 119, 2017–2043. doi: 10.1080/00207450903139671

Beneventi, H., Tonnessen, F. E., Ersland, L., and Hugdahl, K. (2010a). Executive working memory processes in dyslexia: behavioral and fMRI evidence. *Scand. J. Psychol.* 51, 192–202. doi: 10.1111/j.1467-9450.2010.00808.x

Beneventi, H., Tonnessen, F. E., Ersland, L., and Hugdahl, K. (2010b). Working memory deficit in dyslexia: behavioral and FMRI evidence. *Int. J. Neurosci.* 120, 51–59. doi: 10.3109/00207450903275129

Booth, J. R., Bebko, G., Burman, D. D., and Bitan, T. (2007). Children with reading disorder show modality independent brain abnormalities during semantic tasks. *Neuropsychologia* 45, 775–783. doi: 10.1016/j.neuropsychologia.2006.08.015

Brambati, S. M., Termine, C., Ruffino, M., Danna, M., Lanzi, G., Stella, G., et al. (2006). Neuropsychological deficits and neural dysfunction in familial dyslexia. *Brain Res.* 1113, 174–185. doi: 10.1016/j.brainres.2006.06.099

Brunswick, N., McCrory, E., Price, C. J., Frith, C. D., and Frith, U. (1999). Explicit and implicit processing of words and pseudowords by adult developmental dyslexics: a search for Wernicke's Wortschatz? *Brain* 122(Pt 10), 1901–1917. doi: 10.1093/brain/122.10.1901

Cao, F., Bitan, T., and Booth, J. R. (2008). Effective brain connectivity in children with reading difficulties during phonological processing. *Brain Lang.* 107, 91–101. doi: 10.1016/j.bandl.2007.12.009

Cao, F., Bitan, T., Chou, T. L., Burman, D. D., and Booth, J. R. (2006). Deficient orthographic and phonological representations in children with dyslexia revealed by brain activation patterns. *J. Child Psychol. Psychiatry* 47, 1041–1050. doi: 10.1111/j.1469-7610.2006.01684.x

Cattinelli, I., Gallucci, M., Borghese, N. A., and Paulesu, E. (2013a). Reading the reading brain: a new meta-analysis of functional imaging data on reading. *J. Neurolinguistics* 26, 214–238. doi: 10.1016/j.jneuroling.2012.08.001

Cattinelli, I., Valentini, G., Paulesu, E., and Borghese, A. N. (2013b). A novel approach to the problem of non-uniqueness of the solution in hierarchical clustering. *IEEE Trans. Neural Netw. Learn. Syst.* 24, 1166–1173 doi: 10.1109/TNNLS.2013.2247058

Cohen, L., Jobert, A., Le Bihan, D., and Dehaene, S. (2004). Distinct unimodal and multimodal regions for word processing in the left temporal cortex. *Neuroimage* 23, 1256–1270. doi: 10.1016/j.neuroimage.2004.07.052

Cohen, L., Lehericy, S., Chochon, F., Lemer, C., Rivaud, S., and Dehaene, S. (2002). Language-specific tuning of visual cortex? Functional properties of the visual word form area. *Brain* 125(Pt 5), 1054–1069. doi: 10.1093/brain/awf094

Conway, T., Heilman, K. M., Gopinath, K., Peck, K., Bauer, R., Briggs, R. W., et al. (2008). Neural substrates related to auditory working memory comparisons in dyslexia: an fMRI study. *J. Int. Neuropsychol. Soc.* 14, 629–639. doi: 10.1017/S1355617708080867

Corbetta, M., and Shulman, G. L. (2011). Spatial neglect and attention networks. *Annu. Rev. Neurosci.* 34, 569–599. doi: 10.1146/annurev-neuro-061010-113731

Cornelissen, P. L., Hansen, P. C., Gilchrist, I., Cormack, F., Essex, J., and Frankish, C. (1998). Coherent motion detection and letter position encoding. *Vision Res.* 38, 2181–2191. doi: 10.1016/S0042-6989(98)00016-9

Cornelissen, P., Richardson, A., Mason, A., Fowler, S., and Stein, J. (1995). Contrast sensitivity and coherent motion detection measured at photopic luminance levels in dyslexics and controls. *Vision Res.* 35, 1483–1494.

Crepaldi, D., Berlingeri, M., Cattinelli, I., Borghese, N. A., Luzzatti, C., and Paulesu, E. (2013). Clustering the lexicon in the brain: a meta-analysis of the neurofunctional evidence on noun and verb processing. *Front. Hum. Neurosci.* 7:303. doi: 10.3389/fnhum.2013.00303

Danelli, L., Berlingeri, M., Bottini, G., Ferri, F., Vacchi, L., Sberna, M., et al. (2013). Neural intersections of the phonological, visual magnocellular and motor/cerebellar systems in normal readers: implications for imaging studies on dyslexia. *Hum. Brain Mapp.* 34, 2669–2687. doi: 10.1002/hbm.22098

Dehaene, S., Pegado, F., Braga, L. W., Ventura, P., Nunes Filho, G., Jobert, A., et al. (2010). How learning to read changes the cortical networks for vision and language. *Science* 330, 1359–1364. doi: 10.1126/science.1194140

Demb, J. B., Boynton, G. M., and Heeger, D. J. (1998). Functional magnetic resonance imaging of early visual pathways in dyslexia. *J. Neurosci.* 18, 6939–6951.

Demonet, J. F., Taylor, M. J., and Chaix, Y. (2004). Developmental dyslexia. *Lancet* 363, 1451–1460. doi: 10.1016/S0140-6736(04)16106-0

Desroches, A. S., Cone, N. E., Bolger, D. J., Bitan, T., Burman, D. D., and Booth, J. R. (2010). Children with reading difficulties show differences in brain regions associated with orthographic processing during spoken language processing. *Brain Res.* 1356, 73–84. doi: 10.1016/j.brainres.2010.07.097

Dufor, O., Serniclaes, W., Sprenger-Charolles, L., and Demonet, J. F. (2007). Top-down processes during auditory phoneme categorization in dyslexia: a PET study. *Neuroimage* 34, 1692–1707. doi: 10.1016/j.neuroimage.2006.10.034

Eckert, M. A., Leonard, C. M., Wilke, M., Eckert, M., Richards, T., Richards, A., et al. (2005). Anatomical signatures of dyslexia in children: unique information from manual and voxel based morphometry brain measures. *Cortex* 41, 304–315. doi: 10.1016/S0010-9452(08)70268-5

Eden, G. F., Jones, K. M., Cappell, K., Gareau, L., Wood, F. B., Zeffiro, T. A., et al. (2004). Neural changes following remediation in adult developmental dyslexia. *Neuron* 44, 411–422. doi: 10.1016/j.neuron.2004.10.019

Eden, G. F., VanMeter, J. W., Rumsey, J. M., Maisog, J. M., Woods, R. P., and Zeffiro, T. A. (1996). Abnormal processing of visual motion in dyslexia revealed by functional brain imaging. *Nature* 382, 66–69. doi: 10.1038/382066a0

Eickhoff, S. B., Laird, A. R., Grefkes, C., Wang, L. E., Zilles, K., and Fox, P. T. (2009). Coordinate based activation likelihood estimation meta-analysis of neuroimaging data: a random effects approach based on empirical estimates of spatial uncertainty. *Hum. Brain Mapp.* 30, 2907–2926. doi: 10.1002/hbm.20718

Facoetti, A., Paganoni, P., Turatto, M., Marzola, V., and Mascetti, G. G. (2000). Visual-spatial attention in developmental dyslexia. *Cortex* 36, 109–123. doi: 10.1016/S0010-9452(08)70840-2

Finn, E. S., Shen, X., Holahan, J. M., Scheinost, D., Lacadie, C., Papademetris, X., et al. (2013). Disruption of functional networks in dyslexia: a whole-brain, data-driven analysis of connectivity. *Biol. Psychiatry* 76, 397–404. doi: 10.1016/j.biopsych.2013.08.031

Fisher, R. A. (1970). *Statistical Methods for Research Workers*. Edinburgh: Oliver & Boyd.

Fox, P. T., Parsons, L. M., and Lancaster, J. L. (1998). Beyond the single study: function/location metanalysis in cognitive neuroimaging. *Curr. Opin. Neurobiol.* 8, 178–187. doi: 10.1016/S0959-4388(98)80138-4

Frith, U. (1999). Paradoxes in the definition of dyslexia. *Dyslexia* 5, 192–214.

Gaab, N., Gabrieli, J. D., Deutsch, G. K., Tallal, P., and Temple, E. (2007). Neural correlates of rapid auditory processing are disrupted in children with developmental dyslexia and ameliorated with training: an fMRI study. *Restor. Neurol. Neurosci.* 25, 295–310.

Galaburda, A. M., and Livingstone, M. (1993). Evidence for a magnocellular defect in developmental dyslexia. *Ann. N.Y. Acad. Sci.* 682, 70–82. doi: 10.1111/j.1749-6632.1993.tb22960.x

Galaburda, A. M., Sherman, G. F., Rosen, G. D., Aboitiz, F., and Geschwind, N. (1985). Developmental dyslexia: four consecutive patients with cortical abnormalities. *Ann. Neurol.* 18, 222–233.

Georgiewa, P., Rzanny, R., Hopf, J. M., Knab, R., Glauche, V., Kaiser, W. A., et al. (1999). fMRI during word processing in dyslexic and normal reading children. *Neuroreport* 10, 3459–3465. doi: 10.1097/00001756-199911080-00036

Grande, M., Meffert, E., Huber, W., Amunts, K., and Heim, S. (2011). Word frequency effects in the left IFG in dyslexic and normally reading children during picture naming and reading. *Neuroimage* 57, 1212–1220. doi: 10.1016/j.neuroimage.2011.05.033

Grunling, C., Ligges, M., Huonker, R., Klingert, M., Mentzel, H. J., Rzanny, R., et al. (2004). Dyslexia: the possible benefit of multimodal integration of fMRI- and EEG-data. *J. Neural Transm.* 111, 951–969. doi: 10.1007/s00702-004-0117-z

Hari, R., and Renvall, H. (2001). Impaired processing of rapid stimulus sequences in dyslexia. *Trends Cogn. Sci.* 5, 525–532. doi: 10.1016/S1364-6613(00)01801-5

Heim, S., Grande, M., Pape-Neumann, J., van Ermingen, M., Meffert, E., Grabowska, A., et al. (2010). Interaction of phonological awareness and 'magnocellular' processing during normal and dyslexic reading: behavioural and fMRI investigations. *Dyslexia* 16, 258–282. doi: 10.1002/dys.409

Heim, S., Tschierse, J., Amunts, K., Wilms, M., Vossel, S., Willmes, K., et al. (2008). Cognitive subtypes of dyslexia. *Acta Neurobiol. Exp. (Wars)* 68, 73–89.

Hoeft, F., Hernandez, A., McMillon, G., Taylor-Hill, H., Martindale, J. L., Meyler, A., et al. (2006). Neural basis of dyslexia: a comparison between dyslexic and nondyslexic children equated for reading ability. *J. Neurosci.* 26, 10700–10708. doi: 10.1523/JNEUROSCI.4931-05.2006

Horwitz, B., Rumsey, J. M., and Donohue, B. C. (1998). Functional connectivity of the angular gyrus in normal reading and dyslexia. *Proc. Natl. Acad. Sci. U.S.A.* 95, 8939–8944. doi: 10.1073/pnas.95.15.8939

Hu, W., Lee, H. L., Zhang, Q., Liu, T., Geng, L. B., Seghier, M. L., et al. (2010). Developmental dyslexia in Chinese and English populations: dissociating the effect of dyslexia from language differences. *Brain* 133(Pt 6), 1694–1706. doi: 10.1093/brain/awq106

Ingvar, M., Trampe, P., Greitz, T., Eriksson, L., Stone-Elander, S., and von Euler, C. (2002). Residual differences in language processing in compensated dyslexics revealed in simple word reading tasks. *Brain Lang.* 83, 249–267. doi: 10.1016/S0093-934X(02)00055-X

Johannes, S., Kussmaul, C. L., Munte, T. F., and Mangun, G. R. (1996). Developmental dyslexia: passive visual stimulation provides no evidence for a magnocellular processing defect. *Neuropsychologia* 34, 1123–1127. doi: 10.1016/0028-3932(96)00026-7

Kandel, E., Schwartz, J., Jessell, T., Siegelbaum, S., and Hudspeth, A. J. (2012). *Principles of Neural Science.* 5th Edn. New York, NY: McGraw Hill Professional.

Kast, M., Bezzola, L., Jancke, L., and Meyer, M. (2011). Multi- and unisensory decoding of words and nonwords result in differential brain responses in dyslexic and nondyslexic adults. *Brain Lang.* 119, 136–148. doi: 10.1016/j.bandl.2011.04.002

Klingberg, T., Hedehus, M., Temple, E., Salz, T., Gabrieli, J. D., Moseley, M. E., et al. (2000). Microstructure of temporo-parietal white matter as a basis for reading ability: evidence from diffusion tensor magnetic resonance imaging. *Neuron* 25, 493–500. doi: 10.1016/S0896-6273(00)80911-3

Kober, H., and Wager, T. D. (2010). Meta-analysis of neuroimaging data. *Wiley Interdiscip. Rev. Cogn. Sci.* 1, 293–300. doi: 10.1002/wcs.41

Kovelman, I., Norton, E. S., Christodoulou, J. A., Gaab, N., Lieberman, D. A., Triantafyllou, C., et al. (2011). Brain basis of phonological awareness for spoken language in children and its disruption in dyslexia. *Cereb. Cortex* 22, 754–764. doi: 10.1093/cercor/bhr094

Koyama, M. S., Di Martino, A., Kelly, C., Jutagir, D. R., Sunshine, J., Schwartz, S. J., et al. (2013). Cortical signatures of dyslexia and remediation: an intrinsic functional connectivity approach. *PLoS ONE* 8:e55454. doi: 10.1371/journal.pone.0055454

Kronbichler, M., Hutzler, F., Staffen, W., Mair, A., Ladurner, G., and Wimmer, H. (2006). Evidence for a dysfunction of left posterior reading areas in German dyslexic readers. *Neuropsychologia* 44, 1822–1832. doi: 10.1016/j.neuropsychologia.2006.03.010

Kronschnabel, J., Schmid, R., Maurer, U., and Brandeis, D. (2013). Visual print tuning deficits in dyslexic adolescents under minimized phonological demands. *Neuroimage* 74, 58–69. doi: 10.1016/j.neuroimage.2013.02.014

Landi, N., Mencl, W. E., Frost, S. J., Sandak, R., and Pugh, K. R. (2010). An fMRI study of multimodal semantic and phonological processing in reading disabled adolescents. *Ann. Dyslexia* 60, 102–121. doi: 10.1007/s11881-009-0029-6

Levy, J., Pernet, C., Treserras, S., Boulanouar, K., Aubry, F., Demonet, J. F., et al. (2009). Testing for the dual-route cascade reading model in the brain: an fMRI effective connectivity account of an efficient reading style. *PLoS ONE* 4:e6675. doi: 10.1371/journal.pone.0006675

Liddle, E. B., Jackson, G. M., Rorden, C., and Jackson, S. R. (2009). Lateralized temporal order judgement in dyslexia. *Neuropsychologia* 47, 3244–3254. doi: 10.1016/j.neuropsychologia.2009.08.007

MacSweeney, M., Brammer, M. J., Waters, D., and Goswami, U. (2009). Enhanced activation of the left inferior frontal gyrus in deaf and dyslexic adults during rhyming. *Brain* 132(Pt 7), 1928–1940. doi: 10.1093/brain/awp129

Maisog, J. M., Einbinder, E. R., Flowers, D. L., Turkeltaub, P. E., and Eden, G. F. (2008). A meta-analysis of functional neuroimaging studies of dyslexia. *Ann. N.Y. Acad. Sci.* 1145, 237–259. doi: 10.1196/annals.1416.024

Maurer, U., Schulz, E., Brem, S., der Mark, S., Bucher, K., Martin, E., et al. (2011). The development of print tuning in children with dyslexia: evidence from longitudinal ERP data supported by fMRI. *Neuroimage* 57, 714–722. doi: 10.1016/j.neuroimage.2010.10.055

Mazziotta, J. C., Toga, A. W., Evans, A., Fox, P., and Lancaster, J. (1995). A probabilistic atlas of the human brain: theory and rationale for its development. The International Consortium for Brain Mapping (ICBM). *Neuroimage* 2, 89–101. doi: 10.1006/nimg.1995.1012

McCrory, E. J., Frith, U., Brunswick, N., and Price, C. (2000). Abnormal functional activation during a simple word repetition task: a PET study of adult dyslexics. *J. Cogn. Neurosci.* 12, 753–762. doi: 10.1162/089892900562570

McCrory, E. J., Mechelli, A., Frith, U., and Price, C. J. (2005). More than words: a common neural basis for reading and naming deficits in developmental dyslexia? *Brain* 128(Pt 2), 261–267. doi: 10.193/brain/awh340

Menghini, D., Finzi, A., Benassi, M., Bolzani, R., Facoetti, A., Giovagnoli, S., et al. (2010). Different underlying neurocognitive deficits in developmental dyslexia: a comparative study. *Neuropsychologia* 48, 863–872. doi: 10.1016/j.neuropsychologia.2009.11.003

Menghini, D., Hagberg, G. E., Caltagirone, C., Petrosini, L., and Vicari, S. (2006). Implicit learning deficits in dyslexic adults: an fMRI study. *Neuroimage* 33, 1218–1226. doi: 10.1016/j.neuroimage.2006.08.024

Meyler, A., Keller, T. A., Cherkassky, V. L., Gabrieli, J. D., and Just, M. A. (2008). Modifying the brain activation of poor readers during sentence comprehension with extended remedial instruction: a longitudinal study of neuroplasticity. *Neuropsychologia* 46, 2580–2592. doi: 10.1016/j.neuropsychologia.2008.03.012

Monzalvo, K., Fluss, J., Billard, C., Dehaene, S., and Dehaene-Lambertz, G. (2012). Cortical networks for vision and language in dyslexic and normal children of variable socio-economic status. *Neuroimage* 61, 258–274. doi: 10.1016/j.neuroimage.2012.02.035

Morgan, B. J. T., and Ray, A. P. G. (1995). Non-uniqueness and inversions in cluster analysis. *Appl. Stat.* 44, 117–134. doi: 10.2307/2986199

Nicolson, R. I., Fawcett, A. J., Berry, E. L., Jenkins, I. H., Dean, P., and Brooks, D. J. (1999). Association of abnormal cerebellar activation with motor learning difficulties in dyslexic adults. *Lancet* 353, 1662–1667. doi: 10.1016/S0140-6736(98)09165-X

Nicolson, R. I., Fawcett, A. J., and Dean, P. (2001). Developmental dyslexia: the cerebellar deficit hypothesis. *Trends Neurosci.* 24, 508–511. doi: 10.1016/S0166-2236(00)01896-8

Olulade, O. A., Gilger, J. W., Talavage, T. M., Hynd, G. W., and McAteer, C. I. (2012). Beyond phonological processing deficits in adult dyslexics: atypical FMRI activation patterns for spatial problem solving. *Dev. Neuropsychol.* 37, 617–635. doi: 10.1080/87565641.2012.702826

Olulade, O. A., Napoliello, E. M., and Eden, G. F. (2013). Abnormal visual motion processing is not a cause of dyslexia. *Neuron* 79, 180–190. doi: 10.1016/j.neuron.2013.05.002

Paulesu, E., Connelly, A., Frith, C. D., Friston, K. J., Heather, J., Myers, R., et al. (1995). Functional MR imaging correlations with positron emission tomography. Initial experience using a cognitive activation paradigm on verbal working memory. *Neuroimaging Clin. N. Am.* 5, 207–225.

Paulesu, E., Demonet, J. F., Fazio, F., McCrory, E., Chanoine, V., Brunswick, N., et al. (2001). Dyslexia: cultural diversity and biological unity. *Science* 291, 2165–2167. doi: 10.1126/science.1057179

Paulesu, E., Frith, C. D., and Frackowiak, R. S. (1993). The neural correlates of the verbal component of working memory. *Nature* 362, 342–345. doi: 10.1038/362342a0

Paulesu, E., Frith, U., Snowling, M., Gallagher, A., Morton, J., Frackowiak, R. S., et al. (1996). Is developmental dyslexia a disconnection syndrome? Evidence from PET scanning. *Brain* 119(Pt 1), 143–157. doi: 10.1093/brain/119.1.143

Paulesu, E., McCrory, E., Fazio, F., Menoncello, L., Brunswick, N., Cappa, S. F., et al. (2000). A cultural effect on brain function. *Nat. Neurosci.* 3, 91–96. doi: 10.1038/71163

Pecini, C., Biagi, L., Brizzolara, D., Cipriani, P., Di Lieto, M. C., Guzzetta, A., et al. (2011). How many functional brains in developmental dyslexia? When the history of language delay makes the difference. *Cogn. Behav. Neurol.* 24, 85–92. doi: 10.1097/WNN.0b013e318222a4c2

Pekkola, J., Laasonen, M., Ojanen, V., Autti, T., Jaaskelainen, I. P., Kujala, T., et al. (2006). Perception of matching and conflicting audiovisual speech in dyslexic and fluent readers: an fMRI study at 3 T. *Neuroimage* 29, 797–807. doi: 10.1016/j.neuroimage.2005.09.069

Pennington, B. F., Van Orden, G. C., Smith, S. D., Green, P. A., and Haith, M. M. (1990). Phonological processing skills and deficits in adult dyslexics. *Child Dev.* 61, 1753–1778. doi: 10.2307/1130836

Pernet, C., Andersson, J., Paulesu, E., and Demonet, J. F. (2009). When all hypotheses are right: a multifocal account of dyslexia. *Hum. Brain Mapp.* 30, 2278–2292. doi: 10.1002/hbm.20670

Pernet, C., Schyns, P. G., and Demonet, J. F. (2007). Specific, selective or preferential: comments on category specificity in neuroimaging. *Neuroimage* 35, 991–997. doi: 10.1016/j.neuroimage.2007.01.017

Peyrin, C., Demonet, J. F., N'Guyen-Morel, M. A., Le Bas, J. F., and Valdois, S. (2011). Superior parietal lobule dysfunction in a homogeneous group of dyslexic children with a visual attention span disorder. *Brain Lang.* 118, 128–138. doi: 10.1016/j.bandl.2010.06.005

Price, C. J., Gorno-Tempini, M. L., Graham, K. S., Biggio, N., Mechelli, A., Patterson, K., et al. (2003). Normal and pathological reading: converging data from lesion and imaging studies. *Neuroimage* 20(Suppl. 1), S30–S41. doi: 10.1016/j.neuroimage.2003.09.012

Pugh, K. R., Mencl, W. E., Jenner, A. R., Katz, L., Frost, S. J., Lee, J. R., et al. (2000). Functional neuroimaging studies of reading and reading disability (developmental dyslexia). *Ment. Retard. Dev. Disabil. Res. Rev.* 6, 207–213. doi: 10.1002/1098-2779(2000)6:3<207::AID-MRDD8>3.0.CO;2-P

Radua, J., and Mataix-Cols, D. (2012). Meta-analytic methods for neuroimaging data explained. *Biol. Mood Anxiety Disord.* 2:6. doi: 10.1186/2045-5380-2-6

Ramus, F., Rosen, S., Dakin, S. C., Day, B. L., Castellote, J. M., White, S., et al. (2003). Theories of developmental dyslexia: insights from a multiple case study of dyslexic adults. *Brain* 126(Pt 4), 841–865. doi: 10.1093/brain/awg076

Reid, A. A., Szczerbinski, M., Iskierka-Kasperek, E., and Hansen, P. (2007). Cognitive profiles of adult developmental dyslexics: theoretical implications. *Dyslexia* 13, 1–24. doi: 10.1002/dys.321

Reilhac, C., Peyrin, C., Demonet, J. F., and Valdois, S. (2013). Role of the superior parietal lobules in letter-identity processing within strings: fMRI evidence from skilled and dyslexic readers. *Neuropsychologia* 51, 601–612. doi: 10.1016/j.neuropsychologia.2012.12.010

Richards, T. L., and Berninger, V. W. (2008). Abnormal fMRI connectivity in children with dyslexia during a phoneme task: before but not after treatment. *J. Neurolinguistics* 21, 294–304. doi: 10.1016/j.jneuroling.2007.07.002

Richlan, F., Kronbichler, M., and Wimmer, H. (2009). Functional abnormalities in the dyslexic brain: a quantitative meta-analysis of neuroimaging studies. *Hum. Brain Mapp.* 30, 3299–3308. doi: 10.1002/hbm.20752

Richlan, F., Kronbichler, M., and Wimmer, H. (2011). Meta-analyzing brain dysfunctions in dyslexic children and adults. *Neuroimage* 56, 1735–1742. doi: 10.1016/j.neuroimage.2011.02.040

Richlan, F., Kronbichler, M., and Wimmer, H. (2013). Structural abnormalities in the dyslexic brain: a meta-analysis of voxel-based morphometry studies. *Hum. Brain Mapp.* 34, 3055–3065. doi: 10.1002/hbm.22127

Richlan, F., Sturm, D., Schurz, M., Kronbichler, M., Ladurner, G., and Wimmer, H. (2010). A common left occipito-temporal dysfunction in developmental dyslexia and acquired letter-by-letter reading? *PLoS ONE* 5:e12073. doi: 10.1371/journal.pone.0012073

Rimrodt, S. L., Clements-Stephens, A. M., Pugh, K. R., Courtney, S. M., Gaur, P., Pekar, J. J., et al. (2009). Functional MRI of sentence comprehension in children with dyslexia: beyond word recognition. *Cereb. Cortex* 19, 402–413. doi: 10.1093/cercor/bhn092

Rorden, C., and Brett, M. (2000). Stereotaxic display of brain lesions. *Behav. Neurol.* 12, 191–200. doi: 10.1155/2000/421719

Ruff, S., Cardebat, D., Marie, N., and Demonet, J. F. (2002). Enhanced response of the left frontal cortex to slowed down speech in dyslexia: an fMRI study. *Neuroreport* 13, 1285–1289. doi: 10.1097/00001756-200207190-00014

Rumsey, J. M., Andreason, P., Zametkin, A. J., Aquino, T., King, A. C., Hamburger, S. D., et al. (1992). Failure to activate the left temporoparietal cortex in dyslexia. An oxygen 15 positron emission tomographic study. *Arch. Neurol.* 49, 527–534. doi: 10.1001/archneur.1992.00530290115020

Rumsey, J. M., Donohue, B. C., Brady, D. R., Nace, K., Giedd, J. N., and Andreason, P. (1997a). A magnetic resonance imaging study of planum temporale asymmetry in men with developmental dyslexia. *Arch. Neurol.* 54, 1481–1489. doi: 10.1001/archneur.1997.00550240035010

Rumsey, J. M., Nace, K., Donohue, B., Wise, D., Maisog, J. M., and Andreason, P. (1997b). A positron emission tomographic study of impaired word recognition and phonological processing in dyslexic men. *Arch. Neurol.* 54, 562–573. doi: 10.1001/archneur.1997.00550170042013

Salimi-Khorshidi, G., Smith, S. M., Keltner, J. R., Wager, T. D., and Nichols, T. E. (2009). Meta-analysis of neuroimaging data: a comparison of image-based and coordinate-based pooling of studies. *Neuroimage* 45, 810–823. doi: 10.1016/j.neuroimage.2008.12.039

Sandak, R., Mencl, W. E., Frost, S. J., Rueckl, J. G., Katz, L., Moore, D. L., et al. (2004). The neurobiology of adaptive learning in reading: a contrast of different training conditions. *Cogn. Affect. Behav. Neurosci.* 4, 67–88. doi: 10.3758/CABN.4.1.67

Schulz, E., Maurer, U., van der Mark, S., Bucher, K., Brem, S., Martin, E., et al. (2008). Impaired semantic processing during sentence reading in children with dyslexia: combined fMRI and ERP evidence. *Neuroimage* 41, 153–168. doi: 10.1016/j.neuroimage.2008.02.012

Schulz, E., Maurer, U., van der Mark, S., Bucher, K., Brem, S., Martin, E., et al. (2009). Reading for meaning in dyslexic and young children: distinct neural pathways but common endpoints. *Neuropsychologia* 47, 2544–2557. doi: 10.1016/j.neuropsychologia.2009.04.028

Schurz, M., Wimmer, H., Richlan, F., Ludersdorfer, P., Klackl, J., and Kronbichler, M. (2014). Resting-State and task-based functional brain connectivity in developmental dyslexia. *Cereb. Cortex.* doi: 10.1093/cercor/bhu184. [Epub ahead of print].

Shaywitz, B. A., Shaywitz, S. E., Pugh, K. R., Mencl, W. E., Fulbright, R. K., Skudlarski, P., et al. (2002). Disruption of posterior brain systems for reading in children with developmental dyslexia. *Biol. Psychiatry* 52, 101–110. doi: 10.1016/S0006-3223(02)01365-3

Shaywitz, S. E., Escobar, M. D., Shaywitz, B. A., Fletcher, J. M., and Makuch, R. (1992). Evidence that dyslexia may represent the lower tail of a normal distribution of reading ability. *N. Engl. J. Med.* 326, 145–150. doi: 10.1056/NEJM199201163260301

Shaywitz, S. E., Shaywitz, B. A., Pugh, K. R., Fulbright, R. K., Constable, R. T., Mencl, W. E., et al. (1998). Functional disruption in the organization of the brain for reading in dyslexia. *Proc. Natl. Acad. Sci. U.S.A.* 95, 2636–2641. doi: 10.1073/pnas.95.5.2636

Silani, G., Frith, U., Demonet, J. F., Fazio, F., Perani, D., Price, C., et al. (2005). Brain abnormalities underlying altered activation in dyslexia: a voxel based morphometry study. *Brain* 128(Pt 10), 2453–2461. doi: 10.1093/brain/awh579

Smith, E. E., Jonides, J., Marshuetz, C., and Koeppe, R. A. (1998). Components of verbal working memory: evidence from neuroimaging. *Proc. Natl. Acad. Sci. U.S.A.* 95, 876–882. doi: 10.1073/pnas.95.3.876

Snowling, M. J. (2001). From language to reading and dyslexia. *Dyslexia* 7, 37–46. doi: 10.1002/dys.185

Stein, J. (2001). The magnocellular theory of developmental dyslexia. *Dyslexia* 7, 12–36. doi: 10.1002/dys.186

Stein, J., and Walsh, V. (1997). To see but not to read; the magnocellular theory of dyslexia. *Trends Neurosci.* 20, 147–152. doi: 10.1016/S0166-2236(96)01005-3

Steinbrink, C., Groth, K., Lachmann, T., and Riecker, A. (2012). Neural correlates of temporal auditory processing in developmental dyslexia during German vowel length discrimination: an fMRI study. *Brain Lang.* 121, 1–11. doi: 10.1016/j.bandl.2011.12.003

Talairach, J., and Tournoux, P. (1988). *Co-planar Stereotaxic Atlas of the Human Brain: 3-D Proportional System: An Approach to Cerebral Imaging.* New York, NY: Thieme Medical Publishers.

Taylor, J. S., Rastle, K., and Davis, M. H. (2013). Can cognitive models explain brain activation during word and pseudoword reading? A meta-analysis of 36 neuroimaging studies. *Psychol. Bull.* 139, 766–791. doi: 10.1037/a0030266

Temple, E., Poldrack, R. A., Protopapas, A., Nagarajan, S., Salz, T., Tallal, P., et al. (2000). Disruption of the neural response to rapid acoustic stimuli in dyslexia: evidence from functional MRI. *Proc. Natl. Acad. Sci. U.S.A.* 97, 13907–13912. doi: 10.1073/pnas.240461697

Temple, E., Poldrack, R. A., Salidis, J., Deutsch, G. K., Tallal, P., Merzenich, M. M., et al. (2001). Disrupted neural responses to phonological and orthographic processing in dyslexic children: an fMRI study. *Neuroreport* 12, 299–307. doi: 10.1097/00001756-200102120-00024

Turkeltaub, P. E., Eden, G. F., Jones, K. M., and Zeffiro, T. A. (2002). Meta-analysis of the functional neuroanatomy of single-word reading: method and validation. *Neuroimage* 16(3 Pt 1), 765–780. doi: 10.1006/nimg.2002.1131

Turkeltaub, P. E., Eickhoff, S. B., Laird, A. R., Fox, M., Wiener, M., and Fox, P. (2012). Minimizing within-experiment and within-group effects in activation likelihood estimation meta-analyses. *Hum. Brain Mapp.* 33, 1–13. doi: 10.1002/hbm.21186

Turkeltaub, P. E., Gareau, L., Flowers, D. L., Zeffiro, T. A., and Eden, G. F. (2003). Development of neural mechanisms for reading. *Nat. Neurosci.* 6, 767–773. doi: 10.1038/nn1065

Vallar, G., Bottini, G., and Paulesu, E. (2003). "Neglect syndromes: the role of the parietal cortex," in *The Parietal Lobe (Advances in Neurology)*, eds A. M. Siegel, R. A. Andersen, H. J. Freund, and D. D. Spencer (Philadelphia, PA: Lippincott Williams & Wilkins), 293–319.

van der Mark, S., Bucher, K., Maurer, U., Schulz, E., Brem, S., Buckelmuller, J., et al. (2009). Children with dyslexia lack multiple specializations along the visual word-form (VWF) system. *Neuroimage* 47, 1940–1949. doi: 10.1016/j.neuroimage.2009.05.021

van der Mark, S., Klaver, P., Bucher, K., Maurer, U., Schulz, E., Brem, S., et al. (2011). The left occipitotemporal system in reading: disruption of focal fMRI connectivity to left inferior frontal and inferior parietal language areas in children with dyslexia. *Neuroimage* 54, 2426–2436. doi: 10.1016/j.neuroimage.2010.10.002

Vanni, S., Uusitalo, M. A., Kiesila, P., and Hari, R. (1997). Visual motion activates V5 in dyslexics. *Neuroreport* 8, 1939–1942. doi: 10.1097/00001756-199705260-00029

Vasic, N., Lohr, C., Steinbrink, C., Martin, C., and Wolf, R. C. (2008). Neural correlates of working memory performance in adolescents and young adults with dyslexia. *Neuropsychologia* 46, 640–648. doi: 10.1016/j.neuropsychologia.2007.09.002

Wager, T. D., Lindquist, M., and Kaplan, L. (2007). Meta-analysis of functional neuroimaging data: current and future directions. *Soc. Cogn. Affect. Neurosci.* 2, 150–158. doi: 10.1093/scan/nsm015

Ward, J. H. J. (1963). Hierarchical grouping to optimize an objective function. *J. Am. Stat. Assoc.* 58, 236–244. doi: 10.1080/01621459.1963.10500845

Wimmer, H., Schurz, M., Sturm, D., Richlan, F., Klackl, J., Kronbichler, M., et al. (2010). A dual-route perspective on poor reading in a regular orthography: an fMRI study. *Cortex* 46, 1284–1298. doi: 10.1016/j.cortex.2010.06.004

Wolf, R. C., Sambataro, F., Lohr, C., Steinbrink, C., Martin, C., and Vasic, N. (2010). Functional brain network abnormalities during verbal working memory performance in adolescents and young adults with dyslexia. *Neuropsychologia* 48, 309–318. doi: 10.1016/j.neuropsychologia.2009.09.020

World Healt Organization. (1993). *The International Classification of Deseases.* Geneve: World Healt Organization.

Zorzi, M., Barbiero, C., Facoetti, A., Lonciari, I., Carrozzi, M., Montico, M., et al. (2012). Extra-large letter spacing improves reading in dyslexia. *Proc. Natl. Acad. Sci. U.S.A.* 109, 11455–11459. doi: 10.1073/pnas.1205566109

11

What does the brain of children with developmental dyslexia tell us about reading improvement? ERP evidence from an intervention study

Sandra Hasko*, Katarina Groth, Jennifer Bruder, Jürgen Bartling and Gerd Schulte-Körne

Department of Child and Adolescent Psychiatry and Psychotherapy, University Hospital Munich, Munich, Germany

Correspondence:
Sandra Hasko, Department of Child and Adolescent Psychiatry and Psychotherapy, University Hospital Munich, Pettenkoferstr. 8a, 80336 Munich, Germany
e-mail: sandra.hasko@med.uni-muenchen.de

Intervention is key to managing developmental dyslexia (DD), but not all children with DD benefit from treatment. Some children improve (improvers, IMP), whereas others do not improve (non-improvers, NIMP). Neurobiological differences between IMP and NIMP have been suggested, but studies comparing IMP and NIMP in childhood are missing. The present study examined whether ERP patterns change with treatment and differ between IMP and NIMP. We investigated the ERPs of 28 children with DD and 25 control children (CON) while performing a phonological lexical decision (PLD) task before and after a 6-month intervention. After intervention children with DD were divided into IMP ($n = 11$) and NIMP ($n = 17$). In the PLD–task children were visually presented with words, pseudohomophones, pseudowords, and false fonts and had to decide whether the presented stimulus sounded like an existing German word or not. Prior to intervention IMP showed higher N300 amplitudes over fronto-temporal electrodes compared to NIMP and CON and N400 amplitudes were attenuated in both IMP and NIMP compared to CON. After intervention N300 amplitudes of IMP were comparable to those of CON and NIMP. This suggests that the N300, which has been related to phonological access of orthographic stimuli and integration of orthographic and phonological representations, might index a compensatory mechanism or precursor that facilitates reading improvement. The N400, which is thought to reflect grapheme-phoneme conversion or the access to the orthographic lexicon increased in IMP from pre to post and was comparable to CON after intervention. Correlations between N300 amplitudes pre, growth in reading ability and N400 amplitudes post indicated that higher N300 amplitudes might be important for reading improvement and increase in N400 amplitudes. The results suggest that children with DD, showing the same cognitive profile might differ regarding their neuronal profile which could further influence reading improvement.

Keywords: developmental dyslexia, intervention, treatment, improvement, non-improvement, electrophysiology, N400, N300

INTRODUCTION

Developmental dyslexia (DD) is characterized by severe problems in learning to read properly and is often accompanied by a comorbid spelling disorder. These difficulties arise unexpectedly, because affected children and adults possess the intelligence, motivation, and educational opportunities required for language acquisition and they do not suffer from neurological or sensory deficits (DSM-5: APA, 2013). With prevalence rates around 4–9%, DD is one of the most common specific developmental disorders (Shaywitz et al., 1990; Katusic et al., 2001; Esser et al., 2002). DD accompanies the individuals throughout their lifespan and interferes with academic achievement and professional success (Shaywitz et al., 1999; Daniel et al., 2006; Willcutt et al., 2007). In addition around 40% of children with DD suffer from comorbid psychiatric disorders, especially from externalizing disorders, low school-related self-esteem, and depressive symptoms, as a consequence of their failure in acquiring adequate reading and spelling skills (Willcutt and Pennington, 2000; Arnold et al., 2005; Daniel et al., 2006; Goldston et al., 2007; Willcutt et al., 2007; Mugnaini et al., 2009). Therefore, the attainment of sustainable intervention effects in children with DD is crucial.

In contrast, the empirical state of research for evidence-based evaluation of interventions for children with DD is low. Current meta-analyses quantified the effectiveness of treatment approaches on reading and spelling disabilities and reported only marginal to average effect sizes (Ise et al., 2012; Galuschka et al., 2014). Because DD has a neurobiological basis (e.g., Shaywitz et al., 2007; Shaywitz and Shaywitz, 2008; Caylak, 2009; Richlan, 2012; Richlan et al., 2013) it is important to understand how interventions work on the neuronal level. Does intervention normalize neuronal activity of children with DD? Or does intervention lead to an enhancement of compensatory mechanisms?

A better understanding of treatment related changes on the neuronal level might help to refine intervention programs in order to make treatment more effective.

In addition, meta-analyses reported high heterogeneity between the effect sizes of different studies for both reading and spelling interventions (National Institute of Child Health and Human Development, 2000; Ise et al., 2012; McArthur et al., 2012; Galuschka et al., 2014). Weak and inconsistent effect sizes might amongst others arise by inclusion of participants who do not improve during intervention (non-improvers; NIMP). This assumption is supported by studies indicating that up to 30% of struggling readers do not benefit from intervention (Shanahan and Barr, 1995; Vaughn et al., 2003). A better understanding of neuronal differences between children who improve during intervention (improvers; IMP) and children who continue to struggle might help to predict treatment response and to further establish intervention programs adapted to the special needs of the latter.

Against this background, the aim of the present study was twofold. On the one hand we were interested in investigating which neurophysiological changes occur during treatment. A further goal was to explore whether there might be any pre-existing neurophysiological differences, between IMP and NIMP.

Over the past decade researchers began to focus on the neuronal processes related to inefficient reading and spelling abilities to understand the efficacy of reading and spelling interventions. Treatment-related functional changes have been observed in the neuronal reading network. Aberrant activation patterns in the subsystems of the neuronal reading network including posterior occipito-temporal and parieto-temporal regions as well as inferior-frontal areas in DD have been established (Shaywitz et al., 2007; Shaywitz and Shaywitz, 2008; Caylak, 2009; Richlan, 2012; Richlan et al., 2013). Compared to typically developing children, children with DD show a hypoactivation in the posterior subsystems of the left hemispheric reading network, which was found to be accompanied by an overactivation in homolog right hemispheric regions during performing language tasks (Simos et al., 2002; Demonet et al., 2004; Kronbichler et al., 2007; Shaywitz and Shaywitz, 2008; Richlan et al., 2009). With respect to the inferior-frontal subsystem results are less homogeneous. Some studies report hypoactivation (Paulesu et al., 1996; Wimmer et al., 2010; for meta-analyses see Richlan et al., 2009, 2011) whereas others observed hyperactivation in subjects with DD (Salmelin et al., 1996; Shaywitz et al., 1998; Brunswick et al., 1999; for review see Pugh et al., 2000; Sandak et al., 2004). Furthermore, disconnectivity between posterior and frontal subsystems (Paulesu et al., 1996) as well as the two posterior subsystems (Shaywitz et al., 2002) of the neuronal reading network has been described. After intervention a normalization of activation in the neuronal reading network has been observed in English speaking children (Simos et al., 2002, 2006, 2007b; Aylward et al., 2003; Temple et al., 2003; Shaywitz et al., 2004; Richards et al., 2007; Meyler et al., 2008) and adults with DD (Eden et al., 2004). Furthermore, it has been described that the connectivity between reading-related areas is normalized after treatment (Richards and Berninger, 2008; Keller and Just, 2009). Treatment-related changes have been also found using electrophysiology. Researchers observed changes in several reading-related event-related potential (ERP) measures (MMN: Kujala et al., 2001; Huotilainen et al., 2011; Lovio et al., 2012; P100: Mayseless, 2011; N170: Jucla et al., 2009; Spironelli et al., 2010; P300: Santos et al., 2007; Jucla et al., 2009) as well as in EEG frequency bands (Penolazzi et al., 2010; Weiss et al., 2010) after intervention.

It has been suggested that different neurobiological processing disorders might cause DD and that these differences in brain development within the group of children with DD might further influence improvement in literacy skills during treatment (Noble and McCandliss, 2005). However, studies examining whether there might be neurophysiological differences prior to receiving intervention between IMP and NIMP are less common. To the best of our knowledge only eight studies differentiated between IMP and NIMP (Simos et al., 2005, 2007a; Odegard et al., 2008; Davis et al., 2011; Farris et al., 2011; Rezaie et al., 2011a,b; Molfese et al., 2013).

Six out of these eight studies focused on neuronal differences between IMP and NIMP after intervention. In most studies this was the consequence of applying a cross-sectional design, which investigated neurophysiological activity only after intervention (Odegard et al., 2008; Davis et al., 2011; Farris et al., 2011; Molfese et al., 2013). These cross-sectional studies reported on normal activation patterns throughout the reading network in IMP after intervention or on brain mechanisms which are known to have a compensatory function (Odegard et al., 2008; Davis et al., 2011; Farris et al., 2011; Molfese et al., 2013). In contrast, NIMP who had persistent deficits in reading performance were marked by aberrant activation patterns throughout the reading network (Odegard et al., 2008; Davis et al., 2011), deficiencies in ERP measures (Molfese et al., 2013) and lower functional connectivity between reading-related brain areas (Farris et al., 2011). Furthermore, two longitudinal studies conducted by Simos et al. (2005, 2007a) reported on similar spatial and temporal brain activation patterns in normal developing children and 6–8-year-old (Simos et al., 2005) and 8–10-year-old (Simos et al., 2007a) IMP after intervention, which was not observed in NIMP. However, Simos et al. (2005, 2007a) did not report on pre-existing differences between IMP and NIMP. Small sample sizes and confounding variables such as wide age range probably mask pre-existing differences, which might be expected if different neurobiological processing disorders underlie DD and influence improvement during intervention (Noble and McCandliss, 2005). In line with this assumption, Rezaie et al. (2011a,b) reported on pre-existing differences between adolescent IMP and NIMP using MEG. In contrast to control children (CON) and IMP, children, who did not improve in reading ability displayed reduced activity in left middle- and superior-temporal gyri, left supramarginal and angular gyrus and ventral occipito-temporal regions as well as in the right parahippocampal gyrus (Rezaie et al., 2011a,b). Furthermore, NIMP displayed reduced activity in the superior- and medial-temporal gyrus of both hemispheres compared to CON (Rezaie et al., 2011b). No differences in these areas were found between CON and IMP. Interestingly, the degree of activation in these regions predicted improvement during intervention, suggesting that pre-existing neuronal activity might influence improvement during treatment.

To summarize, neuronal differences between IMP and NIMP have been reported before (Rezaie et al., 2011a,b) and after intervention (Simos et al., 2007a; Odegard et al., 2008; Davis et al., 2011; Farris et al., 2011; Molfese et al., 2013). Even though these studies provide interesting information about IMP and NIMP their informative value is limited due to methodological difficulties. First the cross-sectional design of most studies (Odegard et al., 2008; Davis et al., 2011; Farris et al., 2011; Rezaie et al., 2011a,b; Molfese et al., 2013) makes clear interpretation of the results difficult. Second the inclusion criterion for DD within most of the studies was not very strict (below the 25th for Rezaie et al., 2011a,b; below the 30th percentile for Simos et al., 2007a) or DD was assessed by non-standardized tests (Davis et al., 2011). This suggests that also normally developing children with somewhat poorer reading skills might have participated in previous studies. Third, differentiation between IMP and NIMP was not strict in most studies using either the median split or performance above and below of arbitrary defined percentile ranges in order to group IMP and NIMP (Simos et al., 2005, 2007a; Davis et al., 2011; Rezaie et al., 2011a,b; Molfese et al., 2013). Moreover small sample sizes, wide age ranges (Simos et al., 2007a; Odegard et al., 2008; Farris et al., 2011), differences in reading ability between IMP and NIMP before intervention (Simos et al., 2007a; Odegard et al., 2008; Davis et al., 2011; Farris et al., 2011), partly rehabilitated NIMP (average skills in phonological awareness but not in word reading) and a big time lag between completion of the intervention and participation in the experiments (Odegard et al., 2008; Farris et al., 2011) are further methodological problems which have to be taken into account. In addition to the best of our knowledge, so far nothing has been reported about preexisting neurophysiological differences between IMP and NIMP in childhood. However, keeping the high number of children, who don't improve during interventions (Shanahan and Barr, 1995; Vaughn et al., 2003; Groth et al., 2013) and the therapy costs involved (Georgii et al., in review) in mind it is absolutely essential to better understand possible markers of improvement and non-improvement.

In order to investigate electrophysiological differences between IMP and NIMP before and after intervention in the present study we took advantage of the phonological lexical decision (PLD)—task. In this task subjects are presented with real words (W), pseudohomophones (PH), pseudowords (PW), and false fonts (FF) and indicate whether the visually presented stimulus sounds like a real word or not (Kronbichler et al., 2007; van der Mark et al., 2009, 2011; Schurz et al., 2010; Wimmer et al., 2010; Hasko et al., 2013). One major advantage of the PLD—task, is the fact, that it is a continuous reading task, which allows to study both orthographic and phonological processing in one experiment (Hasko et al., 2013). The PLD—task taps orthographic processing on two levels. Firstly, by comparing the letter string material (W; PH; PW) to the visual control stimuli (FF) print sensitivity will be examined. Secondly, the contrast between orthographic familiar (W) and unfamiliar (PH; PW) word material, while controlling for phonology in the case of the contrast between W and PH provides information about the subjects' familiarity with orthographic representations. Furthermore, according to dual route models of reading (e.g., Coltheart et al., 1993, 2001) contrasting of unfamiliar (PH; PW) with familiar (W) word material also taps phonological processing because grapheme-phoneme correspondence (GPC) rules need to be applied in order to sound out the orthographic unfamiliar word material (see Hasko et al., 2013).

Using this task we recently proposed a temporal model of reading processes (Hasko et al., 2013) based on the assumption of dual route models of reading (Coltheart et al., 1993, 2001) in normal developing children and we found processing differences in children with DD. According to dual route models of reading (Coltheart et al., 1993, 2001) reading processes take place in a hierarchical manner. After identification of visual features (contrast, color, spatial frequency) of a letter string the first step of reading processes comprises the identification of letters (Coltheart et al., 1993, 2001). Our results show that the first component which is sensitive to print in contrast to non-orthographic stimuli (FF) is the N170 over occipito-temporal electrodes. At about 220 ms CON's N170 mean peak amplitudes are higher for orthographic material compared to FF indicating that letters are identified in this time window. After the identification of letters phonology of a letter string can be accessed in two different ways depending on the orthographic familiarity of the letter string. Familiar known words are read via the lexical route by accessing the orthographic representations in the orthographic lexicon and directly retrieving the corresponding phonological representations from the phonological lexicon. Whereas unfamiliar word forms, such as pseudohomophones and pseudowords or words for which the reader does not possess an entry in the orthographic lexicon are read by applying GPC rules in order to access the phonological representation (Coltheart et al., 1993, 2001). According to dual route models of reading these processes proceed in a parallel manner (Coltheart et al., 1993, 2001) and they occur at about 400 ms (Hasko et al., 2013). In normal developing children N400 amplitudes over centro-parietal electrodes were comparable high for W, PH, and PW suggesting that children rely on comparable reading processes for all letter strings. Thus, with respect to dual route models of reading the N400 might index the process of GPC or the searching process within in the orthographic lexicon. Access to the phonological lexicon in the PLD—task is indexed between 600 and 900 ms by a late positive complex (LPC) over left centro-parietal electrodes, which was higher for phonological familiar W and PH in contrast to PW in normally developing children. Processing differences dependent on the linguistic material in CON were observed only in the LPC, suggesting that similar reading processes were adopted independent of orthographic familiarity. With respect to children with DD our results indicated deficits on all processing steps. Firstly, a diminished mean area under the curve for the word material—FF contrasts in the time window of the N170 indicated that the degree of print sensitivity was reduced in the brain of children with DD. Secondly, reduced N400 amplitudes in children with DD pointed to less specified orthographic representations or impairments in accessing the orthographic lexicon or applying GPC rules. Lastly, the difference between phonological familiar and phonological unfamiliar word material was not found in children with DD suggesting an impaired access to phonological representations or an underspecification of phonological representations.

With respect to the first research question of the present study, namely which neurophysiological changes occur during treatment in children with DD we hypothesized to find effects on the N400. This was expected because the applied intervention programs worked on either orthographic knowledge or GPC, which is reflected by the N400. As found previously (see Hasko et al., 2013) we hypothesized to find higher N400 mean peak amplitudes before intervention for CON in contrast to IMP and NIMP. After intervention we expected that IMP might show an increase in N400 mean peak amplitudes, with the result that differences in N400 mean peak amplitudes between IMP and CON are diminished. No changes in N400 mean peak amplitudes over time were expected for CON and NIMP.

To answer our second research question whether there might be any neurophysiological differences between IMP and NIMP our analysis strategy was exploratory, as to the best of our knowledge there is no study, which allows deriving specific hypotheses regarding ERPs. However, previous MEG studies give us hints that differences between IMP and NIMP might be expected over temporo-parietal areas before intervention.

METHODS

PARTICIPANTS

As part of a longitudinal study 29 children without DD and 40 children with DD participated in the present study (for detailed description of recruitment procedure see Hasko et al., 2013). All children were tested regarding their reading and spelling abilities before and after intervention by means of German standardized tests. Common word and pseudoword reading fluency was assessed by using the one-minute-fluent reading-test (German: Ein-Minuten-Leseflüssigkeitstest [SLRT-II]; Moll and Landerl, 2010). In this measure, children are presented with a list of common words and pseudowords and are given one minute to read as many items as possible. Spelling was assessed with a basic vocabulary spelling test for grades 2–3 before intervention (German: Weingartener Grundwortschatz Rechtschreib-Test für zweite und dritte Klassen [WRT2+]; Birkel, 1994) and for grades 3–4 after intervention (German: Weingartener Grundwortschatz Rechtschreib-Test für dritte und vierte Klassen [WRT3+]; Birkel, 2007). In addition, reading comprehension was measured with a reading comprehension test for grades 1–6 (German: Leseverständnistest für Erst- bis Sechstklässler [ELFE 1-6]; Lenhard and Schneider, 2006). Moreover, measures of phonological awareness, rapid automatized naming (RAN) of numbers, letters, colors, and objects and working memory (digit span forwards and backwards from the Wechsler Intelligence Scale for Children IV; German: Hamburg-Wechsler-Intelligenztest für Kinder- IV [HAWIK-IV]; Petermann and Petermann, 2007) were taken.

In order to be included into the study the CON's common word reading fluency and spelling performance had to exceed the 25th percentile for both measures. Before intervention both the reading and the spelling score of children with DD had to diverge from the mean T-value for at least 1 SD (cutoff criteria was therefore set to a T-value of 40) and 1 SD from the IQ according to the regression criterion (Schulte-Körne et al., 2001). Thus, both a discrepancy of reading and spelling abilities from the class or age level, but also from the level expected on the basis of the child's intelligence was required for diagnosing DD. Children with DD were pseudorandomly assigned to one of two intervention programs. Three CON did not take part in the post treatment measurement and one CON had to be excluded from further analyses due to technical problems during EEG recording, resulting in 25 CON. From the children with DD one child started another intervention before our intervention period began and therefore recalled study participation resulting in a sample size of 39 children with DD. In the present study we were interested in the investigation of reading improvement during intervention. Therefore, children with DD were classified as IMP or NIMP after intervention according to their gain in common word reading fluency measured with the SLRT-II. Children were assigned to the group of IMP if their reading ability increased at least half SD from pre to post. We oriented our classification criteria based on results from current meta-analyses reporting effect sizes of $g = 0.31$ and $g = 0.33$ for reading interventions (Ise et al., 2012; Galuschka et al., 2014). Children whose ability did not change at all over time or did decrease from pre to post were classified as NIMP. According to this classification 12 children were identified as IMP, 21 as NIMP and 6 could not be assigned to one of the groups because their gain in common word reading fluency was between 1 and 4 T-values. One child from IMP and a total of 4 children from NIMP were excluded from further analyses due to excessive EEG artifacts, resulting in a sample size of 11 IMP and 17 NIMP.

Before intervention all groups had an average age of about 8 years (see **Table 1**). Gender was distributed similarly in all groups [$\chi^2 = 1.35, p = 0.51$] and apart from 1 IMP and 4 NIMP all subjects were right-handed [$\chi^2 = 6.56$, $p = 0.04$; see **Table 1**]. As can be seen in **Table 1** all children had an IQ within the normal range ($\geq$ 85 IQ points; as measured with the Culture Fair Intelligence Test; CFT 1; Cattell et al., 1997), the IQ of CON was significantly higher than the IQ of IMP and NIMP ($p < 0.05$). Attention was assessed with the subscale "Attention Problems" of the Child-Behavior-Checklist (CBCL/1–4; Achenbach, 1991). The CBCL-score of all children was below the cut-off score (CBCL-score < 7 for girls and CBCL-score < 8 for boys, see **Table 1**). In all reading and spelling tests IMP and NIMP performed significantly worse than CON before and after intervention ($p < 0.001$; see **Table 1**). Furthermore, CON outperformed IMP and NIMP before and after intervention in phoneme deletion, all subtests of the RAN and working memory ($p < 0.05$). The only difference between IMP and NIMP, was found in reading comprehension where IMP performed significantly better than NIMP pre and post ($p < 0.05$). As expected due to group assignment the common word reading fluency increased significantly over time for IMP ($p < 0.001$) and IMP outperformed NIMP in this measure after intervention ($p < 0.001$). Reading comprehension increased in all groups over time ($p < 0.001$). In addition all children improved their performance from pre to post ($p < 0.05$) in phoneme deletion and segmentation and all subtests of the RAN (apart from IMP in the subtest RAN—objects). In order to control for a confounding influence of IQ, handedness and text comprehension on the ERP results the groups were matched according to these variables resulting in sample sizes of 20, 10,

Table 1 | Descriptive statistics of CON, IMP, and NIMP.

	CON ($n = 25$)		IMP ($n = 11$)		NIMP ($n = 17$)	
Age	8.18 (0.32)		8.28 (0.39)		8.27 (0.35)	
Sex (male:female)	13:12		8:3		10:7	
Handedness (right:left)	24:1		10:1		13:4	
IQ[a]	112.04 (10.78)		101.55 (6.33)		104.94 (7.57)	
Attention[b]	2.88 (1.83)		4.82 (2.23)		4.35 (2.06)	
	Pre	**Post**	**Pre**	**Post**	**Pre**	**Post**
Word reading (T)[c]	56.36 (6.37)	54.28 (5.65)	31.55 (4.13)	38.27 (3.90)	32.24 (3.68)	29.65 (3.39)
Word reading (RS)[c]	58.28 (13.81)	73.76 (13.79)	19.36 (3.14)	39.00 (5.29)	18.53 (3.54)	27.76 (4.71)
Pseudoword reading (T)[c]	54.68 (7.66)	54.56 (9.99)	36.45 (1.51)	37.36 (5.37)	36.29 (3.90)	34.59 (3.71)
Pseudoword reading (RS)[c]	35.44 (7.34)	42.60 (8.58)	17.91 (2.84)	24.64 (5.54)	18.29 (4.07)	21.88 (3.08)
Reading comprehension (T)[d]	57.58 (8.04)	62.42 (4.75)	37.53 (2.68)	44.90 (3.99)	34.65 (2.41)	37.33 (5.55)
Spelling (T)[e]	52.28 (5.34)	55.48 (10.20)	35.27 (2.97)	33.27 (5.80)	33.94 (3.98)	32.76 (4.60)
Phoneme deletion[f]	21.16 (2.98)	23.32 (2.23)	17.09 (4.76)	19.18 (2.99)	17.65 (5.94)	19.35 (4.81)
Phoneme segmentation[g]	4.56 (2.16)	6.32 (2.10)	5.00 (2.10)	5.36 (1.57)	4.88 (2.62)	5.47 (2.38)
RAN – numbers[h]	100.24 (20.69)	114.15 (20.17)	82.20 (10.58)	89.73 (15.49)	78.94 (14.00)	85.51 (14.14)
RAN – letters[h]	104.72 (18.15)	120.33 (18.28)	53.67 (13.41)	59.74 (13.98)	52.07 (17.33)	63.50 (15.79)
RAN – colors[h]	60.03 (10.55)	65.45 (11.69)	49.06 (7.83)	54.62 (8.95)	47.71 (8.49)	52.63 (10.51)
RAN – objects[h]	51.97 (9.30)	60.34 (11.91)	40.99 (11.22)	41.15 (6.98)	37.93 (6.51)	42.43 (7.06)
Working memory, SS[i]	8.36 (2.53)	9.00 (2.72)	7.09 (1.81)	6.55 (1.64)	7.35 (1.54)	6.59 (2.35)

CON, control group; IMP, improvers; NIMP, non-improvers; n, sample size; T, T-values, T-values have a mean of 50 (SD ± 10); RS, raw scores; SS, standard scores, SS have a mean of 10 (SD ± 3); [a]CFT 1; [b]CBCL/1–4; [c]SLRT-II; [d]ELFE 1-6; [e]WRT 2+/WRT 3+; [f]number of correct items, max. 27; [g]number of correct items, max. 10; [h]items per minute; [i]HAWIK-IV.

and 16 children for CON, IMP, and NIMP, respectively. The Analyses of Variance (ANOVAs) presented below were also run with matched groups and significant results reported below were also observed within these calculations.

Parents and children were informed about the aim, purpose, and procedure of the study and gave their written consent prior to inclusion in the study. Before and after intervention children received a present as acknowledgement for their participation in the testing session. Experimental procedures were approved by the Ethical Committee of the Faculty of Medicine at the University of Munich, Germany.

INTERVENTION

Children with DD received intervention twice a week for 6 month in an individual setting in our clinic. Intervention started in the beginning of the third grade. All children completed 40 units each lasting 45 min. Both intervention programs (IP1 and IP2) were highly structured thus assuring a consistent proceeding between therapists. Furthermore, to ensure fidelity of treatment, therapists, basically students of linguistics and speech therapy, were extensively trained before and regularly supervised during intervention by psychologists and speech and language therapists. In addition video recordings as well as the observation of single treatment sessions were used to assure treatment fidelity.

As mentioned in the section Participants children with DD were pseudorandomly assigned to the treatment groups. IP1 is based on orthographic knowledge and systematic, rule-based strategies (Schulte-Körne and Mathwig, 2007; Ise and Schulte-Körne, 2010; Schulte-Körne et al., 2012). It focuses on the transfer of correct phoneme discrimination and the according orthographic knowledge (e.g., in German orthography long vowels are often marked by a following silent /h/ or another vowel, whereas short vowels are often marked by two following consonants; therefore perceiving the correct vowel length is important for deducing the right orthographic rule). IP2 belongs to the group of phonics trainings (Dummer-Smoch and Hackethal, 2007). Words are read aloud in syllables and phonemes are used instead of letter pronunciation. It focuses on the acquisition of GPC. For this reason only words with a 1-1 GPC are used (for further information see Groth et al., 2013). Six IMP and 8 NIMP did receive IP1 and 5 IMP and 9 NIMP participated in IP2.

ERP PARADIGM AND PROCEDURE

All children underwent ERP recording before and after intervention (6 month later). During ERP acquisition children performed a PLD—task (Hasko et al., 2013). In this task participants had to decide whether a visually presented stimulus sounded like a real word or not ("Does … sound like a real word?" see **Figure 1**). Children were presented either with W (orthographically and phonologically familiar forms of German nouns), PH (phonologically correct but orthographically unfamiliar forms of the same words) or PW (phonologically and orthographically unfamiliar forms). W and PH required a "yes" response and PW should be responded with "no." For each item type (W; PH; PW) 60 stimuli were presented and every item was presented once only. To

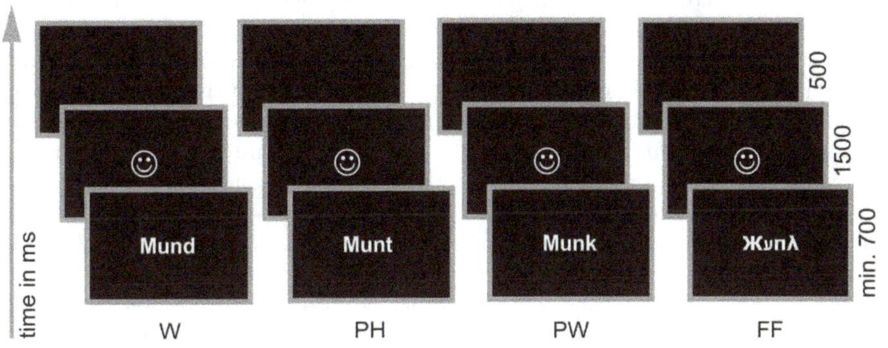

FIGURE 1 | Phonological lexical decision task. Words (W; e.g., Mund /mʊnt/, engl.: mouth), pseudohomophones (PH; e.g., Munt /mʊnt/), pseudowords (PW; e.g., Munk /mʊŋk/) and false fonts (FF; e.g., Жυ π λ) were presented individually in white on black background in the center of a 17 inch screen. Participants were instructed to decide via button press whether a presented stimulus sounded like a real word or not. Figure taken from Hasko et al. (2013).

avoid a response bias toward "yes" responses we included a fourth condition, consisting of 60 FF and requiring a "no" response. FF were created by assigning a FF to each upper and lower case letter. To avoid effects due to item length and complexity all stimuli were matched for number of characters (3–7 characters). In addition W, PH, and PW were controlled for bigram frequency (see Hasko et al., 2013, for a complete list of all stimuli used in the PLD task and for further description of item selection).

All stimuli were presented in white font on black background in the center of a 17″ screen using E-Prime® 2.0 software (Psychology Software Tools, Inc.). The computer screen was placed 70 cm in front of the children resulting in a vertical visual angle of 1.23° and in an average horizontal angle of 3.44°. The 240 stimuli were presented pseudorandomized in four blocks. After each block there was a short break. To ensure that the subjects fully understood the task, the experiment was preceded by a short practice-block (24 trials). Trials utilized in the practice-block did not occur in the experiment. The task was self-paced in order to make sure that even the poorest reader had enough time to read the letter string stimuli. However, all children were presented with the stimuli for a minimum of 700 ms to guarantee that all participants saw the same in the first milliseconds, which is important for ERP analysis. Participants had to decide by button press whether the presented stimulus sounded like a real word or not. Half of the children used their right hand for giving a "yes" response and the left hand for giving a "no" response, the other half used the left hand for "yes" and the right hand for "no" responses. Depending on correct or incorrect response children were provided with a feedback in form of a happy or sad face (1500 ms). The next trial appeared automatically after a blank screen of 500 ms (see **Figure 1**).

ERP RECORDING AND ANALYSIS

EEG was recorded during the stimulus presentation with an Electrical Geodesic Inc. 128-channel-system (see **Figure 2**, for a schematic illustration of the electrode net). The impedance was kept below 50 kΩ. EEG-data was recorded continuously with Cz as the reference electrode and sampled at 500 Hz. Further analysis steps were performed with Brainvision Analyzer (Brain Products GmbH).

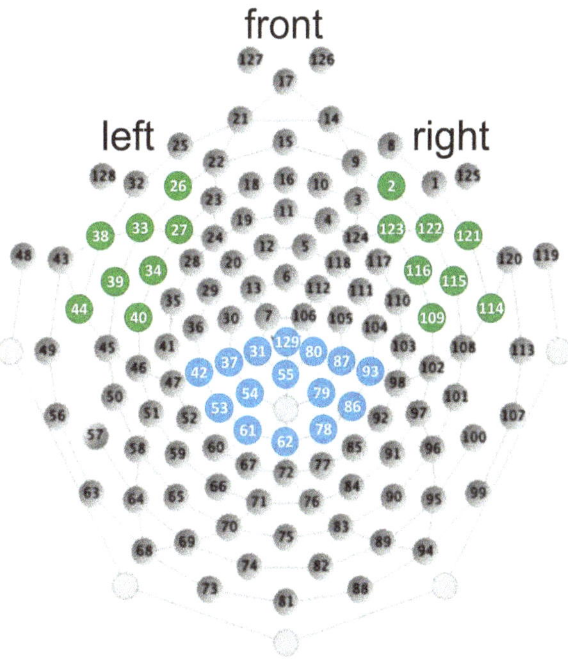

FIGURE 2 | Illustration of the 128-channel-system and electrode position taken from Electrical Geodesics Inc. (2007). Filled blue circles depict electrodes included in the ROI of the N400. Filled green circles depict electrodes included in the LH and RH ROIs of the N300.

After filtering (low cutoff: 0.5 Hz, time constant 0.3, 12 dB/octave; high cutoff: 40 Hz, 24 dB/octave; Notch filter: 50 Hz; filtered continuous on raw data to avoid discontinuities and transient phenomena), removing EOG-artifacts with Independent Component Analysis (Zhou et al., 2005; Hoffmann and Falkenstein, 2008) and exclusion of other artifacts (gradient criteria: more than 50 μV difference between two successive data points or more than 150 μV in a 200 ms window; absolute amplitude criterion: more than ±150 μV; low activity: less than 0.5 μV in a 100 ms time window), the EEG was re-referenced to the average reference.

The data was then segmented into 1100 ms epochs including 100 ms pre-stimulus baseline and the ERP data was baseline corrected. For inclusion in the statistical analysis a minimum of 20 artifact free trials was necessary. Only correct trials were analyzed. Grand averages of all conditions were computed by averaging separately for each subject group (CON; IMP; NIMP) and each point in time (pre; post).

Based on our hypothesis we were interested in changes of the N400, which reflects GPC or the searching process in the orthographic lexicon. Based on the electrophysiological activity for W in CON before intervention the time window for the N400 was set 330–460 ms using running t-tests against zero ($p < 0.05$) at each electrode and the following centro-parietal electrodes were selected for the region of interest (ROI): 31, 37, 42, 53, 54, 55, 61, 62, 78, 79, 80, 86, 87, 93, 129 (see **Figure 2**, e.g., Deacon et al., 2004; Hasko et al., 2013; for review see Lau et al., 2008; Kutas and Federmeier, 2011).

The analyses run to answer our second research question (whether we could identify any pre-existing electrophysiological differences between IMP and NIMP) was exploratory. During the visual inspection of electrodes and unpaired t-tests comparing the electrophysiological activity of IMP and NIMP we observed a hyperactivation over left and right hemispheric (LH and RH) fronto-temporal electrodes starting around 300 ms (see **Figure 4**). According to the timing and the topography we identified a N300 in the time window of 300–400 ms. Based on the electrophysiological activity for W in CON before intervention using running t-tests against zero ($p < 0.05$) at each electrode we selected LH and RH ROIs. Electrodes included in the LH were 26, 27, 33, 34, 38, 39, 40, 44 and electrodes included in the RH were 2, 109, 114, 115, 116, 121, 122, 123 (see **Figure 2**).

Mean peak amplitude measures capturing data 20 ms before and 20 ms after the individual peak and peak latencies were exported for each electrode of the N400 and N300 ROIs using the defined time windows. The values of individual mean peak amplitudes and peak latencies were averaged after peak export for every ROI.

STATISTICAL ANALYSIS

To test for significant changes over time regarding the N400 mean peak amplitudes and peak latencies we computed ANOVAs. The ANOVAs included the within-subject factors *condition* (W; PH; PW) and *time* (pre; post) and the between-subject factor *group* (CON; IMP; NIMP). For clean ERP data at least 10–20 participants are recommended (Luck, 2005), therefore a further specification of the groups by IP1 and IP2 was not reasonable. In order to test the main hypotheses, namely changes of the N400 during treatment dependent and independent t-tests were calculated. Firstly, we hypothesized that CON show higher mean peak amplitudes compared to IMP and NIMP before intervention. Therefore, independent t-tests were tested one-sided. Furthermore, we hypothesized that N400 mean peak amplitudes should increase over time in IMP and should remain stable in CON and NIMP, which was also evaluated using one-sided alpha-level.

The expected effect that N400 mean peak amplitudes should increase over time for IMP was moderate to large but only marginally significant. The small sample size ($n = 11$) might be the main reason why the effect did not reach significance on the 5% level. Therefore, we decided to simulate the data for a larger group of IMP. The simulation was done in two steps. Firstly, we estimated the required sample size with g*power using the observed effect size of $d = 0.54$, alpha of 0.05 and beta of 0.95. This estimation resulted in a sample size of 39 IMP. Secondly, the data of 39 IMP was generated with R using normal distribution sampling with the mean and SD of the original IMP group. For each simulated child, 1000 observations were randomly generated and the mean of these observations was calculated.

Similar ANOVAs for repeated measures were computed to analyze the N300 mean peak amplitudes and peak latencies including the additional within-subject factor *hemisphere* (LH; RH). The resulting fourfold interaction between group*time*condition*hemisphere for the N300 mean peak amplitudes was analyzed by stratifying the data on time as we were interested in exploring pre-existing differences between IMP and NIMP. Therefore, two further ANOVAs for repeated measures were calculated separately for pre and post measures. Resulting threefold interactions were analyzed by combining two of the three factors in further ANOVAs for repeated measures. To interpret twofold interactions we ran *post-hoc* t-tests for independent and dependent samples.

The behavioral data (reaction times and accuracy on the PLD—task) was analyzed using ANOVAs for repeated measures including the within-subject factors *condition* (W; PH; PW; FF) and *time* (pre; post) and the between-subject factor *group* (CON; IMP; NIMP). Trials were excluded from analysis if the response times were lower than 200 ms and deviating more than 2.5 SD from the individual group mean within a condition type. This procedure resulted in a loss of 2.65 and 2.96% of the trials for pre and post, respectively. Furthermore, for the reaction time analysis only correct trials were included. Resulting threefold interactions were analyzed by combining two of the three factors in further ANOVAs for repeated measures. To interpret twofold interactions we ran *post-hoc* t-tests for independent and dependent samples.

If sample sizes are equal, ANOVAs are unsusceptible against violations of homogeneity of variance. Given that the sample of CON was bigger than the sample of IMP and NIMP the F_{max}—test was applied in case of violations of the homogeneity of variances (Bühner and Ziegler, 2009). According to the F_{max}—test an adjustment of the alpha-level is necessary if the critical value of $F_{max} > 10$ is exceeded (Bühner and Ziegler, 2009). In none of the variables the critical value was exceeded. If necessary the Greenhouse-Geisser correction was applied to correct for violations of the sphericity assumption. The alpha level for all analyses was 0.05. In order to avoid alpha-error-inflation due to multiple comparisons the alpha level of 0.05 for follow-up tests was corrected using the Bonferroni-Holm correction (Bühner and Ziegler, 2009). Bonferroni-Holm correction was applied separately for each set of dependent and independent t-tests and for each follow-up ANOVA.

In addition to the p-values, effect sizes η_p^2 for ANOVAs with repeated measures and Cohen's d for independent and dependent t-tests are reported for significant results (Cohen, 1988; Bühner and Ziegler, 2009). Regarding the ERP data for follow-up tests detailed statistical values will be presented only for significant results, whereas non-significant results are indicated by $p > 0.05$. For the behavioral data significant and non-significant results of the follow-up analyses will be indicated by $p < 0.05$ and $p > 0.05$ without reporting detailed statistical values.

Additionally, in order to better understand the significance of the N300 for improvement during treatment we computed correlations across the whole group of children with DD and for IMP and NIMP separately. Correlations were calculated between N300 mean peak amplitudes before intervention and the gain in common word reading fluency and the N400 after intervention. For common word reading fluency we used the post minus pre differences' of raw scores (see **Table 1**). Raw scores were used in order to enhance variance. As we did not observe differences between W, PH, and PW in the N400 we decided to use mean values calculated across the three letter string types for the correlation analysis. Because of the small sample size in the IMP group Cook's d was calculated for significant correlations in order to check for undue influence of single cases. All cases had a Cook's $d < 1$ indicating that none of the participants had an excessive influence on the correlational results. The correlational analysis was exploratory, therefore Bonferroni-Holm correction was not applied. Significant results on the 5% and tendencies toward significance (10% alpha level) will be reported.

RESULTS

N400

Mean peak amplitudes

The analysis of the N400 mean peak amplitudes revealed only a main effect group. No main effect time, condition and no interactions could be observed (see **Table 2**, first column). As no effect of condition could be observed independent and dependent t-tests to test our N400 hypotheses were computed across conditions (see **Table 3**, for N400 mean peak amplitudes).

In line with our hypothesis independent t-tests revealed higher N400 amplitudes for CON compared to IMP and for CON in contrast to NIMP before intervention (see **Figure 3A**). No difference was found between IMP and NIMP before intervention (see **Figure 3A**).

Consistent with our expectation a clear trend towards increased N400 mean peak amplitudes in IMP after 6 month of intervention could be observed (see **Figure 3B**). In agreement with our assumptions N400 mean peak amplitudes remained stable over time in CON and NIMP (see **Figure 3B**). Mean peak amplitudes were comparable between CON and IMP after intervention but still diminished for NIMP in contrast to CON (see **Figure 3C**). Even though **Table 3** and **Figure 3C** suggest higher N400 amplitudes in IMP in comparison to NIMP after intervention this effect does not reach significance (see **Figure 3C**).

Simulation of the intervention effect in IMP. Although the increase of the N400 amplitude from pre to post in IMP was moderate to large ($d = 0.54$), this effect was only marginally significant ($p = 0.052$, see **Figure 3B**). The small sample size ($n = 11$) is probably the main reason why the effect did not reach significance on the 5% alpha level. Therefore, data was simulated for a larger sample size ($n = 39$). Dependent t-tests of the simulated data revealed a significant increase in N400 mean peak amplitudes from pre ($-0.30\,\mu V \pm 1.36$ SD) to post ($-1.81\,\mu V \pm 0.77$ SD), $t_{(38)} = 6.99, p < 0.001, d = 1.12$.

Peak latencies

The analysis of the N400 peak latencies revealed a main effect group (see **Table 2**, second column). No further effects were observed. Independent *post-hoc* t-tests showed shorter peak latencies for NIMP compared to CON, $t_{(40)} = 2.97$, $p = 0.005$, $d = 0.96$, before and after intervention and no differences in peak latencies were observed between CON and IMP as well as between IMP and NIMP before and after intervention ($p > 0.05$; see **Table 3**).

N300

Mean peak amplitudes

The analysis of the N300 mean peak amplitudes revealed a main effect group, time, and condition, as well as an interaction condition*hemisphere. Furthermore, the four-way interaction group*time*condition*hemisphere reached significance (see **Table 4**, first column).

Table 2 | Results of the ANOVAs for repeated measures with F-values (df), p-values, and effect sizes η_p^2 for the N400 mean peak amplitudes and latencies including the between-subject factor *group* (CON; IMP; NIMP) and the within-subject-factor *time* (pre; post) and *condition* (W; PH; PW).

Effect	Mean peak amplitudes			Peak latencies		
	F	p	η_p^2	F	p	η_p^2
Group (G)	5.39 (2, 50)	**0.008**	0.18	4.95 (2, 50)	**0.011**	0.17
Time (T)	0.68 (1, 50)	0.413	–	1.27 (1, 50)	0.265	–
Condition (C)	2.60 (2, 100)	0.080	–	0.49 (2, 100)	0.612	–
G*T	2.59 (2, 50)	0.085	–	2.26 (2, 50)	0.115	–
G*C	0.44 (4, 100)	0.783	–	1.73 (2, 100)	0.150	–
T*C	0.96 (2, 100)	0.388	–	0.50 (2, 100)	0.608	–
G*T*C	1.02 (4, 100)	0.402	–	1.35 (4, 100)	0.258	–

CON, control children; IMP, improvers; NIMP, non-improvers; pre, before intervention; post, after intervention; W, words; PH, pseudohomophones; PW, pseudowords. Significant results are indicated in bold.

Table 3 | N400 mean peak amplitudes in μV (SD) and latencies in ms (SD).

		CON		IMP*		NIMP	
		pre	post	pre	post	pre	post
Amplitudes	W	−2.68 (1.94)	−1.72 (1.51)	−0.37 (2.43)	−1.23 (1.50)	−0.90 (2.18)	−0.80 (2.20)
	PH	−2.67 (1.98)	−2.53 (2.11)	−1.19 (2.74)	−1.91 (1.51)	−0.85 (2.55)	−1.22 (1.72)
	PW	−2.33 (1.95)	−2.27 (2.05)	−0.32 (2.11)	−1.85 (1.39)	−1.26 (1.70)	−0.94 (1.95)
	Mean across conditions	−2.56 (1.63)	−2.17 (1.65)	−0.62 (2.03)	−1.66 (1.18)	−1.01 (1.88)	−0.99 (1.72)
Latencies	W	394.78 (17.32)	397.55 (20.09)	387.52 (17.86)	386.47 (16.76)	387.17 (16.60)	381.92 (14.23)
	PH	392.29 (18.49)	401.15 (23.60)	392.73 (10.84)	385.94 (13.52)	392.76 (21.38)	381.35 (19.09)
	PW	399.17 (21.32)	399.36 (24.33)	395.96 (18.03)	387.07 (22.83)	383.06 (16.68)	377.88 (18.39)

*W, words; PH, pseudohomophones; PW, pseudowords; CON, control children; IMP, improvers; NIMP, non-improvers; pre, before intervention; post, after intervention. *IMP had significantly shorter peak latencies for all conditions before and after intervention (M = 397.38, SD = 16.40) compared to CON (M = 384.02, SD = 10.39).*

In order to explore this four-way interaction two separate ANOVAs were conducted for each point in time. The analysis of the N300 mean peak amplitudes before intervention revealed a significant interaction group*condition*hemisphere, $F_{(4,\ 100)} = 3.84$, $p = 0.006$, $\eta_p^2 = 0.13$. No main effects and no further interactions could be observed ($p > 0.05$). In order to interpret this three-way interaction separate follow-up ANOVAs were run by combining two of the three factors.

Follow-up ANOVAs for each hemisphere. For the LH we found a main effect condition, $F_{(1,\ 50)} = 3.84$, $p = 0.015$, $= 0.08$, and an interaction group*condition, $F_{(2,\ 50)} = 3.05$, $p = 0.020$, $\eta_p^2 = 0.11$. No main effect group could be observed ($p > 0.05$). Independent *post-hoc* t-tests revealed that IMP had higher amplitudes for PW in contrast to CON and NIMP in the LH (see **Figure 4A**). In CON and NIMP amplitudes for PW were comparable high (see **Figure 4A**). No group differences were found for W and PH (see **Figure 4A**). Mean amplitudes for W, PH, and PW did not differ within CON, IMP, and NIMP ($p > 0.05$).

For the RH the main effect group, $F_{(2,\ 50)} = 4.59$, $p = 0.015$, $\eta_p^2 = 0.16$, was significant. No main effect condition and interaction group*condition could be observed ($p > 0.05$). Independent *post-hoc* t-tests calculated across conditions revealed higher mean peak amplitudes for IMP in contrast to CON and NIMP (see **Figure 4B**). No difference was found between CON and NIMP ($p > 0.05$, see **Figure 4B**).

Follow-up ANOVAs for each condition. As could be expected from the ANOVAs run separately for each hemisphere (see above) the analysis revealed a main effect group for PW, $F_{(2,\ 50)} = 5.99$, $p = 0.005$, $\eta_p^2 = 0.19$. No hemisphere effect as well as no interaction group*hemisphere could be observed ($p > 0.05$). Independent *post-hoc* t-tests revealed higher N300 mean peak amplitudes for IMP in contrast to CON, $t_{(34)} = 2.97$, $p = 0.005$, $d = 1.11$ and NIMP, $t_{(26)} = -3.29$, $p = 0.003$, $d = 1.32$, bilaterally and no difference was found between CON and NIMP ($p > 0.05$, see **Figures 4A,B**). For W and PH no main effects and no interactions were found ($p > 0.05$).

Follow-up ANOVAs for each group. A twofold interaction condition*hemisphere did occur within the IMP group, $F_{(2,\ 20)} = 5.10$, $p = 0.016$, $\eta_p^2 = 0.34$, and no main effect condition or hemisphere was observed for the IMP group ($p > 0.05$). This interaction suggests that mean peak amplitudes are higher for PW in contrast to W and PH specifically in the LH (see **Figure 4A**). However, dependent *post-hoc* t-tests did not reveal amplitude differences between conditions in the LH and RH ($p > 0.05$). Furthermore, mean peak amplitudes were comparable high between the LH and RH for W, PH, and PW ($p > 0.05$). For CON and NIMP no main effects and no interactions were found ($p > 0.05$).

To summarize IMP in contrast to CON and NIMP are marked by higher N300 mean peak amplitudes for all conditions in the RH and additionally for PW in the LH.

After intervention no significant main effect group, time, condition and no significant interactions between these factors could be observed for the N300 mean peak amplitudes ($p > 0.05$, see **Table 5** and **Figure 5**).

Peak latencies

The analysis of the N300 peak latencies revealed a twofold interaction condition*hemisphere and a threefold interaction group*condition*hemisphere (see **Table 4**, second column). Because the twofold interaction was modulated by the factor group follow-up ANOVAs were conducted for each group over both points in time by combining the factors condition and hemisphere.

The follow-up ANOVAs revealed a significant interaction condition*hemisphere for the NIMP group, $F_{(2,\ 32)} = 7.59$, $p = 0.002$, $\eta_p^2 = 0.32$, the main effect condition and the main effect hemisphere were not significant ($p > 0.05$). In the LH NIMP had shorter peak latencies for PW in contrast to W, $t_{(16)} = -3.35$, $p = 0.004$, $d = 0.81$, and PH, $t_{(16)} = -3.19$, $p = 0.006$, $d = 0.77$, peak latencies between W and PH were comparable ($p > 0.05$, see **Table 5**). No difference between conditions was found in the RH and peak latencies did not differ for none of the conditions between LH and RH ($p > 0.05$). No significant main effect condition, hemisphere and no significant interaction

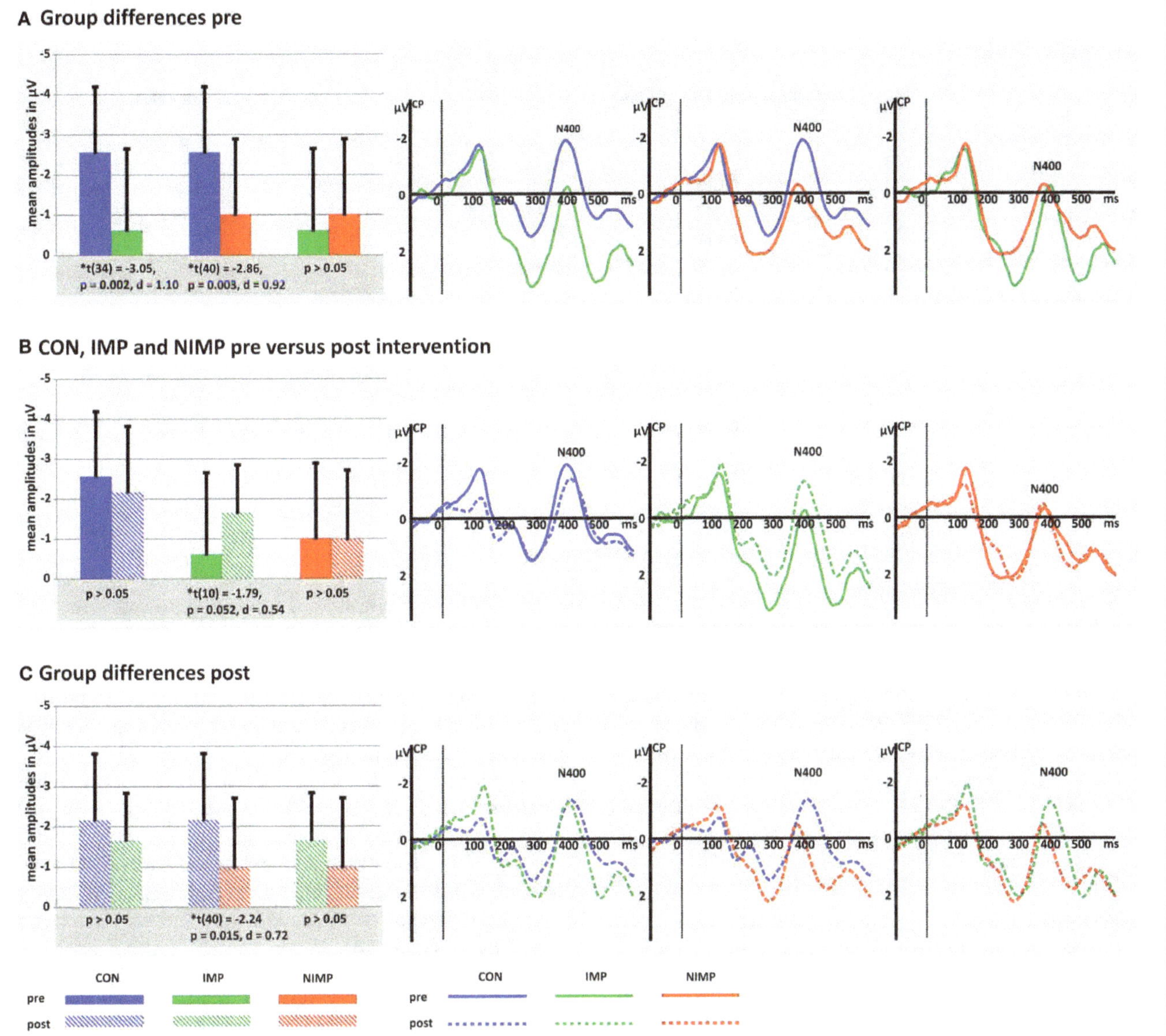

FIGURE 3 | N400 mean peak amplitudes for control children (CON), improvers (IMP), and non-improvers (NIMP). (A) Illustrates group differences before intervention (pre). **(B)** Depicts treatment effects. **(C)** Shows group differences after intervention (post). CP = centro-parietal electrodes included in the ROI of the N400. Negativity is depicted upwards. Error bars illustrate standard deviation. *one-sided alpha-level.

condition*hemisphere could be observed for CON and IMP ($p > 0.05$).

BEHAVIORAL RESULTS

Accuracy

Performance on the PLD—task revealed a main effect group, time and condition, as well as the twofold interactions group*condition and time*condition ($p < 0.05$, see **Table 6**, first column).

In order to better understand the two-way interaction between the factors time and condition dependent *post-hoc* t-tests were calculated. Accuracy rates increased over time for W and PH ($p < 0.05$) and slightly decreased for FF ($p < 0.05$). No difference between pre and post was found for PW ($p > 0.05$; see **Figure 6A**). Furthermore, dependent *post-hoc* t-tests revealed that all children gave more correct answers to FF compared to the linguistic material (W, PH, and PW) before and after intervention ($p < 0.05$). In addition, accuracy rates were pre and post higher for W compared to PH and PW ($p < 0.05$). And all children had higher accuracy rates for PH compared to PW before intervention and after intervention ($p < 0.05$, see **Figure 6A**).

Dependent *post-hoc* t-tests in order to explain the twofold interaction between group and condition revealed the accuracy pattern FF > W > PH > PW ($p < 0.05$) as described above for IMP and NIMP. In CON, however, no difference between correct

Table 4 | Results of the ANOVAs for repeated measures with *F*-values, *p*-values, and effect sizes η_p^2 for the N300 mean peak amplitudes and latencies including the between-subject factor *group* (CON; IMP; NIMP) and the within-subject-factor *time* (pre; post), *condition* (W; PH; PW), and *hemisphere* (LH; RH).

Effect	Mean peak amplitudes			Peak latencies		
	F	p	η_p^2	F	p	η_p^2
Group (G)	4.76 (2, 50)	**0.013**	0.16	3.11 (2, 50)	0.054	–
Time (T)	4.15 (1, 50)	**0.047**	0.08	0.10 (1, 50)	0.748	–
Condition (C)	4.74 (2, 100)	**0.011**	0.09	0.32 (1.75, 87.58)	0.322	–
Hemisphere (H)	2.11 (1, 50)	0.152	–	0.01 (1, 50)	0.936	–
G*T	1.90 (2, 50)	0.161	–	0.59 (2, 50)	0.556	–
G*C	1.19 (4, 100)	0.319	–	0.76 (3.5, 87.58)	0.537	–
G*H	1.05 (2, 50)	0.358	–	0.08 (2, 50)	0.920	–
T*C	0.35 (2, 100)	0.158	–	0.11 (2, 100)	0.897	–
T*H	3.11 (1, 50)	0.084	–	0.42 (1, 50)	0.521	–
C*H	3.11 (2, 100)	**0.049**	0.06	4.31 (1.78, 89.35)	**0.020**	0.08
G*T*C	0.71 (4, 100)	0.589	–	1.41 (4, 100)	0.236	–
G*T*H	0.13 (2, 50)	0.883	–	0.20 (2, 50)	0.820	–
G*C*H	1.81 (4, 100)	0.132	–	3.01 (3.57, 89.35)	**0.027**	0.11
T*C*H	0.95 (2, 100)	0.389	–	0.79 (2, 100)	0.459	–
G*T*C*H	3.70 (4, 100)	**0.008**	0.13	2.32 (4, 100)	0.062	–

CON, control children; IMP, improvers; NIMP, non-improvers; pre, before intervention; post, after intervention; W, words; PH, pseudohomophones; PW, pseudowords; LH, left hemisphere; RH, right hemisphere. Significant results are indicated in bold.

answers for PH and PW ($p > 0.05$) could be detected resulting in an accuracy pattern with FF > W > PH = PW (see **Figure 6A**). Independent *post-hoc t*-tests revealed that over both, pre and post, CON's performance was better to all linguistic stimuli compared to IMP and NIMP ($p < 0.05$). No difference in none of the conditions was found between IMP and NIMP and no group differences were found for FF ($p > 0.05$ see **Figure 6A**).

Reaction times

Performance on the PLD—task revealed a significant main effect group, time and condition, as well as the significant interactions group*time, group*condition, time*condition and group*time*condition (see **Table 6**, second column). In order to better understand the threefold interaction separate follow-up ANOVAs were run by combining two of the three factors.

Follow-up ANOVAs for each point in time. The analysis before and after intervention revealed a significant main effect group and condition as well as the interaction group*condition ($p < 0.05$).

Follow-up ANOVAs for each condition. For W, PH, and PW the ANOVAs revealed a significant main effect group and time as well as the interaction group*time ($p < 0.05$). No significant effects were found for FF ($p > 0.05$).

Follow-up ANOVAs for each group. For CON the analysis revealed a significant main effect condition as well as the interaction condition*time ($p < 0.05$) but no main effect time ($p > 0.05$). For IMP and NIMP a significant main effect time and condition and the interaction condition*time occurred ($p < 0.05$).

In the following the results of the independent and dependent *post-hoc t*-tests calculated in order to examine the twofold interactions will be summarized.

Independent *post-hoc t*-tests indicated that CON had shorter reactions times to W, PH, and PW compared to IMP and NIMP before intervention and after intervention ($p < 0.05$). No differences for W, PH, and PW were found for the comparison between IMP and NIMP before and after intervention ($p > 0.05$). For FF no group differences were found before and after intervention ($p > 0.05$, see **Figure 6B**).

Dependent *post-hoc t*-tests within each group revealed the same pattern of reaction times for all groups before and after intervention. CON, IMP, and NIMP had longer reaction times for all linguistic stimuli compared to FF before intervention and after intervention ($p < 0.05$). Furthermore, all groups showed shorter reaction times for W compared to PH and for W compared to PW before and after intervention ($p < 0.05$). And all groups responded slower to PW compared to PH before and after intervention ($p < 0.05$, see **Figure 6B**).

Reaction times did not change over time in CON for W, PH, PW, and FF ($p > 0.05$). However, IMP and NIMP had faster reaction times after intervention for W, PH, and PW ($p < 0.05$). No changes from pre to post were observed for FF in IMP and NIMP ($p > 0.05$, see **Figure 6B**).

CORRELATIONAL RESULTS

When interpreting the correlation results, please note that N300 and N400 mean peak amplitudes have negative values. Larger increase in common word reading fluency was significantly correlated to higher N300 mean peak amplitudes before intervention for W and PH in the RH and PW in the LH and by trend for PW in the RH. Furthermore, a larger increase in pseudoword reading

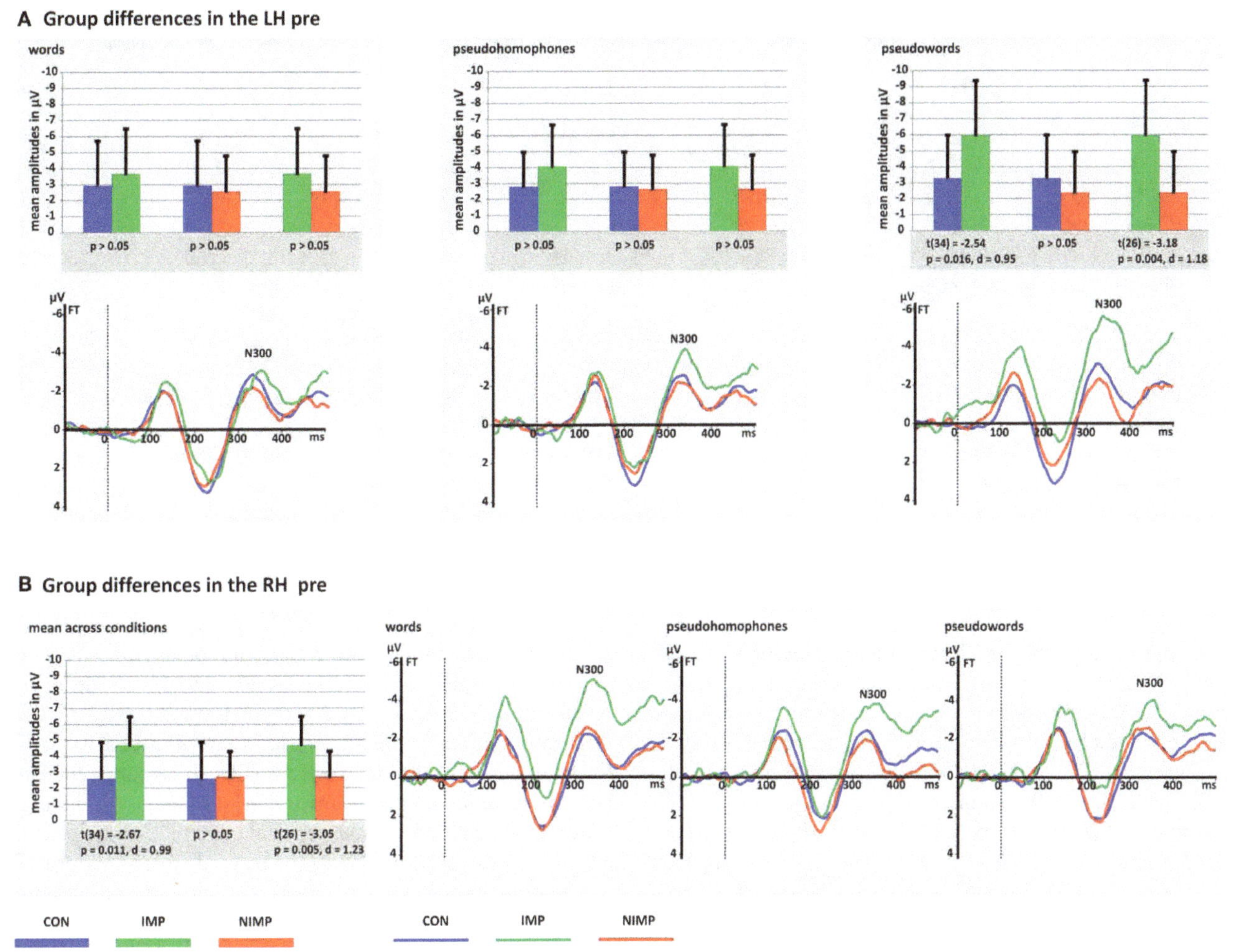

FIGURE 4 | N300 mean peak amplitudes for control children (CON), improvers (IMP), and non-improvers (NIMP) before intervention. (A) Illustrates group differences in the left hemisphere (LH). **(B)** Depicts group differences in the right hemisphere (RH). FT = fronto-temporal electrodes included in the LH and RH ROI of the N300. Negativity is depicted upwards. Error bars illustrate standard deviation.

fluency was correlated significantly to higher N300 mean peak amplitudes for W in the RH and by trend for PW in the LH. The linear relationship between N300 before intervention in the RH and gain in common word reading fluency remained stable only in the group of IMP (please see **Table 7**). Even though only the correlation between N300 mean peak amplitudes before intervention for PH in the RH and increase in common word reading fluency reached significance in the IMP group, the resulting correlations were large, ranging from $r = -0.54$ to $r = -0.59$ (see **Table 7**). Furthermore, higher N400 mean peak amplitudes after intervention were related to higher N300 mean peak amplitudes before intervention for PW in the LH and by trend for W and PH in the LH in children with DD. In the IMP group higher N400 mean peak amplitudes after intervention were related to higher N300 mean peak amplitudes before intervention for PH and PW in the LH (see **Table 7**).

DISCUSSION

The aim of the present study was twofold. On the one hand we wanted to clarify whether growth in common word reading fluency during treatment is related to changes in the N400. Furthermore, we were interested whether we could identify pre-existing differences on the neurophysiological level between IMP and NIMP. In order to achieve our aims we investigated a PLD—task before and after children with DD were trained in literacy skills over 6 months. We investigated the ERPs of IMP, who did improve in common word reading fluency for at least half a SD, NIMP who did not show any increase in common word reading fluency and normally developing children.

READING IMPROVEMENT IS REFLECTED IN AN INCREASE OF N400

As both trainings worked on either orthographic knowledge or GPC we hypothesized to find changes in the N400 (see Introduction), which reflects GPC or the searching process in the orthographic lexicon (Hasko et al., 2013). In line with our previous study (Hasko et al., 2013) we were able to show that both groups of children with DD (IMP and NIMP) had reduced N400 mean peak amplitudes compared to CON before intervention. The reduced N400 amplitudes in IMP and NIMP point to less specified orthographic representations or impairments

Table 5 | N300 mean peak amplitudes in μV (SD) and latencies in ms (SD).

		CON		IMP		NIMP	
		Pre	**Post**	**Pre**	**Post**	**Pre**	**Post**
Amplitudes	W; LH	−2.94 (2.77)	−2.70 (2.01)	−3.67 (2.81)	−3.72 (1.94)	−2.55 (2.23)	−2.67 (2.54)
	PH; LH	−2.79 (2.17)	−3.07 (1.89)	−4.07 (2.58)	−2.86 (1.97)	−2.63 (2.12)	−2.55 (2.11)
	PW; LH	−3.27 (2.70)	−2.95(2.12)	−5.96 (3.42)	−3.98 (1.56)	−2.37 (2.56)	−3.20 (2.24)
	W; RH	−2.46 (2.62)	−1.92 (2.03)	−5.25 (2.06)	−3.26 (1.78)	−2.89 (1.56)	−2.39 (1.88)
	PH; RH	−2.56 (2.82)	−1.62 (1.59)	−4.43 (1.89)	−2.42 (1.77)	−2.20 (2.27)	−2.71 (2.20)
	PW; RH	−2.72 (2.25)	−1.71 (1.69)	−4.32 (2.18)	−2.98 (1.86)	−2.96 (2.03)	−2.66 (2.00)
Latencies	W; LH	341.62 (13.31)	346.53 (15.53)	349.18 (21.15)	344.57 (17.88)	339.82 (19.27)	339.79 (12.94)
	PH; LH	341.26 (16.24)	340.65 (20.18)	339.50 (13.99)	340.68 (12.32)	339.52 (17.01)	340.31 (15.78)
	PW; LH	336.87 (17.41)	341.51 (21.42)	346.14 (12.89)	348.10 (15.99)	331.20 (12.71)*	336.09 (15.63)*
	W; RH	340.09 (13.21)	337.49 (20.00)	347.21 (11.69)	344.86 (15.07)	329.88 (16.45)	337.72 (14.19)
	PH; RH	338.77 (14.83)	342.37 (19.32)	348.64 (17.45)	348.25 (19.78)	339.86 (14.94)	336.24 (12.70)
	PW; RH	337.71 (15.60)	346.76 (17.01)	347.47 (15.04)	338.75 (18.66)	341.32 (20.79)	336.88 (12.47)

*W, words; PH, pseudohomophones; PW, pseudowords; LH, left hemisphere; RH, right hemisphere; CON, control children; IMP, improvers; NIMP, non-improvers; pre, before intervention; post, after intervention. *In NIMP PW in the LH over pre and post (M = 333.64, SD = 11.31) are significantly smaller compared to W (M = 339.81, SD = 11.50) and PH (M = 339.91, SD = 11.28).*

in accessing the orthographic lexicon or in applying GPC rules (Hasko et al., 2013). As hypothesized a clear trend towards increased N400 amplitudes over time in IMP only was observed. This might indicate an alteration of the process reflected by this component. Thus, in line with previous electrophysiological (Kujala et al., 2001; Santos et al., 2007; Jucla et al., 2009; Penolazzi et al., 2010; Spironelli et al., 2010; Huotilainen et al., 2011; Mayseless, 2011; Lovio et al., 2012) and neuroimaging studies (Simos et al., 2002; Aylward et al., 2003; Temple et al., 2003; Eden et al., 2004; Shaywitz et al., 2004; Simos et al., 2006, 2007b; Richards et al., 2007; Meyler et al., 2008; Richards and Berninger, 2008; Keller and Just, 2009) we found evidence for neurophysiological changes during treatment. This suggests that specific deficient processes in DD, in our case processes related to the N400, are malleable in children with DD. The design of the present study does not allow testing which proportion of reading improvement is related to the applied treatments and which proportion is due to other factors not related to the treatment. Probably due to the small sample size in the IMP group ($n = 11$) the increase in N400 amplitudes, which was moderate to large failed to reach significance. Simulation of the data for a larger sample of IMP revealed a significant increase in the N400 confirming our assumption that the small sample size is the main reason for why the effect does not reach significance.

Due to our classification criterion the common word reading fluency of IMP increased significantly but was still below average after intervention. Therefore, we expected to find increased N400 amplitudes for IMP and thus diminished differences between IMP and CON in N400 amplitudes. However, the differences between IMP and CON were not only diminished after intervention, but absent. N400 amplitudes of CON slightly decreased over time and thus contribute to the absence of differences between IMP and CON, even though this effect does not reach significance. Although no condition effect could be observed, **Table 3** shows that the slight decrease in N400 amplitudes is mainly the result of a reduction of the N400 component for W, whereas amplitude means remain stable for PH and PW. A decrease of N400 amplitudes for W in CON is what might be expected with maturation of the reading network. In line with this, it has been found that N400 amplitudes were smaller to orthographic familiar word forms compared to unfamiliar word forms in adults (e.g., Braun et al., 2006; Briesemeister et al., 2009). This suggests that adults in contrast to children (Hasko et al., 2013) adopt different reading strategies for orthographic familiar and unfamiliar word material. In the framework of dual route models of reading (Coltheart et al., 1993, 2001) less effort is needed in order to find a fitting orthographic representation for familiar words in the orthographic lexicon, whereas the search in the orthographic lexicon is prolonged and GPC rules have to be applied in case of unfamiliar word forms resulting in enhanced N400 amplitudes (Hasko et al., 2013). Thus, the observations in the present study might denote the beginning development of the orthographic familiarity effect for the N400 suggesting that some of the W do already possess an entry in the orthographic lexicon and are read via accessing the phonological lexicon directly from the orthographic lexicon in typically developing children. It might be interesting to further investigate when the maturation of the orthographic familiarity effect is fully developed as it indicates the point in time when children steadily use orthographic representations to access phonological representations for familiar word forms.

As expected, children who continued to struggle with common word reading fluency after intervention in our study did not show neurophysiological changes over time. This is consistent with previous research reporting that NIMP continuously display abnormal activation patterns throughout the neuronal reading network (Simos et al., 2007a; Odegard et al., 2008; Davis et al., 2011; Farris et al., 2011; Molfese et al., 2013). One question which remains unanswered is why some children with DD improve during intervention, whereas other do not. This leads directly to our second research question, namely whether there might be any

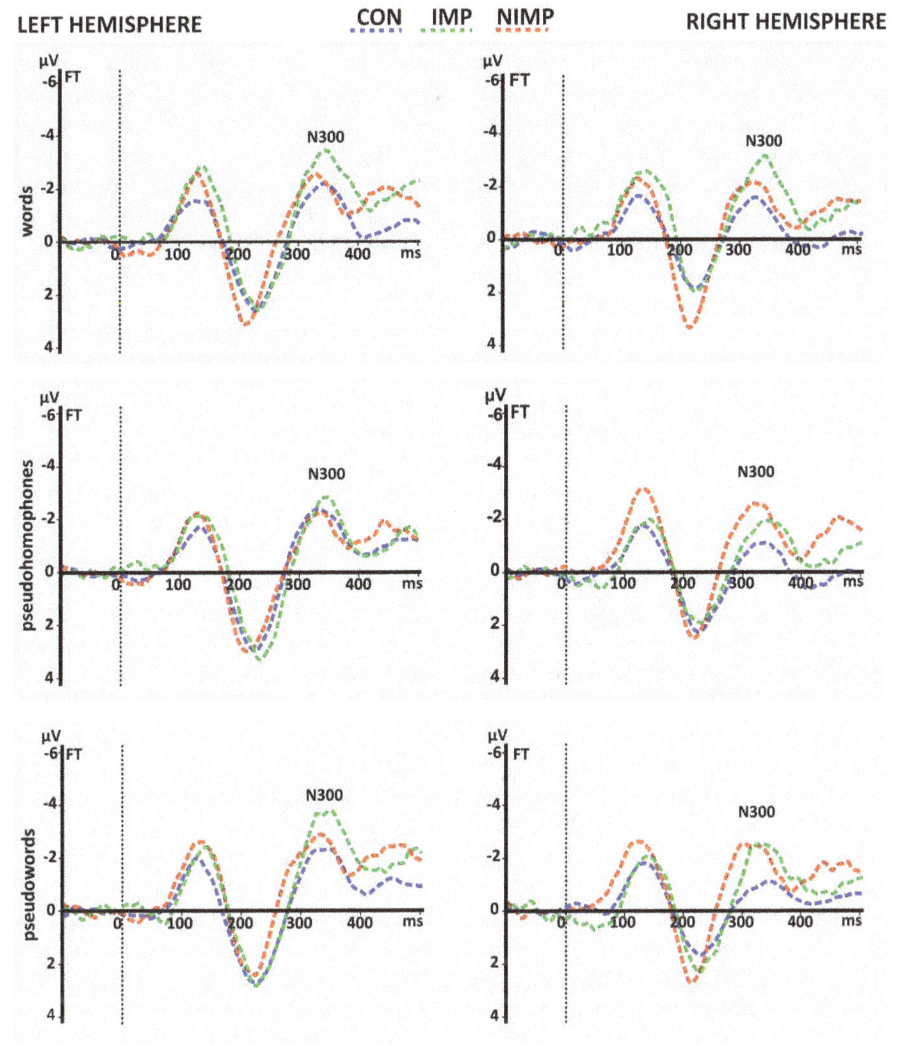

FIGURE 5 | Illustration of the N300 after intervention. FT = fronto-temporal electrodes included in the left hemispheric and right hemispheric ROI of the N300 for control children (CON), improvers (IMP), and non-improvers (NIMP). Negativity is depicted upwards.

pre-existing differences between IMP and NIMP, which could give insight into improvement and non-improvement.

PROFILING IMPROVER AND NON-IMPROVER

Surprisingly, although the hypothesis of neurodiversity within DD has been raised several times (McCandliss and Noble, 2003; Shaywitz et al., 2004; Noble and McCandliss, 2005) neurobiological differences and their influence on improvement in literacy skills during treatment have been neglected in previous intervention studies, thus the analysis run to answer this question in the present study was exploratory. During the inspection of single electrodes and t-maps comparing the topographical distribution between IMP and NIMP we observed a hyperactivation distributed over left and right temporo-frontal electrodes starting around 300 ms after stimulus onset (see **Figure 4**). Based on the topographical distribution and latency the negative potential was identified as N300. The N300 was investigated employing different tasks and was attributed as being related to grapheme-phoneme conversion (Bentin et al., 1999; Penolazzi et al., 2006), phonological word analysis (Spironelli and Angrilli, 2007, 2009) and the integration of orthographic and phonological representations (Hasko et al., 2012).

In the present study IMP revealed before intervention higher N300 amplitudes for W, PH, and PW in the RH and additionally for PW in the LH compared to NIMP and CON. This suggests that enhanced N300 amplitudes might play an important role for improvement in common word reading fluency, which was further strengthened by our correlational results. Correlations calculated across the whole group of children with DD largely reflected the group differences found for IMP and NIMP, i.e., children who improved in common word reading fluency were those who had higher N300 amplitudes for W, PH, and PW (only marginal significant) in the RH and for PW in the LH before intervention. Especially, higher N300 amplitudes over the

RH seem to play an important role for reading improvement as the same pattern of correlation between N300 amplitudes over the RH before intervention and improvement in common word reading fluency was found for IMP only. Children with the highest N300 amplitudes over the RH before intervention displayed also the strongest improvement in common word reading fluency. Even though only the correlation between N300 mean peak amplitudes before intervention for PH in the RH and increase in common word reading fluency reached significance in the IMP group, the resulting correlations were large, ranging from $r = -0.54$ to $r = -0.59$ and are therefore noteworthy.

In previous fMRI studies investigating the PLD—task (Kronbichler et al., 2007; Wimmer et al., 2010) it has been found that this task induces activation throughout the neural reading network including the inferior-frontal subsystem. As mentioned in the introduction evidence for aberrant activation patterns in this subsystem in DD was not as clear as for the left hemispheric posterior subsystem, where hypoactivation was reported repeatedly (Simos et al., 2002; Demonet et al., 2004; Kronbichler et al., 2007; Shaywitz and Shaywitz, 2008; Richlan et al., 2009). With regard to the inferior-frontal subsystem some studies report an hypoactivation (Paulesu et al., 1996; Wimmer et al., 2010; for meta-analyses see: Richlan et al., 2009, 2011); whereas others observed an hyperactivation (Salmelin et al., 1996; Shaywitz et al., 1998; Brunswick et al., 1999; for review see: Pugh et al., 2000; Sandak et al., 2004) in subjects with DD. In line with these inhomogeneous results children with DD in the present study varied with respect to their N300 amplitudes over right and left fronto-temporal electrodes depending on reading improvement or non-improvement with IMP showing significantly higher N300 amplitudes before intervention. It has been suggested that the inferior-frontal subsystem might be involved in articulation processes (Shaywitz and Shaywitz, 2008). Maybe IMP try to adopt different not efficient reading strategies via articulation processes in order to compensate for less specified orthographic representations, impairments in accessing the orthographic lexicon or in applying GPC rules as reflected by reduced N400 amplitudes. This strategy is probably not being applied in the NIMP group, for what reason is unsolved so far.

The observance of pre-existing differences on the neurophysiological level between IMP and NIMP in the present study is in line with the results of Rezaie et al. (2011a,b) who also reported differences between adolescent IMP and NIMP prior to intervention. In contrast to the present study, however, activation profiles of IMP in the studies of Rezaie et al. (2011a,b) seemed to resemble the activation profile of CON. Whereas NIMP were marked by aberrant activation patterns throughout the reading network in contrast to CON, the only difference between IMP and CON was observed in higher activity within the pars opercularis for CON in contrast IMP (Rezaie et al., 2011a,b). This suggests that poor reading skills in NIMP might be stronger influenced by neurobiological factors, whereas for low reading skills in IMP environmental factors like home literacy or socioeconomic status might play an important role. In addition, our results contrast the outcome of Simos et al.'s (2005, 2007a) studies who did not observe differences depending on improvement before intervention. One possible explanation for the absence of neurobiological differences in the study of Simos et al. (2007a) could be the wide age range, as children from 8 to 10 years were included. As this is a very sensitive age for reading development this might probably mask pre-existing differences between IMP and NIMP. Furthermore, in the 2005 study of Simos et al. the NIMP group consisted only of three children allowing to make only descriptive comparisons between IMP and NIMP and thus failing to find pre-existing differences.

Due to the cross-sectional design of the studies of Rezaie et al. (2011a,b), assessing neurobiological activity only before treatment, no statement can be made about neurobiological differences between IMP and NIMP after intervention. And studies comparing IMP and NIMP only after intervention (Odegard et al., 2008; Davis et al., 2011; Farris et al., 2011; Molfese et al., 2013) are limited as it cannot be resolved whether group differences between treatment IMP and NIMP is a cause or the result of improvement. An advantage of the present study is that we have assessed electrophysiological correlates before and after treatment. Interestingly, together with the improvement in reading ability and the increase in the N400 component the N300 amplitudes are higher in IMP compared to CON and NIMP only before intervention. This suggests that the N300 might index a compensatory mechanism or precursor, which facilitates reading improvement as well as the development of the N400 and is given up in favor of the more efficient process reflected by the N400. This is in line with a previous study by Shaywitz et al. (2004) showing that efficient activations throughout the neural reading network were enhanced and compensatory mechanisms were abandoned after a reading intervention. An important role of enhanced N300 amplitudes over the RH for improvement in common word reading fluency as suggested by the correlational results has been hypothesized above. Furthermore, the correlational results indicate that N300 amplitudes over the LH might be related to the increase in the N400. IMP with higher N300 amplitudes over the LH for PH and PW before intervention were those who had higher N400 amplitudes after intervention. Thus, the engagement of the LH seems to be of particular importance for the increase in the N400. At first sight this stands in contrast to our finding that especially the N300 amplitudes over the RH before intervention might be related to reading improvement. In a previous study it has been found that IMP in contrast to NIMP were marked by significantly higher functional connectivity between left and right inferior frontal regions (Farris et al., 2011). The authors suggested that IMP might use the connectivity from LH to RH in order to engage the RH when tasks are difficult. Therefore, with respect to the present study we might hypothesize that enhanced N300 amplitudes over the RH are the result of higher connectivity from LH to RH allowing the engagement of the RH. Thus, it might be concluded that children with highest amplitudes over the LH and highest connectivity between LH and RH show the strongest improvement as indexed by enhanced N400 amplitudes and growth in common word reading fluency. Another explanation might be that the higher LH N300 amplitudes just reflect some additional compensatory mechanism, which is present in IMP only. Because the whole correlational analyses were exploratory no terminal conclusions can be drawn about the relation between the N300 and the increase

Table 6 | Results of the ANOVAs for repeated measures with *F*-values (df), *p*-values, and effect sizes η_p^2 for the accuracy and reaction times of the behavioral task including the between-subject factor *group* (CON; IMP; NIMP) and the within-subject-factor *time* (pre; post) and *condition* (W; PH; PW; FF).

Effect	Accuracy			Reaction times		
	F	*p*	η_p^2	*F*	*p*	η_p^2
Group (G)	31.26 (2, 50)	**<0.001**	0.56	38.06 (2, 50)	**<0.001**	0.60
Time (T)	4.64 (1, 50)	**0.036**	0.09	56.21 (1, 50)	**<0.001**	0.53
Condition (C)	150.76 (2.08, 104.05)	**<0.001**	0.75	382.44 (1.70, 85.10)	**<0.001**	0.88
G*T	0.21 (2, 50)	0.814	–	12.97 (2, 50)	**<0.001**	0.34
G*C	16.89 (4.16, 104.05)	**<0.001**	0.40	37.18 (3.40, 85.10)	**<0.001**	0.60
T*C	6.00 (2.30, 115.21)	**0.002**	0.11	35.05 (2.63, 131.33)	**<0.001**	0.41
G*T*C	1.82 (4.61, 115.21)	0.120	–	6.06 (5.25, 131.33)	**<0.001**	0.20

CON, control children; IMP, improvers; NIMP, non-improvers; pre, before intervention; post, after intervention; W, words; PH, pseudohomophones; PW, pseudowords; FF, false fonts. Significant results are indicated in bold.

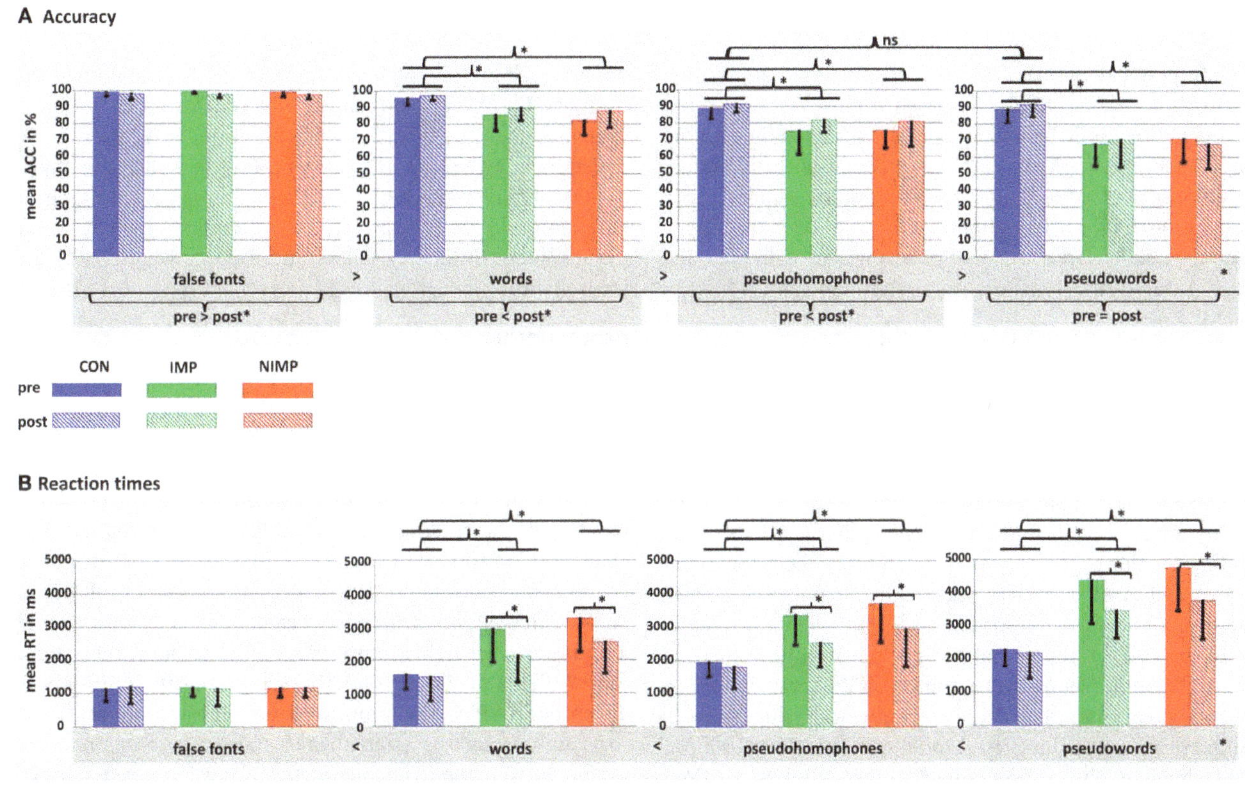

FIGURE 6 | Behavioral results for the PLD—task for control children (CON), improvers (IMP), and non-improvers (NIMP) before (pre) and after (post) intervention. (A) Depicts accuracy data and **(B)** illustrates reaction time data. Error bars illustrate standard deviation. $^*p < 0.05$; ns, non-significant.

in common word reading fluency and N400 amplitudes. Future research should further investigate whether the N300 truly has a predictive quality for reading improvement.

When interpreting the above mentioned data it is important to control for group differences on a behavioral level, as these too might influence improvement in literacy skills. Previous studies have reported, that especially, word-reading skills before intervention, phoneme awareness, rapid naming, IQ, and attention have an influence on improvement in literacy skills (Wise et al., 2000; Torgesen et al., 2001). However, in the present study IMP and NIMP had a very similar cognitive profile (see **Table 1**) suggesting that these factors might play a subordinate role for reading improvement in the present study. Only with respect to reading comprehension IMP differed from NIMP with the latter showing significantly lower reading comprehension skills before and after intervention. Lower performance in reading comprehension might point to deficits in oral language skills. It has been argued that reading comprehension deficits probably arise from poor vocabulary knowledge, weak grammatical skills, and difficulties in oral language comprehension (Snowling and Hulme, 2012a).

Table 7 | Pearson correlations across the whole group with DD and within the group of IMP and NIMP between the N300 before intervention and the gain in word and pseudoword reading fluency and the N400 after intervention.

Pre	Children with DD ($n = 28$)			IMP ($n = 11$)			NIMP ($n = 17$)		
	Post – Pre		Post	Post – pre		Post	Post – pre		Post
N300 (μV)	W reading	PW reading	N400 (μV)	W reading	PW reading	N400 (μV)	W reading	PW reading	N400 (μV)
W; LH	−0.13	−0.02	**0.34(*)**	0.32	−0.02	0.33	−0.02	0.13	0.30
PH; LH	−0.32	−0.29	**0.35(*)**	0.19	−0.13	**0.85****	−0.36	−0.41	0.04
PW; LH	**−0.39***	**−0.34(*)**	**0.38***	0.37	−0.40	**0.65***	−0.02	−0.07	0.15
W; RH	**−0.58****	**−0.41***	0.21	**−0.54(*)**	**−0.59(*)**	0.03	0.05	0.02	0.16
PH; RH	**−0.46***	−0.11	0.15	**−0.62***	−0.05	0.02	0.15	0.16	0.07
PW; RH	**−0.36(*)**	−0.17	−0.03	−0.41	−0.10	−0.01	−0.02	−0.03	−0.15
Mean; RH	**−0.53****	−0.26	0.13	**−0.58(*)**	−0.31	0.01	−0.08	−0.06	0.02

*DD, developmental dyslexia; IMP, improvers; NIMP, non-improvers; pre, before intervention; post, after intervention; post – pre, difference between pre and post measures; W reading, common word reading fluency from the SLRT II; PW reading, pseudoword reading fluency from the SLRT-II; W, words; PH, pseudohomophones; PW, pseudowords; LH, left hemisphere; RH, right hemisphere; ** $p < 0.001$; * $p < 0.05$; (*) $p < 0.10$.*

Furthermore, it has been found that general verbal ability predicts growth in reading ability (Torgesen et al., 2001). Thus, our results suggest that NIMP in addition to deficits in common word reading fluency are marked by stronger impairments in oral language skills in contrast to IMP, impeding reading improvement, and suggesting that NIMP might probably profit from training of oral language skills. Unfortunately, oral language skills were not assessed in this study, therefore this assumption cannot fully be answered.

Previous studies reported that up to 30% of struggling readers do not benefit from intervention (Shanahan and Barr, 1995; Vaughn et al., 2003). With a proportion of 50% our study shows that this number might be even larger. As has been reported above several factors, including word-reading skills before intervention, phoneme awareness, rapid naming, IQ, attention and general verbal ability might influence improvement in literacy skills. Thus, depending on the cognitive profile of children included in the respective studies improvement rates might vary between studies. Furthermore, and most important differences in improvement rates also depend on the operationalization of improvement in literacy skills. Improvement rates will be differing depending on which ability (e.g., phonological awareness, reading fluency, reading comprehension, spelling, etc.) and which cut-off criteria (0.5 SD, 1 SD, median, observation of therapists) is used. So far there are no guidelines or suggested criteria how to define improvement. With respect to the present study we oriented our cut-off criteria on results from current meta-analyses reporting effect sizes of $g = 0.31$ and $g = 0.33$ for reading interventions (Ise et al., 2012; Galuschka et al., 2014).

LIMITATIONS

One limitation of the present study was the quite small sample size of our IMP group, albeit greater (often two times larger) in contrast to many previous studies. Probably due to the small sample size some of the observed effects were only marginally significant. This limits the degree to which the results can be generalized and interpretations have to be drawn cautiously. Therefore, the study needs replications with larger sample sizes. Furthermore, due to small sample sizes, splitting our groups according to type of intervention (IP1 vs. IP2) was not reasonable. Therefore, the present study does not allow discriminating intervention effects depending on the type of treatment. Future studies investigating treatment IMP and NIMP need to take into account that groups will be divided in two and that depending on the definition of improvement in literacy skills some children might be excluded from the study, meaning very large sample sizes are needed.

CONCLUSION

In the present study we attempted to investigate the ERPs related to reading improvement. To summarize, children who significantly improve in reading during intervention are marked by an increased N400 component, which reflects GPC or the searching process within the orthographic lexicon. Children who continue to struggle in reading do not exhibit any neurophysiological changes over time. Furthermore, IMP and NIMP can be discriminated according to their neurophysiological profile already before intervention. Only IMP display higher N300 mean peak amplitudes over right fronto-temporal electrodes when processing W, PH, and PW and additionally over left fronto-temporal electrodes for PW. The importance of N300 amplitudes for reading improvement is strengthened by the correlational results in the IMP group. The higher the N300 amplitudes over the RH before intervention the larger the improvement in common word reading fluency. Furthermore, IMP with higher N300 amplitudes over the LH before intervention have higher N400 amplitudes after intervention. After intervention the N300 of IMP is equally high to the N300 of CON and NIMP suggesting that the N300 might index a compensatory mechanism or precursor, which facilitates the development of the N400 as well as reading improvement.

Future research should concentrate on the examination of the special needs of NIMP. What are the factors that make them more resistant to environmental change? Do they exhibit a different type of DD and therefore have to be treated in a different way? But how can this be identified? Which role play genetic differences for reading improvement? With respect to the present study NIMP seem to be a special group, who might benefit from another type of training. Lower reading comprehension skills in NIMP in the present study point to more pronounced impairments in oral language skills in contrast to IMP. Therefore, the NIMP in the present study might possibly profit from an additional training in oral language skills (Snowling and Hulme, 2011, 2012b). Answering these questions would help enormously to improve and adjust intervention for children with DD.

Important for all future studies, is to keep in mind that children with DD, even though matched with respect to their cognitive profile might differ regarding their neuronal profile. In fact, it is extremely difficult to categorize children on the behavioral level when the underlying cause of their DD might be very different with contributions from neurophysiology, neurobiology, genetics and environment. Future intervention studies should carefully distinguish between IMP and NIMP as the mixture of these children might even distort the results.

One of the main future goals is to further examine the N300 effects and to verify whether they can be replicated and hold true for a large sample size. Furthermore, future research should investigate whether the N300 might be a predictor for reading improvement in response to treatment. If the N300 truly has a predictive quality for response to intervention then it would be possible to streamline therapies for certain children.

ACKNOWLEDGMENTS

This research was supported by grant of the Bundesministerium für Bildung und Forschung (Grant Number 01GJ1001). Special thanks to all of the children and their parents who were so kind and willing to participate in this study and who continue to take part in many important studies.

REFERENCES

Achenbach, T. M. (1991). *Manual for the Child Behavior Checklist/4–18 and 1991 Profile.* Burlington: University of Vermont, Department of Psychiatry.

APA. (2013). *Diagnostic and Statistical Manual of Mental Disorders, 5th Edn., DSM-5.* Washington, DC: American Psychiatric Association.

Arnold, E. M., Goldston, D. B., Walsh, A. K., Reboussin, B. A., Daniel, S. S., Hickman, E., et al. (2005). Severity of emotional and behavioral problems among poor and typical readers. *J. Abnorm. Child Psychol.* 33, 205–217. doi: 10.1007/s10802-005-1828-9

Aylward, E. H., Richards, T. L., Berninger, V. W., Nagy, W. E., Field, K. M., Grimme, A. C., et al. (2003). Instructional treatment associated with changes in brain activation in children with dyslexia. *Neurology* 61, 212–219. doi: 10.1212/01.WNL.0000068363.05974.64

Bentin, S., Mouchetant-Rostaing, Y., Giard, M. H., Echallier, J. F., and Pernier, J. (1999). ERP manifestations of processing printed words at different psycholinguistic levels: time course and scalp distribution. *J. Cogn. Neurosci.* 11, 235–260. doi: 10.1162/089892999563373

Birkel, P. (1994). *Weingartener Grundwortschatz Rechtschreib-Test für Zweite und Dritte Klassen (WRT2+).* Göttingen: Hogrefe.

Birkel, P. (2007). *Weingartener Grundwortschatz Rechtschreib-Test für Dritte und Vierte Klassen (WRT3+).* Göttingen: Hogrefe.

Braun, M., Jacobs, A. M., Hahne, A., Ricker, B., Hofmann, M., and Hutzler, F. (2006). Model-generated lexical activity predicts graded ERP amplitudes in lexical decision. *Brain Res.* 1073–1074, 431–439. doi: 10.1016/j.brainres.2005.12.078

Briesemeister, B. B., Hofmann, M. J., Tamm, S., Kuchinke, L., Braun, M., and Jacobs, A. M. (2009). The pseudohomophone effect: evidence for an orthography-phonology-conflict. *Neurosci. Lett.* 455, 124–128. doi: 10.1016/j.neulet.2009.03.010

Brunswick, N., McCrory, E., Price, C. J., Frith, C. D., and Frith, U. (1999). Explicitly and implicit processing of words and pseudowords by adult developmental dyslexics. *Brain* 122, 1901–1917. doi: 10.1093/brain/122.10.1901

Bühner, M., and Ziegler, M. (2009). *Statistik für Psychologen und Sozialwissenschaftler.* München: Pearson.

Cattell, R. B., Weiß, R. H., and Osterland, J. (1997). *Grundintelligenztest Skala 1 (CFT 1).* Göttingen: Hogrefe.

Caylak, E. (2009). Neurobiological approaches on brains of children with dyslexia: review. *Acad. Radiol.* 16, 1003–1024. doi: 10.1016/j.acra.2009.02.012

Cohen, J. (1988). *Statistical Power Analysis for the Behavioural Sciences.* Hillsdale, NJ: Lawrence Erlbaum.

Coltheart, M., Curtis, B., Atkins, P., and Haller, M. (1993). Models of reading aloud: dual-route and parallel-distributed-processing approaches. *Psychol. Rev.* 100, 589–608. doi: 10.1037/0033-295X.100.4.589

Coltheart, M., Rastle, K., Perry, C., Langdon, R., and Ziegler, J. (2001). DRC: a dual route cascaded model of visual word recognition and reading aloud. *Psychol. Rev.* 108, 204–256. doi: 10.1037/0033-295X.108.1.204

Daniel, S. S., Walsh, A. K., Goldston, D. B., Arnold, E. M., Reboussin, B. A., and Wood, F. B. (2006). Suicidality, school dropout and reading problems among adolescents. *J. Learn. Disabil.* 39, 507–514. doi: 10.1177/00222194060390060301

Davis, N., Barquero, L., Compton, D. L., Fuchs, L. S., Fuchs, D., Gore, J. C., et al. (2011). Functional correlates of children's responsiveness to intervention. *Dev. Neuropsychol.* 36, 288–301. doi: 10.1080/87565641.2010.549875

Deacon, D., Dynowska, A., Ritter, W., and Grose-Fifer, J. (2004). Repetition and semantic priming of nonwords: implications for the theories of N400 and word recognition. *Psychophysiology* 41, 60–74. doi: 10.1111/1469-8986.00120

Demonet, J. F., Taylor, M. J., and Chaix, Y. (2004). Developmental dyslexia. *Lancet* 363, 1451–1460. doi: 10.1016/S0140-6736(04)16106-0

Dummer-Smoch, L., and Hackethal, R. (2007). *Kieler Leseaufbau.* Kiel: Veris.

Eden, G. F., Jones, K. M., Cappell, K., Gareau, L., Wood, F. B., Zeffiro, T. A., et al. (2004). Neural changes following remediation in adult developmental dyslexia. *Neuron* 44, 411–422. doi: 10.1016/j.neuron.2004.10.019

Electrical Geodesics Inc. (2007). *Geodesic Sensor Net Technical Manual.* Available online at: http://ganesha.uoregon.edu/images/8/8c/Gsn_013107.pdf?bcsi_scan_64377d2312a1e457=0andbcsi_scan_filename=Gsn_013107.pdf (Accessed January 24, 2014).

Esser, G., Wyschkon, A., and Schmidt, M. H. (2002). Was wird aus Achtjährigen mit einer Lese-Rechtschreibstörung. *Z. Klin. Psychol. Psychother.* 31, 235–242. doi: 10.1026/1616-3443.31.4.235

Farris, E. A., Odegard, T. N., Miller, H. L., Ring, J., Allen, G., and Black, J. (2011). Functional connectivity between the left and right inferior frontal lobes in a small sample of children with and without reading difficulties. *Neurocase* 17, 425–439. doi: 10.1080/13554794.2010.532141

Galuschka, K., Ise, E., Krick, K., and Schulte-Körne, G. (2014). Effectiveness of treatment approaches for children and adolescents with reading disabilities: a meta-analysis of randomized controlled trials. *PLoS ONE* 9:e89900. doi: 10.1371/journal.pone.0089900

Goldston, D. B., Walsh, A., Mayfield Arnold, E., Reboussin, B., Sergent Daniel, S., Erkanli, A., et al. (2007). Reading problems, psychiatric disorders, and functional impairment from mid- to late adolescence. *J. Am. Acad. Child Adolesc. Psychiatry* 46, 25–32. doi: 10.1097/01.chi.0000242241.77302.f4

Groth, K., Hasko, S., Bruder, J., Kunze, S., and Schulte-Körne, G. (2013). Interventionseffekte bei Lese-Rechtschreibstörung: evaluation von zwei Förderkonzepten unter besonderer Betrachtung methodischer Aspekte. *Lernen und Lernstörungen* 2, 161–175. doi: 10.1024/2235-0977/a000038

Hasko, S., Bruder, J., Bartling, J., and Schulte-Körne, G. (2012). N300 indexes deficient integration of orthographic and phonological representations in children with dyslexia. *Neuropsychologia* 50, 640–654. doi: 10.1016/j.neuropsychologia.2012.01.001

Hasko, S., Groth, K., Bruder, J., Bartling, J., and Schulte-Körne, G. (2013). The time course of reading processes in children with and without dyslexia: an ERP study. *Front. Hum. Neurosci.* 7:570. doi: 10.3389/fnhum.2013.00570

Hoffmann, S., and Falkenstein, M. (2008). The correction of eye blink artefacts in the EEG: a comparison of two prominent methods. *PLoS ONE* 3:e3004. doi: 10.1371/journal.pone.0003004

Huotilainen, M., Lovio, R., Kujala, T., Tommiska, V., Karma, K., and Fellman, V. (2011). Could audiovisual training be used to improve cognition in extremely low birth weight children? *Acta Paediatr.* 100, 1489–1494. doi: 10.1111/j.1651-2227.2011.02345.x

Ise, E., Engel, R. R., and Schulte-Körne, G. (2012). Was hilft bei Lese-Rechtschreibstörung? Ergebnisse einer Metaanalyse zur Wirksamkeit deutschsprachiger Förderansätze. *Kindheit und Entwicklung* 21, 122–136. doi: 10.1026/0942-5403/a000077

Ise, E., and Schulte-Körne, G. (2010). Spelling deficits in dyslexia: evaluation of an orthographic spelling training. *Ann. Dyslexia* 60, 18–39. doi: 10.1007/s11881-010-0035-8

Jucla, M., Nenert, R., Chaix, Y., and Demonet, J. F. (2009). Remediation effects on N170 and P300 in children with developmental dyslexia. *Behav. Neurol.* 22, 121–129. doi: 10.1155/2010/913692

Katusic, S. K., Colligan, R. C., Barbaresi, W. J., Schaid, D. J., and Jacobsen, S. J. (2001). Incidence of reading disability in a population-based birth cohort, 1976-1982, Rochester, Minn. *Mayo Clin. Proc.* 76, 1081–1092. doi: 10.4065/76.11.1081

Keller, T. A., and Just, M. A. (2009). Altering cortical connectivity: remediation-induced changes in the white matter of poor readers. *Neuron* 64, 624–631. doi: 10.1016/j.neuron.2009.10.018

Kronbichler, M., Bergmann, J., Hutzler, F., Staffen, W., Mair, A., Ladurner, G., et al. (2007). Taxi vs. taksi: on orthographic word recognition in the left ventral occipitotemporal cortex. *J. Cogn. Neurosci.* 19, 1584–1594. doi: 10.1162/jocn.2007.19.10.1584

Kujala, T., Karma, K., Ceponiene, R., Belitz, S., Turkkila, P., Tervaniemi, M., et al. (2001). Plastic neural changes and reading improvement caused by audiovisual training in reading-impaired children. *Proc. Natl. Acad. Sci. U.S.A.* 98, 10509–10514. doi: 10.1073/pnas.181589198

Kutas, M., and Federmeier, K. D. (2011). Thirty years and counting: finding menaing in the N400 component of the event-related brain potential (ERP). *Annu. Rev. Psychol.* 62, 621–641. doi: 10.1146/annurev.psych.093008.131123

Lau, E. F., Philips, C., and Poeppel, D. (2008). A cortical network for semantics: (De)constructiong the N400. *Nat. Rev. Neurosci.* 9, 920–933. doi: 10.1038/nrn2532

Lenhard, W., and Schneider, W. (2006). *Ein Leseverständnistest für Erst- bis Sechstklässler (ELFE1-6).* Göttingen: Hogrefe.

Lovio, R., Halttunen, A., Lyytinen, H., Näätänen, R., and Kujala, T. (2012). Reading skill and neural processing accuracy improvement after a 3-hour intervention in preschoolers with difficulties in reading-related skills. *Brain Res.* 1448, 42–55. doi: 10.1016/j.brainres.2012.01.071

Luck, S. J. (2005). *An Introduction to Event-Related Potential Technique.* Cambridge, London: The MIT Press.

Mayseless, N. (2011). Can intervention programs influence how the dyslexic brain processes low-level visual stimuli? *Dev. Neuropsychol.* 36, 949–954. doi: 10.1080/87565641.2011.606421

McArthur, G., Eve, P. M., Jones, K., Banales, E., Kohnen, S., Anandakumar, T., et al. (2012). Phonics training for English-speaking poor readers. *Cochrane Database Syst. Rev.* 12:CD009115. doi: 10.1002/14651858.CD009115.pub2

McCandliss, B.-D., and Noble, K.-G. (2003). The development of reading impairment: a cognitive neuroscience model. *Ment. Retard. Dev. Disabil. Res. Rev.* 9, 196–204. doi: 10.1002/mrdd.10080

Meyler, A., Keller, T. A., Cherkassky, V. L., Gabrieli, J. D., and Just, M. A. (2008). Modifying the brain activation of poor readers during sentence comprehension with extended remedial instruction: a longitudinal study of neuroplasticity. *Neuropsychologia* 46, 2580–2592. doi: 10.1016/j.neuropsychologia.2008.03.012

Molfese, P. J., Fletcher, J. M., and Denton, C. A. (2013). Adequate versus inadequate response to reading intervention: an event-related potentials assessment. *Dev. Neuropsychol.* 38, 534–549. doi: 10.1080/87565641.2013.825260

Moll, K., and Landerl, K. (2010). *SLRT-II. Lese- und Rechtschreibtest. Weiterentwicklung des Salzburger Lese- und Rechtschreibtests (SLRT).* Bern: Hans Huber.

Mugnaini, D., Lassi, S., La Malfa, G., and Albertini, G. (2009). Internalizing correlates of dyslexia. *World J. Pediatr.* 5, 255–264. doi: 10.1007/s12519-009-0049-7

National Institute of Child Health and Human Development. (2000). *Report of the National Reading Panel. Teaching Children to Read: an Evidence-Based Assessment of the Scientific Research Literature on Reading and its Implications for Reading Instruction: Reports of the Subgroups (NIH Publication No. 00-4754).* Washington, DC: Government Printing Office.

Noble, K. G., and McCandliss, B. D. (2005). Reading development and impairment: behavioral, social, and neurobiological factors. *J. Dev. Behav. Pediatr.* 26, 370–378. doi: 10.1097/00004703-200510000-00006

Odegard, T. N., Ring, J., Smith, S., Biggan, J., and Black, J. (2008). Differentiating the neural response to intervention in children with developmental dyslexia. *Ann. Dyslexia* 58, 1–14. doi: 10.1007/s11881-008-0014-5

Paulesu, E., Frith, U., Snowling, M., Gallagher, A., Morton, J., Frackowiak, R. S. J., et al. (1996). Is developmental dyslexia a disconnection syndrome?: evidence from PET scanning. *Brain* 119, 143–157. doi: 10.1093/brain/119.1.143

Penolazzi, B., Spironelli, C., Vio, C., and Angrilli, A. (2006). Altered hemispheric asymmetry during word processing in dyslexic children: an event-related potential study. *Neuroreport* 17, 429–433. doi: 10.1097/01.wnr.0000203350.99256.7d

Penolazzi, B., Spironelli, C., Vio, C., and Angrilli, A. (2010). Brain plasticity in developmental dyslexia after phonological treatment: a beta EEG band study. *Behav. Brain Res.* 209, 179–182. doi: 10.1016/j.bbr.2010.01.029

Petermann, F., and Petermann, U. (2007). *Hamburg-Wechsler-Intelligenztest für Kinder- IV - HAWIK-IV.* Bern: Hans Huber.

Pugh, K. R., Mencl, W. E., Jenner, A. R., Katz, L., Frost, S. J., Lee, J. R., et al. (2000). Functional neuroimaging studies of reading and reading disability (developmental dyslexia). *Ment. Retard. Dev. Disabil. Res. Rev.* 6, 207–213. doi: 10.1002/1098-2779(2000)6:3<207::AID-MRDD8>3.0.CO;2-P

Rezaie, R., Simos, P. G., Fletcher, J. M., Cirino, P. T., Vaughn, S., and Papanicolaou, A. C. (2011a). Engagement of temporal lobe regions predicts response to educational interventions in adolescent struggling readers. *Dev. Neuropsychol.* 36, 869–888. doi: 10.1080/87565641.2011.606404

Rezaie, R., Simos, P. G., Fletcher, J. M., Cirino, P. T., Vaughn, S., and Papanicolaou, A. C. (2011b). Temporo-parietal brain activity as a longitudinal predictor of response to educational interventions among middle school struggling readers. *J. Int. Neuropsychol. Soc.* 17, 875–885. doi: 10.1017/S1355617711000890

Richards, T., Berninger, V., Winn, W., Stock, P., Wagner, R., Muse, A., et al. (2007). Functional MRI activation in children with and without dyslexia during pseudoword aural repeat and visual decode: before and after treatment. *Neuropsychology* 21, 732–741. doi: 10.1037/0894-4105.21.6.732

Richards, T. L., and Berninger, V. W. (2008). Abnormal fMRI connectivity in children with dyslexia during a phoneme task: before but not after treatment. *J. Neurolinguist.* 21, 294–304. doi: 10.1016/j.jneuroling.2007.07.002

Richlan, F. (2012). Developmental dyslexia: dysfunction of a left hemisphere reading network. *Front. Hum. Neurosci.* 6:120. doi: 10.3389/fnhum.2012.00120

Richlan, F., Kronbichler, M., and Wimmer, H. (2009). Functional abnormalities in the dyslexic brain: a quantitative meta-analysis of neuroimaging studies. *Hum. Brain Mapp.* 30, 3299–3308. doi: 10.1002/hbm.20752

Richlan, F., Kronbichler, M., and Wimmer, H. (2011). Meta-analyzing brain dysfunctions in dyslexic children and adults. *Neuroimage* 56, 1735–1742. doi: 10.1016/j.neuroimage.2011.02.040

Richlan, F., Kronbichler, M., and Wimmer, H. (2013). Structural abnormalities in the dyslexic brain: a meta-analysis of voxel-based morphometry studies. *Hum. Brain Mapp.* 34, 3055–3065. doi: 10.1002/hbm.22127

Salmelin, R., Kiesilä, P., Uutela, K., Service, E., and Salonen, O. (1996). Impaired visual word processing in dyslexia revealed with magnetoencephalography. *Ann. Neurol.* 40, 157–162. doi: 10.1002/ana.410400206

Sandak, R., Mencl, W. E., Frost, S. J., and Pugh, K. R. (2004). The neurobiological basis of skilled and impaired reading: recent findings and new directions. *Sci. Stud. Read.* 8, 273–292. doi: 10.1207/s1532799xssr0803_6

Santos, A., Joly-Pottuz, B., Moreno, S., Habib, M., and Besson, M. (2007). Behavioural and event-related potentials evidence for pitch discrimination deficits in dyslexic children: improvement after intensive phonic intervention. *Neuropsychologia* 45, 1080–1090. doi: 10.1016/j.neuropsychologia.2006.09.010

Schulte-Körne, G., Bruder, J., Ise, E., and Rückert, E. (2012). "Spelling disability - neurophysiologic correlates and intervention," in *Reading, Writing, Mathematics and the Developing Brain: Listening to Many Voices. Literacy Studies,* eds Z. Breznitz, O. Rubinsten, V. J. Molfese, and D. L. Molfese (Dordrecht; Heidelberg; New York; London: Springer), 157–175. doi: 10.1007/978-94-007-4086-0_9

Schulte-Körne, G., Deimel, W., and Remschmidt, H. (2001). Zur Diagnostik der Lese-Rechtschreibstörung. *Z. Kinder Jugendpsychiatr. Psychother.* 29, 113–116. doi: 10.1024/1422-4917.29.2.113

Schulte-Körne, G., and Mathwig, F. (2007). *Das Marburger Rechtschreibtraining. Ein Regelgeleitetes Förderprogramm für Rechtschreibschwache Kinder.* Bochum: Winkler.

Schurz, M., Sturm, D., Richlan, F., Kronbichler, M., Ladurner, G., and Wimmer, H. (2010). A dual-route perspective on brain activation in response to visual words: evidence for a length by lexicality interaction in the visual word form area (VWFA). *Neuroimage* 49, 2649–2661. doi: 10.1016/j.neuroimage.2009.10.082

Shanahan, T., and Barr, R. (1995). Reading Recovery: an independent evaluation of the effects of an early instructional intervention for at-risk learners. *Read. Res. Q.* 30, 968–996. doi: 10.2307/748206

Shaywitz, B. A., Shaywitz, S. E., Blachman, B. A., Pugh, K. R., Fulbright, R. K., Skudlarski, P., et al. (2004). Development of left occipitotemporal systems for skilled reading in children after a phonologically- based intervention. *Biol. Psychiatry* 55, 926–933. doi: 10.1016/j.biopsych.2003.12.019

Shaywitz, B. A., Shaywitz, S. E., Pugh, K. R., Mencl, W. E., Fulbright, R. K., Skudlarski, P., et al. (2002). Disruption of posterior brain systems for reading in children with developmental dyslexia. *Biol. Psychiatry* 52, 101–110. doi: 10.1016/S0006-3223(02)01365-3

Shaywitz, S. E., Fletcher, J. M., Holahan, J. M., Schneider, A., Marchione, K. E., Stuebing, K. K., et al. (1999). Persistence of dyslexia: the connecticut longitudinal study at adolescence. *Pediatrics* 104, 1351–1359. doi: 10.1542/peds.104.6.1351

Shaywitz, S. E., Gruen, J. R., and Shaywitz, B. A. (2007). Management of dyslexia, its rationale, and underlying neurobiology. *Pediatr. Clin. North Am.* 54, 609–623. doi: 10.1016/j.pcl.2007.02.013

Shaywitz, S. E., and Shaywitz, B. A. (2008). Paying attention to reading: the neurobiology of reading and dyslexia. *Dev. Psychopathol.* 20, 1329–1349. doi: 10.1017/S0954579408000631

Shaywitz, S. E., Shaywitz, B. A., Fletcher, J. M., and Escobar, M. D. (1990). Prevalence of reading disability in boys and girls results of the Connecticut longitudinal study. *J. Am. Med. Assoc.* 264, 998–1002. doi: 10.1001/jama.1990.03450080084036

Shaywitz, S. E., Shaywitz, B. A., Pugh, K. R., Fulbright, R. K., Constable, R. T., Mencl, W. E., et al. (1998). Functional disruption in the organization of the brain for reading in dyslexia. *Proc. Natl. Acad. Sci. U.S.A.* 95, 2636–2641. doi: 10.1073/pnas.95.5.2636

Simos, P. G., Fletcher, J. M., Bergman, E., Breier, J. I., Foorman, B. R., Castillo, E. M., et al. (2002). Dyslexia-specific brain activation profile becomes normal following successful remedial training. *Neurology* 58, 1203–1213. doi: 10.1212/WNL.58.8.1203

Simos, P. G., Fletcher, J. M., Denton, C., Sarkari, S., Billingsley-Marshall, R., and Papanicolaou, A. C. (2006). Magnetic source imaging studies of dyslexia interventions. *Dev. Neuropsychol.*, 30, 591–611. doi: 10.1207/s15326942dn3001_4

Simos, P. G., Fletcher, J. M., Sarkari, S., Billingsley, R. L., Denton, C., and Papanicolaou, A. C. (2007a). Altering the brain circuits for reading through intervention: a magnetic source imaging study. *Neuropsychology* 21, 485–496. doi: 10.1037/0894-4105.21.4.485

Simos, P. G., Fletcher, J. M., Sarkari, S., Billingsley, R. L., Francis, D. J., Castillo, E. M., et al. (2005). Early development of neurophysiological processes involved in normal reading and reading disability: a magnetic source imaging study. *Neuropsychology* 19, 787–798. doi: 10.1037/0894-4105.19.6.787

Simos, P. G., Fletcher, J. M., Sarkari, S., Billingsley-Marshall, R., Denton, C. A., and Papanicolaou, A. C. (2007b). Intensive instruction affects brain magnetic activity associated with oral word reading in children with persistent reading disabilities. *J. Learn. Disabil.* 40, 37–48. doi: 10.1177/00222194070400010301

Snowling, M. J., and Hulme, C. (2011). Evidence-based interventions for reading and language difficulties: creating a virtuous circle. *Br. J. Educ. Psychol.* 81, 1–23. doi: 10.1111/j.2044-8279.2010.02014.x

Snowling, M. J., and Hulme, C. (2012a). Annual research review: the nature and classification of reading disorders a commentary on proposals for DSM-5. *J. Child Psychol. Psychiatry* 53, 593–607. doi: 10.1111/j.1469-7610.2011.02495.x

Snowling, M. J., and Hulme, C. (2012b). Interventions for children's language and literacy difficulties. *Int. J. Lang. Commun. Disord.* 47, 27–34. doi: 10.1111/j.1460-6984.2011.00081.x

Spironelli, C., and Angrilli, A. (2007). Influence of phonological, semantic and orthographic tasks on the early linguistic components N150 and N350. *Int. J. Psychophysiol.* 64, 190–198. doi: 10.1016/j.ijpsycho.2007.02.002

Spironelli, C., and Angrilli, A. (2009). Developmental aspects of automatic word processing: language lateralization of early ERP components in children, young adults and middle-aged subjects. *Biol. Psychol.* 80, 35–45. doi: 10.1016/j.biopsycho.2008.01.012

Spironelli, C., Penolazzi, B., Vio, C., and Angrilli, A. (2010). Cortical reorganization in dyslexic children after phonological training: evidence from early evoked potentials. *Brain* 133, 3385–3395. doi: 10.1093/brain/awq199

Temple, E., Deutsch, G.-K., Poldrack, R.-A., Miller, S., Tallal, P., Merzenich, M.-M., et al. (2003). Neural deficits in children with dyslexia ameliorated by behavioral remediation: evidence from functional MRI. *Proc. Natl. Acad. Sci. U.S.A.* 100, 2860–2865. doi: 10.1073/pnas.0030098100

Torgesen, J. K., Alexander, A. W., Wagner, R. K., Rashotte, C. A., Voeller, K. K. S., and Conway, T. (2001). Intensive remedial instruction for children with severe reading disabilities: immediate and long-term outcomes from two instructional approaches. *J. Learn. Disabil.* 34, 35–58. doi: 10.1177/00222194010 3400104

van der Mark, S., Bucher, K., Maurer, U., Schulz, E., Brem, S., Buckelmüller, J., et al. (2009). Children with dyslexia lack multiple specializations along the visual word-form (VWF) system. *Neuroimage* 47, 1940–1949. doi: 10.1016/j.neuroimage.2009.05.021

van der Mark, S., Klaver, P., Bucher, K., Maurer, U., Schulz, E., Brem, S., et al. (2011). The left occipitotemporal system in reading: disruption of focal fMRI connectivity to left inferior frontal and inferior parietal language areas in children with dyslexia. *Neuroimage* 54, 2426–2436. doi: 10.1016/j.neuroimage.2010.10.002

Vaughn, S., Linan-Thompson, S., and Hickman, P. (2003). Response to instruction as a means of identifying students with reading/learning disabilities. *Except. Children* 69, 391–409.

Weiss, S., Grabner, R. H., Kargl, R., Purgstaller, C., and Fink, A. (2010). Behavioral and neurophysiological effects of morphological awareness training on spelling and reading. *Read. Writ.* 23, 645–671. doi: 10.1007/s11145-009-9177-7

Willcutt, E., and Pennington, B. (2000). Psychiatric comorbidity in children and adolescents with reading disability. *J. Child Psychol. Psychiatry* 41, 1039–1048. doi: 10.1111/1469-7610.00691

Willcutt, E. G., Betjemann, R. S., Pennington, B. F., Olson, R. K., Defries, J. C., and Wadsworth, S. J. (2007). Longitudinal study of reading disability and attention-deficit/ hyperactivity disorder: implications for education. *Mind Brain Educ.* 1, 181–192. doi: 10.1111/j.1751-228X.2007.00019.x

Wimmer, H., Schurz, M., Sturm, D., Richlan, F., Klackl, J., Kronbichler, M., et al. (2010). A dual-route perspective on poor reading in a regular orthography: an fMRI study. *Cortex* 46, 1284–1298. doi: 10.1016/j.cortex.2010.06.004

Wise, B. W., Ring, J., and Olson, R. K. (2000). Individual differences in gains from computer-assisted remedial reading. *J. Exp. Child Psychol.* 77, 197–235. doi: 10.1006/jecp.1999.2559

Zhou, W., Zhou, J., Zhao, H., and Ju, L. (2005). Removing eye movement and power line artifacts from the EEG based on ICA. *Conf. Proc. IEEE Eng. Med. Biol. Soc.* 6, 6017 6020. doi: 10.1109/IEMBS.2005.1615863

12

Visual and auditory synchronization deficits among dyslexic readers as compared to non-impaired readers: a cross-correlation algorithm analysis

Itamar Sela *

Edmond J. Safra Brain Research Center for the Study of Learning Disabilities, University of Haifa, Haifa, Israel

Correspondence:
Itamar Sela, Edmond J. Safra Brain Research Center for the Study of Learning Disabilities, University of Haifa, Mount Carmel, Haifa 31905, Israel
e-mail: isela01@campus.haifa.ac.il

Visual and auditory temporal processing and crossmodal integration are crucial factors in the word decoding process. The speed of processing (SOP) gap (Asynchrony) between these two modalities, which has been suggested as related to the dyslexia phenomenon, is the focus of the current study. Nineteen dyslexic and 17 non-impaired University adult readers were given stimuli in a reaction time (RT) procedure where participants were asked to identify whether the stimulus type was only visual, only auditory or crossmodally integrated. Accuracy, RT, and Event Related Potential (ERP) measures were obtained for each of the three conditions. An algorithm to measure the contribution of the temporal SOP of each modality to the crossmodal integration in each group of participants was developed. Results obtained using this model for the analysis of the current study data, indicated that in the crossmodal integration condition the presence of the auditory modality at the pre-response time frame (between 170 and 240 ms after stimulus presentation), increased processing speed in the visual modality among the non-impaired readers, but not in the dyslexic group. The differences between the temporal SOP of the modalities among the dyslexics and the non-impaired readers give additional support to the theory that an asynchrony between the visual and auditory modalities is a cause of dyslexia.

Keywords: dyslexia, asynchrony, crossmodal integration, EEG, ERP, cross-correlation analysis

INTRODUCTION

According to a widely accepted definition of developmental dyslexia, a dyslexic reader is one who exhibits slow and inaccurate reading performance unrelated to his/her IQ level or educational opportunities (British Psychological Society, 1999; Lyon and Shaywitz, 2003; Shaywitz and Shaywitz, 2008). An abundance of research into phonological deficits has indicated that the primary source of the difficulties experienced by dyslexic readers lies in word decoding accuracy (Liberman and Shankweiler, 1991; Badian, 1997). Some studies have found that disabled readers demonstrate a fundamental orthographic deficit (Stanovich and West, 1989; Cunningham and Stanovich, 1990; Zecker, 1991; Barker et al., 1992; Morris et al., 1998).The reading deficits of developmental dyslexia persist into adulthood (Bruck, 1992; Leonard et al., 2001). A large number of studies have shown deficient phonological processing as a core deficit in developmental dyslexia. The leading theory, the phonological deficit theory of developmental dyslexia (Stanovich, 1988; Share, 1994; Snowling, 1995), suggests that dyslexic readers may suffer from an (unspecified) dysfunction in peri-sylvian brain regions, which leads to difficulties in generating and processing accurate and efficient phonological representations of speech sounds (Stanovich, 1988; Temple et al., 2001).

In addition, researchers are still debating whether dyslexic readers are characterized by impairment in basic auditory and/or visual processing (Amitay et al., 2002a,b; Vellutino et al., 2004; Lachmann et al., 2005; Groth et al., 2011). In the auditory domain, data has indicated dyslexics' inability to discriminate between temporal rapidly changing tones and consecutive acoustic events (Tallal, 1980; Tallal et al., 1993, 1998). Difficulties locating the origin of sounds and blending them were also found (Stein, 1993). In the visual domain, findings have indicated that dyslexic readers have smaller and fewer neurons in the magnocellular layers of the Lateral Geniculate Nucleus (LGN) (Livingstone, 1991) suggesting fundamental deficiencies of the magnocellular system and pathways of the visual cortex that are responsible for motion, contrast sensitivity (Stein and Walsh, 1997; Stein and Talcott, 1999; Stein, 2001; Stein et al., 2001) and fast sequential processing (Ben-Yehudah and Ahissar, 2004). Based on the aforementioned studies regarding the presumed low-level visual and/or auditory sensory deficit among dyslexic readers, it was recently demonstrated, using the Pair Associate Learning paradigm (Hulme et al., 2007), that dyslexic readers exhibited a crossmodal association difficulty (Jones et al., 2013). Previous data (Breznitz, 2002, 2003, 2006) has found that the gap in the speed of processing (SOP) between the visual and auditory modalities is wider among dyslexic readers than non-impaired readers. This gap prevents the precise integration over time (Berninger et al., 1990; Wolf and Bowers, 2000) of the cross-modal information necessary for accurate word decoding and leads to the asynchrony phenomenon. Breznitz (2006) suggested that the asynchrony phenomenon in the word-decoding process occurs when there is time gap resulting in a mismatch between the grapheme and its phoneme correspondent.

It was previously suggested that different frequency ranges are important to speech perception (Luo and Poeppel, 2007; Ghitza and Greenberg, 2009). The temporal sampling framework for developmental dyslexia (Goswami, 2011) proposes that at the basic level of auditory perception processing, dyslexic readers have difficulties distinguishing between different frequency ranges, an impairment that leads to a slower and less accurate speech perception (Goswami et al., 2010). It is reasonable to assume that an impairment in sensory temporal processing that can be identified at the frequency domain may be also expressed at the time domain. Thus, it is important to study whether dyslexic readers exhibit an abnormal basic sensory (auditory or visual) information processing. Here, the dyslexic readers' ability to process fundamental sensory input is investigated by using a time-based cross-correlation analysis.

The synchronization hypothesis proposes that for accurate information processing to occur, it is crucial that the information that arrives from more than one modality be integrated in both content (Fujisaki and Nahida, 2005; Ghajar and Ivry, 2008; Neil et al., 2011) and time (Llinas, 1993; Breznitz, 2001, 2002, 2003, 2006; Breznitz and Misra, 2003; Breznitz et al., 2013). The act of reading relies on the information processing system and during the word decoding process both the visual and the auditory modalities are activated. Word decoding accuracy can be achieved only when the activation within and between modalities is synchronized (Breznitz, 2008). It was found that the time gap between the visual and auditory Event Related Potential (ERP) component of P1 of the dyslexic readers was larger than 100 ms, whereas the non-impaired readers exhibited an insignificant time gap of 15–30 ms only (Breznitz, 2008). A similar trend of results was found when the time gap between the auditory and visual ERP of N1 was analyzed. Moreover, it was shown that the between-modalities time gap has developmental constraints: while the auditory components of N1 and P1 had shorter latency as compared to visual ones among dyslexic children, the opposite was found among adult dyslexic readers (Breznitz, 2008). The author argued that these results support the notion that a deficit within the visual modality affects decoding ability, a claim that was supported by evidence of a significant correlation between the between-modalities time gap and reading performance (fluency and reading errors).

The visual-orthographic and auditory-phonological systems are the core systems activated temporally during the word-decoding process. However, during a normal course of processing, both systems differ not only in the structure and length of their neural networks, but are also located in different parts of the brain (Saito et al., 2005) and operate in a different manner and at different speeds (Breznitz, 2002, 2003, 2006). Data has indicated that auditory information arrives (Mishra et al., 2007) at the auditory cortex, about 30 ms after stimulus presentation (Heil et al., 1999), whereas visual information arrives (Mishra et al., 2007) at the visual cortex about 70 ms after stimulus presentation (Schmolesky et al., 1998). This suggests that when a stimulus includes both visual and auditory representations, the auditory stimuli arrive in the brain faster than the visual stimuli. However, at the word-decoding level, the auditory-phonological channel perceives and processes the information in a temporal-serial manner (Rosenzweig and Bennet, 1996), whereas the visual-orthographic channel process information in a spatial, holistic manner (Breznitz, 2006). This suggests that visual processing at this level might be faster than auditory processing. Yet, an effective word decoding process requires an exact integration of graphemes and phonemes (Adams, 1990; Berninger, 2001). In other words, the two systems need to be synchronized for appropriate crossmodal integration to occur. The focus of the current study is to quantify the synchronization of the two modalities among non-impaired and dyslexic readers.

Earlier studies that verified the relationships between visual and auditory processing among non-impaired readers suggested that presenting a visual pattern prior to an auditory one eases inter-sensory correspondence while the presentation of an auditory pattern prior to a visual one increases correspondence errors (Botuck and Turkewitz, 1990). It has been suggested that either the information might be received more accurately through the visual as opposed to the auditory modality, or it is more difficult to register information arranged temporally than information arranged spatially in memory (Botuck and Turkewitz, 1990). Furthermore, Ben-Artzi and Marks (1995) examined whether and how stimulus type influences visual-auditory interaction. In Ben-Artzi and Marks' study (1995), participants were asked to classify sound levels and spatial locations on two types of tasks: uni-dimensional and bi-dimensional. Data indicated that visual identification is not only faster (see also Melara and O'Brien, 1987) but also dominant (Egeth and Sager, 1977) over the auditory identification. Posner et al. (1976) suggested that visual dominance is, in fact, a compensation for the visual system's limited capacity to arouse internal attention. According to this approach, the increases in sound level in the auditory system arouse attention automatically. However, the arousal of attention in the visual system requires specific controlled effort and the brain learns to allocate attention to visual stimuli. Furthermore, it has been suggested that the existence of the visual system, which can allocate attention to spatial stimuli, enables the ear to relate to its relevant stimuli (Posner et al., 1976). By using fMRI imaging techniques, recent studies have indicated that during crossmodal activation, when both visual and auditory information are presented, the visual modality is dominant at the pre- response level whereas the auditory is more dominant at the response level (i.e., Koppen et al., 2009; Chen and Zhou, 2013). Thus, all the above support the notion that a deficit in the visual modality might be involved in dyslexia. In light of the assumption that the visual modality has dominancy over the auditory modality, it is important to investigate the relationship and interaction between the two sensory modalities.

The basic assumption of this study is that exposing a participant to either a visual or an auditory stimulus triggers sequential information processing which has an effect on ongoing ERP activity. Furthermore, visual-only or auditory-only information processing is carried out in a similar fashion irrespective of whether the stimulus is solely visual or accompanied by an auditory stimulus presented at the same time (crossmodal presentation). Therefore, the first hypothesis of this study is that the ongoing

ERP of the crossmodal condition will contain visual and auditory elements that will also be found in each of the unimodal conditions (Marchant and Driver, 2013). It should be noted that the current study does not assume that an apparent correlation between the unimodal and crossmodal ERPs stems solely from the presence of the unimodal element within the crossmodal ERP. It is proposed that to a certain extent, the two datasets share a common factor which may be explained as a specific unimodal brain reaction.

The second hypothesis asserts that although the information processing of a unimodality (specific-visual or auditory) will be similar under the two conditions of the unimodal stimulus type and under the two modalities stimulus type, the crossmodal processing will affect the SOP of the uni (specific) modality. Thus, if the data were to be looked at in an individual time window for the unimodal condition, it is assumed that a similar pattern of the component (factor) will be found in a corresponding time window for the crossmodal condition, but not necessarily in exactly the same time location, as it may appear earlier or later [this is defined as Delta Time (DT)]. The polarity of DT indicates either an acceleration (negative DT) or deceleration (positive DT) in one modality's SOP as a result of the presence of the second modality.

As the SOP of the two different modalities was shown to differ (Saito et al., 2005) the third hypothesis of the current study is that differences will be found between the size of the interaction between the visual and auditory modalities and the influence of one modality on the other. Moreover, as dyslexic readers' ability to process uni (visual or auditory) and crossmodal sensory information was found deficient (Lachmann et al., 2005; Breznitz, 2006; Jones et al., 2013), the fourth hypothesis of the current study is that differences between the two-reading-level groups will be found. Specifically, it is assumed that the results of the current study would show a negative effect of one modality (visual or auditory) on the SOP of the other modality among the dyslexic readers.

METHODS

PARTICIPANTS

Nineteen dyslexic readers (age 25.5 ± 2.91) and 17 non-impaired readers (age: 24.52 ± 2.29) were included in the study [$t_{(35)} = 0.191, p = 0.242$]. None of the participants had a history of neurological or emotional disorders, and no differences were found between dyslexics and non- impaired readers in attention ability as measured by the d2 test for adults [$t_{(35)} = -0.222, p = 0.825$] (Brickenkamp, 1981). The dyslexic readers were diagnosed with dyslexia during childhood, and their diagnosis was confirmed as adults by achieving one standard (−1) score or below on the Hebrew "MATAL" normative reading test (MATAL Battery, 2007). The non-impaired readers were recruited via notices posted on campus bulletin boards. Individuals with dyslexia were recruited through the Student Support Service at the University of Haifa. All participants were native Hebrew speakers from a middle-class background, right-handed, and screened for normal hearing. All participants displayed normal or corrected-to-normal vision in both eyes. All participants gave their informed written consent prior to inclusion in the study, and all were paid as compensation for their time. The experiment was approved by the University of Haifa Ethics Committee (Number, 1991) according to the Helsinki Declaration.

The classification of participants into non-impaired readers and dyslexic readers groups was based on the following behavioral measures (For more details see Breznitz and Misra, 2003; Breznitz et al., 2013).

Intelligence

Intelligence was tested by the *Block Design* (performance) and the Similarities sub-tests (verbal) from the WAIS-III (Wechsler, 1997).

Decoding skills

One Minute Tests (Breznitz and Misra, 2003) comprised a battery of two subtests one for words and the other for pseudowords in which the participants were asked to read single words or pseudowords as quickly and as accurately as possible within the space of 1 min.

Reading rate and accuracy of connected text

Oral reading time and accuracy of a narrative text comprising 247 words (MATAL Battery, 2007. See also Breznitz and Misra, 2003). Reading time was defined as the mean reading time for each word read correctly.

Reading rate and comprehension

A Reading Comprehension Test (MATAL Battery, 2007), comprising 412 words. The participants were asked to silently read a passage as quickly as possible and then answer 18 comprehension questions. Reading time was based on the mean reading time per word. Comprehension scores were based on the total number of correct answers.

Memory

In the Digit Span (WAIS III, Wechsler, 1997), the standard scores of each participant were recorded.

Speed of processing (SOP)

Two tests were used to assess SOP: The Digit Symbol Task and Coding Task-Speed Factor (WAIS III, Wechsler, 1997).

Table 1 presents the means, standard deviations, and *t* values for the reading and the cognitive background measures. The dyslexic readers achieved significantly lower scores than the non-impaired readers in reading accuracy and time parameters but not for silent reading comprehension. In addition the dyslexic readers also obtained significantly lower scores compared to the non-impaired readers in the SOP and working memory measures but not in the intelligence measures (see **Table 1**).

APPARATUS

Two computer sets were used in this study. The first computer was used to present the task stimuli (visual as well as auditory, using a screen, and a pair of speakers) and to record participant's responses. The electrophysiological data was collected using a Bio-Logic Brain Atlas IV computer system (2nd computer set) with 20 electroencephalographic (EEG) activity reception channels. The data collection from the scalp began at approximately

Table 1 | Reading and cognitive measures for dyslexic and non-impaired readers.

	Non-impaired readers group		Dyslexic readers group		*t*
	Mean	*SD*	Mean	*SD*	
One minute test—number of words read correctly	111.04	16.99	65.63	20.71	−8.87***
Pseudowords per minute—number of correct Pseudowords read	59.89	15.68	27.50	11.05	−8.70***
Oral reading (per letter reading rate)	0.69	0.18	0.41	0.09	6.19***
Silent text reading rate—total reading time	212.05	54.69	128.83	30.12	−6.89***
Reading comprehension (correct answers out of 18 questions)	16.67	2.40	15.54	4.70	1.06
Digit symbol SD score	12.60	10.75	8.23	15.16	−2.63**
Coding SD Score	13.87	10.86	8.90	5.98	5.57***
General ability similarities	12.01	3.86	11.90	2.91	1.57
Block design	12.67	2.29	12.85	1.66	1.21
Digit span—standard score	12.42	3.08	9.00	2.76	−4.38***

$^{**}p < 0.01$; $^{***}p < 0.001$.

1000 ms prior to the beginning of the experimental task. The sample rate was 256 Hz and was carried out using a full array of electrodes placed according to the International 10/20 system (Jasper, 1958) utilizing an Electro-cap (a nylon cap fitted over the head with 9 mm tin electrodes sewn within).An electro-oculogram (EOG) was recorded with an electrode extension that was located under the left eye. A ground electrode was placed on the left mastoid. All electrodes were maintained at an impedance of 5 KΩ or less. Brain activity was sampled directly from 19 scalp electrodes (Fp1, Fp2, F7, F3, Fz, F4, F8, T3, C3, Cz, C4, T4, T5, P3, Pz, P4, T6, O1, O2).

TASK DESIGN

A visual, auditory, and crossmodal processing task (Breznitz and Misra, 2003; Meyler and Breznitz, 2003) was administered. This task consisted of 150 stimuli presented to the participants in three different conditions: auditory alone (50 tones occurring at 1000 Hz with a time length of 200 ms), visual alone (50 white rectangle shape stimuli, presented at the middle of a black screen for duration of 200 ms), and crossmodal (50 tones and flashes occurring simultaneously). The 150 stimuli were presented in a randomized order. The between trials interval, i.e., the time from the beginning of one trial to the beginning of the next trial was set to 2 s. The participants were asked to press one of three computer keys—One key to indicate the appearance of an auditory tone stimulus alone, one key for the visual rectangle-like flash, and the another key to indicate when the two stimuli occurred simultaneously. Off-line analysis differentiated between the auditory, visual, and simultaneous segments. All stimuli were presented to the participants on a PC computer. Participants were seated 0.5 m from the computer screen and heard the tones via speakers.

PROCEDURE

During data collection, participants were seated in a sound attenuated room. The experiment took place during two sessions of about 2 h each. The first part of data collection consisted of gathering the behavioral measures, and in the second part the experimental tasks ERP measures were incorporated.

DATA ANALYSIS

For each participant and for each of the three task conditions, both the mean value of Reaction Time (RT) for correct responses and accuracy were computed. The EEG data were segmented into 1945 ms epochs (one per trial) and by three different conditions based on the trial type (1-visual-only, 2-auditory-only, 3-crossmodal stimulus). Data of one trial started 445 ms prior to stimulus presentation and ended 650 ms following presentation. The data was corrected for eye movements using the Orgil Medical Equipment (1997), normalized by comparing cognitive activity time with inactive time for each electrode, separately, for each participant, filtered using a low pass 20–24 Hz filter, and averaged by stimulus type (Orgil software, 1997) prior to beginning the cross-correlation analysis.

CROSS-CORRELATION ANALYSIS

In order to verify the research hypotheses, a cross-correlation analysis was obtained. Cross-correlation analysis is a procedure used in signal processing by which the similarity between two signals is measured. The algorithm analysis output is a series of correlation coefficients between two signals according to time, i.e., one correlation coefficient is calculated for successive time points according to a specific temporal increment (Woody, 1967; Nelson-Wong et al., 2009). Previously, the cross-correlation technique was used as part of a tool aimed at overcoming the limitations of the traditional ERP averaging method and to categorize participants based on their ERP data (Sela et al., 2008). Similar to the work of Sela et al. (2008), the current study algorithm obtained and compared data time windows taken from participants' ERPs. These data time windows included all 19 electrodes within the selected time areas. In the following algorithm, the term "unimodal" refers to either visual- or auditory-only ERP datasets. The term "crossmodal" refers to the synchronized visual-auditory stimulus's ERP.

TIME WINDOW ANALYSIS—CREATION OF A CROSS-CORRELATION GRAPH

The following algorithm was used on three different datasets: visual-only ERP, auditory-only ERP, and crossmodal ERP. The explanation below describes the process in which a cross-correlation graph is computed.

1. A unimodal time window was constructed by taking the values (amplitude) of all electrodes from the unimodal dataset across a certain time window (**Figure 1**). Thus, a time window is defined as a two-dimensional dataset with electrodes as rows and time samples as columns. The time window's location is defined as the center of the specific time window. For example, a time window taken at the time area of 150 ms

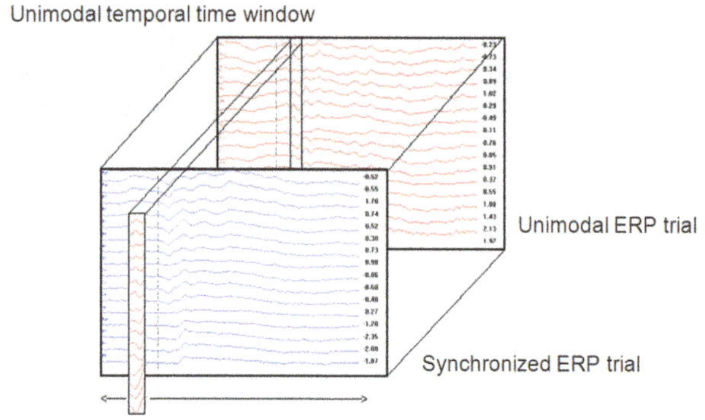

FIGURE 1 | Cross-correlation analysis between a unimodal time window throughout the crossmodaltrial.

is defined as the amplitude data of all electrodes between 100 and 200 ms (see Temporal implementation of Phases A and B for an explanation of the choice of time window location).

2. A cross-correlation loop between the above time window and the crossmodal ERP was applied as follows:
   a. A crossmodal ERP time window of the same duration of the unimodal ERP time window constructed in Phase 1 was computed. The first crossmodal ERP time window used in the algorithm was from 0 to 100 ms. Note that the algorithm takes into account a time window of all electrodes altogether.
   b. The correlation strength between the two time windows was calculated and resulted in a number within the range of −1 and 1. A value of zero indicates no correlation. A correlation value that approaches −1 indicates a strong negative correlation and a value that approached 1 indicates a strong positive correlation.
   c. A new crossmodal ERP time window was then constructed which was located one successive time frame (3.9 ms) after the crossmodal ERP time window constructed in Phase 2a.
   d. This procedure was repeated until the end of the crossmodal ERP trial duration (see **Figure 1**).
3. The result of the algorithm is a series of correlation coefficients computed for each unimodal ERP time window location every 10 ms, from the beginning of the ERP trial to the end.
   If assumption 1 is correct, then the cross-correlation graph should appear as in **Figure 2**.
   Thus, for most of the iterations (Phases 2b to 2d) the correlation between the unimodal ERP window and the crossmodal ERP should be relatively low, but at a particular time, the correlation strength should increase and reach a relatively high peak. The peak's location is the point in time at which the ERP data of the unimodal window have their maximum similarity to the crossmodal ERP. This notion can be understood as two pictures that look almost the same.
4. The DT between the peak time and the center of the unimodal window was measured. DT is the parameter used as the basis for the next phase of analysis.

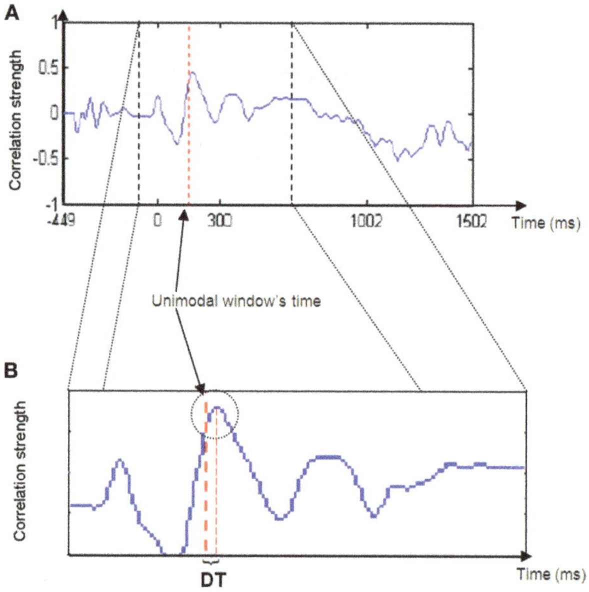

FIGURE 2 | Cross-correlation strength graph. Note the peak in graph strength in the area of the unimodal time window (right red dashed line in **B**) and the delta time (DT) between the line and the peak maximum.

DELTA TIME (DT) PARAMETER

The dependent variable in the proposed algorithm consists of the DT between the unimodal window's location and the correlation peak's time location. If the unimodal time window represents a temporal fraction of information processing and there is a relatively strong correlation between the window and a window similar in size from the crossmodal ERP, then the algorithm suggests that the same temporal fraction of information processing occurred in both ERPs. In addition, if there is a DT between the peak location and the unimodal window, then the fraction of information processing occurred earlier or later, depending upon the DT polarity. Thus, a negative DT indicates early occurrence of the information processing fraction, or in other words, the second modality influenced and accelerated the process of the first modality. In contrast, a positive DT indicates late occurrence of the information processing fraction, which means that the second modality decelerated the SOP of the first modality.

The algorithm found the DT for each participant between the peak's location and the center of the unimodal time window. A *t*-test assessed whether there was a significant difference on DT values between the two groups of participants.

TEMPORAL IMPLEMENTATION OF PHASES A AND B

The phases described above (A and B) focus on a particular time window (for example, between 100 and 200 ms). However, SOP rate can change throughout time. In addition, it is reasonable to assume that the second modality's degree of influence is varied at different time locations. Therefore, the last phase of the algorithm runs across the entire unimodal time course. In other words, the DT for each time window's location for each participant was calculated between the location of the unimodal window and the location of the correlation peak with the crossmodal ERP. For each of the time windows, an average DT was computed for each group. It has been suggested (Goswami, 2011) that dyslexic individuals suffer from difficulties at processing information presented at rates corresponding to the occurrence of syllabic information in speech, and critical for speech comprehension (4–7 Hz, Giraud and Poeppel, 2012). Information at these frequencies arrive to the brain every 142–250 ms. Therefore, it is reasonable to assume that in the current study, where the task was to react to a single event stimulus (visual, auditory, or crossmodal type), the DT of each of the groups would differ statistically within this time area. To verify this assumption, a series of *t*-test analyses was run on the DT parameter (that was computed based on each of the time windows taken from the time area of 140–250 ms) to assess whether there was a significant difference between the two groups.

IMPLEMENTATION OF PHASE C ON BOTH MODALITIES

The procedure was run twice, once for each modality. The window locations were set between 50 and 650 ms. Each successive time window was moved in increments of 10 ms (i.e., the second time span was centered at 60 ms, the third at 70 ms, etc.; see **Figure 3** for a full flowchart description of the cross-correlation algorithm).

RESULTS

EXPERIMENTAL BEHAVIORAL MEASURES:

In order to investigate task accuracy and RT when processing visual, auditory and crossmodal integration, an analysis of variance (ANOVA) in a 2 × 3 design (Group (dyslexic

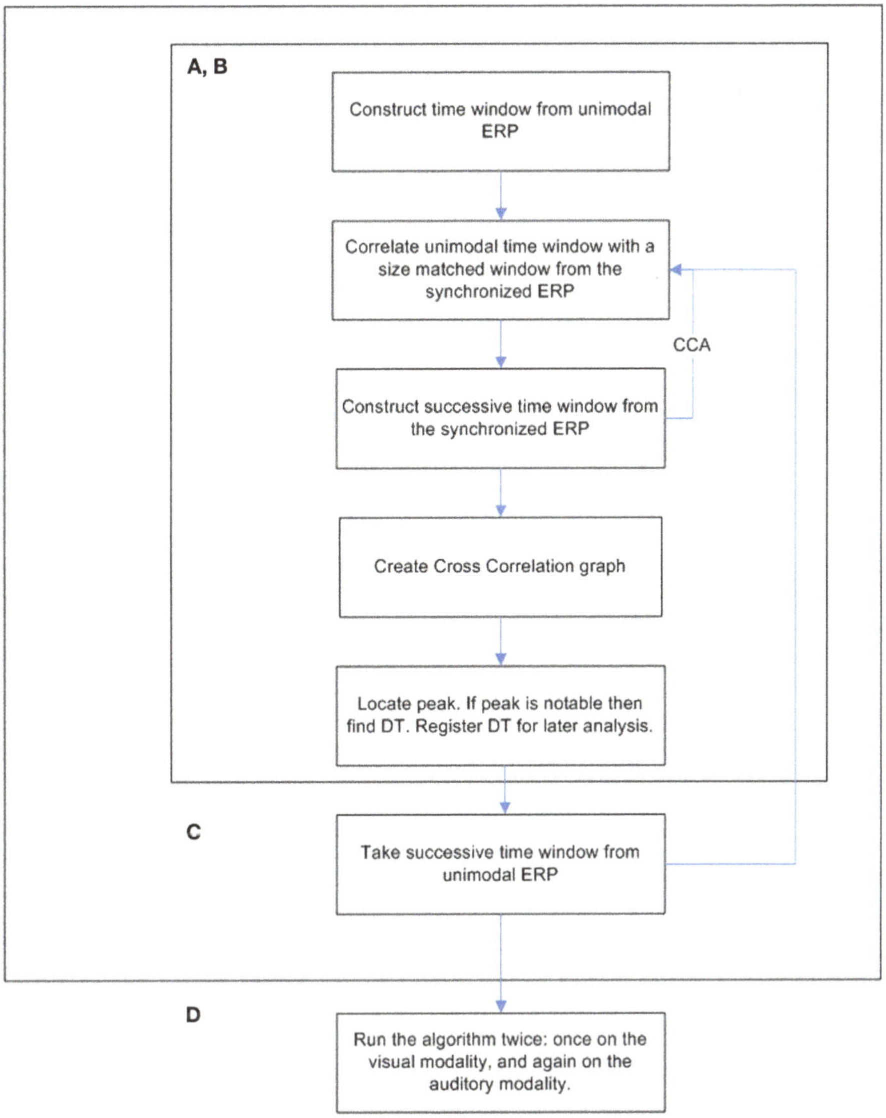

FIGURE 3 | The cross-correlation algorithm flow chart.

Xnon-impaired readers) × conditions (visual-only × auditory-only × crossmodal) was employed for RT and Accuracy separately. No significant between-group differences were found in accuracy [$F_{(1, 34)} = 2.48$, $p > 0.05$]. A significant Condition effect was obtained [$F_{(2, 68)} = 50.2$, $p < 0.001$] which stemmed from a lower performance under the auditory only condition for both groups (**Table 2**). No significant group by Condition interaction was found [$F_{(2, 68)} = 0.22$, $p > 0.05$].

The analysis of the RT data revealed a significant group effect [$F_{(1, 34)} = 4.45$, $p < 0.05$], but no significant condition effect [$F_{(2, 68)} = 1.2$, $p > 0.05$] and no significant group by condition interaction [$F_{(2, 68)} = 1.44$, $p > 0.05$].

ERP CROSS-CORRELATION ANALYSIS RESULTS

In order to investigate the influence of the presence of one modality on the SOP of the other modality, several cross-correlation analyses were obtained on averaged on-going ERP. The first analysis was obtained in order to investigate the influence of the auditory modality on the SOP of the visual one and the second analysis investigated the influence the visual modality on SOP of the auditory one. The cross-correlation analysis was run between sequential time windows taken from each unimodal condition and the crossmodal condition. The cross-correlation analysis outcome measure, the visual and auditory DT, was then used to compare between-modalities' influence and between group differences.

Table 2 | Mean (and Standard Deviation) for the dyslexic and non-impaired readers of the behavioral reading and experimental measures.

	Dyslexic readers	Non-impaired readers	*t*	*p*
Visual correct responses (%)	73 (20.8)	83 (16)	1.43	n.s
Auditory correct responses (%)	65 (19.5)	73 (16.3)	1.02	n.s
Visual + Auditory correct responses (%)	71.8 (18.7)	83.3 (14.2)	1.68	n.s
Visual reaction time (ms)	669 (115)	565 (122)	2.23	<0.05
Auditory reaction time (ms)	692 (110)	586 (129)	2.29	<0.05
Visual + auditory reaction time (ms)	639 (136)	587 (66)	1.12	n.s

Based on the size of the correlation between the unimodal data and the crossmodal ERP data within an allotted time frame, it can be inferred that a given time window from the unimodal condition exists in the crossmodal ERP data (see **Figure 4**).

For most participants, a notable peak could be identified (see **Figure 4A**), though results should be interpreted with caution as the graph's shape did not always indicate successful correlation strength (see **Figures 4B,C**). For example, iteration B's dataset is too noisy to determine the peak's location because of an artificial waveform and iteration C's is very local and low. Therefore, inclusion conditions were developed and applied: only cross-correlation graphs which had a peak which was located no more than 50 ms before or after the time of the unimodal window were included in the computation of the DT average. The time window total width of 100 ms (50 ms before and after the time window location) was based on previous evidence that asserted that the variance of ERP component time locations is normally distributed in a time area of less than 50 ms before and after the component mean time location (for example, see Simon et al., 2007; Maurer et al., 2008; Spironelli and Angrilli, 2009). In addition, the graphs could not contain more than 3 additional local peaks within the given time window. These criteria kept distorted datasets out of the further analysis (see Phase B). **Figure 5** shows the percentage of participants included in the process in every time window location. **Figures 5A,B** reveal the percentage of participants included in each time window analysis throughout the visual and auditory information process analysis, respectively. Overall, a relatively low number of participants from both groups were included in the visual analysis in the time areas of 50–150 and 450 ms to the end (**Figure 5A**). It is interesting to note that toward the end of the trial, the percentage of dyslexic readers included in the analysis decreased more slowly than the percentage of included non-impaired readers. In the auditory analysis (**Figure 5B**), the percentage rate of included participants in both groups remained constant from the beginning of the trial until about 500 ms.

In order to investigate the influence of one modality's activation on the SOP of the other modality, a DT for each of the participants and for each of the time windows was computed (**Figure 6**). A *t*-test analysis was applied for time windows located within the time area of 140–250 ms (**Table 3**), to determine if there was a between-group difference in each of the

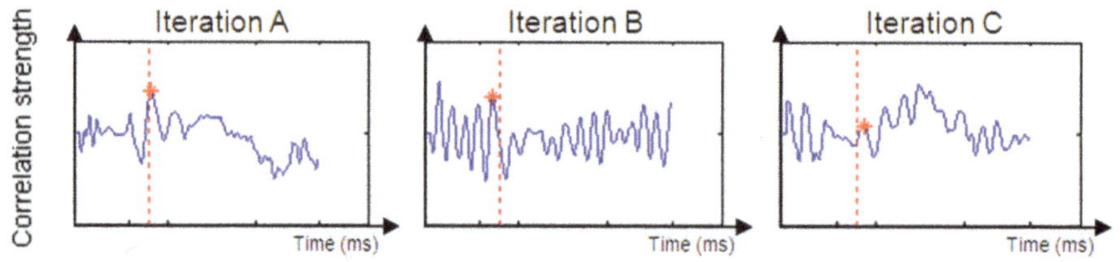

FIGURE 4 | Examples of a successful correlation result (Iteration A) and unsuccessful correlation result (Iterations B and C). Iteration **(A)** produced a positive peak near the original time of the unimodal window. Iteration **(B)**'s dataset is too noisy to suppose that the value of DT is reliable. Iteration **(C)**'s peak is to low and expresses a weak correlation between the two datasets.

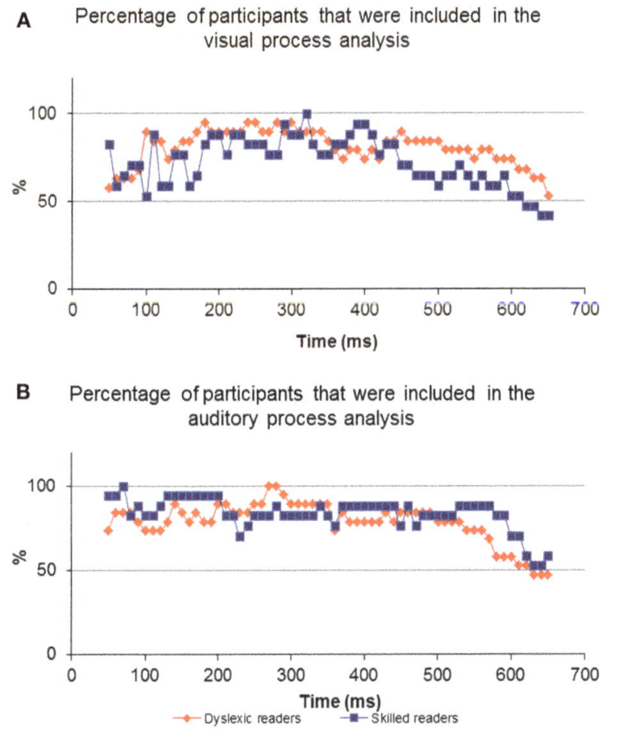

FIGURE 5 | The percentage of participants included in every comparison. Note the inverted 'U' shape of the visual process graph where at the beginning and end of the process the percentage of participants is relatively low compared to the middle. In contrast to the visual process's graph, the auditory graph is stable at the beginning.

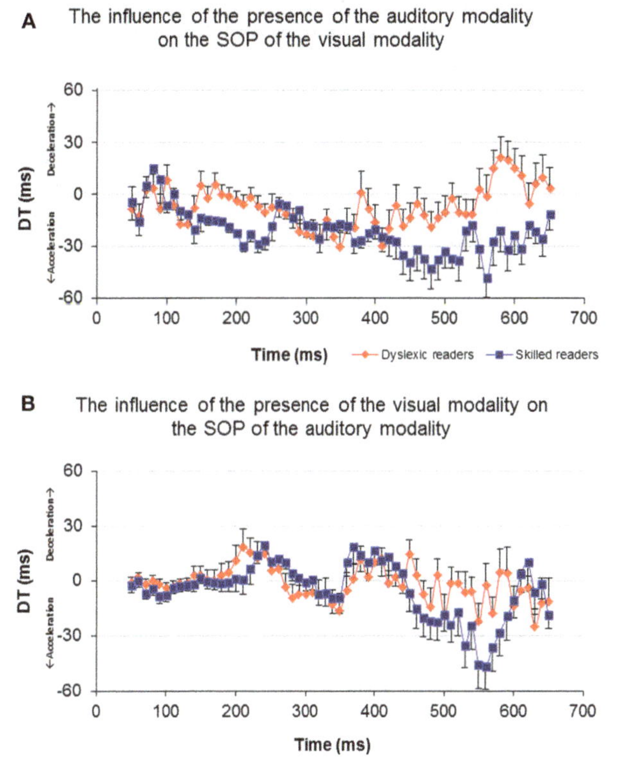

FIGURE 6 | Average DT of the two groups for each time window. Axis X represents time and axis Y represents DT. **(A)** The DT results of the visual-only and the crossmodal ERPs. **(B)** The DT results of the auditory-only and the crossmodal ERPs.

time windows (it is important to note here that a *t*-test was used to assess between-group differences rather than repeated measures analysis of variance (rmANOVA) due to the number of degrees of freedom and the relatively insufficient number of participants in this study). When the DT was based on the influence of the auditory modality on the SOP of the visual modality, significant between-group differences were found in the time area of 170 ms through 240 ms (**Figure 6A**, **Table 3**). In contrast, no significant between-group differences were found when the DT was based on the influence of the visual modality on the SOP of the auditory modality (**Figure 6B**). Nevertheless, note the positive peak (de-acceleration) in the value of the non-impaired readers' DT in the time area of 240 ms, and of the dyslexic readers' similarly shaped peak occurring at 210 ms.

Table 3 | The comparison between the groups' DT computed from the Visual modality time windows taken from the time area of 140–250 ms.

Window location (ms)	$t_{(35)}$	*p*
140	1.157	0.258
150	1.595	0.122
160	1.426	0.167
170	2.506	0.019
180	2.553	0.016
190	2.872	0.007
200	3.033	0.005
210	3.645	0.001
220	3.022	0.005
230	2.7	0.011
240	2.199	0.036
250	1.022	0.315

DISCUSSION

The purpose of this experiment was to investigate the effect of one modality on the SOP of the second modality. Stimuli of visual and auditory modalities were employed in a unimodal and crossmodal presentation. Overall, our results support the notion that there is in fact an interaction between modalities during information processing, consistent with previous research. Furthermore, the significant differences that were found between dyslexic and non-impaired readers highlight the difficulty which dyslexic readers face in synchronizing processing between the visual and auditory modalities.

Hypothesis 1 suggested that the ERP data of the crossmodal condition would contain unimodal visual and auditory elements. It is suggested that the peak in the correlation graph results supports this assumption (**Figure 2A**). As described previously, a cross-correlation analysis computing successive correlation coefficients between unimodal ERP within a specific time window and successive crossmodal ERP time windows sliding along the entire crossmodal trial was implemented. More specifically, the current algorithm took a fraction (i.e., 100 ms) of the temporal information processing from a unimodal ERP trial and searched for a matching fraction of information processing throughout the crossmodal ERP trial. It is apparent from **Figure 2A** that throughout the sequence, the correlation strength was mainly low and randomized. However, at a particular point in time, an increase in the correlation strength appeared, usually a short distance in time from the time location of the unimodal window. It may be argued that this constitutes evidence for the presence of the same fraction of information processing that occurs in the crossmodal ERP. A short while after the correlation strength reaches its peak, it starts to decline as the unimodal window passes its identical fraction of information processing and continues toward the time area in which low and randomized similarity appear.

Hypothesis 2 implied that the presence of a second modality will have an effect on the SOP of a first modality. **Figure 2B** reveals that the correlation graph's peak location is not in the exact location of the unimodal time window. Furthermore, data analysis across the entire time domain and across participants revealed that the correlation peak location may appear shortly before or after the unimodal window's time location. It is suggested that the time difference between the two locations (i.e., DT) is a reflection of the degree of influence of the second modality on the first modality's SOP when presented simultaneously. If the closest matching fraction of information processing taken from a unimodal ERP was found at a later time location (i.e., DT is positive), then this comparison indicates that there was a delay in the processing of the modality in the crossmodal ERP, meaning that SOP decelerated. Conversely, if the DT was negative, then the location of the same fraction of information processing existed at an earlier point of time in the crossmodal ERP compared to the unimodal ERP. Consequently, this constitutes evidence of SOP acceleration in the modality.

The neurobiology of the visual system is considered to be constructed from two major pathways (the dorsal and ventral), where visual information enters the retina and travels to the visual cortex. Information reaches the visual cortex about 100–150 ms post visual stimulus presentation. Auditory processing begins at the ear and initial auditory information reaches the auditory cortex through several pathways about 70–100 ms post stimulus presentation (see Breznitz, 2006 for review). Both modality pathways prepare initial sensory information for higher cognitive processing. As the pathways process information rapidly and in areas deep within the brain, it is expected that their operations will not have a strong impact on EEG data. Therefore, comparing the visual-only ERP and the crossmodal ERP during the first 150 ms of data collection will result in a relatively lower "success" rate when locating the visual information processing fraction in the crossmodal ERP (**Figure 5A**). However, as time progresses and processing moves from deeper brain areas to higher cortical structures, the size of the common components in the two ERP sets increases. Therefore, the algorithm has more success in finding common visual components 150 ms post stimulus presentation. As a result, a higher percentage of participants are included in the analysis from 150–450 ms. When finding the common components between the auditory-only ERP and crossmodal ERP, a higher "success" rate was found at an earlier time frame (50 ms post stimulus presentation) as initial auditory processing is faster than initial visual processing (**Figure 5B**).

Shifting our focus to the end of processing within the visual modality, a differential between the dyslexic reading group and non-impaired readers is apparent beginning at around 450 ms post stimulus presentation (**Figure 5A**). The differential begins at this point in time due to the decrease in the percentage of non-impaired readers included in the analysis. The percentage of dyslexic readers included in the analysis remains high for a longer period of time. The decrease in the percentage rate of included participants for analysis implies that among the non-impaired readers, the shared elements of the two ERPs end at that point. Thus, the duration of visual information processing is approximately 450 ms, and, as such, the ERP data appearing after 450 ms no longer deals with visual information, which results in a lower "success" rate of finding a sufficient correlation between the two datasets. However, visual information processing lasts longer in the dyslexic group and as such, the percentage of participants starts to decrease approximately 50 ms later. This is an important difference between the two groups as it provides evidence for slow speed of visual processing among the dyslexic readers as compared to non-impaired readers.

As can be seen in **Figure 6A**, non-impaired readers' visual processing "benefits" from the presence of the auditory synchronized stimulus as the value of DT is negative almost throughout the entire timeline (i.e., their SOP of visual information is accelerated). A similar but lower effect was observed among the dyslexic readers. Furthermore, a significant difference was found between the values of DT appearing around 170 and 240 ms where the DT of the non-impaired readers was more negative than that of the dyslexic readers. This time area is considered to be related to perception and has been suggested by previous research to be related to the dyslexia phenomenon (Maurer et al., 2006, 2008). On the other hand, processing within the auditory modality was not affected by the presence of a visual stimulus appearing from about 50–200 ms in both groups (**Figure 6B**). The non-impaired readers began to decelerate their auditory SOP around 210 ms. Similar deceleration was observed among the dyslexic readers but 40 ms earlier. Based on the reasoning that visual processing is slower than auditory processing, we provide additional evidence that in the normal information processing sequence, whenever there is a need to synchronize the two modalities, the brain accelerates processing within the visual modality and decelerates processing within the auditory modality. Unlike the non-impaired readers, the dyslexic readers do not accelerate their visual SOP to the same degree (**Figure 6A**). Moreover, they decelerated their auditory processing too early (**Figure 6B**). It is possible that this leads to asynchrony within the two modalities and to an overall slowness of information processing.

Failure at the level of lower sensory processing, which was the focus of the present study, may accumulate in the higher order levels of processing such as processing letters, syllables, words, sentences, and general reading comprehension. As reading activates sequential parallel visual and auditory processes, synchronization between the two modalities is necessary for successful reading accuracy and rate. The results obtained in the current study concerning common elements between single modality and crossmodal processing lend support to the synchronization hypothesis (Breznitz and Misra, 2003).

Prior studies in the field of temporal processing have been focused on the ability of the brain to process input at different frequencies (Buzsaki and Draghun, 2004; Luo and Poeppel, 2007; Power et al., 2012). Specifically, the temporal sampling framework of dyslexia (Goswami, 2011) suggests that the dyslexic reader may suffer from atypical processing of information occurring at frequencies between 4 and 7 Hz, i.e., every 142–250 ms (theta band, and possibly lower frequencies). The current results indicate an apparent failure of dyslexic readers in processing information occurring within the specific time area of 150–250 ms following a single event stimulus (**Figure 6**). The non-impaired readers demonstrated a non-symmetric effect of one modality on the other, in which the occurrence of bimodal information processing accelerated the SOP of the visual modality and decelerated the SOP of the auditory modality at the time area of 170–250 ms. This concurrent change in the two modalities' SOP was not obtained among the dyslexic readers as their visual modality's SOP did not accelerate in the presence of auditory information processing (**Figure 6**). It could be that, as proposed by the temporal sampling framework of dyslexia (Goswami, 2011), atypical neural oscillations at the theta frequency band for auditory processing among the dyslexic readers impact negatively the SOP of their visual modality processing, by preventing it from accelerating adequately. Thus, it may be suggested that these results provide additional support for the difficulty of the dyslexic individual to process a 4–7 Hz inflow of information and moreover, support the temporal sampling framework of dyslexia (Goswami, 2011; Power et al., 2012).

ACKNOWLEDGMENT

This research was funded by the Edmond J. Safra Philanthropic Foundation.

REFERENCES

Adams, M. J. (1990). *Beginning to Read: Learning and Thinking About Print.* Cambridge, MA: MIT Press.

Amitay, S., Ben-Yehuda, G., Banai, K., and Ahissar, M. (2002a). Disabled readers suffer from visual and auditory impairments but not from a specific magnocellular deficit. *Brain* 125, 2272. doi: 10.1093/brain/awf231

Amitay, S., Ben-Yehudah, G., and Nelken, I. (2002b). Auditory processing deficits in reading disabled adults. *J. Assoc. Res. Otolaryngol.* 3, 302. doi: 10.1007/s101620010093

Badian, N. A. (1997). Dyslexia and the double deficit hypothesis. *Ann. Dyslexia* 47, 69. doi: 10.1007/s11881-997-0021-y

Barker, T. A., Torgeson, J. K., and Wagner, R. K. (1992). The role of orthographic processing skills on five different reading tasks. *Read. Res. Q.* 335. doi: 10.2307/747673

Ben-Artzi, E., and Marks, L. E. (1995). Visual-auditory interaction in speeded classification: role of stimulus difference. *Percept. Psychophys.* 57, 1151. doi: 10.3758/BF03208371

Ben-Yehudah, G., and Ahissar, M. (2004). Sequential spatial frequency discrimination is consistently impaired among adult dyslexics. *Vision Res.* 44, 1047. doi: 10.1016/j.visres.2003.12.001

Berninger, V. (1990). Multiple orthographic codes: key to alternative instructional methodologies for developing the orthographic-phonological connections underlying word identification. *School Psych. Rev.* 19, 518.

Berninger, V. (2001). Understanding the 'Lexia'in dyslexia: a multidisciplinary team approach to learning disabilities. *Ann. Dyslexia* 51, 21. doi: 10.1007/s11881-001-0004-3

Botuck, S., and Turkewitz, G. (1990). Intersensory functioning: auditory visual pattern equivalence in younger and older children. *Dev. Psychol.* 26, 115. doi: 10.1037/0012-1649.26.1.115

Breznitz, Z. (2001). "The determinants of reading fluency: a comparison of dyslexic and average readers," in *Dyslexia, Fluency and the Brain,* ed M. Wolf (Timonium, MD: York Press), 245–276.

Breznitz, Z. (2002). Asynchrony of visual-orthographic and auditory-phonological word recognition processes: an underlying factor in dyslexia. *Read. Writ.* 15, 15. doi: 10.1023/A:1013864203452

Breznitz, Z. (2003). Speed of phonological and orthographic processing as factors in dyslexia: electrophysiological evidence. *Genetic Soc. Gen. Psychol. Monogr.* 129, 183–206.

Breznitz, Z. (2006). *Fluency in Reading: Synchronization of Brain Processes.* Mahwah: Lawrence Erlbaum Associates.

Breznitz, Z. (2008). Special issue on the use of electrophysiological measures in reading research. *J. Neurolinguistics* 21, 277. doi: 10.1016/j.jneuroling.2007.02.001

Breznitz, Z., and Misra, M. (2003). Speed of processing of the visual–orthographic and auditory–phonological systems in adult dyslexics: The contribution of "asynchrony" to word recognition deficits. *Brain Lang.* 85, 486. doi: 10.1016/S0093-934X(03)00071-3

Breznitz, Z., Shaul, S., Horowitz-Kraus, T., Sela, I., Nevat, M., and Karni, A. (2013). Enhanced reading by training with imposed time-constraint in typical and dyslexic adults. *Nat. Commun.* 4:1486. doi: 10.1038/ncomms2488

Brickenkamp, R. (1981). *Test d2: Aufmerk-sankeits-delastungf-test.* Gottingen: Varlag fur Psychology.

British Psychological Society. (1999). "Dyslexia literacy and psychological assessment," in *Report by a Working Party of the Division of Educational and Child Psychology* (Leicester: British Psychological Society).

Bruck, M. (1992). Persistence of dyslexics' phonological awareness deficits. *Dev. Psychol.* 28, 874–886. doi: 10.1037/0012-1649.28.5.874

Buzsaki, G., and Draghun, A. (2004). Neuronal oscillations in cortical networks. *Science* 304, 1926–1929. doi: 10.1126/science.1099745

Chen, Q., and Zhou, X. (2013). Vision dominates at the preresponse level and audition dominates at the response level in cross-modal interaction: behavioral and neural evidence. *J. Neurosci.* 33, 7109–7121. doi: 10.1523/JNEUROSCI.1985-12.2013

Cunningham, A. E., and Stanovich, K. E. (1990). Assessing print exposure and orthographic processing skill in children: a quick measure of reading experience. *J. Educ. Psychol.* 82, 733. doi: 10.1037/0022-0663.82.4.733

Egeth, H. E., and Sager, L. C. (1977). On the locus of visual dominance (vision over audition). *Percept. Psychophys.* 22, 77. doi: 10.3758/BF03206083

Fujisaki, W., and Nahida, S. (2005). Temporal frequency characteristics of synchrony–asynchrony discrimination of audio-visual signals. *Exp. Brain Res.* 166, 455–464. doi: 10.1007/s00221-005-2385-8

Ghajar, J., and Ivry, R. B. (2008). The predictive brain state: asynchrony in disorders of attention? *Neurorehabil. Neural Repair* 22, 217–227. doi: 10.1177/1545968308315600

Ghitza, O., and Greenberg, S. (2009). On the possible role of brain rhythms in speech perception: intelligibility of time-compressed speech with periodic and aperiodic insertions of silence. *Phonetica* 66, 113–126. doi: 10.1159/000208934

Giraud, A. L., and Poeppel, D. (2012). Cortical oscillations and speech processing: emerging computational principles and operations. *Nat. Neurosci.* 15, 511–517. doi: 10.1038/nn.3063

Goswami, U., Gerson, D., and Astruc, L. (2010). Amplitude envelope perception, phonology and prosodic sensitivity in children with developmental dyslexia. *Read. Writ.* 23, 995–1019. doi: 10.1007/s11145-009-9186-6

Goswami, U. (2011). A temporal sampling framework for developmental dyslexia. *Trends Cogn. Sci.* 15, 3–10. doi: 10.1016/j.tics.2010.10.001

Groth, K., Lachmann, T., Riecker, A., Muthmann, I., and Steinbrink, C. (2011). Developmental dyslexics show deficits in the processing of temporal auditory information in German vowel length discrimination. *Read. Writ.* 24, 285–303. doi: 10.1007/s11145-009-9213-7

Heil, M., Rolke, B., Engelkamp, J., Roesler, F., Oezcan, M., and Hennighausen, E. (1999). Event-related brain potentials during recognition of ordinary and bizarre action phrases following verbal and subject-performed encoding conditions. *Eur. J. Cogn. Psychol.* 11, 261. doi: 10.1080/713752313

Hulme, C., Goetz, K., Gooch, D., Adams, J., and Snowling, M. J. (2007). Paired-associate learning phoneme awareness, and learning to read. *J. Exp. Child Psychol.* 96, 150–166. doi: 10.1016/j.jecp.2006.09.002

Jasper, H. H. (1958). The 10-20 electrode system of the international federation. *Electroencephalogr. Clin. Neurophysiol. Evoked Potentials* I, 371.

Jones, M. W., Branigan, H. P., Parra, M. A., and Logie, R. H. (2013). Cross-modal binding in developmental dyslexia. *J. Exp. Psychol. Learn. Mem. Cogn.* 39, 1807–1822. doi: 10.1037/a0033334

Koppen, C., Levitan, C. A., and Spencer, C. (2009). A signal detection study of the Colavita visual dominance effect. *Exp. Brain Res.* 196, 353–360. doi: 10.1007/s00221-009-1853-y

Lachmann, T., Berti, S., Kujala, T., and Schroger, E. (2005). Diagnostic subgroups of developmental dyslexia have different deficits in neural processing of tones and phonemes. *Int. J. Psychophysiol.* 56, 105–120. doi: 10.1016/j.ijpsycho.2004.11.005

Leonard, C., Eckert, M., Lombardino, L. J., Oakland, T., Kranzler, J., Mohr, C. M. et al. (2001). Anatomical risk factors for phonological dyslexia. *Cerebral Cortex* 11, 148–157. doi: 10.1093/cercor/11.2.148

Liberman, I. Y., and Shankweiler, D. (1991). "Phonology and beginning to read: a tutorial," in *Learning to Read: Basic Research and its Implications,* eds L. Reiben and C. A. Perfetti (Hillsdale, NJ: Lawrence Erlbaum Associates), 3–18.

Livingstone, M. S. (1991). Physiological and anatomical evidence for a magnocellular defect in developmental dyslexia. *Proc. Natl. Acad. Sci. U.S.A.* 88, 7943. doi: 10.1073/pnas.88.18.7943

Llinas, R. (1993). Is dyslexia a dyschronia? *Ann. N.Y. Acad. Sci.* 682, 48. doi: 10.1111/j.1749-6632.1993.tb22958.x

Luo, H., and Poeppel, D. (2007). Phase patterns of neuronal responses reliably discriminate speech in human auditory cortex. *Neuron* 54, 1001–1010. doi: 10.1016/j.neuron.2007.06.004

Lyon, G. R., and Shaywitz, S. E. (2003). Defining dyslexia, comorbidity,teachers' knowledge of lLanguage and reading: a definition of dyslexia. *Ann. Dyslexia* 53, 1–14. doi: 10.1007/s11881-003-0001-9

Marchant, J. L., and Driver, J. (2013). Visual and audiovisual effects of isochronous timing on visual perception and brain activity. *Cereb. Cortex* 23, 1290–1298. doi: 10.1093/cercor/bhs095

MATAL Battery. (2007). *Diagnostic Battery for the Assessment of Learning Functions.* Jerusalem: The Council for Higher Education and the Center for Psychometric Tests.

Maurer, U., Brem, S., Brem, F., Kranz, K., Bucher, R., Benz, P., et al. (2006). Coarse neural tuning for print peaks when children learn to read. *Neuroimage,* 33, 749–758. doi: 10.1016/j.neuroimage.2006.06.025

Maurer, U., Rossion, B., and McCandliss, B. D. (2008). Category specificity in early perception: face and word N170 responses differ in both lateralization and habituation properties. *Front. Hum. Neurosci.* 2:18. doi: 10.3389/neuro.09.018.2008

Melara, R. D., and O'Brien, T. P. (1987). Interaction between synesthetically corresponding dimensions. *J. Exp. Psychol.* 116, 323.

Meyler, A., and Breznitz, Z. (2003). Processing of phonological, orthographic and cross-modal word representations among adult dyslexic and normal readers. *Read. Writ.* 16, 785.

Mishra, J., Martinez, A., Sejnowski, T. J., and Hillyard, S. A. (2007). Early cross-modal interactions in auditory and visual cortex underlie a sound-induced visual illusion. *J. Neurosci.* 27, 4120–4131. doi: 10.1523/JNEUROSCI.4912-06.2007

Morris, J. S., Ohman, A., and Dolan, R. J. (1998). Conscious and unconscious emotional learning in the human amygdala. *Nature* 393, 467–470. doi: 10.1038/30976

Neil, W., Roach, N. W., Heron, J., Whitaker, D., and McGraw. P. V. (2011). Asynchrony adaptation reveals neural population code for audio-visual timing *Proc. R. Soc. B* 278, 1314–1322. doi: 10.1098/rspb.2010.1737

Nelson-Wong, E., Howarth, S., Winter, D., and Callaghan, J. (2009). Application of autocorrelation and cross-correlation analyses in human movement and rehabilitation research. *J. Orthop. Sports Phys. Ther.* 39, 287–295. doi: 10.2519/jospt.2009.2969

Orgil Medical Equipment. (1997). *Analysis Software User's Manual for the Brain Performance Measurement System.* Ein Ayala.

Posner, M. I., Nissen, M. J., and Klein, R. M. (1976). Visual dominance: an information-processing account of its origins and significance. *Psychol. Rev.* 83, 157. doi: 10.1037/0033-295X.83.2.157

Power, A. J., Mead, N., Bames, L., and Goswami U. (2012). Neural entrainment to rhythmically presented auditory, visual, and audio-visual speech in children. *Front. Psychol.* 3:216. doi: 10.3389/fpsyg.2012.00216

Rosenzweig, M. R., and Bennet, E. L. (1996). Psychobiology of plasticity: effects of training and experience on brain and behavior. *Behav. Brain Res.* 78, 57. doi: 10.1016/0166-4328(95)00216-2

Saito, D. N., Yoshimura, K., Kochiyama, T., Okada, T., Honda, M., and Sadato, N. (2005). Cross-modal binding and activated attentional networks during audio-visual speech integration: a functional MRI study. *Cereb. Cortex* 15, 1750–1760. doi: 10.1093/cercor/bhi052

Schmolesky, M. T., Wang, Y., Hanes, D. P., Thompson, K. G., Leutgeb, S., Schall, J. D., et al. (1998). Signal timing across the macaque visual system. *J. Neurophysiol.* 79, 3272–3278.

Sela, I., Breznitz, S., and Breznitz, Z. (2008). The correlation-based model: An alternative system for analyzing ERP data in cognitive research. *J. Neurlinguistics* 21, 305–332. doi: 10.1016/j.jneuroling.2007.07.003

Share, D. L. (1994). "Deficient phonological processing in disabled readers implicates processing deficits beyond the phonological module," in *Current Directions in Dyslexia Research,* eds K. P. van den Bos, L. S. Siegel, D. J. Bakker, and D. L. Share (Lisse: Swets and Zeitlinger), 149–167.

Shaywitz, S., and Shaywitz, B. (2008). Paying attention to reading: the neurobiology of reading and dyslexia. *Dev. Psychopathol.* 20, 1329–1349. doi: 10.1017/S0954579408000631

Simon, G., Rebai, M., Petit, L., and Bernard, C. (2007). N170 ERPs could represent a logographic processing strategy in visual word recognition. *Behav. Brain Func.* 3, 21. doi: 10.1186/1744-9081-3-21

Snowling, M. J. (1995). Phonological processing and developmental dyslexia. *J. Res. Read.* 18, 132–138. doi: 10.1111/j.1467-9817.1995.tb00079.x

Spironelli, C., and Angrilli, A. (2009). Developmental aspects of automatic word processing: language lateralization of early ERP components in children, young adults and middle-aged subjects. *Biol. Psychol.* 35–45. doi: 10.1016/j.biopsycho.2008.01.012

Stanovich, K. E. (1988). Explaining the differences between the dyslexic and the garden-variety poor reader: the phonological-core variable-difference model. *J. Learn. Disabil.* 21, 590–612. doi: 10.1177/002221948802 101003

Stanovich, K. E., and West, R. F. (1989). Exposure to print and orthographic processing. *Read. Res. Q.* 24, 402. doi: 10.2307/747605

Stein, J. (1993). Dyslexia-impaired temporal information processing? *Ann. N.Y. Acad. Sci.* 682, 83–86. doi: 10.1111/j.1749-6632.1993.tb22961.x

Stein, J. (2001). The magnocellular theory of developmental dyslexia. *Dyslexia* 7, 12. doi: 10.1002/dys.186

Stein, J., and Talcott, J. (1999). Impaired neuronal timing in developmental dyslexia—the magnocellular hypothesis. *Dyslexia* 5, 59–77. doi: 10.1002/(SICI) 1099-0909(199906)5:2<59::AID-DYS134>3.0.CO;2-F

Stein, J., Talcott, J., and Witton, C. (2001). "The sensorimotor basis of developmental dyslexia," in *Dyslexia: Theory and Good Practice,* ed A. J. Fawcett (London: Whurr), 65–88.

Stein, J., and Walsh, V. (1997). To see but not to read; the magnocellular theory of dyslexia. *Trends Neurosci.* 20, 147–152. doi: 10.1016/S0166-2236(96) 01005-3

Tallal, P. (1980). Language and reading: some perceptual prerequisites. *Bull. Orton Soc.* 30, 170. doi: 10.1007/BF02653716

Tallal, P., Merzenich, M. M., Miller, S., and Jenkins, W. (1998). Language learning impairments: Integrating basic science, technology, and remediation. *Exp. Brain Res.* 123, 210. doi: 10.1007/s002210050563

Tallal, P., Miller, S., and Fitch, R. S. (1993). Neurobiological basis of speech: a case for the preeminence of temporal processing. *Ann. N.Y. Acad. Sci.* 682, 27. doi: 10.1111/j.1749-6632.1993.tb22957.x

Temple, E., Poldrack, R. A., Salidis, J., Deutsch, G. K., Tallal, P., Merzenich, M. M. et al. (2001). Disrupted neural responses to phonological and orthographic processing in dyslexic children: An fMRI study. *Neuroreport* 12, 299–307. doi: 10.1097/00001756-200102120-00024

Vellutino, F. R., Fletcher, J. M., Snowling, M. J., and Scanlon, D. M. (2004). Specific reading disability (dyslexia): What have we learned in the past four decades? *J. Child Psychol. Psychiatry* 45, 2. doi: 10.1046/j.0021-9630.2003.00305.x

Wechsler, D. (1997). *WAIS-III Administration and Scoring Manual.* San Antonio, TX, The Psychological Corporation.

Wolf, M., and Bowers, P. (2000). The question of naming-speed deficits in developmental reading disability: an introduction to the Double-Deficit Hypothesis. *J. Learn. Disabil.* 33, 322–324. doi: 10.1177/002221940003300404

Woody, C. D. (1967). Characterization of an adaptive filter for the analysis of variable latency neuroelectric signals. *Med. Biol. Eng.* 5, 539. doi: 10.1007/BF02474247

Zecker, S. G. (1991). The orthographic code: developmental trends in reading-disabled and normally-achieving children. *Ann. Dyslexia* 41, 178. doi: 10.1007/BF02648085

13

A similar correction mechanism in slow and fluent readers after suboptimal landing positions

Benjamin Gagl*, Stefan Hawelka and Florian Hutzler

Department of Psychology, Centre for Neurocognitive Research, University of Salzburg, Salzburg, Austria

***Correspondence:**
Benjamin Gagl, Department of Psychology, Centre for Neurocognitive Research, University of Salzburg, Hellbrunnerstrasse 34, Salzburg 5020, Austria
e-mail: benjamin.gagl@sbg.ac.at

The present eye movements study investigated the optimal viewing position (OVP) and inverted-optimal viewing position (I-OVP) effects in slow readers. The basis of these effects is a phenomenon called corrective re-fixations, which describes a short saccade from a suboptimal landing position (word beginning or end) to the center of the word. The present study found corrective re-fixations in slow readers, which was evident from the I-OVP effects in first fixation durations, the OVP effect in number of fixations and the OVP effect in re-fixation probability. The main result is that slow readers, despite being characterized by a fragmented eye movement pattern during reading, nevertheless share an intact mechanism for performing corrective re-fixations. This correction mechanism is not linked to linguistic processing, but to visual and oculomotor processes, which suggests the integrity of oculomotor and visual processes in slow readers.

Keywords: eye movements, reading, landing position, slow readers, corrective re-fixations

INTRODUCTION

The initial landing position of the eyes on a word affects the speed of word recognition (e.g., O'Regan and Jacobs, 1992; Hutzler et al., 2008). Typically, a fixation position slightly left to the word center, which is termed as the optimal viewing position (OVP), allows fast word recognition. In contrast, landing on the initial or the final letters of a word increases word processing times (see **Figure 1**). This is a classical finding from visual word recognition research, which could be replicated in different languages (Finnish: Hyönä and Bertram, 2011; German: Hutzler et al., 2008; French: O'Regan and Jacobs, 1992; Vitu et al., 2007) and different age groups (e.g., Aghababian and Nazir, 2000). Eye movement evidence suggests that increased reading times at suboptimal landing positions are the result of a correction mechanism that precedes visual word recognition to provide high quality visual information to the reading system. **Figure 1A** (bottom) presents a schematic example of a corrective re-fixation. Also, in **Figure 1B**, a schematic description of the OVP effect in reading time is presented and effects on eye movements that are described in the following.

In reading paradigms, for example, silent sentence or passage reading, word processing measures such as the number of fixations and the percentage of re-fixations typically show an OVP effect. The number of fixations and the percentage of re-fixations are lowest after landing at the word center when compared to suboptimal landing positions (**Figure 1B**; e.g., McConkie et al., 1989; Vitu et al., 2001; Nuthmann et al., 2005). Similar OVP effects were found for gaze duration. In addition, the study of Vitu et al. (2001) described the influence of landing position on the first fixation duration. The initial fixation duration showed an inverted-optimal viewing position effect (I-OVP) with the longest fixation durations at the center of the word and shorter fixations at suboptimal landing positions, that is, the word beginning or end (see **Figure 1B**). This finding was replicated in different languages (e.g., Vitu et al., 2001; Nuthmann et al., 2005; Hyönä and Bertram, 2011), age groups (Vitu et al., 2001; Huestegge et al., 2009; Joseph et al., 2009), and successfully modeled for adults (Reichle et al., 2003; Engbert et al., 2005) and children (Reichle et al., 2013).

At first sight, the I-OVP effect was counterintuitive since the initial fixation duration showed the opposite pattern compared to reading times (**Figure 1B**). To understand the I-OVP effect, the complementary OVP effects on the number of fixations and the probability of re-fixating a word, have to be taken into account. The first line of **Figure 1A** shows a standard case where a word is fixated at a preferred central location (Rayner, 1979) and recognized by a single fixation. In this case the fixation durations are the longest and influenced by linguistic word characteristics (e.g., Vitu et al., 2001). In the second line of **Figure 1A** the word *Maler* is initially fixated at the word end. After such a suboptimal fixation position the duration is typically short and accompanied by a re-fixation at the word center. The initial short fixations are not influenced by word characteristics such as word frequency (Vitu et al., 2001; Vergilino-Perez et al., 2004) or the lexicality of the letter string (i.e., word vs. pseudoword; Hutzler et al., 2008). To summarize, when readers land optimally, the initial fixation durations are longer, influenced by the linguistic properties of the word and less likely followed by an additional fixation. In case of landing at the beginning or the end of a word, initial fixation durations are shorter, not influenced by linguistic word characteristics and highly likely followed by a re-fixation.

The mechanism underlying the I-OVP–OVP effect combination is a correction process that initiates a saccade from unfavorable landing positions to the center of a word (see **Figure 1A**).

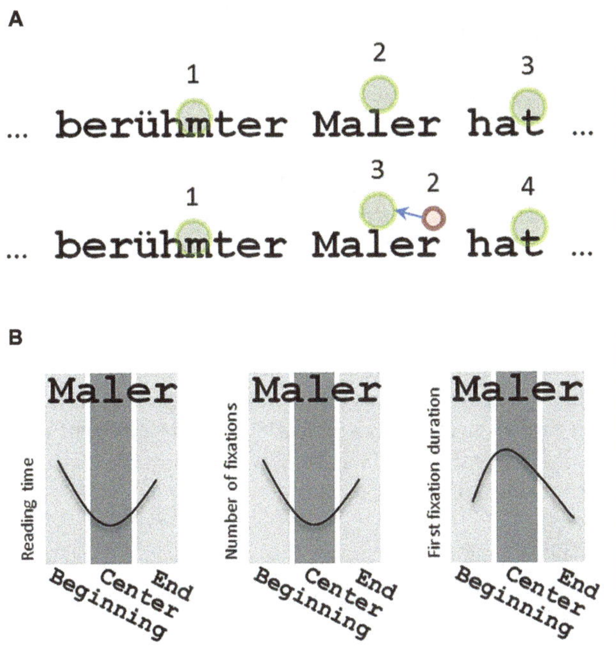

FIGURE 1 | (A) Schematic illustration of eye movements during reading. Standard reading fixations are presented as green circles and the numerals indicate the sequential order. In the lower line a corrective re-fixation occurs after suboptimal landing at the end of the word *Maler*. The initial fixation on *Maler*, presented in a smaller red circle (indicating a shorter fixation duration), is followed by a saccade (blue arrow) to set up a fixation near the word center (Hutzler et al., 2008). **(B)** The optimal viewing position effects (OVP effect) for reading times and the number of fixations for landing positions at the beginning, the center and the end of the word *Maler*. The right panel depicts the inverted optimal viewing position effect (I-OVP effect) for first fixation durations. The OVP effect shows longer reading times and a higher number of fixations after landing at the word beginning or the word end. In contrast, the I-OVP effect on first fixation durations shows the shortest fixation durations at word beginnings or ends and the longest durations at the word center. Note that, after landing at the word center of a short to medium length word (e.g., smaller than eight letters) only one fixation is typically required for word recognition (e.g., Vitu et al., 2001).

This initial information processing and saccade programming is independent from linguistic processing (Hutzler et al., 2008). In other words, after landing at an unfavorable landing position the brain recognizes that the position is off target (i.e., word center) and corrects the position by means of a fast eye movement towards the preferred location near the word center. In a study by Hutzler et al. (2008), this mechanism was labeled as corrective re-fixations and might allow the investigation of non-linguistic processing, such as visual and oculomotor processing of slow readers.

Landing position effects on slow readers (e.g., dyslexic readers) were seldom reported and, to our knowledge, there is no existing report of an I-OVP effect in fixation durations and OVP effects in the number of fixations and the re-fixation probability. Two eye movement studies (MacKeben et al., 2004; Hawelka et al., 2010) reported landing position data of dyslexic readers. These readers tend to target the word beginning more often than fluent readers. In addition, the relation between initial landing position and word length was investigated. Here the classical finding is that a fluent reader tries to initially fixate a position near the word center (Rayner, 1979). This means that for a short word of four letters the preferred viewing location is near the second letter but on an eight-letter word the preferred viewing location would be around the fourth letter. In the dyslexic readers of Hawelka et al. (2010) the influence of word length on the initial landing position was smaller than in the fluent readers. They landed more towards the word beginning (at the second letter of words with four to seven letters) than the fluent readers (who landed on the third letter; see also MacKeben et al., 2004). To our knowledge, no further investigation of, for example, a reading time measure in relation to landing position is present in the literature.

The participants of the Hawelka study were German dyslexic readers. In German, dyslexia is mainly characterized by massively impaired reading speed (e.g., Wimmer, 1993). The speed impairment is reflected in prolonged fixation durations as well as in a higher number of fixations per word in comparison to fluent readers (Hutzler and Wimmer, 2004; Dürrwächter et al., 2010; Hawelka et al., 2010). Furthermore, the slow readers exhibited markedly increased word length and frequency effects on number of fixations. In combination, the strong word length effect (e.g., in gaze durations), the high number of fixations and the initial landing position at the word beginnings of slow readers were interpreted as a serial reading strategy. Serial reading is typically present in beginning readers and reflects letter to sound conversion (e.g., Share, 1995; Ziegler and Goswami, 2005). The converted sounds are then assembled to allow access to phonological representations. After the initial phase of literacy acquisition the length effect typically decreases which is interpreted as reflecting the emergence of whole word recognition (see Rau et al., 2014, for a recent eye movement study).

Dyslexic and slow readers might stick to serial reading. From this perspective, word beginnings are reasonable targets for the initial fixation. The most prominent theory, the phonological deficit hypothesis, suggests that in dyslexic individuals the representation, storage, and retrieval of speech sounds is impaired (e.g., Snowling, 2000). Other hypotheses assume impairments in the process of connecting letters and orthographic information (e.g., an orthographic word unit) to the respective phonological representation (e.g., Wolf and Bowers, 1999; Wimmer and Schurz, 2010). These hypotheses are concerned with cognitive processes that are specific for linguistic processing during reading. Another type of deficit theories is concerned with processes during reading apart from the core linguistic processes. Examples would be deficits in visual processing (e.g., magnocellular vision; Stein and Walsh, 1997) or oculomotor processes (e.g., Pavlidis, 1981; Bucci et al., 2008; but see Kirkby et al., 2011). These processes are non-linguistic processes that accompany the core linguistic processes but are not exclusive to reading.

The main aim of the study is investigating the phenomenon of corrective re-fixations in slow readers. In particular, it is investigated whether or not slow readers also show corrective re-fixations along with OVP and I-OVP effects. If slow readers correct for unfavorable landing positions, then they should show an (1) OVP effect in the re-fixation probability, (2) OVP effect in the number of fixations and (3) an I-OVP effect on first fixation durations. In case the pattern of effects suggests such a correction procedure, it is of interest if the first fixation durations at suboptimal landing positions are (4) comparable between groups and if they are (5) influenced by word frequency or predictability. An absence of a correction mechanism as well as differences to the normal corrective pattern such as longer fixation durations at suboptimal landing positions would indicate an impairment in the non-linguistic visuo-oculomotor components of reading. For landing positions at the word center, slower readers are expected to show increased fixation durations and stronger effects of frequency and predictability in contrast to fluent readers. With regard to the deficit theories, a comparable correction mechanism would support theories which assume deficient linguistic processing. In contrast, differences in corrective re-fixations would support theories suggesting deficits in non-linguistic processes. Final analyses will investigate the OVP and I-OVP effects for each individual reader (see e.g., Ramus et al., 2003). These analyses will inform whether deficits can be generalized for slow readers or whether there is a distinct subgroup of slow readers who exhibit evidence for a visuo-oculomotor deficit.

MATERIALS AND METHODS

PARTICIPANTS

We recorded eye movements from 46 slow readers (18 adolescent dyslexic readers were from Hawelka et al., 2010; 16 student dyslexic readers and 12 academic slow readers from previously unpublished datasets) and 99 fluent readers (18 adolescent fluent readers were from Hawelka et al., 2010 and 49 from Gagl et al., 2011; 28 fluent reading students, from previously unpublished datasets). All readers were either adolescents or adults (16–47 years old) and native speakers of German. All slow readers scored below a percentile of 10 on a reading speed test, which is an adaptation of a reading speed test for children (Auer et al., 2004) and our group is currently collecting the norming samples. The preliminary norms of the test are based on a sample of 309 students. In this test, readers are instructed to mark sentences as semantically correct or incorrect and the number of correctly marked sentences within 3 min was used as a measure of reading speed. For example sentences like "*People with pale skin and blond hair have an enhanced risk of sunburn*" or "*A weighing-machine measures the height of a person*" were included. In addition, all adult slow readers had achieved a high level of education and all adolescent dyslexics had a normal to high IQ. For 34 slow readers (i.e., the two dyslexic groups) two non-verbal subtests of German version of the Wechsler Adult intelligence scale (WAIS-R; German Version: Tewes, 1991) were administered. The group scores (standard deviations) were 12.3 (2.7) and 13.3 (2.8) for block design and object assembly, respectively. Note both scores were higher than the norm mean of 10 (3). This is a typical profile for a group of developmental dyslexics (e.g., Snowling, 2000). In addition, the adolescent dyslexic readers of Hawelka et al. stem from two large scale longitudinal studies from Salzburg (e.g., Wimmer et al., 2000) and most of the student dyslexic readers were diagnosed with developmental dyslexia before (10/16). The third group of 12 adult slow readers achieved at least a higher education entrance qualification. They were students or already hold an academic degree and therefore it is highly unlikely that their reading speed deficit is due to an intellectual handicap. To be conservative we refer to the whole group as slow (rather than as dyslexic) readers.

Fluent readers were included, if they exhibited a reading score above percentile 35. As an additional measure for the group selection we calculated a word per minute measure (wpm) from the eye movement sentence reading task. Similar to Rayner et al. (2010) we set a *wpm* criterion, which was 200 wpm. Eight slow readers (seven from the student dyslexics and one slow reading academic) and 17 fluent readers performed above and below the criterion, respectively. Thus they might be inadequately assigned to their reading group. To be conservative, we discarded these participants from further analysis. As a result 38 slow and 82 fluent readers ($M = 139$ wpm; SD = 38 and 277 wpm; SD = 55, respectively) were included in the final analysis.

MATERIALS

Participants read the 144 sentences with various grammatical structures of the Potsdam sentence corpus (PSC; Kliegl et al., 2004), which were presented in a mono-spaced, bold Courier New font (14 pt; 0.3° character width). Eye movements were analyzed on all words with four to seven letters ($n = 495$ words; $M = 5.5$ letters; SD = 1.1; four-letter words: $n = 121$; five-letter: 135; six-letter: 125; seven-letter: 114). We note that more than one word per sentence were included in the analysis. For example, in the sentence "*Der **Gehilfe** des Gärtners sät **Kresse** und Radieschen.*" the words in bold letters met the criteria. However, the initial word of a sentence was not considered for analyses. Predictability measures were provided by the Potsdam group and word frequency values were obtained from the SUBTLEX frequency norms (Brysbaert et al., 2011). The mean log SUBTLEX frequency of the target words was 3.36 (SD = 1.17) per million and the mean predictability was 0.19 (SD = 0.29) in the whole set of the corpus sentences. The dyslexic student readers and their control group ($n = 9$ and $n = 22$, respectively) read a reduced set of the Potsdam sentence corpus ($n = 36$ sentences). In this short version, 157 words of four to seven letters were analyzed ($M = 5.5$ letters; SD = 1.1; $n = 32$, 48, 41, and 36 for the levels of words lengths, respectively). These words had a very similar frequency and predictability as those from the entire corpus ($M = 3.36$; SD = 1.10; $M = 0.19$; SD = 0.28, respectively).

APPARATUS AND PROCEDURE

The eye movement recordings and the sentence reading paradigm are described in detail in Hawelka et al. (2010) and in Gagl et al. (2011). In short, an Eyelink 1000 tower mount system (SR-Research, Ontario, Canada) was used to record the eye movements of the right eye. The participant's heads were placed in a head and a chin rest in front of a 21' cathode ray tube monitor (Belinea, Germany, 1024 × 768 screen resolution; 120 Hz refresh rate). The sentence reading task was preceded by a monocular calibration procedure and 10 practice sentences. The participants were instructed to read the sentences silently. The presentation of the sentences was triggered by a fixation at a fixation point at the left side of the screen (vertically centered). After the detection of a fixation at the fixation point, a sentence was presented in such a way that the fixation landed at the OVP of the first word of the sentence. To terminate the sentence presentation a cross at the bottom right corner of the screen had to be fixated whereupon a new trial was initiated. After about a quarter of the sentences a comprehension question was orally presented. These questions could mostly be answered with a single word. To ensure high eye tracking quality and a low number of recalibrations (in both groups on average four times) the chin rest was placed in such a way that the utterance was not hampered. Both groups had no problems comprehending the sentences, which was reflected in their nearly perfect performance on the comprehension questions (>98% in both groups).

DATA TREATMENT AND ANALYSIS

First fixation durations, the re-fixation probability and the number of fixations were analyzed during the first pass reading of all 4–7 letter words in relation to the initial landing position. All fixation durations shorter than 80 ms and longer than 800 ms were removed from analysis (<2% of the fixation durations in each group). In sum 14,994 and 27,865 fixations were analyzed for slow and fluent readers, respectively, of which 4,597 and 6,043 landed at the beginnings of words and 1,028 and 5,054 landed at the ends of words. The re-fixation probability is estimated by setting the probability to one in case a word was re-fixated (i.e., more than one fixation) and to zero in single fixation cases. The re-fixation probability of, for example, a specific word would then be the mean of the probability values from each participant for this word excluding cases in which the word was skipped.

Data analysis was performed with linear mixed effect models (LMM) with the *lme4* package (Bates et al., 2007) in *R*. The LMM analysis is suitable for investigating sentence corpus data since LMMs deal well with missing data and they allow treating items and participants as random effects in a single analysis. For fixation durations, we analyzed both untransformed and log-transformed durations. The result of such a transformation usually lead to a better fit between observed and predicted data (i.e., to smaller residuals). However, we did not observe differences in the pattern of effects for the two analyses. Thus, we report the coefficients and statistics of the untransformed data from which one can more readily perceive the effect sizes. For the analyses of re-fixations and number of fixations the binomial and the Poisson distributions were used for modeling the LMMs, respectively.

To capture the parabolic shape of the I-OVP and the OVP effects we centered the first fixation position measure and added in the LMM the second order polynomial term of the centered position (i.e., the squared centered first fixation position). To illustrate, a centered initial landing position of zero relates to either the middle letter of a word or to the space between the two middle letters (in words with an even number of letters). Thus, zero would relate to the third letter in five-letter words or to the position in between the second and the third letter in four letter words. A first fixation position at the second and third letter of a five-letter word is one for both instances (the square of -1 and $+1$, respectively) and a fixation at the first and the last letter is four (the square of -2 and 2). This convention made possible to capture the parabolic shape of the OVP/I-OVP effects by accounting for the decrease or the increase of the eye movement measures with increasing distance of the fixation position from the word center (see also McConkie et al., 1989; Nuthmann et al., 2005).

To summarize, the main LMM analysis contains a first and second order polynomial of centered first fixation position (i.e., the linear and the squared effect of first fixation position) and the factor reading group. For these three fixed effects all possible interactions were modeled. In addition, we added word frequency, predictability and length as fixed effects to account for the effects of these word characteristics. Participants and items were treated as random effects.

RESULTS

GLOBAL EYE MOVEMENT CHARACTERISTICS

The global eye movement characteristics of the slow and the fast readers for all words of the sentence corpus are presented in **Table 1**. As evident from the Table, the slow readers exhibited longer first fixation durations, longer gaze durations and a higher number of fixations. The higher number of fixations was due to a lower percentage of word skippings (7%; fast readers: 20%) and a higher percentage of instances in which words receive multiple fixations (52 vs. 24%). Importantly, for the analysis of re-fixation cases, the total number of cases in which words were fixated more than once is similar in both groups (around 7,500 cases). The initial and second landing position was closer to the word beginnings in the slow readers compared to the fast readers.

LANDING POSITION EFFECTS

Figure 2 presents the landing position distributions of the initial and the second fixation for the four to seven-letter words. Slow readers preferentially targeted the beginning of the words (**Figure 2A**). In contrast, the fluent readers' initial landing position was, on average, closer to the word center. However, the peak of the distribution was still slightly left of center. Fluent readers did not only target the word beginning less often, they also showed a higher preference for landing positions between the center and the end of a word when contrasted to slow readers. In **Figure 2B**, the distribution of the second fixation position is presented. Here the group differences are more subtle, but still reliable (see **Table 1**). A detailed inspection revealed that the slow readers still tend to fixate slightly more to the left of the center than the fluent readers. The latter fixated more often to the right of the center. Overall however, the second fixation distribution of both groups has its maximum at a position slightly left to the center of the words. Thus, we may assume that the target of the first re-fixation in both groups is near the center of a word.

Figure 3 shows all eye movement measures in relation to centered first fixation position for both groups and all four word length levels. Visual inspection of the I-OVP and OVP effects for each word length indicate that the shape, of the largely overlapping effects, was comparable between length levels. To decrease complexity word length was only added as fixed effect to the LMMs as a control variable without the interactions. The word

Table 1 | Means (standard errors) of global eye movement measures and group comparisons.

	Slow Readers	Fluent Readers	Group comparisons	
			t(118)	p
First fixation position (letter)	2.32 (0.05)	2.92 (0.03)	9.2	<0.001
First fixation duration (ms)	236 (5)	193 (2)	9.4	<0.001
Second fixation position (letter)	3.20 (0.11)	3.63 (0.07)	3.4	<0.001
Second fixation duration (ms)	217 (7)	178 (2)	9.4	<0.001
Gaze duration (ms)	512 (40)	284 (11)	7.3	<0.001
Number of fixations	2.37 (0.18)	1.27 (0.05)	7.7	<0.001
Word skipping	7%	20%		
Single fixation cases	41%	56%		
Multiple fixation cases	52%	24%		

Fixation positions are presented in absolute letter position and fixation probabilities in percentages.

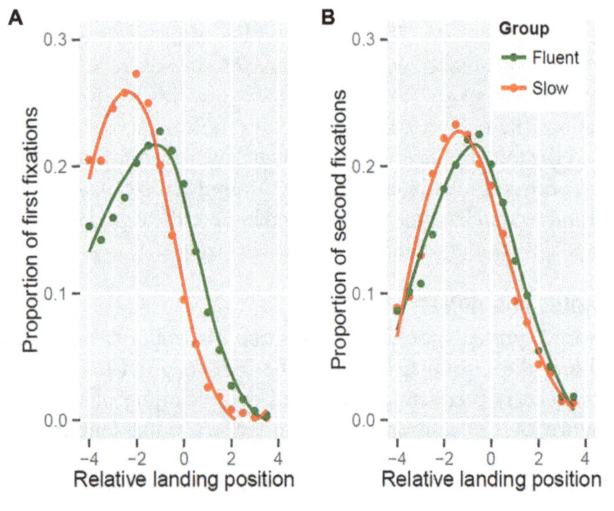

FIGURE 2 | Landing position distributions of the initial (A) and second fixation position (B) for slow and fluent readers. The initial landing position is presented in relation to the center of the words.

length effect, on top of the effects of group, the linear and the squared effect of first fixation position, was not reliable for first fixation durations ($t < 1$), re-fixation probability and number of fixations (both Z's < 1.9). **Figures 3A,B** shows the re-fixation probability and the number of fixations in relation to the initial landing position. Increased re-fixation probabilities and number of fixations were found after landing at the word beginning or after landing at word ends. This OVP effect was present for slow and fluent readers. However, the slow readers exhibited more fixations and a higher probability for re-fixations than the fluent readers. The LMM analysis (**Table 2**) confirmed this observation for number of fixations and the re-fixation probability with a reliable effect of group and reliable effects of the linear and squared first fixation position. In addition, both measures showed a reliable interaction of group and linear landing position, which were due to more pronounced linear effects of landing position for the slow than for the fast readers. To be specific, the slow readers, in contrast to the fast readers, exhibited a higher number of fixations and a higher re-fixation probability at word beginnings than at word ends. Critically, no reliable interaction of group and the squared first fixation position was found which indicates that the quadratic effects were similar in both groups.

The right panels of **Figure 3** show the first fixation durations in relation to landing position. Note that, we distinguished between the first fixation durations of all cases and first fixation durations of cases in which the initial fixation was followed by at least one re-fixation indicating corrective re-fixations at unfavorable landing positions. In general, fixation durations of the slow readers were prolonged when compared to fluent readers. In relation to the landing position, the fixation durations of both groups were shorter after landing at the beginning or the end of a word in contrast to landing at the word center. Thus we observed an I-OVP effect for both measures and both groups. The main finding in **Figure 3** is that landing at the word end resulted in short fixation durations and, most critically, the durations were not different in the slow and the fast readers which was particularly the case for the fixation durations in multiple fixation cases.

The slow readers showed longer fixation durations than the fast readers for landing positions at the beginning and the center of the words. The LMM analysis (**Table 2**) confirms this observation. For both fixation duration measures, reliable effects of group and of the squared landing position were found. In addition, both first fixation duration measures showed a reliable interaction between the quadratic effect of landing position and group which was due to a more pronounced I-OVP effect in the slow than in the fast readers. The interaction between the linear and the quadratic landing position was also reliable indicating that an increase in the linear landing position effect was accompanied with an increase in the

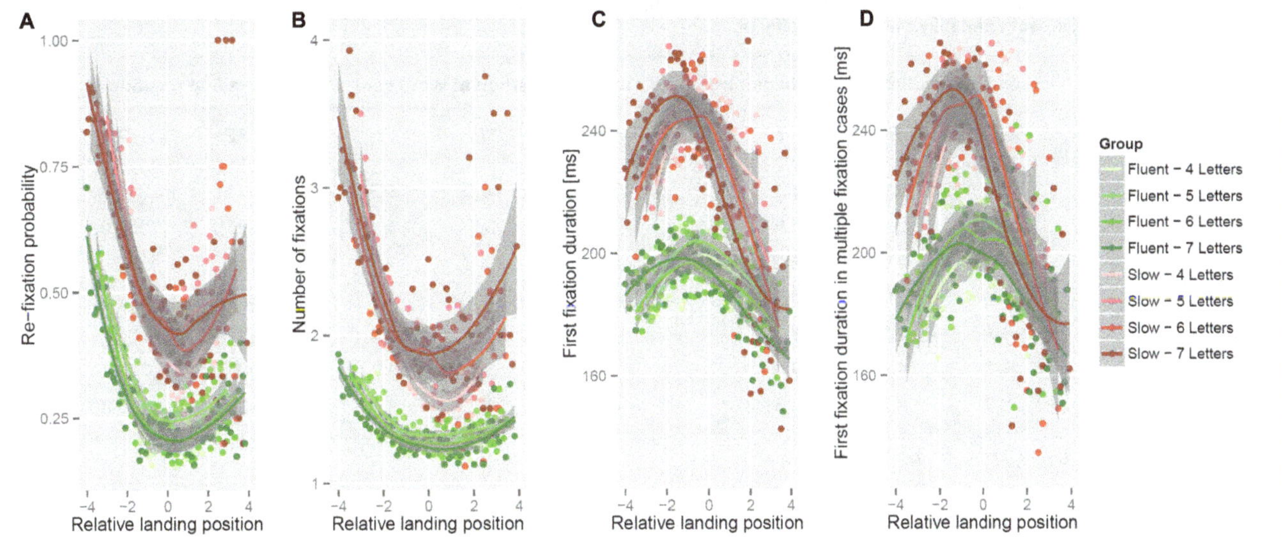

FIGURE 3 | Re-fixation probability (A) number of fixations (B), first fixation duration (C) and the first fixation duration of multiple fixation cases (D) in relation to centered initial landing position for both groups and all four word length levels. The lines depicts smoothed means; the gray areas confidence intervals as provided by the ggplot2-package (Wickham and Chang, 2013).

Table 2 | Results from the LMM analysis for the percentage of re-fixations, number of fixations, first fixation durations and first fixation durations of multiple fixation cases.

	Percentage of re-fixations			Number of fixations			First fixation duration			First fixation duration of multiple fixations		
	FE	*SE*	*z*	*FE*	*SE*	*z*	*FE*	*SE*	*t*	*FE*	*SE*	*t*
Group (G)	**−1.450**	**0.4**	**3.5**	**−0.37**	**0.07**	**5.8**	**−46.3**	**4.4**	**10.5**	**−38.2**	**5.1**	**7.5**
First fixation position (FP)	**−0.271**	**0.03**	**9.5**	**−0.04**	**0.01**	**5.0**	−0.9	0.7	1.2	−0.6	1.1	0.5
First fixation position squared (FP^2)	**0.133**	**0.01**	**12.6**	**0.02**	**0.00**	**6.4**	**−4.9**	**0.3**	**18.2**	**−6.5**	**0.4**	**16.8**
G × FP	**0.098**	**0.04**	**2.7**	**−0.03**	**0.01**	**2.3**	−0.7	0.9	0.8	1.5	1.5	1.0
G × FP^2	0.006	0.01	0.5	0.00	0.00	0.6	**3.6**	**0.3**	**11.9**	**3.5**	**0.5**	**6.6**
FP × FP^2	−0.002	0.01	0.4	−0.00	0.00	0.1	**−0.5**	**0.1**	**3.9**	**−0.6**	**0.2**	**3.0**
G × FP × FP^2	−0.001	0.01	0.2	−0.00	0.00	0.6	**−0.6**	**0.2**	**3.6**	0.5	0.3	1.7

Reliable effects are shown in bold. FE: fixed effect; SE: standard error; z relates to Wald z which is a non-parametric statistic for the binomial or Poisson distributions of the re-fixation probability and the number of fixations, respectively.

quadratic landing position effect. For first fixation duration only, a three-way interaction of reading group with the linear and the squared landing position was found. The interaction was due to fact that the slow readers exhibited both, a more pronounced linear reduction of fixation durations towards the word end and a more pronounced quadratic effect, than the fast readers.

In an additional LMM analysis (**Table 3**; **Figure 4**), we investigated the influence of word frequency and predictability on fixation durations of multiple fixation cases separately for landing position (beginning, middle, end). This analysis is concerned with the question whether the short fixations after landing on the end of words are influenced by word frequency and predictability. The focus of this analysis was on the durations of the first fixation of multiple fixation cases. The rationale is that these fixations are the most sensitive measure to investigate corrective re-fixations. The analyses was a combined one for all levels of word length. A landing position of smaller than −2 was defined as landing at the word beginning and a landing position greater than +2 was defined as landing at word end. Landing positions between −2 and +2 were defined as landing at the word center. As evident from the regression lines in **Figure 4** (right panel) and the LMM analysis in **Table 3**, no reliable main effects or interactions of group, word frequency and word predictability were found when readers landed on the end of the words. This is a strong indication that linguistic processes did not influence fixation durations after landing on word ends. In contrast, if fixations landed at the beginning or the center of a word (left panel of **Figure 4**), then the slow readers exhibited longer fixation durations and we

Table 3 | Results from LMM analysis for first fixation durations of multiple fixation cases with reading group, word frequency and predictability as fixed effects and participants and items as random effects.

	Landing position at word beginning			Landing position at word center			Landing position at word end		
	FE	*SE*	*t*	*FE*	*SE*	*t*	*FE*	*SE*	*t*
Group (G)	**−49.9**	**8.7**	**5.7**	**−69.1**	**7.4**	**9.3**	−14.6	13.5	1.1
Word predictability (P)	−42.1	23.2	1.8	−39.0	23.1	1.7	−62.1	52.0	1.2
Word frequency (F)	**−9.7**	**1.5**	**6.3**	**−11.0**	**1.5**	**7.6**	−2.2	3.3	0.7
G × P	54.4	31.7	1.7	35.5	29.5	1.2	25.2	58.3	0.4
G × F	**6.1**	**2.2**	**2.8**	**9.3**	**1.7**	**5.4**	−2.4	3.6	0.7
P × F	**14.3**	**6.2**	**2.3**	10.0	5.9	1.7	11.2	12.1	0.9
G × P × F	−11.4	8.7	1.3	−10.3	7.6	1.4	−3.0	13.6	0.2

Reliable effects are shown in bold. FE: fixed effect; SE: standard error.

observed a reliable interaction of word frequency with group. This interaction was due to a more pronounced effect of word frequency in the slow compared to the fast readers. The predictability of the word influenced fixation durations only after landing on the word beginnings. A reliable predictability by frequency interaction which was due to a more pronounced effect of frequency in case of predictable words could be found at word beginnings.

INDIVIDUAL EFFECTS

In addition to the group analysis, we conducted an individual estimation of the effect of squared landing position on fixation durations of multiple fixations, number of fixations and refixation probability. Separately, for each group, a simplified model was computed that included the centered linear and squared landing positions as fixed effects and participants and items as random effects on the intercept. In addition, the random effect of participants on the slope of the linear and squared landing position was included in the model. The additional random effects made possible to estimate the individual linear and quadratic effects of landing position. However, we will focus on the quadratic effects. The I-OVP effect on first fixation durations (i.e., a negative effect of the squared landing position) was found in 37 out of the 38 slow readers (97%) with a mean of −5.7 ms (SE = 1.9 ms; range: −10.1 to 1.6 ms). This effect was found in each of the fluent readers with a mean of −2.6 ms (SE = 1.0 ms; range: −4.9 to −0.1 ms). The OVP effect on number of fixations (i.e., a positive effect of the squared landing position) was found in 92% of slow (35/38) and 99% of fast readers (81/82) with means of 0.05 (SE = 0.5; range: −0.009 to 0.21 fixations) and 0.03 (SE = 0.2; range: −0.002 to 0.09 fixations), respectively. For the re-fixation probability, which showed the lowest quadratic effects of all three measures, only 71% (27/38) and 74% (61/82) of the slow and the fast readers showed an OVP effect. Mean values were 0.3% (SE = 1.3; range: −1.9 to 2.2 fixations) and 0.8% (SE = 1.3; range: −1.8 to 2.8 fixations), respectively.

A second analysis was conducted for each slow reader in respect to the first fixation durations of multiple fixation cases that landed on the word end. For these fixation durations the group analysis showed no reliable differences between the groups but this result might mask several slow readers that may still show increased fixation durations. In this analysis one sample t-tests were realized that compared the individual means of the slow readers compared with the fixation durations of the group of fluent readers (M = 201 ms; SD = 30). This analysis showed that 27 of the 38 slow readers exhibited first fixation durations which were not reliably different from the fluent readers. In other words, 71% of slow readers showed fixation durations (i.e., corrective re-fixations) comparable to those of the fluent readers.

DISCUSSION

The present study investigated landing position effects in slow and fluent readers during sentence reading. We found (1) an OVP effect in re-fixation probability, (2) OVP in number of fixations and (3) an I-OVP effect on first fixation durations in slow readers. The main finding was that we found (4) no difference between slow and fluent readers in fixation durations at word end. Furthermore, the fixation durations of both groups were (5) not influenced by linguistic word characteristics, when the fixation landed at the end of a word. Thus, we can conclude that both groups exhibited a similar correction process (i.e., corrective re-fixations) after landing at unfavorable positions within words. However, the total number of fixations and the percentage of re-fixations were higher in slow readers compared to the fluent readers. Furthermore, we replicated the finding that slow readers initially fixate closer to word beginnings than fluent readers (MacKeben et al., 2004; Hawelka et al., 2010). A further group difference was that the I-OVP effect was stronger in the slow readers, which was reflected by prolonged fixation durations at the word center (and at word beginnings) accompanied by a steep decrease of fixation durations towards the word ends.

The I-OVP effect in fluent readers showed the expected pattern with the longest fixation durations at the center and shorter of fixation durations at suboptimal landing positions, that is, at the end and beginnings of words. In both groups the I-OVP effect was most pronounced in first fixation duration of multiple fixation cases and similar for all word lengths. Therefore, we speculate that in most of the multiple fixation cases at a suboptimal position the

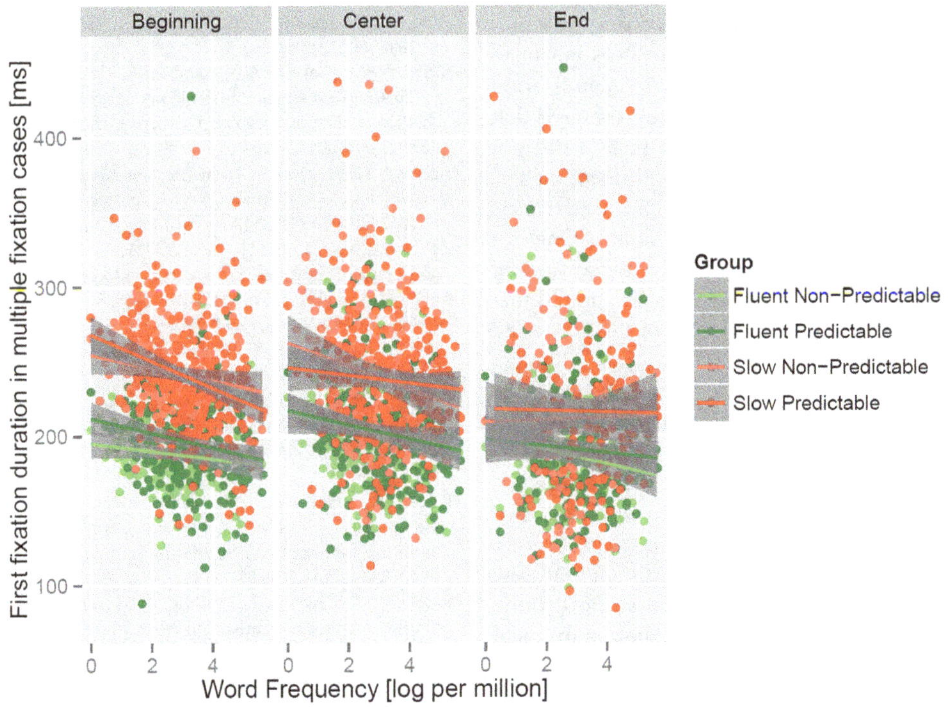

FIGURE 4 | The first fixation duration of multiple fixation cases in relation to word frequency for both groups, landing position and respective regression lines with confidence intervals for predictable (predictability > 0) and unpredictable words (predictability = 0). The categorical distinction of predictability was only used for displaying the interaction of frequency and predictability; for the analysis the continuous predictability measure was used.

fixation duration reflect the visuo-oculomotor processes preceding a corrective re-fixation. These corrective re-fixations are the main objective of the study and hence we will focus on them forth on.

The group differences in fixation durations at the word center (i.e., the OVP) and word beginning (the preferred landing position in the slow readers) reflect linguistic processing. For these landing positions we found reliable effects of word frequency. The frequency effect was substantially more pronounced in the slower than in the fluent readers (replicating, e.g., Hawelka et al., 2010). After landing at the end of words, the fixation durations of both groups were similar and were not influenced by word frequency or word predictability. Therefore, fixation durations after landing at the end are not influenced by linguistic processes and the increased number of fixations and higher percentage for a re-fixation indicates that these fixations are highly likely followed by a corrective saccade towards the word center. When inspected in detail, these fixations were followed by a saccade towards the word center in 78 and 83% of the cases for fast and slow readers, respectively. Thus, one can assume that the pattern after landing at word end reflects corrective re-fixations, a mechanism which is intact in (the majority of) slow readers.

We observed group differences in fixation duration when the initial fixation was at the beginning of the words. The slow readers' fixation durations were prolonged and more affected by word frequency than those of the fluent readers. This finding suggests that slow readers habitually target word beginnings (MacKeben et al., 2004). In fluent readers the preferred viewing location is slightly left to the word center (Rayner, 1979). However, even in the slow readers the fixation duration at word beginnings were, on average, shorter than fixations at the word center. Thus, the cohort of fixations at the beginnings of words might include two cohorts of fixations of different type: one small cohort in which the slow readers correct for suboptimal landing positions and a second, larger cohort which initialized the process of visual word recognition instantaneously (i.e., serial decoding; see below), that is, without correction of the landing position.

The differences in the fixation pattern might stem from differences in cognitive processes that lead to word recognition. In the study by Hawelka et al. (2010), the landing positions of dyslexic readers at the word beginning, in combination with their higher number of fixations and their strong word length effect, was interpreted as a reflection of word processing by means of serial decoding. In fluently reading adults, only words of very low frequency and pseudowords elicit a word length effect (Weekes, 1997). The present finding of the tendency of initially fixating at word beginnings accompanied with a second fixation at the word center, suggests that, at least in a considerable amount of cases, serial decoding is still present in our adolescent and adult slow readers.

The pattern of group differences suggests that slow readers show comparable corrective re-fixations than fluent readers, especially at word end; anyway, when linguistic processing is present, indicated by the frequency and predictability effects, their slow reading speed is reflected in massively prolonged fixation durations. On an individual level, the group pattern does not fit to all of the slow readers. The individual I-OVP effects on fixation duration and the OVP effect of number of fixations showed that a small number of slow readers (a maximum of 8%) did not show I-OVP and OVP effects. In comparison, all fluent readers showed an I-OVP effect and only one out of 82 fluent readers did not show an OVP effect on number of fixations. Only for the re-fixation probability OVP effect, which was the weakest of the three effects, a larger number of individuals were found that did not show a positive OVP effect. Here 26% of the fluent and 29% of the slow readers did not show an OVP effect. Although these percentages are high, they were comparable between the groups. Thus, the main finding from the individual analysis is that the vast majority of the slow readers do not exhibit visuo-oculomotor deficits and that deficient linguistic processing is the cause of their impaired reading speed. Studies, which assessed this issue with non-linguistic tasks, came to similar conclusions. Especially, sophisticated search tasks that used stimuli that were very similar to reading stimuli (e.g., consonant strings) found that slow and fluent readers showed comparable eye movement patterns (Hutzler et al., 2006; Prado et al., 2007) indicating that visual and oculomotor processing of the slow readers is intact. For the few slow readers who exhibited deviant I-OVP and OVP effects one could assume that non-linguistic processes be the proximal cause or an additional source for their slow reading speed. Although the prevalence of this type of deficit was very low in the present sample of slow readers, it deserves attention particularly with regard to individual diagnostic and individually tailored therapies.

To sum up, the present study on the I-OVP effect in first fixation durations and accompanying effects (e.g., OVP of number of fixations) informed about the influence of landing position on the eye movement characteristics of slow readers. In case of sub-optimal landing positions both groups used a similar corrective mechanism, a fast corrective re-fixation to the word center. Similar corrective re-fixations in fluent and slow readers allow drawing the conclusion that visual and oculomotor processes cannot be the primary cause of the reading speed impairment.

ACKNOWLEDGMENTS

We thank Heinz Wimmer, Julia Crone, Christina Marx, Fabio Richlan, and Mathias Schurz for helpful discussions and comments on an earlier version of the article. This work was supported by the Austrian Science Fund (FWF P 25799-B23).

REFERENCES

Aghababian, V., and Nazir, T. A. (2000). Developing normal reading skills: aspects of the visual processes underlying word recognition. *J. Exp. Child Psychol.* 76, 123–150. doi: 10.1006/jecp.1999.2540

Auer, M., Gruber, G., Mayringer, H., and Wimmer, H. (2004). *Salzburger Lesescreening 5–8. Handbook.* Salzburg: Mimeo.

Bates, D., Maechler, M., and Bolker, B. (2007). *The lme4 Package (R Package, Version 2).* Available at: http://CRAN.R-project.org/package_lme4

Brysbaert, M., Buchmeier, M., Conrad, M., Jacobs, A. M., Bölte, J., and Böhl, A. (2011). The word frequency effect: a review of recent developments and implications for the choice of frequency estimates in German. *Exp. Psychol.* 58, 412–424. doi: 10.1027/1618-3169/a000123

Bucci, M. P., Brémond-Gignac, D., and Kapoula, Z. (2008). Latency of saccades and vergence eye movements in dyslexic children. *Exp. Brain Res.* 188, 1–12. doi: 10.1007/s00221-008-1345-5

Dürrwächter, U., Sokolov, A. N., Reinhard, J., Klosinski, G., and Trauzettel-Klosinski, S. (2010). Word length and word frequency affect eye movements in dyslexic children reading in a regular (German) orthography. *Ann. Dyslex.* 60, 86–101. doi: 10.1007/s11881-010-0034-9

Engbert, R., Nuthmann, A., Richter, E., and Kliegl, R. (2005). SWIFT: a dynamical model of saccade generation during reading. *Psychol. Rev.* 112, 777–813. doi: 10.1037/0033-295X.112.4.777

Gagl, B., Hawelka, S., and Hutzler, F. (2011). Systematic influence of gaze position on pupil size measurement: analysis and correction. *Behav. Res. Methods* 43, 1171–1181. doi: 10.3758/s13428-011-0109-5

Hawelka, S., Gagl, B., and Wimmer, H. (2010). A dual-route perspective on eye movements of dyslexic readers. *Cognition* 115, 367–379. doi: 10.1016/j.cognition.2009.11.004

Huestegge, L., Radach, R., Corbic, D., and Huestegge, S. M. (2009). Oculomotor and linguistic determinants of reading development: a longitudinal study. *Vision Res.* 49, 2948–2959. doi: 10.1016/j.visres.2009.09.012

Hutzler, F., Braun, M., and Jacobs, A. M. (2008). On the specificities of the inverted-optimal viewing position effect and their implications on models of eye movement control during reading. *Brain Res.* 1239, 152–161. doi: 10.1016/j.brainres.2008.08.065

Hutzler, F., Kronbichler, M., Jacobs, A. M., and Wimmer, H. (2006). Perhaps correlational but not causal: no effect of dyslexic readers' magnocellular system on their eye movements during reading. *Neuropsychologia* 44, 637–648. doi: 10.1016/j.neuropsychologia.2005.06.006

Hutzler, F., and Wimmer, H. (2004). Eye movements of dyslexic children when reading in a regular orthography. *Brain Lang.* 89, 235–242. doi: 10.1016/S0093-934X(03)00401-2

Hyönä, J., and Bertram, R. (2011). Optimal viewing position effects in reading Finnish. *Vision Res.* 51, 1279–1287. doi: 10.1016/j.visres.2011.04.004

Joseph, H. S., Liversedge, S. P., Blythe, H. I., White, S. J., and Rayner, K. (2009). Word length and landing position effects during reading in children and adults. *Vision Res.* 49, 2078–2086. doi: 10.1016/j.visres.2009.05.015

Kirkby, J. A., Blythe, H. I., Drieghe, D., and Liversedge, S. P. (2011). Reading text increases binocular disparity in dyslexic children. *PLoS ONE* 6:e27105. doi: 10.1371/journal.pone.0027105

Kliegl, R., Grabner, E., Rolfs, M., and Engbert, R. (2004). Length, frequency, and predictability effects of words on eye movements in reading. *Eur. J. Cogn. Psychol.* 16, 262–284. doi: 10.1080/09541440340000213

MacKeben, M., Trauzettel-Klosinski, S., Reinhard, J., Dürrwächter, U., Adler, M., and Klosinski, G. (2004). Eye movement control during single-word reading in dyslexics. *J. Vis.* 4, 388–402. doi: 10.1167/4.5.4

McConkie, G. W., Kerr, P. W., Reddix, M. D., Zola, D., and Jacobs, A. M. (1989). Eye movement control during reading: II. Frequency of refixating a word. *Percept. Psychophys.* 46, 245–253. doi: 10.3758/BF03208086

Nuthmann, A., Engbert, R., and Kliegl, R. (2005). Mislocated fixations during reading and the inverted optimal viewing position effect. *Vision Res.* 45, 2201–2217. doi: 10.1016/j.visres.2005.02.014

O'Regan, J. K., and Jacobs, A. M. (1992). Optimal viewing position effect in word recognition: a challenge to current theory. *J. Exp. Psychol. Hum. Percept. Perform.* 18, 185. doi: 10.1037/0096-1523.18.1.185

Pavlidis, G. (1981). Do eye movements hold the key to dyslexia? *Neuropsychologia* 19, 57–64. doi: 10.1016/0028-3932(81)90044-0

Prado, C., Dubois, M., and Valdois, S. (2007). The eye movements of dyslexic children during reading and visual search: impact of the visual attention span. *Vision Res.* 47, 2521–2530. doi: 10.1016/j.visres.2007.06.001

Ramus, F., Rosen, S., Dakin, S. C., Day, B. L., Castellote, J. M., White, S., et al. (2003). Theories of developmental dyslexia: insights from a multiple case study of dyslexic adults. *Brain* 126, 841–865. doi: 10.1093/brain/awg076

Rau, A. K., Moeller, K., and Landerl, K. (2014). The transition from sublexical to lexical processing in a consistent orthography: an eye-tracking study. *Sci. Stud. Read.* 18, 224–233. doi: 10.1080/10888438.2013.857673

Rayner, K. (1979). Eye guidance in reading: fixation locations within words. *Perception* 8, 21–30. doi: 10.1068/p080021

Rayner, K., Slattery, T. J., and Bélanger, N. N. (2010). Eye movements, the perceptual span, and reading speed. *Psychon. Bull. Rev.* 17, 834–839. doi: 10.3758/PBR.17.6.834

Reichle, E. D., Liversedge, S. P., Drieghe, D., Blythe, H. I., Joseph, H. S., White, S. J., et al. (2013). Using EZ reader to examine the concurrent development of eye-movement control and reading skill. *Dev. Rev.* 33, 110–149. doi: 10.1016/j.dr.2013.03.001

Reichle, E. D., Rayner, K., and Pollatsek, A. (2003). The E-Z Reader model of eye movement control in reading: comparisons to other models. *Behav. Brain Sci.* 26, 445–476. doi: 10.1017/S0140525X03000104

Share, D. L. (1995). Phonological recoding and self-teaching: sine qua non of reading acquisition. *Cognition* 55, 151–218. doi: 10.1016/0010-0277(94)00645-2

Snowling, M. J. (2000). *Dyslexia,* 2nd Edn. Oxford: Blackwell.

Stein, J., and Walsh, V. (1997). To see but not to read; the magnocellular theory of dyslexia. *Trends Neurosci.* 20, 147–152. doi: 10.1016/S0166-2236(96)01005-3

Tewes, U. (1991). *Hamburger-Wechsler Intelligenztest für Erwachsene Revision,* 2nd Edn. Bern: Huber.

Vergilino-Perez, D., Collins, T., and Doré-Mazars, K. (2004). Decision and metrics of refixations in reading isolated words. *Vision Res.* 44, 2009–2017. doi: 10.1016/j.visres.2004.03.012

Vitu, F., Lancelin, D., and Marrier d'Unienville, V. (2007). A perceptual-economy account for the inverted-optimal viewing position effect. *J. Exp. Psychol. Hum. Percept. Perform.* 33, 1220–1249. doi: 10.1037/0096-1523.33.5.1220

Vitu, F., McConkie, G. W., Kerr, P., and O'Regan, J. K. (2001). Fixation location effects on fixation durations during reading: an inverted optimal viewing position effect. *Vision Res.* 41, 3513–3533. doi: 10.1016/S0042-6989(01)00166-3

Weekes, B. S. (1997). Differential effects of number of letters on word and nonword naming latency. *Quart. J. Exp. Psychol. A* 50, 439–456. doi: 10.1080/713755710

Wickham and Chang. (2013). *Package 'ggplot2'.* Available at: http://cran.r-project.org/web/packages/ggplot2/

Wimmer, H. (1993). Characteristics of developmental dyslexia in a regular writing system. *Appl. Psycholinguist.* 14, 1–33. doi: 10.1017/S0142716400010122

Wimmer, H., Mayringer, H., and Landerl, K. (2000). The double-deficit hypothesis and difficulties in learning to read a regular orthography. *J. Educ. Psychol.* 92, 668. doi: 10.1037/0022-0663.92.4.668

Wimmer, H., and Schurz, M. (2010). Dyslexia in regular orthographies: manifestation and causation. *Dyslexia* 16, 283–299. doi: 10.1002/dys.411

Wolf, M., and Bowers, P. G. (1999). The double-deficit hypothesis for the developmental dyslexias. *J. Educ. Psychol.* 91, 415. doi: 10.1037/0022-0663.91.3.415

Ziegler, J. C., and Goswami, U. (2005). Reading acquisition, developmental dyslexia, and skilled reading across languages: a psycholinguistic grain size theory. *Psychol. Bull.* 131, 3–29. doi: 10.1037/0033-2909.131.1.3

14

Spatial and temporal attention in developmental dyslexia

Milena Ruffino[1]*, Simone Gori[1,2], Daniela Boccardi[2], Massimo Molteni[1] and Andrea Facoetti[1,2]

[1] Child Psychopathology Unit, Scientific Institute, IRCCS Eugenio Medea, Lecco, Italy
[2] Developmental and Cognitive Neuroscience Lab, Department of General Psychology, University of Padua, Padua, Italy

***Correspondence:**
Milena Ruffino, Child Psychopathology Unit, Scientific Institute, IRCCS Eugenio Medea, Via Don Luigi Monza, 20, Bosisio Parini, Lecco 23842, Italy
e-mail: milena.ruffino@bp.lnf.it

Although the dominant view posits that developmental dyslexia (DD) arises from a deficit in phonological processing, emerging evidence suggest that DD could result from a more basic cross-modal letter-to-speech sound integration deficit. Letters have to be precisely selected from irrelevant and cluttering letters by rapid orienting of visual attention before the correct letter-to-speech sound integration applies. In the present study the time-course of spatial attention was investigated measuring target detection reaction times (RTs) in a cuing paradigm, while temporal attention was investigated by assessing impaired identification of the first of two sequentially presented masked visual objects. Spatial and temporal attention were slower in dyslexic children with a deficit in pseudoword reading ($N = 14$) compared to chronological age ($N = 43$) and to dyslexics without a deficit in pseudoword reading ($N = 18$), suggesting a direct link between visual attention efficiency and phonological decoding skills. Individual differences in these visual attention mechanisms were specifically related to pseudoword reading accuracy in dyslexics. The role of spatial and temporal attention in the graphemic parsing process might be related to a basic oscillatory "temporal sampling" dysfunction.

Keywords: spatial attention, temporal attention, temporal sampling, phonological decoding, reading disorder

INTRODUCTION

Developmental dyslexia (DD) is a neurodevelopmental disorder identified in about 10% of children which refers to a pattern of learning difficulties characterized by problems with accurate or fluent word recognition, poor decoding and poor spelling abilities, despite normal intelligence, and adequate access to conventional instruction (American Psychiatric Association, 2013).

According to the dual-route model (see Perry et al., 2007 for a review), written words can be processed either by the sub-lexical route, based on grapheme-to-phoneme correspondences, allowing us to read unfamiliar words and pseudowords, or by the lexical route, based on lexical unit correspondences, crucial for reading familiar and irregular words only. Phonological dyslexics show great difficulties in reading unfamiliar words and pseudowords compared to known words, and this is thought to arise from damage to the sub-lexical route. In contrast, surface dyslexia is characterized by impaired reading of irregular words, and this is thought to arise from a damage in the lexical route (e.g., Castles and Coltheart, 1993), potentially linked to an under-stimulation of the visual word recognition system resulting from low experience with literacy. However, in shallow orthographies such as Italian, spelling-sound irregularity is limited to the supra-segmental level (that is, to stress assignment). Thus, in Italian dyslexic children the increased weighting of sub-lexical processing does not permit precise measurement of the efficiency of the lexical-route (see also Gori et al., under revision). It is crucial to note that—regardless of spelling-sound regularity—for a beginning reader all words are at first pseudowords because the lexical-orthographic representations have still to be developed. Accordingly, most longitudinal studies have shown that beginning readers use primarily the sub-lexical route (see Sprenger-Charolles et al., 2003, for a review). Phonological decoding, which is typically measured by examining children's pseudoword reading performance, is one of the most critical skills for successful reading acquisition (e.g., Share, 1995). Interestingly, Ziegler et al. (2003) showed that dyslexics with both regular (German-speaking children) and irregular (English-speaking children) spelling-to-sound correspondences present an extremely slow and serial phonological decoding mechanism. Consequently, an efficient learning to read is crucially mediated by an accurate and fluent use of the sub-lexical route (e.g., Goswami et al., 2000; see Vellutino et al., 2004, for a review).

The underlying neurocognitive mechanisms that lead to the observed reading impairments are still hotly debated (see Vidyasagar and Pammer, 2010; Goswami, 2011). Impaired auditory and speech-sound processing is assumed to characterize the core deficit in DD (e.g., Tallal, 1980; Bradley and Bryant, 1983; Chandrasekaran et al., 2009; Vandermosten et al., 2010; Hornickel et al., 2012; see Wright et al., 2000; Goswami, 2003, 2011; Tallal, 2004; Gabrieli, 2009; Peterson and Pennington, 2012, for reviews). However, the hypothesis that DD arises specifically from a deficit of phonological awareness is still debated because of the circular relationship between reading ability and phonological skills acquisition (e.g., Blau et al., 2009; Dehaene et al., 2010; see Castles and Coltheart, 2004, for a review).

Emerging evidence suggested that DD could arise from a more basic cross-modal letter-to-speech sound integration deficit (e.g., Blau et al., 2009, 2010; Dehaene et al., 2010; see Blomert, 2011, for a recent review). A recent study has also shown that cross-modal binding is impaired at the very early stages of associative learning (Jones et al., 2013). Those authors suggested that dyslexic readers' difficulties in binding may be characterized by inadequate attentional deployment to spatial location. Letters have to be precisely selected from irrelevant and cluttering letters (Bouma, 1970; Bouma and Legein, 1977) by rapid orienting of visual attention (Yeshurun and Rashal, 2010) before the correct letter-to-speech sound integration applies (e.g., Hari and Renvall, 2001; Facoetti et al., 2010a; Vidyasagar and Pammer, 2010; Zorzi et al., 2012). Accordingly, recent studies have shown that visual attention is impaired not only in dyslexic children (e.g., Facoetti et al., 2010a; Lallier et al., 2010), but also in pre-readers at familial risk for DD. These results indicate that visual attention disorders are present before reading acquisition (e.g., Plaza and Cohen, 2007; Facoetti et al., 2010b) and that they are predictors of future reading acquisition skills controlling not only for age, IQ, and phonological processing, but also for non-alphabetic, visual-to-phonological mapping (Franceschini et al., 2012). Moreover, recent findings have shown that attentional training—not involving phonological or orthographic learning—by using action video games can improve reading abilities in children with DD (Franceschini et al., 2013). Visual attention can be oriented in space and time as a spotlight (i.e., attentional shifting; Posner, 1980; Yantis and Jonides, 1984; Jonides and Yantis, 1998). The spotlight of attention (i.e., attentional focus) can also be expanded or contracted in spatial extent to encompass large or small objects, respectively (e.g., Castiello and Umiltà, 1990; LaBerge, 1995; Ronconi et al., 2014). When attention is spatially concentrated in a small portion of the visual field it is called focused attention, while when it is spread across a large part of the visual field it is called distributed attention.

A specific relationship between non-linguistic deficits referred to as attentional shifting has been proposed by Hari and Renvall (2001). According to their multisensory "Sluggish Attentional Shifting" (SAS) framework, when dyslexics deal with rapid stimulus sequences, their automatic attention system cannot disengage fast enough from one item to the next one, yielding slow and degraded processing. SAS is assumed to distort cortical networks, more specifically those which support sub-lexical auditory-phonological (e.g., syllables and/or phonemes) and visual-orthographic (e.g., syllables and/or grapheme) representations. Attentional shifting and rapid processing deficits have been proposed as a more basic problem yielding to the phonological impairment observed in DD (e.g., Breznitz et al., 2013; see Farmer and Klein, 1995; Tallal, 2004, for reviews). This hypothesis is supported by a number of studies showing evidence for temporal processing of brief stimuli within both visual and auditory modalities in dyslexic populations (e.g., Hari and Kiesilä, 1996; Helenius et al., 1999; Hari et al., 1999, 2001; Renvall and Hari, 2002). Consequently, it has been suggested that non-linguistic deficits in dyslexics can be linked to a generally inefficient multi-sensory processing of perceptual stimuli (e.g., perceptual noise exclusion deficit; Sperling et al., 2005; Ziegler et al., 2009; Facoetti et al., 2010a) that impairs the ability to detect relevant stimuli (i.e., signals) when encountering signal interference induced by spatially (Geiger and Lettvin, 1987; Sperling et al., 2005; Geiger et al., 2008; Ruffino et al., 2010) or temporally close noise (Di Lollo et al., 1983; Visser et al., 2004; Montgomery et al., 2005; Facoetti et al., 2008). Notably, attentional deficits in children with DD, with specific language impairment and with autism spectrum disorder (e.g., Ronconi et al., 2012, 2013a) arise from a difficulty in the visual noise exclusion process that specifically requires more time between two stimuli to identify accurately the target as compared to typically developing children (e.g., Ruffino et al., 2010; Dispaldro et al., 2013; Ronconi et al., 2013b).

It is important to highlight that spatial attention is involved in perceptual noise exclusion (e.g., Carrasco et al., 2000, 2002, 2004), by optimizing the perceptual filter so that the signal is further processed and noise is excluded (Dosher and Lu, 2000). The major effect on perceptual functions is that spatial attention appears to enhance the neural representation of stimuli at the attended location (see Reynolds and Chelazzi, 2004, for a review). This signal enhancement manifests itself in a variety of ways, including faster reaction times (RTs) (Posner, 1980), improved sensitivity (lowered thresholds; Carrasco et al., 2002) and reduced interference exerted by flanking stimuli (Carrasco et al., 2000; Facoetti and Molteni, 2000; Boyer and Ro, 2007). An important unresolved issue is whether spatial attention can also speed up the rate at which information is processed. Spatial attention not only improves the spatial resolution, but also accelerates the rate of information processing (Carrasco and McElree, 2001). Moreover, it allows decisions to be based on information at the selected location alone, while disregarding any distracting stimuli (Dosher and Lu, 2000; Braun, 2002). On the basis of these perceptual effects, spatial attention influences all post-sensorial processes, such as the content of short-term memory, perceptual decisions and voluntary responses.

SAS may be a crucial factor behind difficulties in learning to read (Hari and Renvall, 2001; Facoetti et al., 2005) and may be one important factor involved in perceptual difficulties, mostly in tasks requiring an efficient noise exclusion mechanism. Moreover, spatial attention deficits have been repeatedly shown in DD (e.g., Cestnick and Coltheart, 1999; Facoetti et al., 2005, 2006; Bosse et al., 2007; see Hari and Renvall, 2001; Vidyasagar and Pammer, 2010, for reviews) and more specifically in dyslexics with poor pseudoword reading ability (Cestnick and Coltheart, 1999; Buchholz and McKone, 2004; Facoetti et al., 2006, 2008; Roach and Hogben, 2007; Jones et al., 2008; Ruffino et al., 2010). The efficient learning of sub-lexical spelling-sound mappings requires not only accurate representations at the phoneme or syllabic level (Snowling, 2000; Goswami, 2003, respectively), but also an efficient graphemic parsing mechanism (Facoetti et al., 2006, 2010a; Perry et al., 2007; Ruffino et al., 2010; Vidyasagar and Pammer, 2010). These visual attentional processes are hypothesized to be crucially involved in spelling-to-sound conversion mechanisms. Computational models of silent or oral reading assume that graphemic parsing requires the serial engagement of visual attention onto, and its disengagement from, each sub-lexical unit. Among the processes necessary for adequate processing along the sub-lexical route, a graphemic parsing mechanism may be critically linked to the selection mechanism of visual attention (Zorzi, 2005; Perry et al., 2007; Zorzi et al., 2012; Schneps et al., 2013a,b).

Although it has already been demonstrated that visual spatial and temporal attention deficits could contribute independently to the poor reading outcome of dyslexic individuals, as yet, no studies have shown that both spatial and temporal attentional deficits co-occur in the same group of children with DD. These findings indicate that a sluggish shifting of spatial attention is specifically related to a perceptual noise exclusion deficit in DD.

Thus, in the current study, we investigated whether both spatial and temporal attention are impaired in DD with poor phonological decoding, and if they have a specific predictive relationship with phonological decoding skill.

We measured the time-course of visual spatial attention (VSA) and visual temporal attention (VTA) in two groups of dyslexic children, classified on the basis of their phonological decoding (dis)ability, and one group of controls matched for chronological age and IQ.

VSA has been extensively studied by using spatial cuing paradigms (Posner, 1980), in which covert attention (without eye movements) is engaged across two locations of a forthcoming target stimulus by a peripheral, informative spatial cue (i.e., cue location predicts target location) at two variable cue-target intervals (100 and 350 ms). Stimuli presented at the valid location are detected faster than stimuli appearing at the invalid location (the cuing effect reflects facilitation and inhibitory mechanisms of attention; see **Figure 1**). These attentional effects have been interpreted as a consequence of enhanced sensory processing of stimuli appearing at attended locations (Posner, 1980; Carrasco et al., 2000, 2002, 2004), and indicate that VSA has been efficiently engaged. Processing facilitation in VSA is usually found at short cue-target delays only (e.g., 50–150 ms; see Klein, 2000, for a review; see also Facoetti et al., 2010a). Therefore, sluggish VSA might be revealed by a delay in the normal time-course of VSA, i.e., this attentional processing facilitation should be present at longer but not at shorter cue-target delays.

VTA was measured by using an identification task in which the first of two sequentially and centrally presented, forward and backward masked objects had to be recognized (i.e., signal + noise condition; Duncan et al., 1994), and it was compared to the identification of a single displayed object (signal condition). The first visual object (O1) preceded the onset of the second visual object (O2), by a short stimulus-onset-asynchrony (150 ms O1–O2 SOA; Facoetti et al., 2008). However, in order to highlight the O2 perceptual segregation and simplify the task for children, it was displayed in a different color from O1 (see **Figure 2A**). The accuracy to identify O1 allowed us to measure the efficiency of temporal engagement onto a centrally presented visual object.

MATERIALS AND METHODS

PARTICIPANTS

Participants were 32 Italian children with DD recruited at the Child Psychopathology Unit, Scientific Institute, IRCCS Eugenio Medea, Bosisio Parini, Lecco. Chronological age ranged from 8 to 14 (mean = 10, *SD* = 1.85). Reading performance, in terms of accuracy and/or speed, was 2 SDs below the norm on at least one of the age-standardized Italian tests included in the clinical battery (single word and pseudoword reading; Sartori et al., 1995). Dyslexics were selected on the basis of: (i) a full scale IQ greater than 85, as measured by the Wechsler Intelligence Scale for Children-Revised (WISC-R, Wechsler, 1993); (ii) normal or corrected-to-normal vision and hearing; (iii) the absence of neurological and/or psychiatric disorders; and (iv) the absence of attention deficit disorder with or without hyperactivity (because of its high co-morbidity with DD), as evaluated through DSM-IV diagnostic criteria (American Psychiatric Association, 1994). None of the dyslexic children followed an intensive nor a specific training based on well-documented efficacy. Forty-three typically reading children (NR), matched on age and IQ, were also selected. They were aged between 7 and 14 years (mean = 10, *SD* = 2.31) and were recommended as typical readers by their parents, confirmed by individual evaluation in a quiet room in their school. Reading performance was considered typical when accuracy and speed were higher than 1 SD below the norm of the age-standardized Italian tests included in the clinical battery

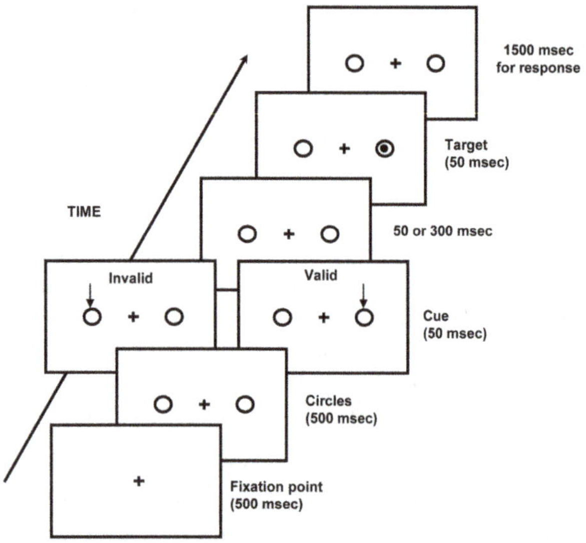

FIGURE 1 | Schematic representation of the display used in the visual spatial attention task.

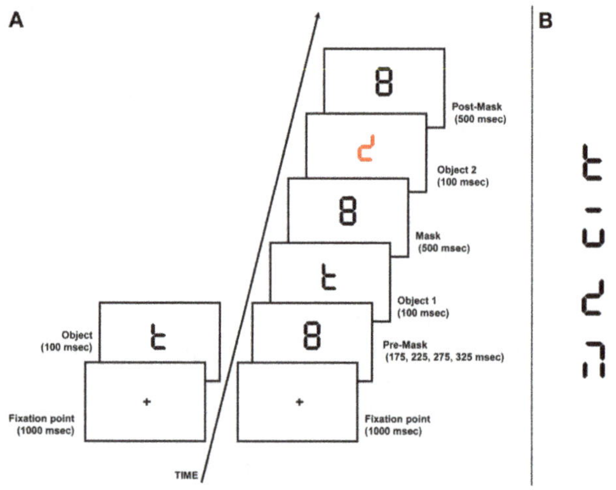

FIGURE 2 | Schematic representation of the display used in the visual temporal attention task (A); Stimuli used in the visual temporal attention task (B).

(single word and pseudoword reading task; Sartori et al., 1995). Informed written consent was obtained from the parents of each child, and the Scientific Institute, IRCCS "Eugenio Medea" ethics committee approved the research protocol. The entire research process was conducted according to the principles expressed in the Declaration of Helsinki. Dyslexic and normally reading children were comparable for chronological age (two-tailed *t*-test, $p = 0.96$) and Performance IQ (Figure Completion subtest, WISC-R, Wechsler, 1993; two-tailed *t*-test, $p = 0.09$), but they were significantly different for both accuracy and speed of word and pseudoword reading (two-tailed *t*-test, all $ps < 0.0001$).

DYSLEXIA SUB TYPING

In order to study the sub-lexical route efficiency, dyslexic children were divided into two groups on the basis of their accuracy in phonological decoding. In particular, their ability to read aloud was measured on a list of 50 Italian regular and 50 Italian irregular[1] words and 50 pseudowords, in order to assess phonological decoding ability. We measured only accuracy in our study because low accuracy is frequently a problem observed even in Italian dyslexics (e.g., Facoetti et al., 2006, 2010a; Ruffino et al., 2010). Specifically, a dyslexic child was assigned to the DDP− group (where P- indicates severe pseudoword reading) if pseudoword reading accuracy was below the 5th percentile in comparison to normally reading children. We selected this criterion in order to find an inefficient sub-lexical route. All dyslexic children who did not meet the criterion for inclusion in the DDP− group were assigned to the DDP+ group (where P+ indicates less severe pseudoword reading). The percentage mean of pseudoword reading accuracy was 64% ($SD = 10.14$) for the DDP− and 79% ($SD = 14.83$) for the DDP+ group ($p < 0.0001$).

PHONOLOGICAL TASKS

We administered a Pseudowords Phoneme Blending (PPB) task and a Pseudoword Short-Term Memory (PSTM) task to the participants.

In the PPB task, single phonemes were presented, and participants were asked to pronounce the resulting pseudowords from their synthesis (i.e., G-A-S-T-I-B-O = GASTIBO). Performances were calculated on the basis of the number of pseudowords correctly pronounced (the number of words administered were one for familiarization, nine experimental; the number of phonemes included in each pseudoword ranged from 7 to 10). The PSTM task consisted of repeating lists of pseudoword trigrams orally presented (i.e., two items ranging from 2 to 8 trigrams) in the same order as originally presented. Performances were indexed as the number of phonemes correctly repeated in the correct position (the maximum score was 210 phonemes). The number of list items increased with correct responses until participants made an error in both list items administered of the same length. For additional details see Supplementary Material.

[1] Italian irregular words are defined as words stressed at third or fourth syllable from last (e.g., rùvido, dòllaro, àbitano, dèlegano).

VISUAL ATTENTIONAL TASKS

Spatial attention

Testing was carried out in a dimly lit (luminance of 1.5 cd/m^2) and quiet room (approximately 50 dB SPL). Participants were seated in front of a computer screen (background luminance of 0.5 cd/m^2), with their head positioned on a chinrest so that the eye-screen distance was 40 cm. Stimuli were white on a black background and had a luminance of 24 cd/m^2. Each trial started with the onset of the fixation point (1° visual angle; 500 ms). Two circles (2.5°) were displayed peripherally (8° eccentricity, one to the left and one to the right of the fixation point) and 500 ms later the visual cue was shown, consisting of an arrow (1.5° visual angle) displayed for 50 ms above one of the circles. In response trials, a target (dot, 0.5°; duration 50 ms) was presented after one of two cue-target stimulus onset asynchronies (SOA, 100 or 350 ms) in one of the two possible locations. The probability that the cue was presented in the target location was about 80% (i.e., the cue location was predictive of target location). In contrast, in catch trials the target was not presented and participants did not have to respond. Catch trials were intermixed with response trials. Participants were instructed to react as quickly as possible to the onset of the visual targets by pressing the spacebar on the computer keyboard (detection task). Simple RTs and error rates were recorded by the computer. The maximum time allowed to respond was 1500 ms. The inter-trial interval was 1000 ms, after that time the trial started automatically. The experimental session consisted of 128 trials divided into two blocks of 64 trials each, which were distributed as follows: 40 valid trials (20 targets in the right visual field and 20 in the left visual field, 10 for each SOA), 12 invalid trials (6 targets in the right visual field and 6 in the left visual field, 3 for each SOA), and 12 catch trials (6 for each SOA; see **Figure 1**).

Temporal attention

The experimental environment was the same as described above for the spatial attention task. Each trial began with the onset of the fixation mark (0.3° of visual angle; duration 500 ms). Participants were instructed to keep their eyes on the fixation mark throughout the duration of the trial. Two conditions, a "signal alone" (O) and "signal + noise" (O+noise), were randomly presented to each participant. In the O condition a single object (duration 100 ms) was displayed and the aim was to measure the participants' ability to identify the experimental stimuli. In the O+noise condition an 8 digital clock-face font comprising seven line segments was displayed for a variable time exposure (175, 225, 275, or 325 ms) acting as a pre-mask, two successive objects (black O1 and red O2) were presented for 100 ms by removing some of the line segments (see **Figure 2B**, for stimuli used), each followed by a post-mask (8-digital clock-face font) of different duration (i.e., for O1 = 50 and for O2 = 500 ms). This condition was designed to maximize the load of the perceptual noise exclusion mechanism. All visual stimuli displayed had a luminance of 0.6 cd/m^2, the background appeared white and had a luminance of 119 cd/m^2. Participants viewed the sequence of stimuli binocularly and they were instructed to identify, at the end of each trial, O and O1 as accurately as possible, measuring the attentional engagement onto the target (O and O1).

Before the start of the experimental session, participants viewed each of the four different stimuli one by one with no time constraint (familiarization phase). After each trial all four possible targets were presented on the screen together (two targets per line). Participants responded by pointing on the screen. These responses were registered by the experimenter by pressing the corresponding key on a computer keyboard and no feedback was provided. The experimental session consisted of 40 trials (16 for the O condition and 24 for the O+noise condition; see **Figure 2**).

RESULTS

AGE, IQ, READING, AND PHONOLOGICAL SKILLS: GROUPS ANALYSIS

The differences between the three groups in age, Performance IQ, experimental reading paradigm (the accuracy in regular, irregular word, and pseudoword reading) and phonological tasks (pseudowords and phonemes correctly reported in the PPB and PSTM task, respectively) were analyzed. Results showed no significant differences in age or Performance IQ [$F < 1$ and $F_{(1, 72)} = 1.94$, $p > 0.05$, respectively], whereas significant differences were shown in all reading indexes [Regular words: $F_{(1, 72)} = 9.77$, $p < 0.0001$; Irregular words: $F_{(1, 72)} = 9.86$, $p < 0.0001$; and Pseudowords: $F_{(1, 72)} = 54.14$, $p < 0.0001$] and in the two phonological tasks. The NR group demonstrated a significantly higher number of correctly pronounced pseudowords in the PPB task [$F_{(1, 72)} = 15.08$, $p < 0.0001$] and correctly pronounced phonemes in the PSTM task [$F_{(1, 72)} = 12.31$, $p < 0.0001$] compared to the two groups of dyslexic children. Planned comparisons demonstrated that, although both dyslexic groups were significantly different from NR in all reading and phonological abilities, DDP− and DDP+ were different only in pseudoword reading accuracy (see **Table 1**). Thus, the selective deficit in phonological decoding skills observed in the DDP− group is difficult to explain with respect to differences in their phonological processing, which did not significantly differ between the two dyslexic groups (see **Table 1**).

VISUAL ATTENTIONAL TASKS: GROUPS ANALYSIS

Spatial attention

Mean correct detection RTs were analyzed with a mixed ANOVA that had target condition (valid and invalid) and SOA (100 and 350 ms) as within-subject factors, and group (NR, DDP+, and DDP−) as between-subject factor. The target condition main effect was significant, $F_{(1, 72)} = 69.85$, $p < 0.0001$; RTs were slower in the invalid condition (460 ms) than in the valid condition (423 ms; cuing effect = 37 ms). No other main effects were significant. Notably, the critical three-way interaction group × SOA × target condition interaction was significant, $F_{(2, 72)} = 3.77$, $p < 0.05$ (see **Figure 3**), indicating a different time-course of attentional orienting in the three groups. At short SOA, both dyslexic groups, in the valid condition, appear to detect targets more slowly in comparison to the normal readers. These results show an apparently reduced facilitation effect in both dyslexic groups. In the invalid condition the DDP− group was similar to the NR group suggesting an unimpaired inhibition mechanism in the DDP− group. The DDP− group was faster than the DDP+ in the invalid cue condition suggesting an abnormal inhibition mechanism in the DDP+ group. All three groups showed a significant cuing effect (i.e., invalid-valid RT differences) at 350 ms SOA [NR = 37 ms ($SD = 39.26$), DDP+ = 32 ms ($SD = 67.74$), and DDP− = 59 ms ($SD = 62.91$); all $ps < 0.005$], demonstrating that they are able to orient spatial attention at the longer time interval. In contrast, only the DDP− group did not show a significant cuing effect at the 100 ms SOA [NR = 37 ms ($SD = 38.15$), DDP+ = 32 ms ($SD = 44.50$), and DDP− = 13 ms ($SD = 44.51$)], demonstrating a sluggish VSA in DDP− in comparison to NR and DDP+ (see **Table 2**). Moreover, the DDP− group showed and amplified cuing effect in comparison to NR and DDP+ grouped together at 350 ms SOA ($p < 0.05$; see **Figure 4**).

In summary, the data highlighted a marked offset of the time-course of visual attention in DDP−, which suggests a sluggish VSA, because differences were selectively present only for the

Table 1 | Mean (M) and standard deviation (SD) of age (months), Performance IQ (Figure Completion, Wechsler, 1993), Reading abilities (Regular, Irregular words, and Pseudowords), pseudowords phoneme blending (number of correct pseudowords), and a pseudoword short-term memory (number of correct phonemes) in normally reading children (NR) and developmental dyslexics without (DDP+) and with (DDP−) phonological decoding deficit.

	NR ($N = 43$)		DDP+ ($N = 18$)		DDP− ($N = 14$)		Comparison NR vs. DDP+			Comparison NR vs. DDP−			Comparison DDP+ vs. DDP−		
	M	*SD*	*M*	*SD*	*M*	*SD*	$t_{(59)}$	*P*	*C.'s d*	$t_{(55)}$	*P*	*C.'s d*	$t_{(30)}$	*P*	*C.'s d*
Age (months)	122.23	27.87	122.50	20.00	122.57	25.45	−0.04	>0.05	−0.01	−0.04	>0.05	−0.01	0.01	>0.05	−0.003
Performance IQ (ss)	13.65	2.61	12.11	3.41	13.07	2.43	1.17	>0.05	0.51	0.76	>0.05	0.23	−0.93	>0.05	−0.32
Regular words reading (%)	99.67	0.75	90.56	15.76	93.57	3.16	2.45	**<0.05**	0.82	7.17	**<0.001**	2.66	−0.80	>0.05	−0.26
Irregular words reading (%)	98.28	2.64	88.94	16.77	89.00	7.51	2.35	**<0.05**	0.78	4.53	**<0.001**	1.65	−0.01	>0.05	−0.005
Pseudowords reading (%)	93.77	6.02	78.78	14.83	64.43	10.14	4.15	**<0.002**	1.32	10.25	**<0.001**	3.52	−3.24	**<0.001**	1.13
Number of correct pseudowords	5.44	1.76	3.50	2.75	2.18	1.99	2.77	**<0.02**	0.84	5.46	**<0.001**	1.73	−1.57	>0.05	0.55
Number of correct phonemes	56.74	17.20	40.61	15.41	35.86	11.97	3.60	**<0.002**	0.99	5.05	**<0.001**	1.41	−0.98	>0.05	0.34

The effect size (Cohen's d) is reported as C.'s d.

shorter SOA. DDP− group show that for the longer SOA, VSA was abnormally oriented.

Temporal attention

The identification accuracy mean in the O condition was analyzed by a One-Way ANOVA with Group as the between subjects factor. The group main effect was not significant [$F_{(2, 72)} = 1.34$, $p > 0.05$], highlighting that signal identification in the DDP− group did not differ from either the NR or DDP+ groups. In contrast, the mean O1 accuracy rate[2] ANOVA showed a significant group effect [$F_{(2, 72)} = 3.23$, $p < 0.05$], demonstrating that signal identification in presence of noise was significantly impaired in DDP− (47%), in comparison to NR (64%) and DDP+ (64%). Planned comparisons showed that the DDP− group, as compared to NR [$t_{(72)} = 5.93$, $p < 0.005$] and DDP+ [$t_{(72)} = 4.84$, $p < 0.05$], was significantly impaired in signal identification when presented with noise (see **Table 3**). In order to test perceptual-noise exclusion mechanism, "intrusion" errors for the identity of the second target were analyzed by a 1-tailed Independent Sample Test, showing a higher incidence of identity intrusions in the DDP− group (mean = 42%, $SD = 11.22$) compared to NR (mean = 36%, $SD = 12.19$), $p < 0.05$ and DDP+ (mean = 34%, $SD = 10.97$), $p < 0.05$ (details are reported in **Table 4**). In summary, our results showed that only dyslexics with phonological decoding deficit present difficulties in their perceptual-noise exclusion mechanism (see **Figure 5**).

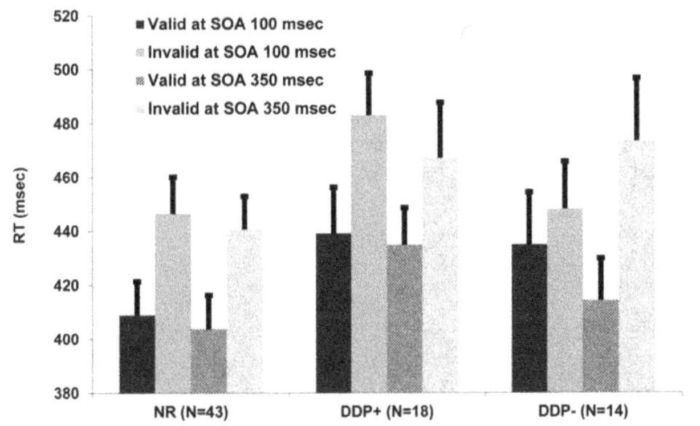

FIGURE 3 | Mean RT and standard error as a function of group (NR, DDP+, and DDP−), target condition (valid vs. invalid cue), and cue-target SOA (100 and 350 ms).

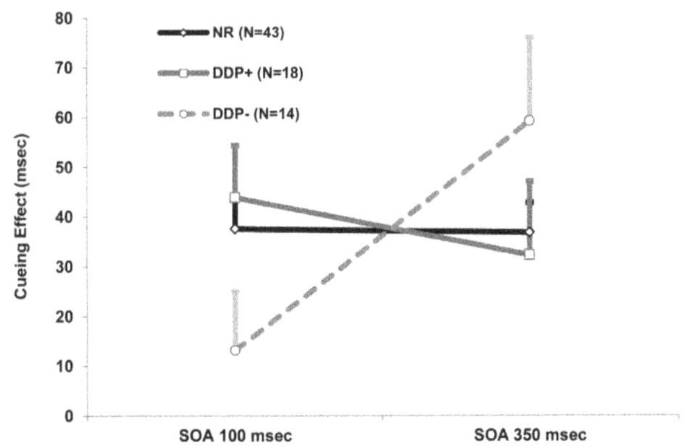

FIGURE 4 | Mean of cuing effect (i.e., invalid – valid RT differences) and standard error as a function of cue-target stimulus onset asynchrony (SOA; 100 and 350 ms) and group (NR, DDP+, and DDP−).

RELATIONSHIP BETWEEN VISUAL ATTENTION AND PHONOLOGICAL DECODING IN DYSLEXIC CHILDREN

Our results demonstrate a specific VSA and VTA deficit in the DDP− group. In order to investigate a possible relationship between individual measures of the cuing effect (VSA) time-course, the perceptual noise exclusion mechanism (VTA), and phonological decoding skill across our entire sample of dyslexic children ($N = 32$), bivariate correlations were computed. Reading abilities were measured on regular words, irregular words and pseudowords. The time-course of VSA was indexed by the difference between the cuing effects at 350 and 100 ms SOA. The efficiency of the VTA corresponded to the identification

[2]The main effect of the O1 pre-mask variable time exposure (175, 225, 275 or 325 msec) and the interaction effect with the group were not significant ($ps > 0.05$).

Table 3 | Mean (M) and standard deviation (SD) of single object (O) and signal+noise (O+noise).

	NR (*N* = 43)		DDP+ (*N* = 18)		DDP− (*N* = 14)	
	M	*SD*	*M*	*SD*	*M*	*SD*
O	94	8.27	93	10.53	89.50	9.30
O+noise	64	21.09	64	21.66	47	23.83

Table 2 | Mean (M) and standard deviation (SD) of cuing effect at 100 and 350 ms cue-target delay.

	NR (*N* = 43)		DDP+ (*N* = 18)		DDP− (*N* = 14)		Comparison NR vs. DDP+			Comparison NR vs. DDP−			Comparison DDP+ vs. DDP−		
	M	*SD*	*M*	*SD*	*M*	*SD*	$t_{(59)}$	*P*	*C.'s d*	$t_{(55)}$	*P*	*C.'s d*	$t_{(30)}$	*P*	*C.'s d*
100 ms cue-target delay	37.56	38.15	43.83	44.50	12.74	44.51	−0.52	>0.05	−0.01	2.03	**<0.05**	0.88	1.96	**<0.05**	0.96
350 ms cue-target delay	36.79	39.26	32.25	67.74	59.19	62.91	0.27	>0.05	0.08	−1.26	>0.05	−0.43	−1.15	>0.05	−0.41

The Effect Size (Cohen's d) is reported as C.'s d.

Table 4 | Mean (M) and standard deviation (SD) of "intrusion" errors for the identity of the second target in the temporal attention task (O+noise condition).

	NR ($N = 43$)		DDP+ ($N = 18$)		DDP− ($N = 14$)		Comparison NR vs. DDP+					Comparison NR vs. DDP−					Comparison DDP+ vs. DDP−				
	M	*SD*	*M*	*SD*	*M*	*SD*	$t_{(59)}$	*P*	*C.'s d*	*l.C.L*	*u.C.L.*	$t_{(55)}$	*P*	*C.'s d*	*l.C.L*	*u.C.L.*	$t_{(30)}$	*P*	*C.'s d*	*l.C.L*	*u.C.L.*
"intrusion" errors (O+noise condition)	35.81	12.19	34.44	10.97	42.14	11.22	0.43	>0.05	0.003	−5.3	8.03	−1.79	**<0.05**	0.051	−*13.71*	1.05	−1.94	**<0.05**	0.113	−*15.76*	0.36

The effect size (Cohen's d) is reported as C.'s d. The confidence limits are reported as l.C.L (lower Confidence Limit), u.C.L (upper Confidence Limit).

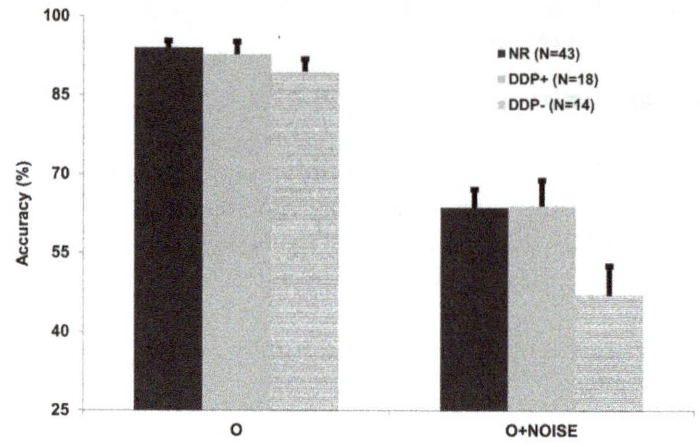

FIGURE 5 | Mean O and standard error as a function of group (NR, DDP+, and DDP−), signal accuracy (O), and signal + noise accuracy (O+noise).

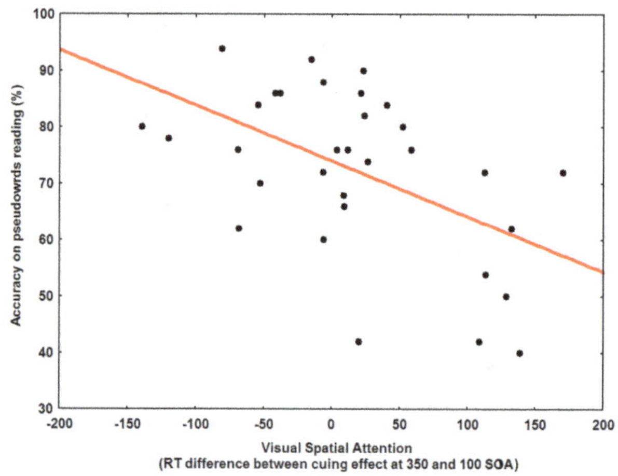

FIGURE 6 | Scatter plot of the relationship between time-course of visual spatial attention (RT difference between cuing effect at 350 and 100 ms SOA) and pseudoword reading accuracy across our entire sample of dyslexic children ($N = 32$).

accuracy mean in the O+noise condition. Phonological abilities were measured by using the efficiency in the PPB and PSTM tasks.

The main results showed that phonological decoding was significantly correlated with both spatial and temporal attention as well as phoneme blending (see **Figures 6, 7**). In addition, irregular word reading was correlated with both phonological tasks and VSA. Finally, temporal and spatial attention were highly correlated to each other (see **Table 5A**). The same bivariate correlations were computed in our entire sample ($N = 75$), including the NR children, confirming the relationship between visual attention and phonological decoding (see **Table 5B**).

To determine predictive relationships between visual attention and reading (pseudoword and irregular) accuracy, we computed two four-step fixed-entry multiple regression analyses on the individual data of the dyslexic children to control for the effects of age, Performance IQ, attentional mechanisms, and phonological processing.

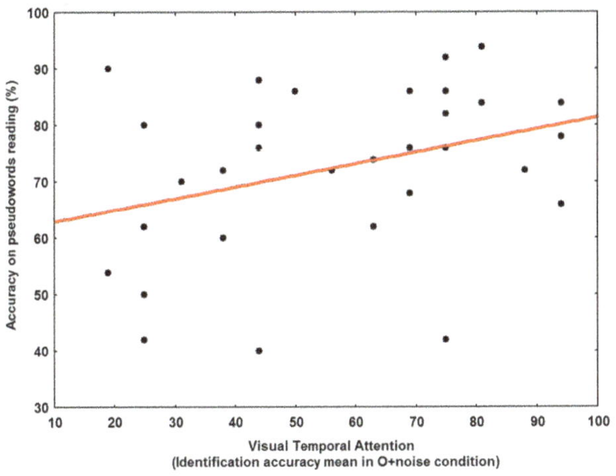

FIGURE 7 | Scatter plot of the relationship between visual temporal attention (identification accuracy mean in O+noise condition) and pseudoword reading accuracy across our entire sample of dyslexic children (*N* = 32).

Descriptive statistics of variables included in the multiple regression analysis are reported in **Table 6**. Because attentional graphemic parsing precedes phonemic blending during the reading process and VSA precedes the perceptual noise exclusion mechanism, we selected the following order of steps. In the first multiple regression analysis the dependent variable was pseudoword reading accuracy and the predictors entered at the four steps were: (i) age and Performance IQ, (ii) VSA, (iii) VTA, and (iv) PPB. Results showed that the time-course of spatial attention accounted for 17% ($p < 0.02$) of unique variance in sub-lexical reading accuracy. Only the PPB entered at the last step accounted for 14% ($p < 0.05$) of unique variance in lexical reading accuracy (see **Table 7**).

In the second multiple regression analysis the dependent variable was irregular word reading accuracy and the predictors entered at the four steps were the same as in the first analysis. Only the PPB entered at the last step accounted for 12% ($p < 0.05$) of unique variance in lexical reading accuracy (see **Table 8**).

DISCUSSION

Our results demonstrate that both spatial and temporal attention were impaired only in dyslexics with a poor phonological decoding (DDP−), confirming the relationship between visual attentional mechanisms and graphemic parsing processes. It is important to note that attentional graphemic parsing precedes the letter-to-speech sound integration.

The attentional cuing effect was present at the shortest cue-target delay (100 ms) in both NR and DDP+, as predicted by automatic capture theories (for a review, see Klein, 2000). In contrast, DDP− children showed a slower visual-spatial attentional orienting, because the cuing effect was not present at the short cue-target delay (distributed attention) whereas it appears at the long cue-target delay, as predicted by the "SAS" theory (Hari and Renvall, 2001; Facoetti et al., 2010a; Lallier et al., 2010; see Facoetti, 2012, for a recent review). We note that in DDP− the cuing effect was stronger than in DDP+ and NR grouped together at the long cue-target delay, suggesting that poor phonological decoders present a more concentrated focus of attention on the cue. These findings could reconcile apparent contradictory results in the literature regarding the different size of the attentional focus in dyslexics. For example, according to some evidence the attentional focus appears more distributed in dyslexics in comparison to normally reading children (e.g., Geiger et al., 1994, 2008; Facoetti et al., 2000). In contrast, other studies have shown more focused attention in dyslexics in comparison to normally reading children (e.g., Bosse et al., 2007). In general, before the cue onset, the attentional focus—controlled by the right frontal eye fields (Ronconi et al., 2014)—is probably distributed across the possible target locations indicated by the two circles. The attentional focus of the poor phonological decoders will be on the cue location for long cue-target delay (cuing effect), whereas their attentional focus will not be there for short cue-target delay (absence of cuing effect), suggesting a sluggish attentional orienting (Facoetti et al., 2010a; see Hari and Renvall, 2001; Facoetti, 2012, for reviews). Once on the cue, the attentional focus appears more focused in comparison to the other two groups. This combination of spatial attention disorders probably impairs the serial letter processing during graphemic parsing.

Moreover, object identification in the object task without noise was not impaired in poor phonological decoders, excluding a possible general visual perception deficit. In contrast, DDP− showed a specific identification deficit in comparison to NR and DDP+ when the object was displayed with noise (i.e., masks and a second object), demonstrating an inefficient perceptual-noise exclusion mechanism. Although the DDP− group showed a larger second object substitution, it would be important for future research to incorporate a baseline measure including O1+mask, but excluding O2, which would better isolate the role of specific O2 interference on O1. This condition could be relevant to even better isolate the pure role of the O2 interference, otherwise it would be difficult to exclude that unknown processing speed differences between the groups may play a role in the results.

According to the phonological hypothesis, it is important to note that poor pseudoword reading accuracy is strongly related to impaired phonological awareness (Frith, 1997; Snowling, 2000; Goswami, 2003, 2011; Vellutino et al., 2004). However, the two samples of dyslexics were not different in general phonological processing (i.e., phoneme blending and short-term memory of pseudowords). Only in DDP− both spatial and temporal attentional tasks were specifically disturbed, consistent with the hypothesis that SAS (Hari and Renvall, 2001) contributes to difficulties in phonological decoding, and it is at least partially independent from phonological skills (Bosse et al., 2007; Facoetti et al., 2010a,b; Franceschini et al., 2012, 2013; Zorzi et al., 2012; see Vidyasagar and Pammer, 2010, for a review).

Our attention indices allowed us to discriminate between dyslexics with poor phonological decoding and dyslexics with unimpaired phonological decoding or normal readers. Our results suggest that visual attention impairments are the core

Table 5 | Bivariate correlations between abilities were measured on Regular and Irregular words and Pseudowords, time-course of visual spatial attention (VSA; RT difference between cuing effect at 350 and 100 ms SOA), time-course of visual temporal attention (VTA; identification accuracy mean in O+noise condition), pseudowords phoneme blending (number of correct pseudowords), and a pseudoword short term memory (number of correct phonemes).

	Regular words reading (%)	Irregular words reading (%)	Pseudowords reading (%)	Number of correct pseudowords	Number of correct phonemes	VTA
(A)						
Irregular words reading (%)	**0.937****	–				
Pseudowords reading (%)	**0.691****	**0.739****	–			
Number of correct pseudowords	0.336	**0.436***	**0.463****	–		
Number of correct phonemes	0.172	**0.350***	0.159	**0.574****	–	
VTA	0.056	0.120	**0.333***	−0.063	0.012	–
VSA	−0.322	**−0.374***	**−0.476****	−0.239	−0.325	**−0.517****
(B)						
Irregular words reading (%)	**0.932****	–				
Pseudowords reading (%)	**0.717****	**0.743****	–			
Number of correct pseudowords	**0.430****	**0.502****	**0.543****	–		
Number of correct phonemes	**0.301****	**0.439****	**0.372****	**0.613****	–	
VTA	0.117	0.206	**0.310****	0.168	0.181	–
VSA	**−0.267****	**−0.347****	**−0.267***	−0.203	**−0.255***	**−0.295***

*Bivariate correlations computed in dyslexic children (N = 32) are reported in the **A**. Bivariate correlations computed in the entire sample (N = 75) are reported in the **B**.*

**Correlation is significant at the 0.05 level.*

***Correlation is significant at the 0.01 level.*

Table 6 | Descriptive Statistics of variables included in the multiple regression analysis: age (month), Performance IQ (Figure Completion, Wechsler, 1993), pseudoword reading accuracy, time-course of visual spatial attention (VSA; RT difference between cuing effect at 350 and 100 ms SOA) and time-course of visual temporal attention (VTA; identification accuracy mean in O+noise condition), and pseudowords phoneme blending (PPB; number of correct pseudowords) in dyslexic children (*N* = 32).

	DD (*N* = 32)	
	M	***SD***
Age (months)	122.53	22.16
Performance IQ (ss)	12.53	3.02
Pseudowords reading (%)	72.5	14.70
VSA	13.81	79.50
VTA	56.59	23.84
Number of correct phonemes	38.53	14

deficit in dyslexics characterized by poor (i.e., inaccurate) phonological decoding. This finding was supported by the predictive relationship of reading performance and visual attentional tasks, even after controlling for age and Performance IQ. Attentional graphemic parsing was significantly related to phonological decoding because it represents the first step that precedes not only letter-to-speech sound integration but also phonemic blending (significantly related to pseudoword reading) during the reading process.

It is important to stress that the predictive relationship between attention and reading skills held across the entire sample of dyslexics, independently of any a priori classification or subtyping of the dyslexic children. Thus, regardless of whether children in the DDP+ group constitute a specific subtype in shallow orthographies (Wimmer, 1993) or have partly compensated their reading deficit, rapid and efficient orienting of spatial attention seems to be related to phonological decoding. We suggest that this relationship might be causal because: (i) VSA is impaired in preschoolers at risk of DD (Facoetti et al., 2010b); (ii) it represents a significant predictor of future reading abilities (Franceschini et al., 2012); and (iii) attentional video games training has been proven to increase reading skills (Franceschini et al., 2013).

Our findings are consistent with previous results (e.g., Roach and Hogben, 2007; Facoetti et al., 2010a), and with the predictions of the CDP+ computational model of reading aloud (Perry et al., 2007). Efficient focused attention—indicated by a cuing effect at the short cue-target delay—is necessary for serial letter processing during phonological decoding, limiting the perceptual noise. In the DDP− group the cuing effect was absent at short cue-target delay, increasing the interference produced by perceptual noise during letter processing. Accordingly, several studies suggest that a general disorder in ignoring task-irrelevant information characterizes dyslexia perceptual processing (e.g., Badcock et al., 2008, 2011; Roach and Hogben, 2008). The sluggish attentional orienting index (spatial attention, task 1) is linked to a perceptual noise exclusion mechanism (temporal attention, task 2). The CDP+ assumes that focused attention is specifically involved in the sub-lexical spelling-to-sound mapping process (i.e., the sub-lexical route). Visual attentional tasks

Table 7 | Multiple regression analysis with pseudoword reading accuracy as dependent variable and the following predictors entered at the four steps: (i) age and Performance IQ, (ii) time-course of visual spatial attention (VSA; RT difference between cuing effect at 350 and 100 ms SOA), (iii) time-course of visual temporal attention (VTA; difference between signal accuracy and signal + noise accuracy), and (iv) pseudowords phoneme blending (PPB; number of correct pseudowords) in dyslexic children ($N = 32$).

Predictors	R	R^2	Change Statistics				
			R^2 Change	F Change	$df1$	$df2$	Sig. F Change
Age and performance IQ	0.283	0.080	0.080	1.265	2	29	>0.05
VSA	0.501	0.251	0.171	6.380	1	28	**<0.02**
VTA	0.506	0.256	0.005	0.187	1	27	>0.05
PPB	0.628	0.394	0.138	5.908	1	26	**<0.05**

Table 8 | Multiple regression analysis with irregular word reading accuracy as the dependent variable and the following predictors entered at the four steps: (i) age and Performance IQ, (ii) time-course of visual spatial attention (VSA; RT difference between cuing effect at 350 and 100 ms SOA), (iii) time-course of visual temporal attention (VTA; difference between signal accuracy and signal + noise accuracy), and (iv) pseudowords phoneme blending (PPB; number of correct pseudowords) in dyslexic children ($N = 32$).

Predictors	R	R^2	Change Statistics				
			R^2 Change	F Change	$df1$	$df2$	Sig. F Change
Age and performance IQ	0.266	0.071	0.071	1.102	2	29	>0.05
VSA	0.402	0.162	0.072	0.091	1	28	>0.05
VTA	0.438	0.192	0.030	1.006	1	27	>0.05
PPB	0.556	0.309	0.117	4.381	1	26	**<0.05**

accounted almost for 20% of unique variance in phonological decoding, representing an excellent predictor of pseudoword reading. Moreover, irregular word reading accuracy was not significantly predicted by the visual attentional variables, but only by the phonological ones (which accounted for 12%).

Clearly, these results are inconsistent with the hypothesis that DD is an exclusively phonological deficit. The present link between deficits in spatial and temporal attention and impaired phonological decoding is consistent with the hypothesis that visual selection (i.e., the perceptual-noise exclusion mechanism) operates on graphemes as the basic component of the phonological assembly process (Cestnick and Coltheart, 1999; Perry et al., 2007, Gori et al., under revision in the same issue). Both spatial (Geiger and Lettvin, 1987; Sperling et al., 2005; Geiger et al., 2008) and temporal (Di Lollo et al., 1983; Visser et al., 2004; Montgomery et al., 2005; Facoetti et al., 2008) processing windows in which noise interferes with the signal appear to be broader in dyslexics than normally reading children. In this study, we demonstrated that these deficits are specific in poor phonological decoders, and this can be attributed to the perceptual-noise exclusion deficit (Sperling et al., 2005). The link between deficits in VSA and impaired phonological decoding is also consistent with the results of recent studies in dyslexics that used visual search paradigms (e.g., Buchholz and McKone, 2004; Roach and Hogben, 2007; Jones et al., 2008; Facoetti et al., 2010a; Vidyasagar and Pammer, 2010, for a review). Furthermore, our results demonstrate, for the first time, that the relationship between visual attention and phonological decoding skills in dyslexia is explained by a sluggish shifting of spatial attention rather than a general perceptual noise exclusion mechanism. We suggest that inefficient spatial attention could specifically impair the graphemic parsing mechanism in dyslexic children. Although our spatial attention task involves also a temporal component, several studies have shown that the rapid shift of spatial attention modulates the speed of processing and consequentially the temporal aspects of attention (e.g., Carrasco and McElree, 2001; Carrasco et al., 2002, 2004; see Enns and Di Lollo, 2000, for a review). However, further studies are necessary to investigate the specific relationship between spatial and temporal attention. The results of the present study do not speak to the issue of visual vs. auditory and phonological processing deficits in DD. Several authors have argued that the core problem in DD is a deficit in phonological representation (Snowling, 2000; Ramus, 2003). It is important to note that efficient learning of sub-lexical spelling-sound mappings requires not only graphemic parsing but also accurate auditory and speech-sound segmentation mechanisms (see Goswami, 2003, 2011, for reviews). In particular, rise times are crucial events in the speech signal, as they reflect the patterns of amplitude modulation that facilitates the temporal segmentation of the acoustic signal into syllables. Rise time discrimination is impaired in dyslexia in English, French, Hungarian, Spanish, Chinese, and Finnish (Goswami, 2011). Rise time is a significant predictor of phonological awareness. However, efficient acoustic processing and segmentation of the speech signal are likely to require the rapid engagement of auditory attention (Renvall and Hari, 2002; Facoetti et al., 2003, 2005, 2010a). Auditory attention is, indeed, necessary for speech segmentation based on statistical learning (Toro et al., 2005) and for learning phonetic discriminations based on acoustic cues (Gordon et al., 1993; Francis et al., 2008; but see also Seitz et al., 2010). Moreover, auditory spatial attention has been shown to be defective in children with specific language impairment (SLI; Stevens et al., 2006) and reading DD (Asbjørnsen and Bryden, 1998; Renvall and Hari, 2002; Facoetti et al., 2003, 2005, 2010a,b).

Neural coding by brain oscillations is a major focus in neuroscience (e.g., Buzsaki and Draghun, 2004; Schroeder et al., 2008), with important implications for DD research (see Goswami, 2011, for a recent review). The results could be interpreted inside the oscillatory "temporal sampling" framework which is a compelling and robust theoretical framework (Goswami, 2011). Temporal sampling of speech-sound by neuroelectric oscillations that encode incoming information at different frequencies could explain the perceptual and phonological difficulties with syllables, rhymes and phonemes found in individuals with DD. A temporal sampling framework based on oscillations that entrain to sensory input could also have implications for other sensory theories of DD such as the magnocellular-dorsal (M-D) deficit theory (see Stein and Walsh, 1997; Gori and Facoetti, 2013, for a recent review). Thus, we conclude that a temporal sampling disorder of neural oscillations could characterize DD, suggesting innovative training programs not only for treatment but also for the possible prevention of DD at the pre-reading stage.

ACKNOWLEDGMENTS

This work was supported by a grant from University of Padua ("Progetto di Ateneo 2009 and 2011" to Andrea Facoetti and "Assegni di Ricerca 2009 and 2011" to Simone Gori). The contributions of the staff members of Eugenio Medea Scientific Institute as well as of the children and their families are gratefully acknowledged. We thank Marc Pomplun for his reading of the manuscript.

REFERENCES

American Psychiatric Association. (1994). *Diagnostic and Statistical Manual of Mental Disorders, 4th Edn.* Washington, DC: DSM-IV.

American Psychiatric Association. (2013). *Diagnostic and Statistical Manual of Mental Disorders, 5th Edn.* Arlington, VA: American Psychiatric Publishing.

Asbjørnsen, A. E., and Bryden, M. P. (1998). Auditory attentional shifts in reading-disabled students: quantification of attentional effectiveness by Attentional Shift Index. *Neuropsychologia* 36, 143–148. doi: 10.1016/S0028-3932(97)00090-0

Badcock, N. A., Hogben, J. H., and Fletcher, J. F. (2008). No differential attentional blink in dyslexia after controlling for baseline sensitivity. *Vision Res.* 48, 1497–1502. doi: 10.1016/j.visres.2008.03.008

Badcock, N. A., Hogben, J. H., and Fletcher, J. F. (2011). Dyslexia and practice in the attentional blink: evidence of slower task learning in dyslexia. *Cortex* 47, 494–500. doi: 10.1016/j.cortex.2010.03.002

Blau, V., Reithler, J., van Atteveldt, N., Seitz, J., Gerretsen, P., Goebel, R., and Blomert, L. (2010). Deviant processing of letters and speech sounds as proximate cause of reading failure: a functional magnetic resonance imaging study of dyslexic children. *Brain* 133, 868–879. doi: 10.1093/brain/awp308

Blau, V., van Atteveldt, N., Ekkebus, M., Goebel, R., and Blomert, L. (2009). Reduced neural integration of letters and speech sounds links phonological and reading deficits in adult dyslexia. *Curr. Biol.* 19, 503–508. doi: 10.1016/j.cub.2009.01.065

Blomert, L. (2011). The neural signature of orthographic-phonological binding in successful and failing reading development. *Neuroimage* 57, 695–703. doi: 10.1016/j.neuroimage.2010.11.003

Bosse, M. L., Tainturier, M. J., and Valdois, S. (2007). Developmental dyslexia: The visual attention span deficit hypothesis. *Cognition* 104, 198–230. doi: 10.1016/j.cognition.2006.05.009

Bouma, H. (1970). Interaction effects in parafoveal letter recognition. *Nature* 226, 177–178. doi: 10.1038/226177a0

Bouma, H., and Legein, C. P. (1977). Foveal and parafoveal recognition of letters and words by dyslexics and by average readers. *Neuropsychologia* 15, 69–80. doi: 10.1016/0028-3932(77)90116-6

Boyer, J., and Ro, T. (2007). Attention attenuates metacontrast masking. *Cognition* 104, 135–149. doi: 10.1016/j.cognition.2006.06.001

Bradley, L., and Bryant, P. (1983). Categorizing sound and learning to read: a casual connection. *Nature* 301, 419–421. doi: 10.1038/301419a0

Braun, J. (2002). Visual attention: light enters the jungle. *Curr. Biol.* 12, 599–601. doi: 10.1016/S0960-9822(02)01103-X

Breznitz, Z., Shaul, S., Horowitz-Kraus, T., Sela, I., Nevat, M., and Jarni, A. (2013). Enhanced reading by training with imposed time constraint in typical and dyslexic adults. *Nat. Commun.* 4, 1486. doi: 10.1038/ncomms2488

Buchholz, J., and McKone, E. (2004). Adults with dyslexia show deficits on spatial frequency doubling and visual attention tasks. *Dyslexia* 10, 24–43. doi: 10.1002/dys.263

Buzsaki, G., and Draghun, A. (2004). Neuronal oscillations in cortical networks. *Science* 25, 1926–1929. doi: 10.1126/science.1099745

Carrasco, M., Ling, S., and Read, S. (2004). Attention alters appearance. *Nat. Neurosci.* 7, 308–313. doi: 10.1038/nn1194

Carrasco, M., and McElree, B. (2001). Covert attention accelerates the rate of visual information processing. *Proc. Natl. Acad. Sci. U.S.A.* 98, 5363–5367. doi: 10.1073/pnas.081074098

Carrasco, M., Penpeci-Talgar, C., and Eckstein, M. (2000). Spatial covert attention increases contrast sensitivity across the CSF: support for signal enhancement. *Vision Res.* 40, 1203–1215. doi: 10.1016/S0042-6989(00)00024-9

Carrasco, M., Williams, P., and Yeshurum, Y. (2002). Covert attention increases spatial resolution with or without masks: support for signal enhancement. *J. Vis.* 2, 467–479. doi: 10.1167/2.6.4

Castiello, U., and Umiltà, C. (1990). Size of the attentional focus and efficiency of processing. *Acta Psychol. (Amst)* 73, 195–209. doi: 10.1016/0001-6918(90)90022-8

Castles, A., and Coltheart, M. (1993). Varieties of developmental dyslexia. *Cognition* 47, 148–180. doi: 10.1016/0010-0277(93)90003-E

Castles, A., and Coltheart, M. (2004). Is there a causal link from phonological awareness to success in learning to read? *Cognition* 91, 77–111. doi: 10.1016/S0010-0277(03)00164-1

Cestnick, L., and Coltheart, M. (1999). The relationship between language-processing and visual processing deficit in developmental dyslexia. *Cognition* 71, 231–255. doi: 10.1016/S0010-0277(99)00023-2

Chandrasekaran, B., Hornickel, J., Skoe, E., Trent, N., and Kraus, N. (2009). Context-dependent encoding in the human auditory brainstem relates to hearing speech in noise: implications for developmental dyslexia. *Neuron* 64, 311–319. doi: 10.1016/j.neuron.2009.10.006

Dehaene, S., Pegado, F., Braga, L. W., Ventura, P., Nunes Filho, G., Jobert, A., et al. (2010). How learning to read changes the cortical networks for vision and language. *Science* 330, 1359–1364. doi: 10.1126/science.1194140

Di Lollo, V., Hanson, D., and McIntyre, J. S. (1983). Initial stages of visual information processing in dyslexia. *J. Exp. Psychol. Hum. Percept. Perform.* 6, 923–935. doi: 10.1037/0096-1523.9.6.923

Dispaldro, M., Laurence, B. L., Corradi, N., Ruffino, M., Bronte, T., and Facoetti, A. (2013). Visual attentional engagement deficits in children with Specific Language Impairment and their role in real-time language processing. *Cortex* 49, 2126–2139. doi: 10.1016/j.cortex.2012.09.012

Dosher, B. N., and Lu, Z. (2000). Noise exclusion in spatial attention. *Psychol. Sci.* 11, 139–146. doi: 10.1111/1467-9280.00229

Duncan, J., Ward, R., and Shapiro, K. (1994). Direct measurement of attentional dwell time in human vision. *Nature* 369, 313–315. doi: 10.1038/369313a0

Enns, J. T., and Di Lollo, V. (2000). What's new in visual masking? *Trends Cogn. Sci.* 4, 345–352. doi: 10.1016/S1364-6613(00)01520-5

Facoetti, A. (2012). "Spatial attention disorders in developmental dyslexia: towards the prevention of reading acquisition deficits," in *Visual Aspect of Dyslexia,* eds J. Stein and Z. Kapoula (Oxford, UK: Oxford University Press). doi: 10.1093/acprof:oso/9780199589814.003.0008

Facoetti, A., Corradi, N., Ruffino, M., Gori, S., and Zorzi, M. (2010b). Visual spatial attention and speech segmentation are both impaired in preschoolers at familial risk for developmental dyslexia. *Dyslexia* 16, 226–239. doi: 10.1002/dys.413

Facoetti, A., Lorusso, M. L., Cattaneo, C., Galli, R., and Molteni, M. (2005). Visual and auditory attentional capture are both sluggish in children with developmental dyslexia. *Acta Neurobiol. Exp.* 65, 61–72.

Facoetti, A., Lorusso, M. L., Paganoni, P., Umiltà, C., and Mascetti, G. G. (2003). The role of visuospatial attention in developmental dyslexia: evidence from a rehabilitation study. *Cogn. Brain Res.* 15, 15–164. doi: 10.1016/S0926-6410(02)00148-9

Facoetti, A., and Molteni, M. (2000). Is attentional focusing an inhibitory process at distractor location? *Cogn. Brain Res.* 10, 185–188. doi: 10.1016/S0926-6410(00)00031-8

Facoetti, A., Paganoni, P., and Lorusso, M. L. (2000). The spatial distribution of visual attention in developmental dyslexia. *Exp. Brain Res.* 132, 531–538. doi: 10.1007/s002219900330

Facoetti, A., Ruffino, M., Peru, A., Paganoni, P., and Chelazzi, L. (2008). Sluggish engagement and disengagement of non-spatial attention in dyslexic children. *Cortex* 44, 1221–1233. doi: 10.1016/j.cortex.2007.10.007

Facoetti, A., Trussardi, A. N., Ruffino, M., Lorusso, M. L., Cattaneo, C., Galli, R., et al. (2010a). Multisensory spatial attention deficits are predictive of phonological decoding skills in development dyslexia. *J. Cogn. Neurosci.* 22, 1011–1025. doi: 10.1162/jocn.2009.21232

Facoetti, A., Zorzi, M., Cestnick, L., Lorusso, M. L., Molteni, M., Paganoni, P., et al. (2006). The relationship between visuo spatial attention and nonword reading in developmental dyslexia. *Cogn. Neuropsychol.* 23, 841–855. doi: 10.1080/02643290500483090

Farmer, M. E., and Klein, R. M. (1995). The evidence for a temporal processing deficit linked to dyslexia. *Psychon. Bull. Rev.* 2, 469–493. doi: 10.3758/BF03210983

Franceschini, S., Gori, S., Ruffino, M., Pedrolli, K., and Facoetti, A. (2012). A causal link between visual spatial attention and reading acquisition. *Curr. Biol.* 22, 814–819. doi: 10.1016/j.cub.2012.03.013

Franceschini, S., Gori, S., Ruffino, M., Viola, S., Molteni, M., and Facoetti, A. (2013). Action video games make dyslexic children read better. *Curr. Biol.* 23, 1–5. doi: 10.1016/j.cub.2013.01.044

Francis, A. L., Kaganovich, N., and Driscoll-Huber, C. (2008). Cue-specific effects of categorization training on the relative weighting of acoustic cues to consonant voicing in English. *J. Acoust. Soc. Am.* 124, 1234–1251. doi: 10.1121/1.2945161

Frith, U. (1997). "Brain, mind and behaviour in dyslexia," in *Dyslexia: Biology, Cognition and Intervention*, eds C. Hulme and M. Snowling (London: Whurr), 1–19.

Gabrieli, J. D. (2009). Dyslexia: a new synergy between education and cognitive neuroscience. *Science* 325, 280–283. doi: 10.1126/science.1171999

Geiger, G., Cattaneo, C., Galli, R., Pozzoli, U., Lorusso, M. L., Facoetti, A., et al. (2008). Wide and diffuse perceptual modes characterized dyslexics in vision and audition. *Perception* 37, 1745–1764. doi: 10.1068/p6036

Geiger, G., and Lettvin, J. Y. (1987). Peripheral vision in persons with dyslexia. *N. Engl. J. Med.* 316, 1238–1243. doi: 10.1056/NEJM198705143162003

Geiger, G., Lettvin, J. Y., and Fanhle, M. (1994). Dyslexic children learn a new visual strategy for reading: a controlled experiment. *Vision Res.* 34, 1223–1233. doi: 10.1016/0042-6989(94)90303-4

Gordon, P. C., Eberhardt, J. L., and Rueckl, J. G. (1993). Attentional modulation of the phonetic significance of acoustic cues. *Cogn. Psychol.* 25, 1–42. doi: 10.1006/cogp.1993.1001

Gori, S., and Facoetti, A. (2013). Perceptual learning as a possible new approach for remediation and prevention of developmental dyslexia. *Vision Res.* doi: 10.1016/j.visres.2013.11.011. [Epub ahead of print].

Goswami, U. (2003). Why theories about developmental dyslexia require developmental designs. *Trends Cogn. Sci.* 7, 534–540. doi: 10.1016/j.tics.2003.10.003

Goswami, U. (2011). A temporal sampling framework for developmental dyslexia. *Trends Cogn. Sci.* 15, 3–10. doi: 10.1016/j.tics.2010.10.001

Goswami, U., Thomson, J., Richardson, U., Strainthorp, R., Hughes, D., Rosen, S., et al. (2000). Amplitude envelope onsets and developmental dyslexia: A new hypothesis. *Proc. Natl. Acad. Sci. U.S.A.* 99, 10911–10916. doi: 10.1073/pnas.122368599

Hari, R., and Kiesilä, P. (1996). Deficit of temporal auditory processing in dyslexic adults. *Neurosci. Lett.* 23, 138–140. doi: 10.1016/0304-3940(96)12393-4

Hari, R., and Renvall, H. (2001). Impaired processing of rapid stimulus sequences in dyslexia. *Trends Cogn. Sci.* 5, 525–532. doi: 10.1016/S1364-6613(00)01801-5

Hari, R., Renvall, H., and Tanskanen, T. (2001). Left minineglect in dyslexic adults. *Brain* 124, 1373–1380. doi: 10.1093/brain/124.7.1373

Hari, R., Valta, M., and Uutella, K. (1999). Prolonged attentional dwell time in dyslexic adults. *Neurosci. Lett.* 271, 202–204. doi: 10.1016/S0304-3940(99)00547-9

Helenius, P., Uutela, K., and Hari, R. (1999). Auditory stream segregation in dyslexic adults. *Brain* 122, 907–913. doi: 10.1093/brain/122.5.907

Hornickel, J., Zecker, S. G., Bradlow, A. R., and Kraus, N. (2012). Assistive listening devices drive neuroplasticity in children with dyslexia. *Proc. Natl. Acad. Sci. U.S.A.* 109, 16731–16736. doi: 10.1073/pnas.1206628109

Jones, M. W., Branigan, H. P., Parra, M. A., and Logie, R. H. (2013). Cross-modal binding in developmental dyslexia. *J. Exp. Psychol. Learn. Mem. Cogn.* 39, 1807–1822. doi: 10.1037/a0033334

Jones, M. W., Branigan, H. P., and Kelly, M., L. (2008). Visual deficits in developmental dyslexia: relationships between non-linguistic visual tasks and their contribution to literacy. *Dyslexia* 14, 95–115. doi: 10.1002/dys.345

Jonides, J., and Yantis, S. (1998). Uniqueness of abrupt visual onset in capturing attention. *Percept. Psychophys.* 43, 346–354. doi: 10.3758/BF03208805

Klein, R. M. (2000). Inhibition of return. *Trends Cogn. Sci.* 4, 138–147. doi: 10.1016/S1364-6613(00)01452-2

LaBerge, D. (1995). *Attentional Processing: The Brain's Art of Mindfulness.* Cambridge, MA: Harvard University Press. doi: 10.4159/harvard.9780674183940

Lallier, M., Tainturier, M. J., Dering, B., Donnadieu, S., Valdois, S., and Thierry, G. (2010). Behavioral and ERP evidence for amodal sluggish attentional shifting in developmental dyslexia. *Neuropsychologia* 48, 4125–4135. doi: 10.1016/j.neuropsychologia.2010.09.027

Montgomery, C. R., Morris, R. D., Sevcik, R. A., and Clarkson, M. G. (2005). Auditory backward masking deficits in children with reading disabilities. *Brain Lang.* 95, 450–456. doi: 10.1016/j.bandl.2005.03.006

Perry, C., Ziegler, J. C., and Zorzi, M. (2007). Nested incremental modeling in the development of computational theories: the CDP+ model of reading aloud. *Psychol. Rev.* 114, 273–315. doi: 10.1037/0033-295X.114.2.273

Peterson, R. L., and Pennington, B. F. (2012). Developmental dyslexia. *Lancet* 379, 1997–2007. doi: 10.1016/S0140-6736(12)60198-6

Plaza, M., and Cohen, H. (2007). The contribution of phonological awareness and visual attention in early reading and spelling. *Dyslexia* 13, 67–76. doi: 10.1002/dys.330

Posner, M. I. (1980). Orienting of attention. *Q. J. Exp. Psychol.* 32, 3–25. doi: 10.1080/00335558008248231

Ramus, F. (2003). Developmental dyslexia: specific phonological deficit or general sensorimotor dysfunction? *Curr. Opin. Neurobiol.* 13, 212–218. doi: 10.1016/S0959-4388(03)00035-7

Renvall, H., and Hari, R. (2002). Auditory cortical responses to speech-like stimuli in dyslexic adults. *J. Cogn. Neurosci.* 14, 757–768. doi: 10.1162/08989290260 138654

Reynolds, J. H., and Chelazzi, L. (2004). Attentional modulation of visual processing. *Annu. Rev. Neurosci.* 27, 611–647. doi: 10.1146/annurev.neuro.26.041002. 131039

Roach, N. W., and Hogben, J. H. (2007). Impaired filtering of behaviourally irrelevant visual information in dyslexia. *Brain* 130, 771–785. doi: 10.1093/brain/awl353

Roach, N. W., Hogben, J. H. (2008). Spatial cueing deficits in dyslexia reflect generalised difficulties with attentional selection. *Vision Res.* 48, 193–207. doi: 10.1016/j.visres.2007.11.001

Ronconi, L., Basso, D., Gori, S., and Facoetti, A. (2014). tms on right frontal eye fields induces an inflexible focus of attention. *Cereb. Cortex* 24, 396–402. doi: 10.1093/cercor/bhs319

Ronconi, L., Gori, S., Giora, E., Ruffino, M., Molteni, M., and Facoetti, A. (2013b). Deeper attentional masking by lateral objects in children with autism. *Brain Cogn.* 82, 213–218. doi: 10.1016/j.bandc.2013.04.006

Ronconi, L., Gori, S., Ruffino, M., Franceschini, S., Urbani, B., Molteni, M., and Facoetti, A. (2012). Decreased coherent motion discrimination in autism spectrum disorder: the role of attentional zoom-out deficit. *PLoS ONE* 7:e49019. doi: 10.1371/journal.pone.0049019

Ronconi, L., Gori, S., Ruffino, M., Molteni, M., and Facoetti, A. (2013a). Zoom-out attentional impairment in children with autism spectrum disorder. *Cortex* 49, 1025–1033. doi: 10.1016/j.cortex.2012.03.005

Ruffino, M., Trussardi, A. N., Gori, S., Finzi, A., Giovagnoli, S., Menghini, D., et al. (2010). Attentional engagement deficits in dyslexic children. *Neuropsychologia* 48, 3793–3801. doi: 10.1016/j.neuropsychologia.2010.09.002

Sartori, G., Job, R., and Tressoldi, P. E. (1995). *Batteria per la Valutazione Della Dislessia e Della Disortografia Evolutiva.* Firenze: Giunti O.S. Organizzazioni Speciali.

Schneps, M. H., Thomson, J. M., Chen, C., Sonnert, G., and Pomplun, M. (2013a). E-readers are more effective than paper for some with dyslexia. *PLoS ONE* 18:e75634. doi: 10.1371/journal.pone.0075634

Schneps, M. H., Thomson, J. M., Sonnert, G., Pomplun, M., Chen, C., and Heffner-Wong, A. (2013b). Shorter lines facilitate reading in those who struggle. *PLoS ONE* 5:e71161. doi: 10.1371/journal.pone.0071161

Schroeder, C. E., Lakatos, P., Kajikawa, Y., Partan, S., and Puce, A. (2008). Neuronal oscillations and visual amplification of speech. *Trends Cogn. Sci.* 12, 106–113. doi: 10.1016/j.tics.2008.01.002

Seitz, A. R., Protopapas, A., Tsushima, Y., Vlahou, E. L., Gori, S., Grossberg, S., et al. (2010). Unattended exposure to components of speech sounds yields same benefits as explicit auditory training. *Cognition* 115, 435–43. doi: 10.1016/j.cognition.2010.03.004

Share, D. L. (1995). Phonological recoding and self-teaching: sine qua non of reading acquisition. *Cognition* 55, 151–218. doi: 10.1016/0010-0277(94)00645-2

Snowling, M. J. (2000). *Dyslexia.* Oxford: Blackwell.

Sperling, A. J., Lu, Z. L., Manis, F. R., and Seidenberg, M. S. (2005). Deficits in perceptual noise exclusion in developmental dyslexia. *Nat. Neurosci.* 8, 862–863. doi: 10.1038/nn1474

Sprenger-Charolles, L., Siegel, L. S., Bechennec, D., and Serniclaes, W. (2003). Development of phonological and orthographic processing in reading aloud, in silent reading, and in spelling: a four-year longitudinal study. *J. Exp. Child Psychol.* 84, 194–217. doi: 10.1016/S0022-0965(03)00024-9

Stein, J., and Walsh, V. (1997). To see but not to read; the magnocellular theory of dyslexia. *Trends Neurosci.* 20, 147–152. doi: 10.1016/S0166-2236(96)01005-3

Stevens, C., Sanders, L., and Neville, H. (2006). Neurophysiological evidence for selective auditory attention deficits in children with specific language impairment. *Brain Res.* 1111, 143–152. doi: 10.1016/j.brainres.2006.06.114

Tallal, P. (1980). Auditory temporal perception, phonetic, and reading disabilities in children. *Brain Lang.* 9, 182–198. doi: 10.1016/0093-934X(80)90139-X

Tallal, P. (2004). Improving language and literacy is a matter of time. *Nat. Rev. Neurosci.* 5, 721–728. doi: 10.1038/nrn1499

Toro, J. M., Sinnet, S., Soto-Faraco, S. (2005). Speech segmentation by statistical learning depends on attention. *Cognition* 97, 25–34. doi: 10.1016/j.cognition.2005.01.006

Vandermosten, M., Boets, B., Luts, H., Poelmans, H., Golestani, N., Wouters, J., et al. (2010). Adults with dyslexia are impaired in categorizing speech and non-speech sounds on the basis of temporal cues. *Proc. Natl. Acad. U.S.A.* 107, 10389–10394. doi: 10.1073/pnas.0912858107

Vellutino, F. R., Fletcher, J. M., Snowling, M. J., and Scanlon, D. M. (2004). Specific reading disability (dyslexia): what have we learned in the past four decades? *J. Child Psychol. Psychiatry* 45, 2–40. doi: 10.1046/j.0021-9630.2003.00305.x

Vidyasagar, T. R., and Pammer, K. (2010). Dyslexia: a deficit in visuo-spatial attention, not in phonological processing. *Trends Cogn. Sci.* 14, 57–63. doi: 10.1016/j.tics.2009.12.003

Visser, T. A. W., Boden, C., and Giaschi, D. E. (2004). Children with dyslexia: evidence for visual attention deficits in perception of rapid sequences of objects. *Vision Res.* 44, 2521–2535. doi: 10.1016/j.visres.2004.05.010

Wechsler, D. (1993). *Wechsler Intelligence Scale for Children-Revised (WISC-R).* Firenze: Giunti O. S. Organizzazioni Speciali.

Wimmer, H. (1993). Characteristics of developmental dyslexia in a regular writing system. *Appl. Psycholinguist.* 14, 1–33. doi: 10.1017/S0142716400010122

Wright, B. A., Bowen, R. W., and Zecker, S. G. (2000). Nonlinguistic perceptual deficits associated with reading and language disorders. *Curr. Opin. Neurobiol.* 10, 482–486. doi: 10.1016/S0959-4388(00)00119-7

Yantis, S., and Jonides, J. (1984). Abrupt visual onsets and selective attention: evidence from visual search. *J. Exp. Psychol. Hum. Percept. Perform.* 10, 601–621. doi: 10.1037/0096-1523.10.5.601

Yeshurun, Y., and Rashal, E. (2010). Precueing attention to the target location diminishes crowding and reduces the critical distance. *J. Vis.* 10, 1–12. doi: 10.1167/10.10.16

Ziegler, J., Pech-Georgel, C., George, F., and Lorenzi, C. (2009). Speech perception in noise deficits in dyslexia. *Dev. Sci.* 12, 732–745. doi: 10.1111/j.1467-7687.2009.00817.x

Ziegler, J. C., Perry, C., Wyatt, A. M., Ladner, D., and Schülte-Korne, G. (2003). Developmental dyslexia in different languages: language-specific or universal? *J. Exp. Child Psychol.* 86, 169–193. doi: 10.1016/S0022-0965(03)00139-5

Zorzi, M. (2005). "Computational models of reading," in *Connectionist Models in Cognitive Psychology,* ed G. Houghton (London, UK: Psychology Press), 403–444.

Zorzi, M., Barbiero, C., Facoetti, A., Lonciari, I., Carrozzi, M., Montico, M., et al. (2012). Extra-large letter spacing improves reading in dyslexia. *Proc. Natl. Acad. Sci. U.S.A.* 109, 11455–11459. doi: 10.1073/pnas.1205566109

15

Dissociations between developmental dyslexias and attention deficits

Limor Lukov, Naama Friedmann*, Lilach Shalev, Lilach Khentov-Kraus, Nir Shalev, Rakefet Lorber and Revital Guggenheim

School of Education and Sagol School of Neuroscience, Tel Aviv University, Tel Aviv, Israel[1]

***Correspondence:**
Naama Friedmann, Language and Brain Lab, School of Education and Sagol School of Neuroscience, Tel Aviv University, Ramat Aviv, Tel Aviv 69978, Israel
e-mail: naamafr@post.tau.ac.il

We examine whether attention deficits underlie developmental dyslexia, or certain types of dyslexia, by presenting double dissociations between the two. We took into account the existence of distinct types of dyslexia and of attention deficits, and focused on dyslexias that may be thought to have an attentional basis: letter position dyslexia (LPD), in which letters migrate within words, attentional dyslexia (AD), in which letters migrate between words, neglect dyslexia, in which letters on one side of the word are omitted or substituted, and surface dyslexia, in which words are read via the sublexical route. We tested 110 children and adults with developmental dyslexia and/or attention deficits, using extensive batteries of reading and attention. For each participant, the existence of dyslexia and the dyslexia type were tested using reading tests that included stimuli sensitive to the various dyslexia types. Attention deficit and its type was established through attention tasks assessing sustained, selective, orienting, and executive attention functioning. Using this procedure, we identified 55 participants who showed a double dissociation between reading and attention: 28 had dyslexia with normal attention and 27 had attention deficits with normal reading. Importantly, each dyslexia with suspected attentional basis dissociated from attention: we found 21 individuals with LPD, 13 AD, 2 neglect dyslexia, and 12 surface dyslexia without attention deficits. Other dyslexia types (vowel dyslexia, phonological dyslexia, visual dyslexia) also dissociated from attention deficits. Examination of 55 additional individuals with both a specific dyslexia and a certain attention deficit found no attention function that was consistently linked with any dyslexia type. Specifically, LPD and AD dissociated from selective attention, neglect dyslexia dissociated from orienting, and surface dyslexia dissociated from sustained and executive attention. These results indicate that visuospatial attention deficits do not underlie these dyslexias.

Keywords: developmental dyslexia, attention, letter position dyslexia, attentional dyslexia, dissociation, neglect dyslexia, surface dyslexia

INTRODUCTION

One of the paths that the research of developmental dyslexia takes is the quest for a cognitive underlying source for developmental dyslexia. In this research we examine whether attention deficits are a source for developmental dyslexia, by searching for dissociations between the two. In our investigation we applied a neuropsychological perspective that treats both reading and attention as multifaceted constructs and as a result differentiates between types of dyslexia and between types of attention difficulties. Namely—beyond examining whether double dissociations can be found between developmental dyslexia and attention deficits, we ask more specific questions: we take specific dyslexias, analyze their possible relations to specific attention functions, and ask whether they can be dissociated from deficits in the relevant attention functions.

Dyslexia is a reading impairment that can result from brain damage (acquired dyslexia) or be present already before reading acquisition (developmental dyslexia). More than 10 types of developmental dyslexia have been identified, each resulting from deficits in different components of the reading process, and each having different characteristics (Marshall, 1984; Castles and Coltheart, 1993; Temple, 1997; Castles et al., 1999, 2006; Jones et al., 2011; Coltheart and Kohnen, 2012; Friedmann and Haddad-Hanna, 2014). Similarly, the neuroscience literature treats attention as a multifaceted system composed of several different attention networks (Posner and Petersen, 1990; Parasuraman, 2000; Tsal et al., 2005; Petersen and Posner, 2012). Tsal et al. (2005) describe four attentional subsystems (or functions) that are independent to some degree and can be localized in different anatomical loci. Therefore, in the current research we wish to explore the nature of the relation between specific types of

[1]This article is dedicated to the precious memory of Limor Lukov, our much-loved and appreciated student and teacher, an avid proponent of the dissociability of dyslexias from attention disorders and from phonological disorders. The article is mainly based on Limor's PhD research.

dyslexia and specific types of attention deficits and to learn about their shared and/or separate bases.

In what follows, we briefly describe the process of normal reading that we assume and the different types of dyslexia that stem from deficits in its different components, then discuss the different attention functions and different types of attention deficits that stem from deficits in its different components, and then discuss the relation between specific types of dyslexia and specific attention deficits.

THE PROCESS OF SINGLE WORD READING AND THE VARIOUS DYSLEXIA TYPES

According to the dual-route model for single word reading (Patterson et al., 1985; Ellis and Young, 1996; Coltheart et al., 2001; Jackson and Coltheart, 2001; Castles et al., 2006; Coltheart and Kohnen, 2012, and others, see **Figure 1**), the early stage of reading is responsible for orthographic-visual analysis, including the identification of the abstract identity of letters in the word, the encoding of the relative position of letters within the word, and binding of letters to a word. The output of these components is held in a graphemic input buffer until it is processed in the next stages.

Each of the functions of the orthographic-visual analyzer is susceptible to a selective deficit, causing a different type of dyslexia, with different pattern of errors and effects on reading. A deficit in letter identification results in visual dyslexia, letter identification dyslexia, or letter agnosia (Nielsen, 1937; Marshall and Newcombe, 1973; Lambon Ralph and Ellis, 1997; Cuetos and Ellis, 1999; Brunsdon et al., 2006; Friedmann et al., 2012); a deficit in the encoding of letter position within words results in letter position dyslexia, characterized by letter migrations within the word (Friedmann and Gvion, 2001, 2005; Friedmann and Rahamim, 2007, 2014; Friedmann et al., 2010a; Friedmann and Haddad-Hanna, 2012, 2014; Kohnen et al., 2012).

A deficit in letter-to-word binding gives rise to attentional dyslexia, in which letters migrate between words (Shallice and Warrington, 1977; Price and Humphreys, 1993; Saffran and Coslett, 1996; Hall et al., 2001; Humphreys and Mayall, 2001; Davis and Coltheart, 2002; Friedmann et al., 2010b). A further type of dyslexia that results from a deficit at the visual analysis stage, neglect dyslexia at the word level, is characterized by neglect of one side of the word, resulting in omissions, substitutions, or additions of letters on one of the sides of the word, typically on the left side (Bisiach et al., 1986; Ellis et al., 1987, 1993; Caramazza and Hillis, 1990; Cubelli et al., 1991; Haywood and Coltheart, 2001; Arduino et al., 2002, 2003; Vallar et al., 2010).

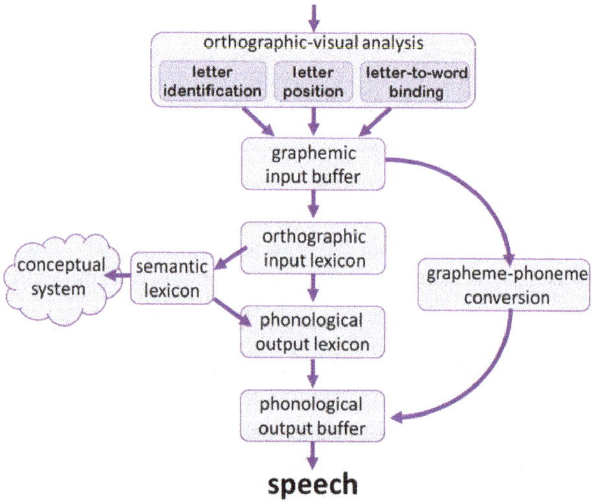

FIGURE 1 | The dual route model of single word reading.

From the orthographic-visual analysis stage, the information flows in two routes: a lexical route and a sublexical route. The lexical route starts with an orthographic input lexicon, which stores the orthographic form of words the reader is acquainted with. The information that arrives from the orthographic-visual analyzer activates an entry of a word in the orthographic input lexicon. This entry, in turn, activates an entry in the phonological output lexicon, where information about the phonology of the word is stored, including consonants, vowels, stress position, and number of syllables. This phonological information then activates the phonological output buffer, which constructs the phonological representation from the consonants, vowels, and their order, and holds the phonological information until the word is spoken. The lexical route is the fast and accurate route for reading aloud. Another branch of the lexical route arrives from the orthographic input lexicon to the semantic-conceptual system, where the information about the meaning of the written word is stored.

The other route, the sublexical route, allows the reading of unfamiliar words, by converting graphemes into phonemes. This route may cause regularization in reading irregular words (such as reading *love* to rhyme with cove and *listen* with a pronounced "t"). The correct reading aloud of such irregular words requires reading through the lexical route. Recent studies of dyslexia teach us that the sublexical route converts consonants and vowels separately (Khentov-Kraus and Friedmann, 2011), and converts graphemes with sensitivity to phonological features (Gvion and Friedmann, 2010).

Again, different types of dyslexia result from deficits in various loci in these two routes. A deficit in the lexical route results in surface dyslexia (Marshall and Newcombe, 1973; Newcombe and Marshall, 1981, 1984, 1985; Coltheart et al., 1983; Coltheart and Funnell, 1987; Howard and Franklin, 1987; Castles and Coltheart, 1993, 1996; Weekes and Coltheart, 1996; Ellis et al., 2000; Judica et al., 2002; Castles et al., 2006; Friedmann and Lukov, 2008). Because readers with surface dyslexia cannot use the lexical route to read aloud, they read via grapheme-to-phoneme conversion. As a result, their reading is slower (Zoccolotti et al., 1999), and, in the case of irregular words and words for which grapheme-to-phoneme conversion is ambiguous, also inaccurate.

An impairment in the sublexical route gives rise to phonological dyslexia, in which readers can read only via the lexical route, so they are only able to read correctly words that are already in their orthographic input lexicon, whereas they experience great difficulty in reading aloud nonwords and new words (Temple and Marshall, 1983; Glosser and Friedman, 1990; Coltheart, 1996; Friedman, 1996; Southwood and Chatterjee,

1999, 2001). This dyslexia can result from a deficit in grapheme-to-phoneme conversion or from a deficit in the phonological output buffer (Guggenheim and Friedmann, 2014). Given the special nature of the sublexical route described above, specific types of dyslexia can result from a selective deficit in reading vowel letters (Khentov-Kraus and Friedmann, 2011; Friedmann and Haddad-Hanna, 2014), or a selective deficit in some phonological features like voicing (Gvion and Friedmann, 2010).

A deficit to both the lexical and the sub-lexical reading routes results in *deep dyslexia*, which causes semantic errors in reading (reading *smile* as "laugh," and *swam* as "swimming"), and inability to read nonwords and function words.

Thus, various types of dyslexia exist, with different patterns of errors in reading, which result from damage to different components of the reading process. Most of the subtypes of dyslexia were initially identified only in acquired dyslexia. In recent years we see more and more studies that provide robust evidence for the existence of subtypes of developmental dyslexia, which show striking similarity to subtypes of acquired dyslexia. This has been reported for developmental *surface dyslexia* (Broom and Doctor, 1995a; Temple, 1997; Masterson, 2000; Castles et al., 2006; Friedmann and Lukov, 2008), developmental *phonological dyslexia* (Broom and Doctor, 1995b; Temple, 1997; Guggenheim and Friedmann, 2014), developmental *deep dyslexia* (Stuart and Howard, 1995; Friedmann and Haddad-Hanna, 2014), developmental *letter position dyslexia* (Friedmann and Rahamim, 2007, 2014; Kohnen et al., 2012; Friedmann and Haddad-Hanna, 2014), developmental *visual dyslexia* (McCloskey and Rapp, 2000), developmental *attentional dyslexia* (Rayner et al., 1989; Shvimer et al., 2009; Friedmann et al., 2010b), developmental vowel dyslexia (Khentov-Kraus and Friedmann, 2011), and developmental *neglect dyslexia* (Friedmann and Gvion, 2002; Friedmann and Nachman-Katz, 2004).

ATTENTION FUNCTIONING

Within the neuropsychological perspective, attention is also treated as a multifaceted construct. In the present study we adopted the model of four functions of attention proposed by Tsal et al. (2005). This model is derived from Posner and Petersen's (1990) influential theory of attention networks. The four-functions-of-attention model refers to four distinct functions within the attention regime: (a) sustained attention - the ability to allocate attentional resources to a non-attractive task over time while maintaining a constant level of performance; (b) selective (spatial) attention—the ability to focus attention on a relevant target while ignoring adjacent distracters; (c) orienting of attention—the ability to direct attention over the visual or auditory field according to sensory input, and to disengage and reorient efficiently; (d) executive attention - the ability to resolve conflicts of information and/or responses.

In a study that compared the attention functioning of children with and without ADHD (Attention Deficit Hyperactivity Disorder), Tsal et al. (2005) reported that sustained attention deficits were the most frequent deficit, which characterized many of the participants in the ADHD sample, whereas each of the deficits in selective, orienting and executive attention characterized approximately half of participants in the ADHD sample. Importantly, Tsal et al.'s study showed that ADHD can entail deficits in any single (or combination of) attention function/s. Thus, different children with ADHD can have divergent clusters of attention deficits.

ON THE RELATION BETWEEN DYSLEXIA AND ATTENTION DEFICITS

Attention disorders and reading disorders are often reported to co-occur (e.g., August and Garfinkel, 1990; Semrud-Clikeman et al., 1992; Snider et al., 2000; Willcutt and Pennington, 2000). Some researchers suggest that this co-occurrence is principled, and that attention lies at the basis of reading, and hence, attention deficits may underlie dyslexia. For example, Clark (1999) suggested that attention should be engaged at the word-target location before a saccade can be made to that location. Hoffman and Subramaniam (1995) have shown that spatial attention is a crucial mechanism in generating voluntary saccadic movements. Thus, visuospatial attention initiates the saccade, and the programming of the next saccade begins when visual attention shifts from the fovea toward the next word into the parafoveal area (Clark, 1999).

Other researches provide less-specific approaches to the relation between attention and reading but claim that attention is crucial for reading. For example, Reynolds and Besner (2006) suggest that attention is critical for translating print into speech, and Shaywitz and Shaywitz (2008) claim that attention has a role in reading, and that deficient attention may cause reading difficulties. Several previous studies reported certain attention deficiencies in children with dyslexia compared with typically developed children (Slaghuis et al., 1993; Casco and Prunetti, 1996; Casco et al., 1998; Vidyasagar and Pammer, 1999). For instance, Facoetti and his colleagues found that children with dyslexia (without specifying the types of dyslexia) did not benefit from exogenous (peripheral) precues although they did demonstrate improved performance when endogenous (central) precues were introduced (Facoetti et al., 2000, 2003a,b). According to these studies, difficulties in spatial attention (orienting and/or selective) may serve a causal role in dyslexia.

However, comorbid occurrence of two deficits is still not necessarily indicative of a principled relation between them. In the current study we aim to examine whether co-occurrences of reading and attention difficulties indicates a causal relation between the two. The way neuropsychology usually approaches questions of relations between modules and functions is by searching for dissociations and double dissociations: if a double dissociation between dyslexia and attention deficits is found, then reading and attention are independent modules that can be selectively impaired, and an impairment in one does not result from an impairment in the other. Thus, this study searched, first, for double dissociations between developmental dyslexia and attention deficit in general. The next stage is aimed to explore the finer relations between specific types of dyslexia and attention, asking whether in cases of comorbid impairments, specific dyslexias are linked to certain specific attention deficits. To the best of our knowledge, no study has tested the relations between subtypes of developmental dyslexia and subtypes of attention difficulties.[2]

DYSLEXIAS SUSPECTED TO HAVE ATTENTIONAL BASIS

Three types of peripheral dyslexia that affect many Hebrew readers with developmental dyslexia present characteristics that seem to be related to attention, and are hence the best candidates for having attention deficits of some sort at their basis. One is *letter position dyslexia* (LPD, Friedmann and Gvion, 2001, 2005; Friedmann and Rahamim, 2007, 2014; Friedmann et al., 2010a; Friedmann and Haddad-Hanna, 2012, 2014; Kohnen et al., 2012; Kezilas et al., 2014). LPD is characterized by transpositions of middle letters within words. According to some analyses, it results from a difficulty in attention allocation to letters, whereby attention is allocated to the first and final letters in the word, and then to all middle letters together. This creates illusory conjunctions between middle letters and their positions (Friedmann and Gvion, 2001). The question that immediately arises is whether this is a general visuo-spatial attention of the type that is measured in attention tasks, or whether this is an orthographic-specific attention function that is specifically harnessed to reading.

Attentional dyslexia is another dyslexia that might stem from a deficit in attention (as the title that Shallice and Warrington selected for the 1977 article in which they first reported this type of dyslexia already suggests: "The possible role of selective attention in acquired dyslexia"). Attentional dyslexia is an impairment in binding letters to words, which results in migrations of letters between words (Shallice and Warrington, 1977; Warrington et al., 1993; Saffran and Coslett, 1996; Hall et al., 2001; Humphreys and Mayall, 2001; Davis and Coltheart, 2002; Mayall and Humphreys, 2002; Friedmann et al., 2010b). A possible attentional approach for attentional dyslexia would ascribe it to a deficit in selective attention that hampers the ability to glue letters to words, or the ability to focus on the target word and attenuate neighboring words.

Another theoretically possible point of contact between dyslexia and attention is *neglect dyslexia*, in which the deficit is related to a specific difficulty in shifting attention to one of the sides of the word, usually its left side. The main types of errors in this dyslexia are omissions, substitutions, and additions of letters in the neglected side (Vallar et al., 2010; and see Friedmann and Nachman-Katz, 2004; Nachman-Katz and Friedmann, 2007, 2008, 2009, 2010; Friedmann and Haddad-Hanna, 2014, for the developmental form of this dyslexia). A natural place to look for an attentional source of this dyslexia would be in orienting of attention. And again, the question is whether this is a general visuo-spatial attention or an orthographic-specific one.

Finally, a different sort of relation between attention and dyslexia may characterize *surface dyslexia*. As explained above, surface dyslexia is a deficit in reading via the lexical route that results in reading via the sublexical route. One may imagine several mechanisms in which attention deficits may give rise to surface dyslexia errors. One is a general one - given difficulties in sustained attention during childhood and during the time of learning to read, children may not be able to attend to classes and devote resources to learning to read, reading, and doing homework. As a result, they might not be familiar with many written words, their lexicon would be impoverished, and their reading would have to rely on the sublexical route[3]. Similar indirect reduction of time allotted to reading may be caused by deficits in other attention functions such as selective attention, which affect the ability or motivation of a child to cope with the situation of reading in general. A more specific effect was suggested by Valdois and collegues (Valdois et al., 2004; Bosse et al., 2007). According to Valdois et al., an impairment of visual attention that reduces the visual attention span – the number of elements that can be identified in parallel—could also lead to reading letter-by-letter in a way typical to surface dyslexia[4]. Finally, it is also possible to imagine a more specific mechanism related to executive attention, assuming that executive attention is responsible for keeping the reader on the lexical route and resolving conflicting inputs that come from the output of the parallel sublexical route.

In the second part of this research we therefore assessed these specific questions on the fine relations between different types of dyslexia and specific attentional functions.

SOME EVIDENCE TO THE DISSOCIABILITY OF DEVELOPMENTAL DYSLEXIA AND ATTENTION DEFICITS

One source of evidence to the dissociability of dyslexia and ADHD comes from the differential effect that methylphenidate (MPH) has on the two. MPH is the most commonly used drug treatment for ADHD. Keidar and Friedmann (2011) assessed whether individuals with developmental dyslexia and ADHD whose attention deficits are relieved by MPH also show reduced rates of errors in reading with MPH. They tested 20 Hebrew-speaking participants with attentional-based dyslexia (mainly LPD and attentional dyslexia) and ADHD, once with and once without MPH. The results were that even though MPH positively affected their performance in at least one of the attentional functions (sustained, selective, orienting, or executive attention), it did *not* improve their reading accuracy. All of these participants had LPD, and many of them also had attentional dyslexia, but still their rate of migrations between words and within words was not affected by MPH. This study already provides some

[2] In this study we focus on dyslexia, and hence on reading at the single word (and nonword) level. Another type of relation between reading and attention pertains to text reading and reading comprehension. Individuals with attention disorders may read an entire chapter and have no idea about its content (Levine, 1987), as a result they often have to read the same paragraph repeatedly in order to grasp its meaning (Robin, 1998, p. 284. See also Cherkes-Julkowski et al., 1995; Brock and Knapp, 1996; Stern and Shalev, 2013, for impairments of children with ADHD on comprehension at the text level).

[3] It is also possible that a deficit in sustained attention would induce a more general reading impairment, leading to garden variety of errors: letter substitution, addition, omission and migration, as well as possibly reading via grapheme-to-phoneme conversion.

[4] Notice that even if reduced attention span can account for surface dyslexia, it cannot account for other dyslexias, such as LPD, attentional dyslexia, and the others.

evidence that reading and attention systems are separate, and that the deficit that underlies LPD and attentional dyslexia is orthographic-specific rather than resulting from a general attentional deficit. Had the attention deficit been the source of the reading impairment, we would have expected improved attention to also reduce reading errors.

Another type of evidence suggesting that the deficit in LPD and in neglect dyslexia is orthographic-specific rather than resulting from a general attentional deficit comes from the differential effect of dyslexia on the reading of words and numbers. Friedmann et al. (2010a) reported on ten individuals with LPD who made many migration errors of letters within words, but their performance on multi-digit number reading was good: they read numbers without migration errors, and not differently from the control participants. Had attention been the source of the deficit in reading, we would expect all kinds of stimuli to be affected by it, including numbers, and not only words. Similarly, Friedmann and Nachman-Katz (2004) and Nachman-Katz and Friedmann (2008) reported on 21 individuals with developmental neglect dyslexia who made neglect errors on the left side of words, but not on the left side of multi-digit numbers. Such a dissociation between word and number reading is inconsistent with a general visuo-spatial attention deficit, which should have affected both types of stimuli.

Finally, Collis et al. (2013) recently examined the performance in a partial report task of adults with developmental dyslexia who make letter position errors and migrations between words (parallel to LPD and attentional dyslexia). They compared the participants' performance on strings of letters and symbols (as well as digits), and found that the participants with developmental dyslexia performed poorer than the control participants, but their deficit was limited to letter strings, and did not affect symbol strings. These findings suggest that the dyslexic participants did not suffer from a general visuo-spatial deficit in the visual attentional window, but rather from a deficit that was limited to orthographic material.

In this study we examined the relation between developmental dyslexia and attention deficits from another perspective, by systematically examining developmental dyslexia types and specific attention difficulties. We aimed to identify, at the cognitive level, the bases of different types of reading difficulties and different types of attention deficits. We assessed the reading and attention of all the participants. Firstly, we asked whether reading and attention are separate cognitive modules. Then, we asked whether participants with specific types of dyslexia share a specific attention deficit. The rationale was that if we can identify cases of dissociation between dyslexia and attention deficits, and specifically, if we can identify individuals with dyslexia that has a suspected attentional cause who do not have a visuo-spatial attention deficit, attention cannot be the underlying cause for this dyslexia.

METHODS

PARTICIPANTS

The participants we report below are 110 Hebrew-readers with either dyslexia or attention deficit, 65 of them are children and adolescents (age ranges 10;0–17;0, $M = 13;2$, 35 girls and 30 boys) and 45 are adults (with ages ranging 18;1–42;0, $M = 28;2$, 23 women and 22 men). We only included children older than 10 years of age, to make sure that they have already had enough time to fully acquire reading and to establish an orthographic lexicon. For all of the participants, the reading and attention deficits were developmental: none of them had history of brain lesion, neurological disease, or loss of consciousness. For all of them Hebrew was the first language, and the first language in which they learned to read.

Most of the participants responded to ads that invited volunteers with both reading and attention deficits and a few of them responded to ads that looked for individuals with difficulties in at least one of the above domains. The Tel Aviv University and the Ministry of Education Ethics Committees approved the experimental protocol.

All participants completed two extensive test batteries: a reading battery and an attention functioning battery. Because we were only interested in dissociations between reading and attention deficits, we only included in the study participants who had a deficit in at least one of the domains: dyslexia, or attention deficits, or both.

READING ASSESSMENT

To evaluate the oral reading of each participant and to determine which type of dyslexia each participant had, we tested each of the participants using the TILTAN screening test (Friedmann and Gvion, 2003), which was developed to identify subtypes of dyslexia in Hebrew. The screening test includes oral reading of 136 single Hebrew words (2–11 letters long), 30 word pairs (3–6 letters long), and 40 nonwords (3–6 letters long). According to the error types in the screening test, we ran additional tests to each participant for the types of dyslexia that emerged from the reading aloud test. These tests are described below for each type of dyslexia.

The word list in the screening test included words of various types that can reveal the different types of dyslexia: 65 migratable words—words in which middle letter migration creates another existing word, for the identification of letter position dyslexia; 104 words for which omission, substitution, migration, or addition of a vowel letter creates another existing word, for the identification of vowel letter dyslexia; 136 words for which neglect of the left side of the word yields another existing word, for the identification of neglect dyslexia, and 108 words for which right neglect errors create an existing word; 84 irregular words and potentiophones for the identification of surface dyslexia; 57 morphologically complex words for deep dyslexia and phonological dyslexia; and 26 abstract nouns and 28 function words, for deep dyslexia. All the words were sensitive to visual dyslexia, as each words had more than six orthographic neighbors.

The 40 nonwords were included for the identification of impairments in the sublexical route, in phonological dyslexias or vowel dyslexia, and deep dyslexia, but also contained migratable nonwords and words that created existing words by substitution, omission, or addition of letters, and where hence also sensitive to various impairments at the orthographic-visual analyzer (letter position dyslexia, visual dyslexia, neglect dyslexia). The list of 30 word pairs was created so that between-word migrations created other existing words, for the identification of attentional dyslexia.

On the basis of this test, we determined whether a participant had normal reading or whether s/he had dyslexia, and if s/he had dyslexia, which types of dyslexia were suspected based on the error pattern s/he showed and the factors that affected her/his reading (frequency effect, word length effect, lexicality effect, etc.). Impaired performance in the screening task, as well as on each of the further reading tasks, was determined according to the comparison of the participant's reading to an age-matched control group. The control groups were collected in previous studies and throughout the development of the test batteries. The control group for the adult participants included 372 adults, the children control groups included at least 20 children in each age group. Skilled readers after 8th grade showed identical reading pattern to the adult control group. Each participant's performance was compared to the control group using the Crawford and Howell's (1998) *t*-test for the comparison of the performance of a participant with a control group. An impaired performance was defined as performance that was significantly below the control, with $p < 0.05$. The type of dyslexia was determined using the same procedure and statistical test, applied to the various types of errors. We determined that a participant had a certain dyslexia if s/he made significantly more errors of the relevant type compared to the control group, and performed significantly poorer than the control group in the relevant reading tests. We only included in the no-dyslexia group individuals who performed within the normal range in all the reading tests. Unclear cases, with performance that was marginally different from that of the control group, and hence could not form a clear case of dissociation, were excluded from the study.

Letter position dyslexia was determined according to the number of letter position errors in reading migratable words (See Appendix C for Hebrew examples of the words of the various types and types of errors).

Attentional dyslexia was determined according to the number of between-word errors, including between-word migrations and between-word letter omissions, in reading migratable word pairs.

Left neglect dyslexia was determined according to letter errors (substitutions, omissions, and additions) that occurred predominantly on the left side of the words (see Friedmann and Nachman-Katz, 2004; Friedmann and Gvion, 2005; Nachman-Katz and Friedmann, 2007, 2008, 2009, 2010; Reznick and Friedmann, 2009, for a description of the manifestation of neglect dyslexia in Hebrew readers).

Surface dyslexia was determined according to the number of reading errors that resulted from reading via the sublexical route rather than via the lexical route, which caused regularization errors in irregular words and potentiophones.

Vowel dyslexia was determined according to the number of vowel letter errors (migrations, substitutions, omissions, and additions) in words and nonwords.

We then further tested the participants' reading in additional tests from the TILTAN battery that were specific to different types of dyslexia that emerged from the screening test, in order to establish decisively the type of dyslexia each participant had. In these additional tests, reading aloud was done without time limit, and the participants were requested to read aloud as accurately and as quickly as possible. The first responses were counted, even when they were later self-corrected. In the lexical decision and the comprehension tasks, the participants were requested to perform the tasks in silent reading, without sounding out the words they read.

The results of each participant in each of the further reading tasks was compared to those of age-matched controls. In the reading aloud tasks, the number of errors of each type (reading via the sublexical route, vowel omission, substitution, addition, migration, consonant omission, substitution, addition, migration, letter neglect on the left, migrations between words, voicing errors, semantic errors) was compared to the number of these errors in the control group. In the lexical decision and comprehension tasks, the percentage of correct responses was compared to that of the control group.

Letter position dyslexia

To establish the diagnosis of letter position dyslexia, which is characterized by letter migrations within words, we used tasks that tested the participants' oral and silent reading of words that are most sensitive to this dyslexia—migratable words. These are words in which migration of middle letters within the words creates another existing word (such as cloud-could, parties-pirates, casual-causal).

The *reading aloud* task for LPD included 232 migratable words of 4–7 letters ($M = 4.9$, $SD = 0.9$). In 87 of these words, a middle migration that involves a vowel letter and a consonant letter creates another existing word, and in 163 words a middle migration that involves two consonant letters creates another word. (For an English example, the word *stops* has a potential for transposition of two consonant letters- *t* and *p*, creating the words *spots*, and the word *form* has a potential for migration that involves a vowel—a transposition of *o* and *r* would create the word *from*).

Additional tasks involved *same-different decision* in which the participant was presented with 60 word pairs, half of which differed in middle letter order (clam-calm), and was requested to determine whether the words in the pair are same or different; *lexical decision task*, in which the participants saw 60 items, half of them words and half migratable nonwords (pecnil) and were requested to determine whether the item was a word; and a *reading comprehension task* that included 50 triads. Each triad consisted of a target migratable word, and two words to choose from: one word that is semantically associated with the target word, and one that is semantically associated with a word that can result from a transposition of middle letter (dairy → milk, notebook). The participants were requested to circle the word that is semantically associated with the target word.

Attentional dyslexia

To establish the diagnosis of attentional dyslexia, characterized by migrations of letters between neighboring words (and by omissions of an instance of a letter that appears in two neighboring words in the same position), the participants read aloud additional lists of word pairs and a list of nonword pairs.

The *word pair* list included 120 word pairs of 2–7 letters ($M = 4.8$, $SD = 1$). All these word pairs were migratable, namely, for each of them, migration of a letter from one word to the other, preserving the within-word position, creates another existing word (e.g., *mild wind* in which between-word migration can create *wild mind*). The *migratable nonword pair* list included 30 3-letter nonword pairs in which letter migration between words would result in existing words.

Neglect dyslexia

Identification of neglect dyslexia was based on an analysis of the position of consonant letter errors (substitutions, additions, and omissions) in the three subtests of the reading aloud screening task, as well as three additional tasks: reading aloud of words and nonwords that share the right side with other words, and lexical decision.

The *oral reading of words* for neglect dyslexia included 100 words in which substitution, omission, or addition of a letter on the left side created another existing word (*rice*→ nice, price, ice). The list for *oral reading of nonwords* for neglect dyslexia included 30 nonwords that differ from existing words in the left letter (*netter*). The *lexical decision* task included 50 nonwords that differ from existing words in the left letter (*diraffe*), as well as 40 existing words.

Surface dyslexia

Surface dyslexia test: Reading aloud of potentiophones. To establish surface dyslexia, which is characterized by reading via the sublexical route, the participants read aloud 78 potentiophonic words, 2–6 letters long ($M = 3.7$ letters, $SD = 0.8$). Potentiophones are words whose reading via grapheme-to-phoneme conversion creates another existing word (like *now*, which can be read via grapheme-to-phoneme conversion to sound like "know," Friedmann and Lukov, 2008). Such words are the most sensitive stimuli to detect surface dyslexia because, like irregular words, their correct reading requires the lexical route. They are more sensitive to surface dyslexia than other irregular words because reading them via the sublexical route results in another word, and hence the reader cannot know that the word was read erroneously.

Pseudo-homophone lexical decision. The lexical decision task for surface dyslexia contained 66 word pairs. Each pair included a word spelled correctly and its pseudo-homophone (e.g., knife-nife). For each pair, the participants were requested to circle the word that was spelled correctly.

Homophone-potentiophone written word comprehension. The reading comprehension task included 40 triads. Each triad consisted of a target word, and two words to choose from: one word that is semantically associated with the target word, and a homophone or a potentiophone of the associated word (e.g., bottle—bear beer). The participants were requested to circle the word that is semantically associated with the target word.

Vowel dyslexia

To establish the diagnosis of vowel dyslexia, characterized by substitutions, omissions, additions and migrations of vowel letters, the participants performed two additional tasks of lexical decision and word comprehension.

Lexical decision. The vowel dyslexia lexical decision task contained 80 items: 45 nonwords in which a vowel error creates existing Hebrew words and 35 existing words—16 of which included a vowel letter and 19 without vowel letters. The items in the task were 2–8 letters ($M = 4.8$, $SD = 1.13$). The participants were requested to silently read each word and to circle the words that exist in Hebrew.

Written word comprehension. The reading comprehension task for vowel dyslexia included 52 triads. Each triad consisted of a target word (3–6 letters long, $M = 4.4$, $SD = 0.75$), and two to four words to choose from: one word that is semantically associated with the target word, and the rest are words that are semantically associated with words that can result from a vowel error in the target word (form → shape, to, ranch). The participants were requested to circle the word that is semantically associated with the target word.

ATTENTION ASSESSMENT

Attention functioning was assessed by using four computerized neuropsychological tasks, serving as indicators of performance in each of the attention functions (Tsal et al., 2005). The four attention tasks enable us to assess the attentional profile of each participant. The performance of each participant in each of the above tests was compared to that of an age-matched control group. The control group for the adult participants included 300 adults, and the children control groups included at least 30 children in each age group collected throughout the development of the test battery. A deficit in sustained, selective, or executive attention was defined in cases where an individual's performance was located in the lowest five percentages of the distribution of her/his age-matched control group, that is, when ≤ -1.645. In orienting attention there are two different possible deficits: a deficit in disengagement of attention (when invalid cue caused a large decrease in performance) and a deficit in automatic orienting of attention (when a valid cue was not effective and did not improve performance). The former was defined in cases where the performance was located in the lowest 5% of the distribution, that is, when ≤ -1.645 and the latter was defined when the performance was located in the highest 5% of the distribution, that is, when ≥ 1.645. Each attention test starts with a short practice block and the test lasts approximately 12 min. The task that assessed sustained attention was always administered as the first task. The other three attention tasks were administered in a counter-balanced order.

Sustained attention

For sustained attention, we used a Conjunctive Continuous Performance Test (CCPT). Participants were presented with a long series of stimuli but were instructed to respond to a single reoccurring pre-specified target (a red square) while withholding responses to all other, non-target stimuli. There were four possible shapes (square, circle, triangle, and star) and four possible colors (red, blue, green, and yellow). As soon as a target appeared the participant was requested to press the spacebar. Using a low rate of target stimuli (30%) and varying the inter-stimulus interval (ISI), this task maintains a high demand on sustained attention but minimizes the involvement of other cognitive factors. Standard deviation of mean RT of target trials served as the measure of sustained attention (Shalev et al., 2011; Stern and Shalev, 2013).

Selective (spatial) attention

For selective attention, we used a conjunctive search task (Tsal et al., 2005). Participants were instructed to search for a target stimuli appearing among distracters. The displays varied in their set size (i.e., the number of distractors), enabling estimation of the effect of attentional load on performance. The participant was instructed to fixate on a central fixation point which was followed by a display of items. The participant was requested to decide whether the display contained the target—a blue square among the distractors (blue circles and red squares). The target appeared in 50% of the displays. If a target was detected the participant had to press the "L" key and if the target was absent then s/he had to press the "A" key. The slope of the search graph reflected the efficiency of spatial selective attention.

Orienting attention

For orienting of attention, we used a peripheral cueing paradigm (Posner et al., 1980) with an exogenous cue (Jonides, 1981). Participants had to discriminate a stimulus—a triangle or a circle—preceded by an abrupt onset at either the target's location (valid cue) or the opposite side of fixation (invalid cue). When the target was a triangle the participant had to press the "L" key and when the target was a circle s/he had to press the "A" key. The difference in performance between valid and invalid trials indicates the ability to orient attention and efficiently disengage from irrelevant locations (Tsal et al., 2005).

Executive attention

For executive attention, we used a Location-Direction Stroop-like task (Stroop, 1935) with a spatial aspect. Participants had to respond either to the location or the direction of an arrow (in different blocks) appearing on the screen, while ignoring the other irrelevant dimension. Half of the stimuli were congruent trials (that is, the location on the screen and the direction of the arrow match; i.e., an arrow presented below fixation pointing downwards) and half of them were incongruent (i.e., an arrow presented above fixation pointing downwards). In the first two blocks of the tasks participants were requested to judge the location of the arrow (relative to the fixation point; if it is presented above the fixation they had to press "L" and if it is presented below the fixation they had to press "A") and in the last two blocks they were requested to judge its direction (Tsal et al., 2005). The widely-used interference effect in such tasks reflects the extent to which conflicting irrelevant information is being effectively suppressed.

RESULTS

PART A: DISSOCIATIONS BETWEEN DYSLEXIA AND ATTENTION DEFICITS

One of the most fundamental tools in the neuropsychological toolbox is that of double dissociation. Such a condition in which one person has impairment in cognitive ability A but has normal performance on B, and another person with the opposite dissociation, impairment in cognitive ability B but with normal performance on A, suggests that A and B are separate modules. Thus, if we are able to identify a double dissociation between dyslexia and attention deficits, we can demonstrate that neither of them underlies the other. Specifically for this special issue, we will be able to answer the question as to whether attention deficits underlie developmental dyslexia in "NO."

As shown in **Tables 1, 2**, we identified 55 participants who showed a double dissociation between reading and attention functions: As summarized in **Table 1**, 28 had dyslexia with normal attention functioning (12 children and 16 adults), and 27 had deficits in at least one attention function, with normal reading (10 children and 17 adults). Importantly, various types of dyslexia showed dissociations with attention: among the participants with dyslexia who had spared attention abilities there were 21 individuals with letter position dyslexia, 13 with attentional dyslexia, and 2 with neglect dyslexia, all dyslexias that have been linked by some to attention functions, as well as 12 participants with surface dyslexia, 11 with vowel dyslexia, and one woman with phonological buffer dyslexia. Appendix A details the relevant error rates in reading aloud for each of these participants- for each participant, errors of each type that occurred at a rate significantly ($p < 0.05$) higher than that of an age-matched control group appear under the relevant dyslexia type. Empty cells in Appendix A indicate no errors or a small percentage of error within the normal range for the relevant error (average percentage and *SD* of each type of error for each control age group appear in the bottom of each dyslexia column).

These results suggest that each of these types of dyslexia can be dissociated from attention deficits, indicating that reading and attention are separate, and that attention deficits do not underlie these dyslexias.

As summarized in **Table 2**, it is also clear that each of the four tested attention functions could be impaired without giving

Table 1 | The types of dyslexia among individuals with intact attention and impaired reading ($n = 28$).

Dyslexia	Number of participants with intact attention who showed these dyslexias
LPD	5
LPD, attentional dyslexia	3
LPD, attentional dyslexia, surface dyslexia	4
LPD, attentional dyslexia, vowel dyslexia, surface dyslexia	3
LPD, attentional dyslexia, vowel dyslexia	1
LPD, attentional dyslexia, neglect dyslexia, vowel dyslexia, surface dyslexia	1
LPD, surface dyslexia	2
LPD, vowel dyslexia	1
LPD, vowel dyslexia, surface dyslexia	1
Attentional dyslexia, neglect dyslexia	1
Vowel dyslexia	4
Surface dyslexia	1
Phonological buffer dyslexia	1

Table 2 | The various attention deficits among individuals with intact reading and impaired attention ($n = 27$).

Attention deficits	Number of participants with intact reading who showed these attention deficits
Sustained	5
Orienting	3
Executive	1
Selective	1
Sustained and orienting	4
Sustained and executive	4
Sustained and selective	3
Orienting and executive	2
Selective and executive	1
Sustained, orienting, and executive	1
Sustained, selective, orienting, and executive	2

rise to dyslexia. Among the 27 participants with attention deficit whose reading was intact there were 19 with deficient sustained attention, 7 with deficient selective attention, 12 with deficient orienting attention and 11 with executive attention deficit (the detailed Z-scores for each of these participants in each of the tasks are presented in Appendix B). Importantly, we demonstrated that individuals who suffer from a deficit in any of the four functions of attention (sustained, selective, orienting, and executive) may still show preserved reading. These findings further support the claim that attention deficits are not necessarily related to dyslexia.

PART B: FINER GRAINED OBSERVATIONS: TYPES OF DYSLEXIA AND TYPES OF ATTENTION DEFICITS

Considering the possible connections between specific dyslexias and specific attention deficits, one can ask whether when an individual has both dyslexia and attention deficit, there are consistent relations between the type of dyslexia and the type of attention function that is impaired.

As we explained in the Introduction, several possible specific relations between dyslexia and attention deficits can be inferred from the assumption that reading and attention deficits are the result of the same core deficit. The possible connections that we examined were between letter position dyslexia and selective attention, between attentional dyslexia and selective attention, between neglect dyslexia and orienting of attention, and between surface dyslexia and sustained or executive attention. We have already seen in Section A that dyslexia can be dissociable from attention deficits altogether, and hence, we can also conclude that these types of dyslexia can be dissociated from attention deficits. In the data summarized in **Table 3** we are able to explore, for individuals who have both dyslexia and attention deficit, whether the witnessed attention function that was impaired was the one suspected under a general attentional hypothesis for each dyslexia with possible attentional bases.

Starting with letter position dyslexia, where we look for relations to a selective attention deficit, **Table 3** shows that even in cases where both reading and attention are impaired, LPD does not necessarily appear with selective attention deficit. In our results, summarized in **Table 3**, 30 individuals had LPD but no selective attention deficit. A broader look at the other attention functions indicates that there was no single attention function that was impaired for all the individuals with LPD who also had an attentional deficit.

Similarly, attentional dyslexia can also be thought to stem from a deficit in selective attention. **Table 3**, however, reports on 18 individuals with attentional dyslexia who had an attention deficit but no selective attention deficit.

As for neglect dyslexia, the suspected attention function would be orienting of attention. However, the results in **Table 3** include three individuals with developmental neglect dyslexia, and neither of them had a deficit in orienting of attention.

Finally, considering surface dyslexia, we suggested that a deficit in sustained attention can cause a chain of events following which children will have more limited exposure to reading, and read via grapheme-to-phoneme conversion, rather than via the lexical route. This mechanism as a basis for surface dyslexia is also not supported by our results: In **Table 3** we report 15 individuals with surface dyslexia who had an attention deficit but intact sustained attention, and 13 individuals with sustained attention deficit, who did not have surface dyslexia. As for the hypothesis according to which executive attention underlies surface dyslexia, there were 10 participants with executive attention deficit without surface dyslexia, and 21 participants with surface dyslexia without executive attention deficit.

Additionally, three participants had phonological dyslexia. It may be suggested that a deficit in grapheme-to-phoneme conversion may be related to a difficulty in the serial shift of attention from one letter to the next. Such attention function may be supported by orienting of attention. This suggestion is not supported by the findings, however. There were two phonological dyslexics who also had attention disorders: one had only selective attention deficit and one had only sustained attention deficit. More importantly, in Part A we reported a woman who had phonological (buffer) dyslexia with completely normal attention functions. Similarly, no specific attention deficit was found for vowel dyslexia or visual dyslexia.

DISCUSSION

An important part of the quest into the nature of developmental dyslexia is the search for underlying causes for dyslexia. Often such causes are searched within the general cognitive abilities, and one such candidate is attention. In this research we explored the question of the relation between attention deficit and dyslexia from a neuropsychological perspective that takes into account the existence of various types of dyslexia and of various types of attention deficits. As a first step, we established a double dissociation between dyslexia in general and attention deficits in general in 55 individuals. We showed children, adolescents, and adults who had dyslexia (of any type) without attention deficits (all four attention functions were normally functioning). We then showed children, adolescents, and adults who had attention deficits (of any of the four types) without dyslexia (reading at

Table 3 | Types of dyslexia and types of attention deficit for the participants who had both dyslexia and attention deficits.

Participant	Age (years), gender	Dyslexia (% errors)							Attention deficits			
		LPD	Attentional	Neglect	Vowel	Surface	Phonological	Visual	Sustained	Selective	Orienting	Executive
ARD	10, F	10	15		16	26			−2.08	0.61	0.99	1.18
AXA	10, M	11	13			21			−3.26	0.79	−1.06	2.27
LHV	10, M	16	18	4	10	27			−5.13	1.84	1.12	0.02
LDS	10, M	7				19			−2.05	−0.05		2.78
NMR	11, M					29		50	−2.58	0.29	1.08	−2.50
OHT	11, M	16							−14.88	0.40	7.55	−22.25
NSU	12, F	13	11						−7.59	−0.04	−0.18	−2.14
VEH	12, F	15			18	10			−2.76	−4.02	0.35	−1.36
LMF	12, F	11	12						−2.06	−3.14	−0.29	−2.05
ORF	12, F	16	15		12				1.10	−3.36	0.92	−2.53
VAL	12, F	23			20				0.29	0.27	1.05	−4.25
VDA	12, M	30	27		8	17			−4.30	0.49	2.00	−10.96
VIV	12, M	17				11			−0.52	−1.82	−0.17	−2.20
RSU	12, M	9	15						−2.92	1.57	3.12	1.64
NML	12, M	15			9				−3.51	0.98	−1.42	−0.76
AAU	12, M		14			8			−3.10	0.06	2.88	0.65
VBR	12, M				20	13			−1.25	−6.49	0.07	−0.73
NSH	13, F	10			8	10		4	−0.95	−0.69	0.12	−5.43
VOH	13, F	28			23	13			−0.25	−1.69	−1.08	−3.48
VSP	13, F	12			13	15			−0.29	−0.22	0.86	−2.65
VLR	13, F	22			10	20		3	−0.24	−1.50	0.25	−1.74
AGA	13, F	12			13	12			0.14	0.48	1.24	−1.71
NLU	13, F		8						−6.45	0.21	1.38	0.79
YSH	13, F						20		−1.54	−3.44	1.13	−0.95
AAZ	13, F	16	22			18			−3.28	−4.38	2.32	1.34
AVA	13, M	14	13		16	27			−12.78	−1.33	1.99	−0.61
LXZ	13, M	19	32			19			−4.85	−1.20	3.12	0.85
VMM	13, M	36	23		20	26		5	0.50	−2.54	1.24	−0.96
LOF	13, M	9		18		31			−0.31	−1.90	1.07	−1.19
VNH	14, F		20		50				−9.66	−1.01	0.67	−4.14
VMV	14, F	13			13				−0.69	−1.34	1.52	−6.61
VDL	14, M	9			35	11			0.13	0.40	0.97	−5.63
VKK	14, M	13			10				−12.17	−1.45	1.21	−8.71
VDY	14, M				33	10			−4.09	−5.73	0.87	2.30
LNA	14, M	23				7			−1.64	−1.95	0.41	−1.62
VEB	15, F	22	23		18	25		4	0.93	−3.48	1.34	−5.28
VNN	15, F				18	20		4	−0.95	−1.56	−0.49	−3.88

(Continued)

Table 3 | Continued

Participant	Age (years), gender	Dyslexia (% errors)							Attention deficits			
		LPD	Attentional	Neglect	Vowel	Surface	Phonological	Visual	Sustained	Selective	Orienting	Executive
LOA	15, M	9	7			7			−3.38	−0.54	−0.12	−2.00
LDK	15, M	26	50	4	30	10			−10.65	−0.94	−0.94	−1.83
VBF	15, M	13			13				−2.10	−1.00	−0.45	0.69
ASH	16, F	30			9				−1.82	−0.20	−1.50	−1.16
LPD	16, F	7	9						0.52	−0.04	−1.86	−0.12
LEA	17, F	13			10				−0.77	−2.11	0.51	0.32
LPD	25, F	13							0	−1.02	1.92	0.51
ONA	26, F		20			8			−1.54	−2.68	−0.78	1.01
REM	28, F	6	15						−1.95	−0.75	−0.68	−2.96
NGM	28, M	12							0.37	−2.09	−1.38	−0.27
ASM	30, F	12	9		7	6			−6.42	−0.06	−2.33	1.05
AAM	30, M	17	23			4			−3.55	−1.77	0.50	1.70
ZOT	31, F						22		−9.52	−1.34	0.63	−1.19
ZGS	37, M	6			12	9			−6.86	0.69	0.57	1.44
ARM	38, M	18	23		17	14			−4.82	−1.03	0	0.37
LIA	41, F	15	24						−6.17	−12.28	−2.40	−2.96
SGM	42, F	9	11		13	17			−6.32	−0.94	−1.34	0.37
ZYK	42, M	30				14			−0.98	−1.85	0.02	0.57
CONTROL GROUPS: %M (*SD*)												
4th–5th grade		1.8 (2.7)	3.8 (4.1)	0.0 (0.0)	1.3 (2.1)	3.2 (2.3)	4.2 (3.0)	0.05 (0.2)				
7th grade		1.6 (2.2)	2.8 (3.5)	0.03 (0.14)	1.4 (1.7)	3.8 (2.0)	4.0 (2.9)	0.14 (0.4)				
15 year olds-adults		0.6 (1.1)	1.9 (2.7)	0.03 (0.2)	1.0 (1.9)	1.3 (1.4)	2.7 (3.3)	0.05 (0.2)				

Each row represents a different participant (n = 55).

[a] *In the attention tasks, Z scores smaller than −1.645 reflect deficient functioning. In the case of orienting attention Z scores smaller than −1.645 reflect deficient disengagement of attention and Z scores larger than +1.645 reflect deficient automatic orienting. That is, the colored cells represent performance level below the cutoff of 0.05.*

[b] *In the reading tasks, all the error rates of the various types presented in the table are significantly larger than the age-matched control groups and indicate a dyslexia of the relevant type. Empty cells indicate that there were no relevant errors at all or that the relevant error rate was within the normal range, in most cases less than 1%. The percentages of errors that appear in the table for each dyslexia are: for LPD—migrations in migratable words (except LEA, VIV, LNA, and ZYK whose error rates refer to their migrations in nonwords), for attentional dyslexia- migrations between words in migratable word pairs, for neglect—consonant omission and substitution on the left of the word, for vowel dyslexia—vowel letter omission, substitution, migration, or addition in nonwords (except NML, ASH, VKK, ORF, AVA, ARD, and LDK whose error rates refer to their vowel letter errors in words), for surface dyslexia—sublexical reading in irregular words and potentiophones, for phonological dyslexia—errors in nonwords, and for visual dyslexia—consonant omission, substitution, or addition (for NMR, who has visual-analyzer-output dyslexia, the error rates also included vowel letter errors and letter migrations).*

[c] *As can be seen when comparing the error rates of the dyslexics to those of the controls, although, 4% neglect errors seem like a low error rate, unimpaired readers make almost no such errors and hence 4% errors (5 or 6 consonant errors on the left out of the 136 words) already signifies a significant deficit, which is supported by the additional reading tests. The same holds also for visual dyslexia, where 3% visual errors (4 consonant omission, substitution or addition errors out of the 136 words) already indicates a significant deficit.*

the single word level was completely normal). Such double dissociation already indicates that attention cannot be the source of dyslexia.

However, we sought to be more specific in this study, and looked for the fine relations, or lack thereof, between specific types of dyslexia and specific attention functions.

Starting with *letter position dyslexia*, an imaginable attentional source would be selective attention: if an individual cannot focus attention on a restricted area, several letters could be perceived together in the attended area, and as a result their positions may be misperceived. The results, however, do not support such account. We have seen 21 individuals with LPD who had no attention deficits, and 7 individuals with a deficit in selective attention who had no dyslexia, including no LPD. Even in cases where both reading and attention are impaired, LPD does not necessarily appear with selective attention deficit. In our results, 30 individuals had LPD but no selective attention deficit. A broader look at the other attention functions indicates that there was no single attention function that was impaired for all the individuals with LPD who also had an attentional deficit.

Similarly, *attentional dyslexia* can be thought to stem from a deficit in selective attention. Here the suspected mechanism would be that a deficit in attenuation of the neighboring words would result in letters from the neighboring words being perceived with the target words. Here, again, our results do not support such an underlying basis for attentional dyslexia: firstly, in Section A we reported on 13 individuals who had attentional dyslexia without any attention deficit, and 7 individuals with selective attention deficit without attentional dyslexia. Secondly, we reported on 18 individuals with attentional dyslexia who did have an attentional deficit but no selective attention deficit.

In fact, these findings indicate that even the dyslexia that Shallice and Warrington (1980) termed "attentional dyslexia," is actually not attentional in nature, and can occur in individuals with no general visuo-spatial attention deficit.

Additionally, one may take the dissociations found between letter position dyslexia and attentional dyslexia as an additional indication that a general deficit in selective attention cannot be the source of these dyslexias. Had selective attention deficit been the source of both these dyslexias, we would expect them to always appear together. However, in this study there are 23 individuals with letter position dyslexia who did not have attentional dyslexia, and 4 individuals with attentional dyslexia who did not have letter position dyslexia. This double dissociation was also found in previous studies of these dyslexias: Friedmann and Rahamim (2007) and Keidar and Friedmann (2011) reported on individuals with LPD without attentional dyslexia and Friedmann et al. (2010b) reported on individuals with attentional dyslexia without LPD. Thus, this is an additional evidence that these dyslexias cannot stem from the same attentional source[5].

When we think of *neglect dyslexia*, the imaginable connections to attention are different. One can think of neglect dyslexia as resulting from a deficit in orienting of attention to the left visual field. In fact, data from adults with acquired dyslexia already show that neglect dyslexia at the word level can appear without visuo-spatial neglect (Kinsbourne and Warrington, 1962; De Lacy Costello and Warrington, 1987; Patterson and Wilson, 1990; Haywood and Coltheart, 2001; see a summary and discussion in Cubelli et al., 1991 and Young et al., 1991). Such dissociation was also reported from Hebrew-speaking children and adolescents with developmental neglect dyslexia (Friedmann and Nachman-Katz, 2004; Nachman-Katz and Friedmann, 2007, 2010). The other direction of dissociation has also been reported: Primativo et al. (2013) reported seven patients with unilateral spatial neglect who did not have word-level neglect dyslexia. Such double dissociations already suggest that there are two different mechanisms underlying visuo-spatial neglect (and omissions of words on one side of text) and neglect dyslexia at the word level. The current results support these conclusions (as well as Haywood and Coltheart's, 2001 perception of word-level neglect dyslexia as separate from visuospatial neglect) from additional angle: Part A reported two individuals with developmental neglect dyslexia with no attention deficits, and 8 individuals with a deficit in orienting of attention without any dyslexia, including no neglect dyslexia. The results of part B include three additional individuals with developmental neglect dyslexia, none of whom had a deficit in orienting of attention and eleven participants with deficient orienting of attention who suffer from different types of dyslexia, none of which is neglect dyslexia.

Finally, let us consider the non-specific effect that a deficit in sustained attention may have on reading. One hypothesis we raised in the Introduction was that a deficit in *sustained* attention would cause a chain of events following which children will have more limited exposure to reading. In this case, many words will not be represented in the orthographic lexicon, and they will be read via grapheme-to-phoneme conversion, leading to *surface dyslexia*-like errors. This mechanism as a basis for surface dyslexia is also not supported by our results: we saw in part A 12 individuals who had surface dyslexia but no attention deficits, and 27 individuals who had attention deficits (including 19 with sustained attention deficit) without surface dyslexia. Part B added to these results by showing 15 individuals with surface dyslexia who had an attention deficit but intact sustained attention, and 12 individuals with sustained attention deficit, but without surface dyslexia. We also found results that do not support *executive* attention as the basis for surface dyslexia: we suggested that executive attention may be responsible for keeping the reader on the lexical route and resolving conflicts in the output buffer between inputs from the lexical and sublexical routes. However, this mechanism is not borne out, as in part A there were 12 individuals who had surface dyslexia but no attention deficits, and 27 individuals who had attention deficits (including 11 with executive attention deficit) without surface dyslexia. Part B added to these results by showing 20 participants with surface dyslexia who had an attention deficit but intact executive attention, and 10 individuals with executive attention deficit and dyslexia, but without surface dyslexia.

[5]The double dissociation between LPD and attentional dyslexia indicates that it cannot be the case that selective attention underlies both dyslexias but only one of them is affected in some cases because it is more sensitive to the attention deficit.

The other hypothesis, according to which sustained attention deficit would lead to a garden variety of errors in reading is also not supported by our results, especially given the 19 participants in part A who had sustained attention deficit but no dyslexia at all.

In addition, it was found that the different attention deficits are dissociable from one another (i.e., there were participants who were impaired in a single attention function). Most importantly, it seems that selective attention and orienting of attention—two spatial attention functions that sometimes are treated as interchangeable functions, are separate. We reported (in **Tables 2, 3**) 22 participants who showed no significant orienting deficit yet demonstrated selective attention deficit and 15 participants who showed the opposite pattern.

Thus, we saw double dissociations between letter position dyslexia and attention, including a double dissociation with selective attention; between attentional dyslexia and attention, including a double dissociation with selective attention; between word-based left neglect dyslexia and attention, including a double dissociation with orienting of attention; and between surface dyslexia and attention, including a double dissociation with sustained attention and with executive attention, as well as dissociations between vowel dyslexia and phonological dyslexia and attention. These results show that each of these dyslexias can occur with intact attention, indicating that attention deficits do not underlie these dyslexias. These results may suggest that the impairment in dyslexias such as letter position dyslexia, attentional dyslexia, or neglect dyslexia lies in an attention component that is specific to reading, an *orthographic-attention*. Such approach is also consistent with previous findings that describe letter migrations in words without digit migrations in numbers (Friedmann et al., 2010a); neglect of the left side of words without neglect of the left side of numbers (Friedmann and Nachman-Katz, 2004; Nachman-Katz and Friedmann, 2008); findings according to which MPH improves visuo-attention functions but not reading errors in letter position dyslexia or attentional dyslexia (Keidar and Friedmann, 2011); and findings according to which adults with developmental dyslexia perform poorer than controls on partial report task only in letter strings but not in symbol strings (Collis et al., 2013).

The differences between the findings of the current study and previous studies that reported comorbidities between reading and attention can be ascribed to several factors. Firstly, whereas previous studies focused on the group level and looked for correlations, we examined the question at the individual level and focused on the search for dissociations as a tool to examine whether attention deficit underlies dyslexia. Another difference relates to the level at which reading disorders were examined. We examined dyslexia and hence tested errors in reading at the single word (and nonword) level, whereas some of the previous studies that found relation between attention and reading tested reading speed, which may be affected by attention, and reading comprehension at the text level.

This research is the first to assess the intricate relations between types of dyslexia and types of attention deficits, and it has demonstrated how important it is to assess reading and attentional personal profiles of children and adults with reading and/or attention deficits. We have demonstrated that the different types of dyslexia are dissociated from the different attention deficits and that individuals who suffer from a reading disorder, attention deficit or both can be characterized by various reading and attention profiles. The sensitive identification of detailed reading and attention profiles may improve significantly the ability to select personalized tailor-made interventions that will aim at facilitating reading as well as other everyday functioning.

ACKNOWLEDGMENTS

This article is dedicated to the precious memory of Limor Lukov, our much-loved and appreciated student and teacher, an avid proponent of the dissociability of dyslexias from attention disorders and from phonological disorders. The article is mainly based on Limor's PhD research. This research was supported by the Israel Science Foundation (grant no. 837/04, Shalev; 1066/14, Friedmann), by the Lieselotte Adler Laboratory for Research on Child Development, and by the Australian Research Council Centre of Excellence for Cognition and its Disorders (CE110001021).

REFERENCES

Arduino, L. S., Burani, C., and Vallar, G. (2002). Lexical effects in left neglect dyslexia: a study in Italian patients. *Cogn. Neuropsychol.* 19, 421–444. doi: 10.1080/02643290244000013

Arduino, L. S., Burani, C., and Vallar, G. (2003). Reading aloud and lexical decision in neglect dyslexia patients: a dissociation. *Neuropsychologia* 41, 877–885. doi: 10.1016/S0028-3932(03)00015-0

August, G. J., and Garfinkel, B. D. (1990). Comorbidity of ADHD and reading disability among clinic-referred children. *J. Abnorm. Child Psychol.* 18, 29–45. doi: 10.1007/BF00919454

Bisiach, E., Perani, D., Vallar, G., and Berti, A. (1986). Unilateral neglect: personal and extra-personal. *Neuropsychologia* 24, 759–767. doi: 10.1016/0028-3932(86)90075-8

Brunsdon, R., Coltheart, M., and Nickels, L. (2006). Severe developmental letter processing impairment: a treatment case study. *Cogn. Neuropsychol.* 23, 795–821. doi: 10.1080/02643290500310863

Bosse, M. L., Tainturier, M. J., and Valdois, S. (2007). Developmental dyslexia: the visual attention span deficit hypothesis. *Cognition* 104, 198–230. doi: 10.1016/j.cognition.2006.05.009

Brock, S., and Knapp, P. (1996). Reading comprehension abilities of children with attention deficit hyperactivity disorder. *J. Atten. Disord.* 1, 173–186. doi: 10.1177/108705479600100305

Broom, Y. M., and Doctor, E. A. (1995a). Developmental surface dyslexia: a case study of the efficacy of a remediation programme. *Cogn. Neuropsychol.* 12, 69–110. doi: 10.1080/02643299508251992

Broom, Y. M., and Doctor, E. A. (1995b). Developmental phonological dyslexia: a case study of the efficacy of a remediation programme. *Cogn. Neuropsychol.* 12, 725–766. doi: 10.1080/02643299508251400

Caramazza, A., and Hillis, A. E. (1990). Levels of representation, co-ordinate frames, and unilateral neglect. *Cogn. Neuropsychol.* 7, 391–445. doi: 10.1080/02643299008253450

Casco, C., and Prunetti, E. (1996). Visual search of good and poor readers effects with target having single and combined features. *Percept. Mot. Skills* 82, 1155–1167. doi: 10.2466/pms.1996.82.3c.1155

Casco, C., Tressoldi, E. P., and Dellantoni, A. (1998). Visual selective attention and reading efficiency are related in children. *Cortex* 34, 531–546. doi: 10.1016/S0010-9452(08)70512-4

Castles, A., Bates, T. C., and Coltheart, M. (2006). John Marshall and the developmental dyslexias. *Aphasiology* 20, 871–892. doi: 10.1080/02687030600738952

Castles, A., and Coltheart, M. (1993). Varieties of developmental dyslexia. *Cognition* 47, 149–180. doi: 10.1016/0010-0277(93)90003-E

Castles, A., and Coltheart, M. (1996). Cognitive correlates of developmental surface dyslexia: a single case study. *Cogn. Neuropsychol.* 13, 25–50. doi: 10.1080/026432996382051

Castles, A., Datta, H., Gayan, J., and Olson, R., A (1999). Varieties of developmental reading disorder: genetic and envioromental influences. *J. Exp. Child Psychol.* 72, 73–94. doi: 10.1006/jecp.1998.2482

Cherkes-Julkowski, M., Stolzenberg, J., Hatzes, N., and Madaus, J. (1995). Methodological issues in assessing the relationship among ADD, medication effects and reading performance. *Learn. Dis. A Multidiscip. J.* 6, 21–30.

Clark, J. J. (1999). Spatial attention and latencies of saccadic eye movements. *Vision Res.* 39, 585–602. doi: 10.1016/S0042-6989(98)00190-4

Collis, N. L., Kohnen, S., and Kinoshita, S. (2013). The role of visual spatial attention in adult developmental dyslexia. *Q. J. Exp. Psychol.* 66, 245–260. doi: 10.1080/17470218.2012.705305

Coltheart, M. (1996). Phonological dyslexia - past and future issues. *Cogn. Neuropsychol.* 13, 749–762. doi: 10.1080/026432996381791

Coltheart, M., and Funnell, E. (1987). "Reading and writing: one lexicon or two?" in *Language Perception and Production*, eds A. Allport, D. Mackay, W. Prinz, and E. Sheerer (London: Academic Press), 313–339.

Coltheart, M., and Kohnen, S. (2012). "Acquired and developmental disorders of reading and spelling," in *The Handbook of the Neuropsychology of Language*, ed M. Faust (New York, NY: Wiley), 892–920.

Coltheart, M., Masterson, J., Byng, S., Prior, M., and Riddoch, J. (1983). Surface dyslexia. *Q. J. Exp. Psychol.* 35, 469–495. doi: 10.1080/14640748308402483

Coltheart, M., Rastle, K., Perry, C., Langdon, R., and Ziegler, J. (2001). DRC: A dual route cascaded model of visual word recognition and reading aloud. *Psychol. Rev.* 108, 204–256. doi: 10.1037/0033-295X.108.1.204

Crawford, J. R., and Howell, D. C. (1998). Comparing an individual's test score against norms derived from small samples. *Clin. Neuropsychol.* 12, 482–486. doi: 10.1076/clin.12.4.482.7241

Cubelli, R., Nichelli, P., Bonito, V., De Tanti, A., and Inzaghi, M. G. (1991). Different patterns of dissociation in unilateral spatial neglect. *Brain Cogn.* 15, 139–159. doi: 10.1016/0278-2626(91)90023-2

Cuetos, F., and Ellis, A. W. (1999). Visual paralexias in a Spanish-speaking patient with acquired dyslexia: a consequence of visual and semantic impairments? *Cortex* 35, 661–674. doi: 10.1016/S0010-9452(08)70826-8

Davis, C. J., and Coltheart, M. (2002). Paying attention to reading errors in acquired dyslexia. *Trends Cogn. Sci.* 6, 359–361. doi: 10.1016/S1364-6613(02)01950-2

De Lacy Costello, A., and Warrington, E. K. (1987). The dissociation of visuospatial neglect and neglect dyslexia. *J. Neurol. Neurosurg. Psychiatry* 50, 1110–1116. doi: 10.1136/jnnp.50.9.1110

Ellis, A. W., Flude, B., and Young, A. W. (1987). Neglect dyslexia and the early visual processing of letters in words and nonwords. *Cogn. Neuropsychol.* 4, 439–464. doi: 10.1080/02643298708252047

Ellis, A. W., Lambon Ralph, M. A., Morris, J., and Hunter, A. (2000). "Surface dyslexia: description, treatment, and interpretation," in *Case Studies in the Neuropsychology of Reading*, ed E. Funnell (Hove: Psychology Press), 85–119.

Ellis, A. W., and Young, A. W. (1996). *Human Cognitive Neuropsychology*. Hillsdale, NJ: Erlbaum.

Ellis, A. W., Young, A. W., and Flude, B. M. (1993). "Neglect and visual language," in *Unilateral Neglect: Clinical and Experimental Studies*, eds I. H. Robertson and J. C. Marshall (Hillsdale, NJ: Erlbaum), 233–255.

Facoetti, A., Lorusso, M. L., Paganoni, P., Cattaneo, C., Galli, R., and Mascetti, G. G. (2003a). The time course of attentional focusing in dyslexic and normally reading children. *Brain Cogn.* 53, 181–184. doi: 10.1016/S0278-2626(03)00105-2

Facoetti, A., Lorusso, M. L., Paganoni, P., Cattaneo, C., Galli, R., Umiltà, C., et al. (2003b). Auditory and visual automatic attention deficits in developmental dyslexia. *Brain Res. Cogn.* 16, 185–191. doi: 10.1016/S0926-6410(02)00270-7

Facoetti, A., Paganoni, P., Turatto, M., Marzola, V., and Mascetti, G. G. (2000). Visual-spatial attention in developmental dyslexia. *Cortex* 36, 109–123. doi: 10.1016/S0010-9452(08)70840-2

Friedman, R. B. (1996). Recovery from deep alexia to phonological alexia: points on a continuum. *Brain Lang.* 52, 114–128. doi: 10.1006/brln.1996.0006

Friedmann, N., Biran, M., and Gvion, A. (2012). Patterns of visual dyslexia. *J. Neuropsychol.* 6, 1–30. doi: 10.1111/j.1748-6653.2011.02000.x

Friedmann, N., Dotan, D., and Rahamim, E. (2010a). Is the visual analyzer orthographic-specific? Reading words and numbers in letter position dyslexia. *Cortex* 46, 982–1004. doi: 10.1016/j.cortex.2009.08.007

Friedmann, N., and Gvion, A. (2001). Letter position dyslexia. *Cogn. Neuropsychol.* 18, 673–696. doi: 10.1080/02643290143000051

Friedmann, N., and Gvion, A. (2002). Modularity in developmental disorders: evidence from SLI and peripheral dyslexias. *Behav. Brain Sci.* 25, 756–757. doi: 10.1017/S0140525X02270132

Friedmann, N., and Gvion, A. (2003). *TILTAN: A Test Battery for Dyslexias*. Tel Aviv: Tel Aviv University.

Friedmann, N., and Gvion, A. (2005). Letter form as a constraint for errors in neglect dyslexia and letter position dyslexia. *Behav. Neurol.* 16, 145–158. doi: 10.1155/2005/635634

Friedmann, N., and Haddad-Hanna, M. (2012). Letter position dyslexia in Arabic: from form to position. *Behav. Neurol.* 25, 193–203. doi: 10.1155/2012/296974

Friedmann, N., and Haddad-Hanna, M. (2014). "Types of developmental dyslexia in Arabic," in *Handbook of Arabic Literacy: Insights and perspectives. Language and Literacy Series*, eds E. Saiegh-Haddad and M. Joshi (Dordrecht; Heidelberg; New York; London: Springer), 119–152. doi: 10.1007/978-94-017-8545-7_6

Friedmann, N., Kerbel, N., and Shvimer, L. (2010b). Developmental attentional dyslexia. *Cortex* 46, 1216–1237. doi: 10.1016/j.cortex.2010.06.012

Friedmann, N., and Lukov, L. (2008). Developmental surface dyslexias. *Cortex* 44, 1146–1160. doi: 10.1016/j.cortex.2007.09.005

Friedmann, N., and Nachman-Katz, I. (2004). Developmental neglect dyslexia in a Hebrew-reading child. *Cortex* 40, 301–313. doi: 10.1016/S0010-9452(08)70125-4

Friedmann, N., and Rahamim, E. (2007). Developmental letter position dyslexia. *J. Neuropsychol.* 1, 201–236. doi: 10.1348/174866407X204227

Friedmann, N., and Rahamim, E. (2014). What can reduce letter migrations in letter position dyslexia? *J. Res. Read.* 37, 297–315. doi: 10.1111/j.1467-9817.2011.01525.x

Glosser, G., and Friedman, R. B. (1990). The continuum of deep/phonological alexia. *Cortex* 26, 343–359. doi: 10.1016/S0010-9452(13)80085-8

Guggenheim, R., and Friedmann, N. (2014). *Previously Undescribed type of Developmental Phonological Dyslexia. To be Presented at the International Neuropsychological Society Meeting.* Jerusalem.

Gvion, A., and Friedmann, N. (2010). Dyscravia: voicing substitution dysgraphia. *Neuropsychologia* 48, 1935–1947. doi: 10.1016/j.neuropsychologia.2010.03.014

Hall, D. H., Humphreys, G. W., and Cooper, A. C. G. (2001). Neuropsychological evidence for case-specific reading: multi-letter units in visual word recognition. *Q. J. Exp. Psychol.* 54, 439–467. doi: 10.1080/713755978

Haywood, M., and Coltheart, M. (2001). Neglect dyslexia with a stimulus-centered deficit and without visuospatial neglect. *Cogn. Neuropsychol.* 18, 577–615. doi: 10.1080/02643290042000251

Hoffman, J. E., and Subramaniam, B. (1995). The role of visual attention in saccadic eye movements. *Percept. Psychophys.* 57, 787–795. doi: 10.3758/BF03206794

Howard, D., and Franklin, S. (1987). "Three ways for understanding written words, and their use in two contrasting cases of surface dyslexia," in *Language Perception and Production: Relationships Between Listening, Speaking, Reading and Writing*, eds A. Allport, D. MacKay, W. Prinz, and E. Scheerer (London: Academic Press), 340–366.

Humphreys, G. W., and Mayall, K. A. (2001). Peripheral reading deficit under conditions of diffuse visual attention. *Cogn. Neuropsychol.* 18, 551–576. doi: 10.1080/02643290042000242

Jackson, N. E., and Coltheart, M. (2001). *Routes to Reading Success and Failure*. Hove: Psychology Press.

Jones, K., Castles, A., and Kohnen, S. (2011). Subtypes of developmental reading disorders: Recent developments and directions for treatment. *ACQ. Knowledge Speech Lang. Hear.* 13, 79–83. Available online at: http://hdl.handle.net/1959.14/315817

Jonides, J. (1981). "Voluntary vs. automatic control over the mind's eye movement," in *Attention and Performance IX*, eds J. B. Long and A. D. Baddeley (Hisdale, NJ: Erlbaum), 187–204.

Judica, A., De Luca, M., Spinelli, D., and Zoccolotti, P. (2002). Training of developmental surface dyslexia improves reading performance and shortens eye fixation duration in reading. *Neuropsychol. Rehabil.* 12, 177–197. doi: 10.1080/09602010244000002

Keidar, R., and Friedmann, N. (2011). Does Methylphenidate help readers with letter position dyslexia and attentional dyslexia? *Lang. Brain* 10, 195–214.

Kezilas, Y., Kohnen, S., McKague, M., and Castles, A. (2014). The locus of impairment in English developmental letter position dyslexia. *Front. Hum. Neurosci.* 8:356. doi: 10.3389/fnhum.2014.00356

Khentov-Kraus, L., and Friedmann, N. (2011). Dyslexia in vowel letters. *Lang. Brain* 10, 65–106.

Kinsbourne, M., and Warrington, E. K. (1962). A variety of reading disability associated with right hemisphere lesions. *J. Neurol. Neurosurg. Psychiatry* 25, 339–344. doi: 10.1136/jnnp.25.4.339

Kohnen, S., Nickels, L., Castles, A., Friedmann, N., and McArthur, G. (2012). When 'slime' becomes 'smile': developmental letter position dyslexia in English. *Neuropsychologia* 50, 3681–3692. doi: 10.1016/j.neuropsychologia.2012.07.016

Lambon Ralph, M. A., and Ellis, A. (1997). "Patterns of paralexia" revisited: Report of a case of visual dyslexia. *Cogn. Neuropsychol.* 14, 953–974. doi: 10.1080/026432997381312

Levine, M. (1987). *Developmental Variation and Learning Disorders.* Cambridge, MA: Educators Publishing Service.

Marshall, J. C. (1984). "On some relationships between acquired and developmental dyslexias," in *Dyslexia: A Neuroscientific Approach to Clinical Evaluation*, eds E. H. Duffy and N. Geschwind (Boston, MA: Little, Brown and Co).

Marshall, J. C., and Newcombe, F. (1973). Patterns of paralexia: a psycholinguistic approach. *J. Psycholinguist. Res.* 2, 179–199. doi: 10.1007/BF01067101

Masterson, J. (2000). "Developmental surface dyslexia," in *Neuropsychology of Reading*, ed E. Funnell (Hove: Psychology Press), 123–148.

Mayall, K., and Humphreys, G. W. (2002). Presentation and task effects on migration errors in attentional dyslexia. *Neuropsychologia* 40, 1506–1515. doi: 10.1016/S0028-3932(01)00175-0

McCloskey, M., and Rapp, B. (2000). A visually based developmental reading deficit. *J. Mem. Lang.* 43, 157–181. doi: 10.1006/jmla.2000.2724

Nachman-Katz, I., and Friedmann, N. (2007). Developmental neglect dyslexia: characteristics and directions for treatment. *Lang. Brain* 6, 75–90.

Nachman-Katz, I., and Friedmann, N. (2008). Developmental neglect dyslexia and its effect on number reading. *Lang. Brain* 7, 83–96.

Nachman-Katz, I., and Friedmann, N. (2009). Writing words in developmental neglect dyslexia. *Lang. Brain* 9, 119–141.

Nachman-Katz, I., and Friedmann, N. (2010). An empirical evaluation of treatment directions for developmental neglect dyslexia. *Proc. Soc. Behav. Sci.* 6, 248–249. doi: 10.1016/j.sbspro.2010.08.124

Newcombe, F., and Marshall, J. C. (1981). On psycholinguistic classifications of the acquired dyslexias. *Bull. Orton Soc.* 31, 29–46. doi: 10.1007/BF02658599

Newcombe, F., and Marshall, J. C. (1984). Varieties of acquired dyslexia: a linguistic approach. *Semin. Neurol.* 4, 181–195. doi: 10.1055/s-2008-1041548

Newcombe, F., and Marshall, J. C. (1985). "Reading and writing by letter sounds," in *Surface Dyslexia: Cognitive and Neuropsychological Studies of Phonological Reading*, eds K. E. Patterson, J. C. Marshall, and M. Coltheart (London: Erlbaum), 15–34.

Nielsen, J. M. (1937). Unilateral cerebral dominance as related to mind blindness: minimal lesion capable of causing visual agnosia for objects. *Arch. Neurol. Psychiatry* 38, 108–135. doi: 10.1001/archneurpsyc.1937.02260190118009

Parasuraman, R. (2000). "The attentive brain: issues and prospects," in *The Attentive Brain*, ed R. Parasuraman (Cambridge, MA: MIT Press), 3–15.

Patterson, K. E., Marshall, J. C., and Coltheart, M. (1985). *Surface Dyslexia.* London: Erlbaum.

Patterson, K., and Wilson, B. (1990). A rose is a rose or a nose: a deficit in initial letter identification. *Cogn. Neuropsychol.* 7, 447–477. doi: 10.1080/02643299008253451

Petersen, S. E., and Posner, M. I. (2012). The attention system of the human brain: 20 years after. *Ann. Rev. Neurosci.* 35, 73–89. doi: 10.1146/annurev-neuro-062111-150525

Posner, M. I., and Petersen, S. E. (1990). The attention system of the human brain. *Ann. Rev. Neurosci.* 13, 25–42. doi: 10.1146/annurev.ne.13.030190.000325

Posner, M. I., Snyder, C. R., and Davidson, B. J. (1980). Attention and the detection of signals. *J. Exp. Psychol. Gen.* 109, 160. doi: 10.1037/0096-3445.109.2.160

Price, C. J., and Humphreys, G. W. (1993). Attentional dyslexia: the effect of co-occurring deficits. *Cogn. Neuropsychol.* 10, 569–592. doi: 10.1080/02643299308253474

Primativo, S., Arduino, L. S., De Luca, M., Daini, R., and Martelli, M. (2013). Neglect dyslexia: a matter of "good looking." *Neuropsychologia* 51, 2109–2119. doi: 10.1016/j.neuropsychologia.2013.07.002

Rayner, K., Murphy, L. A., Henderson, J. M., and Pollatsek, A. (1989). Selective attentional dyslexia. *Cogn. Neuropsychol.* 6, 357–378. doi: 10.1080/02643298908253288

Reynolds, M., and Besner, D. (2006). Reading aloud is not automatic: processing capacity is required to generate a phonological code from print. *J. Exp. Psychol. Hum. Percept. Perform.* 32, 1303–1323. doi: 10.1037/0096-1523.32.6.1303

Reznick, J., and Friedmann, N. (2009). Morphological decomposition in the early stages of orthographic-visual analysis: evidence from neglexia. *Lang. Brain* 8, 31–61.

Robin, A. (1998). *ADHD in Adolescents: Diagnosis and Treatment.* New York, NY: Guilford Press.

Saffran, E. M., and Coslett, H. B. (1996). "Attentional dyslexia" in Alzheimer's disease: a case study. *Cogn. Neuropsychol.* 13, 205–228. doi: 10.1080/026432996382006

Semrud-Clikeman, M., Biederman, J., Sprich-Buckminster, S., Lehman, B. K., Faraone, S. V., and Norman, D. (1992). Comorbidity between ADDH and learning disability: a review and report in a clinically referred sample. *J. Am. Acad. Child Adolesc. Psychiatry* 31, 439–448. doi: 10.1097/00004583-199205000-00009

Shalev, L., Ben-Simon, A., Mevorach, C., Cohen, Y., and Tsal, Y. (2011). Conjunctive Continuous Performance Task (CCPT)-A pure measure of sustained attention. *Neuropsychologia* 49, 2584–2591. doi: 10.1016/j.neuropsychologia.2011.05.006

Shallice, T., and Warrington, E. K. (1977). The possible role of selective attention in acquired dyslexia. *Neuropsychologia* 15, 31–41. doi: 10.1016/0028-3932(77)90112-9

Shallice, T., and Warrington, E. K. (1980). "Single and multiple component central dyslexic syndromes," in *Deep Dyslexia*, eds M. Coltheart, E. K. Patterson, and J. C. Marshall (London: Routledge and Kegan Paul), 119–145.

Shaywitz, S. E., and Shaywitz, B. A. (2008). Paying attention to reading: the neurobiology of reading and dyslexia. *Dev. Psychopathol.* 20, 1239–1349. doi: 10.1017/S0954579408000631

Shvimer, L., Kerbel, N., and Friedmann, N. (2009). An empirical evaluation of various treatment directions in developmental attentional dyslexia. *Lang. Brain* 8, 87–118.

Slaghuis, W. L., Lovegrove, W. J., and Davidson, J. A. (1993). Visual and language processing deficits are concurrent in dyslexia. *Cortex* 29, 601–615 doi: 10.1016/S0010-9452(13)80284-5

Snider, V. E., Frankenburger, W., and Aspenson, M. R. (2000). The relationship between learning disabilities and attention deficit hyperactivity disorder: a national survey. *Dev. Dis. Bull.* 28, 19–37. doi: 10.1177/074193250302400105

Southwood, M. H., and Chatterjee, A. (1999). Simultaneous activation of reading mechanisms: evidence from a case of deep dyslexia. *Brain Lang.* 67, 1–29. doi: 10.1006/brln.1998.2046

Southwood, M. H., and Chatterjee, A. (2001). The simultaneous activation hypothesis: explaining recovery from deep to phonological dyslexia. *Brain Lang.* 76, 18–34. doi: 10.1006/brln.2000.2384

Stern, P., and Shalev, L. (2013). The role of sustained attention and text's conditions in reading comprehension among adolescents with ADHD and without it. *Res. Dev. Disabil.* 34, 431–439. doi: 10.1016/j.ridd.2012.08.021

Stroop, J. R. (1935). Studies of interference in serial verbal reactions. *J. Exp. Psychol.* 18, 643–662. doi: 10.1037/h0054651

Stuart, M., and Howard, D. (1995). KJ: A developmental deep dyslexia. *Cogn. Neuropsychol.* 12, 793–824. doi: 10.1080/02643299508251402

Temple, C. M. (1997). *Developmental Cognitive Neuropsychology.* Hove: Psychology Press.

Temple, C. M., and Marshall, J. C. (1983). A case study of developmental phonological dyslexia. *Br. J. Psychol.* 74, 517–533. doi: 10.1111/j.2044-8295.1983.tb01883.x

Tsal, Y., Shalev, L., and Mevorach, C. (2005). The diversity of attention deficits in ADHD: the prevalence of four cognitive factors in ADHD versus controls. *J. Learn. Disabil.* 38, 142–157. doi: 10.1177/00222194050380020401

Valdois, S., Bosse, M. L., and Tainturier, M. J. (2004). The cognitive deficits responsible for developmental dyslexia: review of evidence for a selective visual attentional disorder. *Dyslexia* 10, 339–363. doi: 10.1002/dys.284

Vallar, G., Burani, C., and Arduino, L. S. (2010). Neglect dyslexia: a review of the neuropsychological literature. *Exp. Brain Res.* 206, 219–235. doi: 10.1007/s00221-010-2386-0

Vidyasagar, T. R., and Pammer, K. (1999). Impaired visual search in dyslexia relates to the role of the magnocellular pathway in attention. *Neuroreport* 10, 1283–1287. doi: 10.1097/00001756-199904260-00024

Warrington, E. K., Cipolotti, L., and McNeil, J. (1993). Attentional dyslexia: a single case study. *Neuropsychologia* 31, 871–885. doi: 10.1016/0028-3932(93)90145-P

Weekes, B., and Coltheart, M. (1996). Surface dyslexia and surface dysgraphia: treatment studies and their theoretical implications. *Cogn. Neuropsychol.* 13, 277–315. doi: 10.1080/026432996382033

Willcutt, E. G., and Pennington, B. F. (2000). Comorbidity of reading disability and attention-deficit/hyperactivity disorder differences by gender and subtype. *J. Learn. Disabil.* 33, 179–191. doi: 10.1177/002221940003300206

Young, A. W., Newcombe, F., and Ellis, A. W. (1991). Different impairments contribute to neglect dyslexia. *Cogn. Neuropsychol.* 8, 177–191. doi: 10.1080/02643299108253371

Zoccolotti, P., De Luca, M., Di Pace, E., Judica, A., Orlandi, M., and Spinelli, D. (1999). Markers of developmental surface dyslexia in a language (Italian) with high grapheme–phoneme. *Appl. Psycholinguist.* 20, 191–216. doi: 10.1017/S0142716499002027

APPENDIX A

Table A1 | Percentage of relevant errors in reading aloud of each of the 28 participants with dyslexia and with normal attention functions (summarized in Table 1).

Participant	Age (years), gender	LPD	Attentional	Neglect	Vowel	Surface	Phonological
		%Migrations in migratable words	%Migrations between words in migratable word pairs	%Consonant omission and substitution on the left of the word	%Vowel letter omission, substitution, migration, or addition	%Sublexical reading in irregular words/ potentiophones	%Errors in nonwords
LGB	10, F	18%	13%		14%		
SXA	10, F	9%	7%			10%	
KSH	10, F		27%	4%			
SHL	11, F	17%	17%	3%	13%	12%	
LTM	11, M	15%				17%	
VBO	13, F	7%	13%		23%	12%	
AXA	13, M	10%	6%				
DXZ	13, M	6%					
AAX	14, M	15%	19%			8%	
MML	15, F					19%	
SHR	15, F	9%					
KGA	16, M	13%	10%			8%	
NOL	23, F	13%					
OLA	25, M	6%	10%				
NLK	25, M	9%					
ZET	26, M	10%			36%	7%	
ZYH	26, M	12%	16%			8%	
ZRS	26, F				13%		
ZGA	26, M	10%				18%	
NLK	26, M	15%			11%		
ZAF	26, F	8%					
ALM	28, M	11%	15%		15%	8%	
NKV	28, M				13%		
KSH	29, F						31%
NAK	30, F				17%		
ZRB	32, M	8%	11%		23%	9%	
ALU	36, M	6%	12%				
ZRC	38, M				10%		
Control groups: %M (SD)							
4th–5th grade		1.8 (2.7)	3.8 (4.1)	0.0 (0.0)	1.3 (2.1)	3.2 (2.3)	4.2 (3.0)
7th grade		1.6 (2.2)	2.8 (3.5)	0.03 (0.1)	1.4 (1.7)	3.8 (2.0)	4.0 (2.9)
15 year olds—adults		0.6 (1.1)	1.9 (2.7)	0.03 (0.2)	1.0 (1.9)	1.3 (1.4)	2.7 (3.3)

[a] *All the error rates of the various types presented in the table are significantly larger than the age-matched control groups for this error type ($p < 0.05$), and indicate a dyslexia of the relevant type. Empty cells indicate that there were no relevant errors at all or that the relevant error rate was within the normal range, in most cases less than 1%. The percentages of errors that appear in the table for each dyslexia are: for LPD—migrations in migratable words, for attentional dyslexia—migrations between words in migratable word pairs, for neglect—consonant omission and substitution on the left of the word, for vowel dyslexia—vowel letter omission, substitution, migration, or addition for surface dyslexia—sublexical reading in irregular words and potentiophones, and for phonological buffer dyslexia—errors in non-words.*

[b] *The percentage of vowel errors of LGB, SHL, NLK, ALM, and NKV refer to their percentage errors in reading words, for the other vowel dyslexic participants the percentages are from nonwords.*

APPENDIX B

Table B1 | Percentage of relevant z-scores in the attention tasks of each of the 27 participants with attention disorders and with normal reading (summarized in Table 2).

Participant	Age (years), gender	Sustained	Selective	Orienting	Executive
LLM	21, F	−3.43	−0.87	−0.21	−0.43
LEB	12, F	0.07		1.17	−2.73
LGB	18, M	−2.08	−2.10	−1.17	0.37
LAV	25, M	−4.83	0.10	−1.47	−2.00
LXP	15, M	−2.06	−1.25	0.64	−6.84
LSS	17, F	−7.36	−1.92	0.46	−0.12
LNV	17, F	−8.39	0.30	0.97	1.71
LYA	11, F	−2.28	−1.34	2.96	−5.10
LMA	16, F	−12.69	−1.26	1.31	−0.45
USG	19, M	1.40	−0.74	2.67	−1.94
THL	23, F	−0.86	0.32	−3.09	−1.88
SHM	15, F	−4.31	−0.05	0.69	1.07
SHS	15, M	−1.83	−1.19	−0.78	−2.60
YG	15, F	−1.88	−1.93	0.50	−1.17
ZEZ	30, M	−1.65	−0.18	1.20	1.02
ZON	24, M	−3.07	−0.4	0.47	−0.14
ZYS	28, F	−7.18	−11.40	−6.81	−6.69
ZTL	31, F	−3.42	0.56	−6.64	−0.62
ZJO	31, M	−0.77	0.54	−2.74	0.34
ZSY	27, F	−5.31	3.46	3.26	−1.09
ZMS	27, F	−7.18	−11.40	−6.81	−6.69
NHP	26, F	0.85	−2.24		−2.45
NPL	24, F	1.12	−6.01	0.77	−1.00
NMH	22, F	−1.76	−1.56	2.51	−1.63
NHO	22, F	−0.32	−0.3	−1.90	−0.53
NLO	22, F	0.51	−0.4	1.97	0.09
LNL	13, M	−3.60	2.19	−0.63	−6.69

LEB did not participate in a selective attention task; NHP did not complete the orienting attention task.

APPENDIX C

Table C1 | Examples for the various types of Hebrew stimuli used in the reading tasks.

Stimulus type, the dyslexia it was used to detect, and the error type	Target word	Relevant error
Migratable words—for letter position dyslexia (an example of a letter migration error)	מדענים md?nim mad'anim scientists	מעדנים m?dnim maadanim delicacies
Migratable nonwords—for letter position dyslexia and phonological dyslexia (an example of a letter migration error)	מרדגות mrdgot mardegot nonword	מדרגות mdrgot madregot stairs
Migratable word pair—for attentional dyslexia	חצב מגב xcb mgb xacav magav squill wiper	מצב חגב mcb xgb macav xagav situation grasshopper
Potentiophone—for surface dyslexia (an example of a sublexical reading)	כתף Ktf katef shoulder	קטף kTf kataf picked
Irregular word—for surface dyslexia (an example of a sublexical reading)	זאת zat zot this	זאת zat zat nonword
Words with a lexical potential for errors on the left—for neglect dyslexia (examples of letter errors on the left: substitution, addition, omission)	שלח Slx shalax sent	של/ שלחת/ שלט SlT/ Slxt/ Sl shelet/ shalaxt/ shel sign/ you-sent/ of
Words with a lexical potential for vowel errors—for vowel dyslexia (examples of vowel letter migration, omission)	חלוק xlok xaluk gown	חלק/ חולק xolk/xlk xolek/xalak shares/smooth
Nonwords with a lexical potential for vowel errors—for vowel dyslexia (examples of vowel letter errors omission, substitution)	לושון loSon lushon nonword	לישון/ לשון lSon/liSon lashon/ lishon tongue / to-sleep

Each example shows the Hebrew target word and the word or words created by the relevant error, followed by orthographic transliteration, phonological transcription, and translation.

Permissions

All chapters in this book were first published by Frontiers; hereby published with permission under the Creative Commons Attribution License or equivalent. Every chapter published in this book has been scrutinized by our experts. Their significance has been extensively debated. The topics covered herein carry significant findings which will fuel the growth of the discipline. They may even be implemented as practical applications or may be referred to as a beginning point for another development.

The contributors of this book come from diverse backgrounds, making this book a truly international effort. This book will bring forth new frontiers with its revolutionizing research information and detailed analysis of the nascent developments around the world.

We would like to thank all the contributing authors for lending their expertise to make the book truly unique. They have played a crucial role in the development of this book. Without their invaluable contributions this book wouldn't have been possible. They have made vital efforts to compile up to date information on the varied aspects of this subject to make this book a valuable addition to the collection of many professionals and students.

This book was conceptualized with the vision of imparting up-to-date information and advanced data in this field. To ensure the same, a matchless editorial board was set up. Every individual on the board went through rigorous rounds of assessment to prove their worth. After which they invested a large part of their time researching and compiling the most relevant data for our readers.

The editorial board has been involved in producing this book since its inception. They have spent rigorous hours researching and exploring the diverse topics which have resulted in the successful publishing of this book. They have passed on their knowledge of decades through this book. To expedite this challenging task, the publisher supported the team at every step. A small team of assistant editors was also appointed to further simplify the editing procedure and attain best results for the readers.

Apart from the editorial board, the designing team has also invested a significant amount of their time in understanding the subject and creating the most relevant covers. They scrutinized every image to scout for the most suitable representation of the subject and create an appropriate cover for the book.

The publishing team has been an ardent support to the editorial, designing and production team. Their endless efforts to recruit the best for this project, has resulted in the accomplishment of this book. They are a veteran in the field of academics and their pool of knowledge is as vast as their experience in printing. Their expertise and guidance has proved useful at every step. Their uncompromising quality standards have made this book an exceptional effort. Their encouragement from time to time has been an inspiration for everyone.

The publisher and the editorial board hope that this book will prove to be a valuable piece of knowledge for researchers, students, practitioners and scholars across the globe.

List of Contributors

Pierluigi Zoccolotti
Department of Psychology, Sapienza University of Rome, Rome, Italy
Neuropsychology Unit, IRCCS Fondazione Santa Lucia, Rome, Italy
Neuropsychology Research Centre, IRCCS Santa Lucia, Rome, Italy

Maria De Luca
Neuropsychology Unit, IRCCS Fondazione Santa Lucia, Rome, Italy

Donatella Spinelli
Neuropsychology Unit, IRCCS Fondazione Santa Lucia, Rome, Italy
Department of Human Movement Sciences and Health, University of Rome "Foro Italico", Rome, Italy

Pamela Varvara
Neuroscience Department, Children's Hospital Bambino Gesù, Rome, Italy
Psychology Department, Libera Università Maria Ss. Assunta, Rome, Italy

Cristiana Varuzza, Anna C. P. Sorrentino, Stefano Vicari and Deny Menghini
Neuroscience Department, Children's Hospital Bambino Gesù, Rome, Italy

Elsje van Bergen
Department of Experimental Psychology, University of Oxford, Oxford, UK

Aryan van der Leij and Peter F. de Jong
Research Institute of Child Development and Education, University of Amsterdam, Amsterdam, Netherlands

Kristen Pammer
The Research School of Psychology, The Australian National University, Canberra, ACT, Australia

Rosa K. W. Kwok and Andrew W. Ellis
Department of Psychology, University of York, York, UK

Marie Lallier
Basque Center on Cognition Brain and Language, Donostia-San Sebastian, Spain

Sophie Donnadieu
Laboratoire de Psychologie et NeuroCognition, UMR CNRS 5105, Grenoble-Chambéry, France
Faculté de Psychologie, Université de Savoie, Chambéry, France

Sylviane Valdois
Laboratoire de Psychologie et NeuroCognition, UMR CNRS 5105, Grenoble-Chambéry, France
Centre National pour la Recherche Scientifique, Paris, France

Hua-Chen Wang, Eva Marinus, Lyndsey Nickels and Anne Castles
Department of Cognitive Science, ARC Centre of Excellence in Cognition and its Disorders, Macquarie University, Sydney, NSW, Australia

Chiara V. Marinelli
Neuropsychology Research Centre, IRCCS Santa Lucia, Rome, Italy
Neuropsychology Unit, IRCCS Fondazione Santa Lucia, Rome, Italy

Daniela Traficante
Department of Psychology, Catholic University of Milan, Milan, Italy
NeuroMI – Milan Center for Neuroscience, Milan, Italy

Alan J. Power, Natasha Mead, Lisa Barnes and Usha Goswami
Department of Psychology, Centre for Neuroscience in Education, University of Cambridge, Cambridgeshire, UK

Eraldo Paulesu
Department of Psychology, University of Milano-Bicocca, Milan, Italy
NEUROMI- Milan Center for Neuroscience, University of Milano-Bicocca, Milan, Italy
fMRI – Unit, Istituto di Ricovero e Cura a Carattere Scientifico Galeazzi, Milan, Italy

Laura Danelli and Manuela Berlingeri
Department of Psychology, University of Milano-Bicocca, Milan, Italy
NEUROMI- Milan Center for Neuroscience, University of Milano-Bicocca, Milan, Italy

Sandra Hasko, Katarina Groth, Jennifer Bruder, Jürgen Bartling and Gerd Schulte-Körne
Department of Child and Adolescent Psychiatry and Psychotherapy, University Hospital Munich, Munich, Germany

Itamar Sela
Edmond J. Safra Brain Research Center for the Study of Learning Disabilities, University of Haifa, Haifa, Israel

Benjamin Gagl, Stefan Hawelka and Florian Hutzler
Department of Psychology, Centre for Neurocognitive Research, University of Salzburg, Salzburg, Austria

Milena Ruffino and Massimo Molteni
Child Psychopathology Unit, Scientific Institute, IRCCS Eugenio Medea, Lecco, Italy

Simone Gori and Andrea Facoetti
Child Psychopathology Unit, Scientific Institute, IRCCS Eugenio Medea, Lecco, Italy
Developmental and Cognitive Neuroscience Lab, Department of General Psychology, University of Padua, Padua, Italy

Daniela Boccardi
Developmental and Cognitive Neuroscience Lab, Department of General Psychology, University of Padua, Padua, Italy

Limor Lukov, Naama Friedmann, Lilach Shalev, Lilach Khentov-Kraus, Nir Shalev, Rakefet Lorber and Revital Guggenheim
School of Education and Sagol School of Neuroscience, Tel Aviv University, Tel Aviv, Israel

Index

www.ingramcontent.com/pod-product-compliance
Lightning Source LLC
LaVergne TN
LVHW082219200926
848484LV00008B/2276
* 9 7 9 8 8 8 7 4 0 0 4 5 7 *